BAJA
HANDBOOK

MEXICO'S WESTERN PENINSULA, INCLUDING CABO SAN LUCAS

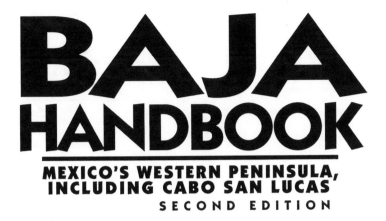

BAJA
HANDBOOK

MEXICO'S WESTERN PENINSULA, INCLUDING CABO SAN LUCAS'

SECOND EDITION

JOE CUMMINGS

MOON
PUBLICATIONS INC.

BAJA HANDBOOK
SECOND EDITION

Published by
Moon Publications, Inc.
P.O. Box 3040
Chico, California 95927-3040, USA

Printed by
Colorcraft Ltd., Hong Kong

Please send all comments,
corrections, additions,
amendments, and critiques to:

**BAJA HANDBOOK
MOON PUBLICATIONS, INC.
P.O. BOX 3040
CHICO, CA 95927-3040, USA**

Printing History
1st edition — February 1992
2nd edition © September 1994

Library of Congress Cataloging-in-Publication Data
Cummings, Joe
   Baja Handbook / Joe Cummings. — 2nd ed.
         p.   cm.
   Includes bibliographical references and index.
   ISBN 1-56691-052-8
   1. Baja California (Mexico) — Guidebooks.   I. Title.
F1246.C99   1994   94-8408
   917.2'204835 — dc20   CIP

Editor: Kevin Jeys
Copy Editors: Mark Arends, Asha Johnson
Production & Design: Carey Wilson, David Hurst, Chris Parmenter
Cartographers: Bob Race, Brian Bardwell
Index: Mark Arends

Front cover photo: Terrence Moore
All photos by Joe Cummings unless otherwise noted.

Distributed in the U.S.A. by Publishers Group West
Printed in Hong Kong

Although the author and publisher have made every effort to ensure that the information was correct at
the time of going to press, the author and publisher do not assume and hereby disclaim any liability to any
party for any loss or damage caused by errors, omissions, or any potential travel disruption due to labor or
financial difficulty, whether such errors or omissions result from negligence, accident, or any other cause.

The very air here is miraculous,
and outlines of reality change with the moment.

—John Steinbeck,
The Log from the Sea of Cortez

CONTENTS

MAPS

MAP SYMBOLS

⬡	MEX. FEDERAL HIGHWAY	− − −	INTERNATIONAL BORDER	■	POINT OF INTEREST
◯	MEX. STATE HIGHWAY	·−·−·	STATE BORDER	●	ACCOMMODATION
◠	U.S. STATE HIGHWAY	▬▬▬	FREEWAY	○	TOWNS / VILLAGES
▢	U.S. HIGHWAY	▬▬▬	MAIN HIGHWAY	○	CITIES
▽	U.S. INTERSTATE	− − −	OTHER ROADS	⅃L	TOLL GATE
		= = =	UNPAVED ROADS	✝	MISSION
⛽	PEMEX GAS STATION	=	BRIDGE	Λ	CAMPSITE
		■▬■	RAILROAD	▲	MOUNTAIN
		〜〜〜	WATER		

CHARTS

SPECIAL TOPICS

ABBREVIATIONS

a/c—air conditioned
d—double occupancy
km—kilometer

RV—recreation vehicle
s—single occupancy
t—triple occupancy

ACKNOWLEDGMENTS

Gringos and *mexicanos* near and far were of immeasurable assistance during the updating process for this new edition of *Baja Handbook,* including Becky Aparecio, Bill Baffert and Bajahoteles, Amy Bortz and Edelman Public Relations Worldwide, María Esther Cabuto, Betsy Carpenter, Mario Cruz, Dorothy Eller, Cecilia Haugen, Hugh Kramer, Bo Landress, Roy Mahoff, Elena Moreno, Michael Mortenson, Patricia Hernandez Mota, Cesar Meza Palomares, Jesús Montañez Roman, Angel López Sotelo, Dwight Stiles, Dale Townsend de Parra, Jane Perkins, and William Wolf.

I must also thank research assistants Tom Huhti, Chris Humphrey, and Richard Sterling for their valuable contributions; readers Peter Harmathy, Michael Mortenson, Janice Peterson, Doug Swords, and Wayne Tolmachoff for taking the time to write such informative letters; and both Lynne Cummings and Riley Binford for providing on-the-road companionship.

As always, the national and state representatives of the Secretaría de Turismo (SECTUR) were of invaluable assistance in providing information on Baja California destinations and ongoing logistical support.

IS THIS BOOK OUT OF DATE?

Between the time this book went to press and the time it reached the shelves, hotels have opened and closed, restaurants have changed hands, and roads have been repaired or fallen into disrepair. Also, prices have probably increased; therefore, all prices herein should be regarded as approximations and are not guaranteed by the publisher or author.

We want to keep this book as accurate and up to date as possible and would appreciate hearing about any errors or omissions you encounter while using *Baja Handbook.*

If you have any noteworthy experiences (good or bad) with establishments listed in this book, please pass them along to us. If something is out of place on a map, tell us; if the best restaurant in town is not included, we'd like to know. Found a new route to a mission ruins site or palm oasis? Share it with other Baja travelers. All contributions will be deeply appreciated and properly acknowledged. Address your letters to:

Baja Handbook
c/o Moon Publications
P.O. Box 3040
Chico, California 95927
USA

COMBATTING CALIFORNIA CONFUSION

Following common usage, this book uses "Baja California" and "Baja" interchangeably. For clarity's sake, all references to the U.S. state will appear as "Alta California" or "the U.S. state of California."

FOREWORD

If you're thinking of visiting Baja California and are hesitating . . . don't! There will never be a better time than now. Certainly, don't be put off by the thought of bandidos, Mexi--- jails or *turista*. Before I ventured into Baja 14 years ago I was subjected to every horror story imaginable—mostly from Southern Californians who had never been there.

Now a veteran of a score of Baja adventures, and having spent two years walking alone around the peninsula's beautiful coastline, I have to look back and wonder at the origin of the "stories" and declare that in all my time below the border I have never had a problem with anyone. My abiding memories are of incredible vistas, fascinating wildlife, and a people as warm and hospitable as any in the world.

Whatever attracts you to Baja—fishing, surfing, seafood, desert flora, cave paintings, whales, Spanish missions, sun-filled days—you won't be disappointed. Although this "forgotten peninsula" has been discovered and every year brings more development and better facilities, much if it remains a true frontier with an attendant frontier ethos. Don't be surprised to find a seemingly impoverished fisherman or rancher coming to your aid and then politely refusing a fistful of pesos in return, declaring sincerely, "Out here we are all brothers."

Joe Cummings's impressively researched and comprehensive *Baja Handbook* will not only assist you around Baja's border cities and down the main highways, but will also open your eyes to the "real" Baja of remote villages, fish camps, empty beaches, and rugged islands. Together with courtesy and common sense, this excellent guide will go a long way toward getting you safely to wherever you want to go; then, as many of us have found, the biggest danger is you may not want to come back.

Graham D Mackintosh

Graham Mackintosh, author
Into A Desert Place

BOB RACE

INTRODUCTION

The first maps of Baja California, drawn by 16th-century Spanish explorers, depicted it not as a peninsula but as an island. Lured by tales of gold cities and a kingdom of warrior women, the conquistadors were among the first in a long line of seekers who have approached Baja's shores with a sense of mystery. Though the maps have long since been corrected, a legion of explorers—Latinos and gringos alike—continue to tramp the peninsula with dreams of finding Shangri-la in a hidden canyon or secluded cove.

Scattered along Baja's natural and artificial borders are outward concessions to the modern world (including Mexico's fifth-largest city), as well as sufficient recreational opportunities to satisfy the most hedonistic refugees from that same world. This is one Baja; a peninsula wedged between one of the world's wealthiest and most technologically advanced countries and one struggling to develop with dignity.

But another Baja remains an island, in spite of 20th-century mapping. For four centuries, this Baja has stubbornly resisted the efforts of conquistadors, missionaries, miners, developers, and tourist boards to bring "civilization" into its rugged interior. The intrepid few who make it to the cultural and geographic heart of the peninsula will find it belongs to an era long ago lost to most of North America.

THE LAND

BIRTH OF A PENINSULA

Baja California is the fourth-longest peninsula in the world after the Kamchatka, Malay, and Antarctic, but its landmass wasn't always scissored from the rest of Mexico. At one time its entire length was attached to a broad tropical plain along Mexico's Pacific coast; about two-thirds of the area lay beneath the ocean. The 23-ton duck-billed hadrosaur roamed the region (its fossilized bones have been found near El Rosario) as did mammoth, bison, hyracotherium (a small, primitive horse), and camel.

The peninsula's eventual divergence from the mainland came about as a result of the continual shifting of massive sections of the earth's surface, a process known as plate tectonics.

Like much of coastal Alta California to the north, Baja California is part of the North Pacific Plate, while the rest of the North American continent belongs to the North American Plate. The boundary line between these two plates is the San Andreas Fault, which extends northward through the center of Mexico's Sea of Cortez and into Alta California, where it parallels the California coast on a southeast-northwest axis before veering off into the Pacific Ocean near San Francisco. The North Pacific and North American plates have shifted along this gap for millions of years, with the Pacific plate moving in a northwesterly direction at a current rate of about one to two inches a year.

This movement eventually tore basins in the earth's crust which allowed the Sea of Cortez to form, thus separating the land area west of the fault zone from land to the east. At one time the Sea of Cortez extended as far north as Palm Springs in Alta California; the sea would have continued moving northward at a gradual pace had it not met with the Colorado River. Silting in the Colorado River delta reversed the northward movement of the basins, holding the northern limit of the Sea of Cortez at a point well below what is now the U.S.-Mexican border. Alta California's Salton Sea is a remnant of the northernmost extension of the Sea of Cortez, cut off by delta sedimentation.

As the peninsula moved slowly northwestward (257 km from the mainland by the time the Sea of Cortez became a stable feature—about five million years ago), the coastal plains tipped toward the west, creating a series of fault-block mountain ranges that now form one of Baja California's most outstanding topographic features. Volcanism further contributed to the peninsular and island geography, as seen in the massive lava flows east of San Ignacio (where the Tres Vírgenes volcanos erupted as recently as 1746), the basaltic geology south of Bahía de los Angeles, the various cinder cones near San Quintín, and the volcanic islands of Isla Raza, Isla Guadalupe, and Isla San Luis. At Laguna de los Volcánes in northeastern Baja,

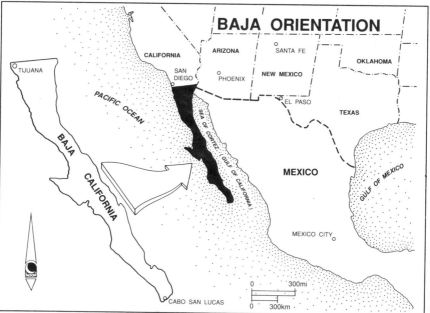

BAJA ORIENTATION

CALIFORNIA
TIJUANA
PACIFIC OCEAN
BAJA CALIFORNIA
ARIZONA
SANTA FE
CALIFORNIA
SAN DIEGO
PHOENIX
NEW MEXICO
OKLAHOMA
EL PASO
TEXAS
SEA OF CORTEZ (GULF OF CALIFORNIA)
MEXICO
GULF OF MEXICO
MEXICO CITY
CABO SAN LUCAS
0   300mi
0   300km

boiling mud pits and steam vents are the most visible signs of recent volcanic activity.

A third topographical contributor, sedimentation, has created the salient features of Baja's larger valleys and southwestern coastal plains. Prehistoric Mexican rivers, cut off from their mainland sources upon the creation of the Sea of Cortez, deposited sediments west of Mexicali to form the vast Laguna Salada. The fertile Valle de Mexicali, like Alta California's Imperial Valley, holds silt from the Colorado River—much of it comprised of geologic elements once contained in the Grand Canyon. The low coastal plain that forms the western portion of the Vizcaíno Desert region features sedimentary deposits up to 16 km thick, a combination of sierra river deposits and material left over from the period 15 million years ago when this area lay beneath the Pacific Ocean.

GEOGRAPHY

Size And Area
Baja California extends 1,300 km (806 miles) from the U.S.-Mexico border to the peninsula's southernmost tip—a hundred miles longer than Italy and twice the length of Florida. If the coastline could be straightened, it would reach a distance equivalent to that between Tijuana and Juneau, Alaska. Its widest girth, measured across land only, is at the 193-km (120-mile) border. Measuring across land and water to include Bahía de Sebastian Vizcaíno, the widest point is about 230 km (144 miles), from Punta Eugenio on the west coast to Punta San Francisquito on the east. The peninsula reaches its narrowest point at a section 161 km (100 miles) above the southern tip, where it's only 45 km (28 miles) between the Pacific Ocean and Bahía de La Paz.

The total land area of the states of Baja California (or Baja California Norte) and Baja California Sur is about 144,000 square km (55,000 square miles)—add another 2,460 square km (930 square miles)

for the dozens of islands and islets nearby. The coastline created by the Pacific Ocean, the Sea of Cortez, and the dozens of bays, lagoons, coves, and inlets totals about 4,800 shore km (3,000 miles).

Mountain Ranges
Baja's most striking geographical feature is the spine of mountain ranges, or sierras, that run down its center from northwest to southeast. For the most part, Baja's sierras are a continuation of a mountain system that stretches southward from Alaska's Aleutian Islands to the spectacular rock formations at Cabo San Lucas. There are 23 named ranges in all; most are of fault-block origin, a scattered few are volcanic.

Because of the way in which the underground fault blocks tipped to create these sierras, the mountains tend to slope gradually toward the west and fall off rather dramatically toward the east. The Cape Region's Sierra de la Laguna is the major exception. Like Alta California's Sierra Nevada, Baja's high sierras typically feature granitic peaks topped by conifer forests. The eastern escarpment, facing the Sea of Cortez, is dissected by stream-eroded canyons and *arroyos*, stream beds that are dry most of the year.

The four most substantial mountain ranges are the **Sierra Juárez** and **Sierra de San Pedro Mártir** in the north, the volcanic **Sierra de la Giganta** in the upper south, and the **Sierra de la Laguna** in the center of the southern cape.

BAJA CALIFORNIA MOUNTAIN RANGES OVER 1,500 METERS (5,000 FEET)

RANGE AND HIGHEST PEAK(S)

Sierra Juárez—Cerro Torre Blanco 1,794 meters (5,904 feet)

Sierra de San Pedro Mártir—Picacho del Diablo 3,086 meters (10,154 feet)

Sierra la Asamblea—Cerro Dos Picachos 1,653 meters (5,438 feet)

Sierra San Borja—Pico Echeverria 1,902 meters (6,258 feet)

Sierra de San Francisco—Pico Santa Monica 2,098 meters (6,904 feet)

Sierra de Guadalupe—Monte Thetis 1,635 meters (5,380 feet)

Sierra de la Giganta—Cerro la Giganta 1,760 meters (5,792 feet)

Sierra de la Laguna—Picacho de la Laguna 2,155 meters (7,090 feet)

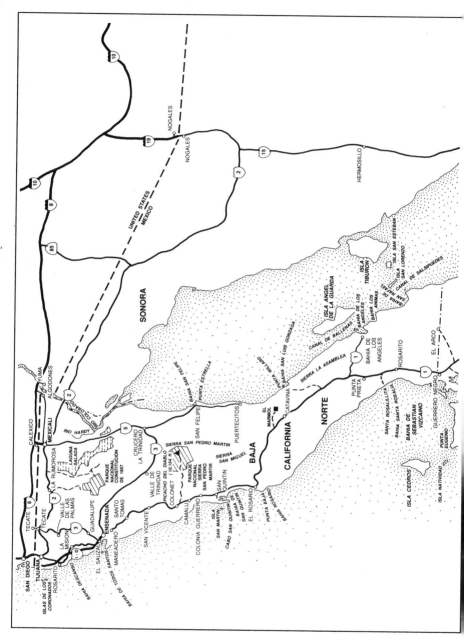

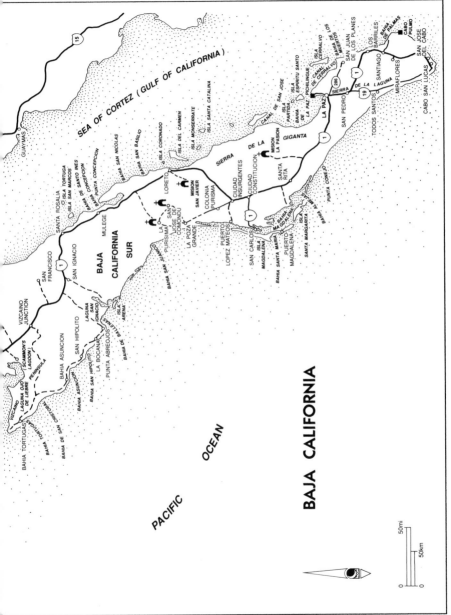

BAJA CALIFORNIA

© MOON PUBLICATIONS, INC.

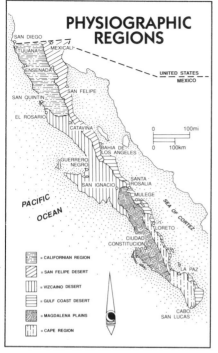

PHYSIOGRAPHIC REGIONS

SAN DIEGO
TIJUANA — MEXICALI
ENSENADA
SAN QUINTIN
SAN FELIPE
EL ROSARIO
CATAVINA
BAHIA DE LOS ANGELES
GUERRERO NEGRO
SAN IGNACIO
SANTA ROSALIA
MULEGE
LORETO
CIUDAD CONSTITUCION
LA PAZ
CABO SAN LUCAS

UNITED STATES
MEXICO

PACIFIC OCEAN

SEA OF CORTEZ

0   100mi
0   100km

= CALIFORNIAN REGION
= SAN FELIPE DESERT
= VIZCAINO DESERT
= GULF COAST DESERT
= MAGDALENA PLAINS
= CAPE REGION

© MOON PUBLICATIONS, INC.

Baja's highest peak, **Picacho del Diablo** (3,086 meters/10,154 feet), lies in the Sierra de San Pedro Mártir; during the winter its snowcapped peak can be seen from the Mexican mainland 225 km (140 miles) away.

Deserts

On a simple climatological basis, about 65% of Baja California's total land area can be classified as desert; these portions average less than 25 cm (10 inches) of rain per year. From a botanical perspective, Baja's desert lands belong to the Sonoran Desert, which extends across northwestern Mexico into parts of southeastern Alta California and southern Arizona. However, there are so many endemic plant species in Baja (see "Flora") that these areas probably deserve a classification all their own.

Any visitor who has previously traveled in the Sonoran Desert areas of northern Mexico, southeastern Alta California, or southern Arizona will note many subtle differences in their

Baja counterparts. Because of the peninsula's numerous sierras and its location between two large bodies of water, the aridity of any given area along the peninsula can vary considerably. Following this variation in elevation and aridity, Baja's deserts can be divided into four subregions, each distinguished by its own unique geography and the resultant dominance of one group of plant species over another.

San Felipe Desert: This southwestern extension of Alta California's Colorado Desert is wedged between the eastern escarpment of the northern sierras and the coastal plains of the Sea of Cortez. The peninsula's driest desert, it averages only five cm (two inches) of rainfall a year. Most of the topography is a mixture of saltflats, rocky plains, sand dunes, arroyos, and extinct volcanic craters.

The Valle de Mexicali is part of the San Felipe Desert, but is made productive by an irrigation system fed by the Colorado River. The large Isla Angel de la Guarda and nearby islands also belong to this region. The dominant plant species throughout the sparsely vegetated area are bursage (*huizapol* in Spanish) and creosote bush (*hediondilla*), along with a variety of succulents and hardy trees.

Gulf Coast Desert: This narrow subregion stretches along the Sea of Cortez from just below Bahía de los Angeles to the tip of the peninsula near San José del Cabo. On average, the elevation is substantially higher here (with peaks up to 1,500 meters) than in the San Felipe Desert to the north, and the terrain is marked by several broken sierras of granitic and volcanic rock. These sierras contain numerous arroyos and a few perennial streams that allow for pockets of subsistence farming. The underground stream at Mulegé supports intensive cultivation in the surrounding valley.

The southern reaches of the Gulf Coast Desert receive a bit of extra precipitation from the occasional tropical storm that blows in from the south. As a result of the added moisture and elevation, many more trees and flowering cacti are found here than in the San Felipe Desert, including **torote, palo blanco, ocotillo, cholla,** and **cirio** (the "boojum tree"). Sea of Cortez islands to the east feature similar terrain, although the endemic vegetation varies from island to island.

Vizcaíno Desert: After a worldwide search for the perfect desert habitat, the designers of **Biosphere II,** an ecological research laboratory in Arizona, modeled their dome's desert biome on the Vizcaíno Desert. The largest desert area in Baja, this subregion lies along the Pacific coast from a point just north of El Rosario to the Magdalena Plains some 1,000 km (600 miles) south. Its eastern boundary is the eastern escarpment of the central sierras. This positioning places it just out of reach of the northwestern rains, so important to coastal Alta California and northwestern Baja, as well as the southern tropical storms that bring water to the Cape Region and lower Gulf Coast Desert.

In spite of the lack of measurable precipitation, desert plants proliferate here. The entire region is sparsely populated because of the lack of dependable water sources, but the desert vegetation, especially **yucca,** thrives on night and morning fog from the Pacific Ocean. The whimsical-looking **cirio** is another dominant succulent in the Vizcaíno Desert; toward the Pacific coast it's often draped with ball moss. Other common species here include **agave, mesquite, cholla, prickly pear,** and **pitaya.**

The major coastal feature in this subregion is Laguna Ojo de Liebre, also called Scammon's Lagoon, one of several bays favored by wintering gray whales. The most substantial inland water source is the Río San Ignacio, which flows westward from a large date palm oasis in the heart of the peninsula into the open desert near the coast.

In 1988 a large portion of the Vizcaíno Desert was declared a Biosphere Reserve under the U.N.'s Man and the Biosphere program.

Magdalena Plains (Llano Magdalena): Beginning below the Vizcaíno Desert and bounded by the Pacific coast on the west and by the central and southern sierras on the east, the Magdalena Plains (or Llano Magdalena) extend southward until they come to an abrupt halt at the northwestern escarpment of the Sierra de la Laguna. The main feature of the Pacific side is Bahía Magdalena, Baja's largest bay, which is sheltered by the huge, L-shaped Isla Magdalena to the northwest and the equally large Isla Santa Margarita to the southwest. The Canal Gaviota connects Bahía Magdalena with Bahía Almejas to the immediate south. Other saltwater bays and lagoons along the Pacific coast include Bahía de Ballenas and Laguna San Ignacio; all are used as calving areas by migrating whales.

Other coastal features include mangrove swamps, dunes, and small sandbar islands. The only inland waterway of note is the Río La Purísima, which drops westward from the Sierra de la Giganta to Punta San Gregorio on the Pacific coast. Large underground aquifers in the vicinity of Ciudad Constitución support intensive area agriculture. The aquifer is becoming increasingly saline, however, as fresh water is pumped out faster than it's replenished. A number of arroyos on the west side of the Sierra de la Giganta supply water to the area when rainfall is sufficient.

Cactus varieties are abundant throughout the Magdalena Plains. Stands of **date palm, palo verde, torote, mesquite,** and **palo blanco** line the riverine corridors and upland arroyos.

The Vizcaíno Desert and the Magdalena Plains are sometimes referred to as one entity, the **Central Desert.**

Californian Region

Most of northwestern Baja California features the same topography, climate, and ecosystems as southwestern Alta California. These conditions extend almost as far south as El Rosario, near the Pacific coast, and eastward to the eastern escarpment of the Sierra Juárez and Sierra de San Pedro Mártir. Within this region are four subregions, for the most part defined by changes in elevation from the coast to the highest mountain peaks in the center of the peninsula.

Conifer Forests: This subregion begins at an elevation of about 1,500 meters (4,920 feet) in the Sierra Juárez and from about 2,400 meters (7,872 feet) in the Sierra de San Pedro Mártir. The granitic substrata of these fault-block mountains becomes more apparent the higher you go, as rocky ledges poke through soil and sediment accumulated over the eons. Abundant precipitation supports lush forests and meadows along the flats, ridges, and plateaus of both ranges. During the winter, snow is the most common source of moisture in the higher elevation; peaks are often snowcapped.

Dominant trees in the Sierra Juárez include the **canyon live oak, juniper, piñon pine,** and **Jeffrey pine.** The forests of the Sierra de San Pedro Mártir also feature **incense cedar, white** fir, and **sugar pine,** and at least three tree types not found in either the Sierra Juárez or San Diego County farther north in Alta California: **quaking aspen, lodgepole pine,** and the endemic **San Pedro Mártir cypress.** Along the streams and meadows at slightly lower elevations are **manzanita, Indian paintbrush, hedgehog cactus, snowberry,** and a number of other flowering plants.

Pine-Juniper-Oak Woodlands: On the intermediate slopes of the two sierras, at elevations of about 900 to 1,500 meters (3,000 to 5,000 feet), are stands of pine, oak, and juniper. The lower southern reaches of the Sierra de San Pedro Mártir offer a Darwinian salad of conifer, chaparral, and desert species, mixing pines and juniper with **blue fan palm, Mojave yucca, palmita, sagebrush, sand verbena,** and **barrel cactus.**

Chaparral: At just below 900 meters on either side of the mountain ranges, the woodlands give way to chaparral, a dense shrub community that supports **sagebrush, scrub oak, wild lilac, manzanita, coast live oak, chaparral ash** and other hardy species with deep-branching root systems. Interspersed with the chaparral are boulders of varying size; some of the larger are used as billboards by Baja-californios, who paint them with political slogans, declarations of love, and religious messages.

The **palm canyons** of the eastern slopes lie at chaparral elevation, but because of the abundance of year-round water, they feature unique terrains of their own. Eroded by mountain streams that terminate in the San Felipe Desert, these canyons and steep-walled arroyos shelter picturesque groves of

California fan palm and the endemic **blue fan palm.** Volcanic activity on the eastern side of the peninsula has resulted in underground geothermal reservoirs; hot springs are found in some of the canyons where water seeps to the surface.

Coastal Sage Scrub: On the Sea of Cortez side of the northern mountain ranges, the chaparral subregion gives way to the arid San Felipe Desert. On the Pacific side, chaparral fades into the rolling hills of the coastal plains. The terrain is rocky, with a blend of chaparral vegetation and the low-lying shrubs that dominate the coastal sage-scrub biome. Common species include **chamise, barrel cactus, agave, ash, cholla, flat-top buckwheat, hedgehog cactus, jimson weed, margarita, buckeye, jojoba, saltbush,** and a variety of grasses.

BOB RACE

Cape Region

In many ways, Baja California's Cape Region has the most distinctive geography on the peninsula. The Sierra de la Laguna, in the center of the cape itself, runs north to south rather than northwest to southeast; unlike other ranges in the southern half of the peninsula, it's granitic rather than volcanic. Yet in contrast to the granitic, fault-block ranges of northern Baja, it tips eastward so that its steepest slopes face west. It's also more lushly vegetated than the northern sierras. Arroyos on the eastern slopes of Sierra de la Laguna are filled with water much of the year, enabling this area to support fruit and vegetable farming.

The entire region receives substantially more rainfall than any other part of Baja California, save the Californian Region in the northeast. Most of the rain falls in the highland areas, however, leaving the coastal lowlands fairly dry and highly attractive to beachgoing tourists. About a fourth of the Cape Region falls below the Tropic of Cancer; the combination of dry coastal areas, moist uplands, and tropical latitudes has created two unique subregions.

Cape Oak-Piñon Woodlands: The Sierra de la Laguna has been called an "island in the sky" because of its remarkable isolation from the Central Desert to the north and the Gulf Coast Desert to the east. At its very top, the peaks receive up to 100 cm (40 inches) of annual rainfall; at higher elevations are extensive stands of **Mexican piñon pine** and endemic oaks such as **madroño** and **palmita.** Oaks are also found on the higher slopes of the Sierra de la Giganta to the north, which falls within the Cape Region as well.

Cape Arid Tropical Forest: The coastal areas of the Cape Region as well as the lower slopes of la Laguna and la Giganta sierras share characteristics typical of both tropical and arid biomes, hence the seemingly oxymoronic term "arid tropical forest." Like tropical forests worldwide, the lower Cape forests produce trees, shrubs, and undergrowth of varying heights that create a canopied effect. Mixed with this tangled growth are a profusion of succulents more associated with arid climes, including the **cardón-barbón,** a shorter cousin of the towering cardón found throughout Baja's deserts.

Much of the vegetation in the Cape Arid Tropical Forest is normally associated with the tropical thorn forests of coastal Colima and Guerrero on the Mexican mainland. Prominent marker plants unique to the Cape subregion include the native **Tlaco palm, wild fig** (*zalate*), *mauto,* and the alleged aphrodisiac herb **damiana.**

Coastal Wetlands Region

Wetland pockets exist in numerous spots along the peninsular coast; they lie in shallow areas along bays and lagoons and aren't limited to any particular longitude or latitude. In Baja, these wetlands usually consist of **salt marshes,** which contain high concentrations of salt-tolerant plants such as cordgrass, eelgrass, saltwort, and salt cedar, or **mangrove** (*mangle*) communities containing one or more of the five species common in Baja—black mangrove, white mangrove, red mangrove, buttonwood mangrove, and sweet mangrove. Within any given wetland, there can be considerable variances in salinity, temperature, and wetness; hence, an extensive variety of plants and animals can adapt to wetland areas. Because of this environmental variation, salt marshes and mangrove wetlands represent the most concentrated biomass areas on the planet. For most visitors, the main attraction of the wetlands is the abundance of waterfowl.

Areas with substantial wetlands include Bahía San Quintín (salt marshes), Laguna Ojo de Liebre (saltwater estuarine marshes), Laguna San Ignacio (salt marshes, mangrove forests), Bahía Magdalena (salt marshes, mangrove forests), Bahía

BOB RACE

red mangrove

de la Paz (mangrove forests), Río Mulegé (mixed saltwater/freshwater estuarine marshes), Estero San Bruno (mangrove forests), Bahía de los Angeles (salt marshes, some mangrove), and Bahía San Luis Gonzaga (salt marshes).

Islands

Around 50 islands and islets surround the Baja peninsula, with the great preponderance on the Sea of Cortez side. Many of the Sea of Cortez islands were created as the peninsula broke away from mainland Mexico and hence are "land-bridge" or "continental" islands rather than true oceanic islands. Because of their low elevation, these islands don't snag much of the rain that moves up from the south in summer. As a result, they're quite arid, although the larger islands harbor a number of endemic plant and animal species. Among the largest of these islands are Isla Angel de la Guarda, Isla Espíritu Santo, and Isla Cerralvo. The smaller Isla San Luis and Isla Raza are of volcanic origin.

On the Pacific side, Baja's islands tend to feature semi-moist Californian Region climates on their northwestern (windward) shores and desertic conditions on their southeastern (leeward) shores. Isla Guadalupe, about 250 km (155 miles) west of the Pacific coast, is one of the few islands of volcanic (therefore, oceanic) origin. It's rarely visited by cruising boats because of its steep (up to 450 meters) shores but is an important habitat for the endemic **Guadalupe fur seal** and **northern elephant seal,** as well as various species of endemic pine, cypress, and palm.

Other Pacific islands of note are the much closer Islas de Todos Santos, just 16 km (10 miles) southwest of Ensenada. These twin isles are well-known among surfers for having the highest surf—up to 30 feet high in winter—on the entire North American west coast. Isla Cedros, 24 km (15 miles) north of the Vizcaíno Peninsula, is one of the few Baja islands inhabited by humans. It's used as a transshipment port for salt from the huge Guerrero evaporative saltworks.

THE SEA OF CORTEZ

The Sea of Cortez was apparently named by Francisco de Ulloa after he sailed the entire perimeter of this body of water in 1539 and 1540 at the command of the most infamous of all Spanish conquistadors, Hernán Cortés. Four years previously Cortés had himself sailed the sea in an aborted attempt to colonize the peninsula. The name Mar de Cortés henceforth appeared intermittently on maps of the region, alternating with Mar Vermejo (Vermillion Sea, in reference to the color reflected from huge numbers of pelagic crabs) until the Mexican government officially renamed it the Gulf of California (Golfo de California) early in this century. Sailors, writers, and other assorted romanticists, however, have continued to call it by its older name.

The sea is roughly 1,125 km (700 miles) long, with an average width of 150 km (93 miles). Oceanographers have divided it into four regions based on the prominent characteristics—depth, bottom contours, and marine productivity—of each zone. The northern quarter of the gulf, between the Colorado River delta and the Midriff Islands, is shallow in relation to the zones farther south because of silt deposited by the Colorado River, which has also rounded the bottom contours. The sea here is highly saline due to evaporation and there is a tidal range of up to 10 meters (30 feet). Before the damming of the Colorado River, the tidal bore created when the seaward river currents met the incoming tide was powerful enough to sink ships.

The second region south encompasses the Midriff Islands, where basins reach depths of 820 meters (2,700 feet) and strong currents bring nutrients up from the bottom while aerating the water. This leads to a unusually high level of biological productivity, otherwise known as "good fishin'."

From the Midriff Islands to La Paz, basin depth doubles, silting is minimal, and water temperatures begin decreasing dramatically. The final sea zone below La Paz is oceanic, with trenches and submarine canyons over 3,600 meters (12,000 feet) deep. Around the tip of the cape, the Sea of Cortez meets the Pacific Ocean, a point at which the currents from each meet to produce some wicked riptides. This means that although the tip of the cape is the warmest area on the peninsula during the winter months, beach swimming can be rather treacherous.

Of the 25 named islands in the Sea of Cortez, the largest is Isla Tiburón ("Shark Island"), a geological remnant of the mainland with an area of around 1,000 square kilometers. Because of their isolation, the Cortez islands feature a high number of endemic natural species; at least half of the 120 cactus varieties found on the islands are endemic. The Sea of Cortez is biologically the richest body of water on the planet, with over 800 species of marine vertebrates and over 2,000 invertebrates at last count. The reported number rises with the publication of each new marine study.

CLIMATE

In satellite photographs of the North American continent snapped a hundred miles above the earth, Baja California invariably jumps off the plate. The rest of the continent north and east may be obscured by whorls of clouds while the shores, plains, and mountains of Baja are carved into the photographic image, remarkably clear. In 1991, the truth-in-travel magazine *Condé-Nast Traveler* named Baja California the best dollar value per hour of sunshine for any North American area west of Denver. According to the survey, the chances of a day without rain in the winter are 95% in Baja, beating out Hawaii's 84% and Florida's 87%.

How does Baja California get so much sunshine? The simple answer is that it's positioned almost out of reach of the major weather systems that influence climate in western North America and along the Pacific coast of mainland Mexico. Northwesterly storms from Eurasia and the Arctic bring rain and snow to the American Northwest and Midwest all winter long, while tropical storms roll across the South Pacific from Asia, dumping loads of rainfall along the lower Mexican coast and Central America in the summer.

Baja is only slightly influenced by the outer edges of these systems. Anchored between the warm, fish-filled waters of the Sea of Cortez and the heaving Pacific Ocean, bisected by plains and cordilleras, the peninsula's isolated ecosystems range in climate from Mediterranean to desert to tropical. In some areas, overlapping microclimates defy classification, combining elements of semiarid, arid, subtropical, and tropical climes.

WET AND DRY

The "Land of Little Rain," as Baja has been called by one fanciful author, isn't unique in its aridity since most of the earth's desert areas are found between 15° and 30° latitudes either north or south of the equator; Baja is positioned roughly between 23° N and 31° N latitudes. Global convection currents in the atmosphere create a more or less permanent high-pressure shield over these zones, insulating them from the low-pressure fronts that bring rain clouds.

Only about two-thirds of Baja California can be classified as true desert (less than 25 cm of annual precipitation), and even the driest areas receive occasional rain. In the peninsula's Central Desert this may be as little as 2.5 cm a year, while in the interior of the Cape Region's Sierra de la Laguna annual rainfall may appoach 100 cm (40 inches). Since mountain peaks trap rain clouds, Baja's higher elevations invariably receive more rain than the low-lying coastal zones.

Variation in rainfall also occurs on a seasonal basis. For the northwestern peninsula, the wettest months are Dec.-April (with about 7.5 cm per month in Ensenada, more in the mountains) while in the Cape Region rain usually arrives Aug.-Nov. (an average of 5.8 cm in September for Cabo San Lucas and La Paz). The central peninsula, including both coasts, is relatively dry all year long, receiving only brief spurts of rain from the north in the winter and from the south in the late summer and early fall.

The driest coastal area in all of Baja lies along the northwestern shores of the Sea of Cortez. San Felipe records an average annual precipitation of only five cm, with no measurable rainfall most months. At the other extreme, the peaks of the Sierra de San Pedro Mártir are

ESTIMATING
TEMPERATURE CHANGES

For every degree of latitude farther south you travel, figure a temperature increase of 2° C (3.5° F). For each 100-meter increase in elevation, figure a temperature drop of 2° C.

often covered with a one-meter snowpack during the winter.

HOT AND COLD

Three variables influence temperatures at any given Baja California location: elevation, latitude, and longitude. In plain talk, that means the higher you climb, the cooler it gets; the farther south you go, the warmer it gets; and it's always cooler on the Pacific side of the peninsula and warmer on the Sea of Cortez side.

Pacific Coast
Because of prevailing ocean currents, the Pacific coast shows the least overall variation in temperatures, staying relatively cool year-round. From March to July, the California Current flows southward along the coast, bringing cooler temperatures from the north that moderate seasonal atmospheric warming, while in December and January the coast is warmed by the northward movement of the Davidson Current. These seasonal currents stabilize the air temperatures so that Ensenada, for example, averages 12° C (54° F) in January and 20° C (70° F) in August, a range of only 8° C (16° F). Along much of the central Pacific coast during the summer, the cool air brought by the California Current meets warm air from the interior of the peninsula, resulting in fog masses that can sweep as far inland as 32 km (20 miles).

Sea Of Cortez
The Sea of Cortez has its own set of currents, sometimes lumped together as the Gulf Current, fed by tropical waters of the South Pacific travelling in a counterclockwise direction north along the mainland's upper Pacific coast and then south along the peninsular coast. As a result, the Sea of Cortez enjoys an average annual surface temperature of 24° C (75° F), significantly warmer than the Pacific's 18° C (64° F). The high rate of evaporation at the north end of the sea also contributes to warmer air temperatures; this combination of warm air and water temperatures means the Sea of Cortez can be classified as "tropical" over its entire length.

The weather along this coast is warm and sunny all winter long with average January temperatures ranging from 13° C (55° F) in San Felipe to 18° C (64° F) in Loreto. In August, average temperatures are 28° C (82° F) in San Felipe and 31° C (88° F) in Loreto, although daily high figures in the summer, at either locale, can easily reach 38° C (100° F) or more. La Paz is usually warmer than San Felipe but cooler than Loreto.

Chubascos, Coromuels, And Cordonazos
Monthly average wind velocities for Baja California as a whole are quite low. From mid-May to mid-November, however, tropical storms from the south or east, known as *chubascos,* can bring high winds and rain to the coasts of the Cape Region. Although they usually blow over quickly, local mythology has it that if a chubasco lasts more than three hours, it will last a day; if it lasts more than a day, it will last three days; and if more than three days, it'll be a five-day blow.

Another Sea of Cortez weather pattern is the *cordonazo,* a small but fierce summer storm that originates locally and is usually spent within a few hours. A more welcome weather phenomenon is the *coromuel* of Bahía de La Paz, a stiff afternoon breeze that blows from offshore during the hot summer and early fall months. This wind was named for the English Lord Protector Cromwell, identified with English pirates who took advantage of the wind's regular occurrence for the plunder of ships trapped in the bay.

BEST SEASONS FOR TRAVEL

Northwestern Baja: Tijuana, Tecate, Rosarito, And Ensenada
This area lies within the Californian Region and is affected by the mild Pacific climate. Hence, it's fairly comfortable all year round, very much like Alta California's San Diego County. Although rain is almost never heavy or frequent, even in the winter months, you can usually avoid all rain by planning visits here for anytime from May to October. The beaches between Rosarito and Ensenada are warmest in July, August, and September, when they're most visited by southern Alta Californians. To get away from the crowds and enjoy low-season prices, visit between October and April.

High Sierras

For those who like to travel light, the summer months are best for mountain hiking; even in July everything above 1,500 meters (5,000 feet) will feel like spring. From mid-October to mid-April, come prepared for winter camping for hikes at similar elevations.

To appreciate the beauty of spring flowers, the best hiking season is just after the end of the rainy seasons. For the northern ranges, i.e., Sierra Juárez and San Pedro Mártir, this means April and May. For the Sierra de la Laguna in the Cape Region, October or early November is best. The Cape's rainy season occurs from late summer to early fall.

Deserts

Inland desert explorations should be absolutely avoided May-October when daytime temperatures are fierce. The remaining cooler months are usually fine, although in the Central Desert, January daytime temperatures may be a bit on the cool side in areas exposed to high coastal winds or at higher elevations. The San Felipe and Gulf Coast deserts are usually warm and comfortable throughout the winter. Keep in mind, however, that desert nights can be cold at any time of year.

Sea Of Cortez

Along Baja's Sea of Cortez coasts, temperatures are moderate October through mid-June. High tourist season is November through March, even though for most people the north coast is too cool for swimming during these months. Days and nights grow progressively warmer as you move south, so that water sports are enjoyable from Loreto down, even in the winter.

From mid-June through September, the entire coast can be uncomfortably hot; the fishing, however, is usually very good during these months and out on the sea it's usually breezy. But if you don't fish, forget it. One of the best times to visit the Sea of Cortez coast is April to mid-June, when the weather is balmy and few tourists are about.

Cape Region

The flat end of the peninsula from San José del Cabo to Cabo San Lucas is warm year-round. Pacific influences generally moderate the heat July-September while the tropic waters of the Gulf Current make this stretch the warmest coastal zone on the peninsula during winter months. Except for the occasional chubasco in late summer, the climate seems darn near perfect here, which is why "Los Cabos" has become such a popular vacation destination. Cabo San Lucas receives about 45% of its measurable annual rainfall—a total of 15-18 cm a year—in September, so if there's a month to avoid for weather reasons, that's the one.

The two months when you're least likely to have Los Cabos beaches to yourself are December and January, when large numbers of North Americans come here seeking respite from rainstorms and blizzards.

FLORA

A thorough examination of all the plants and creatures of interest in Baja California would take volumes. The following sections cover only a few of either the most remarkable or most common forms of plant life in Baja. In truth, the peninsula and its islands remain relatively unexplored with regard to the complex interconnecting ecosystems responsible for the high number of solitary species. Several botanists, marine biologists, zoologists, and paleontologists have undertaken solo research in the area, but only in the last four years has the first interdisciplinary team, sponsored by a Canadian university, begun studying the region.

In many ways, these researchers are heir to the Spanish fortune-seeker tradition of nearly five centuries ago. As George Lindsay, director of the California Academy of Sciences, has said, "For the scientist, Baja California is a treasure chest, just barely opened." Botanists estimate that over 4,000 varieties of plants make Baja California their home. The most complete reference available on Baja vegetation, Dr. Ira L. Wiggins's *Flora of Baja California*, lists 2,958 species among 155 families and 884 genera. Another good source of information is Norman C. Roberts' recently published *Baja California Plant Field Guide,* which covers over 550 notable species and provides excellent photos of about half of these.

CACTUS AND SUCCULENTS

Many visitors find the desert plants of Baja the most exciting simply because they're often the most exotic-appearing forms of life in the region. Like Alice in *Through The Looking Glass,* they find that the farther they travel into the interior, the "curiouser and curiouser" the landscape becomes. The seemingly bizarre appearance of many succulents is due to the evolutionary gymnastics they've had to perform to adapt themselves to an environment where water is scarce.

Cactaceae

Around 120 species of cactus have been identified on the peninsula and its surrounding islands, more than anywhere else on the planet. Almost three-fourths are unique to Baja.

One of the most common cacti throughout Baja is the towering **cardón** (*Pachycereus pringlei*), the world's tallest species of cactus. Individuals can reach as high as 18 meters (60

barrel cactus

JOE CUMMINGS

feet) or more and weigh 12 tons, not counting the root system, which can spread up to 50 meters (150 feet) in diameter. More commonly they top out at seven to nine meters. The giant, pale green trunks feature 11-17 vertical ribs and may measure one meter thick. The cardón is often confused with the smaller saguaro cactus of Sonora and Arizona; one major difference is that the branches of the cardón tend to be more vertical than those of the saguaro.

The cardón is near-endemic to Baja California, found throughout the peninsula—except in the Californian Region—and islands, and also along the coast of Sonora. The hardwood cores of cardón columns have been used by Bajacalifornios for centuries as building beams and fence posts. Among Baja residents, a cardón forest is called a *cardonal.* Some individuals live over 400 years.

Another extremely common and highly visible cactus is the **biznaga** or **barrel cactus** (genus *Ferocactus*). There are at least 15 species in Baja, most endemic. Its English name refers to its shape, which is short and squat like a barrel. Most common varieties reach about waist-high. One variety, however, *Ferocactus diguettii*, growing only on a few Sea of Cortez islands, easily reaches four meters (13 feet) in height and a meter (3.28 feet) in diameter. The spines of this cactus are often tinged red; from March to June the tops bloom with gorgeous yellow to red flowers. The indigenous Indians of Baja reportedly used hollowed-out biznaga as Dutch ovens by inserting food into the cavity along with heated stones, then sealing the cactus off till the food was cooked. The sturdy, curved spines also served as fishhooks in native fishing expeditions.

Among Baja's original populations, another of the most important cacti was the **pitahaya dulce,** known among Anglos as **organ pipe cactus.** The spiny, orange-size fruit of the pitahaya (also spelled pitaya) contains a sweet, juicy, pleasant-tasting pulp the color of red watermelon. According to Spanish mission accounts, the Pericú Indians figured their yearly calendar according to the harvest of the ripe fruit in late summer and early fall. During this season, the Indians engaged in a veritable fruit orgy, gorging themselves on the pulp until they fell asleep, then waking to begin eating again. The early Spanish explorers took the fruit along on long sea journeys to prevent scurvy.

The pitahaya dulce has slender, vertical ribs that grow in clusters and is commonly found on the peninsula south of the Sierra de San Borja, on several Sea of Cortez islands, and in Sonora and southern Arizona. A similar species, **pitahaya agria** (*agria* means sour in Spanish; *dulce* is sweet), branches more densely and lower to the ground, hence its English name **galloping cactus.** It grows throughout the peninsula and on most Sea of Cortez islands. The fruit of the pitahaya agria is quite similar in appearance to that of the pitahaya dulce but, as implied by the Spanish name, it's less sweet, more acidic. Both types of pitahaya fruit remain popular among Baja residents and travelers.

Another cactus variety well represented throughout Baja is the genus *Opuntia,* which includes all types known as **cholla** as well as the **nopal,** or **prickly pear.** Cholla are a bane to Baja hikers because they're so prolific, with the spines on any given plant especially numerous. All true chollas belong to the subgenus *Cylindropuntia* and are multibranched, multijointed, and cylindric-stemmed. The typical branch looks somewhat like braided or twisted rope. Historically speaking, cholla has had few domestic uses although a tea made from the roots of the fuzzy-looking **teddy-bear cholla** (also called "jumping cholla" for its propensity to cling to the lower legs of hikers), found along the east coast of the peninsula, is reportedly used by the Seri Indians as a diuretic.

In contrast, the much-loved prickly pear cactus (subgenus *Platyopuntia*) has broad, flat stems and branches and a sparser distribution of spines. In northern Mexico and Baja its fleshy pads are a dietary staple. The most highly prized parts of the nopal are the young stem shoots, called *nopalitos,* and the ripe fruits, dubbed *tuna.* The flavor of the pads is a bit bland, like a cross between bell pepper and okra. The fruit, on the other hand, is juicy and sweet, available in season in many Baja markets. If you want to taste it in the wild, remove the tunas carefully, cut them lengthwise with a sharp knife, and scoop out the insides with a spoon. Nine species of nopal are found in Baja, including the endemic *tuna tapona* found south of Loreto.

Agavaceae

One of the most common and striking desert plants is the **yucca,** which appears in several

yucca

varieties throughout Baja. Yuccas belong to the Agave family, of which Baja has 19 species, including 11 endemics. The largest is the **tree yucca** (*Yucca valida*), called *datilillo* or "little date" for its resemblance to a date palm. The average datilillo grows in clusters three to seven meters tall, the dagger-like blades supported by long woody trunks. This endemic is found throughout the desert plains and chaparral subregions of the peninsula—just about anywhere except in the mountains. The best place to view it in numbers is on the Pacific side of the Vizcaíno Desert where it's the dominant plant.

Yuccas are extremely useful plants for rural Bajacalifornios. The fruit and flowers are edible (a candy called *colache* is made from the cooked flower buds), the roots can be boiled to make soap or leather softener, and the tough leaf fibers are used to make cordage, sandals, baskets, and mats. In some parts of central Baja you may see fences made from packed-together datilillo stalks, which often take root and produce a living fence.

Very similar to yucca is another member of the Agave family called **sotol** (genus *Nolina*). The leaves of a sotol are narrower and softer than those of a yucca; some sotols also produce long flower stalks similar to those of the century plant, though the flower buds occur along the entire length of the stalk instead of only at the top.

Perhaps the most spectacular variety of sotol in Baja is the endemic *Nolina beldingii,* sometimes called *palmita* because of its resemblance to a small palm tree. Taller individuals reach up to seven meters in height, with a complex of thick leaf clusters branching from a short, woody trunk. The palmita grows most commonly along the higher elevations of the Cape Region; isolated stands also exist in mountain areas northwest of Mulegé, north of Bahía de los Angeles, and on Volcán Las Tres Vírgenes.

More common in Baja are the many varieties of **maguey,** commonly called the century plant. Yet another member of the sizable Agave family, the maguey has broad, closely clustered leaves that grow at ground level without a visible trunk. In most species, the plant only flowers once in its lifetime, sending up a tall, slender stalk after maturation—typically at 5-20 years, depending on variety and locale. Early Anglo settlers in the southwestern U.S. spread the myth that agaves bloomed only once in a hundred years, hence the fanciful name "century plant."

The maguey constituted a very important food source to certain aboriginal populations, who harvested the plant just before it bloomed, when it's full of concentrated nutrients. Trimmed of its leaves, the heart of the plant was baked in an underground pit for one to three days, then eaten or stored. Some ranchers still prepare the agave in this manner today; as with datilillo, the leaf fibers are used as cordage for weaving various household goods.

Fouquieriaceae

This family of succulents contains what many travelers consider to be the plant most symbolic of Baja—the **cirio,** or "boojum tree." Most naturalists describe the cirio by likening it to an inverted carrot, since the plant's tall stalk is thickest near the ground and very gradually tapers along its height until it reaches a skinny point at the top. The Spanish name *cirio* ("candle")

seems far more evocative when one compares the plant to the slender wax tapers typically found on mission altars. In times of abundant rain, the cirio even puts forth at its tip a golden bloom resembling a flaring candle flame.

In height, the cirio is second only to Baja's cardón cactus, with mature plants extending 12-15 meters (40-50 feet) high from a base 30 cm or so in diameter. Since a cirio on average grows only three cm a year (or a foot every 10 years), a 15-meter individual is around 500 years old.

The whimsical name "boojum" was bestowed ad hoc upon the cirio by Arizona botanist Godfrey Sykes during a 1922 expedition to Baja. Sykes had apparently been reading Lewis Carroll's *Hunting of the Snark,* a tale which mentioned an imaginary boojum without describing it except to say it inhabited "distant shores." In this sense Sykes's spontaneous epithet was indeed descriptive since the cirio only grows in a relatively narrow, 320-km-wide band between the 30th and 27th parallels on the Baja penin-

cirio

sula; the exception is a small cirio colony near La Libertad in Sonora, at the same latitude. Although the cirio is abundant within this area, the area itself is rather distant from the tourist centers of northwestern Baja, Loreto, and Los Cabos.

Because of its uniqueness, some botanists award the cirio with its own genus, *Idria,* within the Fouquieria family, so the Latin name can appear as either *Fouquieria columnaris* or *Idria columnaris.* Like all plants in this family, the white-barked cirio sprouts tiny leaves over the entire plant surface when there's sufficient rainfall. During long periods of dry weather, the leaves drop off to conserve the internal water supply.

Much more common throughout Baja's desert lands are two other members of the Fouquieria family, the **ocotillo** and *palo adán* ("Adam's tree"). The ocotillo (*Fouquieria splendens*) features long, whip-like branches that radiate directly from the ground in a shape comparable to an exploding shell. In the southwestern U.S., it's sometimes known as a "coachwhip." As with the cirio, tiny leaves come and go on ocotillo stems according to changing weather conditions. After a good rainfall, a mature (two meters or more) plant puts forth droopy red blossoms at the end of each branch.

Ocotillo grows profusely in all the desert regions of Baja north of the 28th parallel and as far northeast as New Mexico and Texas, occasionally appearing as far south as Bahía Concepcíon. A rare endemic species, *Fouquieria burragei,* (*ocotillo de flor*), is distinguished by its salmon-pink flowers and grows between Bahía Concepcíon and La Paz and on a few Sea of Cortez islands. *Rancheros* use ocotillo branches for fencing, shade ramadas, and as bracing in adobe construction.

At about the point on the peninsula where ocotillo begins fading, its cousin the *palo adán* (*Fouquieria diguettii*) begins making an appearance. Looking like a larger ocotillo, the Adam's tree has considerably thicker branches radiating from a short, woody trunk. The leaves, when present, are slightly larger than the ocotillo's, while the flowers are smaller. In the Bahía de los Angeles area, ocotillo and Adam's tree often grow side by side. The latter is also popular as a fencing material and makes excellent firewood when dry.

TREES

Palms

Seven varieties of palm grow wild in Baja California; four are native to the peninsula and islands while three are introduced species. Palms are very important to the local economy in the southern half of the peninsula, where they're most common. The long, straight trunks are used as roof beams, the leaves are used in basketry and for roof and wall thatching, and the fruits provide a source of nutrition.

Among the most handsome Baja palm trees is the endemic **blue fan palm** or *palma azul,* which reaches up to 24 meters (78 feet) tall and sports bluish, fan-shaped leaves at its crown. The 4.5-meter flower stalks, which usually appear February through March, often extend well below the shag, or thatch of dead leaves below the crown. The blue fan palm typically grows in the canyons and arroyos of the Sierra Juárez and in similar locales as far south as San Ignacio.

Another native variety, the **Tlaco palm** (also called *palma palmia* and *palma colorado*), is common in the canyons and arroyos of the Cape Region sierras below Loreto. The smooth, slender trunks, crowned by fan-shaped leaves, stand up to 20 meters (65.5 feet) tall. A closely related species, the **Guadalupe Island palm,** is native to Isla Guadalupe; its self-shedding trunk (leaving little or no shag) has made it highly popular as a cultivated palm in southern Alta California.

Baja's tallest palm variety is the endemic **Mexican fan palm** (also Baja California fan palm, skyduster, or *palma blanca*) which reaches heights of 27-30 meters (90-100 feet). As the name implies, its leaves are fan-shaped; the length of the trunk means the tree is highly productive for local construction use although it's not as durable as the Tlaco palm. The tree's native habitats are the Sierra de la Giganta and Isla Angel de la Guarda, but it's also spread west of Cataviña and reached southern Alta California as an ornamental import. More common in the northern peninsula is the similar, but shorter, **California fan palm.**

Two palm varieties were imported to Baja for their fruit value. The **date palm** was introduced to Baja by Jesuit missionaries and is now common near former mission sites, including Loreto, Comondú, Mulegé, San Ignacio, and San José del Cabo. The tree typically reaches 15-20 meters tall at maturity; the oblong fruit grows beneath feather-shaped leaves in large clusters, turning from pale yellow to dark brown as it ripens. Baja dates are eaten locally and shipped to mainland Mexico but are generally not considered of high enough quality for export. The 30-meter, feather-leafed **coconut palm** commonly grows along coastal areas of the Cape Region as far north as Mulegé and is an important local food source.

Elephant Trees
At least two different species from completely different plant families have received the name "elephant tree." The first, which some Baja experts claim is the only "true" elephant tree, is the sumac family's *Pachycormus discolor,* called either *copalquín* or *torote blanco.* The English name refers to the thick, gray, gnarled-looking trunks and branches. Travelers to East Africa may note a resemblance to the baobab tree.

The papery bark of the elephant tree continually peels off in sheets to reveal the dark green, spongy inner trunk. Drought-deciduous leaves form on the branches when rainfall is sufficient; between May and September small pink flowers may bloom for a few weeks, casting a pink glow over the whole. This endemic species is often seen in the same central desert areas that feature cirios. It's particularly prolific in volcanic soils and lava flows.

The second elephant tree, very similar in appearance to the *Pachycormus* but belonging to the torchwood family, is the *Bursera odorata.* Like the other elephant tree, the *Bursera* has thick, gnarled trunks and branches; the thin bark also peels off in papery sheets. The inner trunk is yellow, however, rather than dark green. This one grows south of Bahía Concepcíon and on the Mexican mainland only. The Spanish name for the tree is the same as for the "true" elephant tree, *torote blanco.* A close relative, the *torote colorado* (another *Bursera*), has a reddish bark. It's found throughout the deserts of Baja and on many Sea of Cortez islands, as well as in Alta California's Anza-Borrego Desert.

Conifers
The high sierras of Baja support a surprising number and variety of conifers, including species of cypress, cedar, juniper, fir, and pine. Among the most interesting because of its relative confinement to the Baja region is the **Tecate cypress,** found on the western slopes of the Sierra Juárez and in the Valle San Vicente, as well as in southern Alta California north to Orange County. Likewise, the **San Pedro Mártir Cypress** is confined to the eastern escarpment of the Sierra de San Pedro Mártir, the **Cedros Island Pine** is found only on Isla Cedros, and the **Guadalupe Island Pine** grows only on Isla Guadalupe.

Other, more common conifer varieties found at higher elevations include **incense cedar, Mormon tea, white fir, piñon pine, Jeffrey pine, sugar pine, bishop pine,** and **lodgepole pine.**

elephant tree

JOE CUMMINGS

Oaks

Varieties of oak (*encino*) abound along the Pacific slopes of the northern sierras and in the canyons, arroyos, and meadows of the two Cape Region sierras. Of the many species found in Baja, four are endemic: the **cape oak,** found in the canyons and arroyos of the Cape Region sierras; **black oak,** confined to the lower slopes of the Cape Region; **Cedros Island oak,** on Isla Cedros, and from San Vicente south to Sierra San Borja; and **peninsular oak,** on the lower slopes of the northern and central sierras. Other common oaks are **coast live oak, canyon live oak, white oak, scrub oak, mesa blue oak,** and **Palmer oak.**

Mimosas

This subfamily of the Leguminosae or pea family represents dozens of genera common to arid and semiarid zones all over the world. Characterized by linear seedpods and double rows of tiny leaves, common varieties in Baja include the **mesquite** and various endemic kinds of **acacia.**

Indians have long used the trunk, roots, leaves, beans, and bark of the mesquite tree for a variety of purposes, from lumber to medicine. Ground mesquite leaves mixed with water form a balm for sore eyes, a remedy still used by *curanderos* (healers) in rural Mexico today. Chewing the leaves relieves toothache. Mesquite gum has also been used by various tribes as a balm for wounds, ceramic glue, dye, and digestive.

Mesquite beans are a good source of nutrition—a ripe bean pod, growing as long as nine inches, contains roughly 30% glucose and is high in protein. Many animals and birds savor the beans; horses will eat them until they're sick. Rural Mexicans grind the dried pods into a flour with which they make bread and a kind of beer. The Seri Indians, who live along the Sonoran coast of the Sea of Cortez, have separate names for eight different stages of the bean pod's development.

One of the prettiest endemic mimosas is the **palo blanco,** which has a tall, slender trunk with silver-white bark and a feathery crown that produces small, white, fragrant blossoms March-May. This tree is found the length of the peninsula although it's most easily seen in the Sierra de la Giganta and in the vicinity of Loreto.

Wild Figs

Three types of *Ficus* trees (*zalate*), one endemic, are common in peninsular Baja. Most are found in rocky areas of the Cape Region. In the village of La Playita, east of San José del Cabo, is a venerable stand of zalates of impressive stature.

Willows

Various cottonwoods (*alamo*) and willows (*sauz*) grow in higher elevations throughout the peninsula. The endemic ***huerivo*** (*Populus brandegeei*) is a beautiful endemic cottonwood found in the canyons and arroyos of the Cape Region Sierras. The tall, straight trunks reach heights of 30 meters and are highly valued as lumber for construction and furniture-making.

An unlikely Baja find is the **quaking aspen** (*Populus tremuloides*), growing in high mountain meadows of the Sierra de San Pedro Mártir and nowhere else in Baja. The name derives from the fluttering of the small leaves as they turn yellow in the fall and shimmer against the white bark of the tree. In Spanish this tree is called *alamillo* or "little cottonwood."

HERBS

Most herbs—those shrubs with culinary, medicinal, or religious value—thrive in arid climates, and in Baja California they grow in some abundance. To get an idea of the variety, visit any peninsula *botánica* (herb shop) and ask to see *yerbas indígenas*. Most likely your query will turn up the following herbs, plus a dozen others.

One of the most common plants in northern Baja is **Great Basin sagebrush,** named for the area of the western United States where it's a dominant species. In Baja it's called *chamizo blanco* and is found in chaparral and piñon-juniper zones throughout the foothills of the northern sierras. Despite its name, the bluish, evergreen shrub isn't a true sage but a member of the mayweed tribe. Like sage, however, its leaves are sometimes used by Mexican herbalists in medicinal teas.

True sages or *salvia* belong to the mint family and are readily identified by the savory aroma of their crushed leaves. **White sage** proliferates on rocky hillsides from southern Alta California to as far south as Puenta Prieta. The grayish-green shrub grows up to three meters tall, and between March and July produces pale lavender flowers along its stalks. Several varieties of white sage are endemic to the peninsula and islands. Sage tea will mitigate the symptoms of a sore throat; the crushed leaves are also used to flavor cooked meats.

The much sought-after *chia* is a species of sage that grows only in the desert areas of Baja, Sonora, and the southwestern United States. The plant produces sizable rose-colored flowers and 2.5-cm-wide nutlets containing seeds valued for their wakefulness-inducing properties.

Another psychoactive plant found in Baja is *datura* or **jimsonweed** (*toloache*). A member of the potato family, a group that also includes nightshade and tobacco, jimsonweed produces large, fragrant, trumpet-shaped flowers that open in the evening and close by noon the following day. According to one folk remedy, the flowers will relieve insomnia if placed beside the pillow at night. All parts of the plant are considered toxic; in certain Yaqui Indian ceremonies, the seeds are eaten for their hallucinatory effect. Datura grows in abundance on rocky and sandy soils below 800 meters (2,600 feet) throughout the peninsula and on some Sea of Cortez islands.

More docile but also widespread in dry, lower elevations Is the **creosote bush** (*gobernadora*), also found in the deserts of northern Mexico, Utah, and Texas. This venerable shrub originated near the lower Colorado River and has been around at least 17,000 years, cloning itself in rings that widen with time. It's a fairly inconspicuous plant, with sparse evergreen branches that reach a maximum height of about 3.5 meters. The English name derives from the creosote-like odor the shrub exudes after rainfall. Dubbed "the smell of the desert" by admirers, this redolence is caused by the reaction of rainwater with a varnish-like resin on the outer skin of the plant. In periods of drought the resin pro-

tects the plant from dehydration.

The indigenous peoples of Baja California and northern Mexico have known about gobernadora's medicinal properties for ages. A tea made from the leaves relieves indigestion, coughs, and colds; a root tea is used to treat ulcers; a root poultice eases arthritis. Rancheros wash their feet in a root solution to prevent foot odor. Pharmacologists are now experimenting with several different chemical components of the plant shown to possess analgesic, diuretic, antihistaminic, expectorant, and antibacterial properties.

damiana

The homely **oregano** plant belongs to the same botanic family (Verbenaceae) as the creosote bush. The crushed leaves of this herb are mainly used in Mexico as a flavoring for stews and tomato sauces; oregano tea is also used by some women to relieve menstrual pain. The small evergreen shrub is found on Isla Magdalena and along the peninsula near Bahía Magdalena, on many Sea of Cortez islands, and along the Sonora/Sinaloa coast on the Mexican mainland.

Probably the most well-known herb native to Baja is **damiana** (*Turnera diffusa*), a small shrub with bright, five-petaled yellow or golden flowers. The plant's aphrodisiac properties are its main claim to fame; these are often derided as nonsense by self-appointed Baja analysts. But according to botanist Norman C. Roberts, damiana "stimulates the genito-urinary tract and is used in the treatment of sexual problems such as impotence, frigidity, sterility, and sexual exhaustion." Other benefits ascribed to the herb include use as a sedative and diuretic.

Damiana grows most commonly in rocky areas of the Cape Region but is also found as far away as Sonora, Texas, and in the West Indies.

The two most common ways of ingesting the herb are in sweetened tea made from the leaves or in a liqueur containing damiana extract. In resort areas a "Baja margarita" substitutes damiana liqueur for triple sec.

KAREN WHITF

FAUNA

LAND MAMMALS

Had Charles Darwin happened to explore the peninsula and islands of Baja California instead of Ecuador's Galapagos Islands, he might well have arrived at the same conclusions about evolution. Baja's unique environment—an arid-to-tropical slice of mountains and plains isolated between two large bodies of water—has led to superlative endemism, or what one naturalist called "a nice degree of freakishness," among its plant and animal species.

Of the hundred or so species of mammals found in Baja California, around 28 are endemic.

Carnivores

One of the most widespread carnivores on the peninsula as well as on some Sea of Cortez islands is the **coyote,** which seems to be able to adapt itself equally well to mountain, desert, and coastal terrains. Anyone venturing into the interior of the peninsula is virtually guaranteed to spot at least one. In some areas they don't seem particularly afraid of humans although they always maintain a distance of at least 15 meters between themselves and larger mammals. A coyote will sometimes fish for crab, placing a furry tail in the water, waiting for a crab to grab on; then, with a flick of the tail, tossing the crab

ERIN DWYER

coyote

onto the beach. Before the crustacean can recover from the shock, the coyote is busy enjoying a fine crab feast.

Rarely sighted is the **mountain lion**—also called cougar, panther, or puma—which, like all cats, is a mostly nocturnal animal. These beautiful creatures occasionally attack humans, so a degree of advance knowledge about their habits is necessary for those hiking in the sierras.

First, if you avoid hiking at night, you're much less likely to encounter a lion. If you do meet up with a lion, wildlife experts suggest you convince the beast you are not prey and may be dangerous yourself. Don't run from the animal, as this is an invitation to chase. Instead, shout, wave your hands, and, if the lion acts aggressively, throw stones at it. If you're carrying a backpack, raise it above your shoulders so that you appear larger to the lion. One or more of these actions is virtually guaranteed to frighten the lion away. If not, grab the biggest, heaviest stick you can find and fight it out to avoid becoming cat food.

Smaller, less intimidating carnivores commonly encountered in Baja include the **kit fox, gray fox, northern fox, ringtail, bobcat, lynx, skunk, raccoon,** and **badger.** Although there haven't been any recent sightings, it is thought the **gray wolf** may still exist in small numbers in the central sierras. Until the middle of this century the gray wolf was fairly common in Baja, but farmers and ranchers made an unfortunate tradition of killing them on sight.

Artiodactyls

This order encompasses all creatures with split hooves, including deer, sheep, pigs, and cattle. One of the largest of these beasts still roaming wild in Baja is the **mule deer,** of which there is an endemic peninsular variety. Mule deer are most commonly seen on mountain slopes below 1,500 meters. A lesser number of **white-tailed deer** is usually found above this elevation. Deer are a popular source of meat for ranchers living in the sierras; they also use deerskin to make soft, homemade boots called *teguas.*

At one time herds of **desert bighorn sheep** (*Ovis canadensis cremnobates*) or *borrego cimmarón* lived throughout the peninsular deserts.

THE BURRO

Long-eared, slow-plodding, dim-witted, the quintessential beast of burden: this is the city person's image of *Equus asinus.* But to rural Mexicans the donkey, or burro, is a beast of strength and sure-footedness. Compared to its taller, more graceful-appearing cousin the horse, the burro is a far more useful animal in mountainous or arid domains. On slopes, rocky surfaces, and sand the burro moves with great agility while balancing any load—whether human or inanimate. Standing only about a meter high at the shoulder, burros can also cover greater distances than horses on less water and food; they actually seem to prefer rough forage such as dead cactus or thorny palo verde over nutrient-rich—and, in Baja, scarce—grasses.

Although a burro's coloring may vary from light to dark brown, its withers are almost always marked with a cross of darker hair. Mexican mythology explains this cross as a symbol of divine protection, the burro's reward for carrying Mary and the infant Christ from Egypt to the Holy Land.

An unknown number of wild burros roams the interior of the peninsula, particularly in the area between the Sierra la Asamblea and Sierra San Borja. Ranchers, or *campesinos,* will occasionally capture a wild burro for domestic use as they're fairly easy to tame. The wild male burro, or "jack," is considered the best stud for producing a mule, so ranchers occasionally turn mares loose to breed with them. Mules produced from such a union are especially hardy.

BOB RACE

The burro's legendary stubbornness can often be attributed to mistreatment by its owner; an animal well cared for is usually quite loyal.

Mountain trekkers occasionally hire burros or mules as pack animals in Baja's sierras. For long forays, it's sometimes cheaper to purchase a burro rather than pay a daily hire rate; prices range from around US$40 for a poor animal to around US$75 for an exemplary burro—if you can find a rancher willing to sell one. If the price doesn't include a *burriqueta,* a saddle-like wooden frame for carrying cargo, you'll have to buy one or have one made; they're quite inexpensive. If possible, have a veterinarian inspect the animal for diseases before agreeing on a purchase.

Big-game hunting in the '20s and '30s as well as overgrazing of domestic livestock reduced their numbers to an estimated 4,500-7,500 individuals. An adult ram measures 81-124 cm (32-49 inches) high at the shoulder, and may weigh around 73 kilograms (160 pounds).

Rams rut during the summer, the only time dominant rams mingle with ewes; the rest of the year they roam only with other rams. During mating season, butting matches between bighorn rams are common. The Mexican government still allows an occasional bighorn hunt for the handful of wealthy hunters who can afford a US$12,000 special permit.

The elegant but endangered **peninsular pronghorn** (*berrendo*), often mistakenly referred to as an antelope, was once found from San Felipe south to Bahía Magdalena. Today less than a hundred pronghorns hang on in the Vizcaíno Desert under the official protection of the Mexican government. Like many life forms on the Vizcaíno Peninsula, pronghorns draw

desert bighorn sheep

moisture from dew left behind by Pacific fogs. The penalties for killing a pronghorn include a large fine plus three years in prison.

In the central Baja sierras roam a smattering of wild horses and many wild cattle. Every five years or so local vaqueros gather in the El Arco area to round up wild, unbranded cattle.

Rabbits

At least four varieties of rabbit hop around Baja: the **brush rabbit, desert cottontail, black-tailed jackrabbit,** and the rare, endemic **black jackrabbit.** Each is especially adapted to its particular habitat. The long, upright ears of the black-tailed jackrabbit, for example, enable it to hear sounds from quite a distance, a necessity for an animal that is prey for practically every larger animal in the Cape Region. The more delicate ears of the desert cottontail act as radiators on hot desert days, allowing the rabbit to release excess body heat into the air.

The endemic black jackrabbit (*Lepus insularis*) is found only on Isla Espíritu Santo. Zoologists haven't yet been able to explain why the fur of this rabbit is mostly black, or why a cinnamon-red coloring appears along the ears and underparts.

Rodents

The Californian Region and the sierras of Baja support a wide variety of common and not-so-common rodents—the **white-tailed antelope squirrel, marsh rice rat, Botta's pocket gopher,** and **piñon mouse,** to name a few. What may surprise some travelers is how many varieties manage to survive in the desert. Among these are the **little desert pocket mouse, cactus mouse, desert wood rat,** and five endemic species of **kangaroo rat.**

The kangaroo rat, which you may see hopping in front of your headlights at night—its long tail acts as a powerful spring—is built so it doesn't need to drink water, ever. It derives moisture from seeds, from the air deep inside its burrows where the relative humidity is 30-50%, and from condensation in its nasal passages (its nostrils are much cooler than the rest of its body). The creature's efficient kidneys excrete uric acid in a concentrated paste, rather than in liquid form. Because its body is so full of moisture, it's prized quarry for larger desert mammals and birds of prey. Backcountry rancheros occasionally trap kangaroo rats for fiesta food.

MARINE MAMMALS

Seals And Sea Lions

Various seals and sea lions flourish along Baja's coasts, including two species, the **elephant seal** (or sea elephant) and the **Guadalupe fur seal,** that only in recent years have come back from the brink of extinction. Both are native to the volcanic Isla Guadalupe, and were heavily hunted in the 19th century, the elephant seal for its oil and the Guadalupe fur seal for its furry skin.

The elephant seal is the largest seal on the planet. Males reach five meters (16 feet) or more and weigh up to two tons, while females are typically around three meters and about half a ton. The male's thick, flexible proboscis resembles a bobbed elephant's trunk. To scare off rivals in breeding season (Dec.-Feb.), the male places the tip of his trunk into his mouth and blows, producing a roaring snort. If the rival doesn't flee, a bloody fight ensues until one bull surrenders.

Lumbering on land but amazingly graceful in water, elephant seals can dive 1,490 meters (4,900 feet) below the sea's surface—deeper than any other seal—to feed on squid, their favorite source of nourishment.

When the seal-hunting era began in the early 19th century, the elephant seal's range extended

BOB RACE

elephant seals

all the way north to Alta California's Point Reyes, near San Francisco. By 1911 seal hunters had wiped out every elephant seal in Alta California waters and reduced the elephant's numbers on Isla Guadalupe to 125. After the Mexican government enacted a ban on seal hunting in 1922, the seals began repopulating Isla Guadalupe and nearby islands. The current population is estimated at around 80,000, most living on Pacific islands of Baja California; the elephant seal is gradually working its way back up the Alta California coast as well.

The smaller Guadalupe fur seal had a more difficult time recovering from the seal-hunting era. It was believed to be extinct by the end of the 1800s but in 1926 a small herd of around 60 living on Isla Guadalupe was discovered by American angler William Clover. Clover captured a pair of the seals and sold them to the San Diego Zoo, but, following a quarrel with the zoo's director, he returned to the island and attempted to kill and skin the entire remaining population. After selling the skins in Panama he met his demise in a barroom brawl. Fortunately he missed some of the seals in his massacre and the current population on the island is estimated at around 500.

California sea lions or *lobos marinas* (*Zapalophus californianus*) number some 145,000, 62% of whom live in the Sea of Cortez—principally around the islands of San Estebán, San Jorge, Angel de la Guarda, San Pedro de Mártir, and Espíritu Santo.

Cetaceans
The protected lagoons of Baja California's Pacific coast and the warm waters of the Sea of Cortez are practically made for whales and dolphins. Twenty-five species of cetaceans frequent Baja water, from the **blue whale,** the largest mammal on earth, to the **common dolphin** (*Delphinus delphis*), which is sometimes seen in the Sea of Cortez in pods as large as 10,000.

Whale species known to visit Baja or make it their year-round habitat include **Minke, fin, Sei, Bryde's, humpback, gray, goose-beaked, sperm, dwarf sperm, false killer, killer,** and **pilot.** Commonly seen dolphins are the **Pacific white-sided, bottle-nosed, spotted, Risso's, spinner,** and **striped.** The *vaquita,* a rare type of harbor porpoise, is endemic to the northern Sea of Cortez.

Gray Whales
The marine mammal usually of most interest to Baja travelers is the gray whale, which migrates some 19,300 km (12,000 miles) a year between its feeding grounds above the Arctic Circle and its calving grounds in the Pacific lagoons of southern Baja California. The gray is the easiest of the whales to view since it frequents shallow coastal waters.

Physiology and Behavior: The *Eschrichtius robustus* or gray whale, often called the California gray whale, reaches 10-15 meters (35-50 feet) in length at maturity (the average length is 13 meters for males, slightly longer for females) and weighs 20-40 tons. Its skin is almost black in color at birth but mottling caused by barnacles and barnacle scars imparts an overall gray tone to the portion of the animal exposed when it breathes, the rostrum, or that area of the head that's a combination upper jaw and nose. Bite scars on flukes and flippers from orca (killer whale) attacks are common—at least 20% of all grays are attacked at one time or another. Most survive; juveniles are the most common fatalities.

Unlike many other whale species that feed on plankton, the gray whale feeds mainly on amphipods, small crustaceans that live on the ocean floor. To get at them, the gray dives to the bottom, scoops water and sand into its mouth cavity, then expels the water through its baleen (a whalebone "sieve" in the mouth), filtering out the amphipods. In spite of an esophagus that's only about four inches wide, one whale can ingest up to a ton of food per day.

Although gray whales may engage in mating behavior at any point along their migration route, females only conceive while at the north end, in the vicinity of the Bering Strait, and give birth at or near the southern end, in Baja's Pacific lagoons. In a remarkable display of tribal rhythm, 90% of all gray whale conceptions take place within three weeks of 5 December. The female grays give birth after a gestation period of about 13 months, by which time the whales have arrived at the lagoons or are well on their way.

The females usually calve in water 3-15 meters deep, which is remarkably shallow considering newborn grays are four to five meters long and weigh up to 1.5 tons. Following birth, the newborns are exercized and fattened up so they'll be strong enough for the migration north. A female gray has recessed nipples on her underside, but the calf doesn't actually suck the milk from the mammaries like other mammals; instead the calf takes the nipple in its mouth, and, after a watertight seal has formed, the mother discharges a stream of milk into the calf's throat.

Since whale milk is about 800% richer in fat than human milk, the calves gain weight rapidly. By the time the return migration begins, roughly three months after birth, the young whales average six meters (20 feet) and 2.5 tons.

Migration: At one time the gray whale swam the Atlantic Ocean, Baltic Sea, and North Sea as well as the Pacific. It was decimated by Dutch, British, and American whalers in the North Atlantic by the beginning of the 19th century and now survives only in the Arctic-Pacific corridor. Currently numbering around 21,000, the grays spend their summers feeding in the Bering, Chukchi, and Beaufort seas in the vicinity of Alaska and Siberia, where the long Arctic days result in highly productive marine growth.

The gray's primary feeding grounds lie in the Chirikof Basin, where they begin their annual migration south in mid- to late fall. Swimming at an average four knots, the whales cover the 9,600-km (6,000-mile) journey to the southern Baja lagoons in about two months. Traveling in pods of three to four whales, they typically rest for a few hours each night. When there's a full moon, they swim all night.

On their way southward the grays follow the North American shoreline closely, taking the outside coast of major islands. By early January they begin arriving at protected bays and lagoons on the Pacific side of Baja, primarily Laguna Ojo de Liebre, Laguna San Ignacio, and Bahía Magdalena. The grays used to winter farther north in Alta California's San Diego Bay, but heavy sea traffic now forces them to stay south.

During the gray's winter sojourn in Baja, the females calve and nurse their young in the interiors of the lagoons, while the males tend to loiter at or near the lagoon entrances. Since female grays are fertile every other year, each available female—those not calving or nursing—has an average of two suitors at each lagoon entry at any given time. When not actively mating, males watch their rivals coupling or seek out other females. Fighting for access to a female is not a known whale behavior.

Calving season extends from December to April, but because of individual differences in pacing, some whales begin migrating north as early as February while others may linger in the lagoons until June. The entire 19,300-km (12,000-mile) migration, the longest of any mammal on the planet, occurs within a period of seven to eight months. Apparently, adult whales don't eat during this entire interval.

The Rise and Fall of Pacific Whaling: The Indians of Alta and Baja California as well as the Eskimos of Alaska were known to hunt whales for tribal consumption. But whaling as an industry didn't begin along the Pacific coast until the 19th century, when American whaleboats from New England and Hawaii began cruising Pacific waters in significant numbers. At first gray whales were left alone; because they're fiercely defensive when under attack, grays are very difficult to kill using traditional harpooning techniques. Often they would destroy attacking whaleboats.

The gray's destiny was altered in 1857 when Boston whaler Charles Melville Scammon followed a pod into Baja's Laguna Ojo de Liebre. Taking advantage of the local geography, Scammon figured out how to bomb the trapped whales with explosive harpoons while his whaleboats remained safely anchored in the shallows, where larger whales couldn't reach them. Scores of whalers followed his example, and within less than 20 years an estimated 10,000 gray whales had been killed.

The slaughter quickened in the 20th century with the introduction of factory boats, which meant whales could be processed on site. By the 1930s the estimated number of grays was down to 250 from a pre-1850s population of 25,000. International fishing agreements signed

WHALEWATCHING

The gray whale is a common target of whalewatching expeditions, its great affinity for land making it one of the more accessible of the large whale species. While other whales tend to frequent deeper parts of the ocean, the gray swims mostly in coastal shallows and seeks out lagoons for calving. Also, because it's a bottom feeder, the gray tolerates areas so shallow its abdomen rests on the sea bottom, something no other large whale can accomplish; most whales would suffocate in such a position. This means large grays are often seen very close to shore.

A visit to a gray calving lagoon can be exciting. Sometimes whales seem to be everywhere you look—"spouting" (clearing their blowholes with pneumatic blasts that send vapor spumes high into the air), "breaching" (leaping out of the sea and arching through the air), "spyhopping" (poking their heads, eyes, and mouths vertically out of the water, possibly to peek at the nonaquatic world), "tail lobbing" (slapping their flukes on the water surface), or just floating by, sleeping on the tide. At other times the whales are relatively inactive. Choppy water seems to occasion more activity.

You can spot grays almost anywhere along Baja's peninsular coast, from Punta Banda near Ensenada right around to the Sea of Cortez. The best place to see them up close and in large numbers is in one of three protected bays in Baja California Sur: Laguna Ojo de Liebre (Scammon's Lagoon) near Guerrero Negro; Laguna San Ignacio, southwest of San Ignacio; and Bahía Magdalena, or adjacent Bahía Almejas, southwest of Ciudad Constitución. Of these three areas, Laguna San Ignacio seems to attract the greatest number of "friendlies," gray whales that actively approach whalewatching boats for human contact.

Although whales can be seen in Baja waters from the beginning of January through the end of March, February is when they're generally present in greatest numbers. At any given lagoon, you can view whales from three vantage points: shore, air, or water. Viewing from shore is sometimes frustrating, since even the closest whales frolic at least 100 meters away; also, since the closest whales usually lie in the shallowest water, they're less likely to perform their more exciting maneuvers, like spyhopping or breaching. Distance is also a problem from the air, since you can't approach too closely without

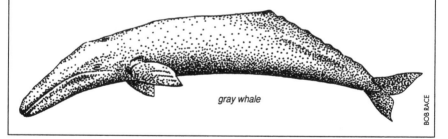

gray whale

BOB RACE

in 1937 and 1946 forbade the killing of gray whales, but American whalers didn't comply until the U.S. government enacted the Marine Mammal Protection Act of 1972, by which time the gray whale was thought to be extinct. The animal's remarkable comeback as a species over the last 20 years has been one of the greatest successes of the environmental movement.

In an ironic historical footnote, whaler Charles Melville Scammon later became a naturalist of some note, and his book, *The Marine Mammals of the Northwestern Coast of North America,* is considered a classic of amateur zoology. It re-

mains one of the most important reference works on whales and the whaling industry.

FISH

The seas surrounding Baja California contain a truly amazing variety of marinelife. In the Sea of Cortez alone, around 800 varieties of fish have been identified. Marine biologists estimate a total of around 3,000 species, including invertebrates, between the Golfo de Santa Clara at the north end of the sea and the southern tip of

endangering the whale's life as well as the lives of those in the plane. And, of course, to consider whale-watching from the air you must either own a small plane, know someone who does, or charter one.

The optimum way to experience the gray whale, then, is from the water. Any boat entering an area where whales are protected—including all three of the bays mentioned above—during calving season must possess a special whalewatching permit issued by the Mexican government on a year-to-year basis. Ordinarily permits are issued only to boat-owners with registered whalewatching concessions and academic researchers from approved institutions.

The least expensive whalewatching trips are those you arrange on your own from the shores of the lagoons. During the season, licensed Mexican boatmen linger with their pangas (skiffs) at approved launching points in each lagoon. All you have to do is drive out there, park your vehicle, and pay the going price, which varies with the distance the boats must travel to reach the whales and the number of hours you stay out.

In Guerrero Negro and San Ignacio, a couple of local hotels arrange trips that include roundtrip ground transport to the lagoons; prices are usually quite reasonable, based on group signups. Next up in price are trips arranged in major tourist towns like Ensenada, Mulegé, Loreto, and Cabo San Lucas. The problem with locally hired whalewatching tours is that the guides are often not very knowledgeable about the whales or can't speak enough English to communicate the knowledge they do possess to non-Spanish-speakers.

Some whalewatchers prefer the convenience and expertise of whalewatching cruises sponsored by scientific or environmental organizations. This sort of trip costs a great deal more than arranging one on your own, but you'll enjoy the advantage of having every contingency planned in advance and will receive the commentary of experienced naturalists. Four well-established organizations in the U.S. that operate Baja whalewatching expeditions are:

Baja Expeditions
2625 Garnet Ave.
San Diego, CA 92109
tel. (619) 581-3311, (800) 843-6967

Biological Journeys
1696 Ocean Dr.
McKinleyville, CA 95521
tel. (800) 548-7555, outside CA;
(707) 839-0178, in CA

Oceanic Society Expeditions
Fort Mason Center, Bldg. E
San Francisco, CA 94123
tel. (415) 441-1106

Sven-Olof Lindblad's Special Expeditions
720 Fifth Ave.
New York, NY 10019
tel. (800) 762-0003, outside NY;
(212) 765-7740, in NY

Biological Journeys, Oceanic Society Expeditions, and Special Expeditions also operate programs in the Sea of Cortez that focus on other marine mammals, including dolphins and humpback, fin, and blue whales.

Cabo San Lucas. This would make the area the richest sea, or gulf, in the world. The wide spectrum of aquatic environments along both coasts is largely responsible for this abundance and has led to Baja's reputation as a mecca for *mariscos* aficionados and fishing and diving enthusiasts.

About 90% of all known Baja fish varieties are found close to the shores of the peninsula or its satellite islands. The Midriff Islands area in the center of the Sea of Cortez is especially rich in life—tidal surges aerate the water and stir up nutrients, supporting a thick food chain from plankton to fish to birds and sea lions. The Cortez, in fact, has acted as a giant fish trap, collecting an assortment of marine species over thousands of years from the nearby Pacific, the more distant equatorial zones of South America, and even the Caribbean, through a now-extinct water link that once existed between the two seas.

The information below represents only a brief overview of the many fish of common, everyday interest to Baja visitors and residents in contact with the aquatic world.

Billfish

Baja is the world capital of sailfish and marlin fishing; just about every serious saltwater angler eventually considers a pilgrimage to La Paz or Cabo San Lucas. Six billfish species exist here in some numbers: **swordfish, sailfish,** and **striped, blue,** and **black marlin.** All are strong fighters, though the sailfish and striped marlin are generally the most acrobatic. Billfish exist in a wide range of offshore Pacific and Sea of Cortez waters south of Bahía Magdalena and the Midriff Islands, although the swordfish is found mostly on the Pacific side.

Corvinas And Croakers
About 30 species in Baja belong to this group of small- to medium-size fish that make croaking sounds. Among the largest is the **totuava,** formerly one of the most famous game fish in the upper Sea of Cortez. Overfishing has led to a scarcity of these silvery 35- to 250-pounders and it's now illegal to take or possess them in Mexico. The totuava is reportedly one of best-tasting of all game fish; others in this category, found inshore to onshore in a variety of coastal waters, include **white seabass, Gulf corvina, yellowfin croaker, orangemouth corvina, spotfin croaker,** and **California corvina.**

Jack
Popular jacks include **yellowtail** (one of the most popular fish for use in *tacos de pescado*), **Pacific amberjack,** various **pompanos, jack crevalle,** and the strong-fighting **roosterfish,** named for its tall dorsal comb. These jacks are most prevalent in inshore to onshore areas in the Sea of Cortez and in the Pacific south of Magdalena.

Dorado, Mackerel, And Tuna
Among the more sought after food fish, found offshore to inshore throughout parts of both seas, are the **dorado,** sometimes called "dolphinfish," though it isn't related to mammalian dolphins or porpoises, or by its Hawaiian name *mahi mahi*; **sierra,** especially good in *ceviche* or marinated seafood salad; the knife-shaped **wahoo,** one of the fastest of all fish, reaching speeds of 50 knots; **Pacific bonito**; and three kinds of tuna, the **bluefin, albacore,** and highly prized **yellowfin.** Yellowfins can reach up to 180 kilograms (400 pounds) and are among the best tasting of all tunas.

Bass
Sea bass are an inshore fish; different species dominate different Baja waters and all commonly find their way into Mexican seafood restaurants.

The larger bass are *garropa* (groupers), the smaller *cabrilla*. Popular varieties are the **leopard grouper,** found in the Sea of Cortez near San Felipe; the **gulf grouper,** which grows up to 90 kilograms (200 pounds) and inhabits waters off San Felipe to the Midriff Islands; **giant sea bass** ranging from San Quintín to above the Midriff Islands; **spotted cabrilla,** Isla Cedros to the upper Sea of Cortez; **flag cabrilla,** lower Sea of Cortez; **kelp bass,** on the northwest Pacific coast; and **spotted sand bass,** Pacific coast north of Magdalena and the upper Sea of Cortez.

Bottomfish
These smaller (13 kilograms or less) bottom-feeding fish favor the inshore Pacific above Magdalena and include the **lingcod, sculpin,** and **rockfish.**

Surf Fish
Most of the 25 or so species of surf fish weigh less than two kilograms and are found along the Pacific coast since there's no surf to speak of in the Sea of Cortez. Popular catches among gringos—this isn't a popular fish with Mexican anglers—are **barred surfperch, rubberlip surfperch,** and **sargo.** The sargo also frequents the upper Sea of Cortez coast.

Flatfish
These include flounder and halibut, usually called *lenguado* in Spanish. The most common variety found on the Pacific side is the **California halibut**; on the other side it's the **Cortez halibut.** Both make good eating and are often used in tourist areas for *tacos de pescado.*

Snapper
Generally found south of Magdalena and round the Cape as far north as the upper Sea of Cortez, locally popular snappers include **red snapper, yellow snapper, barred pargo,** and **dog snapper.** All snappers are called *pargo* in Spanish, except for the red snapper, which is *huachinango.* All are common food fish.

Sharks And Rays
Of the more than 60 species of sharks found in Baja waters, some are rather rare while most stay clear of humans. The more common species are found offshore to inshore from Magdalena to the Midriff, and include the **smooth hammerhead, common thresher, bonito, sand, blue,**

blacktip, and the world's largest fish, reaching up to 18 meters and 3,600 kilograms, the **whale shark.** Shark-fishing is an important activity in Baja, supplying much of the seafood eaten locally. Hammerhead, thresher, bonito (mako), and leopard shark fillets are all very tasty.

Rays are quite common in warmer offshore-to-inshore waters throughout Baja. Many varieties feature barbed tailspines that can inflict a painful wound. Contrary to myth the barb is not actually venomous, although a ray "sting" easily becomes infected. Experienced beachgoers perform the "stingray shuffle" when walking on sandy bottoms. If you bump into a ray resting on the bottom, it will usually swim away; if you step on one, it's likely to give you a flick of the barb.

Common smaller rays found inshore include the **butterfly ray** and the aptly named **shovelnose guitarfish,** a ray with a thick tail and a flat head. Two species of rays are sometimes called "devilfish" because of their horn-like pectoral fins: the **mobula** and the huge **Pacific manta ray.** The Pacific manta posesses a "wingspan" of up to seven meters (23 feet) across and can weigh nearly two tons. Another fairly large ray, the **bat ray,** is sometimes confused with the manta, though it doesn't have the characteristic pectoral fins of the latter. A friendly manta will allow scuba divers to hitch rides by hanging on to the base of the pectorals.

Elongated Fish
These varieties share the characteristics of long, slender bodies and beak-like jaws. The sharp-toothed **California barracuda** swims in the Pacific from the border down to Cabo San Lucas while a smaller, more edible variety is found in the Sea of Cortez. In spite of their somewhat frightful appearance, barracudas rarely attack humans.

The silvery **flying fish** can be seen leaping above offshore waters throughout the Pacific and the lower Sea of Cortez. It is not generally considered a food fish. The most edible of the elongated fish is probably the acrobatic **Mexican needlefish,** or *agujon,* which reaches two meters in length and has green bones.

Shellfish
Baja's shores abound with deep-water and shallow-water shellfish species, including multiple varieties of **clams, oysters, mussels, scallops,** and **shrimp,** many of which have disappeared from coastal Alta California. Baja's most famous shellfish is undoubtedly the **spiny lobster,** which appears on virtually every *mariscos* menu on the peninsula.

Challenges To The Marine Environment
One of the major problems facing Baja fisheries is illegal fishing by unlicensed Japanese and Korean boats. Despite Mexico's ban on the netting of game fish, many foreign vessels still use huge dredge nets and/or longlines to harvest marlin, swordfish, dorado, and other species legally reserved for sportfishing only—not to mention protected species such as porpoises and dolphins.

Novelist John Steinbeck, in his 1941 account of a scientific marine expedition into the Sea of Cortez accompanying marine biologist Ed Ricketts, described how he watched six Japanese shrimpers—weighing at least 600 tons each—purse-dredge the sea bottom, killing hundreds of tons of fish that were merely discarded after each dredging. One of his reactions: "Why the Mexican government should have permitted the complete destruction of a valuable food supply is one of those mysteries which have their ramifications possibly back in pockets it is not well to look into."

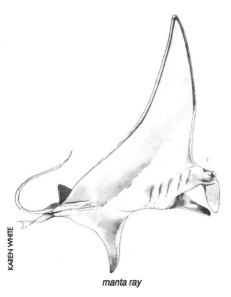

KAREN WHITE

manta ray

With government corruption apparently on the wane, Mexico is taking steps to curtail many of the commercial enterprises on the Sea of Cortez; expanding budgets mean it should become easier to enforce new regulations. One can only hope that intervention is soon enough and strong enough to preserve Mexico's great marine resources.

BIRDS

Hosting around 300 known species of birdlife, the peninsula and islands of Baja California are one of the most concentrated and undisturbed aviary habitats in North America. Ornithological research focusing on Baja, however, is rather difficult to come by as well as incomplete; one of the most up-to-date references available is Peterson and Chalif's *A Field Guide to Mexican Birds,* last published in 1973.

Although numerous varieties thrive in the desert lands, the vast majority of Baja's native and migrating species are either coastal or open-sea (pelagic) birds. The Sea of Cortez islands are particularly rich in birdlife; the Mexican government has designated 49 of the Midriff Islands as wildlife refuges to protect the many rare and endangered species there. The most famous of these islands among birders is Isla San Pedro Mártir, home to the rare and clownish **blue-footed booby** and its more common cousins the **brown booby** and the **masked booby.**

Isla de Raza, a tiny guano-covered Midriff island of only 250 acres, is another birding mecca. Every April this island is the site of territorial "wars" between **Heermann's gulls** and **elegant terns.**

Common throughout the coastal areas of southern Baja is the **magnificent frigate,** called *tijera* (scissors) in Mexico because of its scissor-shaped tail. In spite of their seafood diet, frigates

magnificent frigate

BOB RACE

can't swim or even submerge their heads to catch fish—instead they glide high in the air on boomerang-shaped wings, swooping down to steal fish from other birds, especially slow-witted boobies.

Among the more commonly seen birds along the Sea of Cortez coast is the **brown pelican,** which in global terms is not so common. The pelican species go back 30 million years; paleontologists use the modern pelican as a model for creating visual representations of the pteranodon, an extinct flying reptile with an eight-meter wingspan. Brown pelicans, the only truly marine species among the world's seven pelican species, dive 10-30 meters (30-100 feet) under water to catch fish. Other pelicans only dip their beaks beneath the surface, and tend to frequent inland waterways rather than marine habitats. Browns have disappeared entirely from the U.S. shores of the Gulf of Mexico, and are almost gone from the coastal islands of Alta California—apparently due to the pesticide content of the Pacific Ocean. Baja's Cortez and Pacific coasts are among the last habitats where the brown pelican thrives.

Another rather special bird along the coast is the **fisher eagle,** which, as its name implies, catches and eats fish. The fisher eagle is also occasionally seen along freshwater rivers and around the Pacific lagoons.

Other coastal birds of note are two species of **cormorant,** the **long-billed curlew,** four species of **egret,** four species of **grebe,** 10 species of **gull,** three species of **heron,** the **belted kingbird,** two species of **ibis,** three species of **loon,** the **osprey,** the **American oystercatcher,** six species of **plover,** six species of **sandpiper,** the **tundra swan,** and seven species of **tern.**

Certain fish-eating birds are usually seen only by boaters since they tend to swim over open ocean. These pelagics include two species of **albatross,** the **black-legged kittiwake,** the **red phalarope,** three species of **shearwater,** the **surf scoter,** the **south polar skua,** five species of **storm petrel,** the **black tern,** and the **red-billed tropicbird.**

Another type of waterfowl in Baja frequents only freshwater ponds, *tinajas* (springs), lakes, streams, and marshes. These birds include two species of **bittern,** the **American coot,** two species of **duck,** the **snow goose,** the **northern harrier,** six species of **heron,** the **white-faced ibis,** the **common moorhen,** two species of rail, five species of **sandpiper,** the **lesser scaup,** the **shoveler,** the **common snipe,** the **sora,** the **roseate spoonbill,** the **wood stork,** three species of **teal,** the **northern waterthrush,** and the **American wigeon.** Some of these birds are native, others only winter over.

In Baja's sierras dwell the **golden eagle,** the **western flycatcher,** the **lesser goldfinch,** the **black-headed grosbeak,** the **red-tailed hawk,** two species of **hummingbird,** the **pheasant,** the **yellow-eyed junco,** the **white-breasted nuthatch,** the **mountain plover,** four species of **vireo,** eight species of **warbler,** the **acorn woodpecker,** and the **canyon wren.**

Common over desert and/or open country are three species of **falcon** (peregrine, prairie, and Cooper's), three species of **flycatcher,** six species of **hawk,** the **black-fronted hummingbird,** the **American kestrel,** the **merlin,** two species of **owl,** the **greater roadrunner,** eight species of **sparrow,** two species of **thrasher,** the **vernon,** the **turkey vulture,** the **ladderbacked woodpecker,** and the **cactus wren.**

REPTILES AND AMPHIBIANS

Among the slippery, slimy, scaly, crawly things that live in Baja California are around 30 species of lizards, including two endemics; five species of frogs and toads; six turtles; and around 35 different kinds of snakes, including the endemic rattleless rattlesnake.

Lizards
Four-legged reptilians of note include the **chuckwalla,** which is found on certain islands in the Sea of Cortez; it sometimes grows to nearly a meter in length. The chuckwalla drinks fresh water when available, storing it in sacs that gurgle when it walks; when a freshwater source is not available, the lizard imbibes saltwater, which it processes through a sort of internal desalinator. Another good-sized Baja lizard is the **desert iguana,** found throughout the Gulf Coast Desert and possibly farther north. Larger iguanas are sometimes eaten in ranchero stews and are said to taste better than chicken. The **coast horned lizard,** similar to the horny toad of the American Southwest, is another Baja endemic.

Turtles
Of the six turtle varieties present in Baja, five are sea turtles: the **leatherback, green, hawksbill, western Ridley,** and **loggerhead.** Because their eggs, meat, and shells are highly valued among coastal Mexican populations, all are on the endangered species list. The Mexican government has declared turtle hunting and turtle egg collecting illegal; the decimation of the turtles has slowed considerably but hasn't yet stopped. Bajacalifornios say they're upholding the laws while anglers along the mainland coast of the Sea of Cortez still take sea turtles.

The main culprit has apparently been Japan, which is the world's largest importer of sea turtles—including the endangered Ridley and hawksbill, both of which the Japanese use for meat, turtle leather, and turtle-shell fashion accessories. In 1991 the Japanese government announced a ban on the importation of sea turtles, so perhaps the Sea of Cortez populations will soon make a comeback.

Snakes
The rocky desert lands and chaparrals of Baja are perfect snake country. The bad news is that about half the known species are venomous; the good news is they rarely come into contact with humans. Scorpion bites actually far outnumber the incidents of snakebite in Baja.

Harmless species include the **western blind snake,** the **rosy boa,** the **Baja California rat snake,** the **spotted leaf-nosed**

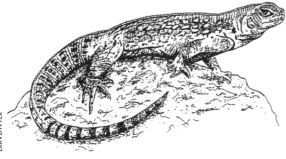

desert iguana

ERIN DWYER

snake, the **western patch-nosed snake,** the **bullsnake,** the **coachwhip,** the **kingsnake,** the **Baja sand snake,** and the **California lyre snake.**

The venomous kinds fall into two categories, one of which contains only a single snake species, the **yellow-bellied sea snake.** Sea snakes usually flee the vicinity when they sense human presence, but as a general precaution don't grab anything in the water that looks like a floating stick—that's how sea snakes deceive their prey.

As for rattlesnakes, there are supposedly 18 species in Baja, the most common of which is the near-endemic **Baja California rattler** (*Crotalus enyo*), with a range that includes the lower three-fourths of the peninsula. Look for scaly mounds over the eyes if you care to make an identification. The **red diamondback** (*Crotalus ruber*) frequents the northern deserts and chaparral and is also fairly common. The most dangerous of Baja rattlers is the **Western diamondback;** it's the largest and therefore has the greatest potential to deliver fatal or near-fatal doses of venom. The diamondback is mostly confined to the canyons of the northern sierras.

All other rattlesnakes in Baja are more a nuisance than an actual threat since they overwhelmingly tend toward the injection of non-fatal doses of venom. For Graham Mackintosh, the Briton who hiked almost the entire perimeter of the Baja peninsula—and wrote a book about his experiences, *Into A Desert Place*—rattlesnake became a welcome part of his desert diet.

The only rattler fully endemic to Baja is also the strangest. The **rattleless rattlesnake** (*Crotalus catalinensis*) was first discovered in 1952 on Isla Santa Catalina, a small mountainous Sea of Cortez island south of Loreto. Fortunately Santa Catalina is the only habitat for this snake; its lack of a warning signal might otherwise keep most of us away from the peninsular deserts forever.

The general all-inclusive Spanish term for snake is *serpiente;* a nonvenomous snake is referred to as *culebra,* the venomous sort *vípera.* A rattlesnake is *un serpiente de cascabel* or simply *un cascabel.* For tips on how to avoid snakebite, see "Snakebite Prevention and Treatment." An encouraging factoid: according to Spanish records, no missionary ever died of snakebite during the 300-year period of Spanish colonization of the New World.

HISTORY

PRE-COLUMBIAN HISTORY

Because Baja California lacks spectacular archaeological remains, such as the Mayan and Aztec ruins in the southern reaches of mainland Mexico, it has largely been ignored by archaeologists. It is highly likely, however, that the Baja California peninsula was inhabited by human populations well before the rest of Mexico. Baja was the logical termination for the coastal migration route followed by Asian groups who crossed the Bering Strait land bridge between Asia and North America beginning around 50,000 B.C.

San Dieguito And La Jolla Cultures

The earliest known Baja inhabitants were members of the San Dieguito culture who migrated southward into northern Baja approximately 7,000 years ago. Evidence of their presence in Alta California dates back 9,000 years. The San Dieguito people spent much of the year wandering in small migratory bands of 15-20, guided by freshwater sources and the availability of game. Their simple economy was based on hunting, fishing, and the gathering of edible wild plants. Archaeological remains include circles of stones, stone tools—choppers, raspers, knives, spear points, axe heads, mortars (*metates*)— and simple pottery.

Evidence suggests the San Dieguitos coexisted, at least for a time, with the Jollanos (or the La Jolla Culture), about whom little is known except that they lived by gathering fish and shellfish, seeds, roots, and wild vegetables.

The Yumanos

The San Dieguito culture either developed into or was superseded by that of the Yumanos, whose archaeological signature of rock paintings and petroglyphs indicates their presence on the peninsula around 2,500 years ago. The Yumanos made use of more sophisticated hunting equipment as well as fishing nets; they also seem to have developed ceramics well before their counterparts in the American Southwest. Upon the arrival of the Spanish in the 16th century A.D.,

some Yumano groups were practicing cultivation in the Río Colorado floodplains of northern Baja. These groups included the Cucapá, Tipai, Paipai (or Pa'ipai), Kumyai, and Kiliwa.

Like many of the less aggressive Indians throughout Mexico and Mesoamerica, the Yumano tribes didn't last very long under the influences of missionization. Those who weren't killed by European-borne diseases or executed for rebelling against the padres were assimilated. All that is left of the Yumano culture today are scattered galleries of petroglyphs and rock paintings.

A Yumano rock painting near La Rumorosa indicates a rudimentary knowledge of astronomy; it depicts a winter solstice celebration. One of the figures in the painting, a 12-inch red human caricature that may represent a shaman, catches light only on 21 December, for about 20 minutes beginning at sunrise.

Yumano Indians, circa 1880s

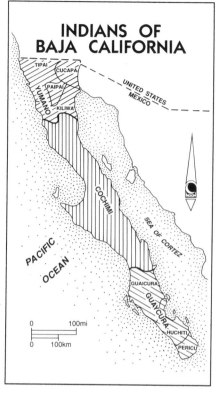

INDIANS OF BAJA CALIFORNIA

© MOON PUBLICATIONS, INC.

The Cochimís And Guaycuras

Indian groups living in the central and southern reaches of the peninsula when the Spanish arrived were apparently much less advanced technologically than the Yumanos. Because of the lack of archaeological research in these areas, the only record we have of these Indians is the one left us by Spanish accounts, which were undoubtedly biased in light of their mission to subordinate the peoples of the New World. Mission histories are full of lurid tales of Indian customs, many probably written to convince the Spanish crown of the desperate need to missionize the natives. Nevertheless, the Indians of central and southern Baja appeared to be among the more "primitive" of the tribes encountered by the Spanish in Mexico or Mesoamerica. In modern archaeological terms, they hadn't progressed beyond the Paleolithic epoch.

According to these accounts, the Cochimís inhabited the central peninsula and Comondú while Guaycuras occupied the Cape Region, divided into the Pericú, Huchiti, and Guaicura tribes. All spent most of their daylight hours searching for food; the men hunted small game or gathered shellfish while the women gathered fruit, seeds, and roots. If game was scarce, the people subsisted on a variety of insects and would even eat dried animal skins, including, according to reports, the leather boots of the conquistadors.

The southern Indians generally lived in the open and sought shelter only in the severest of weather conditions. Men went naked "or nearly so," while women wore leather or yucca-fiber thongs around the waist with woven grasses or twigs suspended from the front and animal skins in the back. These garments were sometimes painted with bright colors. The tips of arrows and spears were generally of sharpened hardwood only, though chipped stone points were occasionally used. The Guaycuras also used a reed blowgun. The most important time of year among these Indians was when the fruit of the pitahaya cactus ripened; the fruit was then so abundant the Indians allegedly abandoned all activities save sleeping and eating.

Neither the Guaycuras nor the Cochimís apparently left behind any artwork. This has been attributed to their harsh living environment; they had little time or energy for artistic pursuits. However, in the inland areas of the peninsula inhabited by the Guaycura/Cochimí tribes are numerous rock-art sites. The Cochimís told the Spanish this rock art was created by a race of giants who'd preceded them. Almost nothing is known about this lost Indian culture, a people Baja rock-art expert Harry Crosby has dubbed "The Painters."

THE SPANISH CONQUEST OF MEXICO

Following 700 years of conflict with the Moors over control of the Iberian peninsula, Spain in the 15th century emerged as the most powerful nation in Europe. Convinced that a Roman Catholic God was destined to rule the world with Spain as His emissary, the Spanish monarchy sent Christopher Columbus in search of a new route to the Far East. His mission was to establish contact with a mythical "Great Khan" in order to develop an alternate trade route with the Orient, since Arabs controlled the overland route through the Middle East. Along the way as many pagans as possible would be converted to Christianity. Once the Arab trade monopoly was broken, the Holy Land would be returned to Christian control.

Columbus's landing in the West Indies in 1492 was followed by Pope Alexander VI's historic 1493 decree which gave the Spanish rights to any new land discovered west of the Azores, as long as the Spanish made "God's name known there." Hence, the Spanish conquest of

WHAT'S IN A NAME?

The name "California," as applied to what was orginally thought to be an island northwest of Mexico, made its first appearance in the diary of a seaman on the 1539-40 Francisco de Ulloa expedition. The term began appearing on maps shortly thereafter, though its derivation was never explained. Until the late 18th century, there were two competing suppositions. One theory said that the oppressive heat of the peninsula led the Spanish to call the place Calida Fornax, Latin for "hot furnace," and that "California" was a corrupted version of this phrase. Another theory claimed the name derived from a mixture of the Spanish *cala,* or "little bay," and the Latin *fornix,* meaning "arch," and that it referred to the arch at Bahía San Lucas. This didn't make much sense either since Bahía San Lucas wasn't a favored harbor in the early days of peninsular exploration.

The true origin of the word wasn't discovered until 1862 when Edward Everett Hale of New England came across the word in a four-part Spanish novel, *Las Sergas de Esplandián* (*The Adventures of Esplandian*), first published in 1500. In the fourth tale of this extremely popular 16th-century novel, the fictional California was:

> *an island on the right hand of the Indies very near the terrestrial Paradise, peopled by black women among whom there was not a single man. They had beautiful, robust bodies, spirited courage and great strength. Their island was the most impregnable in the world with its cliffs and headlands and rocky coasts. Their weapons were all of gold . . . because in all the island there was no metal except gold.*

In the tale the warrior women are known as Amazons—a name later bestowed upon South America's most famous river—and the island's name is a compound of *Califia,* their queen (from the Greek *kalli,*

"beautiful"), and *ornix,* the Greek word for "bird"— a reference to the 500 griffins who supported the Amazons in battles.

Since this novel was widely read during the years of the Spanish conquest of Mexico, the California myth probably joined other gold-tinged stories circulating among the conquistadors. In the novel the Amazons were pagan allies of a Persian king, so the story dovetailed well with the conquistadors' promise to the Vatican to convert the heathen hordes.

At first the name California was applied to all lands west of the Colorado River; the distinction between Baja ("Lower") and Alta ("Upper") California wasn't made until the late 1700s. For the next hundred years or so, if you said "California," it was understood that you meant Baja California, since this was where the first California missions were established. Even after California became a U.S. state in 1850, the "Alta" persisted— in the 1880s, San Franciscans were still publishing a newspaper called the *Daily Alta Californian.*

Today whenever you get a quorum of Baja aficionados around a table of cervezas, you have the raw material for a name debate. Are the peninsula and islands properly called "Baja California" or is just "Baja" okay? What about "the Baja"—which seems to be particularly popular among Canadians, perhaps because they relate it to "the Yukon"? Bajacalifornios (the preferred term for residents of Baja California) will often pretend to be rankled at the abbreviated form, yet you may occasionally catch them using it themselves.

The official names of the two Mexican states separated by the peninsula's 28th parallel are "Baja California" (BC) and "Baja California Sur" (BCS), but many Bajacalifornios refer to the northern state as "Baja California Norte" (BCN) to distinguish it from the southern state. In this book the latter practice will be followed so as not to confuse the northern state with the whole peninsula.

the New World started as a roundabout extension of the Holy Crusades.

A succession of Spanish expeditions into the Caribbean and Gulf of Mexico rapidly achieved the conquest of Mexico and Central America. Conquistador Hernán Cortés subdued the Valley of Mexico Aztecs in three years (1519-21) and the allegiance—or decimation—of other Aztecs and Mayans followed quickly.

Early California Explorations

When the Spanish conquistadors came to the western edge of mainland Mexico and looked beyond toward the landforms they could see above the sea, they concluded that Baja California was a huge island and the as-yet-unnamed Sea of Cortez led to the Atlantic. The idea of a "northwest passage" to the Atlantic persisted for years, even among seasoned explorers like Cabrillo, Drake, and Vizcaíno. Cortés himself directed four voyages from the mainland to the island of La California, although he actually accompanied only the third. The history of these early expeditions exposes the enmity and extreme sense of competition among those conquistadors supposedly working toward a common cause.

The first voyage, launched in 1532, never made it to the peninsula. The ships were captured in the Sea of Cortez by Nuño Guzmán, an arch-rival of Cortés operating farther north in Mexico. The next year a second expedition, under Captain Diego Becerra of the *Concepción,* suffered a mutiny in which the captain was killed. Basque pilot Fortún Jiménez took charge and the ship landed in Bahía de la Paz in early 1534. Thus the first European visitors to reach Baja California, a group of mutineers, arrived there just 42 years after Columbus touched down in the West Indies and nearly a century before the Pilgrims landed at Plymouth Rock.

Before they had much of a chance to explore, Jiménez and 22 of his crew were killed by Indians while filling their water casks at a spring. The survivors managed to sail the *Concepción* back to the mainland, where most were promptly captured by Guzmán. One of the escapees managed to reach Cortés with tales of rich caches of black pearls on a huge island with "cliffs and headlands and rocky coasts," as in the California of popular myth.

Cortés, inspired by these stories, organized and led a third expedition, partially financed by his own personal wealth. His party consisted of three ships and a group of 500 Spanish colonists that included women and children. They landed at the northeast end of Bahía de la Paz—which Cortés named Santa Cruz—in May of 1535, the same year New Spain was officially established. Although Cortés apparently found pearls in abundance, his attempt to colonize the peninsula lasted only two years, by which time disease, hostile Indians, and *chubascos* had driven the colonists back to the mainland.

The fourth attempt by Cortés to establish a Spanish foothold on California soil was led by the highly competent Captain Francisco de Ulloa, who'd accompanied Cortés on the failed Santa Cruz expedition. Cortés stayed behind on this one, hoping Ulloa's expedition would be able to find a more hospitable California beachhead. Ulloa's two ships set sail from Acapulco in July 1539, and over the next eight months he managed to explore the entire perimeter of the Sea of Cortez, reaching the mouth of the Río Colorado and rounding the Cape along the Pacific coast as far north as Isla Cedros.

Upon reaching Isla Cedros, Ulloa reportedly sent one ship back to Acapulco for supplies; it isn't known for certain what happened to the other vessel. According to some historical accounts, Ulloa found his way back to the mainland and was murdered by one of his own crew near Guadalajara; other accounts say he disappeared north of Isla Cedros. At any rate, his written report of the voyage—which indicated Baja was not an island but a peninsula—didn't surface until a hundred years later. His biggest contribution to the geography of the times was the naming of the Mar de Cortés, now the Sea of Cortez, or Gulf of California.

After squandering most of his wealth in futile attempts to explore Baja California, Cortés was recalled to Spain in 1541, never to return to Mexican shores. In his place, Spain dispatched experienced Portuguese navigator Juan Rodríguez Cabrillo in 1542 with orders to explore the Pacific coast. Starting from the southern tip of the peninsula, his expedition made it as far north as the Oregon coast and mapped several major bays along the way, including those of San Diego and Monterey. Cabrillo himself never made it past Alta California's Santa Barbara Islands; he died there following a mysterious fall.

Manila Galleons And Privateers
Meanwhile on the other side of the globe, events were unfolding that would influence Baja California's history for the next 250 years. Although Portuguese navigator Ferdinand Magellan reached the Philippines in 1521, it wasn't until 1565 that Lopez de Legaspi defeated the archipelago's native defenders. Immediately thereafter, Esteban Rodríguez and Padre Andrés de Urdaneta pioneered a ship route from Manila to the New World that took advantage of the 14,500-km (9,000-mile) Japanese Current across the northern Pacific, thus establishing a trade connection between the Orient and New Spain.

The ships making the annual roundtrip voyages between Manila and Acapulco beginning in 1566 came to be called "Manila galleons." The lengthy sea journey was very difficult, however, because of the lack of fresh water during the final weeks of the five- to seven-month eastward crossing. This provided further impetus for establishing some sort of settlement in lower California where ships could put in for water and supplies.

Manila galleon

A California landfall became even more desirable when in 1572 the Manila galleons started carrying shipments of gold, silks, and spices to New Spain. The ships were so heavy they became easy prey for faster pirate vessels. By 1580, England's Sir Francis Drake had entered the Pacific via the Straits of Magellan and circumnavigated the globe, thus ending Spanish dominion over the seas. Drake plundered Spanish ships with regularity, and as news of the treasure-laden ships spread, other English as well as Dutch privateers were lured into the Pacific.

Their raids on Spanish ships became an embarrassment to the crown and a drain on Spanish wealth, so the Spaniards were forced to seek out harbors along Baja's Cape Region where they could hide. Since the first land sighting on the east Pacific leg of the Manila-Acapulco voyage was below the peninsula's midpoint, the Cape Region was the logical choice for a landing. Following much experimentation, Bahía San Lucas and Bahía de la Paz became the two harbors most frequently used.

Eventually, however, the keen privateers figured out how to trap Spanish ships in the very bays their crews sought for protection. Thomas Cavendish plundered the Manila galleon *Santa Ana* at Cabo San Lucas in 1587, and so many ships were captured in Bahía de la Paz that the landfall there, originally called Santa Cruz by Cortés, eventually earned the name Pichilingue, a Spanish mispronunciation of Vlissingen, the provenance of most of the Dutch pirates.

Pirating continued off the Baja coast throughout the entire 250-year history of the Manila-Acapulco voyages. One of the more celebrated English privateers in later years was Woodes Rogers, who arrived in the Pacific in 1709 and captured the Manila galleon *Encarnación* off Cabo San Lucas. On his way to Baja California that same year Rogers rescued Alexander Selkirk, a sailor marooned on an island off the coast of Chile for four years. Selkirk served as shipmaster on Rogers's vessel and later became the inspiration for Daniel Defoe's 1719 novel *Robinson Crusoe*.

Further Exploration And Colonization Attempts
As the need for a permanent settlement in California grew more dire, coastal explorations were resumed after a hiatus of over 50 years. Cabrillo was succeeded by merchant-turned-

admiral Sebastián Vizcaíno, who in 1596 landed at the same bay on the southeast coast chosen by his predecessors, Jiménez and Cortés. This time, however, the natives were friendly—perhaps because it was pitahaya fruit season when they arrived—and Vizcaíno named the site La Paz ("Peace"). Loading up on pitahaya fruit—effective for preventing scurvy—and pearls, Vizcaíno continued northward along the Sea of Cortez coast, stopping to gather more pearls before returning to the mainland.

In 1602 Vizcaíno commanded a second, more ambitious expedition that sailed along the Pacific coast to near present-day Mendocino in Alta California. His names for various points and bays along the coasts of both Californias superseded most of those bestowed by Cabrillo and Cortés.

Upon his return Vizcaíno told his superiors that the Monterey Bay area of Alta California was well suited to colonization. However, because he was no longer in favor with New Spain's fickle viceroys, no one paid much attention to his findings and he was reassigned to an obscure Sinaloa port. The cartographer for the voyage, Gerónimo Martínez, was beheaded for forgery, although his maps of the Californias remained the best available for over 200 years.

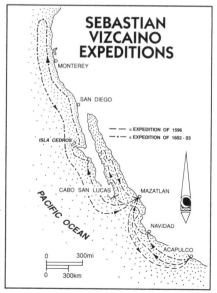

SEBASTIAN
VIZCAINO
EXPEDITIONS

MONTEREY

SAN DIEGO

— — = EXPEDITION OF 1596
— · — = EXPEDITION OF 1602 - 03

ISLA CEDROS

CABO SAN LUCAS   MAZATLAN

PACIFIC OCEAN

NAVIDAD

ACAPULCO

0   300mi
0   300km

This neglect of Alta California's potential enabled an Englishman to put first claim to the territory. Sir Francis Drake, who landed at what is now Drake's Bay in northern Alta California during his 1578-80 voyage, christened the land New Albion on behalf of the English crown. Like the Spanish maps of the time, his maps depicted California as an island.

For a time Spain left both Californias unexplored. In 1615 Captain Juan de Iturbi obtained the first official concession for peninsular pearl diving but no land settlement was established. After two of his ships were captured by Dutch privateers off Cabo San Lucas, de Iturbi's remaining vessel sailed northward in the Sea of Cortez as far as the 28th parallel, harvesting pearls along the way. Because of dwindling provisions, they were forced to turn back to the mainland after only a few months.

The peninsula remained unconquered by the Spanish for another 80 years. In 1683 Spain's Royal Council for the Indies authorized an expedition under Admiral Isidor Atondo y Antillón and Padre Eusebio Francisco Kino which managed to occupy an area of La Paz for 3.5 months before being driven back to the mainland by dwindling provisions and hostile natives. After two months of rest and provisioning on the mainland, they crossed the Sea of Cortez again, this time establishing a mission and presidio just above the 26th parallel at a place they named San Bruno. Supported by a friendly Indian population, the mission lasted 19 months. Lack of water and food—they had to rely on supply ships from the mainland—forced Kino and Atondo back to the mainland.

Kino never returned to Baja California but later became famous for his missionary efforts in northwestern Mexico and Arizona, where he is said to have converted thousands of Indians to Roman Catholicism. In 1701 he accompanied an expedition from the northwest of Sonora to the mouth of the Río Colorado that confirmed Ulloa's claim that Baja California was a peninsula. He died in Sonora in 1711.

THE MISSION PERIOD

The Founding Of The Jesuit Missions

In Baja California Padre Juan María Salvatierra finally succeeded in giving Spain and the Church

MISSIONS (1697 - 1856)

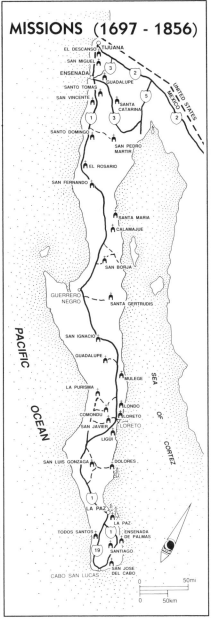

EL DESCANSO TIJUANA
SAN MIGUEL
ENSENADA
3
2
GUADALUPE
SANTO TOMAS
SAN VICENTE
5
SANTA CATARINA
UNITED STATES
MEXICO
1
3
2
SANTO DOMINGO
SAN PEDRO MARTIR
EL ROSARIO
SAN FERNANDO
SANTA MARIA
CALAMAJUE
SAN BORJA
GUERRERO NEGRO
SANTA GERTRUDIS
PACIFIC
SAN IGNACIO
GUADALUPE
MULEGE
SEA
LA PURISMA
OCEAN
LONDO
COMONDU
LORETO
SAN JAVIER
LORETO
LIGUI
OF
SAN LUIS GONZAGA
DOLORES
CORTEZ
1
LA PAZ
LA PAZ
TODOS SANTOS
1
ENSENADA DE PALMAS
19
SANTIAGO
CABO SAN LUCAS
SAN JOSE DEL CABO
0   50mi
0   50km

what they wanted—a permanent Spanish settlement on the peninsula. Backed by the mainland missionary system, a 30,000-peso annual subsidy from the Royal Council of the Indies, and a contingent of Spanish soldiers, Salvatierra landed in San Bruno in October 1697, located a better water source 24 km south of the original presidio, and proceeded to establish the mother of all California missions, Nuestra Señora de Loreto.

The founding of the Loreto mission initiated what Baja historians usually call "the Jesuit missionary period," lasting from 1697 to 1767. During this interval, the Jesuits established 20 missions, stretching from the southern tip of the peninsula to near present-day Cataviña in central Baja. That wasn't a spectacular accomplishment compared with the progress of mainland colonization, but lower California was a much more difficult area to colonize. It had taken 167 years from the time the first Spaniard had set foot on her shores until the first successful settlement was established on Baja California soil.

The Spanish mission system basically worked like this: the padres, always in the company of armed escorts, approached groups of natives and offered them the protection of the Church and the Spanish crown in return for a willingness to undergo religious instruction. Those natives who agreed were congregated at a suitable spot and directed to build a mission. The mission in turn became a refuge for the Indians and a place for them to learn European farming techniques and other trades, as well as Catholic ways. Once pacification was complete, the mission became a secularized church community (*pueblo*) and the missionaries moved on to new areas.

The system worked well with the docile Indians of Central Mexico but was often unsuccessful among the nomadic, fiercely independent Indians of Northern Mexico and Baja. Elsewhere in Mexico and Latin America, the norm was to secularize after 10 years; in Baja, the Spanish Church never voluntarily secularized its missions.

Amateur historians like to say the Californias were missionized by the cross, not the sword. This was actually no more true in Baja than it was for the mainland, although the military presence was indeed less—but only because the

Jesuits were given greater administrative power in Baja and had to finance themselves, and their militia, through Church funds. The conversion techniques were the same: natives who obeyed the padres were rewarded with land and protection, those who rebelled were punished, those who organized rebellions were executed. Apologists claim the padres never endorsed violence, but if this were true, they wouldn't have brought along the militia in the first place.

A contemporary report of the founding of Misión San Juan Bautista describes how Padres Salvatierra and Pedro de Ugarte approached the natives of Liguí in 1703:

The two Padres, the soldier who accompanied them and two Christian Indians were given a real fright by a large band of Indians who fired a shower of arrows toward them, but after the soldier . . . discharged his musket into the air the Indians threw down their weapons and prostrated themselves on the earth, presently sitting up to await the coming of the Padres. Through an interpreter, Padre Salvatierra explained to them the purpose of their visit, and distributed among them some small gifts, expressing the hope that Padre Pedro de Ugarte might return later and be welcomed by them. Before leaving they brought 48 Indian children for baptism.

Indian Revolts, Disease, And The Decline Of The Jesuits

Several times during the Jesuit period, groups of Indians revolted against missionization. The most significant rebellion occurred in 1734-36 among the Pericú Indians of the southern peninsula. Apparently the revolt was triggered by Padre Nicolás Tamaral's injunction against polygamy—long a practice among the Pericús and Guaicuras, tribes in which women outnumbered men. The punishment of a Pericú shaman under the injunction doubled the perceived assault on native culture and a group of disaffected Indians organized themselves against the entire mission structure.

In October 1734, the Pericús attacked and burned the missions at Santiago and San José del Cabo, killing Padre Tamaral and his counterpart at Santiago; they also set fire to the mission in Loreto although the padre there escaped unharmed and was able to send to the mainland for assistance. The provincial governor of Sinaloa, after receiving letters from Loreto describing the uprising, dispatched a ship from the mainland with 60 Yaqui warriors and a number of Spanish soldiers. The troops marched from mission to mission, meeting little resistance from the poorly equipped Pericús.

Unrest among the Pericús continued for another two years, a situation that led to the founding of a large presidio at San José del Cabo. As a further precaution, the garrisons at every mission in the south were expanded by 10 soldiers each. Besides reinforcing the missions, this increased military presence encouraged Manila galleons to make Cabo San Lucas a regular stop on their return voyages from the Orient.

In the years to follow, epidemics of smallpox, syphilis, and measles—diseases borne by Europeans for which Indians had no natural immunity—decimated the Indian population. In 1538 Padre Jacobo Baegert of Misión San Luis Gonzaga estimated the Baja Indian population at about 50,000. In three outbreaks of smallpox in 1742, 1744, and 1748, an estimated 42,000, or five-sixths of the Indian population, perished. Gathering the natives into mission settlements only hastened their demise, intensifying the spread of contagions. A significant number of Indians also lost their lives in continued rebellions against the padres. The La Paz mission was abandoned in 1748; by 1767 only one member of the entire Huchiti branch of the Guaycura nation survived.

As the southern Indians died out, the missionaries moved quickly northward, seeking new sheep for their flocks. The last four missions established by the Jesuits, Santa Gertrudis (1752), San Borja (1762), Calamajué (1766), and Santa María (1767) were scattered widely in northern Baja in an obvious push toward Alta California.

In 1767 King Charles III ordered the expulsion of the Jesuit Order from all Spanish dominions, including Baja California. Accounts of the expulsion disagree as to the reasons behind his action. According to crown representatives, the Jesuits were too power-hungry and would no longer be held accountable for their actions. The Jesuits themselves claimed persecution because they'd dared criticize corruption among the nobility and royalty of Europe. Whatever the reason, in 1768 the 16 Jesuit padres of Baja found themselves herded onto a ship bound for the mainland port of San Blas, where the same ship received a contingent of Franciscan padres sent to replace them.

The Franciscans And Dominicans

The 14 Franciscan padres who arrived in Loreto in 1768 included Padre Junípero Serra, often dubbed the "Father of California." That title really belongs to Padre Salvatierra, who established the first California—Baja California, that is— mission 72 years prior to Serra's arrival at San Diego.

To counter the flow of non-Spanish Europeans toward Alta California—the English across the south and middle of North America, the French across Canada, and the Russians south from Alaska along the coast—Serra was under orders to establish missions and presidios as quickly as possible in a northward direction.

Serra and the Franciscans only established one mission in Baja before moving on to Alta California. This was San Fernando Velicatá, founded in 1769 about 64 km southeast of today's El Rosario. The Velicatá mission was primarily used as a staging area for expeditions to Alta California. There were two initial expeditions, one by sea from La Paz and one by land from Velicatá; both would rendezvous in San Diego Bay. Padre Serra accompanied the land expedition, led by Captain Gaspár de Portolá, and established Alta California's first mission at San Diego, the first in a chain of 20 missions that stretched along the upper California coast as far as Sonoma, north of San Francisco.

The ambitious Serra, realizing that the arid, underpopulated peninsula did not offer the empire-building potential of Alta California, sent to Mexico City a proposal that the administration of the Baja California missions be released to the Dominican Order, who'd been clamoring for a place in California missionary action. The viceroy approved Serra's request in 1772 and the first Dominican priests arrived on the peninsula in 1773 under the direction of Padre Vicente Mora.

The first new Dominican mission, Nuestra Señora del Rosario Viñaraco, was founded in the valley now known as Arroyo del Rosario in

1774. Eight more missions and one visiting chapel were established by the Dominicans between 1774 and 1834, all north of El Rosario. The northernmost was Misión El Descanso, located between modern-day Ensenada and Rosarito and built on the edge of Arroyo del Descanso, the official boundary line separating the respective California domains of the Dominican order to the south and the Franciscan order to the north. This boundary also served to separate the New Spain provinces of Alta and Baja California, as officially designated in 1777. The current border between Baja California and the U.S. state of California was created by the Treaty of Hidalgo at the end of the Mexican-American War in 1848.

By the end of the 18th century it was clear that Spain and the Church could no longer afford to support the Baja missions. The peninsula's Indian population had dwindled to less than 5,000 by 1800, and, without an abundance of free native labor, maintaining a colony wasn't an easy task. The Alta California missions seemed much more promising—water was more available and the Indian labor force was more docile and plentiful. The growing unrest in Mexico placed the peninsula even lower on Spain's list of priorities.

INDEPENDENCE FROM SPAIN

The Catholic Church in Mexico had amassed huge amounts of wealth by the beginning of the 19th century and had become lenders to the colony's growing entrepreneurial class. At the other end of the economic spectrum, the increasing numbers of mestizos—Mexican-born residents of mixed Spanish and Indian ancestry—were denied land ownership and other rights, and were generally treated as second-class citizens.

Fearing the Church was becoming too powerful, King Charles III of Spain decreed in 1804 that all church funds be turned over to the royal coffers. As padres all over Mexico were forced to comply with the decree, calling back large sums of money lent out to entrepreneurs, economic chaos ensued. Mexicans blamed their economic and social problems on Spain's remote rule; when Napoleon invaded Spain in 1808, limiting authority to Spanish loyalists in Mexico City, the disaffected clergy began planning a revolt.

Mexico's struggle for independence from Spain began on 16 September 1810, a date celebrated annually as Diez y Seis or Mexican Independence Day. Padre Miguel Hidalgo y Costilla issued a call for independence entitled the Grito de Dolores ("Dolores Cry") in the mainland province of Guanajato. Although the rebels gathered around Hidalgo soon captured Zacatecas, Valladolid, and San Luis Potosí, Mexico wasn't completely free of Spanish rule for another 11 years. When Hidalgo was captured and executed by loyalists, another padre took his place and the fighting continued until Mexico City acceded to the demands of the rebels in 1821.

The 1821 Plan de Iguala treaty between Spain and Mexico guaranteed three political underpinnings of the new regime: the religious dominance of the Catholic Church, a constitutional monarchy, and equal rights for mestizos as well as Mexican-born Spaniards. Former Viceroy Agustín de Iturbide was appointed emperor of the new republic, but his reign only lasted two years before he was overthrown by another junta that established a short-lived federal republic called Los Estados Unidos de México—the United States of Mexico—in 1824.

Over the next six years the Mexican republic endured two more coups; it wasn't until 1829 that all Spanish troops were expelled from Mexico. In 1832 all non-Dominican missions in Baja were secularized and converted to parish churches. The Dominican missions of the northern peninsula were allowed to remain because they were considered the only outposts of civilization north of La Paz and Loreto and as such were important links with prospering Alta California. Another change in policy involved the encouragement of Anglo-American immigration to the northeastern Mexican state of Coahuila y Texas.

The Mexican-American War

In 1833 Antonio López de Santa Anna, a megalomaniac general in charge of enforcing the expulsion of Spanish troops, seized power and revoked the Constitution of 1824, thus initiating a series of events that eventually led to a war with the U.S. and the resultant loss of huge amounts of territory. During the first 30 years of Mexican independence, Mexico changed governments 50 times; Santa Anna—who called himself the "Napoleon of the West"—headed 11 of these regimes.

Mexican citizens everywhere were angry at the revocation of their republican constitution by a self-appointed dictator. But none were more frustrated than the Anglo-American immigrants who had voluntarily abandoned their U.S. citizenship in order to take Mexican citizenship under the Constitution of 1824 and live in the northern half of Coahuila y Texas. In 1836 the "Texicans" declared an independent Republic of Texas, fought and lost San Antonio's infamous Battle of the Alamo, and then routed Santa Anna's defending troops in San Jacinto, Texas.

Defeated and captured, Santa Anna signed the Velasco Agreement, which guaranteed Texas independence and recognized the Rio Grande as the border between Mexico and the new Texan republic. There matters lay until the U.S. granted statehood to the near-bankrupt republic in 1845. Santa Anna's government refused to recognize the Velasco Agreement, claiming Texas only extended as far south as the Nueces River, about 160 km north of the Rio Grande at the widest gap. When the U.S. Army moved into the area south of the Nueces, Santa Anna retaliated by sending troops across the Rio Grande, thus initiating the Mexican-American War.

After a series of skirmishes along the Rio Grande, U.S. President James Polk ordered the army to invade Mexico. In Baja California, Mexican and American forces engaged at Santo Tomás, Mulegé, La Paz, and San José del Cabo. Mexico City finally fell to U.S. troops in March 1847 and Santa Anna signed the Treaty of Guadalupe Hidalgo in 1848. In the treaty, Mexico conceded not only the Rio Grande area of Texas but parts of New Mexico and Arizona and all of Alta California for a payment of US$25 million and the cancellation of all Mexican debt.

In retrospect, it is likely the annexation of Texas was part of a U.S. plan to provoke Mexico into declaring war so the U.S. could gain more of the Southwest. The war so damaged Mexico's already weakened economy that in 1853 Santa Anna sold southern Arizona and southern New Mexico to the U.S. for another US$10 million. During that same year, American freebooter William Walker sailed to La Paz and declared himself "President of Lower California." He and his mercenary troops fled upon hearing that Mexican forces were on the way.

He was later tried—and acquitted—in the U.S. for violation of neutrality laws. Walker was executed after a similar escapade in Nicaragua two years later.

For the Mexican population, already strongly dissatisfied with Santa Anna, this additional loss and threatened loss of territory was the final straw; in 1855 Santa Anna was overthrown by populist Benito Juárez.

Depopulation Of The Peninsula, Civil War, And Reform

The second half of the 19th century was even more turbulent for Mexico than the first. At the end of the Mexican-American War, the California Gold Rush of 1849 lured many Mexicans and Indians away from the peninsula to seek their fortunes in Alta California, reducing Baja's already scant population even further and transforming it into a haven for bandits, pirates, and an assortment of other outlaws and misfits. Only six Dominican padres remained on the peninsula by the 1880s.

Meanwhile back on the mainland, a civil war (called the "War of Reform" in Mexico) erupted in 1858, following the removal of Santa Anna, in which self-appointed governments in Mexico City and Veracruz vied for national authority. Once again, Church wealth was the principal issue. The liberals, under Zapotec Indian lawyer Benito Juárez, had promulgated a new constitution in 1857 and passed a law further restricting the financial powers of the Church; all Church property save for church buildings had to be sold or otherwise relinquished. A reactionary opposition group took control of Mexico City and fighting continued until 1861, when the liberals won and Juárez was elected president.

Juárez immediately had to deal with the 1862 French invasion of Mexico, which came in response to Mexico's nonpayment of debts to France. The first invading force was defeated at Puebla, but the following year the French captured the port and continued onward to take Mexico City, where they installed Austrian Ferdinand Maximilian as emperor of Mexico. Under U.S. pressure, the French gradually withdrew from Mexico and Juárez was back in power by 1867.

Over the next four years Juárez initiated many economic and educational reforms. Upon his death in 1872, political opponent Porfirio Díaz took over and continued reforms begun by Juárez, albeit in a more authoritarian manner. Díaz and/or his cronies ruled for the next 28 years, suspending political freedoms but modernizing the country's education and transportation systems.

Foreign Investment In Baja California

In Baja, Díaz and the "Porfiriato" encouraged foreign investment on a large scale, and in the 1880s vast land tracts were sold to American or European mining, farming, manufacturing, and railway concessions. All but the mining concessions met failure within a few years, mainly because the investors weren't prepared to deal with the peninsula's demanding climate and lack of transportation. A Connecticut company invested US$5 million as a down payment on US$16 million for extensive land holdings in Ensenada and San Quintín. There it planned to develop farmlands, railways, and seaports. When the first wheat crop succumbed to lack of rain, the company sold out to a similar English development syndicate, which also failed.

KAREN WHITE

Benito Juárez

Mineral excavation in turn-of-the-century Baja enjoyed a boom—gold, silver, copper, and gypsum were the main finds, along with graphite, mercury, nickel, and sulfur. One of the most successful mining endeavors was that of Compañía del Boleo, a French mining syndicate in Santa Rosalía that for many years was the largest copper-mining and smelting operation in Mexico.

INTO THE TWENTIETH CENTURY

The Mexican Revolution

By the early 1900s, it was obvious that the gap between rich and poor was increasing, caused by the extreme pro-capitalist policies of the Díaz regime and the lack of a political voice for workers and peasants. In response to the situation, a liberal opposition group, using Texas as a base, formed in exile, organizing strikes throughout the country. This forced Díaz to announce an election in 1910; his opponent was Francisco Madero, a liberal from Coahuila. As it became clear that Madero was garnering mass support, Díaz imprisoned him on trumped-up charges.

Upon his release, Madero fled to Texas and began organizing the overthrow of the Díaz government. The rebels, with the assistance of the colorful bandit-turned-revolutionary Pancho Villa and peasant-hero Emiliano Zapata, managed to gain control of the northern Mexican states of Sonora and Chihuahua. Unable to contain the revolution, Díaz resigned in May of 1910 and Madero was elected president. The opposition, however, broke into several factions—the Zapatistas, Reyistas, Vasquistas, and Felicistas, named for the leaders of each movement, and Madero was executed in 1913. Baja California had its own faction, the Magonistas, who briefly held Tijuana in 1911.

For the next six years the various factions played musical chairs with national leadership, and Mexico remained extremely unstable until revolutionary leader Venustiano Carranza emerged as president. Carranza held a historic convention that resulted in the Constitution of 1917, the current Mexican constitution. This document established the *ejido* program to return lands traditionally cultivated by the Indian peasantry, but taken away by rich ranch and plantation owners under Díaz, to local communities throughout Mexico. Three years later opponent Álvaro Obregón and his supporters overthrew Carranza.

Obregón managed to hang onto the office for four years, establishing important educational reforms; he was followed in 1924 by Plutarco Elías Calles. Calles instituted wide-reaching agrarian reforms, including the redistribution of three million hectares of land. He also participated in the establishment of the National Revolutionary Party (PNR), the forerunner of the Institutional Revolutionary Party (PRI), Mexico's dominant party today.

U.S. Prohibition

In the same year that Obregón took power in Mexico City, the U.S. government amended its own constitution to make the consumption, manufacture, and sale of alcoholic beverages a federal offense. This proved to be a disastrous experiment for the U.S., ushering in an era of organized crime, but was a boon to Baja California development. Americans began rushing across the border to buy booze from the restaurants, cantinas, and liquor stores of northern Mexico.

Tijuana and Mexicali added casinos and brothels to its assortment of liquor venues and became so prosperous the municipal leadership was able to lobby successfully for the division of Baja California into northern and southern territories. On the negative side, the two cities became renowned as world sleaze capitals. Their reputations persisted long after Prohibition ended in 1933 and the Mexican government outlawed gambling—prostitution remained legal—in 1938. The cities wisely channeled much of their unexpected revenue into manufacturing, agriculture, and other non-tourist-related development.

Nationalist Reforms And World War II

The year 1934 proved a turning point in modern Mexican history as PNR candidate Lázaro Cárdenas ascended to the presidency. Cárdenas, a mestizo with Tarascan Indian heritage, instituted the most sweeping social reforms of any national leader to date, effecting significant changes in education, labor, agriculture, and commerce.

His land reforms included the redistribution of 46 million acres among newly created *ejidos*—a legacy that is as hot a topic for debate today as it was then. Foreign-owned oil interests were expropriated and a national oil company, Petróleos Mexicanos (PEMEX), established. These reforms frightened off foreign investors for many years and it has been only very recently that Mexico has reattracted foreign capital. Cárdenas also reorganized the PNR as the Mexican Revolution Party (PRM—Partido de la Revolución Mexicana), which soon changed its name to the Institutional Revolutionary Party (PRI—Partido Revolucionario Institucional).

During WW II, Mexican troops fought in the Pacific on the Allied side. The Mexican economy grew with the increased demand for materials and labor in the U.S.; the scarcity of imported goods in Mexico forced the nation to increase domestic production. In 1942 the U.S. instituted the Bracero Program, which permitted Mexicans to work north of the border for short periods of time; the program lasted until 1962 and had a profound effect on urban development along the U.S.-Mexico border.

Baja Statehood And
The Transpeninsular Highway

After the war Mexico continued to industrialize and the economy remained relatively stable under one PRI president after another. In 1952 the Territory of (Northern) Baja California was declared Mexico's 29th state as its population moved past the 80,000 required for statehood. Northern Baja was, in fact, better off economically than most of the rest of the country. The boomtowns of Tijuana and Mexicali were servicing a fast-growing border economy and Valle de Mexicali farming competed well with California's Imperial Valley. In 1958 it was determined that Baja was second only to Mexico City in the number of automobiles per capita.

Throughout the 1960s most of Baja south of Ensenada remained benevolently neglected, which led travel writers of the time to employ the famous catchphrase, "the forgotten peninsula." The population of the Territory of Southern Baja California was stagnating, perhaps even decreasing; except for La Paz, it was limited to tiny collections of hardy souls here and there who scratched for cash as rancheros or *pescadores* (fishermen). Even La Paz was just a step above a sleepy backwater port although its status as a duty-free port was beginning to attract a steady trickle of mainland Mexicans.

By the 1970s it was obvious that southern Baja wasn't going to catch up with northern Baja unless transportation between the south, north, and mainland improved. Travel between Tijuana and La Paz took up to 10 days via rough dirt tracks. Construction of the Transpeninsular Highway (Mexico 1) was finally completed in 1973, connecting Tijuana with Cabo San Lucas for the first time. In less than a year, the population of Baja California Sur passed the 80,000 mark and the territory became Mexico's 30th state.

The 1,700-km-long Transpeninsular Highway has greatly contributed to the modernization of one of Mexico's last frontiers. Fishing and agricultural cooperatives can now transport their products to the border or to the ports of Santa Rosalía, Guerrero Negro, and La Paz. The highway has brought Americans, Canadians, and Europeans deep into the peninsula in greater numbers than ever before, and the revenue from their visits provides another means of livelihood for the people of Baja.

Like the border visitors of the Prohibition years, those foreigners who come to Baja in the 1990s are seeking something that's scarce in their own countries. For some it may be the unfenced desert solitude, for others the pristine beaches or historic mission towns. The challenge of the future for Baja's fledgling tourist industry is how to develop and maintain an adequate infrastructure without sacrificing those qualities that make Baja California unique.

GOVERNMENT

POLITICAL BOUNDARIES

The 28th parallel divides the peninsula into two states, officially named Baja California (abbreviated BC) above the parallel and Baja California Sur (BCS) below. Unofficially, the northern state is often called Baja California Norte (BCN); a debate continually simmers as to whether or not to make this version official. In this book, BCN is used so as not to confuse the northern state with the whole peninsula.

Mexicali is BCN's state capital, which governs four *municipios* that are similar to U.S. counties: Tijuana, Ensenada, Mexicali, and Tecate. Besides its southern border with BCS, BCN shares a northern border with the U.S. and an eastern border, formed above the Sea of Cortez by the Colorado River, with the Mexican state of Sonora.

Baja California Sur is divided into five municipios: La Paz, Cabo San Lucas, Mulegé, Loreto, and Comondú. La Paz is the capital.

POLITICAL SYSTEM

As Mexican states, BCN and BCS are part of Mexico's federal system (Estados Unidos Mexicanos, or United Mexican States), which allows for some degree of autonomous rule by state governors and their legislatures. Both states are considered among the most socially progressive in the nation. All of Mexico's 12 orphanages, for example, are located in Baja. BCN is the only state with a non-PRI governor, Ernesto Ruffo Appel, a PAN (Partido Acción Nacional or National Action Party) candidate who defeated PRI's Margarita Ortega Villa in 1989 state elections—the first time in PRI's 60-year history it conceded an electoral loss. In that same election PAN took nine of 19 state legislative seats and the mayoral seats of Tijuana and Ensenada. PAN is sometimes described as a conservative party because it favors private over government ownership, yet in the context of Mexican politics it's more reform-minded than PRI. As elsewhere in the world, political labels and their meanings shift with time.

The PAN victory was considered by some a watershed in Mexican politics, which has been notorious for election fraud since adopting the republican system in 1917. Many Bajacalifornios remain skeptical, however, and see the PRI concession as a one-time occurrence. Hard-boiled cynics insist all high political offices are part of a ruling dynasty extending outward from the presidency in Mexico City; even municipal mayors in Mexico are called *el presidente* and the local seat of government is the *palacio municipal*. Wags point out other symbolic evidence—the President wears an imperial sash and sits upon a throne when making official proclamations—and the fact that political candidates endorsed by the incumbents always win succeeding elections.

The *presidentes municipales* appoint city *delegados* to represent federal power at the local level; smaller communities may have *subdelegados*. These delegados and subdelegados are the highest authority within their jurisdictions and are part of a chain of command that reaches back to the president of Mexico.

ECONOMY

INCOME

Agriculture, fishing, and tourism are Baja's main revenue-earners, followed by manufacturing and services in the border area. Per-capita income figures for BCN and BCS are well above the Mexican national average and second within the nation only to that of Mexico D.F. (Distrito Federal).

Most large-scale farming is centered in the Río Colorado delta (Valle de Mexicali), Valle de Guadalupe, Valle de San Quintín, and the Magdalena Plains surrounding Ciudad Constitución. Fishing boats work both coasts, but the Sea of Cortez produces the largest catch and La Paz is the main fishing center. Tourism is for the most part concentrated in Tijuana, Rosarito-Ensenada, Mulegé-Loreto, La Paz, and Los Cabos (San José del Cabo and Cabo San Lucas).

The stars of the manufacturing sector are the *maquiladoras,* or in-bond industries, which combine third-world labor costs with first-world capital and management. These are predominantly located in special export-processing zones in the Tijuana area, although nearby Tecate and Mexicali are also developing industrial parks. While wages at the maquiladoras are far below comparable wages in the U.S., they're about twice Mexico's current minimum daily wage of US$4.65 a day.

THE SYSTEM

On a macroeconomic level, Baja finds itself caught between two economic systems. Because it's so isolated from the rest of Mexico, the regional economy tends to be American-influenced yet subject to the same economic vicissitudes as the rest of the country, most notably a weak currency and high inflation. Although the country's current-account balance rose from a deficit of US$6.2 billion in 1982 to a surplus of US$4 billion in 1987, the inflation rate that same year hit 146%. Because of its regional ties to the U.S., particularly Alta California, the Baja economy weathered this period better than many areas of Mexico.

Following the election of President Carlos Salinas de Gortari, a Harvard University economics graduate, the nation moved closer to U.S.-style supply-side economics, thus lessening the schizoid nature of Baja's regional economy. In 1988 the Bank of Mexico slowed the runaway devaluation of the Mexican peso almost to a halt; the national currency now loses less than a peso a day against the U.S. dollar, a considerable improvement over the 1976-87 period in which it slid from eight pesos to the dollar to over 2,000.

The Salinas government reprivatized the national banking system and several other state industries; PEMEX is the major exception. The current policy is to open all sectors of the Mexican economy to private investment save for below-ground resources; i.e., petroleum and minerals. The eight largest employers in Mexico are government agencies connected with education, social security, PEMEX, or defense. Among private corporations, the largest employers are General Motors (58,000 employees) and TelMex (49,900).

Inflation is now running at about 12-18% per annum, down from 20-25% two years ago. Foreign exchange reserves are rising; from 1990 to 1991 Mexico's foreign reserves doubled from US$8.4 billion to US$16.7 billion, the highest in the country's history. Exports for 1992 totaled US$27.3 billion; foreign debt as a percentage of exports is 20%, less than half what it was ten years ago. GNP growth is a very respectable four percent per annum and an increase to five or six percent is a reasonable projection. Remarkably, the national budget deficit hit zero in 1992 and by the end of 1993 the budget is expected to run a surplus for the first time in Mexican history.

Some optimistic economists predict that if Mexico continues its current reforms, it may become the world's fastest growing economy by the year 2000. Growth in Baja will probably be slower, however, since much of the current and projected growth is confined to areas of Mexico "catching up" with Baja.

Ejidos

One of the most unique features of the Mexican economy is the *ejido*. An ejido is a land tract, held in common by a peasant community, that includes not only cultivated fields but also school properties, urban zones, water and forest resources, and any other facilities or resources either native to the land or produced by collective efforts. Ejidos are granted to *ejidatarios* by the government without rents or fees of any kind and until recently were nontransferrable, nonattachable, and inalienable—neither state property nor private property but entities of the "social interest sector."

How they're used is solely the concern of the peasant communities that hold them, but around 95% are "individual" ejidos in which common holdings are divided into individual plots and cultivated by individual ejidatarios and their families. The remaining five percent are "collective" ejidos that pool all land resources for collective production.

The ejido came into being under the Constitution of 1917 as a way of restoring Indian lands seized by rich *hacendados* (big ranchers and plantation owners) during Spanish colonization and early Mexican independence. The number and total acreage of Mexico's ejidos is not well documented but by 1970 they encompassed an estimated 46% of all national farmlands.

Various bits of legislation enacted since the ejido's 1917 inception have alternately strengthened and weakened the ejido program. In recent years new laws have allowed ejidatarios to lease land to neighboring private estates for agricultural or livestock purposes. Legislation passed in 1992 now allows ejidatarios to buy and sell ejido land like any real estate.

Has the ejido program been successful? It has kept hereditary lands in the hands of peasant communities who've worked the lands for hundreds of years; without them, many ejidatarios would probably become landless migrant workers. But because ejido production is notoriously low, as are fixed prices for agricultural products, the need for cash has forced many ejidatarios to work as laborers on neighboring private lands. As a result, economists estimate that ejidatarios are among the poorest and most exploited of Mexico's rural workers. All ejidatarios are automatic members of PRI's peasant division, but because of their overall lack of education and political experience, they're easily manipulated by PRI leaders in Mexico City and are hence relatively powerless. The new recognition of property rights gives ejido residents the potential to make money from their lands for the first time since 1917.

THE PEOPLE

The people of Baja California are in many ways a breed apart from their compatriots on the mainland. As Mexico's last frontier, the peninsula continues to attract residents seeking something they haven't been able to find on the mainland, whether it's the rugged, independent life of the interior deserts and sierras, the tropical ambience of La Paz or Cabo San Lucas, or the promising multicultural world in Tijuana and Mexicali, where the two Californias meet.

For the rest of Mexico, Baja California occupies a place in the national psyche somewhat analagous to that of Hawaii for many Americans. It's seen as a place that's part of the nation yet almost out of reach, an exotic destination which most of the population will never have an opportunity to see. Hence, mainlanders typically regard people native to Baja California as somehow "different" from themselves. It works the other way, too.

POPULATION

The current population of the entire peninsula is approximately 2,850,000, about 87% of whom live above the 28th parallel in Baja California Norte. Well over half the people on the peninsula live in Mexicali and Tijuana, with an additional 13% in Ensenada. Obviously, most of the peninsula is very sparsely populated—the average density, even if these and all other Baja cities are included in the estimate, is only 1.5 persons per square km (about four persons per square mile). Outside the three most populated cities it's less than one person per 26 square km (one body per 10 square miles).

Mexico's population growth rate is currently estimated at 1.9% per annum, relatively low for a developing country. The average for Baja California is probably somewhat higher than the national average because of immigration. Baja California Sur is the country's least populated state.

ORIGINS

The residents of Baja California, *bajacalifornios*, are an unusually varied lot. Elsewhere in Mexi-

co, the average citizen is a mix of two heritages, Spanish and Indian. In Baja, the mix is typically more complicated, mainly because the peninsula remained a frontier much longer than most of the mainland, attracting people who arrived in the New World long after the Spanish colonized the Mexican mainland. It was 167 years after the conquest of Mexico before the Spanish were able to maintain a permanent settlement on the peninsula; by this time, tales of the Californias were on the tongues of adventurers throughout the world.

By the end of the 19th century the peninsula had become a favorite spot for sea-weary sailors to jump ship. The eastern shores of the peninsula were placid, and there was little chance deserters would be rounded up and incarcerated by local militia, who were very scarce then, and remain scarce to this day. Most of the ex-sailors who retired to Baja in this manner were English, but during WW I a few Germans and other Europeans came ashore. Their ship captains might have considered them cowardly deserters, but survival in Baja in the 19th and early 20th centuries was possible only for the brave, hardy, and resourceful.

Other immigrants who pioneered the Baja frontier included Chinese workers, who came via the Mexican mainland and eventually flourished in the Mexicali area, Russian viniculturists who settled the Valle de Guadalupe, French miners in Santa Rosalía and Mulegé, and Mexican intellectuals and dissidents fleeing political oppression on the mainland and gravitating toward La Paz, Ensenada, or Tijuana. Many of these newcomers intermarried and their descendants have greatly contributed to the peninsula's multicultural spirit.

Since in a very real sense much of Baja is still a frontier area—with more immigrants wandering in year by year—Baja's demographics have yet to solidify into recognizable pie-graph proportions. About two percent of the population aren't even citizens; many of them are North Americans or Europeans who've retired to Baja. A lesser number are gringos who've simply dropped out of the rat race. With the recent relaxation of investment and trade laws, a growing number of nonnationals are also setting up businesses on the peninsula.

Bajacalifornios

If there's a personality trait common to all true Bajacalifornios, it's a do-or-die spirit that says "I belong here because my family was tough enough to survive in Baja back when this was the toughest place in Mexico to survive." While opinions vary, the popular definition of a "true" Bajacalifornio is someone whose forbears came to and stayed on the peninsula sometime before WW II.

A self-adopted nickname for Bajacalifornios, particularly popular in northern Baja, is *cachanilla* (sometimes spelled *cachania*), taken from a hardy desert plant (*Pluchea sericea,* arrowweed) that produces rose-colored flowers under even the harshest of conditions.

Bajacalifornios love to rant about how the peninsula was neglected by the mainland for centuries, how they cultivated Baja for themselves, without any help from Mexico City. Now that the Transpeninsular Highway is complete and the economic infrastructure is expanding, the Bajacalifornios say, weak mainlanders are coming to harvest the fruits of Baja's development. A special scorn is reserved for *chilangos,* a derogatory term used by Bajacalifornios for Mexico City politicians or businesspeople who come to Baja and tell the cachanillas how to run things.

Indians

Of the estimated 50,000 Indians who inhabited the peninsula when the Spanish established their first Baja mission of any duration in 1697, at least 80% were wiped out by disease or colonial violence within a hundred years. None of the Guaycura tribes of the south—Guaicura, Pericú, Huchiti—survived the Spanish occupation, but small numbers of the central and northern Cochimí and Yumano tribes still reside in the valleys and sierras of BCN.

According to Mexico's 1980 census, the Paipai (Pa'ipai, or "Clever People") are the largest surviving native tribe, numbering around 300; most are concentrated in the vicinity of Santa Catarina and San Isidoro. About 165 Kumyai live in Valle de Guadalupe and Juntas de Neji, 200 Cochimí in Valle Ojos Negros and San Antonio Necua, 200 Kiliwa (Quilihua) in Ejido Tribu Quilihua, and about 200 Cucapá in Cucapá El Mayor in the Río Colorado delta.

The Mexican government has set aside tracts of BCN land for each tribe; the Paipai, for example, own 160,000 acres from the Alamo plain eastward. For the most part, Baja's native tribespeople work on small ranches and farms; the livestock trade in particular has been a primary source of income ever since the Indians acquired horses, burros, cattle, goats, and sheep from Spanish missionaries. It is not known how many *indígenos* preserve tribal traditions, since, as in the American Southwest, many customs and ceremonies have gone underground due to a deep and understandable suspicion of outsiders.

Outnumbering the Indians native to Baja are the thousands of Indians from Sonora, Oaxaca, and Chiapas who've come to Baja to work as migrant laborers. Most numerous in the Valle de San Quintín, they're also commonly found in the Ensenada area. Migrant Indians unable to find agricultural jobs are often seen hawking blankets and other handicrafts on the streets of the tourist districts in Tijuana, Ensenada, and Cabo San Lucas.

LANGUAGE

As in the rest of Mexico, Spanish is the most widely spoken language in Baja California. English is occasionally spoken by merchants, hotel staff, and travel agents in Tijuana, Mexicali, Ensenada, Loreto, La Paz, San José del Cabo, and Cabo San Lucas. Even in these cities, however, you can count on finding English-speaking Mexicans only within each city's tourist districts. Outside of tourist areas, and even in smaller border towns like Tecate, it's somewhat rare to encounter anyone who speaks more than a few words of English.

Hence it's incumbent upon the non-Spanish-speaking visitor to learn at least enough Spanish to cope with everyday transactions. Knowing a little Spanish will not only mitigate communication problems, it will also bring you more respect among the local Mexicans, who quite naturally resent foreign visitors who expect Mexicans to abandon their mother tongue whenever a gringo approaches. A popular sign seen in tourist restaurants reads "We promise not to laugh at your broken Spanish if you won't laugh at our broken English." Out of courtesy, you should at least attempt to communicate in Spanish whenever possible.

The type of Spanish spoken in Mexico is usually referred to as "Latin-American Spanish," in contrast to the Castilian Spanish spoken in Spain. Still, the Spanish here differs significantly from that of even other Spanish-speaking countries in the Western Hemisphere. In Baja California especially, many Anglicisms have crept into the language. For example, the common Latin-American Spanish term for "car" is *coche*, but in Baja you'll more often hear *carro*. Signs at automotive stores may read *auto partes* rather than *refacciones; yonke* (junk) is also commonly seen, and refers to new and used auto parts rather than junked cars.

LANGUAGE STUDY

Dictionaries And Phrasebooks
One of the best portable dictionaries for the Spanish student is the paperback *University of Chicago Spanish-English, English-Spanish Dictionary,* which emphasizes New World usages and contains useful sections on grammar and pronunciation. If even this small volume is too large for your backpack, the *Collins Gem Dictionary: Spanish-English, English-Spanish* comes in a tiny 4-by-3.5-by-1-inch edition with a sturdy plastic cover and over 40,000 entries.

Berlitz's *Latin-American Spanish For Travellers* is a small phrasebook divided by topics and situations (e.g., grammar, hotel, eating out, post office). Not all the phrases and terms it contains are used in Baja, but it's better than nothing.

One of the best references for off-the-road adventurers is Burleson's and Riskind's *Backcountry Mexico: A Traveler's Guide and Phrase Book* (University of Texas Press). Although it's rather bulky for carrying in a backpack and is oriented toward travel in northern mainland Mexico, it contains many words and phrases of value to Baja hikers and campers.

Advanced Spanish learners can improve their command of idiomatic Spanish with Frances de Talavera Berger's *¡Mierda!* (Plume, New York). Subtitled *The Real Spanish You Were Never Taught in School,* the book's copious *vulgarismos* or slang expressions have a decidedly scatological slant and should probably be aired in public only after practice with a trusted native speaker.

Schools In Baja
Those who plan to spend an extended period of time in Baja should seriously consider enrolling in an intensive Spanish course. Night classes at an adult community school or summer university courses are a fine introduction, but the most time- and cost-effective study programs are those that immerse you in the language and culture within the country of the target language. Although there are Spanish language schools at several locations in mainland Mexico, it's also possible to study in Baja. If Baja is your travel focus, it would be prudent to investigate schools on the peninsula.

One well-established school with a good reputation is the family-owned **International Spanish Institute of Ensenada (Colegio de**

Idiomas) (tel. 6-01-09, 6-65-87) at 337 Blvd. J.A. Rodriguez in Ensenada. This school offers a choice of one-day, weekend, and six-day (or longer) courses, with six hours of language class per day. Tuition is US$20 per day, a bargain at less than US$4 an hour. Classes are always limited to five or fewer people. For an additional US$20 per day, the school will arrange a homestay with a local Mexican family that includes a private room and three meals per day. This is considerably cheaper than staying in even the cheapest hotel and eating in restaurants; staying with a Mexican family also gives students plenty of opportunity to practice Spanish after class. You can also contact ISIE through Kathy Luna (tel. 619-472-0600), P.O. Box 536, Bonita, CA 91908.

Another long-running language program is the Spanish conversation course offered by the Glendale Community College Baja California Field Studies Program. This course is held for 12 days in late August at the GCC's rustic field studies center in Bahía de los Angeles. Students sleep on cots in the center itself. The course costs around US$400, including round-trip transport between GCC and Bahía de los Angeles, dormitory-style accommodation, and meals. For further information, contact Dr. José Mercadé, Glendale Community College, 1500 N. Verdugo Rd., Glendale, CA 91209.

RELIGION

Census-takers report that approximately 89% of Baja California's population are Roman Catholics, 4.2% are Protestant, .06% are Jewish, and 4% "have no religion." The original inhabitants of Mexico were indoctrinated in the ways of Roman Catholicism by Spanish missionaries between the 16th and 19th centuries. That Catholicism is now the majority religion in Mexico is an amazing achievement considering it was laid over a vast variety of native belief systems in existence for perhaps thousands of years, and also given the fact the Mexicans eventually forcefully expelled the Spanish.

Mexican Catholics tend to be devout practitioners of their faith. Mexican Catholicism, however, has its own variations that distinguish the religion from its European predecessors. Some are traceable to preexisting Indian spiritual traditions absorbed by the Catholic faith, and as such are localized according to tribe.

One variation common to all of Mexico is the Virgin of Guadalupe cult, which began in 1531 when a dark-skinned Virgin Mary appeared before Indian peasant Juan Diego in a series of three visions at Tepeyac, near Mexico City—which was, coincidentally, a sacred Aztec site dedicated to the goddess Tonantzin. According to legend, in the third vision the Virgin commanded Diego to gather roses and present them to the local bishop, requesting that a church be built in her honor. When the devout Diego unfolded his rose-filled cloak, both he and the bishop beheld an image of the dark-skinned Virgin imprinted on the garment. This was deemed a miracle, and church construction commenced at once.

Today, many Mexican churches are named for Our Lady of Guadalupe, who has become so fused with Mexican identity that the slogan ¡Viva Guadalupe! is commonly used at political rallies. The official feast day for Guadalupe, 12 December, is fervently celebrated throughout the country.

At one time the entire peninsula was under the ecclesiastical jurisdiction of the Guadalajara diocese; now there are regional dioceses centered in Tijuana, Mexicali, and La Paz. Since there are fewer churches per capita in Baja than on the mainland, a church (iglesia) will sometimes hold as many as 18 masses a day. In southern Baja it isn't uncommon for a parish priest to hail from abroad—usually Italy—since there's a chronic shortage of native priests on the peninsula.

Roadside Religion

Along Baja's roadways you'll occasionally see small roadside crosses, sometimes in clusters, or shrines. Often placed at fatal accident sites, each cross marks a soul's point of departure from this world. Larger shrines containing Christ or Virgin figures are erected to confer blessings or protection on passing motorists. These vary from simple enclosures made of vegetable oil cans to elaborate sculptural designs.

In the brush beside the track there was a little heap of light, and as we came closer to it we saw a rough wooden cross lighted indirectly. The cross-arm was bound to the staff with a thong, and the whole cross seemed to glow, alone in the darkness. When we came close we saw that a kerosene can stood on the ground and that in it was a candle which threw its feeble light upward on the cross. And our companion told us how a man had come from a fishing boat, sick and weak and tired. He tried to get home, but at this spot he fell down and died. And his family put the little cross and the candle there to mark the place. And eventually they would put up a stronger cross. It seems good to mark and to remember for a little while the place where a man died. This is his one whole lonely act in all his life. In every other thing, even in his birth, he is bound close to others, but the moment of his dying is his own.

John Steinbeck,
THE LOG FROM THE SEA OF CORTEZ

CUSTOMS AND CONDUCT

CROSS-CULTURAL COMMUNICATION

Time And Appointments

Of the many stereotypes of Mexican culture, the one about the Mexican sense of time being highly flexible is probably the most accurate. The whys and wherefores are too numerous and complex for the context of this book; read Octavio Paz's *The Labyrinth of Solitude* for a glimpse of an explanation. It's important to realize that the so-called *mañana* attitude is nothing more than a generalization; in many cases Mexican individuals are every bit as punctual as North Americans—especially when it comes to doing business with North Americans. Furthermore, Bajacalifornios, it is said, tend to be more punctual than their mainland counterparts.

If you make an appointment with a Bajacalifornio for dinner, a party, or some other social engagement, you should figure the actual meeting time will occur two hours later than verbally scheduled. As with business engagements, if the person involved has dealt frequently with North Americans, this might not always be the case. Also, Mexicans will typically accept an invitation rather than say no, even if they don't plan to attend the scheduled event. This is because, within the Mexican social context, it is usually worse to refuse an invitation than not to show up. To avoid disappointment, prepare yourself for any of these scenarios.

When hiring a fishing boat or any sort of guide

in Baja, you can expect a modicum of punctuality—Mexicans in the tourist industry usually adapt themselves to the expectations of North American and European tourists. Again, note the difference between business and social appointments.

Siesta: The stereotypical siesta, when everyone goes off to sleep for a couple of hours in the afternoon, is fast becoming history throughout Mexico. Nevertheless, a vestige of the siesta is preserved in the operating hours for offices and small businesses, which are typically closed from two to four or three to five in the afternoon. The first hour is reserved for *comida*, the midday meal, while the second hour is for relaxing or taking care of personal business. While to North Americans two hours may seem like a long lunch hour, the fact is that Mexican offices and businesses generally stay open much later than in the U.S. or Canada, until seven or eight in the evening.

No matter what hours are posted for small businesses, the actual opening and closing times may vary with the whims of the proprietors. This is also true for tourist information offices. Banks usually follow their posted hours to the minute.

Meal Times: If you'll be meeting Mexican acquaintances for meals, whether at a restaurant or in their homes, be aware that customary eating times differ from those in North America or northern Europe.

The first meal of the day, *desayuno* (breakfast), is usually taken at about the same time as the average North American breakfast, between 0600 and 0800. On a working weekday, there may be another light breakfast/early lunch at around 1100 called *almuerzo,* which on weekends and holidays may be a much larger feed. Around 1400 or 1500 comes the *comida,* the largest meal of the day. In small towns, workers often go home for this meal, not returning to the workplace until around 1600 or 1700.

After work, at anywhere from around 2000 to 2200, *la cena,* the final meal of the day, is eaten. Cenas are usually as light and informal as desayunos, so it's not often that guests are invited to a home for this meal. On weekends and holidays, the cena can become a grander occasion.

Terms Of Address

Mexicans frequently use titles of respect when addressing one another. At a minimum, "señor" will do for men, "señora" for married women, and "señorita" for unmarried women or girls. When in doubt about a woman's marital status, "seño" can be used.

Professional titles can also be used for variety and to show additional respect. *Maestro* (master) or *maestra* (mistress) are common and can be used to address skilled workers (cobblers, auto mechanics, seamstresses, etc.) and any teacher except those at secondary schools and colleges or universities (who are *profesores*). Attorneys or persons with graduate degrees are *licenciado* (men) or *licenciada* (women), while doctors are *doctor* or *doctora.*

Body Language

Mexicans tend to use their arms and hands more during verbal communication than do their North American or North European counterparts. Learning to read the more common gestures—but not necessarily imitate them—can greatly enhance your comprehension of everyday conversations, even when you don't understand every word being spoken.

One of the more confusing gestures for North Americans is the way Mexicans beckon to other people by holding the hand out, palm down, and waving in a downward motion. This looks similar to a farewell gesture in the U.S. and Canada but means "come here" in Mexico. Holding the palm upward and crooking the fingers toward the body, the typical North American gesture for "come here," is a vaguely obscene gesture in Mexico.

Extending the thumb and forefinger from a closed hand and holding them about a half-inch apart means "a little bit" in North America but in Mexico usually means "just a moment" or "wait a minute," and is often accompanied by the utterance "momentito" or "poquito."

The wagging of an upright forefinger means "no" or "don't do that." This is a good gesture to use when children hanging around at stoplights or gasoline pumps begin wiping your windshield and you don't want them to. Don't overdo it, though—they only need to see a few seconds of the wagging finger—otherwise you'll look out of control.

Handshakes and *Abrazos:* Mexicans commonly greet one another with handshakes, which are used between the sexes and among children and adults—in fact, with everybody. Mexican males who are friends will sometimes greet one another with an *abrazo* (embrace) and urban women may kiss one another on the cheek. Foreigners should stick to the handshake until they establish more intimate relationships with Bajacalifornios. Handshakes are also used upon parting and saying farewell.

Dress

Compared to their mainland counterparts, who tend to be more conservative, Bajacalifornios are relatively tolerant about the way visitors dress. Nonetheless, invisible lines exist which, out of respect for Mexican custom, shouldn't be crossed. Number one is that beachwear is not considered suitable dress for town visits. Rosarito, Cabo San Lucas, and San Felipe are the most obvious exceptions to this general rule since during peak tourist seasons visitors outnumber residents in these towns, so the locals are quite habituated to gringo foolishness. In Ensenada, however, beachwear will result in indignant stares if you wander far from the Avenida López Mateos tourist strip. In La Paz and other Baja towns, you're disrespecting local custom if you wear a bathing suit anywhere other than the beaches.

Churches: Upon entering a church or chapel in Baja, men are expected to remove their hats. Many Mexican males will also remove their hats when passing in front of a church. More traditionminded Bajacalifornio women will cover their heads when inside a church, but younger women usually don't and foreign females aren't expected to. Shorts, sleeveless shirts/blouses, sandals, or bare feet are considered improper dress for both men and women in churches, even for brief sightseeing visits.

OUT AND ABOUT
SPORTS AND RECREATION

Baja California's major attractions largely fall under this heading—from trekking in the Sierra de San Pedro Mártir to scuba diving off Cabo Pulmo. An added bonus is that, for the most part, you can enjoy Baja outdoor recreation at little or no cost. User demand is low, and when fees are involved they're usually quite reasonable.

HIKING AND BACKPACKING

National Parks, Natural Areas, And Wildlife Preserves
Baja has two national parks, Parque Nacional de Sierra San Pedro Mártir and Parque Nacional Constitución de 1857; three natural parks, Parque Natural del Desierto Central de Baja California, Parque Natural Isla Angel de la Guarda, and Parque Natural de la Ballena Gris; two wildlife sanctuaries, Isla Guadalupe and the Midriff Islands; and two underwater marine parks, Arrecife Pulmo and Bahía Cabo San Lucas. At the two national parks, public facilities

are few and rudimentary; in the other government-protected areas they're virtually nonexistent. These public lands are described in some detail in later sections of this guidebook.

Trails
Hiking trails are plentiful in the northern sierras, from fairly wide, 150-year-old paths created by Indians or shepherds to smaller, more recent trails worn by hikers. In the smaller central sierras, which are more arid, trails are scarce—it's a good idea to scout an area first and ask questions locally about the best way to get from point A to point B. Although it's sometimes tempting to venture off established trails, that's a good way to get lost; you might also contribute to the destruction of delicate ecosystems. Light trails that don't seem to go anywhere may be coyote trails, which connect surface water sources.

Maps
Topographic maps, which chart trails and elevation differentials, are essential for extended

hiking and backpacking. **Map Link** (tel. 805-965-4402, fax 805-962-0884, 25 E. Mason, Santa Barbara, CA, 93101) carries a complete line of Baja topo maps in three scales (1:1,000,000, 1:250,000, and 1:50,000) that are sold separately according to region. Costs: around US$6 each. Map Link will mail out a Baja map listing on request.

In 1991 a San Diego publisher issued the useful *Baja Explorer Topographic Atlas Directory*. Besides the 239 topo maps contained therein, the atlas includes several reference sections on accommodations, campgrounds, and other services. Although the atlas has since gone out of print, it's still available through the occasional travel-supply store or Map Link.

Equipment

Day Hikes: For a hike of a day or less, all you need is sturdy footwear (light, high-topped hiking boots are preferable to sneakers in rocky terrains) and whatever food or water you plan to consume for the day (count on at least two liters of water per person for chaparral or lower sierra hiking, more if the weather is hot).

Overnight Hiking/Backpacking: Longer hikes obviously require more preparation and equipment. Whether in the desert or the mountains, bring enough clothing to remain comfortable at both ends of the temperature spectrum; throughout the peninsula days tend to be warm, nights chilly. A light sleeping bag, for temperatures down to 4° C/25° F in the high sierras, and a backpacking tent with plenty of ventilation for camping at lower elevations are necessities for coping with potentially harsh environments.

Good hiking boots are essential. Thick lug soles with steel shanks are preferable, as they provide protection from sharp rocks and desert plants. Bring along a first-aid kit that includes an elastic bandage for sprains and snakebite treatment, and a pair of tweezers for removing thorns and cactus spines. Also pack flashlight, compass, waterproof matches, knife, extra batteries, foul-weather gear, and signal device (mirror or whistle). A handy addition, if you're hiking near Baja's shoreline, is a telescoping fishing rod with light tackle, as surf fish are usually plentiful.

Water and Food: Always carry plenty of water; a minimum of four liters per person per full day of walking during hot weather, three liters in winter. Although springs and tinajas exist in the sierras, the water level varies considerably and you shouldn't count on finding water sources along the way. If you need drinking water from one of these sources, always boil it first for at least 10 minutes or treat it with iodine or a water filter designed to remove impurities. Bring enough food for the duration of your hike, plus one or two days extra.

Campsites: In addition to all the usual rules for choosing campsites, don't camp beneath coconut palms (a falling coconut could knock down your tent or fracture your skull) or in arroyos (danger of flash floods).

Fires and Waste Disposal: Open fires are permitted just about anywhere in Baja except within city limits. Even in the desert, fuel is plentiful, as dried ocotillo and cactus skeletons make excellent fuels. Imitate the locals and keep your fires small. Never leave hot coals or ashes behind; smother with sand—or water, if you can spare it—till cool to the touch.

Pack out all trash that won't burn, including cigarette butts; they take 10-12 years to decompose. Bury human waste six inches down, and don't use soap in streams or springs.

DESERT HIKING

For hikes in Baja's desert lands, special precautions are appropriate. Water is the most important concern; desert hiking requires at least four liters of water per day per person. Some people recommend at least eight liters per day for hikes that span the midday hours. On extended excursions of more than a night or two, the weight of anything beyond eight liters—water weighs about one kilogram per liter—is prohibitive and you'll need to learn in advance where to obtain water from reliable local sources. While hiking, keep your mouth closed and breathe through your nose to keep the mouth and throat from drying out. This will keep you cooler, as the nasal cavities are designed to moderate outside air temperatures as air passes into your lungs.

Sun protection is especially essential in the desert. Wear long- sleeved clothing with light, reflective colors (white is best), sunglasses, a wide-brimmed hat, and sunscreen. Between 1100 and 1500, it's best to take shelter from the sun, especially during the hotter months. Most of Baja's deserts offer plenty of shade in the form of mesquite trees, overhanging cliffs, or leaning boulders. But it's also a good idea to carry your own shade—a light, opaque tarp. A poncho can double as tarp and rain protection; yes, it does occasionally rain in the desert. The Vizcaíno Desert is the most barren of the peninsular deserts, but also the coolest because of the tendency for fog to form when the hot desert air meets cool Pacific breezes.

Anyone contemplating an extended desert hike for the first time might consider reading at least one of the books on desert travel listed in this tome's "Booklist." These contain important information on a variety of desert survival topics, from how to test the edibility of plants to making your own water with an improvised solar still.

FISHING

Baja's reputation as one of the best sportfishing regions in the world is well deserved. Nowhere else will you find as many varieties of fish in an area as compact and accessible as the waters of Baja. Although it's most famous for its acrobatic billfish—marlin, sailfish, and swordfish—and other deep-sea fishing, Baja also offers opportunities for surf casters, small-boaters, and sport divers as well as folks who don't yet know a rod from a reel.

Onshore Fishing
Most accessible to travelers, since it doesn't require a boat, is onshore or surf fishing, which you can enjoy anywhere along the coast you can get a line into the water. In Baja, *Prohibido Pescar* signs are vary rare.

Surf fishing is best along the Pacific coast between El Rosario and Bahía Magdalena, and on the Sea of Cortez between San José del Cabo and La Paz, but fish can be taken just about anywhere along Baja's 4,800-km (3,000-mile) shoreline. Common onshore fish include surfperch, cabezón, sand bass, ladyfish, halibut, corvinas, opaleye, leopard shark, triggerfish, and croakers. Submarine canyons along the shore of the East Cape can actually yield onshore catches of roosterfish, California yellowtail, and yellowfin tuna for anglers using the right tackle; shore-caught dorado (dolphinfish) and

FISH TRANSLATOR

Bajacalifornio guides who lead sportfishing trips often use the local Mexican terms for gamefish; when they don't, the English terms they use aren't always correct. This works the other way, too—many gringos use incorrect Spanish names for Baja fish, which can cause confusion when asking about local fishing conditions. Here is a key to some of the more common translations:

albacore tuna—*albacora*
bluefin tuna—*atún de aleta azul*
blue marlin—*marlín azul*
dolphinfish (mahi mahi)—*dorado*
grouper (generic)—*garropa*
halibut—*lenguado*
hammerhead shark—*cornuda*
jack crevalle—*toro*
ladyfish—*sabalo*
mackerel—*sierra, makerela*
manta ray—*manta*
octopus—*pulpo*
Pacific amberjack—*pez fuerte*
perch (generic)—*mojarra*
puffer (generic)—*bolete*
red snapper—*huachinango*
roosterfish—*papagallo, pez gallo*
sailfish—*pez vela*
sea bass (cabrilla)—*cabrilla*
shark (generic)—*tiburón*
squid—*calamar*
stingray (generic)—*raya*
striped marlin—*marlín rayado*
swordfish—*pez espada*
triggerfish—*cochi*
wahoo—*sierra wahoo, peto*
whale shark—*pez sapo*
white seabass—*corvina blanca*
yellowfin tuna—*atún de aleta; amarilla*
yellowtail—*jurel*

even marlin are not unknown. All of these except the marlin are considered excellent food fish, and even the marlin is edible when smoked.

One fish commonly caught onshore, the puffer, is *not* a good food fish; the meat is toxic to humans and can cause poisoning. The two puffer species common to Baja are easily identified, as their bodies expand like balloons when they're disturbed. Further identifiers: the bullseye puffer features a brownish body with black spots;

WORLD FISHING RECORDS SET IN BAJA

The nonprofit International Game Fish Association (IGFA) tracks world records set for each species of game fish according to weight, weight/test ratio (fish weight to line test), place where the catch was made, and other significant record details. World-record catches achieved by Baja anglers for specific line classes include those for the following fish: Pacific blue marlin, striped marlin, Pacific sailfish, swordfish, roosterfish, dolphinfish (dorado), gulf grouper, California yellowtail, Pacific bonito, bigeye trevally, spotted cabrilla, spearfish, giant sea bass, white sea bass, California halibut, Pacific jack crevalle, black skipjack, yellowfin tuna, Pacific bigeye tuna, and chub mackerel.

Baja anglers hold all-tackle records—highest weight of any fish species regardless of line test—for gulf grouper, roosterfish, Pacific amberjack, white seabass, spotted cabrilla, rainbow runner, black skipjack, yellowfin tuna, Pacific jack crevalle, chub mackerel, and California yellowtail.

For information on IGFA membership and record entries, write to IGFA, 3000 East Las Olas Blvd., Fort Lauderdale, FL 33316. Membership includes a copy of the IGFA's annual *World Record Game Fishes Book*, which contains a list of all current fishing records, as well as the bimonthly *International Angler* newsletter. IGFA members are also eligible for discounts on fishing charters offered by several sportfishing outfitters in Cabo San Lucas.

depending on its stage of maturity, the golden puffer is either all golden or a dark purple-black with white spots and white fin trim. In Mexico this fish is called *bolete*.

Inshore Fishing

Anyone with access to a small boat, either a skiff trailered in or a rented *panga* (an open fiberglass skiff that's usually five to six meters long and powered by a 40-60 hp outboard motor), can enjoy inshore fishing at depths of up to around 50-100 meters. Common inshore catches include many of the surf fishes mentioned above, plus various kinds of groupers, sea bass, bonito shark, sculpin (scorpionfish), barracuda, rockfish, lingcod, sierra, pompano, amberjack, red and yellow snapper, pargo, and cabrilla. Cabrilla, however, must be released when caught.

Larger game fish occasionally taken inshore are the bluefin and yellowfin tuna, yellowtail, dorado, jack crevalle, and roosterfish. Again, all fish mentioned make good eating.

Offshore Fishing

The bigger game fish are found in deeper waters—over 200 meters (100 fathoms)—and require bigger tackle and more technique, including specialized trolling methods prescribed for each type of fish. Larger boats —fishing cruisers—are usually necessary simply because of the distance from shore to fishing area. In the Cape region, however, you can reach depths of over 200 meters in less than 1.5 km. These areas are accessible by skiff or panga, though strong seasonal currents are sometimes a problem, reqiring a larger outboard motor. Contrary to the popular image of Cabo San Lucas sportfishing, it isn't necessary to use a boat equipped with fighting chairs to catch the big ones, although it's undoubtedly more comfortable.

Because of the special tackle and techniques involved in offshore fishing, many Baja visitors hire local fishing guides—who usually provide boats and tackle—to transport them to offshore fishing grounds. A sometimes less expensive alternative involves signing up for fishing cruises which take groups of tourist anglers out on big power boats.

Most offshore anglers go after striped, blue, or black marlin, sailfish, swordfish, wahoo, dorado, roosterfish, yellowtail, and tuna. These fish are large, powerful fighters, requiring a certain skill in handling rod and line. The billfish are the most acrobatic, performing high leaps and pirouettes when hooked; wahoo and roosterfish will also "greyhound," performing a series of long, low jumps while swimming rapidly in one direction.

Of the billfish, none except the swordfish are considered particularly good eating. The rest are traditionally regarded as trophy fish, meant to be stuffed and mounted in the den or living room. To their credit, an increasing number of anglers these days release billfish upon the conclusion of the fight; many outfitters discourage or even forbid the taking of these beautiful creatures unless the fish has been badly damaged in the fight.

The wahoo, dorado, roosterfish, yellowtail, and various tunas all make excellent eating.

Fishing Seasons

Fish are biting somewhere in Baja waters all year round. But water temperature, ocean currents, weather patterns, fish migrations, and other changing variables mean you usually won't find the same type of fish in the same spot in, say, December as in July. Baja presents a complex set of fishing conditions that vary from month to month and year to year. An unusually dry year in the American Southwest, for example, lessens the outflow of nutrients from the Colorado River into the Sea of Cortez, diminishing the store of plankton and other small marine creatures at the bottom of the Cortez food chain. This in turn affects populations of larger fish, from sea bass to whale sharks. All the various "fishing calendars," obviously, can serve only as general guidelines.

But some calendars are more accurate than others. The best is the set devised by Tom Miller in his *Angler's Guide to Baja California,* which divides the Baja coast into 10 fishing zones, with a calendar for each zone. Even with a set of detailed calendars in hand, it's wise to seek the counsel of local fishing guides or other anglers on the scene before investing time and money in trying to catch a particular fish in a particular area.

A few generalizations are possible. The greatest variety and number of offshore, onshore, and inshore fish swim the widest range of Baja waters from April through October, when the water temperatures are relatively warm. During the winter, many species migrate south and are available only off the Cape.

Fortunately for winter anglers farther north, exceptions abound. The widely distributed California yellowtail, for example, is present year-round, migrating up and down the Sea of Cortez—La Paz and the East Cape in the winter, central to northern Cortez in the summer—as well as the lower Pacific coast. Barred perch and rock cod are present year-round on the northern Pacific coast. Sierra peak season is winter, when they're found in abundance near Bahía Magdalena. Wahoo generally spend December through April at the Cape, moving up toward Bahía Magdalena and the southern Cortez in the warmer months.

If your trip occurs between December and April, head for the Cape; from May to November you can angle anywhere along a horseshoe-shaped loop extending from Bahía Magdalena on the Pacific side to Mulegé on the Cortez. You can, if you wish, fish farther north on both coasts, especially in the summer, but if sportfishing is your reason for traveling to Baja, you're more likely to be satisfied by heading to those areas.

As a final caveat, remember that an unusually warm winter means better fishing all over Baja;

pangas

JOE CUMMINGS

likewise a particularly cold winter forces many fish far south, making even Cabo San Lucas, the "fisherman's paradise," less productive.

Equipment

Although bait and tackle are available at shops in Ensenada, San Felipe, Loreto, Mulegé, La Paz, and Cabo San Lucas, you can't count on finding exactly what you want; supplies are variable. Therefore you ought to have your gear assembled before arrival in Baja.

A full fishing kit containing tackle for every conceivable Baja sportfishing possibility would probably weigh in excess of 70 kilograms. Seasoned Baja anglers claim you can get by in just about any situation with four basic rigs: two trolling rods with appropriate reels and 50- to 80-pound test monofilament line for offshore fishing, one medium-duty eight- or nine-foot rod and spinner with 30-pound mono for surf casting and onshore fishing, and a six-foot light spinning rig loaded with four- to eight-pound line for bait fishing, freshwater fishing, or light surf casting. Two trolling rigs are recommended because these are the rods used against fish most likely to yank your outfit into the sea; it's always best to have a spare.

No matter how many rods you bring into Mexico, you're legally permitted to fish with only one at a time. Electric reels are permitted for use by handicapped persons only.

Bait: What a fish will take at any given moment is highly variable, hence the properly equipped angler comes prepared with an array of natural and artificial bait. Live or frozen bait—including everything from squid to mackerel to clams—is usually available near the more frequented fishing areas; you can also catch your own bait quite easily with a light rig. A cooler is necessary for keeping bait fresh; hired boats will usually supply them. Among the vast selection of artificial lures available, the most reliable seem to be those perennials that imitate live bait, such as spoons, leadheads, candybars, swimmers, and, for offshore fishing, trolling heads. Bring along a few of each in different colors and sizes. You can purchase a few highly specialized lures, such as marlin heads and wahoo specials, in Loreto and Cabo San Lucas.

Tide Tables: Serious onshore-inshore anglers should bring along a set of current tide tables so they can decide what time to wake up in the morning.

Legal Requirements

The red tape surrounding fishing in Mexico is minimal. The basic requirement is that anyone over 16 who intends to fish must possess a Mexican fishing license; technically, this includes all persons aboard boats equipped with fishing tackle, whether they plan to fish or not. This is important to remember for anyone going along on fishing trips as a spectator.

A single license is valid for all types of fishing, anywhere in Mexico, and is issued for periods of one day, one week, one month, or one year. A license is usually included in the price of sportfishing cruises, but not necessarily on panga trips—if you don't have a license, be sure to ask if one is provided before embarking on a guided trip. The cost of a Mexican license has risen steadily over the last few years but remains less expensive than most fishing licenses in the U.S. or Canada.

Fishing licenses are available from a number of sources, including tackle shops and Mexican insurance companies near the U.S.-Mexico border. They can be obtained by mail from the **Mexico Department of Fisheries (PESCA)** (tel. 619-233-6956, fax 233-0344, 2550 Fifth Ave., Suite 101, San Diego, CA 92103-6622) or from California branches of the **American Automobile Association. (AAA), Club Mex** (tel. 619-585-3033, P.O. Box 1646, Bonita, CA 92002-1646), and **Discover Baja Travel Club** (tel. 619-275-4225, toll-free 800-727-BAJA, 3065 Clairemont Drive, San Diego, CA 92117).

Mexican Regulations: The general daily bag limit is 10 fish per person, including no more than five of any one species. Certain fish varieties are further protected as follows (per-day limits): one full-grown marlin, sailfish, or swordfish; two dorado, roosterfish, shad, tarpon, or shark. Extended sportfishing by boat is limited to three consecutive days if the daily bag limit is reached each of the three days.

Bag limits are the same for free divers as for rod-and-reelers. Only handheld spears and band-powered spearguns—no gas guns or powerheads—are permitted and no tanks or compressors may be used. A further weight limitation permits no more than 25 kilograms (55 lbs) of fish in a day's catch of five specimens, or one specimen of unlimited weight. Gill nets, purse nets, and every other kind of net except for handling nets are prohibited for use by nonresident aliens, as are traps, explosives, and poisons.

The taking of shellfish—clams, oysters, abalone, shrimp, and lobster—by nonresident aliens is officially prohibited. However, taking a reasonable amount—no more than can be eaten in a meal or two—is customarily permitted. This regulation is in place to protect Mexican fishing unions; even buying shellfish from local sources is prohibited unless you purchase from a public market or *cooperativa*. Obtain a receipt in case of inspection.

Totuava, sea turtles, and cabrilla are protected species that cannot be taken by anyone. Nor can any fish be caught for "ornamental purposes" (e.g., for aquarium use). Mexican fishing regulations are subject to change; check with the Mexico Department of Fisheries for the latest version before embarking on a fishing expedition.

Two areas off limits to all fishing are Bahía Cabo San Lucas harbor and Pulmo Reef, the only official fish sanctuaries along the peninsular coast. Many other areas probably ought to be protected for educational and recreational purposes, since the government-regulated bag limits help to preserve fish species but not fish habitats. Fishing, boating, diving, and other aquatic activities can wreak havoc on lagoons and delicate reef systems—use special care when traversing these areas. Never drop an anchor or a fishing line on a coral reef; such contact can cause irreversible damage to reef systems.

U.S. Customs and California State Regulations: Once you've obeyed Mexican fishing regulations and bagged a load of fish, you still have to conform to U.S. Customs regulations if you wish to cross the border with your catch. Fortunately, U.S. regulations conform with Mexican bag limits, so that whatever you've legally caught south of the border can be transported north. The U.S. state of California further requires anyone transporting fish into the state to present a completed California Declaration of Entry form, available at the border. To facilitate the identification of the transported fish, some part of each fish—head, tail, or skin—must be left intact. In other words, you can't just show up at the border with a cooler full of anonymous fish fillets.

HUNTING

The Mexican government allows licensed hunting in season, as regulated by the Secretaría de Desarrollo Social (SEDESOL). Hunting is popular in Baja among foreigners and Mexicans alike but is for the most part restricted to various species of rabbit, quail, dove, pheasant, and waterfowl (ducks, widgeons, and geese). White-tailed deer and mule deer are also hunted but permits are limited in number and quite expensive by Mexican standards. Occasionally the government sponsors a special hunt for the rare desert bighorn sheep (*borrego cimmarón*); bighorn permits cost around US$12,000 and aren't usually issued to foreigners. Earlier in this century, bighorn hunting by foreigners nearly wiped out the entire population.

Permits come in six types: Type I, waterfowl; Type II, doves; Type III, other birds; Type IV, small mammals; Type V, limited; and Type VI, special. Hunting regulations, which include bag—size and number—limits, are strictly enforced. Signs that say *Prohibido Cazar* mean "Hunting Prohibited." To apply directly to the Mexican government for a permit, contact **SEDESOL** (tel. 61-74-91), Calle Lic. Alfonso Garcia Gonzalez 555, Distrito Profesores Federales, Mexicali, BCN. The office is open Mon.-Fri. 0900-1430 and 1730-2000, Saturdays 0900-1300.

In addition to the SEDESOL hunting permit, foreign hunters need a consular certificate, special visa, and military gun permit. You can obtain the consular certificate from any Mexican consulate upon presentation of a letter from your local law enforcement agency verifying you have no criminal record. This certificate is also necessary for obtaining the military gun permit, issued by the army garrison in Tijuana or Mexicali. Once you possess the consular certificate, gun permit, and hunting permit, you can bring your guns across the border, where you'll receive a special hunter's visa.

If you don't speak Spanish, you might want to arrange all the necessary paperwork through a U.S. broker service. This costs a bit more than applying directly through SEDESOL because you have to pay either membership dues or a surcharge, but the procedure is smoother. One organization dedicated to helping hunters obtain Mexican permits is the **Mexican Hunting Association** (tel. 213-421-1619), 3302 Josie Ave., Long Beach, CA 90808. Another permit broker is **Romero's Mexican Service** (tel. 714-548-8931), 1600 West Coast Hwy., Newport Beach, CA 92663.

Mexican law limits the importation of hunting ammunition to 50 cartridges per registered firearm; weapons are limited to two per person. There are only three stores in all of Baja permitted to sell ammunition to the public. They're located in Tijuana, Mexicali, and La Paz.

BOATING

Recreational boating along Baja's peninsular and island coastlines has been popular since the 1950s. In the days before the Transpeninsular Highway, it was one of the safest, if slowest, ways of traveling from Alta California to the southern peninsula. Despite recent improvements in highway travel, interest in navigating Baja waters has only increased. The main difference now is that smaller vessels can be trailered or cartopped down the peninsula, saving days and weeks that might otherwise be spent just reaching your cruising destination.

An extremely wide range of pleasure boats plies Baja waters, from sea kayaks to huge motor yachts. The most heavily navigated areas lie along the northwest coast between San Diego and Ensenada and in the Cabo San Lucas to La Paz corridor, but even these waters are relatively uncrowded compared to the marinas and bays of Alta California. Cabo San Lucas, the most popular southern Baja harbor, only checks in a thousand foreign-owned vessels or so per year, an average of less than 2.7 arrivals per day.

The Pacific Vs. The Sea Of Cortez
Although a number of visitors circumnavigate the entire Baja peninsula, most boaters select one area for cruising and transport their crafts to that area by land. Because of the relative safety of Sea of Cortez boating, it's the most popular coast, particularly for smaller craft—kayaks, skiffs, and motor- or sail-powered vessels under 10 meters (35 feet). Cortez waters are relatively calm most of the time; late summer and early

fall are the exceptions, when chubascos or hurricanes can whip up sizable and sometimes treacherous swells. The Pacific coast is prone to high winds and challenging swells throughout the year.

The major difference between the two coasts is the number of available, safe anchorages. The Pacific side features about 30 anchorages along the peninsula as well as island shorelines that provide protection when northwest winds prevail; this number is reduced to approximately 12 anchorages during prevailing southwesterlies, common July through September. Over on the Cortez side lie more than 60 protected anchorages—roughly 35 along the peninsula and 30 more on islands just off the coast. The Sea of Cortez offers not only safer waters but a wider selection of places to drop anchor.

Open-ocean Pacific sailing is not for the novice and shouldn't be attempted along Baja's Pacific coast without plenty of prior experience. The relative absence of assistance and boat-repair facilities makes Pacific boating south of Ensenada an especially risky venture.

It's now possible for boaters to navigate from ports in Alta California, British Columbia, or Alaska to the Ensenada marina and then arrange for overland transport of their boats on hired trailers from Ensenada to San Felipe on the Cortez side. Contact the **Ensenada tourist office** (tel. 2-30-22, Blvd. Costero and Calle Las Rocas, Ensenada, BCN) for details on this newly established service.

Cartopping
The most popular boats for short-range cruising, fishing, and diving are those that can be transported on top of a car, RV, or truck—aluminum skiffs in the 12- to 15-foot range. This type of boat can be launched just about anywhere; larger, trailered boats are restricted to boat launches with trailer access. The most appropriate outboard motor size for a boat this size is 15- to 20-horsepower; larger motors are generally too heavy to carry separately from the boat, a necessity for cartopping.

If you decide to transport a skiff or sea kayak on top of your vehicle, be sure to use a sturdy, reliable rack or loader with a bow line to the front bumper and plenty of tie-downs. The rough road surfaces typical of even Baja's best highways can make it difficult to keep a boat in one place; crosswinds are also a problem in many areas. Frequent load checks are necessary.

Inflatables

Rugged inflatable boats, such as those manufactured by Achilles or Zodiac, are also well-suited to Baja travel. You can carry them on top or even in the cargo area of a large car or truck and inflate them with a foot pump or compressor as needed. A small 24-hp outboard motor is the best source of power. Inquire at **Pacific Marine Supply** (tel. 619-223-7194, fax 223-9054, 2084 Canon St., San Diego, CA 92106) for the latest gear.

Trailering

Larger boats that require trailering because of their weight, and must then be floated from the trailer at a launch site, are much less versatile than cartop boats. On the entire peninsula fewer than 20 launches—five or six on the Pacific side, the remainder on the Sea of Cortez—offer trailer access. Another disadvantage to boat trailering is that Baja road conditions make towing a slow, unpleasant task. On the other hand, if one of these spots happens to be your destination and you plan to stay awhile, the added cruising range of a larger vessel might be worthwhile.

Ocean Cruising

The typical ocean cruiser on Baja's Pacific side is a 12- to 24-meter (40- to 80-foot) power boat; on the Cortez side, 10- to 18-meter (35- to 60-foot) sailboats are popular. Properly equipped and crewed, these boats can navigate long distances and serve as homes away from home. Smaller motor-powered vessels are usually prevented from Baja ocean cruising simply because of the lack of available fueling stations—their smaller fuel capacities greatly diminish cruising range. Sailboats smaller than nine meters (30 feet) have a similar problem because of the lack of storage space for food and water.

If you want to try your hand at ocean cruising, contact **Cortez Yacht Charters** (tel. 619-469-4255), 7888 Ostrow St., San Diego, CA 92111.

Charts And Tide Tables

The best nautical charts for Baja waters are those compiled by the U.S. government. They come in two series: the Coastal Series, which covers the entire Pacific and Cortez coastlines in three large charts (numbers 21008, 21014, and 21017) with a scale of around 1:650,000 each; and the Golfo de California Series, which offers much larger-scale maps—from 1:30,000 for La Paz to 1:290,610 for the entire Cape Region—of selected areas along the Cortez coast and around the Cape. The nautical surveys that resulted in both series occured between 1873 and 1901, so many of the place names are out of date.

You can purchase these charts individually from the **Defense Mapping Agency** (tel. 800-826-0342 or 301-227-2495), Washington, DC 20315-0010. Two of the Coastal Series are out of print, however, and others may eventually drop from sight as well. A much better, and less expensive source of these charts is *Charlie's Charts: The Western Coast of Mexico (Including Baja)*, a compilation of all U.S. nautical charts from San Diego to Guatemala, including those currently unavailable from the DMA. The charts have been extensively updated from the DMA originals, with more recent markings for anchorages, boat ramps, hazards, and fishing and diving spots. The spiral-bound volume costs around US$5 and is available from **Charles E. Wood**, Box 1244, Station A, Surrey, BC, Canada V3W 1G0. It's also available in many Alta California marine supply stores. Some outlets may carry an earlier version called *ChartGuide*.

Tide tables are published annually; to cover the entire Baja coastline you'll need two sets, one that pertains to the Pacific tides and one for the Sea of Cortez tides. Either or both are available from **Map Link** (tel. 805-965-4402, fax 805-962-0884, 25 E. Mason, Santa Barbara, CA, 93101) or marine supply stores. You can also order Sea of Cortez tide tables from the **University of Arizona** Printing and Publishing Dept. (tel. 602-621-2572, fax 621-6458), Room 102, West Stadium, Tucson, AZ 85721.

Legal Requirements

Boat Permits: Any nonresident foreigner operating a boat in Mexican waters who intends to fish from that boat is required to carry a Mexican boat permit as well as a fishing permit. Even if you transport a boat to Baja with no fishing tackle and no plans to fish, it's a good idea to obtain a permit; first, because you might change your mind when you see all the fish everyone else is pulling in, and second, because you never know when you might end up carrying a passenger with fishing tackle. *All* boats used for fishing require a permit, whether cartopped, trailered, carried inside a motor vehicle, or sailed on the open seas.

Permits are available by mail from the Mexico Department of Fisheries or from the Discover Baja Travel Club. A boat permit is valid for 12 months; fees vary according to the length of the craft.

Temporary Import Permits: These aren't necessary for Baja but are required if you plan to take a boat to mainland Mexico, whether by land or water. You can obtain the permit from offices in La Paz or Santa Rosalía or from a Registro Federal de Vehiculos office in Tijuana, Mexicali, Ensenada, or La Paz.

Port Check-ins: If you launch a boat at a Mexican port, specifically within the jurisdiction of a Captain of the Port (COTP), you must comply with official check-in procedures. This simply involves reporting to the COTP office and completing some forms. The only time it's a hassle is when the Captain isn't present; you may have to wait around a few hours. Some ports charge filing fees of up to US$15.

Anytime you enter another COTP's jurisdiction, you're required to check in. Checking out is not required except when you leave the port of origin—i.e., the port at which you first launched. Current COTPs in Baja are centered at Ensenada, Guerrero Negro, Bahía Magdalena (San Carlos), Cabo San Lucas, San José del Cabo, La Paz, Puerto Escondido, Loreto, Mulegé, Santa Rosalía, Bahía de los Angeles, and San Felipe.

Fuel, Parts, And Repairs

At present only five permanent marinas offer fuel year-round: Ensenada, Cabo San Lucas, La Paz, Puerto Escondido, and Santa Rosalía. Elsewhere you must count on your own reserves or try your luck at canneries, boatyards, and fish camps, where prices will probably exceed official PEMEX rates. Often at places other than marinas you'll have to go ashore and haul your own fuel back to the boat; come prepared with as many extra fuel containers as you can manage.

Obtaining marine supplies and repairs in Baja is more challenging than finding fuel. Ensenada and La Paz are the best locales for both—there's usually someone around who can work minor miracles. To a limited extent, parts—but not necessarily competent repair work—are also available for established-brand outboard motors in San Felipe, Loreto, Mulegé, and Cabo San Lucas. As with all other motorized conveyances in Baja, it's best to bring along plenty of spare parts, especially props, filters, water pumps, shear pins, hoses, and belts. Don't forget to bring along at least one life jacket per person—statistics show that in 80% of all boating fatalities, the victims weren't wearing personal flotation devices (PFDs).

Watermakers: Ocean cruisers might consider equipping their boats with desalinators. **Recovery Engineering** (tel. 800-548-0406 in the U.S. and Canada) has developed a new line of reverse-osmosis desalinators that run off 12-volt power sources and produce as much

kayaking in Bahía Concepción

JOE CUMMINGS

as 12.5 liters of drinking water per hour from seawater. The company also manufactures a hand-pumped survival version for life rafts that weighs just over one kilogram.

Emergencies

The U.S. Coast Guard monitors VHF radio channel 16 and can pick up transmissions from as far south as Ensenada. In the north end of the Sea of Cortez, the Cholla Bay Sportsmen's Club in Puerto Peñasco, Sonora, will respond to pleas for emergency assistance on VHF 16 with its own search-and-rescue team. Elsewhere along the Baja coastline, many Mexican agencies also monitor this channel, including the Mexican Navy, all COTPs, ferry vessels, and commercial ships.

Citizens-band (CB) radio is commonly used as a substitute for a telephone system in the more remote areas of the peninsula; it's also heavily used by RVers, the Green Angels, CB clubs, and other boaters, and is a quick way to get attention. As in the U.S. and Canada, channel 9 is the most used, but channels 1, 3, 4, 7, 9, and 10 are also monitored. Special radio permits for foreign visitors are no longer required for CB radios with a transmission power of five watts or less.

SEA KAYAKING

Kayaking is one of the best ways to experience coastal Baja. Coves, inlets, water caves, and beaches inaccessible to skiffs or 4WD vehicles are easily approached in a kayak, especially on the Sea of Cortez. The Cortez is, in fact, a truly world-class kayaking environment, as more and more kayakers discover each year. It's also an excellent place to learn sea-kayaking skills, since the seas are generally calm.

The most popular kayaking areas on the Cortez coast lie between Mulegé and Loreto and between Puerto Escondido and La Paz. Bahía Concepción, protected by land on three sides, is a favorite among novice kayakers. The Gulf Current, which runs counterclockwise around the Cortez, favors trips planned in a north-south direction, with pickup arranged at the south end. A few intrepid, experienced kayakers have completed voyages across the

currents from Bahía de los Angeles to the Mexican mainland by using the "Stepping Stones" route from island to island. Seri Indians once followed the same route in reed canoes. Extended Cortez trips are fairly easy when the weather's good, since campsites are available at a huge selection of beaches and coves. If you bring along some light fishing gear, you'll never go without food.

Kayaking on the Pacific side is for the experienced paddler only. Bahía Magdalena is the most popular area; it's large and fairly protected. Whalewatching is also a big attraction here. Gray whales sometimes use their enormous tails to toss kayaks around, however, so your first Magdalena Bay outing in whale season should be in the company of someone who understands whale behavior. Rule one: never paddle directly toward a nearby whale; instead, run parallel to the whale's course. Also, never paddle between a cow and its calf.

Elsewhere on the Pacific coast, high surf and strong currents require equal quantities of strength and expertise. Finding a beach campsite isn't that difficult, but reaching it through the surf might be.

Equipment

There are four basic types of sea-touring kayaks, each with several variations. All fall in the 4.2- to 6.4-meter (14- to 21-foot) range necessary for extended paddling. The traditional closed-cockpit, hardshell boat comes in single (one-person) and double (two-person) models and is made of either molded polyethylene plastic or fiberglass. A "glass" boat is lighter and faster; a polyethylene boat heavier and slower, though it holds up on Baja's rocky beaches much better. This type of kayak is easily cartopped, but a sturdy, secure rack is necessary on Baja's rough roads. Touring models can carry up to 115 kilograms (250 lbs.) of gear in built-in hatches, an attribute that makes them a good choice for extended overnight kayaking. Because of the sealed cockpits, they're also very good in the cold waters of the Pacific and the northern Cortez.

Folding kayaks are much easier to transport and are popular among kayakers who fly to their destinations, or who want to keep boats inside their vehicles rather than on top. The disadvantages are that a folding kayak costs more and is a bit slower because of a wider beam, up to 86 cm (34 inches) compared with a 60-cm (24-inch) beam on a hardshell boat. Assembly and disassembly—the hull is usually hypalon, a synthetic rubber, stretched over aluminum tubing—is not as easy as the sales representative claims. For carrying convenience, however, it can't be beat. The wider beam also means the craft will carry up to twice the payload of a hardshell.

Gaining popularity in recent years, especially in Baja, are open-cockpit kayaks. The advantage to these is that the paddler sits on top of the deck rather than underneath it, which makes it much easier to exit and thus somewhat safer overall. Like the closed-cockpit variety, some models feature hatched stowage compartments that carry up to 115 kilos. Open-cockpit kayaks are easier to paddle and more stable than the traditional kayak; just about anyone can paddle one with little or no practice. An open-cockpit model is also a bit slower because of a wider beam and higher center of gravity. An open-cockpit kayak costs several hundred dollars less than the closed-deck version, making it the ideal kayak for the Baja visitor for whom kayaking is just one among several recreational activities; it also makes an excellent dive station for short scuba- or free-diving trips. A few models, such as the Aquaterra Kahuna or Scupper Scrambler, are designed specifically to carry scuba gear. As with other hardshell kayaks, they're easily cartopped.

Inflatables are the lightest of the touring kayaks, which makes them even easier to transport than folding kayaks. However, inflation requires an air compressor or electric air pump since the craft's rigidity depends on air pressure of two to four pounds per square inch. Like the folding kayak, an inflatable's main advantage is ease of storage and transport.

If you're on your way to Baja by vehicle and need kayaking equipment or supplies, a convenient stop is **Southwest Sea Kayaks** (tel. 619-222-3616) at 1310 Rosecrans St., San Diego, CA 92106. Southwest Sea Kayaks offers rentals as well as sales. In Baja, only **Baja Tropicales** on Bahía Concepción offers reliable year-round equipment rental.

Accessories: Paddle styles are very much a matter of personal choice; as a general rule, Aleuts or asymmetrical paddles are useful on the windy Pacific side, traditional shapes on the Cortez. Whatever you bring, bring a spare. Other essentials include a paddle leash, a 15-meter (50-foot) parachute-cord towline, a waterproof flashlight, and, in the winter, a wetsuit. A detachable two-wheel cart or "skate" for the stern is helpful for transporting a kayak short distances on land; you can easily store it in one of the hatches.

Foot-controlled rudders are really not necessary for Sea of Cortez kayaking for much of the year since winds and currents are usually moderate. The exception is from November to March when wind and swells are up. And since there are no kayaking facilities in Baja, parts and service for a broken rudder are virtually nonexistent. On the Pacific side, or if you're going to attempt a cross-Cortez route to the mainland, a foot-controlled rudder is a good idea. Bring spare parts.

If you can manage the extra weight, include a kayak sail rig to give your arms a rest during a good breeze—common in the Cortez as well as the Pacific.

Maps and Tide Tables: Nautical charts are of little use for kayak navigation. A better choice is 1:50,000-scale topo maps, available from Map Link. Tide tables are also invaluable.

Organized Kayak Trips

A great way to learn sea kayaking in Baja is to join an organized trip led by experienced kayakers. One of the most established is **Sea Trek** (tel. 415-488-1000, P.O. Box 561, Woodacre, CA 94973), which specializes in one-week Sea of Cortez trips December through May. The outfit also occasionally offers special Bahía Magdalena trips during gray whale migrations. **Paddling South** (tel. 707-942-4550 Oct.-May, 942-4796 June-Sept., 4510 Silverado Trail, Calistoga, CA 94515) is another reputable Baja specialist. The venerable standby **Baja Expeditions** (tel. 619-581-3311, 2625 Garnet Ave., San Diego, CA 92109) offers kayaking trips to Magdalena Bay and to the Midriff Islands in the winter. Southwest Sea Kayaks in San Diego also offers guided trips, as does **Aqua Adventures Kayak School** (tel. 619-695-1500, 7985 Dunbrook Rd., Suite H, San Diego, CA 92109).

In Baja, relative newcomer **Baja Tropicales** (tel. 115-3-00-19, fax 115-3-03-40, A.P. 60, Mulegé, BCS, 23900) is the only company offering year-round instruction and guided trips;

prices are quite reasonable since it's head-quartered in Mulegé. Itineraries vary from one-day and overnight Bahía Concepción tours to multi-day paddles north and south along the Sea of Cortez coast from Mulegé. Whale-watching expeditions in the Magdalena and San Ignacio bays are also tentatively planned. The company can also serve as an outfitter for cus-tom-designed trips. For more information on Baja Tropicales programs, see the "Bahía Con-cepción" section under "Vicinity of Mulegé."

Several universities and community colleges in the U.S. state of California sponsor kayak-ing programs in Baja open to nonstudents. The UC Aquatic Center at the University of California, Berkeley, for example, recently began offering a 10-day Sea of Cortez trip for around US$300 less than most private tour companies. Contact **Cal Adventures** (2301 Bancroft Ave., Berke-ley, CA 94720, tel. 510-642-4000) for further information.

WINDSURFING

From November through March, the Sea of Cortez is a windsurfer's paradise, particularly from the central coast southward. Bahía de los Angeles and Bahía Concepción are perfect for beginning and intermediate board-sailors while the high winds of the East Cape will delight those in the advanced class. Any of the channels between the peninsula's east coast and the larg-er offshore islands—Canal de Cerralvo, Canal San José, Canal de Ballenas—usually offer good sideshore wind action, although some-times with strong currents. If you don't see other sailboards out, try to find someone who knows the currents before launching.

La Paz is also a very good area, even in sum-mer, when a strong breeze called El Coromuel comes in just about every afternoon. The best spots here lie along the mostly deserted beach-es of the peninsula northeast of town—Punta Balandra to Punta Coyote. When nothing's blow-ing in the Bahía de la Paz vicinity, dedicated windsurfers can shuttle west across the penin-sula to check out the action at Punta Marquéz on the Pacific side, only 72 km (45 miles) away.

Los Barriles on Bahía de Palmas, along the East Cape, is one of the more accessible wind-surfing areas in southern Baja. The wind is a steady 18-30 knots all winter long and wave-sailing is possible in some spots. During the season, uphauling is usually out of the ques-tion due to chop and high winds, so ability to waterstart is a prerequisite for board-sailing in this area.

Los Barriles is also home to the **Baja Vela Highwind Center** (tel. 800-223-5443 in the U.S. and Canada, or 415-322-0613), which offers highly rated instruction and package deals from mid-November through mid-March. Even if you're not a participant in one of its windsurfing vacations, you may be able to arrange for ser-vice and parts. Every January, Vela cospon-sors—with equipment manufacturer O'Neill— the Baja Windsurfing Championships at Los Barriles.

The Pacific side of Baja generally demands a more experienced board-sailor. Those who can handle high surf and strong winds will love it. Novices and intermediate windsurfers will enjoy the larger bays of Bahía de San Quintín, Bahía Magdalena, and Bahía Almejas, all protected from major swells in all but the worst weather. Board-sailors with sturdy transport—4WD or high-clearance trucks—can choose from dozens of smaller bays connected to Mexico Hwy. 1 by dirt roads of varying quality.

SURFING

Baja is one of the last refuges of "soul surfing," an experience that has all but disappeared from the crowded beaches of Alta California. Instead of fighting for a wave, Baja surfers typically take turns, making sure everyone gets a ride now and then. Baja attracts a lot of older Alta Cali-fornia surfers who are either fed up with the agro scene up north or are simply investigating new territory, or both. Also, there are fewer surfers on Baja beaches, so heated competi-tion is less imperative.

From the border all the way down to Cabo, most of the good surf areas lie below *puntas* (points) that offer right point breaks stoked by prevailing northwesterlies during the winter months. Even without any advance tips, a surfer need only drive down the Transpeninsular with a good road map in hand, turning west wherev-er the map shows a side road leading off to "Punta X." As with all other coastal recreation,

dawn patrol

JOE CUMMINGS

more places are accessible to those with high-clearance vehicles or 4WD, although many good surf spots lie within range of ordinary passenger cars as well.

In the summer the surf's mostly small to flat, except when a tropical storm comes up from the south. When this happens, there's usually high surf at Cabo and at the southern end of many offshore Pacific islands, the most notorious being Isla Natividad and Islas de Todos Santos.

Surf Locations

The number of surfers diminishes as you proceed south of Ensenada or north of Cabo San Lucas; any point between involves some serious road travel. In fact, even when the surf's really pumping in this middle zone, you stand a good chance of sharing monster breaks with only a handful of others—or even having them all to yourself—since there are no "surf hotlines" for central and southern Baja. This means serendipity is a major element in Baja surfing safaris—those who have the most time to scout the coastline will find the best wave action.

In the Ensenada area, the hot spot is San Miguel (also known as "Rincon"), a small bay just south of the last tollgate on the Tijuana-Ensenada toll road. A number of surfers live here year-round and others make weekend trips from southern Alta California, so at times it's a bit on the crowded side. The winter break here is usually quite reliable, pumping for weeks at a time. And when the surf's too small onshore, you can always climb in a panga and cruise 20 km (12 miles) out to Islas de Todos Santos, home of the biggest breaks on the entire west coast of North America. When San Miguel's nearly flat, Todos Santos waves may hit three to four meters (10-12 feet); when San Miguel's ripping at 2.5-3.5 meters (8-10 feet), the pros will be out at northern Todos on their nine-foot guns, tearing down 10-meter (30-foot) Waimea-style walls. The southern island of the twin Islas de Todos Santos produces a good left break during summer swells.

Several spots can also be found between Ensenada and the border in and around La Fonda, La Misión, and Rosarito, especially Punta Descanso, Punta Mesquite, and Punta Salsipuedes. South of Ensenada to the Cape are dozens of places with intermittent point breaks, but the most reputable for accessibility and steady surf are at Punta San José, Punta Baja, Punta Santa Rosalillita, Punta Abreojos, Punta El Conejo, and beaches in the vicinity of Todos Santos (the Baja California Sur town, not the islands).

For important shark information relevant to surfers in Baja waters, see "Sharks: Myth vs. Fact."

Equipment

Surfing is a low-tech sport, so the scarcity of surf shops in Baja is not a major problem. For any extended trip down the coast, carry both a short and a long board—or a gun for the northwest shores of Isla Natividad or Islas de Todos

SHARKS: MYTH VS. FACT

The word "shark" usually evokes a reaction of fear or loathing. This rection is irrational, however, considering that of the 360 identified species of shark, only four—bull, tiger, white, and ocean whitetip—attack humans. Around 60 shark species swim the Pacific and Sea of Cortez waters of Baja California, and of these the most common are smooth hammerhead, common thresher, bonito, sand, blue, and blacktip.

The shark's killer image is based on its quite real, natural prowess as a predator—sharks may, in fact, have been the world's first predators, having first appeared about 400 million years ago, 200 million years before the dinosaurs. Sharks can hear the sounds of other fish in the water from up to a mile away; they can smell blood from a similar distance and sense faint electrical fields transmitted by other animals that indicate whether the creature is in distress. A special lens in the shark's eye intensifies light so it can see prey in almost total darkness. All these attributes combine for quick, silent surprise attacks.

Most sharks feed on small fish. The largest of all, the whale shark, which reaches up to 18 meters (60 feet) long and may weigh as much as four tons, feeds on tiny plankton, and is occasionally seen in the Sea of Cortez.

As animals at or near the top of the marine food chain, sharks play a role in the sea similar to that of lions on land: helping to maintain an ecological balance by weeding out sick or feeble fish that can spread disease or bad genes. As with lions, the shark's greatest natural enemy is humans, whose appetite for shark meat is fast depleting shark populations around the world—especially in the Pacific.

About 100 million sharks a year—about the same quantity as tuna—are taken by hook or net, an amount marine biologists believe is 9,000 tons more than the shark population can endure. As a result, many shark species are on the brink of endangerment, a trend that doesn't bode well for other species in marine ecosystems affected by the shark's important place in the food web.

Shark Attacks

Most sharks are under two meters in length and more likely to flee from a swimmer or diver than attack. The most dangerous is the great white shark, which can reach over six meters and weigh up to 2.5 tons, and is the fastest and most powerful of the species. Its sharp, serrated teeth are set in jaws that hinge widely for the largest possible bite. Although not common, they occasionally cruise the deeper waters of the Pacific and account for most fatal attacks on humans.

Surfers are usually at a greater risk than swimmers or divers because the great white is more likely to confuse the profile of a surfer's dangling limbs with relatively small fish. When a shark can see the entire body of a swimmer, it's more likely to consider the prey too large to attack. Murky waters diminish general visibility and can add to potential confusion; hence, many shark attacks on humans occur in murky waters, often caused by abrupt changes in weather conditions. In an area known for the presence of large sharks (*tiburones*), it's best for surfers to avoid unclear waters, especially at offshore breaks.

Searching the water's surface for shark fins is a relatively useless activity since a shark will pinpoint your location long before you become aware of it. Surfers with open wounds should stay out of the water since blood may attract sharks.

Santos in winter. Besides wax and a cooler, about the only other items you need bring are a fiberglass-patching kit for bad dings and a first-aid kit for routine surf injuries. Most surf spots are far from medical assistance—don't forget butterfly bandages. Boards can be repaired at just about any boatyard on the coast, since most Mexican pangas are made of fiberglass and require a lot of patching.

Small surf shops in Ensenada and Cabo San Lucas sell boards, surfwear, and accessories. You can buy Mexican-made boards—San Miguel and Cactus brands—in Ensenada for about US$50 to US$75 less than what they cost north of the border, about US$100 less than retail for a comparable American or Japanese board.

Organized Trips

Surfers aren't usually big on organized travel but for one destination in Baja, Isla Natividad, some make an exception. Getting to Natividad ordinarily involves driving to Punta Eugenia on the Vizcaíno Peninsula, an ordeal in itself, and then chartering a boat to the island. **Baja Surf**

Adventures (tel. 619-744-5642, toll-free 800-428-7873 in the U.S./Canada) provides a much easier alternative.

BSA offers a special concession for the famous "Open Doors" break at Isla Natividad for six months per year. It offers three- to five-day package surf trips to the island from July through September—peak time for the south swell—that include roundtrip airfare from Ensenada, lodging on Natividad, and two meals per day. Tours are limited to 12 people

SNORKELING AND SCUBA DIVING

The semitropical Sea of Cortez coral reefs at the southern tip of the Cape Region are among the most well-known dive locations in Baja, simply because they're so close to shore. But many spots of interest along much of the 4,800-km coastline are accessible to divers with good boat transportation and the necessary diving skills. For the most part, Pacific diving is for experienced offshore scuba divers only while the Cortez coast and islands are excellent for inshore novice divers as well as snorkelers.

Marinelife is concentrated in Baja among three types of environments: kelp fields, reefs (both rock and hard coral), and shipwrecks. The latter develop artificial reefs with time and are particularly plentiful in Baja waters. Some of the sunken vessels available for exploration are Liberty ships, junks, steamers, tuna clippers, submarines, yachts, ferryboats, tugs, and full-rigged barques.

Pacific Diving
The most popular diving areas are those in the northwest—Islas Todos Santos and Islas Coronados—accessible to daytripping southern Alta Californians. As at most of Baja's Pacific islands, the west and southwest offer the greatest proliferation of sealife, including kelp beds, rock reefs, and encrusted sea pinnacles amid scenic sandflats. Both the Todos Santos and the Coronados are popular among spearfishing enthusiasts because of the large yellowtail populations that feed in the vicinity of these island groups. Halibut, various sea basses, and bonito are also common, as is lobster. The cold, fast-running currents mean visibility is usually quite good in offshore areas.

Farther south at Bahía Rosario, off the coast near the town of El Rosario, are large kelp beds and the Sacramento Reef. Along with an abundance of marinelife, this four-km-long reef features so many shipwrecks it's dubbed the "Graveyard of the Pacific." The reef—named for the paddlewheeler *Sacramento* that ran aground here in 1872—is also home to a population of large lobsters referred to locally as *burros* (donkeys) or *caballos* (horses). Isla San Gerónimo, 2.5 km northwest of the reef, is known as an excellent spearfishing location.

The next diving area south lies off the tip of the Vizcaíno Peninsula at Islas San Benito, Isla Cedros, and Isla Natividad. This group of islands features kelp beds, sea pinnacles, shoals, and rock reefs. Bahía Magdalena, much farther south, is of interest for its shallows teeming with sealife, including sea turtles, sharks, manta rays, seals, and whales. Heavy swells and surging along the Pacific coast mean that it should only be tackled by experienced scuba divers or with an experienced underwater guide. Ensenada has three dive shops; southward along the Pacific coast there are none before Cabo San Lucas.

Sea Of Cortez Diving
The Sea of Cortez offers one of the richest marine ecosystems in the world, and the underwater scenery is especially vivid and varied. Sea lions, numerous whale and dolphin varieties, colorful tropical species, manta rays, and schooling hammerhead sharks are all part of a thick food chain stimulated by cold-water upwellings amid the over 100 islands and islets that dot the Cortez. The largest proportion of Cortez sealife are species of tropical Panamic origins that have found their way north from Central and South American waters.

The northern Cortez is avoided by many divers because of strong tidal surges, speedy currents, and overall lack of underwater marine variety relative to the central and southern Cortez. In general, the northernmost diving area is Bahía de los Angeles, where tidal conditions and visibility are suitable for recreational diving. The offshore islands are the main attractions here; two small hotels service divers and arrange guided trips.

Next south are the Midriff Islands, which require long-range boats and an experienced appraisal of local currents and tidal changes. Rock reefs are abundant throughout these islands. Below the Midriffs, tidal conditions calm down considerably and the water is generally warmer. Marinelife is plentiful and varied, and spearfishing is excellent in many areas.

In the central Cortez, divers are serviced by Mulegé Divers, one of the better dive-shop operations in Baja. Many of the nearby islands, bays, and points are suitable for snorkeling as well as scuba diving; Isla San Marcos, Punta Chivato, Islas Santa Inés, and Bahía Concepción are among the best-known areas. Loreto, a bit farther south, also offers a dive shop and several popular nearby diving areas: Isla Coronado, Punta Coyote, Isla del Carmen, and Isla Danzante. Rock reefs, boulders, volcanic ridges, and sandflats are common throughout. Farther east in the Cortez are vast submarine canyons as well as more remote volcanic and continental islands best explored by experienced scuba divers.

From La Paz south, onshore water temperatures usually hover between 21° C (70° F) and 29° C (85° F) year-round, making the southern Cortez the most popular diving destination on this side of Baja. The area is known for the Pulmo Reef, the only hard coral reef in the Sea of Cortez. Water visibility is best from July through October, when it exceeds 30 meters (100 feet); this is also when the air temperature is warmest, often reaching well over 32° C (90° F).

La Paz features several dive shops; popular local dive sites are numerous and include Playa Balandra (mostly snorkeling), Roca Suwanee, Isla Espíritu Santo, Isla Partida, the *Salvatierra* shipwreck, El Bajito Reef, Los Islotes, and the El Bajo Seamount. El Bajo is famous for its summer population of giant manta rays, who seem unusually disposed toward allowing divers to hitch rides on their *allas* (pectoral fins). Schooling hammerhead sharks are also common during the summer months—they're very rarely aggressive toward divers when swimming in schools, so El Bajo is an excellent observation area.

The Cabo Pulmo and Los Cabos areas are served by several small dive operations in Cabo San Lucas. Pulmo Reef in Bahía Pulmo consists of a series of eight volcanic ridges inhabited by profuse coral life. The coral attracts a wide variety of fish of all sizes and colors; other, smaller reefs as well as shipwrecks lie in the general vicinity. Because most underwater attractions are close to shore, this area is good for diving from small boats or open-cockpit kayaks.

Several coves along the coast toward Cabo San Lucas make good snorkeling sites. Bahía Cabo San Lucas itself is a protected marine park; the rocks and points along the bayshore are suitable for snorkeling and novice scuba diving while the deep submarine canyon just 45 meters offshore attracts more experienced thrillseekers. This canyon is known for its intriguing "sandfalls," streams of falling sand channeled between rocks along the canyon walls. Nearby Playa Santa María, on the way east toward San José del Cabo, is a popular snorkeling area with coral at either end of a large cove.

Equipment

Divers shouldn't count on finding the equipment they need in Baja, even in resort areas. Since most equipment sold or rented in Baja dive shops is imported from the U.S., stocks vary from season to season. Purchase prices are also generally higher in Mexico than north of the border.

For Pacific diving south to Punta Abreojos, a full quarter-inch wetsuit is recommended year-round; from Punta Abreojos south lighter suits are sufficient in the summer. At Cabo San Lucas and around the Cape as far north as the central Cortez, a light suit may be necessary from late November through March; shorties or ordinary swimsuits will suffice the rest of the year. From the Midriff Islands north in the Sea of Cortez, heavier suits are necessary December through early April. In summer, many Sea of Cortez divers wear lycra skins to protect against jellyfish stings.

Because divers and anglers occasionally frequent the same areas, a good diving knife is essential for dealing with wayward fishing line. Bring two knives so you'll have a spare. Include extra CO_2 cartridges for flotation vests, rubber slings for spearguns, O-rings, and a wetsuit patching kit.

Air: Dependable air for scuba tanks is usually available in Ensenada, Mulegé, Loreto, La Paz, and Cabo San Lucas. Always check the compressor first, however, to make sure it's well maintained and running clean. Divers with extensive Baja experience usually carry a portable compressor not only to avoid contaminated air, but for travel to areas where tank refills aren't available.

Recompression Chambers: The nearest full-time, dependable recompression facility is the **Hyperbaric Medicine Center** (tel. 619-543-5222) at the University of California Medical Center in San Diego. The HMC is open Mon.-Fri., 0730-1630, and for emergencies. For emergency air transport to the facility call Life Flight (tel. 619-297-4356) or contact one of the air evacuation organizations servicing Baja. Several commercial diving facilities on the Baja Pacific coast feature recompression chambers but they're often marred by disuse and disrepair.

Organized Diving Trips

Two Alta California outfits operate dive trips in Baja waters: **Baja Expeditions** (tel. 619-581-3311, 2625 Garnet Ave., San Diego, CA 92109) leads scuba diving excursions to the La Paz area in the Sea of Cortez; **Diving Charters** (tel. 619-224-4997, P.O. Box 6374, San Diego, CA 92106) specializes in trips off Baja's Pacific coast—including the Coronados and Isla Guadalupe.

In Baja, divers will find skilled guides in Ensenada, Bahía de los Angeles, Mulegé, Loreto, La Paz, and Cabo San Lucas. Most of the Baja dive outfits also offer instruction and scuba certification at reasonable rates.

RACE AND SPORTS BETTING

During the U.S. Prohibition era of the 1920s, casinos were a major part of Baja high life in Tijuana, Mexicali, the Coronado Islands, and Ensenada. Although the Mexican government outlawed casino gambling in the 1930s, it allows race and sports books in Baja California Norte—a major source of foreign revenue for the state.

The heir to Tijuana's lavish El Casino de Agua Caliente is the **LF Caliente Race and Sports Book,** with locations at the famed Caliente Race Track in Tijuana as well as in Ensenada, Rosarito, Mexicali, San Felipe, La Paz, and Cabo San Lucas. The Caliente Race Track hosts weekly greyhound racing, and at all LF Caliente Race and Sports Book locations you can bet on basketball, football, baseball, and other sports. Caliente has an information hotline in Alta California: (619) 231-1910, or 231-1919. The LF Caliente betting lounges also feature bars and restaurants; betting is not required if patrons just want a drink or a meal while watching sports events on multiple screens.

In Tijuana you can bet on live jai alai matches at the Frontón Jai Alai on Av. Revolución.

ENTERTAINMENT

Most visitors to Baja California come for the beaches, mountains, deserts, fishing, or water sports, not for what would normally be considered "entertainment." Nonetheless it's not necessarily bedtime when the sun goes down, except in the most remote areas. The larger cities—Tijuana, Mexicali, Rosarito, Ensenada, La Paz, and Cabo San Lucas—offer a variety of museums, theaters, cinemas, concert halls, bars, and discos. For specific recommendations regarding these types of entertainment venues, see the destination sections of this book.

MUSIC

When most North Americans think of Mexican music they think of brass-and-violins mariachi music, a style from the state of Jalisco on the Mexican mainland. In Baja, mariachi music is generally reserved for weddings and tourists, as is the music of the so-called Baja Marimba Band. (Marimba music also hails from elsewhere in Mexico.) The most commonly heard music on the peninsula is *la música norteña,* a style that's representative of ranchero life yet has a wide appeal throughout northern Mexico and the southwestern United States. Everyone from urban truckers in Tijuana to *pescadores* in Bahía Agua Verde seems to play norteña tapes on their boomboxes.

Norteña music shares common roots with the Tex-Mex *(tejano)* or *conjunto* music enjoyed in Texas and New Mexico and made famous by Flaco Jimenez, Ramón Ayala, Los Tigres del Norte, and, most recently, the Grammy-winning Texas Tornadoes (a group comprised of Flaco Jimenez, Freddie Fender, and the remnants of Doug Sahm's Sir Douglas Quintet, Doug Sahm and Augie Meyers). It's typically played by an ensemble led by an accordion and *bajo sexto,* a large Mexican 12-string guitar. Originally, these two instruments were supported by a string bass and sometimes a trap drum set; later, electric bass and guitar were occasionally added, along with alto sax and keyboards. Still, most norteña bands maintain the traditional accordion, bajo sexto, and acoustic bass lineup. The music itself encompasses an exciting mix of Latinized polkas and waltzes, *rancheras* (similar to American country and western), and *corridos* (Mexican ballads), as well as modern Latin forms like *cumbias* and salsa.

The most popular norteña band among Bajacalifornios in recent years has been Los Tigres del Norte, who, although based in San Jose, Alta California, are *superestrellas* (superstars) in Mexico. Like many norteña bands, Los Tigres sing songs that reflect the daily lives and sentiments of northern Mexican peasants, often with a political edge. Some of the songs recorded by Los Tigres and other norteña groups are banned by the Mexican government and can only be heard on bootleg tapes that circulate at cantinas or local fiestas. In 1988, Los Tigres won a Grammy award (Mexican music category) in the U.S. for the album *¡Gracias! America Sin Fronteras (Thank You! America Without Borders).*

Live norteña music is often heard at fiestas throughout Baja and in Mexican bars and cantinas in larger towns and cities. Strolling *trovadores,* for example, wander most

norteña musicians

BOB RACE

evenings from bar to bar playing norteña music along Calle Ruíz in Ensenada. It's not the nicest area of town, but it's a place for the musically curious to hear the local sounds.

In more upscale clubs in Tijuana and Mexicali, you may see the latest dance craze to sweep Mexico, the *caballito* ("little horse"). Danced to uptempo norteña *rancheras,* the dance utilizes a set of fancy equestrian-type maneuvers, including a step in which the female dancer briefly mounts the upper leg of the male dancer. Bajacalifornios have developed their own variation of this dance called the *quebradita* ("little break"), which adds a steep bobbing of the head from side to side.

BULLFIGHTS

One type of entertainment you won't find north of the border is the bullfight. Variously called *la corrida de toros* (the running of bulls), *la fiesta brava* (the brave festival), *la lidia de toros* (the fighting of bulls), or *sombra y sol* (shade and sun), the bullfight can be perceived as sport, art, or gory spectacle, depending on the social conditioning of the observer.

To the aficionado, the lidia is a ritual drama which rolls courage, fate, pathos, and death together into a symbolic event. No matter how one may feel toward the bullfight, it is undeniably an integral part of Mexican history and culture. Every town of any size has at least one *plaza de*

toros or bullring; in Baja California you'll find one major stadium in Mexicali and two in Tijuana, including the second largest ring in the world. Occasionally a small bullring is improvised for a rural fiesta.

History
Ritualistic encounters with bulls have been traced as far back as 3000 B.C., when the Minoans on the Greek island of Crete performed ritual dives over the horns of attacking wild bulls. A closer antecedent developed around 2000 B.C. on the Iberian peninsula, where a breed of fierce, wild bulls roamed the plains. Iberian hunters—ancestors of the Spanish and Portuguese—figured out how to evade the dangerous bull at close quarters while delivering a fatal blow with an axe or spear. When the Romans heard about this practice they began importing wild Spanish bulls and accomplished bullfighters for their colosseum games—possibly the first public bullfights.

During the Middle Ages, bullfighting became a royal sport practiced on horseback by both the Spanish and the occupying Moors, who used lances to dispatch the wild bulls. As the *toreros* (bullfighters) began dismounting and confronting the bulls on the ground, the game eventually evolved into the current *corrida* as performed in Spain, Portugal, Mexico, and throughout much of Latin America.

In the early years the only payment the torero received was the bull's carcass. Nowadays bull-

CHRIS PARMENTER

fighters receive performance fees that vary according to their status within the profession.

El Toro

The bulls used in the ring, *toros de lidia* (fighting bulls), are descendants of wild Iberian bulls that have been specially bred for over four centuries for their combative spirit. They're not trained in any way for the ring, nor goaded into viciousness, but as a breed are naturally quick to anger. The fighting bull's neck muscles are much larger than that of any other cattle breed in the world, making the animal capable of tossing a torero and his horse into the air with one upward sweep.

Bulls who show an acceptable degree of bravery by the age of two are let loose in huge pastures—averaging 10,000 acres per animal—to live as wild beasts until they reach four years, the age of combat. By the time *el toro* enters the ring, he stands around 125 centimeters high at the withers and weighs 450 kilograms (a half ton) or more.

The carcass of a bull killed in the ring does not go to waste, at least not from a meat eater's perspective. Immediately after it's taken from the ring, it's butchered and dressed, the meat sold to the public.

El Torero

The bullfighter is rated by his agility, control, and compassion. The torero who teases a bull or who is unable to kill it quickly when the moment of truth arrives is considered a cruel brute. To be judged a worthy competitor by the spectators, el torero must excel in three areas: *parar,* or standing still as the bull charges, with only the cape and the torero's upper body moving; *templar,* or timing and grace, the movements smooth, well timed, and of the right proportion; and *mandar,* or command, the degree to which the torero masters the entire lidia through his bravery, technique, and understanding of the bull, neither intimidating the animal nor being intimidated by it.

Standard equipment for the torero is the *capote de brega,* the large cape used in the first two thirds of the lidia; the *muleta,* a smaller cape used during the final third; the *estoque* or matador's sword; and the *traje de luces* or "suit of lights," the colorful torero's costume originally designed by the Spanish artist Goya.

Although it's usually the bull who dies in a lidia, toreros are also at great risk. Over half of all professional matadors on record worldwide during the last 250 years have been gored to death in the ring.

La Lidia

The regulated procedures (*suertes*) followed in a bullfight date from 18th-century Spain. Anywhere from four to eight bulls may appear in a corrida (typically six), with one torero on hand for every two bulls scheduled. The order of appearance for the toreros is based on seniority. Toreros who've proven their skills in several bullfighting seasons as *novilleros* (novice fighters) are called *matadores de toros* (bull killers). Ordinarily each torero will fight two bulls; if he's gored or otherwise put out of action, another torero will take his place, even if it means facing more than his allotment of bulls.

Each lidia is divided into three *tercios,* or "thirds." In *el tercio de varas,* the bull enters the ring and the matador performs *capeos* (cape maneuvers that don't expose the matador's body to the bull's horns, meant to test the bull or lead it to another spot in the ring) and *lances* (cape maneuvers that expose the matador's body to the horns and bring the bull closer to him) while two horsemen receive the bull's charge with eight-foot *varas* or lances. The varas have short, pyramid-shaped points which are aimed at the bull's neck muscle and do not penetrate very deeply on contact.

The purpose of the encounter is to force the bull to lower his horns and to give him the confidence of meeting something solid so he won't be frustrated by the emptiness of the cape as the lidia proceeds. Usually only two vara blows are administered, but more are permitted if necessary to produce the intended effect: the lowering of the head. The crowd protests, however, when more than two are applied, as they want the matador to face a strong bull.

In *el tercio de banderillas,* the bull's shoulders receive the banderillas, 26-inch wooden sticks decorated with colored paper frills, each tipped with a small, sharp, iron barb. They can be placed by the matador himself or more often by hired assistant toreros, called *banderilleros* when performing this function. The purpose of banderilla placement is to "correct" the bull's posture; the added punishment also makes the bull craftier in his charges. Placed in pairs, up to six banderillas may be applied to the bull, varying in number and position according to the reactions of the individual animal.

At the end of the tercio de banderillas, signaled by a bugle fanfare, the matador takes up his muleta and sword and walks before the box of the *juez* (judge) presiding over the lidia. He looks to the juez for permission to proceed with the killing of the bull and, after receiving a nod, offers his *brindis* (dedication). The brindis may go to an individual spectator, a section of the plaza, or the entire audience. If the dedication is to an individual, he will present his *montera* (matador's hat) to that person, who will return it, with a present inside, to the matador after the lidia. Otherwise, he waves his hat at the crowd and then tosses it onto the sand; he remains hatless for the final tercio, a gesture of respect for the bull.

The final round of the lidia is called *el tercio de muerte* (the third of death). The main activity of this tercio is *la faena* (literally, "the work") involving cape and sword, during which a special set of passes leads to the killing of the bull. The first two tercios have no time limit; for the last, however, the matador has only 15 minutes to kill the bull, or else he is considered defeated and the bull is led from the ring, where it is killed immediately by the plaza butcher.

In a good faena, a matador will tempt fate over and over again, bringing the bull's horns close to his own heart. The time for the kill arrives when the bull has so tired from the faena that he stands still, forelegs squared as if ready to receive the sword. Then, with his cape, the matador must draw the bull into a final charge while he himself moves forward, bringing the sword out from under the cape, sighting down the blade, and driving the blade over the horns

and between the animal's shoulders. A perfect swordthrust severs the aorta, resulting in instant death. If the thrust is off, the matador must try again until the bull dies from one of the thrusts.

It is not necessary to kill the bull in one stroke, which is quite an extraordinary accomplishment; the matador's honor is preserved as long as he goes in over the horns, thus risking his own life, every time. If the bull falls to his knees but isn't dead, another torero immediately comes forward and thrusts a dagger (*puntilla*) behind the base of the skull to sever the spinal cord and put the beast out of his misery. When the bull is dead, the lidia is over. If the matador has shown bravery and artistry, the crowd rewards him with applause; an unusually dramatic performance will see hats and flowers thrown into the ring. In cases of outstanding technique or bravado, the juez awards the bull's ears and/or tail to the matador.

Practicalities

It's usually a good idea to buy tickets for a corrida in advance, since it's not unusual for an event to sell out. Check with the local tourist office to determine if any seats are available. In the event of a sellout, you may still be able to buy a ticket—at higher prices—from a scalper or *revendedor*. In a large stadium, the spectator sections are divided into *sol* (sunny side) and *sombra* (shaded side), then subdivided according to how close the seats are to the bullring itself. Since the corrida doesn't usually begin until around 4 p.m., the *sol* tickets aren't bad, as long as you bring a hat, sunglasses, and sunscreen, plus plenty of pesos to buy beverages. Tequila and beer are usually available, along with soft drinks.

HOLIDAYS, FESTIVALS, AND EVENTS

Mexicans love a fiesta and Bajacalifornios are no exception. Any occasion will suffice as an excuse to hold a celebration, from a birthday to a lobster harvest. Add to all the civic possibilities the vast number of Mexican Catholic religious holidays, and there's potential for some kind of public fiesta at least every week of the year, if not all 365 days. Besides the national religious holidays, Mexico has feast days for 115 Catholic saints per year, nine or 10 each month. Any town, pueblo, ejido, or colonia named for a saint will usually hold a fiesta on the feast day of its namesake. Individuals named for saints, too, will often host parties on their *día de santo* (saint's day).

The primary requisites of a fiesta are plenty of food (especially tamales, considered a festive dish), beer and liquor, music, and dancing. More elaborate celebrations include parades, exhibitions, *charreadas* (Mexican rodeos), and occasional fireworks.

Some of the more memorable yearly events and public holidays observed throughout Baja are highlighted below by month. Smaller festivals and events held locally are mentioned later in the text. Actual dates can vary from year to year, so be sure to check with the appropriate tourist office in advance.

Government offices and some businesses close on national holidays. These closings are not always mentioned in the text; you may want to call ahead to find out.

January
New Year's Day, 1 January, is an official holiday.
Día de los Santos Reyes, 6 January. See *Las Posadas* under December.

February
Constitution Day, 5 February, is an official holiday.
Carnaval: This pre-Lenten festival is held in late February or early March as a last celebration of the carnal pleasures Catholics must forego during the 40-day Lent season preceding Easter. The fiesta's name derives from the Italian *carne vale,* "flesh taken away." In Mexico, Carnaval is traditionally observed only in port towns;

in Baja the festival is celebrated most grandly in La Paz and Ensenada. Like New Orleans's Mardi Gras, Carnaval features lots of music, dancing, costumes, parades, and high-spirited revelry. See "Ensenada" for more information.
Flag Day, 24 February, is an official holiday.

March
Birthday of Benito Juárez, 21 March, is an official holiday.
Spring Break: Not a Mexican holiday at all, but an annual ritual for American college and university students—mostly southern Alta Californians and Arizonans—who go on the rampage in Rosarito, Ensenada, San Felipe, and Los Cabos. The spring break season usually straddles late March and early April. Unless you're one of the revelers, these towns should be avoided during that period.

April
Semana Santa: "Holy Week," or Easter Week (the third week in April), is second only to Christmas as the most important holiday period of the year. One of the most prominent Semana Santa customs is breaking *cascarones,* colored eggs stuffed with confetti, over the heads of friends and family. Besides attending mass on Good Friday and Easter Sunday, many Mexicans take this opportunity to go on vacations. Baja resorts—particularly Rosarito, Ensenada, San Felipe, and Los Cabos—can be overcrowded this week since the peninsula receives a large influx of both Mexican mainlanders and North Americans.
Rosarito-Ensenada 50-Mile Bicycle Ride: The ride takes place on the last Saturday in April and attracts as many as 10,000 participants, making it one of the largest cycling events in the world. The route follows the coast with an elevation differential of around 300 meters. The same ride is repeated in the fall with even larger crowds—up to 16,000. Sponsored by **Bicycling West** (tel. 619-583-3001, P.O. Box 15128, San Diego, CA 92175-0128).
Newport-Ensenada Yacht Race: Reportedly the world's largest international yachting regatta, held the last weekend in April. Boats race from Newport Beach in Alta California to Ensenada.

Sponsored by the Newport Ocean Sailing Association (tel. 714-640-1351, fax 714-640-1628).

May
International Workers' Day, 1 May, is an official holiday.

Cinco de Mayo: Held on 5 May, this festival commemorates the defeat of an attempted French invasion at Puebla de los Angelos, on Mexico's Gulf of Mexico coast, in 1862. Features music, dance, food, and other cultural events.

Mother's Day (Día de las Madres) is held on 10 May.

Feast of Corpus Christi: A religious holiday celebrated 60 days after Easter to honor the Body of Christ and the Eucharist. Corn-husk figurines and miniature mules are displayed in stores and homes.

June
Navy Day, 1 June, is an official holiday.

September
Día de Nuestra Señora de Loreto: Held in Loreto on 8 September to commemorate the founding of the first mission in the Californias. Special masses, processions, music, dancing, and food.

Mexican Independence Day (Fiesta Patria de la Independencia): Also called Diez y Seis, since it falls on 16 September, this holiday celebrates the country's independence from Spain, as announced in 1821 in the town of Dolores. Festivities actually begin on the 15th and last

two days. The biggest celebrations are centered in the state capitals of Mexicali and La Paz, and include fireworks, parades, charreadas, music, and folk-dance performances.

The **Rosarito-Ensenada 50-Mile Bicycle Ride** is held on the last Saturday in September; see description under "April."

October
Día de la Raza: Celebrated as Columbus Day north of the border, 12 October in Mexico commemorates the founding of the Mexican race as heralded by the arrival of Columbus in the New World.

November
Día de los Muertos: The "Day of the Dead" is Mexico's third-most important holiday, corresponding to Europe's All Saints Day except that it's celebrated on the 1st and 2nd of November instead of only the 1st. Some of the festivities are held in cemeteries where children clean the headstones and crucifixes of their deceased relatives (*los difuntos*) and play games unique to this fiesta. Roadside shrines throughout Baja are laid with fresh flowers and other tributes to the dead. Offerings of *pan de los muertos* (bread of the dead) and food and liquor are placed before family altars on behalf of deceased family members, along with papier-mâché skulls and skeletons.

Baja 1000: In the second or third week of November the most famous desert race in North America, the Baja Mil, draws a dedicated crowd

Day of the Dead

JOE CUMMINGS

of off-road fanatics and automotive manufacturers hoping to gain advertising copy like "Baja 1000 Winner" or at least "Baja 1000-Tested." These days the course follows established auto trails to avoid further damage to Baja's fragile desert lands; the course alternates from year to year between a full 1,000-mile (1,600-km) race between Ensenada and La Paz and a 1,000-km race that loops through the northern state only. The race runs in several classes from dirt bikes to 4WD trucks; an average of 300 drivers (about 120 motorcycle and 180 car/truck entries) compete. Sponsored by SCORE (tel. 818-889-9216, 31125 Via Colinas, Suite 908, Westlake Village, CA 91362).

Anniversary of the 1910 Revolution is held on 20 November, and is an official holiday.

December

Día de Nuestra Señora de Guadalupe: The feast day of the Virgin of Guadalupe, Mexico's patron saint, is 12 December; special masses are held that day throughout Mexico. The nearest Sunday to the 12th also features special events such as mariachi masses, food booths, and games. The celebrations at the border town of Tecate are particularly well attended.

Las Posadas: Beginning on 16 December, Mexicans hold nightly *posadas*—candlelight processions terminating at elaborate, community-built nativity scenes—in commemoration of the Holy Family's search for lodging. The processions continue for nine consecutive nights. Other activities include piñata parties where children shatter hanging papier-mâché figures filled with small gifts and candy. Churches large and small hold continuous Christmas masses beginning at midnight on the 25th (Día de la Navidad).

Las Posadas culminates on 6 January, which is Día de los Santos Reyes—literally, "Day of the King-Saints," referring to the story of the Three Wise Men. On this day Mexican children receive their Christmas gifts, and family and friends gather to eat a wreath-shaped fruitcake called *rosca de reyes* (wreath of the kings) baked especially for this occasion. Hidden inside each *rosca* is a small clay figurine (*muñeco*) that represents the infant Jesus. While sharing the rosca on this day, the person whose slice contains the muñeco is obliged to host a *candelaría*, or Candlemas party, on 2 February for everyone present.

At the candelaría—which commemorates the day the newborn Jesus was first presented at the Temple in Jerusalem—the host traditionally displays a larger Christ-infant figure and serves tamales and *atole*, a thick, hot grain drink flavored with fruit or chocolate.

ACCOMMODATIONS

Places to stay in Baja run the gamut from free campgrounds to plush resort hotels. Camping spots are actually more numerous than hotels or motels, so visitors who bring along camping gear will have a greater range of options at any given location. Larger cities—Tijuana, Ensenada, Mexicali, La Paz, and Cabo San Lucas—have dozens of hotels to choose from.

HOTELS AND MOTELS

At many hotels and motels, midweek rates are lower than weekend rates. In northern Baja, some places charge high-season rates from May through October; in southern Baja it's generally the opposite (winter rates are highest). To save money on accommodations, try traveling in the off-season for each region; except for the inland deserts, most of the peninsula is livable year-round. Summer temperatures of 37° C/100° F on the Cortez coast are usually mitigated by sea breezes and relatively low humidity.

Whatever the rack rate, you can usually get the price down by bargaining (except during peak periods, e.g., Christmas, spring break, and Easter). When checking in, be sure to clarify whether the room rate includes meals—occasionally it does. Asking for a room without meals (*sin comidas*) is an easy way to bring the rate down, or simply ask if there's anything cheaper (*Hay algo más barato?*).

Budget

Hotels and motels in Baja are considerably less expensive than their counterparts in the U.S., Canada, or Europe, but slightly more expen-

Hotel Finisterra,
Cabo San Lucas

JOE CUMMINGS

sive than equivalent accommodations in mainland Mexico. In the budget range, you'll find a simple but clean room with private bath and double bed for around US$15-20 a night; up to US$35 in Tijuana, Ensenada, Mexicali, or Cabo San Lucas. Soap, towels, toilet paper, and purified drinking water are usually provided; in some places you may have to ask. Rooms in this price range usually don't offer air conditioners or heaters. In northern Baja you can often obtain a *calentador* or space heater on request for especially cool nights.

Lodging under US$15 per night is rare unless you stay at a youth hostel, *casa de huéspedes*, or *pensión*, where bathrooms are usually shared. The term *baño collectivo* indicates shared bathroom facilities.

Medium-priced
The largest number of hotels and motels in Baja falls into the US$40-60 range. Some are older Mexican-style hotels just a bit larger than those in the budget range while others are American-style motels; most everything in this price range comes with heating and air-conditioning.

La Pinta Chain
Straddling the line between mid-range and luxury hotels is the Hotel La Pinta chain, a joint venture between the Mexican government and Del Prado Inns. In Baja these hotels are located in Ensenada, San Quintín, Cataviña, San Ignacio, and Loreto. Some formerly belonged to the El Presidente chain.

La Pinta hotels are very similar in appearance and facilities; the Las Cazuelas restaurant at each features the same menu, though the food quality varies according to the talents of the local kitchen staff. Room rates are similar throughout the chain, US$55-60 s/d, not including 10% tax. Some rooms at the Loreto La Pinta cost only US$49. These prices assume you're paying in pesos—if you pay in dollars, the low exchange rate will cost you extra.

Like most hotel or motel chains, the most you can say for La Pinta is that there are few surprises. All feature PEMEX pumps conveniently located on the hotel grounds; between Ensenada and Loreto they're the only hotels which accept credit cards for room and meal charges. Mulegé's Hotel Serenidad will also accept credit cards, but adds a 6% surcharge for the service.

Mexico Resorts International can arrange reservations for any La Pinta hotel via a toll-free U.S. number, (800) 336-5454, or you can write MRI, P.O. Box 120637, Chula Vista, CA, 92012. In Baja, reservations can be made by calling the chain's central office in Ensenada at (617) 6-26-01.

Luxury And Resort Hotels
Higher-end places are found in or near Tijuana, Rosarito, Ensenada, San Felipe, La Paz, San José del Cabo, and Cabo San Lucas. Prices in Baja for "international-class accommodation" average around US$80 to US$120. A few Cape resorts charge as high as US$250 for particular rooms or suites. Some of these places are good

values, while others are definitely overpriced. When in doubt, stick to the less-expensive hotels. Or ask about "specials"; the Grand Hotel Tijuana in Tijuana, for example, advertised rooms which normally cost nearly US$100 for just US$49.

Hotel Reservation Services
Most of the hotels and motels mentioned in this guidebook will take advance reservations directly by phone or mail. Some North American visitors may find it more convenient to use reservation services offered in the United States. **Baja Hotel Reservations** (tel. 714-476-5555, toll-free 800-347-2252 in the U.S./Canada, 18552 MacArthur Blvd., Suite 205, Irvine, CA 92715), for example, specializes in luxury hotels, including the Hotel Los Arcos in La Paz and the Hotel Finisterra in Cabo San Lucas. **Baja California Tours** (tel. 619-454-7166, 6986 La Jolla Blvd., La Jolla, CA 92037) handles reservations for the Estero Beach Hotel in Ensenada and Hotel Las Misiones in San Felipe.

In addition to the La Pinta hotels, Mexican Resorts International handles reservations for several other Baja hotels. The exact roster varies from year to year.

GUESTHOUSES AND HOSTELS

Casas De Huéspedes And Pensiones
Aside from free or very basic campgrounds, the casa de huéspedes (guesthouse) and Pensiones (boarding house) are the cheapest places to stay in Baja. Unfortunately for budgeters they aren't very plentiful. They're most numerous in Baja California Sur towns, especially Mulegé and La Paz. The typical casa de huéspedes offers rooms with shared bath (baño colectivo) for US$6-9; US$9-12 with private bath. A pensión costs about the same but may include meals. At either, most lodgers are staying for a week or more but the proprietors are usually happy to accept guests by the night.

The main difference between these and budget hotels/motels—besides rates—is that they're usually located in old houses or other buildings (e.g., convents) that have been converted for guesthouse use. Soap, towels, toilet paper, and drinking water are usually provided, but as with budget hotels and motels you may have to ask.

Youth Hostels
Baja has one youth hostel (villa deportivas juvenile, or youth sports villa) each in Mexicali, La Paz, and Cabo San Lucas. They feature shared dormitory-style rooms where each guest is assigned a bed and a locker. Bathing facilities are always communal and guests must supply their own soap and towels. Rates are US$4 per night in Mexicali, US$5 in BCS (US$5 and US$6 respectively for non-Hostelling International members); temporary memberships can be purchased for US$2. Food is available at hostel cafeterias in BCS only (but not Mexicali) for US$2-3 per meal.

Staying at youth hostels in Baja is a great way to meet young Mexicans and improve your Spanish; English is rarely spoken. About the only drawback is that the hostels tend to be inconveniently located some distance from the center of town, so transport can be a problem. For the fitness-oriented, they're ideal; sports facilities usually include gym, swimming pool, and courts for basketball, volleyball, and tennis.

Hotel Blanco Y Negro, Santa Rosalía

CAMPING

Baja has more campgrounds, RV parks, and other camping areas for its size than anywhere else in Mexico. Because the population density of the peninsula is so dramatically low, it's easy to find hidden campsites offering idyllic settings and precious solitude, often for free. For travelers who like the outdoors, it's also an excellent way to slash accommodation costs. A recent tourist study found that over 50% of Baja's foreign overnight visitors typically camp rather than stay in hotels.

Campgrounds And RV Parks

The Baja peninsula offers roughly 100 campgrounds—perhaps 125 if you count Sea of Cortez fish camps—that charge fees ranging from around US$1.50 for a place with virtually zero facilities to as high as US$15 for a developed RV park with full water, electrical, and sewage hookups plus recreation facilities. Most campgrounds charge around US$3-5 for tent camping, US$6-12 for full hookups. A few RV parks in the Rosarito area actually get away with charging US$25-35 a night—the same price you might pay for a modest hotel room.

If you can forego permanent toilet and bathing facilities you won't have to pay anything to camp in Baja, since there's a virtually limitless selection of free camping spots, from beaches to deserts to mountain slopes. You won't necessarily need 4WD to reach these potential campsites, as plenty of turnouts and graded dirt *ramales* (branch roads) off the main highways can be negotiated by just about any type of vehicle.

FOOD AND DRINK

Much of what Bajacalifornios eat can be considered northern Mexican cuisine. Because northern Mexico is generally better suited to ranching than farming, ranch-style cooking tends to prevail in rural areas, which means that ranch products—meat and dairy foods—are highly favored.

Unlike the northern mainland, however, just about any point in Baja is only a couple of hours' drive from the seashore, so seafood predominates here more than elsewhere in northern Mexico—or anywhere else in Mexico for that matter. In fact, in most places on the peninsula, seafood is more common than meat or poultry. If there's anything unique about Baja cuisine, it's the blending of ranch cooking with coastal culture, which has resulted in such distinctive Baja creations as the *taco de pescado* (fish taco).

WHERE TO EAT

Your selection of eating venues in Baja depends largely on where you are on the peninsula at any given moment. The most populated areas lie at either end of the peninsula, where you'll find the greatest range of places to eat. Baja's larger towns and cities—Tijuana, Mexicali, Ensenada, and La Paz—offer everything from humble sidewalk taco stands to four-star hotel restaurants.

Between Ensenada and La Paz the choices are fewer and more basic. Along certain lengthy stretches of the Transpeninsular Highway in central Baja, about the only places to eat are *ranchos* that serve whatever's on the stone hearth that day. Usually ranchos that take paying diners will hang a sign out front or post an arrow along the highway that says *Lonchería, Café, Comedor, Comida,* Eat, or Food. A few post no signs and are known only by word of mouth.

In small towns there may be only two or three restaurants (*restaurante, restorán*) that serve basic Mexican dishes or, if near the coast, *mariscos* (seafood). Most hotels in Baja have restaurants and in small towns they may be among the best choices. While the Hotel La Pinta chain's restaurants are not known for their culinary excellence, in the town of San Ignacio La Pinta's about the only place where you can count on a full meal. Sometimes the best meals on the road come from what you improvise yourself after a visit to a local *tienda de abarrotes* (grocery store).

Back in the city, one of the main nonrestaurant choices is the *taquería,* a small, inexpensive diner where tacos are assembled before your eyes—sort of the Mexican equivalent to the old-fashioned American hamburger stand. Taquerías tend to be found in areas where there's a lot of foot traffic—near bus terminals, for example. The good ones are packed with taco-eaters in the early evening.

Another economical choice is anything called a *lonchería,* which is a small, café-style place that usually serves *almuerzo* (late breakfast/early lunch) and *comida* (the main, midday meal). Lonchería hours are typically 1100 to 1700. Municipal markets in Baja often feature rows of loncherías where basic meals and *antojitos* (snacks or one-plate dishes) are quite inexpensive. Some loncherías offer *comida corrida,* a daily fixed-price meal that includes a beverage, an entree or two, side dishes, and possibly dessert.

A *comedor* is usually a more basic version of a lonchería; they aren't as common in Baja as on the mainland but are seen occasionally. Cafés are similar to loncherías except that they may open earlier and serve *desayuno* (breakfast) in addition to other meals.

Ordering And Paying
You really don't need much Spanish to get by in a restaurant. Stating what you want, plus *por*

RESTAURANT RATING KEY

$	Less than US$4 per meal
$$	US$4-8 per meal
$$$	US$9-16 per meal
$$$$	Over US$16 per meal

Ratings are based on
the average price of an entree.

favor (please), will usually do the trick (e.g., *dos cervezas, por favor,* "two beers, please"). Don't forget to say *gracias* (thank you). The menu is called *el menú* or, much less commonly in Baja, *la carta*. As a last resort, you can always point to what you want on the menu (if you want to look stupid instead of sounding stupid).

La cuenta is the bill. A tip (*la propina*) of about 15% is expected at any restaurant with table service; look to see if it's already been added to the bill before placing a tip on the table.

WHAT TO EAT

Tortillas

A Mexican meal is not a meal without tortillas, the round, flat, pancake-like disks eaten with nearly any nondessert dish, including salads, meats, seafood, beans, and vegetables. Both wheat-flour and cornmeal tortillas are commonly consumed throughout Baja, although flour tortillas (*tortillas de harina*) are the clear favorite. Corn tortillas (*tortillas de maíz*) are more common in southern Mexico, where Indian populations (the first corn cultivators) are larger, while flour tortillas are more popular in the ranching areas of northern Mexico. Among northern Mexicans, it is said that meat and poultry dishes taste best with flour tortillas while vegetable dishes go best with corn. Most restaurants offer a choice of the two. If you order tortillas without specifying, you may get *¿de harina o de maíz?* as a response.

Although prepackaged tortillas are available in *supermercados* (supermarkets), most Bajacalifornios buy them fresh from neighborhood *tortillerías* or make them at home. Many restaurants and cafés in Baja, and virtually all loncherías and taquerías, serve only fresh tortillas—tortillas made the same day, or the night before. If you're used to prepackaged tortillas—which is what most Mexican eateries in the U.S. or Canada serve—you're in for a pleasurable surprise when you raise a fresh, hot, home-made tortilla to your nose for the first time.

Incidentally, a tortilla has two sides, an inside and an outside, that dictate which direction the tortilla is best folded when wrapping it around food. The side with the thinner layer—sometimes called the *pancita*, or belly—should face the inside when folding the tortilla. If you notice the outside of your tortilla cracking, with pieces

peeling off onto the table, you've probably folded it with the pancita outside instead of inside.

Antojitos

This word literally means "little whims," thus implying snacks to many people. However, the word also refers to any food that can be ordered, served, and eaten quickly—in other words, Mexican fast food. Typical antojitos include tamales, enchiladas, burritos, flautas, chiles rellenos, chalupas, picadillo, quesadillas, tortas, and tacos.

ANTOJITOS

burrito—a flour tortilla rolled around meat, beans, or seafood fillings; Baja's lobster burritos are legendary

chalupa—a crisp, whole tortilla topped with beans, meat, etc. (also known as a *tostada*)

chiles rellenos—mild poblano chiles stuffed with cheese, deep-fried in an egg batter, and served with a *ranchero* sauce (tomatoes, onions, and chiles)

enchilada—a corn tortilla dipped in chile sauce, then folded or rolled around a filling of meat, chicken, seafood, or cheese and baked in an oven

flauta—a small corn tortilla roll, usually stuffed with beef or chicken and fried

picadillo—a spicy salad of chopped or ground meat with chiles and onions (also known as *salpicón*)

quesadilla—a flour tortilla folded over sliced cheese and grilled; ask the cook to add *chiles rajas* (pepper strips) for extra flavor

taco—a corn tortilla folded or rolled around anything and eaten with the hands; *tacos de pescado,* or "fish tacos," are the closest thing Baja has to a regional specialty

tamal—cornmeal (*masa*) dough wrapped in a corn husk and steamed; sometimes stuffed with corn, olives, pork, or turkey

torta—a sandwich made with a Mexican-style roll (*bolillo/birote* or the larger *pan telera*); one of the most popular is the *torta de milanesa,* made with breaded, deep-fried veal or pork

Breakfasts

Menus at tourist restaurants are often confusing because some of the same "breakfast" dishes may end up on more than one section of the menu. Mexicans have two kinds of breakfasts, an early one called *desayuno*, eaten shortly after rising, and a second called *almuerzo* that's usually taken around 1100. To further confuse the issue, Spanish-English dictionaries usually translate almuerzo as "lunch," while bilingual menus often read "breakfast."

The most common Baja desayuno is simply *pan dulce* (sweet pastry) and/or *bolillos* (torpedo-shaped, European-style rolls) with coffee and/or milk. Cereal is also sometimes eaten for desayuno; e.g., *avena* (oatmeal), *crema de trigo* (cream of wheat), or *hojuelas de maíz* (corn flakes).

The heavier eggs-and-frijoles dishes known widely as "Mexican breakfasts" in the U.S. and Canada are usually taken as almuerzo, the late breakfast, which is most typically reserved for weekends and holidays. Eggs come in a variety of ways, including *huevos revueltos* (scrambled eggs), *huevos duros* (hard-boiled eggs), *huevos escafaldos* (soft-boiled eggs), *huevos estrellados* (eggs fried sunny side up), *huevos a la mexicana* (also *huevos mexicanos,* eggs scrambled with chopped tomato, onion, and chiles), *huevos rancheros* (fried eggs served on a tortilla), and *huevos con chorizo* (eggs scrambled with ground sausage), *con tocino* (with bacon), or *con jamón* (with ham). All egg dishes usually come with frijoles and tortillas.

One of the cheapest and tastiest almuerzos is *chilaquiles,* tortilla chips in a chile gravy with crumbled cheese on top. Eggs and/or chicken can be added to chilaquiles as options.

Entrees

The main dish or *el plato fuerte* of any meal can be a grander version of an antojito, a regional specialty from another part of Mexico (*mole poblano,* for example), or something the *cocineros* (cooks) dream up themselves. Typical entrees are centered around meats, seafood, or poultry.

Meat and Poultry: Common meats include *carne de res* (beef), *puerco* (pork), and *cabrito* (kid goat). *Jamón* (ham), *chorizo* (sausage), and *tocino* (bacon) are usually reserved for almuerzo. Steak may appear on menus as *bistec,* *bistek, biftec,* or steak. *Venado* (deer meat or venison) and *conejo* (rabbit) are commonly served on ranchos. Poultry dishes include *pollo* (chicken), *pavo* (turkey), and, less frequently, *pato* (duck) and *codorniz* (quail).

Seafood: Mariscos entrees on the menu are often seasonal or dependent on the "catch of the day." Often just the word *pescado,* along with the method of cooking (e.g., *pescado al mojo de ajo*), will appear. If you need to know exactly what kind of fish, just ask *"¿Hay cuál tipo de pescado?,"* although in some cases the only response you'll get is something generic like *pescado blanco* ("white fish"). For specific fish names, see "Fish Translator."

Baja's number-one seafood specialty is the *taco de pescado* (fish taco). If you haven't ever tried one, you're most likely wondering "What's the big deal—a fish taco?" Eat one, though, and you're hooked for life. Short, tender, fresh fish filets are battered and fried quickly, then folded

---

COOKING METHODS

Entree items, whether meat, poultry, or seafood, are most commonly prepared in one of the following styles:

adobo, adobada—marinated or stewed in a sauce of vinegar, chiles, and spices

a la birria—roasted on a spit (usually goat)

a la parilla—broiled

albóndigas—meatballs

al carbón—charcoal-grilled

a la veracruzana—seafood (often huachinanga, red snapper) cooked with tomatoes, onions, and olives

al mojo de ajo—in a garlic sauce

al pastor—slowly roasted on a vertical spit

al vapor—steamed

asada—grilled

barbacoa—pit-roasted

con arroz—steamed with rice

encebollado—cooked with onions

entomado—cooked with tomatoes

empanizada—breaded

frito—fried

guisado—in a spicy stew

machaca—dried and shredded

into a steaming corn tortilla with a variety of condiments including *salsa fresca* (chopped tomatoes, onions, chiles, and lime juice), marinated cabbage (similar to coleslaw in the States), *guacamole* (a savory avocado paste), and sometimes a squirt of mayonnaise. *¡La última!* Any kind of white-fleshed fish can be used—the best fish tacos are those made from yellowtail (*jurel*) or halibut (*lenguado*).

Shellfish are also quite popular on Baja menus: *ostiones* (oysters), *almejas* (clams), *callos* (scallops), *jaiba* (small crab), *cangrejo* (large crab), *camarones* (shrimp), *langosta* (lobster), *langostina* (crayfish, also called *cucarachas*), and *abulón* (abalone). They can be ordered as *cocteles* (cocktails—steamed or boiled and served with lime and salsa), *en sus conchas* (in the shell), or in many other ways.

Carnitas: This dish belongs in a category all its own and is usually sold only at butcher shops or at restaurants specializing in it. The usual method for producing carnitas is to slowly braise an entire pig in a huge cauldron, along with a variety of flavorings which are a closely guarded secret among carnitas purveyors. The results are chopped into thin slices and eaten with stacks of tortillas, pickled vegetables and chiles, guacamole, and various salsas.

Carnitas are almost always sold by weight. You can order by the *kilo* (one kilogram, about 2.2 pounds), *medio* (half kilo), *cuarto* (one-fourth kilo), or sometimes in 100-gram increments (*cien gramos*). Figure on a quarter kilo (about a half pound) per hungry person and you won't have much left over.

Other Dishes

Beans: The beans most preferred in Baja, as on the northern mainland, are pinto beans, usually dried beans (*frijól*) boiled until soft, then mashed and fried with lard or vegetable oil (usually the former) to make *frijoles*. Often this preparation is called *frijoles refritos,* or "refried beans," although they're not really refried except when reheated. Sometimes the beans are served whole, in their own broth, as *frijoles de olla* (boiled beans) or with bits of roast pork as *frijoles a la charra* (ranch-style beans). Frijoles can be served with any meal of the day, including breakfast.

Cheese: Even the lowliest rancho will usually have some cheese around, so if your appetite isn't stimulated by the *iguana guisada* simmering on the hearth, you can usually ask for *chiles rellenos* (mild poblano chiles stuffed with cheese and fried in an egg batter) or *quesadillas* (cheese melted in folded flour tortillas). A meal of beans, tortillas, and cheese provides a complete source of protein for travelers who choose to avoid meat, poultry, or seafood for health, economic, or moral reasons.

Many ranchos produce their own *queso fresco,* "fresh cheese" made from raw cow's, goat's, or sheep's milk. To make queso fresco, the rancheros first cure the milk with homemade rennet (from a calf's fourth stomach) until the milk separates, then press the curds with weights (sometimes under flat rocks lined with cloth) to remove excess moisture. In more elaborate operations, the initial pressing is then ground up and repressed into small round cakes. If you want to buy some queso fresco, look for *Hay queso* signs as you pass ranchos. If you're very fortunate, you might even come across *queso de apoyo,* an extra-rich cheese made from heavy cream.

Soup: The general menu term for soup is *sopa,* although a thick soup with lots of ingredients is usually a *caldo.*

Vegetables: Although vegetables are sometimes served as side dishes with *comidas corridas,* with restaurant entrees, or in salads (*ensaladas*), they're seldom listed separately on the menu. When they do appear on menus, it's usually at restaurants in towns near farming areas in northern Baja or else in the La Paz-Los Cabos area, where many vegetables come over by boat from the mainland. The best place to add vegetables to your diet is at a market or grocery store.

Salsas And Condiments

Any restaurant, café, lonchería, taquería, or comedor will offer a variety of salsas. Sometimes only certain salsas are served with certain dishes, while at other times one, two, or even three salsas are stationed on every table. Often each place has its own unique salsa recipes—canned or bottled salsas are rarely used.

There are as many types of salsas as there are Mexican dishes—red, green, yellow, brown, hot, mild, salty, sweet, thick, thin, blended, and chunky. It would take a separate book to describe them all. The most typical is the *salsa casera* (house salsa), a simple, fresh concoction of chopped chiles, onions, and tomatoes mixed with salt, lime juice, and cilantro. This is what you usually get with the complimentary basket of *totopos* (tortilla chips) served at the beginning of every Mexican meal. Another common offering is *salsa verde* (green sauce), made with a base of *tomatillos,* a small, tart, green tomato-like vegetable. Some salsas are quite *picante,* or spicy hot (also *picosa*), so it's always a good idea to test a bit before pouring the stuff over everything on your plate.

Whole pickled chiles are sometimes served on the side as a condiment, especially with tacos and carnitas. Salt (*sal*) is usually on the table, although it's rarely needed since Mexican dishes tend to be prepared with plenty of salt. Black pepper is *pimiento negro,* and if it's not on the table it's normally available for the asking. Butter is *mantequilla,* sometimes served with flour tortillas.

In taquerías, *guacamole* (mashed avocado blended with onions, chiles, salt, and sometimes other ingredients), is always served as a condiment. In restaurants it may be served as a salad or with tortilla chips.

BOB RACE

Desserts And Sweets

The most popular of Mexican desserts, or *postres,* is a delicious egg custard called *flan.* It's listed on virtually every tourist restaurant menu, along with *helado* (ice cream). Other sweet alternatives include pastries found in *panaderías* (bakeries) and the frosty offerings at the ubiquitous *paleterías.* Strictly speaking, a paletería serves only *paletas,* flavored ice on sticks (like American popsicles but with a much wider range of flavors), but many also serve *nieve,* literally "snow," flavored ice served in bowls or cones like ice cream.

Another common street vendor food is *churros,* a sweet fried pastry that is something like a donut stick sprinkled with powdered sugar. One of the best places to sample churros is at La Bufadora at Punta Banda, just south of Ensenada. Nowhere else in Baja are there so many churro vendors in one place.

the staff of life

Dulcerías are candy shops that sell a huge variety of sticky Mexican sweets, usually wrapped individually. Often brightly decorated, dulcerías are oriented toward children and sometimes carry inexpensive toys as well as sweets. The larger ones sell piñatas, colorful papier-mâché figures filled with candy and small gifts and hung at parties; on special occasions, children are allowed to break them with sticks, releasing all the goodies inside. Traditionally piñatas are crafted to resemble common animals, but these days you'll see all kinds of shapes, including "Teenage Mutant Tortugas de Ninja."

BUYING GROCERIES

The cheapest way to feed yourself while traveling in Baja is the same way you save money at home, by buying groceries at the store and preparing meals on your own. While it may not have any dining spots to speak of, even the smallest town in Baja will feature a little grocery store or corner market. A ripe avocado, a chunk of queso fresco, and a couple of bolillos can make a fine, easy-to-fix meal.

The humblest stores are the small family-owned *tienda de abarrotes,* usually recognizable by the single word *abarrotes*—"groceries"—printed somewhere on the outside (*tienda* means "store"). These will stock the basics—tortillas, dried beans, flour, herbs and spices, bottled water, a few vegetables, possibly bolillos and queso fresco—as well as limited household goods like soap and laundry detergent. Like the 7-11 back home, the food at the average tienda de abarrotes is not particularly inexpensive.

A better deal, when you can find one, is the government-sponsored CONASUPO (an acronym for Compañía Nacional de Subsistencias Populares). CONASUPOs carry many of the same items as tiendas de abarrotes, but at government-subsidized prices. Not every item is cheaper, however, so it pays to shop around. A large, supermarket-style CONASUPO is called CONASUPER. Even less expensive are markets

Paletería y Nevería

ICE CUMMINGS

operated by ISSSTE (Instituto de Seguridad y Servicios Sociales para Trabajadores del Estado).

Privately run supermarkets like Calimax and Giganta are found in larger towns throughout the peninsula and are usually called *supers* or *supermercados*. Like their North American counterparts, they're usually well stocked with a wide variety of meats, baked goods, vegetables, household goods, and beer and liquor. Supermarket prices are often cheaper than those in smaller grocery stores.

Several towns and cities in Baja feature *mercados municipales* (municipal markets), large warehouse-type structures where meat, fruit, and vegetable producers sell their goods directly to the public. Prices are often very good at these markets but it helps if you know how to bargain. Although they're usually centrally located, sometimes municipal markets are difficult to find simply because they look so inconspicuous; you may have to ask around.

Another common tienda is the *ultramarinos*, which is primarily a place to buy beer and liquor that also usually sells a few deli-style food items.

Panaderías: You can often purchase a few bakery items at all of the above-named stores, but the best place to buy them, naturally, is at their source—a *panadería* (literally, "breadery," i.e., bakery). Many of the panaderías in Baja still use wood-fired *hornos* (ovens), which make the *bolillos* (Mexican rolls), *pastels* (cakes), and *pan dulce* (cookies and sweet pastries) especially tasty. *Pan de barra,* American-style sliced bread, is also occasionally available but never measures up to crusty bolillos. To select bakery items from the shelves of a panadería, simply imitate the other customers—pick up a pair of tongs and a tray from the counter near the cash register and help yourself, cafeteria-style.

Tortillerías: Unless you make them yourself, the best place to buy tortillas is where they make them fresh every day. Restaurants, tiendas, and home cooks will purchase from the local tortillería to avoid spending hours at a *metate* (grinder) and *comal* (griddle). The automated process at a tortillería uses giant electric grinders and conveyor belts to transform whole corn into fresh tortillas, which you purchase by weight, not number. A kilo yields about 40 average, 12-cm tortillas; you can order by the *cuarto* or *medio* (quarter or half kilo). The government-subsidized prices are quite low.

DRINKING

Nonalcoholic Beverages

Cold Drinks: The water and ice served in restaurants in Baja is always purified—it's not necessary to order *agua mineral* (mineral water) unless you need the minerals. Likewise, the water used as an ingredient in "handmade" drinks, e.g., *licuados* or *aguas frescas,* also comes from purified sources.

Licuados are similar to American "smoothies"—fruit blended with water, ice, honey or sugar, and sometimes milk or raw eggs, to produce something like a fruit shake. In Baja, *tuna* (not the fish but the prickly pear cactus fruit) licuados are particularly delicious. Any place that makes licuados will also make orange juice, *jugo de naranja*. Orange juice is very popular in Baja and you'll often see street vendors who sell nothing but fresh-squeezed OJ.

Aguas frescas are the colorful beverages sold from huge glass jars on the streets of larger cities, or at carnivals, usually during warm weather. They're made by boiling the pulp of various fruits, grains, or seeds with water, then straining it and adding large chunks of ice. *Arroz* (rice) and *horchata* (melon-seed) are two of the tastiest aguas.

American soft drinks (*refrescos*) like 7UP, Coke, and Pepsi are common; their Mexican equivalents are just as good. An apple-flavored soft drink called Manzanita is quite popular.

Hot Drinks: Coffee is served in a variety of ways. The best—when you can find it; ranchos sometimes serve it—is traditional Mexican-style coffee, which is made by filtering near-boiling water through fine-ground coffee in a slender cloth sack. Instant coffee (*nescafé*) is often served at small restaurants and cafés; a jar of instant coffee may be sitting on the table for you to add to hot water. When there's a choice, a request for *café de olla* (pot coffee) should bring you real brewed coffee. When you order coffee in a Mexican restaurant, some servers will ask *de grano o de agua?* (literally "grain or water?"), meaning "brewed or instant?" One of the better Mexican brands found in supermarkets is Café Combate.

Café con leche is the Mexican version of café au lait, i.e., coffee and hot milk mixed in near-equal proportions. *Café con crema* (coffee with cream) is not as available; when it is, it usually means a cup of coffee with a packet of nondairy creamer on the side.

Hot chocolate (*chocolate*) is fairly common on Baja menus. It's usually served very sweet and may contain cinnamon, ground almonds, and other flavorings. A thicker version made with cornmeal—almost a chocolate pudding—is called *champurrado*.

Black tea (*té negro*) is not popular among Bajacalifornios although you may see it on tourist menus. Ask for *té helado* or *té frío* if you want iced tea. At home many Mexicans drink *té de manzanilla* (chamomile tea) or *té de yerba buena* (mint tea) in the evenings.

Alcoholic Beverages

Drinking laws in Mexico are quite minimal. The legal drinking age in Mexico is 18 years, and it's illegal to carry open containers of alcoholic beverages in a vehicle. Booze of every kind is widely available in bars, restaurants, grocery stores, and *licorerías* (liquor stores). *Borracho* means both "drunk" (as an adjective) and "drunkard."

Cerveza: The most popular and available beer brand in northern Baja is Tecate, brewed in Tecate, while in the south it's Pacífico, from Mazatlán, just across the Sea of Cortez from Cabo San Lucas. Both are good-tasting, light- to medium-weight brews, with Tecate holding a slight edge (more hops) over Pacífico. You can't compare either of these with their export equivalents in the U.S., since Mexican breweries produce a separate brew for American consumption that's lighter in taste and lighter on the alcohol content. It's always better in Mexico.

Other major Mexican brands such as Corona, Dos Equis (ordered by Mexicans as "Lager"), Superior, Carta Blanca, Bohemia, and Negro Modelo are available in tourist restaurants, but you'll notice the locals stick pretty much to Tecate and Pacífico, perhaps out of regional loyalty.

The cheapest sources for beer are the brewery's agents or distributors. Look for signs saying *agencia, subagencia, cervezería,* or *deposito.* There you can return deposit bottles for cash or credit. You can buy beer by the bottle (*envase*), can (*bote*), six-pack (*canastilla*), or case (*cartón*). Large, liter-size bottles are called *ballenas* ("whales") and are quite popular. When buying beer at an agencia or deposito, specify *fría* if you want cold beer, otherwise you'll get beer *al tiempo* (at room temperature).

Wine: Baja is one of Mexico's major wine-production areas and Baja wines are commonly served in restaurants. Two of the more reliable labels are Domecq and Santo Tomás, both produced in northern Baja. A broad selection of varietals is available, including Cabernet Sauvignon, Chardonnay, Chenin Blanc, Pinot Noir, Barbera, and Zinfandel. These and other grapes are also blended to produce cheaper *vino tinto* (red wine) and *vino blanco* (white wine). When ordering wine in Spanish at a bar, you may want to specify *vino de uva* ("grape wine"), as *vino* alone can refer to distilled liquors as well as wine. *Vino blanco,* in fact, can be interpreted as cheap tequila.

TEQUILA

Mexico's national drink has been in production since at least the time of the Aztecs; the Spaniards levied a tax on tequila as early as 1608. The liquor's name was taken from the Ticuila Indians of Jalisco, who mastered the process of distilling an extract from the *Agave tequiliana,* or **blue agave,** a process still employed by tequila distilleries today. Native to Jalisco, this succulent is the only agave that produces true tequila as certified by the Mexican government. Look for the initials DGN—for *Dirección General de Normas*—on the label.

Much of the tequila-making process is still carried out *a mano* (by hand). In the traditional method, the mature heart of the tequila agave, which looks like a huge pineapple and weighs 20-60 kilograms, is roasted in a pit for 24 hours, then shredded and ground by mule- or horse-powered mills. After the juice is extracted from the pulp and fermented in ceramic pots, it's distilled in copper stills to produce the basic tequila, which is always clear and colorless with an alcohol content of around 40%.

"Gold" tequilas are produced by aging in imported oak barrels. After six months the liquor can be bottled as *reposado* or "rested" tequila; after three years it's truly *añejo* or "aged."

JOE CUMMINGS

José Cuervo, Sauza, and Herradura are well-established tequila labels with international reputations. Of the three, Herradura is said to employ the most traditional methods, and tequila connoisseurs generally prefer it over the other two. But don't take their word for it, try a few *probaditos* (little proofs) for yourself. One of the best places to experiment is Cabo San Lucas' Caballo Blanco Restaurant, where the bar stocks over 35 varieties of tequila. Don't try tasting them all in one night or you'll probably never drink tequila again.

Mezcal And The Worm
The distillate of other agave plants—also known as *magueys* or century plants—is called *mezcal.* The same roasting and distilling process is used for mezcal as for tequila. Actually, tequila, too, is a mezcal, but no drinker calls it that, just as no one in a U.S. bar orders "whiskey" when they mean to specify scotch or bourbon.

The caterpillar-like grub floating at the bottom of a bottle of mezcal is the *gusano de maguey* (maguey worm), which lives on the maguey plant itself. They're safe to eat—just about anything pickled in mezcal would be—but not particularly appetizing. By the time you hit the bottom of the bottle, though, who cares?

Tequila Drinks
The usual way to drink tequila is straight up, followed by a water or beer chaser. Licking a few grains of salt before taking a shot and sucking a lime wedge afterward makes it go down smoother. The salt raises a protective coating of saliva on the tongue while the lime juice scours the tongue of salt and tequila residues.

Tequila con sangrita, in which a shot of tequila is chased with a shot of *sangrita*, is a slightly more elegant method of consumption. Sangrita is a bright red mix of orange juice, lime juice, grenadine, red chile powder, and salt.

An old tequila standby is the much-abused margarita, a tart Tex-Mex cocktail made with tequila, lime juice, and Cointreau (usually "Controy" or triple-sec in Mexico) served in a salt-rimmed glass. A true margarita is shaken and served on the rocks (crushed or blended ice tends to kill the flavor), but just about every gringo in Baja seems to drink "frozen" margaritas, in which the ice is mixed in a blender with the other ingredients. A "Baja margarita" substitutes Baja's own damiana liqueur for the triple-sec. The damiana herb is said to be an aphrodisiac.

BAR LINGO

cantinero—bartender

cerveza—beer

una fría—a cold one

envase, botella—bottle

casco—empty bottle

una copita, uno tragito—a drink

vaso, copa—glass

la cruda—hangover

sin hielo—without ice

con hielo—with ice

botanas—snacks

Liquor: Tequila is Mexico's national drink and also the most popular distilled liquor in Baja. The second most popular is brandy, followed closely by *ron* (rum), both produced in Mexico for export as well as domestic consumption. A favorite rum drink in Baja is the cuba libre (Free Cuba), called cuba for short—a mix of rum, Coke, and lime juice over ice. Similar is the cuba de uva, which substitutes brandy for rum. Other hard liquors—gin, vodka, scotch—may be available only at hotel bars and tourist restaurants.

Cantinas and Bars: Traditionally speaking, a true cantina is a Mexican-style drinking venue for males only, but in modern Mexico the distinction between "bar" and "cantina" is becoming increasingly blurred. Is Hussong's Cantina in En-senada a true cantina? Plenty of women are present each evening holding their own with the best of the machos, yet among locals it still has the reputation of a place where "nice" Mexican girls don't go.

A more typical Baja cantina is the kind of place you'll occasionally stumble upon in a small town, usually on the outskirts, where blinking Christmas lights festoon a palapa roof and palm-thatch or ocotillo walls. Inside are a few tables and chairs and a handful of borrachos; if any women are present, they're either serving the booze or serving as hired "dates." The only drink choices will be beer, Mexican brandy, and cheap tequila or *aguardiente*—moonshine. Often when you order tequila in a place like this, you'll be served a large glass of aguardiente, considered an acceptable substitute.

Bars, on the other hand, are only found in hotels and in the larger cities or resort areas, i.e., Tijuana, Mexicali, Ensenada, San Felipe, La Paz, and Cabo San Lucas. They've developed largely as social venues for tourists or for a younger generation of Mexicans for whom the cantina is passé. A bar, in contrast to a cantina, will offer a variety of beer, wine, and distilled liquor. By Mexican standards, bars are considered very up-market places to hang out, so they aren't extremely popular—many young Mexicans would rather drink at a disco where they can dance, too.

Incidentally, a sign outside a bar reading Ladies Bar almost always means the bar provides ladies for male entertainment, not that it admits women, although it may.

HEALTH

By and large, Baja California is a healthy place. Sanitation standards are relatively high compared to many other parts of Mexico and the tap water quality in many areas is superior to many places in Alta California. The visitor's main health concerns are not food or water sources but avoiding mishaps while driving, boating, diving, surfing, or otherwise enjoying Baja's great outdoor life. Health issues directly concerned with these activities are covered under the relevant sections in this book.

FOOD AND WATER

Visitors who use common sense will probably never come down with food- or water-related illnesses while traveling in Baja. The first rule is not to overdo it during the first few days of your trip—eat and drink in moderation. Shoveling down huge amounts of tasty, often heavy Mexican foods along with pitchers of margaritas or strong Mexican beer is liable to make anyone sick from pure overindulgence. If you're not used to the spices and different ways of cooking, it's best to ingest small amounts at first.

Second, take it easy with foods offered by street vendors, since this is where you're most likely to suffer from unsanitary conditions. Eat only foods that have been thoroughly cooked and are served either stove-hot or refrigerator-cold. Many gringos eat street food without any problems whatsoever, but it pays to be cautious, especially if it's your first time in Mexico. Concerned with the risk of cholera, the Baja California Sur state government banned the sale of ice cream or *ceviche* by street vendors in July 1992; of course enforcing the ban is another matter.

Doctors usually recommend you avoid eating peeled, raw fruit and vegetables in Baja. Once the peel is removed, it is virtually impossible to disinfect produce. Unpeeled fruits and vegetables washed in purified water and dried with a clean cloth are usually okay. After all, plenty of Mexican fruit is consumed daily in Canada and the U.S.

Hotels and restaurants serve only purified drinking water and ice, so there's no need to ask for mineral water or refuse ice. Tap water, however, should not be consumed except in hotels where the water system is purified—if so, you'll be informed by a notice over the washbasin in your room. Most grocery stores sell bottled purified water. Water purification tablets, iodine crystals, water filters, and the like aren't necessary for Baja travel unless you plan on extensive backpacking (see "Sports and Recreation").

Turista
People who've never traveled to a foreign country may undergo a period of adjustment to the new gastrointestinal flora that comes with new territory. There's really no way to avoid the differences wrought by sheer distance. Unfortunately, the adjustment is sometimes unpleasant.

Mexican doctors call gastrointestinal upset of this sort *turista* since it affects tourists but not the local population. The usual symptoms of turista—also known by the gringo tags "Montezuma's Revenge" and "the Aztec Two-Step"—are nausea and diarrhea, sometimes with stomach cramps and a low fever. Again, eating and drinking in moderation will help prevent the worst of the symptoms, whch rarely persist more than a day or two. And if it's any consolation, Mexicans often get sick the first time they go to U.S. or Canada.

Prevention and Treatment: Many Mexico travelers swear by a preventive regimen of Pepto-Bismol begun the day before arrival in country. Opinions vary as to how much of the pink stuff is necessary to ward off or tame the evil flora, but a person probably shoudn't exceed the recommended daily dose. Taper off over the second week until you stop using it altogether.

Another regimen that seems to be effective is a daily tablet of 100-milligram doxycycline (sold as Vibramycin in the U.S.), a low-grade antibiotic that requires a prescription in most countries. It works by killing all the bacteria in your intestinal tract—including the ones that reside there naturally and help protect your bowels. It's available without a prescription in Mexican *farma-*

cias, but you should check with your doctor first to make sure you're not sensitive to it—some people have problems with sunlight while taking doxycycline. Consume with plenty of water and/or a meal. Some physicians believe when you stop taking the drug you're particularly susceptible to intestinal upset because there's no protective bacteria left to fight off infections.

Neither Pepto nor Vibramycin is recommended for travelers planning trips of three weeks or longer.

If you come down with a case of turista, the best thing to do is drink plenty of fluids. Adults should drink at least three liters a day, a child under 37 kilos (80 pounds) at least a liter a day. Lay off tea, coffee, milk, fruit juices, and booze. Eat only bland foods, nothing spicy, fatty, or fried, and take it easy. Pepto-Bismol or similar pectin-based remedies usually help. Some people like to mask the symptoms with a strong over-the-counter medication like Immodium AD (loperamide is the active ingredient), but though this can be very effective, it isn't a cure. Only time will cure traveler's diarrhea.

If the symptoms are unusually severe (especially if there's blood in the stools) or persist more than one or two days, see a doctor. Most hotels can arrange a doctor's visit or you can contact a Mexican tourist office or U.S. Consulate for recommendations.

SUNBURN AND DEHYDRATION

Sunburn probably afflicts more Baja visitors than all other illnesses and injuries combined. The sunlight in Baja can be quite strong, especially in the center of the peninsula and along the Sea of Cortez coast. For outdoor forays, sun protection is a must, whatever the activity. The longer you're in the sun, the more protection you'll need.

A hat, sunglasses, and plenty of sunscreen or sunblock make a good start. Bring along a sunscreen with a sun protection factor (SPF) of at least 25, even if you don't plan on using it all the time. Apply it to *all* exposed parts of your body—don't forget the hands, top of the feet, and neck. Men should remember to cover thinned-out or bald areas on the scalp. Sunscreen must be reapplied after swimming or after periods of heavy perspiration.

If you're going boating, don't leave shore with just a bathing suit. Bring along an opaque shirt, preferably with long sleeves, along with a pair of long pants. Since you can never know for certain whether your boat might get stranded or lost at sea for a period of time (if, for example, the motor conks out and you get caught in an offshore current), you shouldn't be without extra clothing for emergencies.

It's also important to drink plenty of water and/or nonalcoholic, non-caffeinated fluids to avoid dehydration. Alcohol and caffeine—including the caffeine in iced tea and Coke—will increase your potential for dehydration. Symptoms of dehydration include darker-than-usual urine or inability to urinate, flushed face, profuse sweating or an unusual lack thereof, and sometimes headache, dizziness, and general feeling of malaise. Extreme cases of dehydration can lead to heat exhaustion or even heatstroke, in which the victim may become delirious and/or convulse. If either condition is suspected, get the victim out of the sun immediately, cover with a wet sheet or towel, and administer a rehydration fluid that replaces lost water and salts. If you can get the victim to a doctor, all the better—heatstroke can be very serious.

Rehydration Formula: If Gatorade or a similar rehydration fluid isn't available you can mix your own by combining the following ingredients: 1 liter (4 cups or 1 quart) purified water or diluted fruit juice; 2 tablespoons sugar or honey; one quarter teaspoon salt; and one quarter teaspoon bicarbonate of soda. If soda isn't available, use another quarter teaspoon salt. The victim should drink this mixture at regular intervals until symptoms subside substantially. Four or more liters may be necessary in moderate cases, more in severe cases.

MOTION SICKNESS

Visitors with little or no boating experience who join fishing cruises in Baja, especially on the Pacific side, sometimes experience motion sickness caused by the movement of a boat over ocean swells. The repeated pitching and rolling affects a person's sense of equilibrium to the point of nausea. This is known as "seasickness" (*mareado*), and can be a very unpleasant experience not only for those green at the gills but

SNAKEBITE PREVENTION AND TREATMENT

The overall risk of being bitten by a poisonous snake while hiking in Baja California is quite low, mainly because the rattlesnake avoids contact with all large mammals, including humans. Most of the unfortunate few who are bitten by snakes in Baja are local ranchers who spend a great deal of time in snake habitats or small children who may not know to retreat from a coiled rattler.

Nonetheless, anyone spending time in the Baja outback, including campers and hikers, should follow a few simple precautions.

Prevention

First of all, use caution when placing hands or feet in areas where snakes may lie. These include rocky ledges, holes, and fallen logs. Always look first, and if you must move a rock or log, use a long stick or other instrument. Wear sturdy footwear when walking in possible snake habitats. High-top leather shoes or boots are best. *Rancheros* wear thick leather leggings when working in known snake territory; these are sometimes available for purchase at *zapaterías* (shoe stores) or leather and saddle shops.

Most snakes strike only when they feel threatened. Naturally, if you step on or next to a snake, it's likely to strike. If you see or hear a rattlesnake, remain still until the snake moves away. If it doesn't leave, simply back away slowly and cautiously. Sudden move-

ments may cause a snake to strike; rattlers rarely strike a stationary target. A rattler can't strike a target that is farther away than three-fourths of its body length; use this rough measure to judge when it may be safe to move away. Leave plenty of room for error.

Don't attempt to kill a rattler unless you have a genuine need to use it as food. As nasty as they may seem, snakes are as important to the desert ecosystem as the most beautiful flowering cactus.

Treatment

When bitten by a poisonous snake, it's important to remain calm in order to slow the spread of venom, and follow the necessary steps for treatment in a cool-headed manner.

LOUISE FOOTE

---

for fellow passengers anxious lest the victim spew on them.

The best way to prevent motion sickness is to take one of the preventives commonly available from a pharmacist: promethazine (sold as Phenergan in the U.S.), dimenhydrinate (Dramamine), or scopolamine (Transderm Scop). The latter is available as an adhesive patch worn behind the ear—the time-release action is allegedly more effective than tablets. These medications should be consumed *before* boarding the vessel, not after the onset of symptoms. It's also not a good idea to eat a large meal before getting on a boat.

If you start to feel seasick while out on the bounding main, certain actions can lessen the likelihood that it will get worse. First, do not lie down. Often the first symptom of motion sickness is drowsiness, and if you give in to the impulse you'll almost certainly guarantee a wors-

ening of the condition. Second, stay in the open air rather than below decks—fresh air usually helps. Finally, fix your gaze on the horizon; this will help steady your disturbed inner ear, the proximate cause of motion sickness.

BITES AND STINGS

Mosquitoes And *Jejenes*

Mosquitoes breed in standing water. Since standing water isn't that common in arid Baja, neither are mosquitoes. Exceptions include palm oases, estuaries, and marshes when there isn't a strong breeze around to keep them at bay. The easiest way to avoid mosquito bites is to apply insect repellent to exposed areas of the skin and clothing whenever the mossies are out and biting. For most species, this means between dusk and dawn.

First, immediately following the bite, try to identify the snake. At the very least, memorize the markings and physical characteristics so a physician can administer the most appropriate antivenin. If you can kill the snake and bring it to the nearest treatment center, do it. Just remember this could expose you or your fellow hikers to the risk of bite.

Second, examine the bite for teeth marks. A successful bite by a poisonous pit viper will leave one or two large fang punctures in addition to smaller teeth marks; a bite by a nonpoisonous snake will not feature fang punctures. In general, nonpoisonous bites cause relatively small, shallow marks or scratches.

If you suspect the bite is poisonous, immobilize the affected limb and wrap it tightly in an elastic bandage. This will slow the spread of venom through the lymph system and mitigate swelling. Be careful that the bandage isn't wrapped so tightly that it cuts off circulation—you should be able to insert a finger under it without difficulty. Keep the limb below the level of the heart. Avoid all physical activity, since increased circulation accelerates the absorption of the venom. For this same reason, avoid aspirin, sedatives, and alcohol. Do not apply cold therapy—ice packs, cold compresses, and so on—to the bite area or to any other part of the victim's body. The old "slice and suck" method of snakebite treatment has likewise been discredited.

Get the victim to a hospital or physician if possible. Where feasible, carry the victim to restrict physical exertion. Even when wrapping the limb appears successful in preventing symptoms, the bite will need medical attention and a physician may decide antivenin treatment is necessary.

It's possible for a poisonous snake to bite without injecting any venom; up to 20% of all reported bites are "dry bites."

Snakebite victims who require antivenin treatment usually receive the broad-spectrum North American Antisnakebite Serum for pit viper poisoning—where it's available, which is nowhere in Baja outside Tijuana, Mexicali, La Paz, or Cabo San Lucas. Your home physician may be able to provide a prescription for the serum in advance of your trip if convinced you'll visit areas where antivenin is unavailable or medical treatment inaccessible.

In cases where it's been determined a bite is venomous and serum isn't available, the best you can do is follow the treatment outlined above and keep the victim immobile and cool until the symptoms—pain in the affected limb, abdominal cramps, headache—have subsided. For some bites, wrapping the limb in an elastic bandage will avoid all or most of the worst symptoms. The victim should drink plenty of water. Don't panic—remember that few rattlesnake bites are fatal, even when untreated.

The most effective repellents are those containing a high concentration of DEET (N,N-diethyl-metatoluamide). People with an aversion to applying synthetics to the skin can try citronella (lemongrass oil), which is also effective but requires more frequent application.

More common in Baja than mosquitoes are *jejenes*, tiny flying insects known as "no-see-ums" among North Americans—you almost never see them while they're biting. The same repellents effective for mosquitoes will usually do the trick with jejenes.

For relief from the itchiness of mosquito bites, try rubbing a bit of hand soap on the affected areas. Jejene bites will usually stop itching in less than 10 minutes if you refrain from scratching them. Excessive scratching of either type of bite can lead to infection, so be mindful of what your fingers are up to.

In spite of the presence of the occasional mosquito, the U.S. Centers for Disease Control has declared all of Baja California malaria-free.

Wasps, Bees, And Hornets

Although stings from these flying insects can be very painful, they aren't of mortal danger to most people.

If you're allergic to such stings and plan to travel in remote areas of Baja, consider obtaining anti-allergy medication from your doctor before leaving home. At the very least, carry a supply of Benadryl or similar over-the-counter antihistamine. Dramamine (dimenhydrinate) also usually helps mitigate allergic reactions.

For relief from a wasp/bee/hornet sting you can apply a paste of baking soda and water to the affected area.

Liquids containing ammonia, including urine, also help relieve pain. If a stinger is visible, remove—by scraping if possible, or with tweezers—before applying any remedies. If a stung limb becomes unusually swollen or if the victim exhibits symptoms of a severe allergic reaction—difficulty in breathing, agitation, hives—seek medical assistance.

Ticks

If you find a tick embedded in your skin, don't try to pull it out—this may leave the head and pincers under your skin and lead to infection. Covering the tick with petroleum jelly, mineral oil, gasoline, kerosene, or alcohol will usually cause the tick to release its hold in order to avoid suffocation.

Burning the tick with a cigarette butt or hot match usually succeeds only in killing it—when you pull it out, the head and pincers may not come with it. Stick with the suffocation method and if the beast still doesn't come out, use tweezers.

Scorpions

The venom of scorpions (*alacránes*) varies in strength from individual to individual and species to species, but the sting is rarely dangerous to adults. It can be very painful, however, resulting in partial numbness and swelling that lasts several days. In Baja, the small yellow scorpions inflict more painful stings than the larger, dark-colored ones.

The best treatment begins with persuading the victim to lie down and relax to slow the spread of the venom. Keep the affected area below the level of the heart. Ice packs on the sting may relieve pain and mitigate swelling; aspirin also helps.

Children who weigh less than about 13 kilos (30 pounds) should receive medical attention when stung by a scorpion. Doctors in Baja usually have ready access to scorpion antivenin (*anti-alacrán*), but it should only be administered under qualified medical supervision.

Avoiding Scorpions: Scorpions prefer damp, dark, warm places—dead brush, rock piles, fallen logs—so exercise particular caution when placing yourhands in or near such areas. Hands are the scorpion's most common target on the human body; campers should wear gloves when handling firewood in Baja.

Other favorite spots for scorpions are crumpled clothing and bedding. In desert areas of Baja, always check your bedsheets or sleeping bag for scorpions before climbing in. In the same environments, shake out your shoes and clothing before putting them on.

POISONOUS SEA CREATURES

Various marine animals carry poisons in parts of their bodies that can inflict painful stings on humans. In Baja, such creatures include jellyfish, Portuguese men-of-war, cone shells, stingrays, sea urchins, and various fishes with poisonous spines.

The best way to avoid jellyfish and Portuguese men-of-war is to scope out the water before going in—if you see any nasties floating around, try another beach. You can avoid stingrays by shuffling your feet in the sand as you walk in shallow surf, which will usually cause rays resting in the sand to swim away.

To avoid cone shell and sea urchin stings, wear shoes in the water; several sport shoe manufacturers now produce specialized water shoes. You can also often spot cones and urchins in clear water, especially when wearing a diving mask.

Anglers should take care when handling landed fish to avoid poisonous spine wounds. If you don't know how to avoid the spines while handling a fish, let someone more experienced show you how.

The treatment for stings from all of the above is the same: remove all tentacles, barbs, or spines from the affected area; wash with rubbing alcohol or diluted ammonia (urine will do in a pinch) to remove as much venom as possible; and wrap the area in cloth to reduce the flow of oxygen to the wound until pain subsides. If an acute allergic reaction occurs, get the victim to a doctor or clinic as quickly as possible.

scorpion

BOB RACE

MEDICAL ASSISTANCE

The quality of basic medical treatment, including dentistry, is relatively high in Baja's cities and larger towns; ask at a tourist office or at your consulate for recommendations. Hospitals can be found in Tijuana, Mexicali, Ensenada, Guerrero Negro, Ciudad Constitución, and La Paz; there are public clinics or Red Cross (Cruz Roja) stations in nearly every other town. In Tijuana, Ensenada, Mexicali, Rosarito, Tecate, and San Luis Río Colorado, the Red Cross can be reached by dialing 132 (toll-free) from any pay phone.

The best medical care in Baja is available at Ensenada's **Hospital Las Americas** (tel. 6-03-01, Av. Arenas 151), which reportedly has the most modern medical equipment in all of Mexico.

Emergency Evacuation
San Diego's **Air-Evac International** provides emergency 24-hour airlift service (or, in the bor-

der areas, ground ambulance) from Baja to U.S. hospitals in the San Diego area. The emergency number is (619) 278-3822; for inquiries call (800) 254-2569 in the U.S., 95-800-10-09-96 in Mexico. Air-Evac accepts collect calls; payment can be made with a credit card or through your health insurance company. Providing the same service is **Critical Air Medicine** (tel. 619-571-0482, 800-247-8325 in Alta California, 800-633-8326 elsewhere in the U.S., 95-800-10-02-68 in Mexico).

Medical Air Services Association (tel. 817-430-4655, 800-643-9023, 9 Village Circle, Roanoke, TX 76262) offers a yearly membership plan that covers unlimited emergency air transport from anywhere in Mexico to anywhere in the U.S. or Canada. MASA membership rates are US$150 per year per family. The service is also available to Sanborn's Mexico Club members at a discount rate of US$90 annually (US$45 for individuals). For information on club membership, contact Sanborn's (see "Services and Information").

IMMIGRATION AND CUSTOMS

ENTRY REGULATIONS

U.S. And Canadian Citizens
A U.S. or Canadian citizen visiting Mexico solely for tourism, transit, or study purposes is not required to obtain a visa. In fact, for Baja visits of less than 72 hours, all that's needed is proof of citizenship—a birth certificate (or certified copy), voter's registration card, certificate of naturalization, or passport.

All U.S. or Canadian citizens crossing the Mexican border for more than 72 hours or going farther south than Ensenada must carry validated "tourist cards" (Form FMT), which aren't actually cards but slips of paper. These are available free of charge at any Mexican consulate or Mexican tourist office, from many travel agencies, on flights to Mexico, or at the border.

The tourist card is valid for stays of up to 180 days and must be used within 90 days of issuance. Your card becomes invalid once you exit the country—you're supposed to surrender it at the border—even if your 180 days hasn't expired. If you'll be entering and leaving Mexico

more than once during your trip, you should request a multiple-entry tourist card, available from Mexican consulates.

Validation: Once you cross the border, your tourist card must be validated by a Mexican immigration officer. You can arrange this at any *migración* office in Baja (all *municipio* seats have them), but it's accomplished most conveniently at the border crossing itself or at the immigration office in Ensenada (right around the corner from the tourist information booth on Blvd. Costero).

Minors: Before 1991, Mexican regulations required children under the age of 18 crossing the border without one or both parents to carry a notarized letter granting permission from the absent parent, or both parents if both were absent. This regulation is no longer in effect, but we've heard that some Mexican border officers, as well as airline check-in crews, are still asking for the letter, apparently unaware that the regulation has been rescinded. Hence unaccompanied minors or minors traveling with only one parent should be prepared for all situations with notarized letters. In cases of divorce, separation, or death, the minor should carry notarized papers documenting the situation.

In reality, minors with tourist cards are rarely asked for these documents. Children under 15 may be included on their parents' tourist card but this means neither the child nor the parents can legally exit Mexico without the other.

Citizens From Other Countries

Tourists from countries other than the U.S. or Canada may need visas in advance of arrival in Mexico. Citizens of Australia, New Zealand, and most western European countries can usually obtain free, no-photo visas at the border; be sure to check with a Mexican embassy or consulate first, as visa regulations change from year to year.

If you apply in person, the Mexican Consulate General in San Diego can usually issue tourist visas on the day of application.

Pets

Dogs and cats may be brought into Mexico if each is accompanied by a **vaccination certificate** that proves the animal has been vaccinated or treated for rabies, hepatitis, pip, and leptospirosis. You'll also need a **health certificate** issued no more than 72 hours before entry and signed by a registered veterinarian. Upon recrossing the border into the U.S., the U.S. Customs Service will ask to see the vaccination certificate.

Since 1992 the requirement that the health certificate be stamped with a visa at the border or at a Mexican consulate has been repealed. The certificate is still necessary; the visa isn't.

Inmigrante Rentista Visas

Special visas (FM-2 status) are issued to foreigners who choose to reside in Mexico on a "permanent income" basis. This most often applies to foreigners who retire in Mexico, though it's also used by artists, writers, and other self-employed foreign residents. With this visa you're allowed to import one motor vehicle as well as your household belongings into Mexico tax-free.

The basic requirements for this visa are that applicants forego any kind of employment while residing in Mexico and show proof in the form of bank statements of a regular source of foreign-earned income amounting to at least US$1,500 per month, plus US$500 for each dependent over the age of 15, e.g., US$2,000 for a couple. A pile of paperwork, including a "letter of good conduct" from the applicant's local police department, must accompany the initial application, along with an immigration tax payment (currently US$121) and various application fees totaling around US$75. The visa must be renewed annually but the renewal can be accomplished at any immigration office in Mexico—there's one in every municipio. After five years in Mexico, an immigrante rentista is eligible to apply for *inmigrado* status, which confers all the rights of citizenship, including employment in Mexico, save the right to vote.

Similar to the FM-2 but easier to obtain is the FM-3, or *No Inmigrante Visitante,* visa, which requires an income of US$1,000 a month plus US$500 for each dependent. The FM-3 is annually renewable for five years, at which point you must start the application process over again.

Many foreigners who have retired in Baja manage do so on the regular 180-day tourist visa; every six months they dash across the border and return with a new tourist card, issued at the border, on the same day. This method bypasses all the red tape and income requirements of the retirement visa.

Mexican Consulate In San Diego

San Diego's Mexican Consulate General (tel. 619-231-8414, 619-231-8427, 610 "A" St., San Diego, CA 92101) is relatively close to the Tijuana border crossing, about 30-45 minutes by car. These people can assist with visas, immigration problems, special import permits, and questions concerning Mexican customs regulations. The consulate's hours are Mon.-Fri., 0900-1400.

BORDER CROSSINGS

Baja California's U.S.-Mexico border has five official border crossings: Tijuana (open 24 hours a day), Otay Mesa (open 0600-2200), Tecate (0600-midnight), Mexicali (24 hours), and Algodones (0600-2000). Tijuana is the largest and also the most heavily used, connecting Baja with U.S. Interstate 5, which extends all the way up the U.S. west coast to the Canadian border. Border officials are considering longer hours for the nearby Otay Mesa crossing to ease congestion at Tijuana.

At any of the border crossings, you'll find the shortest waits (15-30 minutes at Tijuana) are between 1000 and 1530 or after 1900 or 2000 on weekdays. Weekends are the worst days in either direction, except late at night or before dawn, when traffic is light. If you're on your way out of Baja and find yourself near the border during rush hours, it might be best to find a restaurant and wait it out. A Saturday or Sunday morning wait at the Tijuana crossing can be as long as two hours in either direction; it's always longer going north.

If you're on foot, crossing is usually a breeze. Public and chartered buses also get through more quickly, utilizing special traffic lanes.

CUSTOMS

Entering Mexico
Officially, tourists are supposed to bring only those items into Mexico that will be of use during their trip. This means you can bring in practically anything as long as it doesn't appear in large enough quantities to qualify for resale. Firearms and ammunition, as well as boats, require special permits (see "Sports and Recreation").

Foreign-registered motor vehicles—cars, trucks, RVs, motorcycles, etc.—do not require permits for travel anywhere on the Baja California peninsula. However, if you plan to take a vehicle registered outside Mexico onto one of the vehicle ferries that sail from Baja to the mainland, or if you plan to drive farther east than San Luis Río Colorado in Sonora, you must obtain an auto permit. These are available from any Mexican consulate abroad, at the border, or from the ferry office in La Paz. (For further information on vehicle permits, see "Getting There.")

Into The U.S.
Visitors returning to the U.S. from Mexico may have their luggage inspected by U.S. Customs officials. The hassle can be minimized by giving brief, straight answers to their questions and cooperating with any requests to open your luggage, vehicle storage compartments, or anything else. Occasionally the officers use dogs to sniff vehicles for contraband or illegal aliens.

Customs Duties: Nearly 3,000 items—including all handicrafts—made in Mexico are exempt from any U.S. customs duties. Adults over 21 are allowed one quart of alcoholic beverages and 200 cigarettes (or 100 cigars) per person. All other purchases or gifts up to a total value of US$400 within any 31-day period can be brought into the U.S. duty-free.

Plant And Animal Prohibitions
The following fruits and vegetables cannot be brought into the U.S. from Mexico: oranges, grapefruits, mangoes, avocados (unless the pits are removed), and potatoes (including yams and sweet potatoes). All other fruits are permitted.

Other prohibited plant materials are straw (including packing materials and items stuffed with straw), hay, unprocessed cotton, sugarcane, and any plants in soil, including houseplants.

Animals and animal products that cannot be imported include wild and domesticated birds, pork or pork products, and eggs. Beef, mutton, venison, and other meats are permitted up to 50 pounds total per person.

Customs regulations can change at any time, so if you want to verify the regulations on a purchase before risking duties or confiscation at the border, check with a U.S. consulate in Baja before crossing. Now that NAFTA is a fact, expect sweeping changes in customs regulations—toward more leniency—in both directions.

LEGAL MATTERS

All foreign visitors in Mexico are subject to Mexican legal codes, which are based on Roman and Napoleonic law. The most distinctive features of the Mexican judiciary system, compared to Anglo-American systems, are that the system doesn't provide for trials by jury (the judge decides) nor writs of habeas corpus (though you must be charged within 72 hours of incarceration). Furthermore, bail is rarely granted to an arrested foreigner—for many offenses, not even Mexican nationals are allowed bail. Hence, once arrested and jailed for a serious offense, it can be very difficult to arrange release. The lesson here is: Don't get involved in matters that might result in your arrest. This primarily means anything having to do with drugs or guns.

The oft-repeated saw that in Mexico an arrested person is considered guilty until proven innocent is no more true south of the border than north. As in Canada or the U.S., an arrested person is considered a criminal *suspect* until the courts confirm or deny guilt. You have the right to notify your consulate if detained.

Mexican federal police (*federales*), mostly under pressure from the U.S., occasionally set up roadblocks to conduct searches for drugs. Such roadblocks are increasingly rare in Baja, however, due to complaints from tourists who drive regularly on the peninsula. If your vehicle is stopped by a roadblock, be as cooperative as possible. If there are any irregularities or if you object to the way in which the procedure is carried out, make note of the incident—including whatever badge numbers, names, or license numbers you can obtain discreetly—and later file a report with the Mexican Attorney General for Tourist Protection.

La Mordida

In the past, Mexican police had a reputation for hassling foreigners, especially those who drove their own vehicles in Mexico. Tales of the legendary *mordida* (literally, "bite"), or minor bribe, supposedly a necessary part of navigating one's way around Mexico, swelled way out of proportion to reality but were nonetheless based on real incidents.

For several years now, the Mexican police have for the most part ceased singling out foreigners for arrest, partly as a result of anticorruption efforts by the federal government but more importantly because of a conscious effort to attract more tourists. Most foreign visitors who drive in Baja these days complete their trips without any police hassles. (See "Getting Around" for tips on traffic laws and dealing with traffic police.)

In Case Of Arrest

If you get into trouble with Mexican law, for whatever reason, you should try to contact your nearest consulate in Baja. Embassies and consulates for each town are listed under the respective destination chapters. The state of Baja California Norte has established a special Attorney General for Tourist Protection (Procuraduria de Protección al Turista) with representatives in Tijuana (tel. 85-06-55), Rosarito (tel. 2-02-00), Ensenada (tel. 6-22-22, 6-37-18), Tecate (tel. 4-10-95), Mexicali (tel. 56-11-72, 52-97-95), San Felipe (tel. 7-11-55), San Quintín (tel. 5-

23-76), and San Vicente/Vicente Guerrero (tel. 6-22-16). You can also contact the local offices of the Secretary of Tourism—see the sections on each town for phone numbers and addresses. In Baja California Sur, the Secretary of Tourism office in La Paz may be able to help. These agencies routinely handle emergency legal matters involving visiting foreigners; you stand a much better chance of resolving legal difficulties with their assistance.

SAFETY

Statistics clearly show that violent crime is much less common in Mexico than anywhere in the U.S. In Baja California crime statistics are about 90% lower than the U.S. national average. Yet Americans seem to be the most paranoid of all visitors to Mexico.

Historical reasons, to a large degree, account for this paranoia. Chief among them is the general border lawlessness that was the norm very early in this century. The turn of the century and early 1900s was an era of border disputes and common banditry on both sides of the border, all the way from the Texas gulf coast to California's Pacific coast. Americans living in these areas came to fear *bandidos* who stole livestock and occasionally robbed the Anglo ranchers themselves, while the Mexicans in turn feared American cattle rustlers, horse thieves, gunslingers, and the infamous Texas Rangers, a private militia whose conduct at the time fell somewhere between that of the Hell's Angels motorcycle gang and the Los Angeles Police Department.

Soon after this era had begun to wane, as politics on both sides of the border stabilized, the U.S. Prohibition experiment sent millions of Americans scrambling into Mexican border towns for booze. In the illicit atmosphere, boozers were soon rubbing elbows with gamblers and whoremongers, and it wasn't long before Mexican border towns gained an even more unsavory reputation.

Once Prohibition was lifted, Americans had no reason to come to Mexico solely for drinking purposes and the border towns began cleaning up their acts. Among the uninformed and inexperienced, however, the border-town image remains, sadly mixing with the equally outdated bandido tales to prevent many Americans from enjoying the pleasures of life south of the border.

Neither the author nor anyone of the author's acquaintances has ever been robbed in Baja—or, for that matter, anywhere in Mexico. One morning, however, I left behind two shirts and a pair of slacks in a hotel closet in Loreto, BCS, and didn't remember them until arriving in La Paz that evening. A phone call that night and a visit to the hotel a week later were unsuccessful in retrieving the clothes—the management claimed they were never turned in by the cleaning staff. The moral of the story: try not to leave things behind in hotel rooms.

Precautions: In general, visitors to Baja should take the same precautions they would when traveling anywhere in their own countries or abroad. Keep money and valuables secured, either in a hotel safe or safety deposit box, or in a money belt or other hard-to-reach place on your person. Keep an eye on cameras, purses, etc., to make sure you don't leave them behind in restaurants, hotels, or campgrounds. At night, lock the doors to your hotel room and vehicle.

Private campgrounds usually have some kind of security, if only a night watchman, to keep out intruders. Secluded beach campsites seem to be safe due to their seclusion—in Baja it's rare for crime to occur in such areas. Nonetheless, don't leave items of value lying around outside your tent, camper, or RV at night.

MONEY, MEASUREMENTS, AND COMMUNICATIONS

MONEY

Currency

The unit of exchange in Mexico is the *peso,* which under the "old peso" system appeared in coins of 50, 100, 500, and 1000 pesos, or in bills of 1000, 5000, 10,000, 20,000, 50,000, and 100,000.

In January 1993 the government introduced the *nuevo peso* or "new peso," a currency that simply knocks three zeros off the old peso. Ten new pesos, for example, equals 10,000 old pesos. New peso notes are exact copies of old peso notes without the three zeros. A 10,000-peso note now reads 10 pesos but otherwise looks exactly the same. The new pesos come in denominations of N$10, N$20, N$50, and N$100. Old peso denominations of 50,000 and 100,000 can be difficult to break, so try to get them changed as soon as possible to secure a good supply of smaller notes.

For currency denominations of N$10 and less, new peso and *centavo* coins have been issued in denominations of 5¢, 10¢, 20¢, 50¢, N$1, N$2, N$5, and N$10.

Until the older currency passes from circulation, both kinds of pesos, in any combination, are legal tender throughout Mexico. In remote villages where the new peso isn't yet common, there may be some initial reluctance to accept new pesos. Usually there's someone around who will vouch for the validity of the new currency. As of mid-1994, old pesos were still more common than new pesos, even in larger cities.

The $ symbol is often used for indicating old peso as well as dollar prices. New peso prices are indicated by the symbol N$. While it's highly unlikely you'll ever confuse the two—since the exchange ratio is so high for old pesos—you should ask when in doubt. New peso prices are much closer to what a dollar price might be, hence there's more potential for confusion between dollars and new pesos; but since new peso prices are clearly marked with the symbol N$, this usually isn't a problem. Sometimes the abbreviation m.n. will appear next to a price—this means *moneda nacional* ("national money") and usually refers to old pesos.

When quoting prices verbally, Mexican vendors ordinarily refer to new peso prices. Even under the old peso system, they often abbreviated a verbal price quote by omitting the word *mil* (thousand) since few things cost less than 1000 pesos. Thus *doce cinco* meant *doce mil cinco cien* (12,500 old pesos) and under the new system means 12 new pesos plus fifty centavos or N$12.50. More correctly this would be spoken as *doce cincuenta* or "twelve fifty."

Since the smallest new peso coin is 5¢, all payments are rounded off to the nearest multiple of five centavos. For a marked price of N$8.52 (8,520 old pesos), for example, you actually only pay N$8.50; for a N$8.53 price you pay N$8.55.

Most places in Baja will take U.S. dollars as well as pesos. Paying with pesos, however, usually means a better deal when the price is fixed in pesos; if you pay in dollars, the vendor can determine the exchange rate. If a can of motor oil, for example, is marked at N$6, and the bank rate is N$3 per dollar, you'll pay only US$2 for the oil with pesos changed at the bank. However, if you ask to pay in dollars, the vendor may charge US$2.50 since vendors have the right—by custom rather than law—to charge whatever exchange rate they wish. Then again, if you're bargaining for price, it really doesn't matter what currency you use.

Some stores in smaller towns prefer not to take dollars since this means keeping track of two currencies and makes banking more complicated. PEMEX stations sometimes refuse dollars—attendants are usually too busy to stop and calculate rates.

Deflation

The Mexican peso has been in a deflationary spin since 1976 when the government decided to allow the national currency to "float" on the international money market. From 1976 to 1987 the exchange rate slid from eight pesos to the dollar to over 2,000. In 1988 the Bank of Mexico instituted measures to slow the decline to less than a centavo per day by the end of 1992. Since the switch to the new peso in '93, the peso has actually gained in value against the U.S. dollar. It's too early to say for sure, but all indications point to a stable Mexican currency at least through '95.

The relatively stable exchange rate means that changing money in Baja is much less stressful now than just a few years ago; there's no need to check the exchange rate every day. If the slow devaluation returns, it will work in favor of the dollar-holder; the dollar bought roughly 10% more in 1992 than it did in 1991.

Changing Money

Banks: Banks offer the best exchange rate for buying pesos and they all offer the same rate,

set by the Bank of Mexico. This rate is usually posted behind the counter where foreign exchange is handled. Banks also accept a wide range of foreign currencies, including Swiss francs, German marks, British pounds, Japanese yen, and Canadian dollars. Either cash or traveler's checks are accepted. The main drawbacks with banks are the long lines and short hours (Mon.-Fri. 0900-1330); the foreign-exchange service usually closes at noon or 1230.

Moneychangers: The second best rate is at the *casa de cambio* or private moneychanging office. The casa de cambio either knocks a few pesos off the going bank rate or charges a percentage commission. It pays to shop around for the best casa de cambio rates since some places charge considerably more than others. Rates are usually posted; *compra* refers to the buying rate for US$ (how many pesos you'll receive per dollar), while *venda* is the selling rate (how many pesos you must pay to receive a dollar). As with banks, the difference between the buying and selling rates is the moneychangers' profit, unless they charge commissions on top of it.

Moneychangers are usually open much later than banks; some even work evening hours, which makes them immeasurably more convenient than banks. U.S. dollar currency is generally preferred though many casas will also accept Canadian dollars. However, Canadians should always keep a reserve supply of U.S. dollars for instances when Canadian currency isn't accepted. Moneychangers usually accept traveler's checks; some border-town casas, however, accept only cash.

Only the larger towns and tourist centers offer moneychanging offices. In smaller towns you'll have to resort to a bank or local merchant. Many storekeepers will be happy to buy dollars at a highly variable and sometimes negotiable rate. Few will take traveler's checks, however, unless you make a purchase.

Moneychangers at Mexican airports offer notoriously low rates. Try to buy pesos in advance if arriving by air, or pay with dollars until you can get to a bank or casa de cambio.

Hotels: Hotels, motels, pensiones, and other lodging places generally offer the lowest exchange rates. If you're trying to save money, avoid changing currency where you stay. Pay for your room in pesos if possible, since the same low rate often applies to room charges paid in dollars.

Credit Cards

Plastic money (primarily Visa and MasterCard) is widely accepted in Baja at large hotels, at restaurants catering to tourists or businesspeople, at car rental agencies (you can't rent a car without a credit card), and at shops in tourist centers or large cities. Usually card displays at the cash register or on the door will announce that *tarjetas de credito* (credit cards) are accepted. If in doubt, flash one and ask *"¿Se acepta tarjetas de credito?"* or simply *"¿Está bien?"* A reference to *efectivo* means "cash."

Credit cards are not accepted at PEMEX stations. In 1991 the Mexican government announced plans to introduce a special "tourist credit card" that would be valid at PEMEX outlets; so far, *nada*. If/when the plan is finally realized, travel agencies abroad will know the details.

Paying for goods and services in Baja with credit cards that are paid through U.S. or Canadian banks can save you money since the exchange rate will usually dip farther in the dollar's favor by the time the transaction is posted at your bank. Many shops and some hotels, however, add a 3-6% surcharge to bills paid with a card, which more than offsets the exchange rate differential.

Cash advances on credit card accounts—a very useful service for emergencies—are available at Mexican banks. Banamex will accept MasterCard debit cards ("cash" or "check" cards), a more convenient way to carry travel funds than either cash or traveler's checks.

Estimating Costs

Inflation in Mexico currently runs around 12-18% per annum, in large part due to the continued weakening of the peso on international markets but also because of a slight relaxation of wage and price controls. This means that when estimating travel costs based on prices quoted in this book, some allowance must be made for inflation. Although peso prices will increase in direct proportion to the inflation rate, this isn't necessarily so for prices figured in dollars, since the dollar continues to gain in value against the peso.

Because of fluctuations in the peso-dollar ratio, and in an effort to keep prices up to date, all prices in this book are quoted in dollars. This doesn't mean, however, that there won't be any increase in prices by the time you arrive. A couple of phone calls to hotels for price quotes should give you an idea how much rates have increased, if at all; this difference can be applied as a percentage to all other prices for a rough estimate of costs.

Tipping

A tip of 10-15% is customary at restaurants with table service unless a service charge is added to the bill. Luggage handling at hotels or airports warrants a tip of US$.50, or the equivalent in pesos, per bag. A few hotels maintain a no-tipping policy; details will be posted in your room. The tipping of chambermaids is optional.

You don't need to tip PEMEX station attendants unless they wash your windows, check the oil, or perform other extra services beyond pumping gas. The equivalent of US$.25 to US$.50 in pesos is sufficient. When the change due on a gasoline purchase is less than N$1 it's customary to let the attendant keep the change.

The Mexican government collects an *impuesta al valor agregado* (IVA) or "value added tax" on all goods and services, including hotel and restaurant bills and international phone calls. Before 1992 the IVA was 15% but in an effort to boost consumption the tax has been reduced to 10%. Hotels and restaurants were supposed to pass the five percent tax savings on to the consumer by dropping prices accordingly; as a result you may see menus that read "five percent solidarity discount included."

MEASUREMENTS

Mexico uses the metric system as the official system of weights and measures. This means the distance between Maneadero and San Quintín is measured in kilometers, cheese is weighed in grams or kilograms, a hot day in San Felipe is 32° C, gasoline is sold by the liter, and a big fish is two meters long. A chart at the end of this book converts pounds, gallons, and miles to kilos, liters, and kilometers, and vice versa.

Bajacalifornios used to dealing with American tourists will often use the Anglo-American and metric systems interchangeably. Even rancheros in remote areas occasionally use *millas* (miles) as a measure.

In this book, distances are rendered in kilometers, often followed by miles in parentheses for the benefit of American readers and for checking against American odometers. All road markers in Baja employ the metric system. Dimensions and weights are usually quoted using the metric system, except when feet or pounds are culturally more appropriate, as in prescribing monofilament fishing line.

COMMUNICATIONS

Time

Baja California Norte lies in the Pacific Time Zone, Baja California Sur in the Mountain Time Zone. This means you should set your timepieces an hour ahead when crossing the BCS state line going south and back an hour when crossing north. It isn't necessary to reset your watch from the last Sunday in April to the last Sunday in October, when BCN advances an hour for daylight savings time and thus follows the same time as BCS, which does not observe daylight savings time.

Time in Mexico is commonly expressed according to the 24-hour clock, from 0001 to 2359 (one minute past midnight to 11:59 p.m.). A restaurant posting hours of 1100-2200, for example, is open from 11 a.m. to 10 p.m. To conform to the Mexican system, all times in this guidebook follow the 24-hour clock.

Electricity

Mexico's electrical system is the same as those in the U.S. and Canada: 110 volts, 60 cycles, alternating current (AC). Electrical outlets are of the North American type, designed to work with appliances with standard double-bladed plugs. Small towns in some rural areas may experience brief interruptions of electrical service or periods of brownout (voltage decrease). In a few villages, gasoline-powered generators are the only sources of electricity and they may be turned off during the day.

Postal Service

The Mexican postal service, though quite reliable, is relatively slow. Most towns in Baja have a post office (*oficina de correos*) where you can receive poste restante mail. Have correspondents address mail in your name, last name capitalized, followed by a/c Lista de Correos, the town name, and the state; e.g., Joe CUMMINGS, a/c Lista de Correos, La Paz, Baja California Sur, Mexico.

In small towns and villages, residents often don't use street addresses, simply scrawling the addressee's name followed by *domicilio conocido* ("known residence") and the name of the town or village. Even in large towns and cities, addresses may bear the name of the street without a building number (*sin número*, abbreviated as "s/n"), or will mention the nearest cross streets (e.g., *ent. Abasolo y Revolución*, or "between Abasolo and Revolución").

Many foreigners who are seasonal Baja residents have their mail sent in care of a hotel or RV park. You can rent boxes at larger Mexican post offices but the initial application process often takes several weeks. Tijuana, Tecate, and Mexicali have private mail companies (e.g., Mail Boxes, Etc.) that also rent boxes with minimal red tape.

For mail to the U.S., many residents in towns north of Ensenada or San Felipe save their letters and parcels until a friend or relative makes a trip across the border—the Chula Vista, California post office probably handles more mail from Tijuana than from Chula Vista. A letter mailed to Los Angeles from Tijuana will take a week or more while one mailed from Chula Vista will take only two days. Old Baja hands usually do the same, handing over mail to travelers returning to the States.

Telephone Services

Telmex, the national telephone company, has improved its services considerably over the last few years. In Baja a regional company called TelNor supplements the national system. Local phone calls are relatively cheap—a 10-peso coin, about US$.03, will pay for a phone-booth call—as are long distance calls within Mexico. Connections are usually good, though you may have to wait awhile to get through to the operator during such busy periods as Sundays and holidays.

If you don't want to use a phone booth or a hotel/RV park phone (hotels and RV parks usually add surcharges to both local and long-distance calls), you can make a call during business hours from a TelMex office. Only large towns offer TelMex offices with public telecom-

TELEPHONE CODES

To call a number in Mexico from outside the country, dial 011 + 52 + area code + number. Example: To call the number 2-47-61 in La Paz from the U.S., dial 011 (international dialing code) + 52 (Mexico country code) + 682 (La Paz area code) + 2-47-61 (the phone number in La Paz). Older Baja guidebooks often show a 706 "area code" for the peninsula; this number sequence is no longer functional. You must dial the country code and local area code before the local number.

In Mexico:

Information (national) 01
Long-distance operator (national) 02
Time 03
Information (local) 04
Mexico City area code 05
Police 06
Spanish-English
    emergency information 07
International operator 09

Long-distance Direct Dialing From Mexico:
station to station (in Mexico):
    91 + area code + number
person to person (in Mexico):
    92 + area code + number
station to station (to U.S. and Canada):
    95 + area code + number
person to person (to U.S. and Canada):
    96 + area code + number
station to station (to other countries):
    98 + area code + number
person to person (to other countries):
    99 + area code + number

Baja California Area Codes:

Tijuana 66
Rosarito 661
Ensenada 617
Mexicali 65
Tecate 665
San Felipe 657
Guerrero Negro/Mulegé 115
Loreto 113
La Paz 112
San José del Cabo/Cabo San Lucas . . 114
San Quintín 616

munications facilities; a small town may offer a private telephone office (usually called *caseta de teléfono)*, often set up in the corner of a local shop, where you can make calls. Like hotels, private telephone offices add surcharges to calls.

On the long stretch between Ensenada and Mulegé, few towns or villages possess telephone service, much less a telephone office. There's no phone service in Bahía de los Angeles, for example—residents and visitors alike must drive to Guerrero Negro, some 129 km (80 miles) distant, to place a call. Thus, some residents maintain their own two-way radio stations for communication with the outside world. Mulegé has only two public phone booths; visitors line up on Sundays to phone home.

Making International Calls: To direct dial an international call to the U.S. or Canada, dial 95 plus the area code and number for a station-to-station call or 96 plus area code and number for a person-to-person call. For countries besides Canada and the U.S., dial 98 and 99 respectively. Long-distance international calls are heavily taxed and cost more than equivalent international calls from the U.S. or Canada.

To reach toll-free (800) numbers in Mexico from the U.S. or Canada, dial 91 first. From Mexico, you can reach AT&T by dialing 95-800-462-4240, a toll-free call that connects you with a USADirect system. For MCI the number is 95-800-950-1022, for Sprint 95-800-977-8000. The appropriate long-distance operator can then place a collect call on your behalf or, if you have an AT&T, MCI, or Sprint phone card, charge the call to your account. If you try these numbers from a hotel phone, be sure the hotel operator realizes the call is toll free; some hotel operators use their own timers to assess phone charges. Another way to reach AT&T is to dial **01 on the tan-colored LADATEL phones (the ones which accept LADATEL phone cards) or on blue pay phones.

Collect: For international service, calling collect saves money and hassles. In Spanish the magic words are *por cobrar* (collect), prefaced by the name of the place you're calling (e.g., *"a los Estados Unidos, por favor—por cobrar"*). This will connect you to an English-speaking international operator. You're supposed to be able to obtain an international operator directly by dialing 09, but this number doesn't always work. For best results, speak slowly and clearly.

On some pay phones, or on any private phone, you can dial collect calls to the U.S. and Canada directly by prefixing the area code and number with 92. This is the easiest way to make a collect call.

Local Numbers: Most telephone numbers in Baja consist of five digits (six digits in Tijuana and Mexicali). There's no standard way of hyphenating the numbers; a five-digit number may appear as 211-13, 2-1113, or 2-11-13 while a six-digit number may be written 341720, 341-520, 34-1720, or 34-17-20.

For the sake of consistency, the latter forms are used in this book; they seem to be the most common in Baja.

Business Hours

The typical small business is open Mon.-Fri. (plus Saturday for retail businesses) from 0900 to 1400, closes until 1600 or 1700, then reopens until 1900 or 2000. Official government offices typically maintain an 0830-1530 schedule, although Secretary of Tourism offices usually open again from 1700 to 1900.

Banks are open Mon.-Fri., 0830-1330, but the foreign exchange service usually closes around noon—probably to lock in the exchange rate before afternoon adjustments.

SERVICES AND INFORMATION

Tourist Information

Mexico's federal tourist bureau, the Secretaría de Turismo (SECTUR), staffs state offices in Mexicali and La Paz. These in turn maintain branch offices in Tijuana, Ensenada, Tecate, Rosarito, San Felipe, San Quintín, and Loreto. These offices usually stock a variety of free brochures, maps, hotel and restaurant lists, and information on local activities, but some offices are better staffed to handle visitor queries than others. Tijuana, Ensenada, and Mexicali offer convention and visitors bureaus in addition to state offices, and are particularly well stocked with useful information. The addresses, phone numbers, and hours of each office are listed under the appropriate destination sections of the book.

To contact the national office directly, call or write the **Secretaría de Turismo de México**, Presidente Mazaryk, No. 172, 11570 México, D.F. (tel. 250-01-51, 250-01-23, 250-04-93). In the U.S., SECTUR maintains a toll-free information number, tel. (800) 482-9832.

Outside Mexico the government staffs 12 Mexican Government Tourism Offices (MGTO) to handle requests for tourist information. Seven are located in the United States.

Travel Clubs

Baja's popularity as a boating and RV destination has spawned three Alta California-based travel clubs that specialize in recreational travel on the peninsula and along the Pacific coast of mainland Mexico. Membership benefits include discounts (usually 10-20%) at various hotels, restaurants, and other tourist-oriented establishments in Mexico; discounted group auto and boat insurance; the opportunity to participate in such club events as tours and fiestas; and subscriptions to newsletters containing tips from other club members, short travel features, and the latest information on road conditions and Mexican tourism policy. The clubs can also arrange tourist cards, boat permits, and fishing licenses by mail.

ClubMex and Discover Baja specialize in road (especially RV) travel and publish monthly newsletters, while Vagabundos del Mar is ori-

ented toward boaters and publishes its newsletter every two months. Both ClubMex and Discover Baja invite members or potential members to visit their San Diego area offices on the way to Baja for up-to-date road and weather information. Contact **ClubMex** at 3450 Bonita Rd., Suite 107, Chula Vista, CA 91910 (tel. 619-585-3033, fax 619-420-8133), or write P.O. Box 1646, Bonita, CA 91902-1646. **Discover Baja** can be contacted at 3065 Clairemont Drive, San Diego, CA 92117 (tel. 619-275-4225, toll-free 800-727-BAJA). Write or call **Vagabundos del Mar** at P.O. Box 824, Isleton, CA 95641 (tel. 707-374-5511, fax 707-374-6843).

A fourth travel club, sponsored by Texas-based Sanborn's Mexico Insurance, offers similar benefits for all of Mexico, with the addition of custom-designed itineraries prepared by long-time Mexico travel aficionado, "Mexico" Mike Nelson. For an extra charge Sanborn's Mexico Club members may also subscribe to a medical evacuation service covering all air transportation costs to the U.S. or Canada for medical treatment. For details, contact Sanborn's, P.O. Box 310, McAllen, TX 78502 (tel. 512-686-0711, fax 512-686-0732).

MEDIA

Newspapers

Several Spanish-language newspapers are published in Baja; *El Mexicano,* published daily in Tijuana, has the highest circulation, closely followed by Mexicali's *La Voz de la Frontera* ("Voice of the Border"). Also of considerable interest is the progressive *Zeta* ("Z"), in Tijuana.

Three English-language newspapers and one bilingual newspaper are published monthly in Baja, all heavily oriented toward tourists. Although not exactly pillars of journalism, they nonetheless contain much information of value to the visitor, including up-to-date sketch maps. Typical features include restaurant reviews, cultural primers on upcoming festivals, Spanish language lessons, seasonal fishing recommendations, and the occasional editorial on national or local tourism policies. The content of

BAJA NEWSPAPERS

Baja Sun
Calle Sexta 995
Ensenada, BCN
or P.O. Box 8530
Chula Vista, CA 92012

Baja Times
Centro Comercial
Hotel Rosarito
Rosarito, BCN
(tel. 2-12-44; fax 2-23-66),
or P.O. Box 5577
Chula Vista, CA 91912

Los Cabos Times (El Tiempo Los Cabos)
Blvd. Marina No. 17
Cabo San Lucas, BCS
(tel. 3-19-80; fax 3-19-39)

each is somewhat biased toward the town in which it is published.

Each of the two monthly English-language newspapers based in northern Baja, the *Baja Sun* and the *Baja Times,* offer foreign and local subscriptions. Read the classified ads for information on Baja real estate. The twice-monthly *Los Cabos Times* (*El Tiempo Los Cabos*) is a bilingual newspaper covering the Cape Region, including La Paz.

At newsstands in Tijuana, Ensenada, Mexicali, and La Paz you'll find *The News,* an English-language daily published in Mexico City. In tourist hotels in the north you'll often see day-old copies of the *San Diego Tribune* or the *Los Angeles Times.*

Radio And Television

In the border area of northern Baja, radios and TVs pick up a mix of broadcasts from Tijuana and San Diego. Farther south the San Diego stations begin to fade, then the Tijuana stations. South of Ensenada you'll need shortwave radio to receive anything until you arrive in La Paz or Los Cabos, where TV and radio reception begin again.

Tapes and CDs: Because of the general lack of TV and radio reception in most of Baja, it would be rather foolish to pack an AM/FM radio or portable TV. An audiocassette or portable CD player makes more sense. Many towns in Baja feature shops selling tapes and CDs, for prices generally less expensive than those in the U.S. or Canada. North American and European releases—in addition to Latino recordings—often appear on Mexican labels. Baja is a good place to pick up a selection of *música norteña* tapes.

MAPS

Among the many Baja California maps available to visitors, two are particularly well-suited to general-purpose Baja road travel. One is published by the Automobile Club of Southern California and is available from most AAA offices; maps are free to AAA members. The excellent graphics on this map include topographic shading; it's easy to read, and accurate and detailed enough for any border-to-cape auto trip.

On the AAA map longer distances are marked in miles and kilometers (scale: one inch:12.4 miles or 20 km) but smaller distances are marked only in miles, which makes it convenient for anyone driving a vehicle purchased in the U.S. but frustrating for drivers of vehicles acquired anywhere else in the world. Even for American-market vehicles, it can be confusing trying to match map mileage with the Mexican roadside kilometer markers. The AAA map features a distance table with entries in both miles and kilometers, but this is of little use when trying to figure out distances between points not listed on the table.

International Travel Map Productions (ITM) publishes a well-researched map that's a bit harder to find, especially in the U.S. Map and travel stores may carry it, or it can be ordered from ITM, P.O. Box 2290, Vancouver, BC V6B 3W5, Canada.

In spite of its smaller scale (one inch:15.78 miles or 25.4 km), the ITM map is far more detailed than the AAA map and all distances are entered in kilometers as well as miles. Many dirt roads, trails, and destinations unmarked on the AAA map appear on the ITM map. In addition, the map features contour lines in 200-meter intervals and is annotated with useful historical and sightseeing information. The main drawback of this map is that it's so detailed it's difficult to read. In addition, the map's graphics scheme uses far too much red, a color particularly difficult to read in low light.

Topographical Maps

Since differences in elevation often determine backcountry route selection, hikers, kayakers, mountain bikers, and off-road drivers should consider obtaining topographical maps in advance of their arrival in Baja. Topo maps are very difficult to come by in Baja itself. For information on what's available and where to get it, see the "Hiking and Backpacking" section of "Sports and Recreation."

BUYING OR LEASING PROPERTY IN BAJA

The Mexican government allows both resident and nonresident foreigners to own Mexican real estate—both land and buildings—within certain restrictions. Under the Constitution of 1857, foreign ownership of land by direct title is permitted only in areas more than 100 km (62 miles) from any international border and 50 km (31 miles) from any sea coast. In Baja California, this limits prospective buyers to areas in the interior of the peninsula where services—water, electricity, sewage, telephone—are often nonexistent.

However, since 1973 the Mexican government has offered a way for foreigners to acquire lots that fall outside the geographic limits, including coastal property. For transactions of this nature, the Ministry of Foreign Affairs issues permits to foreigners allowing them to create limited real estate trusts, administered by Mexican banks, with themselves as beneficiaries. Originally, these trusts were valid for 30-year nonrenewable terms only. In 1989 the government further liberalized real estate regulations so that the trusts (called *fideicomisos*) could be renewed at the end of each 30-year term for an additional 30-year term, with no limit on the number of renewals. In December 1993 the basic term for bank trusts was lengthened to 50 years, a period that may be long enough to attract U.S. housing lenders. Until now U.S. lenders have remained aloof from the fideicomiso market. Fideicomisos can be bought and sold among foreigners, at market rates, just like fee-simple property.

Needless to say, Baja real estate prices have increased substantially as a result of this change in policy. An estimated 40,000 foreigners now reside in Baja California Norte alone, some of them Americans who commute to San Diego

for work. The priciest coastal properties are those near the U.S.-Mexico border and on the Cape, but prices are still substantially below what's available in coastal Alta California.

Beach lots large enough for a two- or three-bedroom home in the La Paz area are available for US$15,000 and up. Survivalist types can find beach hideaways with no services for even less; in remote areas, total annual payments are as low as US$500-1000. With a desalinator, generator or solar cells, propane stove and refrigerator, and perhaps an airplane to get in and out, you can live in considerable style.

Precautions: Before you rush off to grab Baja land, you should be aware that a lot of people get burned in Mexican real estate deals. It's best to deal through an established, reputable real estate agent. The American company Century 21 has opened a franchise in Baja, and although it generally represents only the more expensive properties, Century 21 people can be very helpful with information on real estate trusts. Mexican tourist offices in Baja also often carry information on residential property.

Many sellers ask that the full purchase price be paid up front. Because a large number of gringos buy land in Mexico with cash, some Mexicans assume this is customary for all North Americans. Paying up front is not the typical procedure for Mexicans themselves, who usually make down payments and then send in monthly time payments; mortgage terms similar to those found in Canada and the U.S. are available in Mexico. Even if you have the cash, don't hand over more than half the full amount until you have the fideicomiso papers in hand.

Once again, investigate the realtor thoroughly before signing on the dotted line. Mexico doesn't require salespersons or brokers to obtain any sort of real estate license, hence many North Americans who couldn't make the grade in the U.S. or Canada now work in Mexico.

Time Shares

Time-share salespeople are the scourge of Baja resort areas, especially Cabo San Lucas, where they hang out on street corners and in hotel lobbies, hounding every tourist that passes by. These hustlers, who are sometimes gringos, will try almost anything to convince you to sign on the dotted line, on the spot—including denying that what they're selling is a time-share. It pays to hold off on any decision until you've made inquiries among current time-share residents at the development and checked with your consulate to see if there have been any complaints. Time-share developments typically begin selling when construction has just begun—sometimes they don't get finished, or when they do they don't shape up as promised. Also, keep in mind that from an investment perspective, time-shares don't appreciate in value—if they appreciate at all—as much as single-owner properties.

Other Problems: Because time-share owners aren't year-round residents, they usually lack both a sense of community and a sense of responsibility toward the local environment. For the developer, time-shares mean huge profits, as the same space is sold repeatedly in one-week segments. Since land in Baja is relatively inexpensive, considering the charming scenery and climate, it seems to attract get-rich-quick developers who show a decided lack of respect for the fragile Baja environment.

This is not to say there aren't any good time-share opportunities in Baja. But, in general, as with any real estate deal, it pays to proceed very cautiously. Don't be cajoled into buying without considering all the options.

GETTING THERE

BY AIR

International Flights

Baja's most commonly used air gateway for flights from the U.S. (the only country with direct international flights to Baja) is Los Cabos (SJD), a modern airport about 15 km (nine miles) north of San José del Cabo. Daily direct flights to Los Cabos originate in Los Angeles, San Diego, San Francisco, Oakland, and Phoenix.

Loreto (LTO) also fields regularly scheduled flights from the U.S., but via Los Angeles only. International flights to La Paz (LAP) arrive from Los Angeles and Tucson; the Tucson flight is direct with a brief stopover in Guaymas.

Tijuana International Airport (TIJ) is connected to only one U.S. city, Los Angeles. **Air L.A.** (tel. 800-933-5952 in the U.S./Canada, 95-800-10-04-13 in Mexico) flies jet-props four times weekly between Los Angeles and Tijuana. All flights depart from the Los Angeles Airport West Imperial Terminal; fares are US$69 one-way, US$98-138 roundtrip. If you plan to pick up a rental car in Tijuana, arranging a connection through L.A. is considerably easier than flying to San Diego and taking a taxi or bus to Tijuana. Air L.A. is also adding service to Ensenada (US$98-198 RT), and Mexicali (US$138 RT) from L.A.; California points of departures added in early 1994 include Ontario, Burbank, Orange County, and San Diego.

San Felipe and Santa Rosalía each offer airports reportedly equipped to handle international service but so far the only way to fly to either of these places is by chartered plane. Air L.A. recently announced it will begin operating regularly scheduled passenger flights to San Felipe from the L.A. area sometime in 1994 for US$149-199 RT. Another maverick, **Baja Air West Express** (tel. 619-661-6099, toll-free 800-335-2252 in the U.S./Canada, fax 619-661-2597) will schedule flights to Ensenada and San Felipe from Brown Field near San Diego.

Private Planes

Baja is a popular destination among North American light-aircraft pilots. Entry procedures are minimal, air traffic over the peninsula light, and nearly 200 airstrips take pilots and their passengers in a matter of hours to corners of Baja

AIRLINES IN BAJA

Note: All routings subject to change; call the airlines for the latest information.

Aero California (tel. 800-258-3311); to Loreto; nonstop flights from Los Angeles, La Paz and Los Cabos; connecting flights from Los Angeles, Mexico City, Phoenix, and San Diego.

Aero California; (tel. 800-237-6225); to La Paz; nonstop flights from Culiacán, Guaymas, and Los Angeles; connecting flights from Aguascalientes, Colima, Guadalajara, Loreto, Los Angeles, Los Mochis, Mexico City, and Tijuana.

Aeroméxico (tel. 800-237-6639); to La Paz; nonstops from Aguascalientes, Guadalajara, Hermosillo.

Air L.A. (tel. 800-933-5952); to Tijuana, Ensenada, and Mexicali from Los Angeles.

Alaska Airlines (tel. 800-426-0333); to Los Cabos; nonstop flights from Los Angeles and San Diego; connecting flights from Portland, Seattle, and San Francisco.

Mexicana Airlines (tel. 800-531-7921); to Los Cabos; nonstop flights from Los Angeles.

Noroeste (tel. 83-13-36); toTijuana and Mexicali; connecting flights from El Paso, Las Vegas, Mexicali, Phoenix, Tucson, Ciudad Obregón, Hermosillo, Guaymas, La Paz, Mazatlán, and Juárez.

Suntrips (tel. 800-786-8747); to Los Cabos; nonstop flights from Oakland.

United Airlines (tel. 800-538-2929); to Los Cabos; nonstop flights from Los Angeles; connecting flights from major U.S. cities.

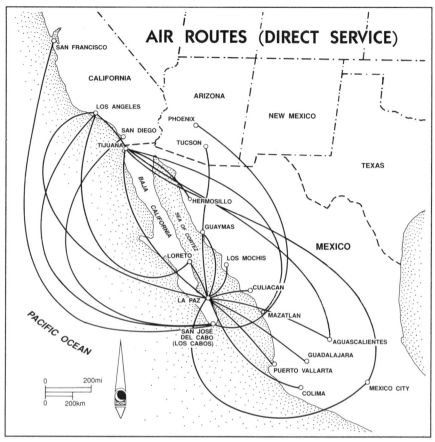

AIR ROUTES (DIRECT SERVICE)

SAN FRANCISCO

CALIFORNIA

ARIZONA

NEW MEXICO

LOS ANGELES

PHOENIX

SAN DIEGO

TIJUANA

TUCSON

TEXAS

BAJA CALIFORNIA

HERMOSILLO

SEA OF CORTEZ

GUAYMAS

LORETO

LOS MOCHIS

MEXICO

CULIACAN

LA PAZ

MAZATLAN

SAN JOSÉ DEL CABO (LOS CABOS)

AGUASCALIENTES

GUADALAJARA

PACIFIC OCEAN

PUERTO VALLARTA

COLIMA

MEXICO CITY

0   200mi
0   200km

© MOON PUBLICATIONS, INC.

usually accessible only by days of driving. Most of these airstrips are unpaved and unstaffed—a significant attraction for those who consider themselves bush pilots.

Private aircraft weighing less than 12,500 kilograms (27,500 pounds) and carrying fewer than 14 passengers are subject to the same customs procedures as automobiles and light trucks. In cases where the plane's owner doesn't accompany the aircraft, flights are further restricted to single-engine craft with five or fewer passengers. Cargo is restricted to the personal belongings of pilots and passengers.

Flight plans must be filed in advance with the Mexican airport nearest the point of entry. Southbound, pilots must clear immigration and customs at the Mexican airport of entry; northbound, a stop on either side of the border is required for pilots and passengers to satisfy both Mexican and U.S. border formalities. For further information on flying regulations in Baja, contact a Mexican consulate or the Departmento de Transport Aéreo Internacional (Edificio Torre, Aeropuerto Internacional de la Ciudad de México, México, D.F.) or Flight Log (see "By Air" under "Getting Around").

For more information on flying conditions in Baja, see "Getting Around."

BY LAND

To San Diego

Whether they reach the U.S.-Baja California border by train, bus, or trolley, most visitors using public transport must first pass through San Diego. From there they can choose from several options in traveling to Tijuana or Mexicali. San Diego is connected to other points in the U.S. by frequent long-distance bus and rail service.

Bus: Intercity buses generally depart more frequently and are less expensive than trains. Greyhound Bus Lines is the major carrier into San Diego. If you're busing a long distance to San Diego, a bus pass may be more economical than single-journey tickets. Outside North America, a Greyhound **Ameripass,** which allows unlimited bus travel within specified dates, can be purchased from travel agencies at a discount (e.g., a seven-day pass bought in the U.S. costs US$250; outside the U.S. US$199). For Greyhound fare and schedule information in the U.S., dial (800) 231-2222.

Rail: The only long-distance passenger rail line to San Diego is Amtrak's San Diegan, which rolls between Los Angeles and San Diego nine times daily (US$30 roundtrip Mon.-Thurs., US$35 roundtrip on weekends, US$23 one way). You can arrange connections with a number of other Amtrak lines to points in the U.S. north or east of Los Angeles. Amtrak offers special one-way, roundtrip, or excursion fares on occasion; always ask before booking.

Outside North America, some international travel agencies sell a **USA Railpass** which allows unlimited rail travel within specified dates. For schedule information or bookings inside the U.S., call (800) 872-7245 (800-USA-RAIL). A rail pass called **All Aboard America** is sold inside the U.S. at slightly higher prices.

Bus To Tijuana

Greyhound Bus Lines (tel. 619-239-9171 in San Diego, 213-620-1200 in L.A.) operates 18 buses a day between 0040 and 2340 from Los Angeles to Tijuana via San Diego. The fare is US$14.50 one way (or US$29 roundtrip) from

L.A., US$4 (or US$7 roundtrip) from San Diego. Buses leave from the downtown Greyhound Trailways terminals in each city and terminate at Tijuana's downtown terminal at Calle Comercio and Avenida Madero. The trip from San Diego is about 35 minutes when traffic is light; in the reverse direction it usually takes around 55 minutes. Mexican Customs doesn't make everyone get off the bus at the border; U.S. Customs does. From Los Angeles, the bus journey is about three hours. Boxed bicycles may accompany paying passengers at no extra charge.

The cheapest bus transport to the border from San Diego is the Metropolitan Transit System's city bus no. 932, which travels from the downtown area (Centre City) to San Ysidro every 30 minutes from 0540 to 2135 (0612 to 2105 weekends and holidays) for just US$1.50. Because it makes several stops along the way, the city bus takes an hour and 20 minutes to reach San Ysidro. For schedule information, call (619) 233-3004.

Mexicoach (tel. 619-232-5049 in San Diego, 800-628-3745 toll free in Alta California, 85-69-13 in Tijuana) runs five buses a day between 0900 and 1900 from the San Ysidro border gateway to the Frontón Jai Alai on Av. Revolución in Tijuana. Drivers will also stop at the Tijuana Cultural Center on request. The fare is US$1.25 one way, US$2 roundtrip.

Tijuana Trolley

The San Diego trolley system's train to San Ysidro, nicknamed the "Tijuana Trolley," is the second-cheapest form of public transport to the border. San Ysidro-bound trains leave every 15 minutes from 0500 to 0100 from downtown San Diego (plus Saturday morning "night owl" service 0200-0500) and cost US$1.75 each way (US$.75 for seniors and disabled passengers, free for children under five). Like the city bus, the trolley makes numerous stops along the way to San Ysidro—figure on about an hour from downtown. Bicycles may be taken on the trolley with certain restrictions (see "Bicycle Transport," under "Getting Around"). Call (619) 231-8549 for general trolley information or (619) 233-3004 for information on scheduling and stops.

Bus To Calexico

Calexico is opposite Mexicali on the U.S. side of the border. Greyhound Trailways operates several buses daily to Calexico from Los Angeles (US$29.65), San Diego (US$19.65), Tucson (US$31.75), Yuma (US$16.45), Phoenix (US $42.35), and El Paso (US$116.20). The Calexico Greyhound terminal is on First St.; from there it's a short walk through the immigration and customs checkpoint into downtown Mexicali.

From Mainland Mexico

Transportes Norte de Sonora and **Auto-transportes del Pacífico** operate long-distance express buses to Mexicali and Tijuana from various towns in Guanajuato, Nayarit, Sonora, Chihuahua, Michoacán, Jalisco, Sinaloa, Zacatecas, Querétaro, and México City.

Green Tortoise

To those who have never traveled by Green Tortoise, it's difficult to describe the experience. Imagine a sort of youth hostel on wheels, with a bit of a '60s spirit, and you'll begin to get the idea. The buses are refurbished Greyhounds with convertible beds and tables, comfortable but a bit of a tight squeeze at night when everyone's lying down. That's also when the bus travels. Great way to meet people.

Green Tortoise operates nine-day (US$249) and 14-day (US$349) trips to Baja Nov.-April that begin in San Francisco (pickups in L.A. are possible) and range as far south as La Paz. Prices are very reasonable—less than full roundtrip fare alone between San Francisco and La Paz—and include roundtrip transport and lodging on the bus, plus guided hikes and side trips to remote Baja beaches. The food fund adds another US$5 per day to the trip; communal meals cover about 70% of the meals—some meals are left to the participants. The trips include an optional windsurfing and sailing program available for an additional fee. All things considered, it's a travel bargain and a novel introduction to Baja.

For further information, contact Green Tortoise Adventure Travel (tel. 800-227-4766), P.O. Box 24459, San Francisco, CA 94124.

Train

Mexico's national rail service has its westernmost terminus in Mexicali. The Mexicali line connects with the Mexico City-Nogales line at Benjamin Hill, hence it's an alternative way to get to Baja from Nogales or Mexico City, or anywhere in between. The ferry from Mazatlán or Topolobampo is a more direct way to southern Baja. For details, see "Mexicali."

Driving To Baja

More people drive private vehicles across the U.S.-Mexico border at Tijuana than at any other point along its 1,600-km (1,000-mile) length—nearly 20 million in 1990. If you find the traffic daunting, you can avoid Tijuana altogether by choosing any of four other Baja border crossings. The red tape for driving into Baja is extremely minimal. In fact, no vehicle permits of any kind are required, no matter how long you stay in Baja, unless you plan to cross to the mainland by road (via San Luis Río Colorado) or ferry (Santa Rosalía or La Paz). For stays of less than 72 hours no farther south than Maneadero, U.S. and Canadian citizens don't even need a tourist permit, just identification.

Insurance: Before driving into Baja, drivers should arrange for Mexican vehicle insurance. No matter what your own insurance company may tell you, Mexican authorities don't recognize foreign insurance policies for private vehicles in Mexico.

Vehicle insurance isn't required by law in Mexico but it's a good idea to carry a Mexican liability policy anyway; without it, a minor traffic accident can turn into a nightmare. Short-term—as little as one day's worth—insurance can be arranged at any of several agencies found in nearly every border town between the Pacific Ocean and the Gulf of Mexico. One of the most popular, and least expensive, is **Oscar Padilla Mexican Insurance**, which has insured North American motorists since 1951. Padilla premiums for a multiple-entry, one-year, comprehensive policy for Baja/Northwest Mexico start at around US$90 for under US$5000 in coverage and rise to US$489 for US$150,000 worth of coverage; liability only costs US$53 per year. The main office is located at 1660 Hotel Circle N., Suite 735, San Diego, CA 92108 (tel. 619-688-1776, toll-free 800-258-8600).

Another good source of Mexican insurance is **International Gateway Insurance Brokers** (tel. 800-423-2646), with rates just a few dollars higher than Padilla's. Its "Tour Aid" service includes US$3,000 accident coverage, emergency towing to US$100 for autos or US$200 for motor homes, emergency road service to

US$100, hospital guarantee to US$500, parts service (they ship parts from the U.S. to Mexico for the cost of parts only), and legal service. Tour Aid is available for US$20 a year or is included with the insurance.

Those in a hurry might prefer **Instant Mexico Insurance Services.** IMIS sits at the last exit before the San Ysidro/Tijuana border crossing (tel. 619-428-4714, toll-free 800-638-0999) at 223 Via de San Ysidro. It's open 24 hours and in addition to insurance offers tourist cards, fishing and boating permits, maps, guidebooks, and other Baja requisites.

Several agencies in Tijuana and Ensenada offer annual policies that charge you only for those days you're actually in Mexico. Of course, this requires a trip south of the border to obtain such a policy, so you'll need a day's worth of border insurance beforehand. One agency north of the border that can arrange Mexican liability insurance on a per-use basis is **Anserv Insurance Services** (tel. 619-233-5444, 800-262-1994 in Alta California, tel. 800-654-7504 elsewhere in the U.S. and Canada). Rates are as low as US$1 a day based on 60 days' minimum use per policy year. The ClubMex, Discover Baja, and Vagabundos del Mar travel clubs (see "Services and Information" for addresses and phone numbers) offer low group insurance rates for members only ranging from US$53 a year for liability only to US$90 a year for US$5000 worth of collision, fire, theft, and glass insurance. Add another US$15-20 for each additional US$5000 in coverage. These group policies are offered on a yearly basis only; they can't be purchased by the day, week, or month.

Some insurance companies try to justify higher premiums by claiming their policies cover repairs performed in the U.S. or Canada, pointing out that less expensive insurance is valid only for repairs in Mexico. In most cases, such an argument is irrelevant; the primary reason you need Mexican insurance is to protect yourself against liability in the event of an accident. In cases where your vehicle is disabled, repairs will have to be performed in Mexico anyway. Even if you obtain a policy that covers U.S./Canada repairs, chances are it won't cover transport of a disabled vehicle to the border. However, North American visitors driving vehicles with difficult-to-obtain parts might want to consider a policy valid for U.S./Canada repairs.

Whichever policy you choose, always make photocopies of it and keep originals and copies in separate, safe places. It's also a good idea to carry a photocopy of the first page—the "declaration" or "renewal of declaration" sheet—of your home country policy as Mexican law requires you cross the border with at least six months' worth of home-country insurance.

Parking In San Ysidro

Another alternative is to drive to San Ysidro, park your vehicle in one of the guarded fee lots, and walk across the border at Tijuana, or take a Mexicoach bus. San Ysidro parking lots charge US$7-8 per day or any portion thereof.

BY SEA

Ferry

Three ferry services currently run to southern Baja from the Mexican mainland—two to La Paz and one to Santa Rosalía. The Cabo San Lucas-to-Puerto Vallarta passenger-vehicle service was terminated in 1989; a jetfoil called *Baja Express* ran between La Paz and Topolobampo in 1992 but ceased operations after less than a year's service due to financial difficulties.

With passenger-vehicle ferries anyone driving on the mainland can reach southern Baja without a time-consuming U-turn at the top of the peninsula. Many drivers from the North American west coast use Baja ferry services as an alternative way of reaching the mainland, since it allows them to avoid Mexico 15 on the way to Mazatlán and points farther south.

Fares and Classes: A few years ago the vehicle ferry system was privatized under the directorship of Grupo SEMATUR (Servicios Marítimos y Turísticos) de California, S.A., and fares are now market-priced rather than subsidized. They've risen substantially each year, except for motorcycle rates, which have dropped over the last two years. The fares listed here were valid as of mid-1993; allow for average inflation, roughly 15% per year, when making ferry plans.

Passenger fares are based on class: *salón* (reclining seats in various general seating areas), *turista* (shared bunk rooms), and *cabina* (private cabins with toilet facilities). Some ferryboats also feature an additional *especial* class with large, deluxe cabins. Vehicle fares are based on the length of the vehicle—the longer the rig, the higher the fare. All fares must be paid in pesos.

Note: Signs at the vehicle ferry ticket offices in Santa Rosalía and La Paz warn that passenger tickets will not be issued to pregnant women.

Reservations: Whether it was the fare increases or the reorganization of management under private auspices, ferry reservations are now much easier to make than they were several years ago. Generally speaking, if you show up at the ferry terminal one day in advance of your desired voyage, you should be able to get passenger tickets; vehicle passage is a little more difficult to arrange.

Salón seats are sold on a first-come, first-served basis; turista can be reserved three days or more in advance; a cabina can be reserved a month or more in advance. During holiday periods—especially Semana Santa, when you might want to avoid ferry service altogether—you should try to pick up your tickets at least a week or two in advance.

Reservations must be confirmed 15 days before departure date for the La Paz-Mazatlán and La Paz-Topolobampo routes, 10 days before departure for the Santa Rosalía-Guaymas route.

SEMATUR operates ticket offices at each of its ferry piers for advance as well as day-of-departure sales. A number of Mexican travel agencies are authorized to handle ticket reservations and sales in Ciudad Constitución, BCS (Viajes Pedrín, tel. 2-01-12), Guerrero Negro, BCS (Viajes Mario's, tel. 7-07-88), La Paz, BCS (Viajes Transpeninsulares, 2-03-99; Viajes Perla, tel. 2-86-66; Viajes Cabo Falso, tel. 2-41-31), Los Mochis (Viajes Paotam, tel. 5-19-14), and Mazatlán (Turismo Coral, tel. 81-32-90; Marza Tours, tel. 86-08-96; Viajes Attiq, tel. 84-24-00). SEMATUR's toll-free information and reservation telephone number in Mexico is 91-800-6-96-96; this number can be dialed from the U.S. and Canada.

Guaymas-Santa Rosalía: Ferries depart Guaymas every Tuesday and Friday at 0800 and arrive at Santa Rosalía at 1500 the same day. In the opposite direction, ferries depart on Sunday and Wednesday at the same hours.

Passenger fares are US$13 salón, US$26.50 turista. Cabina and especial aren't usually available on this route, unless a larger ferry from another route is used. When available, a cabina costs US$40, especial US$53. Vehicle fares range from US$102 for a car, truck, or van under five meters (about 15 feet), up to a whopping US$378 for a full-size bus or motor home (19-meter/62-foot limit). Motorcycles cost US$16.

Topolobampo-La Paz: Topolobampo is a small port town that serves the Los Mochis area. An interesting way to reach Baja from, say, Texas is to take the Chihuahua al Pacífico train via Creel and the Barrancas del Cobre—or "Copper Canyon," Mexico's equivalent of the Grand Canyon—to Los Mochis, then the Topolobampo ferry to La Paz. Ferries on this route are mostly devoted to cargo, with a smaller salón section. During holiday periods, more passenger space is usually available.

The ferry leaves Topolobampo daily (except Sunday) at 0900 and arrives in La Paz about 1800. Eastbound, the ferry departs La Paz daily (except Tuesday) at 2000, arriving at Topolobampo around 0600. Passenger fares are the same as for the Guaymas-Santa Rosalía ferry. Auto, truck, or van fares are US$88; with trailers to nine meters US$160 or to 17 meters US$230; buses and motorhomes US$353; motorcycles US$12.

Mazatlán-La Paz: At the moment this is the most full-service passenger-vehicle ferry available between Baja and the mainland. Each of the three craft that regularly ply this route offer salón, turista, cabina, and especial classes plus a restaurant-bar, disco, video lounge and cafetería.

Ferries depart each port daily at 1500, arriving on the other side at around 0900. Passenger fares are US$20 salón, US$40 turista, US$60 cabina, and US$80 especial. For vehicles, fares are: auto, truck, or van to five meters US$146; with trailers to nine meters US$165; buses and motorhomes 15-19 meters (49-62 feet) US$570; motorcycles US$19.

(previous page) Río Mulegé; (top) agave;
(bottom left) Playa del Amor, Cabo San Lucas; (bottom right) palm and cardón

GETTING AROUND

Most North American visitors to Baja travel the peninsula with their own vehicles—cars, trucks, campers, RVs, or motorcycles. Alternative transportation includes domestic airlines, rented cars, public buses, bicycles, and hitchhiking.

BY AIR

Domestic air travel in Baja is generally less expensive than international flights of comparable distances from the U.S. to Baja. It's cheaper to fly from Tijuana to La Paz than from San Diego to Los Cabos, for example. Hence, especially for San Diego residents, the minor inconvenience of flying out of Tijuana could result in a considerable savings—if your destination is either La Paz or Loreto.

Aero California and Mexicana Airlines each schedule flights between Tijuana and La Paz that cost around US$120 one way, US$215 roundtrip. Aero Mexico also flies between La Paz and Loreto for US$36 one way, US$72 roundtrip.

Local Airlines
Several small airlines in Baja specialize in short flights ("puddle-jumpers") to destinations—usually Pacific islands—inaccessible by land transport. **Aerolineas California Pacíficos** flies between Guerrero Negro, Isla Cedros, and Bahía Tortugas. **Soc. Coop. de Producción Pesquera** (nicknamed "The Cannery") schedules flights from Ensenada's El Ciprés airfield to Isla Cedros and Bahía Tortugas. If enough passengers are on hand to make it profitable—or one passenger is very generous—this company will also fly to Isla Natividad.

Charter Flights
Three companies that can arrange small-plane charters to any airfield in Baja from southern Alta California are: Gunnell Aviation (tel. 310-452-0999, 3100 McDonnell Douglas Loop North, Santa Monica, CA 90405), AeroCargo (tel. 800-335-2252, 619-661-6099, fax 619-661-2597, Brown Field, San Diego, CA 92173), and Lundy Air Charter (tel. 619-562-4181, 1860 Joe Crosson Dr., El Cajon, CA 92020).

Private Flights
With a pilot's license and a plane, you can fly to any of Baja's nearly 200 airstrips. Air traffic over Baja is very light and the paperwork for crossing the border is minimal. At the moment aviation fuel is more expensive in Mexico than in the U.S., so most pilots stop at Brown Field or Calexico to top off before crossing the border. Another reason to take on fuel at the border is because it's only available at or near a fraction of the bush strips; careful planning is required.

A reliable source of information for anyone considering a private flight to Baja is **Flight Log** (tel. 310-391-4464, 714-521-2531, P.O. Box 2465, Fullerton, CA 91623). Flight Log's US$25 membership fee covers a newsletter subscription, a copy of *Flying Baja: A Pilot's Primer,* and a telephone information service. This group also organizes group "adventure" flights to Baja destinations such as Mulegé, Loreto, Punta Chivato, Punta Colorada, and La Paz.

A San Diego area outfit calling itself **Baja Bush Pilots** (tel. 619-297-5587) publishes a 384-page guide, *Airports of Baja California and Northwest Mexico,* by Arnold Senterfitt, which contains aerial photos, sketch maps, and descriptions of virtually every landing strip in Baja. Few pilots fly to Baja without this book.

Nelly's Pilot Supply (tel. 619-661-6099, 1424 Continental St., San Diego, CA 92173) at Brown Field near San Ysidro offers Baja guidebooks, pilot manuals, and flight supplies oriented toward the Baja pilot. Nelly's also claims to be coming out with its own *Baja Nelly's Flight Guide to Mexico,* covering 10 airports in Baja plus Brown Field and Calexico.

Planes that fly into Mexico are required to carry Mexican liability insurance. Lewis and Lewis (tel. 310-657-1112, 8929 Wilshire Blvd. #200, Beverly Hills, CA 90211) offers inexpensive annual aircraft policies. Flight Log recommends Thaddeus Smith & Associates (tel. 714-938-9469, 12443 Lewis St., Suite 201, Garden Grove, CA 92640). Every pilot must show a valid insurance policy at the border to clear customs. In addition, U.S. Customs requires an annual inspection for planes flying into the U.S.

whether American- or foreign-owned; the inspection costs US$25 but is good for an unlimited number of entries per year.

Air Hitching
It's sometimes possible to hitch rides to other points in Baja on private aircraft or small cargo planes. Don't bother asking foreign pilots, who aren't permitted to carry undeclared passengers.

BY BUS OR TAXI

Intercity Bus Service
Intercity bus transportation in Baja is quite reliable and covers the peninsula from Tijuana to Cabo San Lucas. The longest direct ride available is the Tijuana-La Paz route (about 25-28 hours), operated by **Autotransportes Aguila** and **Tres Estrellas de Oro.** For a bus trip all the way to Cabo, you have to disembark in La Paz and change to one of the many La Paz-Cabo San Lucas buses. Central and southern Baja feature two other intercity bus companies, **ABC** (Autobuses Baja California) and **Autotransportes de La Paz. Transportes Norte de Sonora** operates buses between Tijuana, Tecate, Mexicali, and points farther west, including destinations on the Mexican mainland as far away as Mexico City.

Special express buses with hostess service and air-conditioning are used on long-distance trips. Shorter trips may or may not feature air conditioning, but the buses are always tolerably comfortable, with toilets on board and reclining seats that usually work. The infamous "chicken buses" of southern Mexico and Central America don't exist in Baja.

Fares are inexpensive. A Tijuana-La Paz ticket on a *primera* or first-class bus costs about US$42; second class is half that. The La Paz-to-Cabo San Lucas run is around US$9. Reservations aren't accepted for bus travel. Buses usually depart several times daily, so you simply show up at the bus terminal around the time you want to leave. All the Spanish you need for riding a bus is *boleto* (ticket), the name of your destination (have a map handy just in case), and a reasonable command of spoken Spanish numbers for quoted fares (although the fare is always posted somewhere on the ticket office wall).

City Buses
Tijuana, Ensenada, Mexicali, and La Paz offer comprehensive city bus systems with fares averaging US$.15 to US$.33, payable in pesos only. City buses come in a variety of sizes and shapes, from 12-passenger vans to huge modern vessels with automatic doors. In Mexicali, painted school buses are the norm. The destination or general route—typically a street name—is usually painted somewhere on the front of the bus or displayed on a marquee over the front windshield.

Printed bus schedules are either hard to come by or nonexistent. If you can't figure out which bus to take by comparing the destination sign with a map, just ask other waiting bus passen-

intercity bus service in Baja—extensive and reliable

JOE CUMMINGS

gers or, if your Spanish isn't up to that, make inquiries at the tourist office.

Route Taxis
These same cities also feature *taxis de ruta,* specially licensed cars that follow set routes similar to and often paralleling the bus routes. These vehicles are usually large American station wagons that hold up to 12 passengers. Unlike city buses, you can flag them down anywhere along the route. The destination is usually painted in whitewash on the windshield but locals often distinguish the route by the taxis's two-tone color scheme. A *roja y crema* may run from the central bus station to a market on the outskirts of town while a *negro y azul* may travel from the cathedral to the main shopping district. Other than the terminating points of the route at either end, there are no predetermined taxi stops; passengers must let the driver know where they want off. As on city buses, route taxi fares are the same no matter where you disembark. Usually they're only a bit higher than bus fares, around US$.30-.60.

Hire Taxis
Regular hire taxis congregate at hotels and designated taxi stands in Tijuana, Mexicali, Ensenada, Mulegé, Loreto, La Paz, San José del Cabo, and Cabo San Lucas. Sometimes fares are posted at the hotel or taxi stand, but often you must ask for a fare quote. If possible, try to find out the fare from hotel staff or a friendly resident before approaching a taxi driver—you'll feel more secure about not getting ripped off. If the quoted fare doesn't match what you've been told in advance, you can negotiate or try another driver. Fortunately, most Bajacalifornio city taxi drivers will quote the correct fare immediately.

In smaller towns with no buses or route taxis you may sometimes find a few regular hire taxis hanging out by the town plaza. They're generally used for reaching out-of-town destinations, since anyplace in Baja without a city bus system is small enough to wander around on foot. Although the locals pay a set fare based on distance, gringos are sometimes quoted a much higher fare. Dig in and negotiate until it's reasonable. Even if you can afford the higher fare, you owe it to other foreign visitors not to encourage price-gouging.

CYCLING
Among North American cyclists, Baja is the most popular area in all of Mexico. Traffic is relatively light, the scenery is striking, and cyclists can pull over and camp just about anywhere.

Touring or mountain bike? If you're only heading straight down the peninsula and back on the Transpeninsular, or doing the northern loop on Mexico 2, 3, and 5, a touring bike would be the best choice, as it's lighter and faster than a mountain bike. On the other hand, the Baja peninsula offers so many great off-road rides that anyone who really wants to see Baja—and has the time—should consider a mountain bike, since off-road riding requires a stronger frame, higher clearance, and wider tires.

Many interesting trail rides lie within 95 km (60 miles) of the U.S.-Mexico border. Parque Nacional Constitución de 1857—less than 80 km (50 miles) southwest of Mexicali—is called "fat-tire heaven" by cycling editors at *Outside* magazine, offering rides through startling pine forests and subalpine meadows. The Cataviña Boulder Field in the Central Desert also features some excellent trails; don't forget the anti-puncture booting on that one.

Popular paved touring routes include Tecate to Ensenada (116 km) and Ensenada to San Felipe (236 km), both on scenic Mexico 3, as well as the Cape loop on Mexico 1 and Mexico 19 (La Paz-Cabo San Lucas-Todos Santos-La Paz). Because the Baja sun can be particularly strong when you're on paved surfaces, which both reflect and radiate heat, you may find an 1100-1500 siesta necessary no matter what time of year you ride. Don't forget to bring sunglasses and plenty of high-SPF sunscreen.

Equipment And Repairs
Whether you're riding a mountain or touring bike, you'll need the same basic essentials to handle long-distance Baja riding. If you plan to camp along the way, you'll need the usual camping and first-aid gear, selected to fit your panniers. Camping is often your only choice, even on Transpeninsular trips, since cyclists simply can't make the mileage from hotel to hotel in central Baja. Helmets are particularly important; a head injury is even more serious when you're

in the middle of nowhere. A helmet will also keep direct sun off the top of your skull.

A rearview mirror is a must for keeping an eye on motorists coming from behind on narrow roads. A locking cable is preferable to a clunky U-lock for long-distance trips since it weighs less, although bicycle theft isn't much of a problem in Baja. The only other security you might need is a removable handlebar bag for carrying camera and valuables; you can take the bag with you when stopping at restaurants or tiendas and fill it with snacks for eating on the fly.

Water is an uppermost consideration on overnight trips. No matter what the time of year, cyclists should carry four one-liter bottles of water per day. The one-liter bottles used for cycling are more puncture-resistant than water containers designed for camping. Punctures are always a concern in Baja because of all the trees and plants bearing spines.

Tires: The puncture threat means you should outfit your bike with heavy-duty tires and tubes. Bring along two or three spare tubes, one spare tire, a tire gauge, and a complete tire repair kit. You should also carry duct tape and moleskin—or commercial plastic booting—to use as booting material against sidewall cuts caused by sharp rocks or cactus.

Rack: Check nuts and bolts daily and retighten as necessary. Applying Locktite should lessen the need for retightening—carry a small supply along with extra nuts and bolts. Baling wire can be used for improvised repairs; carry two or three meters along with wirecutters.

Other Repairs: Bike shops operate in Tijuana, Ensenada, San Quintín, Ciudad Constitución, La Paz, and Cabo San Lucas. Although the Mexicans who run these shops can sometimes perform miraculous repairs using nothing resembling a bike's original parts, it's safer to come prepared with spares, especially for parts that aren't easily jury-rigged. At a minimum, carry a spare freewheel, a rear derailleur, and all the wrenches and screwdrivers necessary to work on your bike. If in addition you bring along several extra spokes, cables, and a spare chain, you'll be ready for just about any repair scenario.

Bicycle Transport

You can take bikes on the **Tijuana Trolley** to San Ysidro and then walk over the border, but to get the bike on the trolley you first need a pass from the San Diego AYH Travel Store (tel. 619-226-1221) at 335 W. Beach St., about three blocks from the Columbia St. trolley station. The pass costs US$3 and is valid for three years; it requires a photo but can be issued on the spot. Bikes aren't allowed on the trolley on weekdays during the hours of 0500-0900 and 1500-1800 (see "Getting There" for further trolley details).

Mexicoach and **Greyhound** will transport bikes of paying passengers in bus luggage compartments for no additional cost, but bikes should be boxed. For return trips from Baja, you should be able to pick up a box from bicycle shops in Tijuana or Ensenada, or build your own from discarded cardboard boxes.

Guided Bicycle Trips

If you're unsure of your off-road cycling skills, you might want to tackle Baja with an experienced cycle guide. In Northern Baja, **Baja Cycling Adventures** (tel. 617-8-18-79, Blvd. Costero 609-14, Ensenada, BCN) offers one-day guided mountain-biking trips at nearby Punta Banda and in the more remote Parque Nacional Constitución de 1857.

Backroads (tel. 510-527-1555, fax 527-1444, 1616 Fifth St., Berkeley, CA 94710-1740) organizes fully outfitted, six- and seven-day mountain-biking trips in the Cape Region for US$798-1095.

DRIVING IN BAJA

The most heroic procedure for anyone who has decided to get a general idea of what the whole peninsula is like would be to set out from San Diego in a four-wheel-drive truck well loaded with food, water, camping equipment and reserve gasoline to carry him over the long stretches between the border and the Cape, where nothing is available. He should allow a minimum of ten days of hard driving (it may well take more) to cover the thousand road miles to the tip, and he must be prepared to assume all responsibilities for himself and his car.

The famous naturalist Joseph Wood Krutch wrote the above in his classic *The Forgotten Peninsula* as an introduction to a chapter entitled "Seeing Baja the Easy Way." It's obvious that not

HAS THE TRANSPENINSULAR HIGHWAY RUINED BAJA?

Old Baja Hands grieve over the days pre-1973, when Baja was accessible only to the select few macho enough to brave 800 miles of rutted tracks or wealthy enough to own or charter their own planes. These folks will bore you with lengthy tales of iron nerves and crushing hardships. According to these Old Hands, the completion of the Transpeninsular marked Baja's demise as a land of adventure.

In spite of the ranting and raving, Baja is more stubborn than that. A thin strip of asphalt hasn't yet defeated the peninsula—the Old Hands' nightmare of rampant development hasn't made it much farther south than Ensenada or father north than La Paz, and even in these areas it's confined to slim coastal areas. This represents only a small proportion of the peninsula.

Will the rest succumb in the foreseeable future? Probably not, since several obstacles remain—the lack of water is one, along with the fact that engineers just won't quickly tackle many parts of Baja. Most of the peninsula remains unaffected by Big Plans, leaving enough open wilderness for even the greediest Old Hands . . . if only they'd take the time to leave their rigs and do a little hiking.

Proposed Border-Cape Toll Road

A La Paz consortium proposed construction of a privately funded, four-lane toll road from the U.S-Mexico border to the Cape. The highway would closely follow the Pacific Coast rather than parallel the sometimes mountainous route followed by the current Transpeninsular Highway. The proposal suggests either a road-head at Mexicali or a link-up with the current Tijuana-Ensenada toll road— whether it would terminate at La Paz or Cabo San Lucas is still under debate. Funding would come from a variety of Mexican, U.S., and Japanese companies that would recoup their investments with vehicle toll charges on the highway over a period of 15-20 years. Construction of the road would take at least four years.

The Mexican government has already granted a concession to the consortium for engineering studies, but it remains to be seen whether or not this will be another Baja project that remains eternally stalled in the planning stages. Many people hope it will never get off the ground, while business interests are wildly supportive. If it's ever completed, those of us who've only driven post-Transpeninsular-Highway Baja can join the ranks of the cranky Old Hands, saying "You should have seen Baja before they built the Border-Cape Toll Road."

only was this written in a time (1961) when literary license allowed a writer to use masculine pronouns exclusively when speaking of heroic endeavors, but that it was well before the construction of La Carretera Transpeninsular Benito Juárez, otherwise known as the Transpeninsular Highway or Mexico 1.

Skeletons of cars, vans, and trucks that didn't make it, rusting among the ocotillo and cardón alongside Baja's highways, are visible reminders of this era. If you look closely, you'll notice that some of those decaying hulks are post-1973 models, testifying that a certain challenge remains in spite of the long strip of tarmac winding down the peninsula.

For the most part, however, the 1973 completion of the Transpeninsular opened Baja travel to ordinary folks driving ordinary passenger cars, as long as they employ a little ordinary common sense. For the adventurer, there re-

main miles of unpaved roads that will take you as far from civilization as anyone would care to go. Such off-highway digressions are perfect for those who might agree with another of Krutch's fiats:

Baja California is a wonderful example of how much bad roads can do for a country. Bad roads act as filters. They separate those who are sufficiently appreciative of what lies beyond the blacktop to be willing to undergo mild inconvenience from that much larger number of travelers which is not willing. The rougher the road, the finer the filter.

Baja Highways

A 1988 *Car and Driver* magazine story stated that driving in Baja compared with driving in North America "like hiking in the Rocky Mountains compares with walking on Madison Avenue," a more than slight exaggeration. In terms of how it feels to drive in Baja, however, there's more than a small element of truth in this comparison—people who *really* like to drive will love driving in Baja.

In less romantic terms, driving the Transpeninsular Highway is somewhat similar to two-lane driving in some of the less populated areas of the American Southwest. The two main differences are: 1) there tends to be more variance (sometimes a lot) in road conditions from one section of highway to another; and 2) once you're well into the center of the peninsula you're farther from any significant population centers than on any comparable section of American highway, so that accidents or errors of judgment can have more ramifications. Drivers from western Canada may feel more at home than Americans on desolate sections of Baja highway—except that the terrain is completely different from anything in Canada.

Six paved national highways grace the Baja California peninsula: Mexico 1 (the Transpeninsular, from Tijuana to Cabo San Lucas), Mexico 2 (from Tijuana to Sonora), Mexico 3 (Tecate to El Sauzal, near Ensenada, and east to Crucero La Trinidad at Mexico 5), Mexico 5 (Mexicali to San Felipe), Mexico 19 (between Cabo San Lucas and San Pedro, via Todos Santos), and Mexico 22 (Ciudad Constitución to San Carlos). The only state highways are a small cluster of relatively short blacktops in the northeast corner above the Sea of Cortez (BCN

1, 2, 3, 4, and 8, which link farm communities in the Valle de Mexicali with Mexicali and the state of Sonora), BCN 23 (linking Mexico 1 with Punta Banda), and the solitary BCS 286 in the south between La Paz and San Juan de los Planes.

In addition, Mexico 1 features two alternate routings, a four-lane toll road between Tijuana and Ensenada and a two-lane digression to Bahía de los Angeles on the Sea of Cortez coast. All other roads in Baja are gravel, dirt, or some combination thereof.

Off-highway Travel

Like the highways, Baja's unpaved roads vary considerably, from rutted jeep tracks to elevated, graded, gravel boulevards. The trouble with the graded unpaved roads is that they tend to degenerate rather quickly between gradings into washboard surfaces impossible to drive at anything but very low speeds (8-16 kph/5-10 mph)—unless you want to risk crushed vertebrae and a dropped transmission.

The effect of these unpaved roads on you and your vehicle depends a lot on what you're driving. Some off-highway Baja navigators drive pickups with customized shocks and suspension that enable a driver to float over the worst washboard surfaces. Other drivers—like many of the local residents, who can't afford heavy-duty, customized rigs—learn to drive slowly and appreciate the scenery.

The best unpaved roads in Baja are probably

on the road

JOE CUMMINGS

HOW MUCH FARTHER?

Kilometers (miles) from Tijuana, along the Trans-peninsular Highway, using the Tijuana-Ensenada toll road, rounded off to the nearest kilometer (mile):

Ensenada . . . . 109 km (68 miles)
San Quintín . . . . 301 km (187 miles)
El Rosario . . . . 359 km (223 miles)
Cataviña . . . . 481 km (299 miles)
Punta Prieta . . . . 599 km (372 miles)
Bahía de los Angeles . . 654 km (406 miles)
Guerrero Negro . . . . . 714 km (444 miles)
San Ignacio . . . . 856 km (532 miles)
Santa Rosalía . . . . . . 928 km (577 miles)
Mulegé . . . . 990 km (615 miles)
Loreto . . . . 1,125 km (699 miles)
Ciudad Constitución . . 1,268 km (788 miles)
La Paz . . . . 1,483 km (922 miles)
Cabo San Lucas . . . 1,704 km (1,059 miles)

those that have evolved more or less naturally, with little or no grading. When the weather's right (not wet) some of these roads ride better than the Transpeninsular. Of course, unpaved roads may sometimes start out quite nicely but get increasingly worse with each passing mile, to the point where even the most intrepid explorers are forced to turn around. At other times, a road will suddenly improve after a long stretch of cavernous potholes and caved-in sides. Weather is a big determining factor; even the best ungraded, unpaved roads are often impassable during or following a hard rain.

How do you know when to turn around? There's always an element of risk when driving down a dirt road for the first—or even the hundredth—time, but it helps to ask around before embarking on a road that doesn't see much traffic. A good road map can also assist with such decisions. The AAA map (see "Services and Information") classifies unpaved roads into four categories: gravel, graded, dirt, and poor. The annotated ITM map uses a similar but more specific fourfold system: gravel, graded, unimproved dirt, and vehicular track. Although neither of these maps is entirely up to date or 100%

accurate, using one or both in conjunction with local input will greatly improve your decision-making. A topographical map could be of considerable value to a 4WD navigator as well, since sometimes it's the steep canyon grades that mean defeat.

Even with the best planning there's always the possibility of getting stuck in muddy or sandy areas. Anyone engaging in serious off-highway driving should carry along a sturdy shovel for digging out mired wheels. Another handy trick for negotiating soft ground is to let the air out of your tires to a pressure of around 12-15 psi. This really works, but you should also carry along a 12-volt air compressor, one that will plug into the cigarette lighter, for pumping the tires back up after you're on firm ground again.

Organized Trips: 4-Wheeling (tel. 714-707-1340, fax 707-1346, 11 Melody Hill Lane, Aliso Viejo, CA 92653) is a 4WD club that organizes off-highway trips in Baja and Northwest Mexico. Dedicated to safe and ecological off-highway driving, the trips are led by recognized industry expert Harry "Silver Coyote" Lewellyn.

Driving Precautions

The first rule of Baja driving, no matter what kind of road you're on, is *never* take the road for granted. Any highway in Baja, including the Transpeninsular, can serve up 100 meters of smooth, seamless blacktop followed immediately by 100 meters of contiguous potholes or large patches of missing asphalt. A cow, horse, or burro could be right around the next curve, or a large dog can leap out in front of your vehicle just as you fasten your eyes on a turkey vulture drying its wings on top of a tall cardón.

The speed limits set by the Mexican government—80 km per hour (48 mph) on most highways, 110 kph (66 mph) on the Ensenada toll road—are very reasonable for Baja's highway conditions. Obey them and you'll be much safer than if you try to keep the speedometer needle in the spot you're accustomed to. Wandering livestock, relatively narrow highways widths (6-8 meters/19-25 feet max), and inconsistent highway maintenance mean you simply can't drive at U.S.-Canada speeds.

Most Baja roadways also suffer from a conspicuous lack of shoulders. This doesn't mean you won't find any places to pull off, as many Baja writers have implied—gravel turnouts ap-

AUTOMOTIVE EQUIPMENT

Although plenty of visitors drive the length of the Baja peninsula and back without so much as a spare tire, anyone driving long distances in Baja should consider bringing the following extras, regardless of the type of vehicle:

✔ air filters
✔ battery cables
✔ brake, steering, and transmission fluids
✔ fan belts
✔ fuel filters
✔ fuses
✔ lug wrench and jack
✔ radiator hoses
✔ spare tire
✔ spark plugs
✔ water filters
✔ one or two five-gallon gas cans
✔ one five-gallon water container
✔ emergency flares
✔ fire extinguisher
✔ 18-meter (60-foot) tow rope
✔ tire gauge
✔ tube repair kit
✔ 12-volt air compressor

pear fairly regularly, and in many areas you can drive directly onto the roadside from the highway. It just means you can't count on a safe margin in an emergency situation. At the very least, an emergency turnout will raise a lot of rocks and dirt—small dangers in themselves— and in some spots, like the sierras on Mexico 3, leaving the highway can launch you and your vehicle into a thousand-foot freefall. Guardrails are often flimsy or nonexistent.

Yet another reason not to take the road for granted is the high number of sometimes unmarked blind curves and the blind hilltops in areas of varied elevation. Never assume a clear path around a curve or over a hilltop—potential obstructions include an oblivious 18-wheeler or bus passing in the opposite direction, wandering livestock, rockslides, or road washouts. To be on the safe side, keep toward the outside edge of your own lane. Commercial truck drivers in Baja roar down the road as if they're exempt from all speed limits, almost always flying at least 40 kph over the posted limit.

Rule number two is never drive the highways at

night. Except along portions of the Ensenada toll road, Baja highways have no lighting. In addition, reflectors and even painted lines are absent from many highway sections; even if no other vehicles besides your own were on the road at night, you could easily overshoot an unexpected curve. Add to this the fact that many poorly maintained local vehicles have nonfunctioning headlights, taillights, or brakelights and it should be obvious that trying to make highway miles after sundown is crazy. Some Bajacalifornios may do it, but they're used to local conditions and know the roads relatively well. Still, a high proportion of car accidents in Baja—around 80% according to insurance companies—occur at night.

Specific Hazards: When you see road signs marked Vado or Zona De Vados, slow down. The word *vado* is most often translated as "dip," but in Baja it usually means more than a slight depression in the road—it's any place where the road intersects an *arroyo,* or dry stream wash. The danger lies not only in the sudden grade drop but in the potential for running into a recently accumulated body of water. Some vados feature measuring sticks marked in meters; when water is present, you'll know roughly how deep it is. If you come to a vado full of water with no measuring stick, get out of your vehicle and measure the depth yourself using an ocotillo branch or other suitable object.

Vados aren't always signposted, so stay alert—they appear even on relatively flat terrain. Some vados are relatively mild road dips, while others are particularly treacherous, even in dry weather. The vados south of San Felipe on the road to Puertecitos are deadly—crossing them at a high rate of speed can severely damage the undercarriage of a passenger car.

Also watch out for **sand drifts,** which often aren't visible until it's almost too late to avoid them. They're most common in the San Felipe area but can occur anywhere in Baja where a road runs through sandy terrain.

In towns, pueblos, ejidos, or anywhere else people live in Baja, you'll encounter *topes* (speed bumps). Often unpainted and unsignposted, they can really sneak up on you. Some topes are real industrial-strength tire-poppers, so always take it very slow when traversing them.

Highway Signs

One of the pleasures of driving in Baja is the

ROAD SIGNS

stop

railroad crossing

parking

no parking

one way

two way

dip

dip

yield right of way

left turn only

bus stop

keep to the right

relative absence of signs cluttering the roadside. Billboards, in fact, are virtually nonexistent. The Mexican government does have a system of highway signs, however, based on common international sign conventions followed throughout most of the world; these can be very helpful as long as you know what they mean. Most display self-explanatory symbols (e.g., a silhouette of a man holding a shovel means "men working").

Along the Transpeninsular Highway as well as on many secondary roads, you can measure driving progress with the assistance of regularly spaced kilometer markers, usually black lettering on a reflective white background. In northern Baja these markers start at zero (K0) in Tijuana and ascend in number as you proceed southward. Starting at *paralelo* 28, the state borderline between BCN and BCS, the markers descend as you move southward, beginning with K220 in Guerrero Negro. These contrary directions can be traced to the original construction of the Transpeninsular, which started at either end of the peninsula and met in the middle. To further add to the confusion, sometimes the numbers run only as far as the next town, then start over. Still, the markers can be a significant navigational aid, especially when you want to take note of a remote off-highway spot for a future trip.

Cautionary sign captions are especially helpful, including Curva Peligrosa (Dangerous Curve), Despacio (Slow), and Zona de Vados (Dip Zone). Other common highway signs include: Desviación (Detour), No Tire Basura (Don't Throw Trash), Conserve Su Derecha (Keep to the Right), Concida Cambio de Luces (Dim Your Lights), No Rebase (No Passing), and No Hay Paso (Road Closed).

If you're having tire trouble, look for homemade signs reading Llantera, which indicate tire repair shops.

Traffic Offenses

Although Mexican traffic police don't go out of their way to persecute foreign drivers, it may seem that way when you're the foreigner who's stopped. The more cautiously you drive, the less likely you'll inadvertently transgress local traffic codes. This would seem like obvious advice, but for some reason many visiting motorists in Baja drive as if they thought there were no traffic laws in Mexico. Most of these people seem to have California plates.

If you're stopped by a *tránsito* (traffic cop), the first rule is to behave in a patient, civil manner. The officer might then let you off with just a warning. If the officer decides to make a case of it, you'll be asked to proceed to the nearest police post or station, where a fine will be assessed and collected. This is a perfectly legal request. But if the cop suggests or even hints at being paid on the spot, you're being hit up for *la mordida,* the minor bribe.

In Baja, requests for mordida from foreigners—for traffic offenses, at least—have become increasingly rare, and the government is trying hard to stamp the practice out altogether. If confronted with such a situation, you have two choices. Mexico's Attorney General for the Protection of Tourists recommends you insist on going to the nearest station to pay the fine, and that as you pay you request a receipt. Such a request may result in all charges being dropped. If you don't feel like taking the time for a trip to the station, you can choose to negotiate the "fine" on the

spot. Doing so, however, won't contribute to the shrinking of the mordida phenomenon.

Along Mexico 1-D, the toll highway between Tijuana and Ensenada, the federal highway police have recently begun using radar speed detectors. Fines are assessed at a day's Mexican minimum wage (currently about US$5) for each kilometer over the speed limit. The fine is the same for foreigners as for Mexican nationals. The offender's driving license is attached to the citation and delivered to the nearest Baja *transito* station, or to another Baja station chosen by the offender, where the license is returned upon payment of the assessed fine. If you're cited just outside Tijuana, for example, you can elect to settle your citation in Ensenada.

Aside from speeding on Mexico 1-D, driving the wrong direction on one-way streets and running stop signs are the two most common traffic violations among foreign drivers in Baja. In Ensenada, for example, the stop (*Alto*) signs seem almost intentionally hidden in places; also, several intersections display no vertical signs at all, only broad stripes painted on the pavement indicating where vehicles are supposed to stop. The best practice is to assume you're supposed to stop at every single intersection in the city, which is pretty close to the truth. This can be generalized to include most other urban areas on the peninsula.

In Mulegé only two streets in town are open to two-way traffic; all the others are supposed to be one-way, although they're not signposted at every intersection. Always look carefully at the cars driving or parked on a street to determine which direction is legal before turning.

Note to patriotic visitors: In Mexico it's illegal to display any foreign national flag except over an embassy or consulate. A miniature flag flying from a vehicle's radio antenna provides Mexican police with a valid excuse to pull you over. It may also invite vandalism—Mexicans are extremely nationalistic. This is rarely a problem, but don't say you weren't warned.

Insurance

It's very important to carry a Mexican liability-insurance policy on your vehicle while driving in Baja. In case of an accident, such a policy could keep you from going to jail. For details on Mexican insurance, see "Driving to Baja."

Fuel

The only automotive fuel commercially available in Baja is sold at government-owned PEMEX stations. The total number of PEMEX stations in Baja varies from year to year, but they're always scarce outside the large cities. It's best to top off your tank whenever it reaches the half-empty mark and there's a PEMEX station at hand.

Three kinds of fuel are available: leaded ("Nova"), a higher-octane unleaded ("Magna Sin"), and diesel. All three are priced by PEMEX according to standard rates and shouldn't vary from station to station. All three fuels are somewhat more expensive in Mexico than their equivalents in the U.S. or Canada; the price is usually marked in pesos on the pump. The pump readout often accommodates only three or four digits, so a N$25 (25,000-peso) sale may appear as 2500, 25.00, 250, or 25.0. Although this may sound like it could be a problem when paying up, it's not once you're used to seeing it.

It helps to get out of your vehicle to keep an eye on the pumping procedures. If you're confused by the pump readout, currency conversion, or price per liter, carry a handheld calculator to make sure it all adds up; a calculator held in clear view will deter most potential grifters. As new pumps are added they will be calibrated to read in nuevo pesos to conform to the new currency system instituted in January 1992. This should make calculations considerably easier.

As of mid-1994, official government fuel prices per liter were US$.43 for Magna Sin (about US$1.63 per gallon), US$.42 for Nova (US$1.50/gallon), and US$.31 for diesel (US$1.11/gallon). Since PEMEX is government-owned, you don't see the week-to-week price fluctuations common in countries where oil companies are privately owned and rates influenced by small changes in international oil prices. According to recent Mexican government announcements, both Magna Sin and Nova are scheduled to increase by .8% a month in '94, for a total price increase of about 10% by the end of the year. Diesel prices are scheduled to rise just .010 new pesos per month.

Rumors about the quality of PEMEX fuels sometimes suggest an extra fuel filter or additive are necessary. This may have been the case 10 or more years ago, but nowadays PEMEX fuel seems to perform well with all types of vehicles.

The main problem with PEMEX fuel remains its availability. Stations are sometimes widely spaced or abandoned and not all stations carry unleaded gasoline. In a pinch, you can use leaded gas in vehicles intended for unleaded without an appreciative difference in performance. Adding a can of octane booster to each tankful seems to help. You shouldn't be forced to burn more than a tankful of leaded here and there, if at all, since most PEMEX stations in Baja dispense unleaded; in fact, Magna Sin is now more widely available in Baja than in mainland Mexico. All gas stations mentioned in this guidebook generally stock Magna Sin unless otherwise noted.

Other availability-related problems include long lines at small-town stations—the lines at the Mulegé PEMEX are legendary—and the occasional selling out of one or all types of fuel at a particular station. To notify customers, the hose will usually be draped over the top of a pump when it's empty. Major culprits for pump sell-outs are North American RV caravans; if 10 or 15 RVs fuel up at a PEMEX station when it's between deliveries, the station may have to shut down until the next PEMEX tanker arrives.

Liquefied Petroleum Gas (LPG): LPG fuel is available in Baja. The price per liter is about the same as for Magna Sin when bought for vehicular purposes. LPG sold for heating and cooking is subsidized and costs less than in the U.S. or Canada. The difficulty is finding it. Look for signs reading *butano*.

Oil: Motor oil is widely available at tiendas and PEMEX stations throughout Baja. If your vehicle takes anything lower than 30-weight, however, you'd better bring along your own; most places stock only 30- or 40-weight oil.

Parts And Repairs

Good auto shops and mechanics are available in Tijuana, Mexicali, Ensenada, La Paz, and, to a lesser extent, San Quintín, El Rosario, Mulegé, Loreto, and Cabo San Lucas. Elsewhere in Baja, if you have a breakdown, it's either do it yourself or rely on the mercy of passing drivers. In areas where you can find a mechanic, the following makes can usually be serviced: Chevrolet, Dodge, Ford, Nissan, Toyota, and Volkswagen. For anything else, you should carry spare filters, plugs, points, hoses, belts, and gaskets—even for the shortest of trips.

Ensenada Toll Road Assistance: Mexico's federal highway department has installed 29 roadside call boxes at approximate three-km intervals along the Tijuana-Ensenada toll road. Calls are free and bilingual operators are on duty 24 hours a day to help arrange emergency medical or automotive assistance.

Green Angels
The Secretaría de Turismo operates a fleet of 275 green trucks called Angeles Verdes ("Green Angels") that patrol Baja's highways and offer professional assistance to anyone with automotive problems. Each truck carries a first-aid kit, a shortwave radio, gasoline, and a variety of common auto parts. They're usually staffed by two uniformed employees, one of whom may speak some English. The drivers will perform minor repairs for the cost of the parts and can provide towing for distances up to 24 km (15 miles). If they can't remedy the problem or tow your vehicle to a nearby mechanic, they'll give you a lift and/or arrange for other assistance.

The trucks supposedly patrol assigned highway sections at least twice a day; the author's experience is that the Green Angels are much more commonly seen south of Santa Rosalía, where they're most needed due to the longer distances between towns.

Trailers And RVs
Baja is a popular destination for people with trailers and RVs. Not only are there plenty of RV parks with services, but you can pull off the road and camp just about anywhere outside the cities, with few restrictions. Those restrictions that do exist are largely physical; numerous places simply can't accommodate a wide trailer or motor home because of narrow roadways, steep grades, or sharp curves. Even the Transpeninsular is tight in some places. In fact, you shouldn't even attempt a Baja trip in any rig wider than three meters (nine feet).

Caravans: An RV caravan, in which a number of individual RV owners travel as an organized group with a caravan leader, is one way to accomplish an RV trip to Baja. Average costs run about US$100 a day, not including food and gasoline. In theory, RV caravans are a great introduction to Baja for RVers apprehensive about going it alone.

The reality, however, is that everyone else on the road will grow to hate an RV caravan if its members cause traffic jams—especially on winding, mountainous roads—or suck the PEMEX stations dry. Those traveling to Baja in RV caravans must therefore carefully monitor their own behavior to assure they do not become a menace or trial to others on the road. Caravans limited to no more than two or three vehicles are probably best.

Campers And Vans
Probably the rig most suited to Baja travel is a well-equipped camper or van. With a bed, two five-gallon water containers, a small propane stove and refrigerator, and a portable toilet, you can travel just as independently as someone driving a 40-foot motor home. Add a deep-cycle RV battery under the hood and you can run a

automotive angels

JOE CUMMINGS

variety of electrical appliances for at least a week without turning over your engine. For extra power, mount a solar panel on top of the cab or camper.

When tricking out your rig, consider oversize tires for more traction and road clearance, overload shocks to protect your vehicle and its contents on rough roads, and a rollbar over the front seats. Whether or not you have high clearance, skid plates under your fuel tank, engine, and transmission are a good idea if you plan any off-highway driving.

What's the perfect Baja rig? Such a beast doesn't really exist, of course, since we all have individual needs. (How about a kayak with wings?) Probably a near-perfect rig would combine features of the self-sufficient camper as described above with those of a rugged 4WD vehicle featuring a turning circle of six meters (20 feet) or less. Ambitious Baja hands have successfully tried everything from jeeps to three-ton diesel cabs as bases for custom-built campers. **Callen Camper** (tel. 619-442-3305) in El Cajon, Alta California, specializes in custom-outfitting Baja camper rigs.

Car Rental

You can rent cars in Tijuana, Mexicali, Ensenada, Loreto, La Paz, San José del Cabo, and Cabo San Lucas. In general, Tijuana, Cabo San Lucas, and San José del Cabo offer the least expensive rentals, while Ensenada and Loreto feature the most expensive. At many agencies, various Volkswagen models are all that's available; most rental places charge daily rates of around US$25-29 for a VW bug, US$45 for a Jetta, and US$48-55 for a van. Add on fees ranging from US$.18 to US$.30 per kilometer. Rates include Mexican liability insurance, but not collision damage. For added collision coverage, figure an extra US$6-10 a day.

If you're planning on driving long distances, you can save money by arranging a flat rate with no kilometer costs. If you can rent by the week, the savings increase considerably. Currently the best long-distance deal in Baja is from the Avis agency in Tijuana: a new, made-in-Mexico VW bug (no air-conditioning or radio) for US$159 per week, with unlimited free kilometers.

Rentals out of San Diego are sometimes a bit cheaper, but those few agencies that allow their cars into Mexico won't allow them any further

south than Guerrero Negro. They often add mandatory collision damage waivers to the cost as well. The VW bug, incidentally, is one of the best non-4WD passenger cars for Baja travel since the engine is air-cooled (no radiator boilovers) and the road clearance is a bit above average. Should you care to purchase one in Mexico, they're available new for around US$7000; the demand is so high that waiting lists of up to five months aren't uncommon.

Motorcycles

Much of Baja is excellent motorcycle country. The winding sierra roads are especially challenging and since traffic is generally light you can really let it rip. Another advantage of motorcycle travel in Baja is that if your bike gets mired in soft ground, you can almost always extricate it without assistance.

As with automotive travel in Baja, pre-departure planning is important. You should be able to carry enough gear in two panniers and a backpack (tied down on the rear) for a trip all the way down the peninsula. I met a Japanese biker with just such an arrangement heading across the Sea of Cortez by ferry to the mainland and on to the Panama Canal—his second trip along this route.

Motorcycle mechanics in Baja are few and far between—you must be entirely self-reliant to make this trip safely and successfully. Besides the usual camping and first-aid gear, bikers should carry all tools needed for routine maintenance, spare brake shoes, a tire repair kit, spare levers, an extra battery, a clutch cable, spare light bulbs, a four-liter reserve gas can, and a spare helmet visor.

For a transpeninsular trip, any bike smaller than 600cc is too small. A four-stroke gets better mileage than a two-stroke, an important consideration given the Baja gas station situation. Experienced Baja bikers replace standard fuel tanks with larger 20-liter tanks to extend their fuel range.

The same driving precautions that apply to four-wheel driving should be followed by bikers as well. Special care should be taken when negotiating blind curves since buses and trucks in Baja aren't used to seeing motorcycles on the highway. As with bicycle touring, motorcyclists may find that an 1100-1500 siesta is necessary to avoid the sun's worst rays.

BOB RACE

NORTHWESTERN BAJA
TIJUANA

With a population exceeding one million, Tijuana is the fourth largest city in Mexico. It's also one of Mexico's youngest cities, established as a line of defense against *filibusteros* following the Treaty of Guadalupe Hidalgo in 1848. During the U.S. Prohibition era, Tijuana developed a bawdy, rough-and-tumble reputation with its casinos, cantinas, and bordellos; for many North Americans, the image has outlasted the reality.

Today's Tijuana is a rapidly modernizing, bicultural city, with skyscrapers and shopping malls replacing yesterday's shantytowns, and discos outnumbering cantinas. A nearby industrial zone supports over 500 *maquiladora* or in-bond plants where international companies such as Sony, Kodak, and Mattel manufacture export products. Tijuana's colleges and universities (Colegio de la Frontera Norte, Iberoamericana University, Universidad Autonoma de Baja California) attract students from all over the peninsula as well as northwestern Mexico.

For some visitors "TJ" is merely a gateway to Baja while for others—especially San Diegans—it's a destination in its own right. Like the rest of Baja, Tijuana enjoys duty-free status and hence one of its main attractions is shopping—everything from Casas Grandes pottery to Tequila Sauza to Luis Vuitton luggage is available at discount prices. Avenida Revolución, once the city's booze-and-gambling center, is now lined with restaurants, cafes, and boutiques. Bullfights are no longer the only cultural attraction; the Tijuana Cultural Center and other city venues host symphonies, theater, art exhibits, and other events, thus firmly establishing Tijuana as northern Baja's cultural heart.

CLIMATE

As in nearby San Diego, the climate in Tijuana is moderate all year round owing to the confluence of Pacific and desert environments. November through March, temperatures average 15° C (60° F) during the day, 12° C (53° F) at night. Rain is more likely this time of year but generally amounts to less than 25 centimeters (10 inches) per annum—not enough to deter a visit.

June-Sept., daytime temperatures average 22-29° C (72-85° F), nighttime 18-21° C (65-70° F). It rarely rains during the summer months; on still days, however, a thin layer of smog may collect over the city—though never as bad as in Los Angeles, the smog's source. Fall and spring temperatures are in the low 20s C (70s F).

HISTORY

The Frontier
Before the end of the Mexican-American War in 1848, when the Río Tijuana was designated as the westernmost portion of the U.S.-Mexico border, no town as such existed in the shallow river valley. Until the postwar border agreement, the border between Alta and Baja California lay about 20 miles farther south near El Descanso.

San Dieguito and Yumano Indian cultures intermittently occupied the area before the Spanish came in the late 17th century; the Yumano called the valley Ti-wan, meaning "Near-The-Sea." Early 19th-century maps refer to the Río Tijuana as Arroyo de Tijuan, obviously a Spanish rendering of the Yumano name. A local Mexican ranch in existence as early as 1809 was called Rancho Tia Juana—"Tijuan" had no Spanish meaning and "Tia Juana" ("Aunt Jane") was easier to pronounce. Anglo settlers in Alta California somehow latched onto this name and today many North Americans persist in calling the city "Tia-wana." The pronunciation might have remained a southern California colloquialism if it hadn't been for the Kingston Trio's 1959 international hit, "The Tia Juana Jail."

In the 1870s the Mexican government established a small customs house at the border, but Tijuana would probably have remained nothing more than a ranching area if it hadn't been for the development of San Diego across the border. In 1887 a savvy developer built the sprawling Hotel del Coronado, which advertised the locale's favorable year-round climate and quickly became a famous resort. A minor gold rush in the El Alamo area of northern Baja in 1888 brought additional American attention to the border area.

The Mexicans, knowing that wherever Americans congregated there was a danger of losing real estate, created the "Pueblo de Tijuana" or Town of Tijuana in 1889. During the Spanish-American War in 1898, San Diego grew further with the establishment of a U.S. naval base, and following the war many Navy men and their families chose to remain in the San Diego area. By the turn of the century, local entrepreneurs had opened several small resort hotels in Tijuana to compete with those in San Diego. Visitors made the 64-km (40-mile) trip between San Diego and Tijuana by horse or stagecoach; since there was no bridge in those days it was necessary to ford the Río Tijuana.

U.S. attention focused on Tijuana during a local revolution in the early 1900s. Following the 1910 Mexican revolution, a group of International Workers of the World ("Wobblies") affiliated with the Mexican Liberal Party briefly took control of the town under the leadership of Ricardo Magón. Hundreds of San Diegans watched from the U.S. side of the border as Mexican federal troops entered Tijuana on 22 June 1911 to rout the Magonistas, killing 31 rebels. This was the first time many Americans had heard of Tijuana.

Prohibition And Tourism
The town's frontier image was further enhanced in 1915 when the Tijuana Fair proffered bullfights, horse racing, boxing, cockfighting, and casino gambling. Curious San Diegans came in droves for the event, but Tijuana returned to its sleepy state once the fair was over. The city boomed practically overnight, however, when the San Diego city government banned cabaret dancing in 1917; as Tijuana's casinos and cabarets multiplied, the city began drawing visitors from Hollywood—only a three-hour drive away.

The 1920 grand opening of Tijuana's magnificent El Casino de Agua Caliente coincided with the announcement of the 18th Amendment to the U.S. Constitution, which prohibited the sale, manufacture, and consumption of alcoholic beverages. Well-heeled U.S. residents flocked to the plush new casino, which had no peer anywhere in the Americas. The lavish interior blended art deco, Spanish colonial, Moorish, and French provincial designs; Hollywood glitterati such as Douglas Fairbanks, Jean Harlow, Rita Hayworth, Clark Gable, Dolores del Rio, and the Aga Khan danced on its Italian marble floors beneath Louis XV chandeliers.

LA FRONTERA

The U.S. and Mexico share a thousand-mile border that is more than a political boundary. When residents on either side of the border refer to "La Frontera," they're talking about an area that extends as far as a hundred miles north and south of the Rio Grande. This is the center of a hybrid culture that's neither American nor Mexican; here First World meets Third World; north European, Protestant capitalism meets south European, Catholic feudalism.

Despite the fact that Mexico is the U.S.'s third-largest trading partner, La Frontera is one of the poorest areas in either country. The burgeoning twin-plant (*maquila* or *maquiladora*) industry along the border, in which American—or Canadian, European, or Japanese—technology and management exploits cheap Mexican labor, is supposed to be the hope of the future for the borderland. Goods produced at these plants are granted special trade status since they're established in "export processing zones" using U.S. capital. As the number of *maquilas* increases, more unemployed Mexicans migrate to northern Mexico in hopes of landing steady, though low-paying, jobs. Once on the border there's the attraction of higher-paying work just over the river, so labor tends to flow back and forth. Human taxis even wade across carrying passengers on their backs (25 cents a trip) during "commute" hours.

Human Smuggling

A 27-km stretch along the border between the Otay Mountains and the Pacific Ocean, commonly called *la tierra de nadie* (no man's land), is the busiest area of illegal human traffic in the world. Ninety percent of all illegal entries into the U.S. state of California occur here. Visitors driving south just north of the Tijuana international gateway often see Mexicans running in and out of wooded areas alongside the freeway as they make their way into or out of Mexico—part of the daily commute.

For more permanent immigration, and to better avoid the U.S. Border Patrol, "coyotes" or *polleros* regularly lead small groups of seven to 10 *pollos* ("chickens," undocumented immigrants) across the border, delivering them to Los Angeles for fees of around US$300 per Mexican, US$400-500 per Central American; portions of these fees are used to pay safe houses and drivers along the way. Once they've arrived, the immigrants easily blend into the huge, ever-growing Hispanic population in Los Angeles.

A 1980s Rand Corporation report concluded that Mexican immigration, illegal or otherwise, did not pose a true economic or political crisis for the U.S. The evidence, in fact, clearly indicates that the influx of Mexican labor provides strong economic benefits for Southwestern states that greatly outweigh the undocumented immigrants' use of public facilities and services.

As the Tijuana high life boomed, rich American investors poured millions of dollars into developing more racetracks, casinos, hotels, restaurants, and high-class bordellos. Mexicans from the interior of Mexico, hearing that the gutters of Tijuana ran with money (literally true inasmuch as drunk Americans were notorious for dropping change and greenbacks as they stumbled in and out of taxis), rushed to Tijuana as well.

Post-WW II Tijuana

Tijuana's golden days of sin lasted until the repeal of Prohibition in 1933; the ensuing slump became a crash when President Lázaro Cárdenas outlawed casino gambling in 1938. Baja—and the rest of Mexico—was able to reverse its precipitous economic decline with the outbreak of WW II. To aid in alleviating unemployment in

the border area, and to provide needed labor for the wartime U.S. economy, the U.S. and Mexico created the Bracero Program in 1942; this program gave Mexican workers the temporary right to work for American agricultural concerns in Alta California. Another action that prevented Tijuana from becoming a ghost town was the declaration of Baja California as a duty-free zone.

The expansion of San Diego's military presence during WW II brought a new prosperity to the San Diego-Tijuana area, and shopping gradually replaced boozing and gambling as the main Tijuana attraction. Many Alta Californians crossed the border regularly to purchase items rationed in the U.S. during the war—stockings, butter, meat, gasoline. Eventually, Tijuana began to grow even faster than San Diego; between 1950 and 1970 the city's population grew 600%.

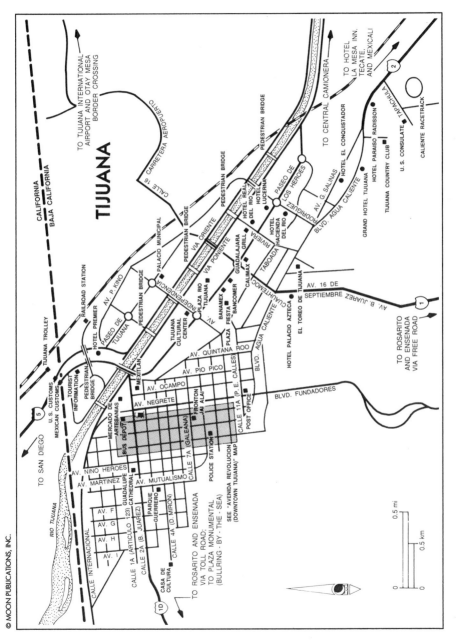

This growth severely taxed the city's infrastructure as Tijuana became ringed by shantytowns practically overnight.

The situation of too many people and too few jobs created problems on both sides of the border. Although the U.S. discontinued the Bracero Program in the early '60s, the flow of migrant labor to Alta California continued. Improper sewage and garbage disposal on both sides of the border threatened to turn the San Diego-Tijuana area into an environmental disaster. Periodic flooding of the Río Tijuana was a bane to communities on either side as unchecked development came ever closer to the river.

Because there was simply no other alternative, U.S.-Mexico cooperation over the last 20 years has begun to deal successfully with these problems. The arrival of the *maquiladoras* in the '70s and '80s alleviated unemployment to some degree, and stricter law enforcement is halting much of the environmental damage caused by uncontrolled waste disposal. Channelization of the Río Tijuana at the border, under the auspices of the International Boundaries and Water Commission (IBWC), solved the flood problem.

More recent economic reform at the national level allowed Tijuana a wider selection of resources, including foreign investment, with which to develop a livable city. Visitors who haven't been to Tijuana for some time may be surprised to find the city has made great strides during the last decade or so and now enjoys one of the highest standards of living of any city in Mexico. Conditions have improved to such a degree that many U.S. citizens who work in San Diego now reside in Tijuana, where living costs are at least a third lower than those north of the border.

SIGHTS

Mexitlán

Tijuana's latest tourist attraction, a new theme park on Av. Ocampo between Calles 2a and 3a, represents a "Mexico-in-miniature" concept. The focus of the 15,000 square-meter complex, built over a huge parking garage, is a permanent exhibit of around 200 scale replicas (1:25) of famous Mexican archaeological monuments, from Mayan to Spanish colonial to modern. The tallest model recreates the Mexicana Airlines building in Mexico City. Designed by Pedro Ramírez Vásquez, architect of the Tijuana Cultural Center as well as Mexico City's Museum of Anthropology and Aztec Stadium, the models are illuminated from sunset until midnight.

Shops on the street level offer ongoing arts-and-crafts demonstrations, while a stage on the terrace features folk dancing and various styles of Mexican music. Facilities include seven Mexican restaurants, purified water fountains, handicapped access to all areas, and locker, stroller, and wheelchair rentals. Garage parking is free for the first two hours.

Although Mexitlán is a premier attraction, visitation hasn't yet approached a profitable level and there are rumors the whole show will move to Mexico City. Apparently the hordes of day visitors to Tijuana are afraid to walk two short blocks east of Av. Revolución to the park. Do yourself a favor if you visit Tijuana and check out Mexitlán before it disappears. Admission to Mexitlán has recently been reduced from US$9.50 to US$3.50 per adult, free for children under 12; the U.S. dollar, pesos, and credit cards are accepted. The exhibits and restaurants are open Tues.-Sun. 1100-2200 during the summer, 1200-2000 the remainder of the year. For more information, call 38-41-01 in Tijuana, (619) 531-1112 in the U.S., or (800) 834-4939 in California.

Centro Cultural Tijuana

This huge, government-built complex at the intersection of Paseo de los Héroes and Av. Independencia is one of the most distinctive monuments in the city, designed by Pedro Ramírez Vásquez, the same architect responsible for Mexico City's Museum of Anthropology. The centerpiece of the complex is the spherical **Space Theater,** meant to resemble the Earth emerging from a broken shell. Three Omnimax-style films are presented daily, with the main attraction *The People of the Sun,* a pan-Mexico travelogue shown daily at 1400 with English narration, and at 1600 on weekends with Spanish narration. Admission to the English version costs US$3.35 adults, US$1.65 children; for the Spanish, US$2.30. The other two films change periodically. A Space Theater ticket entitles the holder to free museum admission.

The center's **Museum of Mexican Identities** features historical, anthropological, and archaeological displays focusing on various Mexican ethnic groups. The exhibits pack a lot of information into a relatively compact area negotiated by an ascending ramp—a pleasant change from the angular stairways found in most museums. Hours are 1100-2000; guided English-language tours are offered at 1400 weekdays, 1300 weekends. Museum admission is US$1.25.

Other Cultural Center facilities include a 1,000-seat performing-arts theater where the National Symphony and Ballet Folklorico perform regularly, exhibit halls with rotating art exhibits, a restaurant serving *platillos típicos,* a bookstore specializing in materials on Baja California, and a shopping arcade with nine shops selling Mexican arts and crafts.

During the summer months an outdoor area features cultural performances by groups such as the Papantla Flyers, a music and dance troupe from Veracruz that performs 1,500-year-old ritual dances from the top of a 30-meter pole.

Tijuana Wax Museum

Opened in 1992, the Wax Museum (tel. 88-24-78, 8281 Calle 1a at Av. Madero) presents a collection of Mexican and international celebrities (Marilyn Monroe, Elvis, Lola Beltrán), horror faves (Jack the Ripper, the Wolfman), and Mexican historical figures such as Pancho Villa and

Miguel Hidalgo y Costilla. This is a good place to kill some time if you're waiting for a bus at the nearby downtown terminal. Admission is US$3 adults, US$2 children 6-12, under six free; open daily 1000-2000.

Catedral Nuestra Señora De Guadalupe

At Calle 2a and Av. Constitución, this large, urban cathedral is only worth a visit if you're Catholic or you've never seen a Mexican cathedral. The interior is perhaps more impressive than the exterior. Vendors on the adjacent sidewalks sell Catholic ritual objects.

Parque Teniente Vicente Guerrero

Tijuana doesn't have a *zócalo* or public square, but four blocks west of Av. Revolución off Calle 3a is a park where late-afternoon strollers may tarry for a few minutes or hours. It's dedicated to the heroes of the 1911 Tijuana battle against the Magonistas; the park's namesake, Lieutenant Guerrero, led the federal troops who quashed the rebellion.

Art Exhibits

Tijuana attracts artists from all over the country and in recent years has become known as an arts center for northern Mexico. The Tijuana Cultural Center is the main showcase for traveling exhibitions but modern artists' works can also be seen at several private galleries in the **Plaza Fiesta** center on Paseo de los Héroes, diagonally opposite the Cultural Center.

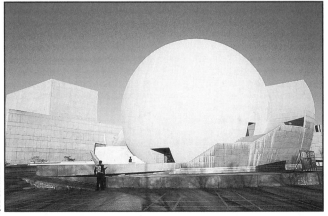

JOE CUMMINGS

Centro Cultural Tijuana

Popular Mexican mural art is found throughout the city; the **Palacio Municipal** (County Hall) on Paseo de Tijuana features several examples. On the third-floor wall is a mural depicting the history of Mexico while on the second floor hangs a *Rebirth of Baja California* mural; other floors have murals as well.

ACCOMMODATIONS

Hotels And Motels

Plenty of rooms are available in Tijuana for those who choose to spend the night. One of the two best hotels in town is the landmark **Grand Hotel**

TIJUANA HOTELS AND MOTELS

Note: Add 10% hotel tax to all rates; some hotels may charge an additional 10% service charge. Area code: 66

Caesar; Av. Revolución 827; tel. 85-16-06; US$30-35; heat, a/c, restaurant

Corona Plaza; Blvd. Agua Caliente 1426; tel. 81-81-83; US$55-63; a/c, pool, restaurants, parking

*****Country Club**; Calle Tapachula 1 (at Blvd. Agua Caliente); tel. 81-77-33, fax 81-70-66; US$53-63; heat, a/c, restaurant, pool, jacuzzi, sauna, parking

Del Mar; Calle 1 1948 (Articulo 123); tel. 85-73-02; US$15-20

El Conquistador; Blvd. Agua Caliente 1777 (P.O. Box 120637, Chula Vista, CA 92012; tel. 800-336-5454); tel. 81-79-55, fax 86-13-40; US$52; heat, a/c, laundry, pool, restaurant, coffee shop, parking

El Rey; Calle 4 (Díaz Miron) 2021; tel. 85-14-26; US$20

Grand Hotel; Blvd. Agua Caliente 4500; tel. 81-70-00, in U.S. tel. 800-343-7825; US$85 up; heat, a/c, laundry, tennis, pool, restaurants, disco, fitness center, jacuzzi, sauna, parking

*****Hacienda del Río**; Blvd. Sanchez Taboada 10606, Zona Río; tel. 84-86-44, fax 84-86-20; US$68-78; restaurant, pool, parking

*****La Mesa Inn**; Blvd. Díaz Ordaz 50; tel. 81-65-22, fax 81-28-71; US$53-65; heating, a/c, restaurants, coffee shop, pool, parking

La Villa de Zaragoza; Av. Madero 1120; tel. 85-18-32; US$33-39; heat, a/c, laundry, parking

Lucerna; Av. Paseo de los Héroes 10902; tel. 34-20-00 (in U.S. & Canada 800-LUCERNA), fax 34-24-00; US$65-75; laundry, restaurants, pool, gardens, car rental

Nelson; Av. Revolución 502; tel. 85-43-03; US$20-35; coffee shop

Padre Kino; Blvd. Agua Caliente 3; tel. 86-42-08; US$23-38; parking

Palacio Azteca; Av. 16 de Septiembre 213; tel. 81-81-00; US$50-55; heat, a/c, laundry, coffee shop, pool, parking, car rental

Paraíso Radisson Tijuana; Blvd. Agua Caliente 1; tel. 81-72-00 (in U.S. & Canada tel. 800-333-3333), fax 86-36-39; US$80 up; heat, a/c, restaurants, pool, jacuzzi, sauna, parking, car rental

*****Plaza de Oro**; Calle 2 & Av. D (Av. Martinez); tel. 85-14-37, fax 85-67-03; US$34-62; a/c, complimentary continental breakfast

Plaza de Oro Revolución; Av. Revolución 277; tel. 38-41-12; US$28-35

Premier; Paseo del Centenario 60, Zona Río; tel. 84-27-10; US$85 up; heating, a/c, laundry, tennis pool, fitness center, business center, bar, restaurants, car rental

Real del Río; Calle J.M. Velasco 1409, Zona Río; tel. 34-31-00, fax 34-50-53; US$60-70; heat, a/c, laundry, business center, bar, coffee shop, snack bar, parking, car rental

San Diego; Av. Madero 761; tel. 85-70-66; US$20-30

*Affiliated with the Best Western chain; reservations can be arranged
in the U.S. or Canada by calling (800) 528-1234

Tijuana (formerly Hotel Fiesta Americana), completed in 1986 as one of the Plaza Agua Caliente twin towers, the city's first skyscrapers. The 22-floor, 430-room, five-star hotel features several restaurants and discos, a race-and-sports betting lounge, and penthouse suites accommodating visiting celebrities and politicos. Completed in 1993, the new 110-room **Hotel Premier** adjacent to the border and the Pueblo Amigo shopping plaza is equally impressive.

Many other tourist hotels and motels are strung out along Blvd. Agua Caliente, especially in the vicinity of the Caliente Race Track. For visitors on a budget, a handful of more economic places to stay can be found downtown—facilities are basic (no heating, a/c, or parking) but adequate. The "Tijuana Hotels and Motels" chart lists room rates and facilities.

Youth Hostel
Tijuana has one *villa juvenil* or youth hostel, located just north of the river between Via Oriente and Av. Padre Kino near the Cuauhtémoc Bridge (tel. 84-75-10). Rates for a bed and locker in a dorm-style room are US$5 a night. From the border, you can reach the hostel by taking any bus marked "Central Camionera"; from the downtown area, take a blue-and-white bus south on Av. Niños Héroes. The hostel is part of a large sports facility (look for the sign Deportivas) off Av. Padre Kino.

Campgrounds And RV Parks
The nearest camping/RV facilities are on the coast between San Antonio del Mar and Rosarito, some 20-25 km south of Tijuana via Mexico 1-D. See "Rosarito."

FOOD

Some of Baja's best food is found in Tijuana; it's worth a stopover just for a meal or two. Menus in La Reforma (Av. Revolución) district list prices in both N$ and US$ or US$ only—if you pay in pesos you'll almost always save a little money. Mexico has very lenient liquor laws, so virtually all the restaurants described below serve at least beer; most offer full bars as well.

Downtown
$-$$ **Bol Corona** (tel. 85-79-40), Calle 2a and Av. Revolución, Plaza Revolución: Origi-

nally opened in 1934, this venerable institution was gutted by fire in 1990 but reopened after several months. The ground floor is now a shopping plaza—gone is the family-style coffee shop—while the upper floor is exclusively a tourist enclave. The menu features a wide selection of northern Mexican specialities, including carne asada and enchiladas verdes, but the restaurant is best known for its burritos—the burrito was probably invented here. Smaller branch restaurants called Burritos del Bol Corona are found all over town. Open daily for breakfast, lunch, and dinner.

$$-$$$ **Caesar's** (tel. 88-27-94), Hotel Caesar, Calle 5a and Av. Revolución: This continental restaurant is famous for its Caesar salad, invented here by Alex and Caesar Cardini in 1924. The original Caesar's recipe uses coddled eggs—eggs boiled for one minute—in the dressing rather than the customary raw egg yolks used in North America. Open daily for dinner.

$-$$ **Denny's** (tel. 85-38-93), Av. Revolución 737, also Plaza Río: Of the several American franchises that have opened in Tijuana in recent years, this remains one of the best. The menu is predominantly Mexican, service is snappy, and it's open 24 hours.

$$ **Pedrin's** (tel. 85-40-62), Av. Revolución 1115: A branch of the long-established Pedrin's in Rosarito, this is one of the most popular seafood places in Tijuana. The cabrilla (sea bass) is particularly reliable. Open daily for lunch and dinner. Pedrin's has two other Tijuana branches, at Calle 7a 150 and at Av. Sánchez Taboada and Blvd. Cuauhtémoc in the Zona Río.

$ **Restaurant Nelson** (tel. 85-77-50), Av. Revolución 100: This nondescript coffee shop on the ground floor of the Hotel Nelson is one of the cheaper sit-down places to eat in La Reforma district, especially for breakfast. Open daily for breakfast, lunch, and dinner.

$$ **Sanborn's** (tel. 88-14-62), Av. Revoluión and Calle 8a, one block south of the Frontón Jai Alai: Not related to Sanborn's insurance or any other American company, this is part of a Mexican department store chain well-known in Mexico for its cafeterías. The food is of high quality, prices are reasonable, and the menu runs the gamut from original-recipe Mexican standards to steaks, seafood, salads, sandwiches, and soups. Breakfasts are particularly

memorable. Open daily for breakfast, lunch, and dinner.

$ **Super Antojitos Jalisco** (tel. 88-08-36), Av. Constitución 1111: The menu here is limited but authentic Mexican fare, and prices are low. Open Mon.-Sat. for lunch and dinner. If Super Antojitos Jalisco is too crowded, plenty of other local favorites are available along Av. Constitución. Another Super Antojitos is located in the Plaza Río shopping center on Paseo de los Héroes, Zona Río.

$$ **Tia Juana Tilly's** (tel. 85-16-12, 85-25-24), Calle 7a and Av. Revolución, part of the Frontón Jai Alai: Tilly's started out as Café de Jai Alai in 1945, later became an elegant restaurant called La Puenta, and in the '70s settled into its current casual-but-polished image. Historic Tijuana photos line the walls, and TV screens to one side of the restaurant broadcast live sports and racing events, so bettors from the adjacent booking lounge can follow their fates. Although basically a tourist scene, the food at Tilly's— Mexican, steak, and seafood—is excellent, especially the *caldos,* served with *chipotle* salsa. The service is fine, too. Open noon-midnight, Fri.-Sat. until 0300.

Tilly's features an outdoor section called **La Terraza** that's open noon-1900 Oct.-May, until midnight the remainder of the year.

$ **Woolworth**, 616 Revolución: Whether the claim that this is the largest Woolworth in the world is true or not, the store's lonchería serves tasty *platillos típicos* and beer at low prices. Open Mon.-Sat. for breakfast, lunch, and dinner.

Zona Río

$$-$$$ **Guadalajara Grill** (tel. 34-30-87), Paseo de los Héroes 17, Zona Río, near Baby Rock disco and Hotel Real del Río: This is one of the more staid enterprises of the Grupo Anderson (of Señor Frog's and Carlos 'n' Charlie's fame), with an emphasis on good eating. Open daily for lunch and dinner.

$-$$ **Lyni's** (tel. 34-12-58), Paseo de los Héroes 50-101: A branch of one of Mexico's top coffee-shop chains, Lyni's offers sparkling service and an extensive menu of *antojitos,* soups, salads, and sandwiches. Open daily for breakfast, lunch, and dinner.

$-$$ **Los Mandilones de Tijuana** (tel. 84-02-60), Plaza Río Tijuana, Paseo de los Héroes: After a visit to this splendid little taco bar, you'll never patronize Taco Bell again. Open daily for lunch and dinner.

$-$$ **Sarita's Place,** Pueblo Amigo Shopping Center: Vegetarians can rejoice in the moderately priced soups, salads, and healthful vegetable dishes here. The pineapple cheesecake, though perhaps not as nutritious as the rest of the menu, is excellent. Open daily 1300-1700 only.

$$ **Victor's** (tel. 84-02-04), Blvd. Sánchez Taboada and Calle Joaquin Clauser: This two-story Mexican restaurant features a full-menu dining room downstairs and a bar with specialty menu upstairs. Both serve good food. Open for breakfast, lunch, and dinner.

Agua Caliente

$$$ **Bocaccio's Nuevo Marianna** (tel. 86-18-45), Blvd. Agua Caliente 2500: A place where the local elite meet to eat, this kitschy Italian restaurant began in 1927 at a downtown location and moved to the racetrack area after a 1957 fire. Some of the best menu items are seafood entrees, including crab claws, lobster, and abalone. Open daily for lunch and dinner.

$-$$ **Carnitas Uruapan** (tel. 81-61-81), Blvd. Díaz Ordaz 550, opposite Plaza Patria: A classic carnitas joint, where the pig is cooked on-site and sold by the kilo along with rice, beans, salsa, and guacamole. Other Mexican specialities as well as steak are on the menu. Breakfasts are good, too. Open 22 hours daily, closed 0500-0700.

$$-$$$ **Mariscos Don Pepe** (tel. 84-90-86), Blvd. Fundadores 688, about three km south of Blvd. Agua Caliente: This restaurant in south Tijuana has one of the most extensive seafood menus in the city; shellfish, freshwater fish, and saltwater fish prepared in a variety of Mexican, American, and continental styles. Don Pedro's *postres* (desserts), including his renowned flan and cheescake, are made on the premises and sold at other Tijuana restaurants. Open daily for lunch and dinner.

$$-$$$ **La Escondida** (tel. 81-44-58), Santa Monica 1, east of the racetrack, off Blvd. Agua Caliente: This converted hacienda serves high-quality seafood, Mexican, and continental specialties in a variety of dining areas, both indoors and outdoors. Open daily 1100-midnight; Wed.-Sat. live music and dancing.

$$ **La Leña** (tel. 86-29-20), Blvd. Agua Caliente 4560: This restaurant near the Grand

Hotel Tijuana and the racetrack specializes in mesquite-grilled Sonoran steaks and carne asada. Mexican plates and seafood are also available. Open daily for lunch and dinner. A second La Leña is located at Av. Revolución 816 (between Calle 4a and 5a) downtown.

$-$$ **Plaza Agua Caliente,** Blvd. Agua Caliente, adjacent to the Grand Hotel Tijuana: The ground floor of this office tower features an array of vendor-style restaurants, including one of the aforementioned Burritos del Bol Corona outlets as well as several other eateries offering Mexican antojitos, burgers, pizza, licuados, ice cream, and enough other alternatives to satisfy most food cravings.

Loncherías

Loncherías are often the least expensive and most colorful sit-down meal spots in Mexico, and Tijuana is full of them. Several are scattered along avenidas Constitución and Madero, often wedged between larger shops. The diagonal bar strip between avenidas Revolución and Constitución also sports a couple of diners. Public markets usually harbor a few—try the **Mercado Hidalgo** opposite the Cultural Center or the **Mercado de Todos** in the 1800 block of Blvd. Agua Caliente. Tacos, tortas, and other antojitos are the usual offerings—sometimes a comida corrida is available.

A few loncherías depart from the usual Mexican standards and serve regional specialities. **Lonchería Rinconcito Yucateco** (tel. 21-60-41) is a bit out of the way at Av. Los Arboles 16 in La Mesa district, but for *comida yucateca* fans it may be worth the trip. Besides food specialties made from Yucatan recipes, the lonchería serves León Negra beer—a rare find anywhere in Mexico outside the Yucatan Peninsula.

Groceries

The northern Baja **Calimax** supermarket chain has several outlets in Tijuana. Food prices at Calimax are often lower than at smaller stores and the selection is huge. Probably the most accessible Calimax for those driving through the city is the one on the south side of Paseo de los Héroes just east of Blvd. Cuauhtémoc.

For bolillos, pan dulce, and other Mexican bakery items, your best choice is **Panificadora Suzette** opposite the Super Antojitos at Plaza Río Tijuana. Although Mexican bakeries don't

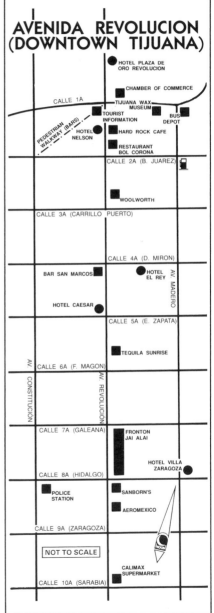

AVENIDA REVOLUCION (DOWNTOWN TIJUANA)

HOTEL PLAZA DE ORO REVOLUCION

CHAMBER OF COMMERCE

CALLE 1A

TIJUANA WAX MUSEUM

TOURIST INFORMATION

BUS DEPOT

HOTEL NELSON

PEDESTRIAN WALKWAY (BARS)

HARD ROCK CAFE

RESTAURANT BOL CORONA

CALLE 2A (B. JUAREZ)

WOOLWORTH

CALLE 3A (CARRILLO PUERTO)

CALLE 4A (D. MIRON)

BAR SAN MARCOS

HOTEL EL REY

AV. MADERO

HOTEL CAESAR

CALLE 5A (E. ZAPATA)

TEQUILA SUNRISE

AV. CONSTITUCION

CALLE 6A (F. MAGON)

AV. REVOLUCION

CALLE 7A (GALEANA)

FRONTON JAI ALAI

HOTEL VILLA ZARAGOZA

CALLE 8A (HIDALGO)

POLICE STATION

SANBORN'S

AEROMEXICO

CALLE 9A (ZARAGOZA)

NOT TO SCALE

CALIMAX SUPERMARKET

CALLE 10A (SARABIA)

usually stock tortillas (they're made and sold at tortillerías), Suzette's does. For decent European-style pastries and baked goods, stop by **La Baguette** at Plaza Fiesta or on Blvd. Agua Caliente southeast of El Toreo bullring.

ENTERTAINMENT

Although Tijuana is considerably tamer now than during Prohibition, it still has some nightlife—albeit of a more polished sort. For the most part, the entertainment center has shifted from La Reforma district round Av. Revolución to the Zona Río along Paseo de los Héroes.

Discos

San Diegans mix with a mostly local crowd at several high-tech discos, most of which are in the Zona Río. The current top draws are: **Baby Rock** (tel. 84-94-38, Calle Diego Rivera 1482), **Mecano** (tel. 82-49-67, Plaza Pueblo Amigo, Via Oriente), **Cascada** (tel. 34-20-88, Paseo de los Héroes 10802, Zona Río), **I's** (tel. 82-83-38, Calle J.M. la Roque 214, Zona Río), **Bacarat** (tel. 81-70-00, Grand Hotel Tijuana), and the world-class **Wild Oh! Laser Club** (tel. 84-02-67, Paseo de los Héroes 56). All these discos maintain dress codes that prohibit blue jeans or sneakers; most nights a cover charge of up to US$10 per person is collected. The recorded music varies from international pop to Latin funk.

Oriented toward young San Diegans, more casual discos along Av. Revolución include the psuedo-Kremlin-style **Red Square** on the corner of Calle 6a and Av. Revolución and **Tequila Sunrise,** between calles 5a and 6a.

Bars

For those who prefer sitting and drinking to dancing, Av. Revolución offers a string of bars and dance halls, from sleazy to posh, attracting an eclectic mix of cholos, punks, tourists, and the occasional American sailor. What was once the longest bar in the world, the Mexicali Beer Bar (also known as La Ballena), ran the entire length of the block between calles 2a and 3a under a tent until the early 1900s. Beer cost five cents a glass. Now the strip consists of a succession of similar-looking discos and a few curtained

go-go bars; in the cheaper places beer costs US$1 a bottle.

Locals patronize a boisterous collection of small bars along a diagonal pedestrian street that cuts between the southwest corner of Calle 1a and Av. Revolución and the northwest corner of Calle 2a and Av. Constitución. Guitar-bass-accordion ensembles wander from bar to bar playing a repertoire of *norteña* and Mexican standards. This is also a spot where mariachi groups wait for pickup gigs.

Bar San Marcos, attached to the Hotel Caesar (tel. 88-27-94, Calle 5a and Av. Revolución), is a classic leftover from Tijuana's pre-WW II boom. A 10-piece mariachi band performs on a semicircular platform over a glistening bar done up in '40s-'50s decor, like a set from the Ricky Ricardo show. The clientele consists of day tourists from San Diego and local businesspeople. The sign on the outside of the building reads Le Drugstore Tijuana.

Riding the line between bar and restaurant is Tijuana's own **Hard Rock Café** (tel. 85-25-13), Av. Revolución and Calle 2a. The decor consists of HRC's trademark rock memorabilia, and the music is modern and loud, though not too loud for conversation. A more elegant drinking establishment is the bar at **No Que No,** at the corner of Av. Sánchez Taboada and Calle Antono Caso in the Zona Río. Attached to a large restaurant, No Que No features live marimba music in a classy, subdued atmosphere.

Miscellaneous

Highbrow evening entertainment takes place at the **Tijuana Cultural Center.** Mexico's National Symphony performs at the center on a regular basis, as do the Ballet Folklorico and other performing-arts groups from around the country.

For lowbrows, a dwindling number of rather tame and expensive strip joints survives along Av. Revolución—vestiges of TJ's former incarnation as a sleaze capital. As for prostitution, the tourist bureau would like everyone to believe it disappeared from Tijuana with the casinos in 1938. The reality is bordello activity has moved to a motley collection of saloons and short-time hotels in the Zona Norte—often known simply as "La Zona"—on the outskirts of town. Definitely not a tourist scene.

SPORTS AND RECREATION

Hipódromo Caliente

Tijuana's first racetrack opened in 1916 just 400 meters south of the current border crossing, in response to a 1909 ban on pari-mutuel betting in Alta California. Business was good right from the start, and when Prohibition sent even greater numbers of Alta Californians south of the border, a larger track was needed. The Hipódromo Agua Caliente was constructed in 1929 following the highly successful 1928 opening of Tijuana's El Casino del Agua Caliente.

In 1931 Caliente became the first track in North America to become a "Hundred Grander," that is, to award US$100,000 to a single race winner. The track remained in operation even after the casino closed, and after the relegalization of pari-mutuel betting in Alta California in 1933, Caliente became an important training ground for young U.S.-owned thoroughbreds. A number of famous horses—Phar Lap (1932), Seabiscuit (1938), and Round Table (1958)—ran at Caliente.

Today, the *cupula* entrance to the Caliente Racetrack, a vestige of Tijuana's Prohibition-era splendor, preserves the 1920s Moorish style that is the epitome of San Diego-Ensenada architecture. Closed for renovations throughout 1990, the refurbished—and renamed, dropping "Agua"—facilities cover 160 acres and feature three tracks for thoroughbred and greyhound racing, three restaurants (Jockey Club, La Cupula, Turf Club), two Caliente Foreign Book Lounges (see "Race and Sports Book," below), and several bars and snack bars. Thoroughbred racing was recently discontinued but greyhound racing still brings in a steady clientele.

The racetrack is 12 km (eight miles) south of the international border on Blvd. Agua Caliente, just east of the Plaza Agua Caliente twin towers. Red-and-black route taxis marked La Mesa pass in front of the entrance, as do green-and-cream city buses.

Greyhounds run at 1400 and 1945 Monday and Wed.-Fri; Sat.-Sunday 1400 only. Grandstand seating is free, while seating in the Jockey Club costs US$5; it's free with purchase of a lunch.

Pari-mutuel wagers include daily doubles, quinielas, trifectas, exactas, pick-six (invented at this track), win, place, and show. Caliente claims to collect the lowest take of any racetrack in North America, 14.86%; the racetrack pays all taxes, so figures shown on the tote board are the actual win amounts. U.S. winners are expected to voluntarily submit the appropriate portion of their winnings to the IRS, unless they spend at least 11 months of the year outside the United States. Bets are accepted in U.S. currency as well as pesos.

Race And Sports Book

Sporting folk don't have to go all the way out to Caliente Racetrack to make a wager, as Tijuana offers several venues for sports and off-track

Hipódromo Caliente

betting. These legal betting lounges feature plush bars and restaurants, plus banks of closed-circuit TV monitors so you can keep up with your wagers or just watch for fun. Sports bets are based on line odds direct from Las Vegas, and all wagers and payoffs are in U.S dollars. Taxes are paid by the booking establishments, so what you see on the tote board represents your take-home winnings.

LF Race and Sports Book occupies locations at the Plaza Pueblo Amigo (Paseo de Tijuana, Zona Río), the Grand Hotel Tijuana, and the Jai Alai palace. The similar **Caliente Foreign Book** is located at the Caliente Race Track and at Av. Revolución and Calle 4a. All book lounges keep the same hours: Wed.-Sun. 0900-2300, Tuesday 0900-2030.

Caliente operates a free minivan shuttle between the border and each of its racing and sports book locations. The shuttle runs every half-hour daily 9 a.m.-10 p.m.

Bullfights

The bullfight season in Tijuana runs from May through September, usually two corridas in May, one in June, and weekly thereafter except for the last week in September. The corridas begin at 1600 on Sundays. Current schedule and ticket information is available in Tijuana by calling 85-22-10. Ticket reservations, often necessary, are obtained by calling the same number. You can purchase tickets at Ticketron outlets in the San Diego (tel. 619-231-3554) and Los Angeles (tel. 213-410-1062) areas; Mexicoach Five Star Tours (tel. 619-232-5049) in San Diego or Tijuana; the Grand Hotel Tijuana (tel. 81-70-00); or the bullfight information booth at Av. Revolución 815 (Sonia Arcade, between Calle 4a and 5a). Depending on the seat and the matador lineup, prices range from US$7 to US$30.

The city contains two permanent bullrings. **El Toreo de Tijuana** (tel. 86-15-10, Agua Caliente Blvd. 100) is the oldest, with more atmosphere; it's located close to the city center. The **Plaza Monumental** (tel. 86-15-10, Paseo Monumental) is approximately 10 km (6 miles) west of the city, in the Playas district next to the Pacific Ocean. Dubbed the "Bullring-by-the-Sea," this huge, stadium-like edifice is reportedly the second-largest bullring in the world; when the

world's top matadors visit Tijuana, they always perform at the Plaza Monumental.

Charreada (Mexican Rodeo)

Although the *charreada* inspired the development of North American rodeo, it differs in significant ways. Competition is generally based on the *charro's* (cowboy's) performance style, rather than timed events, and the atmosphere is considerably more festive, featuring elaborate costumes and music. In Tijuana, occasional charreadas are held Saturdays or Sundays May through September at *lienzos charros* (charreada rings) throughout the city, including the **Lienzo Charro La Misión** (tel. 80-41-85, Av. Braulio Maldonado, Zona Misión). Easier to find are the **Cortijo San José** and **Lienzo Charro Misión del Sol,** both in the Playas Tijuana district near the Plaza Monumental bullring.

Smaller Tijuana lienzos arrange occasional rodeo events during fiestas. For the latest information on charreada schedules, call Tijuana's tourist information number (tel. 83-14-05) or contact the Charro Association secretary at 81-34-01 or 81-26-11.

Jai Alai

Known as "the fastest ballgame in the world," jai alai (a Basque word meaning "merry festival," pronounced "HAI-lai") descended from *pelota,* a 200-year-old Basque game that is also the forerunner of handball, squash, and racquetball. In the Basque country of northern Spain, players originally bounced the pelota—once a goatskin ball, now hard rubber encased in goatskin—against church walls or *frontis;* it moved indoors to the *frontón* (playing court) in the late 18th century.

Jai Alai has come a long way from its humble beginnings as a goatherd's pastime. The Frontón Palacio Jai Alai de Tijuana, a landmark Spanish-style structure in the center of the city, is one of the San Diego-Tijuana area's major attractions. The palacio's facilities include the frontón itself (a three-walled court with hardwood floors and seating for 1500 spectators), one of the city's finest restaurants (Tia Juana Tilly's), a '50s-style burger-and-fries bar (Rock Ola), a sidewalk café (La Terraza), and a disco (Tilly's).

The *pelotaris,* or jai-alai players, who appear at the frontón mostly hail from France, Spain, and Mexico. A pelotari's uniform consists of a numbered, colored jersey, white pants, a red waist sash (*faja*), court shoes, and a helmet. The *cesta* is an elongated wicker basket—imported from Spain at a cost of around US$200 each—strapped to the playing hand and used for throwing and catching the pelota. Using the curvature of the cesta and a skilled throwing technique, the pelotari can launch the pelota against the *frontis, rebote,* and *ayuda* (the front, back and "helper" or side walls) as if shot from a cannon. Ball speeds can reach a blistering 290 km per hour.

The Game: Pelotari teams of six to eight players play in singles or doubles in round-robin fashion. A printed program distributed to spectators contains the name and jersey numbers of the pelotaris in each *juego* (match), along with odds for scoring. The minimum wager is US$2 for win, place, or show; there are also quiniela, exacta, trifecta, and daily-double bets. Twelve juegos are usually played in an evening.

If you've never wagered on jai alai, it might be best to watch a round or two before diving in. Bilingual staff can explain scoring and betting.

Admission: Palacio doors open at 1900. The pelotaris start warming up on the court around 1930, and play begins promptly at 2000. Jai alai matches are played nightly, year-round, except on Wednesdays. General admission, at the top of the seating area, is US$3; reserved seating costs US$4; and seats in the Cancha Club are US$5. Cancha Club seating is closest to the court and offers seated bar service. Bars in the palacio lobby areas (three on the main floor, two on the mezzanine) serve other spectators.

Location and Information: The palacio sits at the intersection of Av. Revolución and Calle 7a. For information call 85-78-33, 85-25-24, or 85-16-12 in Tijuana, (619) 231-1910 in San Diego, or toll-free 800-PIK-BAJA.

El Béisbol

Tijuana can claim its own pro baseball team, Los Potros ("The Colts"), who play other ballclubs in the Mexican-Pacific League as well as the occasional visiting team from North or Central America. Games are played at the exemplary 15,000-seat **Estadio de los Potros** (tel.

25-10-56), off Blvd. Los Insurgentes near the Otay Mesa border crossing. The Mexican baseball season runs from about the end of the American World Series through late January. Game admission is around US$5.

Golf

The **Club Campestre Tijuana,** or Tijuana Country Club (tel. 81-78-55, off Blvd. Agua Caliente near the Caliente Racetrack), offers a decent 6,500-yard, par-72, 18-hole course, an occasional site of the Mexican Open. Nonmembers may tee off at the club for greens fees of US$22 weekdays, US$27 weekends. You can hire carts and caddies at extra cost. A special "fiesta package" is available for US$65 weekdays, or US$78 weekends and holidays, and includes greens fees, cart rental, and lunch at the club for two people.

SHOPPING

For North Americans, shopping is perhaps Tijuana's number-one attraction. Although both Baja California states are designated duty-free zones, Tijuana offers the widest variety of merchandise—everything from Mexican-Indian handicrafts to pharmaceuticals to top-of-the-line European clothing.

Nearly everything is cheaper in Tijuana than it is north of the border. Some of the better bargains are found in leather goods, cosmetics, drugs (prescriptions aren't usually required, even for drugs dispensed by prescription in the U.S.), high-tag import items (e.g., designer fashions), cooking spices (vanilla costs a fraction of the U.S. price), handicrafts (especially blankets, rugs, basketry, and ceramics), and liquor.

Avenida Revolución

For individual shops and boutiques, Av. Revolución between Calle 2a and Calle 9a is one of the best window-shopping areas. **Sanborn's,** at the corner of Av. Revolución and Calle 8a, is a favorite department store among daytripping San Diegans. Although not large, it's divided into book, arts-and-crafts, pharmacy, liquor, and restaurant sections.

For high-quality Mexican handicrafts, **Tolan** (opposite the Frontón Jai Alai on Av. Revolución, between calles 7a and 8a) is among the best shops in the city. **La Fuente,** at Av. Revolución 921-10, offers arts and crafts of similar quality, including masks, woodcarvings, *retablos* (altarpieces), and life-size papier-mâché Day of the Dead skeletons. **Irene's,** at Av. Revolución 921, is a good spot for embroidered dresses at reasonable prices.

Farther north along Av. Revolución, at Calle 2a, is **Plaza Revolución,** a two-story mall with around 65 shops purveying arts and crafts, leather goods, jewelry, and other items. And don't overlook **Woolworth,** at the same intersection, where everyday items are on sale at rock-bottom prices.

Except at department stores, pharmacies, and liquor stores, bargaining for a lower price than marked or quoted is acceptable. U.S. currency is accepted anywhere in the city; some shops take credit cards. Most of the sales staffs in Av. Revolución stores offer someone who can speak some English.

Avenida Constitución

Few visitors seem to know it, but one block west of Av. Revolución is the town's major downtown shopping area. This is where the locals go. Especially for shoes and boots, liquor, and pharmaceuticals, shops on Av. Constitución always beat the prices of their counterparts on Av. Revolución. And unlike at some shops on Revolución, bargaining—or Spanish language mastery—isn't necessary since prices are always marked and fixed.

Shopping Centers

Tijuana was the first city in Mexico to erect North American-style shopping malls; at last count, the city boasted 12 major *centro comerciales* (shopping centers), with more on the way.

The most praised is **Plaza Río Tijuana,** on Paseo de los Héroes between Via Poniente and Blvd. Cuauhtémoc in the Zona Río. Here you'll find over a hundred businesses, including department stores, pharmacies, optometrists, banks, jewelry and gift stores, music shops, clothing stores, a bakery, a florist, a cinema, photo shops, travel agencies, bookstores, sporting-goods stores, and even a chapel, all surrounded by a large parking lot.

Opposite Plaza Río is **Plaza del Zapato,** "Shoe Plaza." This is one of Tijuana's best bargain centers, with over 35 *zapaterías* (shoe stores) in one location. Shoes and boots, especially those made in Mexico, usually cost less than half the prices set north of the border. Next to Plaza del Zapato is **Plaza Fiesta,** a mall featuring old Guanajuato-style architecture. Most of the businesses here are restaurants, bars, or cafés, interspersed with a few specialty shops. **La Herradura de Oro** in Plaza Fiesta sells Mexican, Western, and English riding equipment—chaps, sombreros, rebozos, saddles—and can also produce custom leather work.

The **Tijuana Cultural Center** at Paseo de los Héroes and Av. Independencia offers a shopping area with nine stores specializing in regional arts and crafts, including hand-crafted silver, gold, copper, and brass, with textiles, ceramics, jewelry, paintings, and sculptures.

Other Tijuana shopping centers of note include Plaza Patria (Blvd. Díaz Ordaz, east of Caliente Race Track), Plaza Pueblo Amigo (Av. Via Oriente, near the border crossing), and Plaza Agua Caliente (Av. Agua Caliente, adjacent to the Grand Hotel Tijuana).

Alta Californians who don't want to venture far from home can shop at **Viva Tijuana,** a big indoor-outdoor mall only about 150 meters from the border gate. In fact, all pedestrians entering or exiting the country are forced to walk through this mall. Neither the restaurants nor the shops at Viva Tijuana offer anything very special—it's strictly a place to pick up last-minute souvenirs.

Markets

For a more Mexican shopping experience, seek out Tijuana's public markets. The large **Mercado de Artesanías** at the intersection of Av. Ocampo and Calle 2a offers thousands of pottery items at low prices. Much of what's stacked up in row after row is junk, but you can uncover worthwhile pieces with some diligent searching.

Opposite the Tijuana Cultural Center at Paseo de los Héroes and Av. Independencia is the more atmospheric **Mercado Hidalgo.** This outdoor municipal market features dozens of vendor stalls arranged in a large square. Items for sale vary from year to year but generally include fresh fruits and vegetables, spices, and various other grocery items. A couple of loncherías and crafts shops make the market more than just a grocery stop.

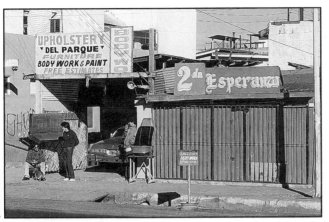

upholstery shop

The **Mercado de Todos**—"Market of Everything"—is out on the 1800 block of Blvd. Agua Caliente/Díaz Ordaz, about four km east of the racetrack. Vendors here offer bargains on clothing, housewares, electronics, and just about anything else you might need to set up house on the peninsula. If you get hungry while strolling from booth to booth, several extra-clean loncherías offer cheap eats. This market doesn't really get rolling until around 1000 on weekdays, or 0900 weekends; it stays open until dark.

Auto Upholstery And Body Work

Tijuana is as legendary for auto work as Hong Kong is for tailoring. As in Hong Kong, patience in arranging for custom work and waiting for completion always pays off. The Tijuana Convention and Visitors Bureau (tel. 84-05-37) maintains a list of reputable upholsterers and body shops—check this list first if you don't already possess a recommendation from someone you know.

Typical of the better upholstery shops is **Richard's Upholstery** at Calle 2a and Av. Madero, which offers tuck-and-roll, diamonds, plaids, squares, and just about any other style in leather, vinyl, or fabric. Prices are half, or less, of what a U.S. auto upholsterer would charge; a complete auto interior starts at around US$225 and requires a full day. Check the quality of the upholstery fill in advance—less reputable shops may use low-quality materials, like newspaper in place of foam. You'll find several other uphol-stery shops along Calle 3a between avenidas Ocampo and Pío Pico. Prices quoted verbally are usually negotiable.

Body shops, or *carroceros*, are mostly located along Ocampo between calles 1a and 4a. Carroceros excel at banging out dents and applying primer, but if you need a fender or door painted, you can usually match the paint better at North American auto dealers. For an all-new paint job, **Javier's Body Shop** (tel. 85-04-40) at Av. Baja California 1347, is recommended; "Pearlescent" is the house specialty. Another quality shop is **Indio** (tel. 85-83-75), Blvd. Agua Caliente 395-A between Ocampo and Pío Pico.

Furniture And Tile

Mexican-made furniture—of wood or wrought iron—and tile are considerably less expensive in Tijuana than in the U.S. or Canada. Most of the larger tile and furniture stores are located along Blvd. Agua Caliente between Av. Revolución and the Caliente Race Track. A few stores specialize in high-quality, handmade wood furniture, but generally the wrought-iron pieces are a better bargain.

One of the widest wall and floor tile selections—including imported tiles from Europe, Brazil, and Japan—is at **Tile Express** (tel. 81-82-87, 81-83-05) at Av. Salinas and Aviacion.

Be sure to check the latest U.S. Customs regulations before buying huge amounts of furniture or tile for U.S. import.

CONSULATES IN TIJUANA

Austria; Blvd. Agua Caliente 3401, desp. 803, Edificio Gallego; tel. 86-36-25

Belgium; Blvd. Díaz Ordaz 700, Int. 421-1; tel. 81-32-94

Canada; Germán Gedoviou 5-202, Zona Río; tel./fax 84-04-61

El Salvador; Av. México 103-1; tel. 85-56-66

Finland; Blvd. Agua Caliente 3401, Edificio Gallego; tel. 86-39-83

France; Av. Revolución 1221; tel. 86-38-83

Germany; Blvd. Sánchez Taboada 9210; tel. 34-13-32

Honduras; Germán Gedoviou 11, Zona Río; tel. 84-01-68

Italy; Calle Santa María 155; tel. 86-23-78, fax 84-78-66

Norway; Calle E, 4, fracc. Rubio, La Mesa; tel. 89-29-86, 89-12-08

People's Republic of China; Av. Jalisco 312, Col. Cacho; tel. 84-27-56, fax 84-09-56

South Korea; Av. H 325; tel. 20-14-14

Spain; Av. de los Olivos, Col. Cubillas; tel. 86-57-80, 81-70-20

Switzerland; Av. Revolución 606-8; tel. 85-45-01, fax 88-10-65

United Kingdom*; Blvd. Salinas 1500, Col. Aviación; tel. 81-73-23

United States; Calle Tapachula 96, Col. Hipódromo; tel. 81-74-00, 86-00-01

*The UK consulate will also serve citizens of Australia and Belize.

The banks in Tijuana aren't accustomed to changing small amounts of foreign currency since just about everyone uses casas de cambio exclusively. If you want to cash traveler's checks, the banks will give you dollars, not pesos. As usual in Mexico, hotels offer low exchange rates but fast service.

Every business and service in Tijuana except public buses and government offices accepts U.S. currency.

Post And Telephone

The **main post office** is at Calle 11a (P.E. Calles) and Av. Negrete; it's open Mon.-Fri. 0800-1700. The **long-distance telephone and telegraph office** is at Calle 10a and Av. Pío Pico; hours are Mon.-Fri. 0800-1400 and 1600-1900.

The **CANACO** office at Calle 1a and Av. Revolución sells stamps and envelopes.

Tijuana's area code is 66.

Hunting Ammunition

Tijuana offers one of only three stores in Baja authorized to sell ammunition to the public. Since Mexican law limits the importation of hunting ammunition to 50 cartridges per registered firearm, with weapons limited to two per person, anything beyond this number must be purchased in Mexico. Prices are slightly higher than in the U.S. or Canada. The store, **Arturo's** (tel. 84-12-77), is at Calle 10a (de Juan Sarabia) 2047.

SERVICES

Changing Money

The best place to exchange foreign currency for pesos is at any of the many casas de cambio found along the pedestrian route from the border to about halfway down Av. Revolución. You'll also find a couple of casas de cambio next to the Calimax supermarket on Paseo de los Héroes in the Zona Río.

Immigration And Customs

Immigration and customs matters are handled at the Tijuana border crossing. These offices are open 24 hours a day. For specific information on visas and tourist permits, see "Immigration and Customs" under "Out and About."

Green Angels

The Green Angels automotive assistance service is headquartered in the Garita Federal Building (Edificio Federal Garita) at the Otay Mesa border crossing. For assistance or information in Tijuana, call 23-38-77.

TIJUANA INFORMATION

Tourist Assistance And Information

The **Tourist Information Booth** (tel. 83-14-05, 83-13-10) at Av. Revolución and Calle 1a distributes maps and useful information brochures on Tijuana and northern Baja; the bilingual staff will also handle simple inquiries about where to go and what to see. The booth is open 0900-1900 daily; similar booths are located at the Tijuana border crossing and Tijuana International Airport. Any questions about Tijuana these people can't answer should be referred to the **Tijuana Tourism and Convention Bureau** (tel. 84-05-37, 84-05-38) at the intersection of Calle Mina and Paseo de los Héroes in the Zona Río. This office is open Mon.-Fri. 0900-1400 and 1600-1900. The **Camara Nacional de Comercio, Servicios y Turismo de Tijuana (CANACO)** (tel. 85-84-72, fax 82-84-86), opposite the SECTUR booth on Av. Revolución at Calle 1a, dispenses tourist information, stamps, and envelopes; it also offers restrooms and a public telephone.

For more tourist information on Baja California Norte, contact the **State Secretary of Tourism** (tel. 81-94-92, 81-94-93, fax 81-95-79) in Plaza Patria, 3rd floor, Blvd. Díaz Ordaz. Legal problems should also be referred to this office.

The Tijuana Chamber of Commerce and Tijuana Tourism and Convention Bureau jointly publish *Baja Visitor,* a free monthly filled with hotel, dining, and sightseeing information. Most of the publication is oriented toward Tijuana.

Every Sunday at noon the "Jan Wood Show," a talk show telecast on San Diego television channel 6, focuses on Tijuana. Discussion topics include the latest info on border waits, art shows, Tijuana restaurants, and coming city events. The program can be picked up by most TVs in both Tijuana and the San Diego area.

GETTING TO TIJUANA

By Air
Four airlines service Tijuana (Abelardo Rodriguez) International Airport (TIJ): Aeromexico, Aero California, Air L.A., and Mexicana. (For more information see "Getting There.") The airport is currently undergoing expansion; lengthened runways and greater capacity will result in more passenger and cargo loads. The airport is an official port of entry for foreign pilots. Fuel is available; the tower frequency is 122.8.

Airport Transport: Taxis from the airport, about eight km east of the city, to anywhere in the city cost a flat US$10 for up to five passengers. Public buses to downtown Tijuana are

---

AIRLINE OFFICES IN TIJUANA

Aero California; Paseo de los Héroes C-19-1, Plaza Río Tijuana; tel. 84-20-06, 84-20-07, toll-free in the U.S. (800) 258-3311

Aeroméxico; Av. Revolución 1236; tel. 85-44-01, 85-44-02, toll-free in the U.S. (800) 237-6639

Air L.A.; Tijuana International Airport; toll-free in Mexico tel. 95-800-01-0413, toll-free in the U.S. (800) 933-5952

Mexicana de Aviacion; Gobernador Balarezo 2800, Col. Davila; tel. 81-72-11; toll-free in the U.S. tel. (800) 531-7921, in Canada tel. (800) 531-7923

Noroeste; Tijuana International Airport; tel. 83-13-36, 82-48-57

---

marked Centro and leave regularly from in front of the airport for about US$.60 per passenger.

By Land
Bus: Several intercity bus lines operate out of Tijuana. The main terminal for Mexico-based lines is the **Central de Autobuses** (tel. 80-90-60, 96-95-15) at Lázaro Cárdenas and Blvd. Arroyo Alamar, about five km east of the city. Taxis from the Central de Autobuses to the downtown area cost a flat US$5 per person; public bus fare is around US$.30. A taxi between the border and the Central de Autobuses costs US$10; the bus rate is US$.60.

The U.S.-based **Greyhound** buses from San Diego and Los Angeles terminate at a downtown depot (tel. 88-07-52) at Av. Madero and Calle 1a. This same terminal also serves Mexican buses (**Autotransportes de Baja California,** or ABC) running between Tijuana and Ensenada (US$2.60), Rosarito (US$.60), and Tecate (US$1.80). Buses to these latter cities depart aproximately every hour 0700-2100 daily.

ABC also runs a deluxe *ejecutivo* bus with air conditioning, movies, and beverage service to Ensenada hourly between 0700 and 2100 for US$4.60. You can board these buses at the Central de Autobuses, the intersection of Av. Madero and Av. México downtown, or the Viva Tijuana complex at the border, near the U.S.

customs/immigration post.

Mexicoach (from San Ysidro) occupies its own depot at the Jai Alai palace at Av. Revolución and Calle 7a.

The larger **Central de Autobuses** (tel. 26-71-01) fields buses (ABC, Transportes del Pacífico, Transportes de Sonora, Tres Estrellas de Oro, Transportes Aguila) eastward to Mexicali (US$9.60, six times daily), Tecate (US$1.60-2, also six times daily), and various points on the Mexican mainland. Buses southward include those to Guerrero Negro (US$27.50, twice daily) and La Paz (US$42, twice daily).

Auto: See "Getting There" under "Out and About" for specifics on driving to Tijuana.

GETTING AROUND TIJUANA

You can see much of downtown Tijuana on foot—avenidas Revolución and Constitución, the cathedral, the Jai Alai palace, the Mercado Artesanías. You can reach outlying attractions like the Zona Río and the racetrack by city bus, or taxi, or in your own car.

Buses

City buses in Tijuana come in several colors, shapes, and sizes. The route destination—usually the name of a district (e.g., Centro or La Mesa)—is displayed on a sign over the windshield or whitewashed directly on it. Fares are around US$.30, payable only in pesos.

Two of the most useful bus lines are the "green and cream" (*verde y crema*), which operates between the city center and the La Mesa district, east of Caliente Race Track; and the "blue and white" (*azul y blanco*), running between the city center and the Playas district (Plaza Monumental). The "Baja P" is the bus to take for jaunts to Zona Río attractions, including the Tijuana Cultural Center, Plaza Fiesta, and Plaza Río Tijuana.

Taxis

Most trips by hired taxi within the *centro* cost US$4-6. From the city center to the Grand Hotel Tijuana/racetrack area costs as much as US$8, while to the airport or Central de Autobuses you can expect to pay up to US$10. Taxis hired from hotels generally cost a bit more than taxis hired on the street; rates are usually posted. If in doubt about a fare, inquire at the tourist information booths at the border or on Av. Revolución at Calle 1a. Drivers are happy to accept U.S. currency.

Bargaining usually isn't necessary—drivers generally quote the standard price immediately, with the exception of the yellow border taxis. You shouldn't have to pay more than US$3 from the border taxistand to Av. Revolución, but drivers often ask gringos for more. A better deal involves taking the Mexicoach bus from San Ysidro on the U.S. side of the border directly to Av. Revolución; only US$1.25.

Route taxis (*taxis de ruta*) in Tijuana are large American-made station wagons holding up to 12 passengers. These taxis operate along set routes, much like city buses, but stop wherever they're flagged down. Fares are US$.50-.60 per person, only a tad higher than city buse fares; as on buses, only pesos are accepted. Route taxis are one of the best ways to get around Tijuana cheaply, since you can tell the drivers exactly where you want off along their route—better than waiting for a bus stop to come along.

Like the city buses, route taxis are painted according to their routes. Red-and-black taxis operate between Calle 2a (between avenidas Revolución and Constitución) and La Mesa, along Blvd. Agua Caliente; brown-and-white route taxis run to the Zona Río and Otay Mesa.

Driving Your Own Vehicle

The traffic in Tijuana is fairly stiff all day long, so it's not one of the most pleasant cities in Baja to drive in. On the other hand, lots of visitors do manage to drive themselves around the city—all it takes is a good map and plenty of patience. Generally speaking, streets in the downtown area are well-marked; the biggest difficulty comes in trying to navigate out of the city to Rosarito, Mexicali, or beyond.

Another problem is parking, although the situation is not nearly as bad as in most larger cities in the United States. In the Av. Revolución area, street parking is hard to come by; it's best to choose one of the fee parking lots (e.g., at the Jai Alai palace/Mexicoach terminal or next door to Woolworth).

Car Rental

Tijuana has seven different car rental operations: AMCA, Avis, Budget, Central, Dollar, Hertz, and National. All offer day, weekend, and weekly

(top) San Felipe; (bottom) Playa Palmilla

(top) mosiac over entrance to Rosarito Beach Hotel;
(bottom left) roadside shrine; (bottom right) olives, Maneadero

TIJUANA
AUTO RENTAL AGENCIES

AMCA; Tijuana International Airport; tel. 83-16-44

AMCA; Av. Madero 1330; tel. 85-89-13, 85-23-12

Avis; Tijuana International Airport; tel. 83-23-10

Avis; Blvd. Agua Caliente 3310, opposite Hotel Paraíso Radisson; tel. 86-37-18, 86-15-07, 86-20-75

Budget; Tijuana International Airport; tel. 83-29-05

Budget; Paseo de los Héroes 77, Zona Río; tel. 84-02-53, 84-02-63

Central; Paseo de los Héroes 104, Zona Río; tel. 84-22-57, 84-22-68

Dollar; Tijuana International Airport; tel. 83-18-61

Dollar; Blvd. Sánchez Taboada 10521, Zona Río; tel. 81-84-84

Hertz; Tijuana International Airport; tel. 83-20-80

Hertz; Hotel Palacio Azteca; tel. 86-22-16, 86-43-71

Hertz; Grand Hotel; tel. 81-70-00

Hertz; Blvd. Agua Caliente 3402; tel. 81-72-20, 81-75-53

National; Tijuana International Airport; tel. 82-44-33

National; Blvd. Agua Caliente 5000; tel. 86-21-03, 82-44-36

---

deals either with per-kilometer charges added in (best rates for local driving only) or as flat rates only (most economical if you plan to drive long distances in Baja). Car rentals are less expensive in Tijuana than anywhere else on the peninsula. Especially for auto tours of northern Baja, you'll enjoy considerable savings if you rent a car here rather than in Ensenada or Mexicali.

Advance reservations are a good idea as most agencies don't maintain large fleets of cars. With or without reservations, a credit card is a prerequisite for car rental.

Leaving Tijuana

To get back across the border, simply drive north on Av. Revolución and follow signs to San Diego. When traffic is stiff, especially on Sundays, you can avoid much of the traffic by circling around to Av. Padre Kino on the north side of town to approach the border crossing from the east lanes. The west lanes are almost always busiest.

To drive to Rosarito, Ensenada, or other destinations south along Mexico 1, you must first decide whether you want to take the toll road or the free road. For the toll road (Mexico 1-D), take Calle 3a west and follow the signs for Ensenada; traffic is often very slow until you reach the toll-road entrance near Playas. The free road is more difficult to find; some visitors say they gave up looking for it and settled for the toll road. There's only one sign indicating the way; if you drive south along Av. Revolución until it curves east into Blvd. Agua Caliente, you'll soon see a sign reading A Rosarito (To Rosarito) with an arrow pointing to the right; watch for a large Calimax store on the right. The next right-hand turn, Blvd. Cuauhtémoc, is the correct turnoff. You can also connect with Blvd. Cuauhtémoc by driving east on Paseo de los Héroes; look for the statue of an Aztec—that's Cuauhtémoc. Once on Blvd. Cuauhtémoc, make no other turns, wade through a seemingly endless succession of stoplights and stop signs, and eventually you'll find yourself on Mexico 1.

For Tecate, Mexicali, and other points east, simply follow Blvd. Agua Caliente southeast out of town until it turns into Blvd. Díaz Ordaz and, finally, Mexico 2.

TIJUANA TO TECATE
(MEXICO 2 EAST)

Once you're beyond the eastern city limits, the scenery along Mexico 2 mostly consists of boulders, rolling hills, and the occasional rancho. At Km 166, the highway crosses over the impressive **Presa Rodriguez** (Rodriguez Dam, usually called simply La Presa, "The Dam"), constructed in 1937. In the vicinity of **El Florido,** a small farm community near Km 158, are several dairy farms; look for Hay Queso signs if you'd like to buy some fresh cheese.

A few kilometers east of El Florido, a scenic unpaved road dating from the Spanish colonial period heads north to Valle Redondo. On the south side of Mexico 2, another road leads to

Presa El Carrizo, a dam with a sizable lake. This gravel road continues south, past a couple of ranchos, to connect with Mexico 3 at Valle de las Palmas. Just before the border town of Tecate, between Km 136 and 135, is the turnoff for **Rancho La Puerta,** one of the world's most highly rated health resorts. Mexico 2 then becomes Av. Juárez, the main west-east thoroughfare through Tecate. Once through Tecate, the highway resumes its eastward direction toward Mexicali and the state of Sonora.

TIJUANA TO ENSENADA

The drive from Tijuana to Ensenada or any points between is fairly straightforward, even for drivers who would never consider navigating the Transpeninsular all the way to the Cape. You can choose between two roadways, a modern, four-lane toll expressway (Mexico 1-D, also called the Carretera Cuota or "Toll Highway") and a slightly more challenging two-lane highway (the original Mexico 1, called along this stretch the Carretera Libre or "Free Highway").

Both are scenic drives of around 100 km (60 miles). Mexico 1, the free road, begins just south of Tijuana and winds through a mountainous area for 18 km before reaching the coast at Rosarito. From Rosarito it hugs the narrow coastal plain for the next 50 km, providing plenty of opportunities for beach stopovers, then turns inland again at La Misión. The final 31 km threads through the mountains before joining Mexico 1-D just north of Ensenada at San Miguel.

Mexico 1-D, the toll highway, parallels the coast the entire distance from Tijuana to Ensenada. The roadbed is set along the slopes and cliffs of the inland sierra, so coastal views provide a higher perspective than along the free road. On the negative side, there are limited opportunities for stopovers since highway exits can be as far as 18 km apart.

Tolls are collected at three tollgates (*casetas de cobro*) along Mexico 1-D: at Playas de Tijuana, Rosarito, and San Miguel. At each gate, the toll is approximately US$2.25 for passenger cars, US$3-5 for cars with trailers, motorhomes, or large trucks. From Tijuana to Ensenada the total runs US$6.75, or US$9-15 for larger vehicles. Both U.S. and Mexican currency is accepted at the tollgates; change is given in pesos, dollars, or a mixture of the two.

ISLAS LOS CORONADOS

The four Los Coronados islands lie only 11 km west of San Antonio del Mar, a mostly American residential area 12 km south of Tijuana. The Spanish explorer Juan Cabrillo passed by in 1542 and called them Las Islas Desiertas ("Desert Islands") because of the apparent lack of vegetation; in 1602 Vizcaíno renamed them Los Cuatros Coronados—"Four Coronados"—after four brothers who died as Christian martyrs during the era of the Roman Empire.

Too steep and rugged for permanent habitation, in ensuing years the islands were briefly used as a pirate hideaway and later as a rendezvous for smugglers bringing rum and Chinese immigrants into the United States. In 1931 a short-lived hotel and casino called the Coronado Islands Yacht Club rose at the edge of a cove on the largest island, Coronado del Sur. The establishment closed in 1933 with the repeal of Prohibition, and little remains of the decaying three-story building. A few Mexican navy personnel live on the island to protect it from intruders.

Geography And Natural History

All four of Los Coronados are the tips of undersea mountain ridges. The largest island, Coronado del Sur, is about three km long and reaches 204 meters at its highest point; the second largest,

Coronado del Norte, is about a kilometer long and 142 meters high. The remaining two, Roca Media ("Middle Rock") and Coronado del Medio ("Middle Coronado"), lie between the larger islands and are little more than rock outcroppings.

The islands and the surrounding immediate area are protected by the Mexican government; commercial

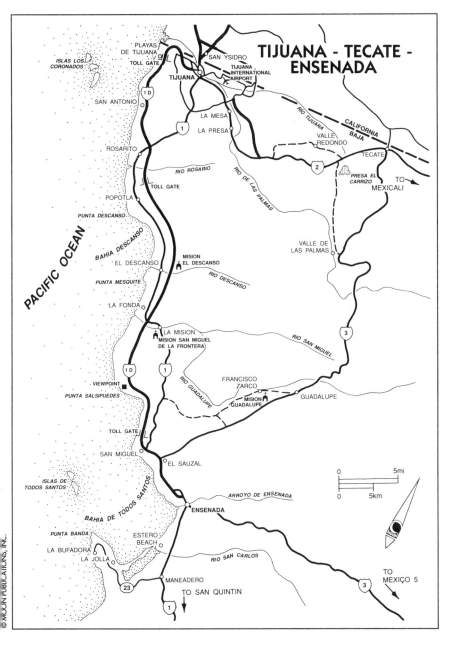

TIJUANA - TECATE - ENSENADA

PACIFIC OCEAN

ISLAS LOS CORONADOS

PLAYAS DE TIJUANA
TOLL GATE
SAN YSIDRO
TIJUANA
TIJUANA INTERNATIONAL AIRPORT

SAN ANTONIO

LA MESA
LA PRESA

ROSARITO

RIO ROSARIO

TOLL GATE

POPOTLA

PUNTA DESCANSO

BAHIA DESCANSO

EL DESCANSO
MISION EL DESCANSO

PUNTA MESQUITE

RIO DESCANSO

LA FONDA

LA MISION
MISION SAN MIGUEL DE LA FRONTERA

VIEWPOINT
PUNTA SALSIPUEDES

RIO GUADALUPE

TOLL GATE

SAN MIGUEL

EL SAUZAL

ISLAS DE TODOS SANTOS

BAHIA DE TODOS SANTOS

ARROYO DE ENSENADA

ENSENADA

PUNTA BANDA
ESTERO BEACH
LA BUFADORA
LA JOLLA

RIO SAN CARLOS

MANEADERO
TO SAN QUINTIN

RIO TIJUANA

CALIFORNIA BAJA

VALLE REDONDO

TECATE

RIO DE LAS PALMAS

PRESA EL CARRIZO
TO MEXICALI

VALLE DE LAS PALMAS

RIO SAN MIGUEL

FRANCISCO ZARCO
MISION GUADALUPE
GUADALUPE

0   5mi
0   5km

TO MEXICO 5

1D 1 2 3 23

fishing, with the exception of a few lobster and sea urchin concessions, isn't permitted, nor can visitors land on any of the islands without government permission. As a result, the islands have become one of the most important brown pelican rookeries on the Pacific coast; over 160 other bird species have been identified as well. Along the west side of Coronado del Norte is a large sea lion colony; harbor seals are common along the same shoreline, with elephant seals occasionally seen. Island plant varieties number around 100, mostly cactus, mimosae, and other species suited to arid climates.

Fishing

Yellowtail fishing is usually excellent in the vicinity of the Coronados, with peak season running from April through October. Rock cod, bonito, halibut, barracuda, calico bass, and white seabass are also frequently taken. Favorite fishing spots lie just north of Roca Media, at the southeast tip of Coronado del Sur, and inshore along the western side of the same island.

Diving

Los Coronados is the most heavily dived area in Baja waters. Many San Diego novices make their first open-water dives here and spearfishers have long extolled the abundance of underwater game. In some places the moray eels are so accustomed to handouts they immediately approach any diver who happens along.

Good sites for divers of all levels include "The Slot," an area of rich marinelife between the two middle islands; a rocky cove called the "Lobster Shack," located along the northeastern coast of Coronado del Norte and named for an old shack onshore used by lobstermen; the large kelp bed just south of the southern tip of Coronado del Sur; and the rock-reef at the northern end of Coronado del Sur. Advanced, open-ocean divers can tackle "Eighty-five-foot Reef," named for the depth at which much of the reef begins. The shallowest portion is about 18 meters (60 feet) below the ocean surface.

Transport And Tours

No regular boat service to Islas Los Coronados exists—most visitors navigate their own craft—although you might find charters in San Antonio del Mar if you ask around.

Several San Diego fishing outfitters offer fishing tours of the islands. **Diving Charters** operates twice-monthly diving trips.

ROSARITO

Rosarito's multiple personality—ranchtown, beachtown, and boomtown rolled into one—reflects a short but varied history. During the mission era, the area was virtually uninhabited—out of the reach of Dominican missions to the south and Franciscan missions to the north. Although the Camino Real ("Royal Road") passed nearby, it wasn't until a parallel road began snaking southward along the coast from Tijuana that anyone but ranchers developed an interest in the area. Early Baja travelers discovered the huge beach at Rosarito—one of the widest and longest on Baja's Pacific coast—in the '20s and it has become more popular with each passing decade.

History

In 1827, as Mexico was gaining its independence from Spain, Juan Machado received a land grant of 407,000 acres in the Rosarito area, then called El Rosario. The Machado family raised cattle and sheep on the property and leased land to other ranchers. In 1914 the family sold 14,000 coastal acres to a land development corporation, which in turn sold them to a New York attorney in 1920.

In 1924 the attorney opened El Rosario Resort and Country Club next to the beach. Initially the resort was little more than a rustic hunting cabin. A dirt road between Tijuana and Ensenada passed El Rosario, however, and it became a popular stopover for North Americans sampling the casinos at either end of the road. The free camping allowed on the property probably didn't hurt its success.

Manuel Barbachano bought the property around 1930 and built the Rosarito Beach Hotel, a 10-room hotel with a small lobby, one bathroom, and a casino to take advantage of the Prohibition boom in gambling. Apparently no record exists as to why Barbachano changed the name from El Rosario to Rosarito—perhaps because "Rosarito" is easier for gringos to pronounce. Another theory claims that he named

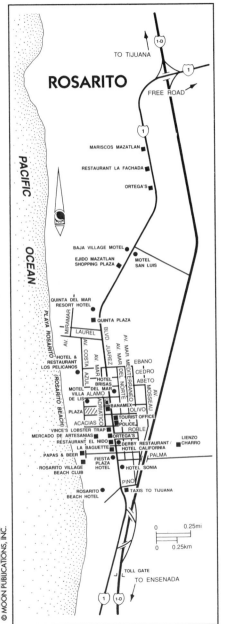

ROSARITO

TO TIJUANA

FREE ROAD

MARISCOS MAZATLAN

RESTAURANT LA FACHADA

ORTEGA'S

PACIFIC OCEAN

BAJA VILLAGE MOTEL

EJIDO MAZATLAN SHOPPING PLAZA

MOTEL SAN LUIS

QUINTA DEL MAR RESORT HOTEL

PLAYA ROSARITO

AV. MIRAMAR

LAUREL

QUINTA PLAZA

BLVD JUAREZ

AV. COSTA AZUL

AV. MAR MEDITERRANEO

AV. MAR DEL NORTE

EBANO

CEDRO

ABETO

AV. MOSSEAU

HOTEL & RESTAURANT LOS PELICANOS

HOTEL BRISAS

MOTEL DEL MAR VILLA ALAMO DE LIS

ADRIATICO

BANAMEX

OLIVO

PLAZA

TOURIST OFFICE

ROSARITO BEACH

ACACIAS

POLICE

ROBLE

VINCE'S LOBSTER TRAP

ORTEGA'S

MERCADO DE ARTESANIAS

RESTAURANT EL NIDO

DERBY RESTAURANT / HOTEL CALIFORNIA

LIENZO CHARRO

LA BAGUETTE

PAPAS & BEER

PALMA

FIESTA PLAZA HOTEL

HOTEL SONIA

ROSARITO VILLAGE BEACH CLUB

PINO

ROSARITO BEACH HOTEL

TAXIS TO TIJUANA

0   0.25mi

0   0.25km

TOLL GATE
TO ENSENADA

the hotel after Lee J. Rose, developer of one of Tijuana's first racetracks.

For most of the next 40 years, all development in Rosarito focused around the Rosarito Beach Hotel. After Prohibition ended and the Mexican government banned casino gambling, Barbachano closed the casino but enlarged the hotel, employing a Belgian architect and Mexican muralist to turn it into a major attraction. During the '40s and '50s, Rosarito became a favorite haunt of Hollywood celebrities, Latin American presidents, and well-heeled international travelers.

The completion of a four-lane toll road to Rosarito in 1967 brought many more Alta Californians into town and modified the exclusive nature of the resort. Other hotels were built and, although the Rosarito Beach Hotel remained the beach centerpiece for some time, the town expanded from a weekend resort to a large residential community of retirees and self-employed expatriates.

Today a four-lane roadway with lighted traffic islands passes through the center of Rosarito, lined with shopping plazas, neon-lit restaurants, highrise hotels, and condominiums. Vacation and retirement homes, an estimated 10,000 owned by North Americans, stretch along the ocean for miles in either direction. Off the impressive main drag, however, many side streets remain unpaved, much to the chagrin of local residents. The city of 80,000 recently received its first central sewage plant, situated in the hills east of the city. During the last two or three years city officials have given some 40,000 trees to local citizens for planting throughout the city.

Many residents would like to see Rosarito become BCN's fifth municipality, an entity roughly analogous to a U.S. county. As part of the municipality of Tijuana—26% of the total area, 5.4% of the population—comparatively wealthy Rosarito provides a large portion of Tijuana's annual budget. If the town could secede from municipal Tijuana, Rosarito residents argue, more money could go towards local urban improvements.

If Rosarito becomes an independent municipality, zoning restrictions might follow. New highrise hotels are added to the Rosarito skyline one by one, pushing the once-sleepy beach town closer and closer toward a fate like that of Miami Beach. The controversial Hotel Festival

Plaza, a bright yellow highrise on the main drag, is meant to look like a giant wooden amusement park—a Coney Island touch.

Sights

Rosarito's main draw is its eight-km-long, sandy beach. Several beachwear and surf shops in town offer swimming, snorkeling, floating, and surfing equipment for rent or purchase.

The **Rosarito Beach Hotel** is an attraction in itself. For nearly a half century it was the only place to stay in Rosarito, and for many repeat visitors it's still the first choice. During its heyday in the '40s and '50s, the hotel gained a reputation among the Hollywood set as a romantic retreat. Frequent guests included Victor Mature, Mickey Rooney, Joan Bennett, Lana Turner, Orson Welles, Rita Hayworth, Debbie Reynolds, Robert Stack, Gregory Peck, Robert Preston, Spencer Tracy, Jack Palance, and Vincent Price. International playboy Ali Khan and actress Gene Tierney, along with an entourage of 24, took over the entire hotel for several weeks in 1955; Kim Novak and Dominican Republic President Rafael Leonidas Trujillo trysted here during the same era. Not all Hollywood rendezvous at the Rosarito were of the illicit variety; Burgess Meredith and Paulette Goddard married here.

The original owner's nephew, Hugo Torres, acquired the property in 1974. Following his uncle's example, Torres continues to expand the facilities and currently offers 300 rooms. Although no longer a celebrity hideaway, a tour of the Belgian-designed architecture, the Matía Santoyo murals, and the seaward-facing Beachcomber Bar is on the itinerary of nearly every Rosarito visitor.

The tiny **Museo Wa-Kuatay,** attached to the hotel and situated next to the pharmacy, houses a collection of historic photos of early ranchers, Hollywood celebrities, and politicos. There is also a display of artifacts left by the Wakutais, the original inhabitants of the Rosarito area. The museum is open Wed.-Mon. noon-1700; admission is free.

Accommodations In Town

Most of Rosarito's hotels are strung out along Blvd. Juárez, the main thoroughfare. Room rates range from US$20 s, US$25 d at the cheapest motels to US$75 at the most expensive hotels—and over US$100 for a suite, condo, or townhouse. These rates are high for Mexico but a bargain for most southern Alta Californians. Rates are usually discounted during the low season, November through April. During high season, July-Aug., reservations are highly recommended; they may also be necessary on weekends.

Currently under construction along Blvd. Juárez is the towering **Villa Corona,** a resort hotel that will offer 500 rooms upon completion.

Time-share condos and vacation homes are also available at the various complexes around town and are often good bargains for four or more people.

Rosarito
Beach Hotel

JOE CUMMINGS

ROSARITO HOTELS AND MOTELS

Note: Rates quoted are for peak season: May through September. Off-season rates drop as much as 30-50%. Add 10% hotel tax to all rates; some hotels may charge an additional 10% service charge. Area code: 661

Baja Village Motel; Blvd. Juárez and Via de las Olas; tel. 2-00-53; US$34-55

Brisas del Mar; Blvd. Juárez 22; tel. 2-25-47, in U.S. tel. (800) 697-5223; US$43-63; restaurant, coffee shop, jacuzzi

Castillas del Mar; 1.6 km (one mile) south of Rosarito Beach Hotel on Blvd. Juárez (P.O. Box 1772, San Ysidro, CA 92073); tel. 2-10-88; US$50-70; ocean view

Hotel Best Western Festival Plaza; Blvd. Juárez north of the Rosarito Beach Hotel

Hotel California; Blvd. Juárez 32; tel. 2-25-50; US$45-65

Hotel Los Pelicanos; Calle Cedros 115; tel. 2-04-45; US$35-55; some rooms with ocean view

Hotel Sonia; Blvd. Juárez next door to Panadería La Espiga; tel. 2-12-60; US$20-25

Marsella's Motel; Calle del Mar 75; tel 2-04-68; US$28-30

Motel Baja del Sol; south end of Blvd. Juárez; tel. 2-13-50; US$35-50

Motel Colonial; Calle 1a de Mayo 71; tel 2-15-75; US$30-40; kitchenettes in some rooms

Motel Don Luis de Rosarito; Blvd. Juárez 11; tel. 2-11-66; US$40-60

Motel Villa de Lis; Calle Alamo and Av. Costa Azul; tel. 2-23-20; US$25-35; beachfront rooms

Quinta del Mar Resort Hotel; north end of Blvd. Juárez, (P.O. Box 184, Rosarito, BCN); tel. 2-13-01, in U.S. tel. (619) 428-5500; US$36-65 s/d, US$75-95 one bedroom, US$115-150 two bedroom, US$160 three bedroom; condos and townhouses, restaurants, pools, tennis, jacuzzi, some rooms with ocean view

Rosarito Beach Hotel; south end of Blvd. Juárez, (P.O. Box 145, San Ysidro, CA 92073); tel. 2-11-06, in California tel. (800) 343-8582; US$55-75, special weekday rates of US$44 available during off-peak periods, US$75-80 junior suites and bungalows with kitchenettes, US$86-126 ocean suites (up to six people); restaurants, pools, tennis and racquetball courts, fitness course, gym, sauna

Accomodations Out Of Town

At **Hotel Las Rocas** (tel. 2-21-40; mailing address: P.O. Box 1948, San Ysidro, CA 92073), is an isolated resort hotel 9.5 km south of Rosarito at Km 37. All rooms have ocean views, fireplaces, and kitchenettes. Other facilities include a restaurant, pool, jacuzzi, and tennis courts. During the week rates range from US$50 for a standard room to US$100 for a deluxe suite, with rates of US$75-150 on weekends and holidays. **Calafia Ocean Resort** (tel. 2-15-80, toll-free 800-CALAFIA) at Km 35.5 is a time-share condo development that frequently has one- or two-bedroom units for rent in the US$100-120 range, plus 16 mobile homes costing US$40-75 a night.

Popotla Trailer Park (tel. 2-15-04), a mobile-home community about 3.5 km south of Rosarito, sometimes has permanently sited trailers for rent for US$25-30 a night.

Camping And RV Parks

Chuy's Trailer Park (tel. 2-16-08), Av. Costa Azul 175 downtown, features 35 beachfront sites with full hookups for US$15 a night; it's often full. Also on Costa Azul, near the Hotel Villa de Lis, **Alamo Trailer Park** (no phone) has a few basic spaces with electricity and water for US$8-10 a night.

About two km north of Rosarito at Km 25 lies the deluxe **Oasis Hotel and RV Resort** (mailing address: P.O. Box 158, Imperial Beach, CA 91933; tel. 3-32-55, 800-462-7472 in the U.S.). Beachfront RV sites cost US$30 a night for up to five people, back row sites are US$20; add US$5 for each additional person plus US$5 for June-Sept. rates. Rooms with refrigerators and microwaves start at US$35 on winter weekdays and reach as high as US$129 on summer weekends. Facilities include two pools, jacuzzis, tennis courts, mini-golf, individual barbecue pits, satellite cable TV at each site, a mini-market, and two restaurants. The beach here is impressive and the park places an emphasis on family-oriented recreational activities.

The **KOA Rosarito** (tel. 86-14-12, A.P. 2082, Tijuana), three km farther north at Km 22, offers tent/ camping/RV sites with full hookups for US$16. Facilities include showers, flush toilets, ice, laundry room, pool, tennis courts, and boat ramp.

About three km south of Rosarito is **Campo Alegre,** with full hookups for US$15 per night. Most of the slots at **Popotla Trailer Park,** in the same vicinity, are occupied by long-term residents; when vacant, a space costs US$12 a night. **Campo Martha,** near Hotel Las Rocas at Km 37.5 on the way to Ensenada, usually has full-hookup spots in the US$12-15 range.

Food

Rosarito's Blvd. Juárez is jammed with restaurants of every description. The area specialties are carnitas and Puerto Nuevo-style lobster; every block seems to contain at least one taco stand and one seafood restaurant. Some of the better choices are listed below.

$ **Los Arcos** (tel. 2-04-91), Blvd. Juárez, next to the Rosarito Beach Hotel gate: An overgrown taco stand serving tasty flautas, tacos, burritos, *queso fundido* (melted cheese), *gorditas* (thick corn tortillas stuffed with meat), and Mexican breakfasts. Open daily 0800-2200.

$$ **Derby Restaurant** (tel. 2-14-22), diagonally opposite the Rosarito Beach Hotel on Blvd. Juárez: This is one of Rosarito's oldest eateries and a favorite among local expats. The mostly ranchero-style Mexican menu features carne asada, chiles rellenos, enchiladas, and steak. An added attraction is the collection of local art on display. Open daily 0800-2200.

$$ **Don Giuseppo's** (tel. 2-16-08), Av. Costa Azul 75, next to Chuy's Trailer Park: Formerly George's, now serving pizza, pasta, seafood, and steak. Open 0800-2300 daily.

$$ **La Fachada** (tel. 2-17-85), Blvd. Juárez 2884: Another expat favorite featuring *parrilladas*—grilled steak, seafood, and Mexican plates. The ravenous can fill up on the "Sky, Sea, and Earth" platter—a quail, lobster, and steak combo. Open daily except Tuesday 0800-2230.

$ **La Flor de Michoacán,** Blvd. Juárez 146: The Ochoa family has been making the best

carnitas in town since 1950. Besides carnitas by the kilo, the menu offers tacos, tortas, burritos, and quesadillas, all served with bowls of fiery salsa, lime sections, and pickled chiles and vegetables. The service is excellent; some nights a roving group of *músicos* performs norteña music on request. A second location is at the Centro Artesanal. Open daily except Wednesday, 1000-2200.

$ **Just For The Halibut Fish Tacos,** opposite the Hotel Festival Plaza, Blvd. Juárez: The owners of this small taco shop catch fresh halibut daily to fold into handmade tortillas. You add the condiments from countertop bowls for the perfect fish taco, at US$.75 each. The walls are adorned with fading autographed magazine photos of famous surfers; on the counter sits a basket of current surf magazines. Open daily from around 1000 to 2200.

$$ **La Leña** (tel. 2-08-26), Quinta Plaza shopping center, Blvd. Juárez: A branch of the well-known Tijuana steak house, specializing in Sonoran-style, mesquite-grilled meats. Most meals come with an appetizer of *machaca* (dried, shredded beef). Open daily noon-2200.

$$ **Mariscos Mazatlán** (tel. 2-23-33), Blvd. Juárez 2223: This is one of the best seafood places in town. Especially good is the *huachinango sarandeado,* barbecued red snapper, though snapper is also available in many other dishes. The extensive menu includes a sampler tray with crab, snapper, octopus, marlin tacos, abalone, rice, vegetables, and salsas. Service is excellent. Open 1000-2300 daily.

$$ **Ortega's Place** (tel. 2-00-22), Blvd. Juárez 200: The Ortega family started out serving lobster dinners to tourists at their home in nearby Puerto Nuevo in 1945. As at the other Ortega's restaurants—seven at last count, five in Puerto Nuevo and two in Rosarito—the house specialty is Puerto Nuevo-style lobster. The creatures are split lengthwise, dropped briefly into hot oil, grilled a few minutes, then served with frijoles, rice, and tortillas for around US$12. There's no better way to eat lobster. Open daily for breakfast, lunch, and dinner.

$-$$ **Palacio Royal** (tel. 2-14-12) Plaza Comercial Ejido Mazatlán, Blvd. Juárez: Of Rosarito's three Chinese restaurants, this is the best. The menu features a variety of southern and northern Chinese cooking styles. Open 1100-midnight.

$$-$$$ **Los Pelicanos** (tel. 2-17-57), Calle

Ebano and Av. Costa Azul: One of the few restaurants in town with an ocean view; good seafood and quail; upscale ambience. Open noon-midnight daily.

$$-$$$ Popotla (tel. 2-15-04), Km 33 (8 km south of Rosarito): Good ocean views; good seafood. Open Mon.-Sat. for lunch and dinner, Sunday for brunch, lunch, and dinner.

$$ Rosarito Beach Hotel: The hotel coffeeshop serves a reasonable Sunday brunch (0730-1400) that includes ceviche, chilaquiles, tamales, seafood, Mexican egg dishes, and fresh fruit. Upstairs, the **Azteca** offers more expensive lunch, seafood, and Mexican fare. Next door the new and elegant **Chabert's** serves steak and continental dishes.

$ Tacos Sonora, Centro Artesanal, next to El Nido: Serves burritos, tacos, carne asada, and quesadillas with large, Sonora-style flour tortillas. Open daily 1000-2200.

$$ Vince's Lobster Trap (tel. 2-12-53), Blvd. Juárez 39: This lobster house/seafood market is a contender for best seafood restaurant in town. Lots of daily specials. A smaller version, **Vince's Grill-Bar El Calamar,** is at Blvd. Juárez 77. Open daily 1100-2300.

Bakeries: Several Rosarito establishments satisfy the pastry cravings of tourists and local residents. **Bibi's Bakery** in the Quinta Plaza shopping center makes breads, cakes, and other North American-style baked goods. **La Baguette** on Blvd. Juárez 137 (between El Nido and the Fiesta Plaza Hotel) is part of a northern Baja chain that bakes European-style fare. For Mexican pastries and bolillos, your best choice is **Panaficadora La Espiga,** across Blvd. Juárez from (and just a bit north of) the Rosarito Beach Hotel. Espiga occupies two other locations—one at the north end of town opposite Ejido Mazatlán shopping plaza and one opposite Ortega's Place.

Entertainment

On weekend nights and any night in July or August, Rosarito throbs with a disco beat. Several clubs are concentrated just north of the Rosarito Beach Hotel, on the beach side of Blvd. Juárez. **Papas and Beer,** at the end of Calle Nogal, features indoor and outdoor bar areas, plus a sand volleyball court; it's packed on warm summer nights, all but deserted during the winter. Opposite Papas and Beer is the similar

Rosarito Village Beach Club. Other dance clubs in the area change names from season to season.

The **Rosarito Beach Hotel** hosts a "Fiesta Mexicana" every Friday evening from 1900 to 0200 in one of the ground-floor lounges. For US$7 guests receive a full Mexican buffet and credible performances of folk dancing, mariachis, and charro rope tricks. The hotel's **Beachcomber Bar** overlooks the beach and is a good place for a quiet sunset drink.

Sports And Recreation

During the winter, intermittent **surf**—usually nothing huge, but surfable—may appear at either end of the beach. Better breaks are usually found south of Rosarito, starting at Km 33, from Punta Descanso to Punta Mesquite. **Tony's Surf Shop** (tel. 2-11-92) at Blvd. Juárez 312 sells surf gear, including boards.

Horseback riding on the beach is a favorite tourist activity. Local wranglers wait for customers on the beach near the Rosarito Beach Hotel and at the north end of Blvd. Juárez. Rates start at around US$5 per hour but are negotiable when business is slow.

Gamblers can indulge in off-track betting and sports book at **LF Race and Sports Book,** La Masia Restaurant, Hotel Quinta del Mar or at **Caliente Race And Sports Book,** Quinta Plaza shopping center.

Charreadas occasionally take place at small charro rings near town—check with the tourist office on Blvd. Juárez for the latest schedule. Once a year, during the summer, there's a *gran charreada*—this is the one to see. Admission is around US$3.

Events

Twice yearly on the last Saturday in April and September, Rosarito kicks off the **Rosarito-Ensenada 50-Mile Bicycle Ride.** Each is reportedly the third-largest biking event in the world, with close to 10,000 cyclists.

Bajacalifornio food fans won't want to miss the **Mexican Food Festival** in early May or the **Rosarito Beach Seafood Fair** in late June—usually on Father's Day—when chefs from the Rosarito area compete for your palate.

For up-to-date information on Rosarito's ongoing schedule of events, call (661) 2-03-96.

Shopping

Rosarito offers a representative sampling of the same kinds of retail outlets found in Tijuana—liquor stores, pharmacies, curio shops, furniture outlets, leather shops, art galleries, and boutiques, all specializing in North American tastes. **Tile Express** (tel. 2-19-13, Blvd. Juárez 54A), for example, is a branch of the larger Tijuana store. An even larger selection of handmade tiles is available at **Artesanías Hacienda** (tel. 2-24-35) at Blvd. Juárez 2500-C. **Interiores de México,** Blvd. Juárez 25500, carries quality furniture and handicrafts; custom orders are accepted.

Among the better art collections in town are **Del Mar** (south end of the Rosarito Beach Hotel complex), **Pabel's** (a block north of the RBH on the opposite side of Juárez), and the gallery in the Derby Restaurant.

On the west side of Blvd. Juárez, about midway between the Quinta del Mar and Rosarito Beach hotels, is the **Mercado de Artesanías,** a crafts market with around 200 vendors selling ceramics, textiles, wood carving, sculpture, and other handmade items. Just south of town is a string of vendor stalls where handicraft prices tend to be a bit lower. Bargaining is expected; most vendors are open 0900-1800.

Many shops are grouped in shopping plazas, e.g., Plaza Ejido Mazatlán, Quinta Plaza, and the arcade attached to the Rosarito Beach Hotel.

Transport

ABC buses from Tijuana (45 minutes, US$.60) and Ensenada (1.5 hours, US$2) arrive hourly from dawn to dusk along Blvd. Juárez. Yellow-and-cream *taxis de ruta* ply the half-hour stretch between Tijuana and Rosarito for US$1 per person.

The drive from Tijuana to Rosarito is 31 km via the toll road, 27 km via the free road. Mexico 1-D, the toll road, is much faster, with four lanes in each direction, no traffic lights, and a maximum speed limit of 110 km per hour (about 65 mph). The toll-road entrance in Tijuana is situated just south of the Río Tijuana; the toll to Rosarito costs about US$2.25.

To take the free road (Mexico 1) from Tijuana you'll need to find Blvd. Cuauhtémoc by driving east on either Paseo de los Héroes or Blvd. Agua Caliente, then turn south on Cuauhtémoc. Coming from San Diego, you can avoid Tijuana altogether by crossing the border at Otay Mesa east

of Tijuana, then following signs for Tecate. Instead of taking the turnoff for Mexico 2 to Tecate, continue straight on Blvd. Lázaro Cárdenas—which becomes Blvd. Independencia or "Libramiento-Oriente"—until the road intersects with Mexico 1. Follow signs reading Ensenada Libre.

Rosarito contains two PEMEX stations, both offering unleaded gas; the one near the Hotel Quinta del Mar is open 24 hours.

Rosarito Information

Tourist Office: The city tourist office (tel. 2-03-69), next to the police station on Blvd. Juárez between Calles Olivo and Acacias, distributes Rosarito area tourist information; the staff can also assist with hotel reservations. If you need information on other destinations in northern Baja, the state tourist office (tel. 2-10-65) at Calle Cipres and Av. Costa Azul may be able to help. There is also an information kiosk at Quinta Plaza on Blvd. Juárez operated by the local visitors and convention bureau.

The monthly *Baja Times,* published out of an office in the Rosarito Beach Hotel shopping arcade, is an excellent source of information on local events. It's distributed free at several shops and hotels in town. The local Spanish-language paper is *Ecos de Rosarito.*

Post and Telephone: Mail Express and Xtras (tel. 2-24-23, fax 2-24-24), at Calle C.R. Cota 853-13 opposite the Rosarito Beach Hotel, offers private mail, UPS, and telephone answering services.

Rosarito's telephone area code is 661.

ROSARITO TO ENSENADA

South of Rosarito along the coast lies a string of beaches, ejidos, and residential communities: Popotla, Las Gaviotas, Puerto Nuevo, Cantamar, El Descanso, La Fonda, La Misión, La Salina, Bajamar, and San Miguel. Real estate developers call this the "Gold Coast," but only the coves and beaches are particularly attractive.

Between Punta Descanso and Punta Mesquite (especially Km 33-38, Km 48, Km 56 on the free road), and as far south as La Misión, are several surfing spots with decent reef or beach breaks. An area of sand dunes near Km 54 south of Cantamar is frequented by hang-gliding enthusiasts.

BAJA CALIFORNIA LOBSTERS

Of the several species of lobster scooting about in Baja seas, the most numerous are *Panulirus interruptus* (known as red lobster or *langosta roja*), found as far south as the 25th parallel on both the Pacific and Sea of Cortez sides, and *P. inflatus* (blue lobster or *langosta azul*) in the Pacific and lower Cortez as far south as Tehuantepec, Oaxaca. None of the lobster species found in Baja waters are related to the cold-water type (genus *Homarus*) found off the coast of the northeastern U.S. and southeastern Canada. Baja's warm-water lobsters are sometimes referred to as "spiny lobsters" because their shells bear spiny projections (the *Homarus* shell is smooth). Spiny lobsters also feature smaller pincers than the cold-water varieties.

Adult spiny lobsters reach up to 61 centimeters (24 inches) in length and weigh as much as six kilo-

grams (13 pounds). Most varieties are nocturnal and tend to frequent depths of five to 30 meters. During the day they stay beneath or between rocks, hiding from natural enemies like sharks, octopus, rays, and a few larger finfish. Their diet consists mostly of crustaceans, mollusks, and other small sea organisms.

Lobstering is a major part of the fishing industry in Mexico, the world's eighth-largest harvester of lobster. In a typical year 700 metric tons are harvested; about half the total catch for export, earning around US$9 million in foreign revenues. The official lobstering seasons are 16 March to 30 September for red lobster and 1 June to 15 September for blue lobster. It's illegal to take lobsters out of Mexico without a receipt proving they were purchased from a store or *cooperativa de pesca* (fishing cooperative).

Puerto Nuevo

This tiny seaside town 19 km (12 miles) south of Rosarito via Mexico 1 is known as Baja's lobster capital. Although the actual lobster harvest in the area isn't what it once was—the lobster served in Puerto Nuevo is mostly harvested in areas south of Ensenada and distributed through San Diego—lobster restaurants are more plentiful than ever. When Baja travelers first discovered Puerto Nuevo in the '50s, they dined in the houses of two or three local families. Now the village offers nearly 30 side-by-side seafood restaurants, some quite modern. An entire village devoted to eating.

The typical Puerto Nuevo-style lobster platter includes lobster, beans, rice, and tortillas. The lobster is usually lightly fried in oil and then briefly grilled before serving, but in some restaurants it is also prepared in a *ranchera* (tomato and chile) sauce, or boiled, new England-style. The Ortega family was the first to serve lobster platters to the public from its home; the original, much-renovated **Ortega's** still stands, along with four other branches nearby and two in Rosarito.

The very first actual restaurant to serve lobster here was **Restaurant Puerto Nuevo,** and judging from the crowds this is still the local favorite. The original Restaurant Puerto Nuevo serves only lobster, shrimp, and fish-fillet platters, and

only cash is accepted. The fancier **Restaurant Puerto Nuevo II** next door features a more extensive menu and accepts credit cards; most of the clientele are visiting gringos. Other family-run favorites include **Miramar, Chela's, La Escondida, El Galeón,** and **La Perlita.** Smaller lobsters with rice, beans, and tortillas cost US$9, medium-sized crustaceans run US$10-12, and a half-kilo (1.5-pound) lobster costs US$15 or more. A few places offer weekday specials as low as US$8 including a complimentary beer or margarita.

Accommodations: The recently completed **Hotel New Port Baja** (tel. 661-4-11-66, toll-free 800-562-1018 in the U.S.) offers deluxe ocean-view rooms starting at US$55 a night midweek, US$95-125 on weekends and holidays. Facilities include pool, jacuzzi, volleyball court, tennis courts, and coffee shop. The **Grand Baja Resort** (tel. 4-14-79, toll-free 800-275-3280) features one-, two-, and three-bedroom condos on a bluff overlooking the Pacific for US$85-125.

RV Parks: Just south of Puerto Nuevo lie two RV facilities, **Cantamar** (P.O. Box 295, San Ysidro, CA 92073), at Cantamar Beach, and **Rancho Reynosa** (A.P. 640, Rosarito, BCN), about 2.5 km north of the Cantamar toll road exit on the free road.

Events: The relatively new **Festival de la Langosta y el Vino** ("Lobster and Wine Festival") occurs in Puerto Nuevo's restaurant zone in mid-October. For US$15 per person participants are welcome to sample all the Baja lobster and wine they can consume.

Transport: Red-and-white route taxis operate between Rosarito and Puerto Nuevo for US$.75 per person. In Rosarito they leave from in front of the Hotel Festival Plaza. In Puerto Nuevo you must stand at the side of the highway opposite the village entrance and flag one down; these taxis actually ply a Rosarito-La Misión route. For evening excursions it's safer to hire a *taxi de ruta* to Puerto Nuevo from Rosarito than to drive it yourself—these drivers know the road very well.

La Fonda And La Misión

To reach this area, approximately 60 km south of the border, take La Misión exit from the toll road. Here you'll find the best beaches between Rosarito and Ensenada. At one time the valley surrounding La Misión sheltered Mission San Miguel Arcángel de la Frontera, founded by Dominican Padre Luis Salles in 1788 and secularized in 1833. The only remains of the mission are two adobe walls standing in a schoolyard on the east side of the free road as it passes through the village.

Accommodations: Two small, comfortable, well-run hotels offer opportunities for overnights. **Hotel La Fonda** (no phone; mailing address: P.O. Box 268, San Ysidro, CA 92073) has rooms for US$35 and ocean-front apartments that accommodate up to four persons for US$50. La Fonda's restaurant serves good seafood with an ocean view. Overlooking the broad beach at La Misión is clean and well-run **Hotel La Misión**, a newer establishment with 10 large rooms, all with fireplace, for US$38 a night Sun.-Thurs. or US$42 on Friday and Saturday. The hotel has a restaurant and a small grocery store.

Outdoor Resorts of Baja (tel. 20-19-83, toll-free 800-356-2252, 1177 Broadway, Suite 2, Chula Vista, CA 91911) at Km 72 is a huge 280-space RV complex with full hookups, sheltered pull-throughs, pool, spa, sauna, tennis courts, restaurant/lounge, and satellite TV for US$24-35 a night for up to four people plus US$3 for each additional adult. Shuttle vans to Ensenada run daily. Several beachfront cottages rent for US$60 a day.

You'll find yet more beach condos at **Plaza del Mar** (tel. 85-91-52, 800-868-0248) at Km 58, about three kilometers (two miles) north of La Misión. Rates are as low as US$27-32 s, US$32-38 d in the winter; US$34-40 s and US$39-46 d in the summer. On the premises are a pool, jacuzzi, basketball and tennis courts, gardens, and a small archaeological museum.

San Miguel

A unique cross between retirement-oriented trailer park and surf camp, San Miguel is the legacy of a Polish-Mexican-American family, the Robertsons, who've lived in northern Mexico and southern Alta California for most of this century. The late Tomás Robertson, who founded the Villa de San Miguel residential community in the '50s, was a mission historian and an active member of the Comité por Conservación de Misións de Baja California. His son Glen now manages the trailer park, bar, and restaurant with aplomb.

The bay formed by Punta San Miguel is the most popular surfing locale in Baja; Mexico's first surfboard manufacturer—San Miguel's—is named after the point. A few hardcore surfers live in San Miguel on a semipermanent basis, and during the winter a small legion takes up residence on the beach or in rented trailers. On winter evenings, those who aren't partying in Ensenada or exhausted by the day's surfing hang out in the San Miguel Restaurant bar swapping war stories about the three-story waves at Islas de Todos Santos.

Accommodations and Food: Camping is permitted on the beach for US$8 per night; full-hookup trailer sites are US$10. Trailers on the hill above the beach can sometimes be rented for US$25-30 a night. Inquire at the restaurant, tel. (617) 4-62-25, or write San Miguel Village, A.P. 55, El Sauzal, BCN. Check to see if the water supply is working before accepting an offer; the water pressure in the trailers near the top of the hill is sometimes low or even absent altogether. For permanent trailers with their own water storage tanks, this isn't a problem; for the rest, the village has plans to upgrade the community system. Occasionally a trailer slot on the hill opens up.

The San Miguel Restaurant serves northern Mexican dishes (including excellent chiles rellenos), steak, seafood, and frog legs. A fireplace adds to the cozy atmosphere on chilly winter evenings.

Another lodging possibility is **Motel Sausalito** (tel. 667-4-61-88) at Km 102 on Mexico 1 in nearby El Sauzal. Although it has no beach or scenic views, the hotel is comfortable enough and includes a pool and restaurant. Rooms are US$27-35 per night. Also in El Sauzal is the **California Trailer Park & Motel** (tel. 617-4-60-33), where RV sites are US$8-10 a night, basic rooms US$30. About four km north of San Miguel at **Playa Saldamando** (tel. 619-285-4289 in the U.S.) is a campground with tent/camper sites (water only) for US$6-8 per night.

Events: The **Flojo Mexican Surf Fiesta,** sponsored by a maker of Mexican fisherman-style sandals, is usually held in San Miguel the last weekend in April and features surfing competitions, food, and bikini contests. The village celebrates **San Miguel's feast day** on the weekend nearest to 29 September; sometimes a group of Paipai Indians from San Miguel Valley joins the festivities. Another big party is held in late October at San Miguel in honor of **Oktoberfest;** the restaurant opens an all-you-can-eat, all-you-can-drink bar and buffet.

Getting There: San Miguel can be difficult to locate. Driving south on the toll road, take the Tijuana Libre exit just past the tollgate at Km 99, then follow the road west across the toll road until it curves south and begins to merge with the toll road a half-km farther. Instead of returning to the highway, follow the short, paved loop to the right and you'll come to San Miguel Village. If you're arriving via the free road, remember to take this road almost immediately before merging with the four-lane highway.

From Ensenada, you can make a U-turn immediately before the tollgate to find the road into the village. To get here by public transport from Ensenada, take a Tijuana-bound bus and disembark at the tollgate; then follow the above directions on foot.

Islas De Todos Santos

These twin islands about 20 km (12 miles) southwest of San Miguel—or west of Ensenada the same distance—offer a variety of recreational opportunities. Fishing is good along the western shores of both islands, especially for yellowtail, halibut, and seabass. For longer visits,

boats can safely anchor in three coves along the eastern shore of the southern island; the middle cove offers the best shelter overall. Local anglers stay at seasonal fish camps at the southern ends of both islands.

For hikers, the southern island offers the most interesting terrain, with cliffs along the perimeter and a hilly interior. The highest elevation, just below the island's midpoint, is approximately 100 meters. Near the northern end of this island are several caves; at the southern tip are a few tidal pools worth exploring. The northern island is mostly flat, with a radio tower and two lighthouses—one abandoned, one in use. Both islands are nesting grounds for brown pelicans, cormorants, blue herons, ospreys, and various other bird species.

Surfing: Islas de Todos Santos is perhaps best known as the site of the Pacific coast's biggest, baddest surf. November through February, a deep-water northwest swell sweeps the skinny northwestern point (partially submerged at high tide) of Isla Norte to produce powerful, eight- to 10-meter (25-30 feet) waves. Dubbed "Killer's," this is a break best attempted only by experienced gunners—unless it's running small. Todos surfers estimate that whatever height the surf at San Miguel is running, waves at Isla Norte will be double plus 2.5 meters (eight feet).

The northwest corner of the southern island also offers an excellent winter break. When the northwest swell is rolling hard, the channel between the two islands conjures up a monumental, long-riding right called Thor's Hammer, formed by the confluence of direct swell movement toward this point and refracted swell as it wraps eastward around the north island, then bounces off the south island and into the channel. This same channel pumps a grinding left break during the summer southwest swell, making the islands a year-round surf destination. Surfers sometimes camp on the flat northern island, but most boat in for the day from San Miguel or Ensenada.

Getting There: All-day *panga rapida* (fast panga) charters to the islands can be arranged for approximately US$25-30 per person at **Juanito's Boats** (tel. 4-09-53) in Ensenada, located behind the Plaza Marina on the waterfront. The trip takes around 30 minutes each way. You can also charter boats at fish camps in Punta Banda south of Ensenada, or sometimes in San Miguel.

San Miguel surfers with their own boats will usually take along a passenger or two if the guests agree to buy gas for the trip and beer for the survivors.

ENSENADA

Every summer an estimated four million visitors—most of them North Americans—pass through Ensenada, far more than any other non-border town on the peninsula. Yet as a busy trade center for northern peninsula fishing and agriculture, the city retains a Bajacalifornio identity in spite of weekend and summer tourism.

Ensenada is the capital of the Municipio de Ensenada, Mexico's largest municipality, extending all the way to the BCS border, comprising 52,511 square km and covering two-thirds of Baja California Norte. The municipality has a population of around half a million; estimates for the city itself vary from 150,000 to 250,000. It's difficult to keep an exact count since there are so many semipermanent residents in the Ensenada area, including an estimated 36,000 North Americans.

Baja California's third-largest city is also the peninsula's largest seaport due to its position on the wide Bahía de Todos Santos. The main industries in the area—aside from tourism—are

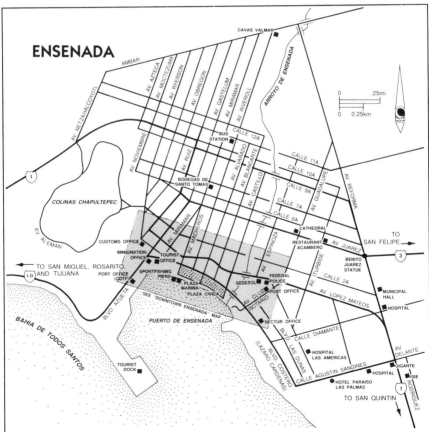

fishing, fish processing, and agriculture, all relying on the bay as a shipping point for sending products to mainland Mexico, the U.S., Canada, and Asia. Olives and grapes are the principal crops produced in the Ensenada area; the huge Oliveres Mexicanos plantation (48 km northeast of Ensenada, near Guadalupe) is the world's largest single olive producer, with over 120,000 trees under cultivation. Yellowtail and halibut are the top fish harvests, followed by various bottom fishes, lobster and other shellfish, and anchovies.

Although some old Baja hands buzz right past Ensenada in a rush to get to the "real Baja" farther south, for many repeat visitors a Baja trip simply doesn't get off to a good start without a ritual *cerveza* at Hussong's or a couple of *tacos de pescado* from the harbor fish market. Is Ensenada Americanized? Though it's undeniably a hybrid culture, Mexican tourists prefer the town to San Felipe or Cabo San Lucas; once you escape the waterfront area, you'll find neighborhood *panaderías,* quiet residential streets, and few tourists of any nationality.

CLIMATE AND TOURIST SEASONS

Ensenada's climate is similar to San Diego's. Yearly rainfall amounts to about 25 centimeters (10 inches), most of which falls Oct.-May. Temperatures are mild year-round, averaging 7-18° C (45-64° F) in January and 17-24° C (63-75° F) in August.

The high tourist season is June-Aug., when the weather is warm and rain is rare. The Christmas-New Year's holidays and spring break in March through early April are also peak periods. To avoid the crowds, consider visiting Ensenada in Oct.-Nov. or April-May.

HISTORY

In pre-Hispanic times, nomadic Yumano Indian tribes occasionally stopped at Bahía de Todos Santos to fish and gather clams, but no permanent Indian settlements existed in the area when the Spanish missionaries arrived in the 18th century. The first Spaniard to lay eyes on the bay was explorer Juan Cabrillo, who in 1542 named it San Mateo. Sebastián Vizcaíno's voyage of 1602 lent a different name to this piece of California coastal geography—Ensenada de Todos Santos, or "All Saint's Cove." Most likely this referred to a smaller cross-section of the bay—possibly the estuary where the Río San Carlos empties into the bay's south end—but eventually the entire bay came to be known as Bahía de Todos Santos.

Following a Spanish land grant to José Manuel Ruíz in 1804, several small farms and ranches were established in the hills east of the bay, including Ruíz's own Rancho Ensenada. A Spanish sergeant, Francisco Gastelum, bought and expanded the ranch in 1824. Following Mexican independence, the discovery of gold at nearby Real del Castillo in 1870 brought miners to the area; the miners needed supplies, and Ensenada, named for Gastelum's ranch, bloomed into a port practically overnight.

In 1882 Ensenada became the capital of the Territory of Baja California. The town continued to attract miners, farmers, and a variety of entrepreneurs who came to take advantage of the town's increasing prosperity. The boom lasted until the early 1900s, when few significant gold deposits remained and the political situation in the border area was becoming increasingly unstable. In order to counter growing Anglo-American influence along the border, the territorial capital was moved to Mexicali in 1915.

Ensenada faded into a farming and fishing village until U.S. Prohibition revived the economy. In the late '20s, heavyweight boxer Jack Dempsey and a number of other Americans opened the Playa Ensenada Hotel and Casino, a grand Spanish-style structure overlooking the bay. Along with Tijuana and Mexicali, Ensenada became a favorite destination for the American drinking-and-gambling set until Prohibition's repeal in 1933 and Mexico's casino closure of 1938. The Playa Ensenada casino-hotel was converted to a resort hotel under a new name, the Riviera del Pacífico, but, unable to attract guests in sufficient numbers, it soon closed. About this same time, following the government's agrarian reforms, Valle de Mexicali agriculture expanded rapidly, and Ensenada's port facilities were steadily upgraded.

Throughout the '40s and '50s the Ensenada area became a favorite destination for sportfishers and earned its title as "Yellowtail Capital of the World." Although increased commercial fishing and shipping decreased the bay's value as a sportfishing destination, overall economic development has fostered a cosmopolitan atmosphere, and Ensenada continues to cultivate its split personality as both tourist center and seaport.

SIGHTS

Ensenada's dual character—half resort, half commercial center—is split into two grids by Av. Juárez in the center of the city. The portion of the city south of Juárez, toward the bay, is mostly given over to tourist-oriented businesses, while the portion to the north consists of local businesses like those found in any Mexican city. Most of the city's hotels, restaurants, and gift shops are found along Blvd. Costero and Av. López Mateos, two parallel streets close to the waterfront.

Many of Ensenada's visual attractions lie out of town—at Estero Beach, Punta Banda, and La Bufadora—but a number of places of interest in the city are accessible by foot.

Riviera Del Pacífico

Ensenada's most impressive edifice opened in 1929 as the Playa Ensenada Hotel and Casino, owned and operated by Jack Dempsey and his financial backers; Al Capone was allegedly a silent partner. The opening act in the hotel ballroom was Bing Crosby, backed by the Xavier Cugat Orchestra; the orchestra included a singer named Margarita Carmen Cansino, a Baja native later known as Rita Hayworth. Facing the bay, the hotel's massive white-walled, red-roofed, palm-encircled exterior became a prime symbol of the city's prosperity.

Like Tijuana's El Casino del Agua Caliente and Rosarito's Rosarito Beach Hotel, Playa Ensenada was a big hit with the Hollywood crowd until the repeal of Prohibition in 1933. Casino management converted it into the Hotel Riviera del Pacífico but, deprived of its gambling clientele and suffering the effects of the '30s Depression, the hotel closed and fell into disrepair shortly thereafter.

In 1977 the city decided to restore the structure and turn it into the **Centro Social Cívico y Cultural de Ensenada** (Social, Civic, and Cultural Center of Ensenada). The various ballrooms and halls of the former hotel are now hired out for civic events, conventions, weddings, art exhibits, and other public and private occasions. One wing houses several municipal agencies, another contains a small Casa de la Cultura with a public library (open Mon.-Fri. 0800-2000, Saturday 0900-1300). The city plans to erect a new convention center adjacent to the former hotel.

Much of the building's original interior tilework, murals, and painted ceilings remain intact. The **Bar Andaluz** in the rear portion of the building, near the large parking lot, is an excellent place for a quiet drink. Visitors are welcome to tour the

Riviera del Pacifico

JOE CUMMINGS

premises daily between 0900 and 1700. The Riviera del Pacífico is located at the corner of Avenidas Costero and Riviera—hard to miss since it's the largest structure along Blvd. Costero.

Wineries

Two Ensenada wineries are open to the public. **Bodegas de Santo Tomás** (tel. 8-25-09, 4-08-36, Av. Miramar 666) is the oldest winery on the peninsula, a direct descendant of the Dominicans' first Valle de San Tomás harvest of 1791. The winery sold its first wine to the public, by the barrel, in 1888. In 1934, Bodegas moved its winemaking operation to Ensenada, where it has remained ever since. The grapes are still grown in the Santo Tomás area as well as in other northern Baja valleys. Today it is Mexico's largest winery.

Current facilities cover 1.5 city blocks in downtown Ensenada and produce over a half-million cases of wine annually. Master vintners employ around 30 different varietals to produce wine, sherry, port, brandy, and champagne-style sparkling wine. Public tours of the winery, in English, are offered daily at 1100, 1300, and 1500. The tours last about an hour and cost US$2 per person; each tour ends in the wood-paneled tasting room, where a variety of vintages are available for tasting. Bread and cheese are served along with the wines. You can purchase bottles of Santo Tomás wine in the tasting room for prices ranging from US$3.50 for a table wine to US$12 for a private-reserve cabernet.

On Friday evenings during the summer, the winery hosts jazz and classical music performances in the **Barrel Room.**

The other Ensenada winery open to the public is **Cavas Valmar** (tel. 8-64-05, Calle Ambar 810), at the northern edge of town. Although Valmar's history and range of wines can't compare with those of Bodegas de Santo Tomás, its wine products are worth investigating. Tasting tours are offered by appointment only.

Nuestra Señora De Guadalupe

This cathedral at Av. Floresta and Calle 6a exhibits a standard-issue, Mexican colonial-style architecture, though the stained-glass windows are well executed. The best times to visit the cathedral are during the Fiesta Guadalupano (Día de Nuestra Señora de Guadalupe, 12-13 December) or Las Posadas (16-25 December), when the interior is filled with candles and worshipers.

El Mirador ("Viewpoint")

The Chapultepec Hills rise along the city's west side and afford a city and bay view. To find the viewpoint, follow Calle 2a west until it termi-

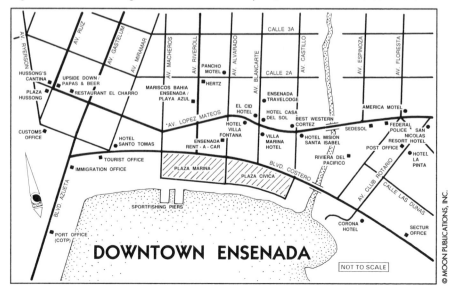

DOWNTOWN ENSENADA

NOT TO SCALE

© MOON PUBLICATIONS, INC.

nates at Av. Alemán; then turn right and follow the road to the top.

ACCOMMODATIONS

Hotels And Motels

Most of Ensenada's hotels are on or off Av. López Mateos and Blvd. Costero. For most of the year—July and August are the exceptions—the supply of hotel rooms outstrips the demand; hence room rates are often negotiable. At any given moment several hotels may stock one or both tourist offices with promotional flyers advertising room specials. For a list of hotels and rates, see the accompanying "Ensenada Hotels and Motels" chart.

Camping And RV Parks

Trailer parks are scattered north and south of the city. Because of competition, rates tend to be a bit lower than at many other tourist centers in Baja; if occupancy is low, or if you plan to stay longer than a night or two, you can negotiate to receive even lower rates.

About two km south of the town center is **Campo Playa RV Park** (tel. 6-29-18), at Av. Lázardo Cárdenas (Blvd. Costero) and Av. Delante (Calle Sangines). Although the nearby boulevards mean this isn't the quietest trailer park in the area, it's the closest to downtown Ensenada—within walking distance, in fact. Tent/RV sites are US$8/10 per night for two people, plus US$1 for each additional person.

The **Joker Hotel and Trailer Park** (tel. 6-72-

ENSENADA HOTELS AND MOTELS

Note: Rates quoted are for midweek, peak season (May through Sept.). Off-season rates may be discounted; weekend and holiday rates may be higher. Add 10% hotel tax to all rates (some hotels may charge an additional 10% service charge). Area code: 617

DOWNTOWN

America; Av. López Mateos 1309; tel. 8-27-15; US$20-30; kitchenettes, parking

Bahia; Av. López Mateos between Riveroll and Alvarado; tel. 8-21-01, fax 8-14-55; US$55, US$75-100 suites, winter midweek rates as low as US$28; restaurant, parking, some rooms with bay view

Balboa; Av. Vicente Guerrero 172; tel. 6-10-77; US$25

Best Western Casa del Sol; Av. López Mateos 1001 (A.P. 557, Ensenada, BCN); tel. 8-15-70, in U.S. tel. (800) 528-1234; US$48 s, US$55-65 d; a/c, restaurant, pool, parking

Best Western Cortez; Av. López Mateos 1089 (A.P. 396, Ensenada, BCN); tel. 8-23-07, in U.S. tel. (800) 528-1234; US$50-60; a/c, restaurant, pool, parking

Corona; Blvd. Costero 1442; tel. 6-09-01, fax 6-40-23; US$55-65; bay view, a/c, heat, restaurant, pool, parking

Coronado; Av. López Mateos 1275; tel. 6-16-16; US$30

El Cid; Av. López Mateos 993; tel. 8-24-01; US$52-72; a/c, refrigerators, restaurant, coffee shop, parking

Ensenada Travelodge; Av. Blancarte 130; tel. 8-16-01, in U.S. tel. (800) 255-3050; US$50; restaurant, pool, parking

Fiesta Inn; Av. Sangines 237; tel. 6-13-61; US$30; pool, parking, discounts for long-term stays

Gonzalez; Av. Pedro Loyola 150; tel. 6-34-77; US$15-18; parking

La Pinta; Av. Floresta and Bucaneros (P.O. Box 120637, Chula Vista, CA 92012); tel. 6-26-01, in U.S. tel. (800) 336-5454; US$58 s, US$69 d; restaurant, pool, parking

Las Palmas; Calle 3a 326; tel. 8-27-88; US$18; kitchenettes in some rooms, restaurant, pool, jacuzzi, parking

Mexico; Av. Ruíz and Calle 4a (P.O. Box 1817, San Ysidro, CA 92073); tel. 8-30-93, 4-05-73, fax 8-32-95; US$36-54; historic building, coffee shop, parking

(continued on next page)

ENSENADA HOTELS AND MOTELS
(continued)

Pancho Motel; Calle Alvarado 211; tel. 8-23-44; US$18-24; parking

Paraíso Las Palmas; Calle Sangines 206; tel. 7-17-01; US$35-45; restaurant, pool, jacuzzi, parking

Rudi's; Av. Hidalgo 450; tel. 6-32-45; US20-30; parking

San Nicolás; Av. López Mateos and Blancarte (P.O. Box 4C, San Ysidro, CA 92073); tel. 6-19-01; US$61-81 s, US$65-97 d; a/c, restaurant, coffee shop, pool, jacuzzi, many rooms with bay view

Santo Tomás; Blvd. Costero 609; tel. 8-15-03; US$51-62; a/c, heat, coffee shop, restaurant, parking

Villa Marina; Av. López Mateos and Blancarte (P.O. Box 727, Bonita, CA 92002); tel. 8-33-21; US$45-88; a/c, heat, coffee shop, pool, parking

Villa Fontana; Av. López Mateos 1050; tel. 8-34-34, 8-38-37; US$45-55; a/c, heat, coffee shop, parking

OUT OF TOWN

Costa Mar; Calle Veracruz 319 (1.5 km south of town); tel. 6-64-25; US$25-35; parking, near beach (Playa Hermosa)

Estero Beach; Estero Beach, 12 km south of town (A.P. 86, Ensenada, BCN); tel. 6-62-35, in U.S. tel. (800) 762-2494, fax 6-69-25; US$38-52 US$58-64 for suites; restaurant, tennis courts, boat ramp, boat rentals, horseback riding, all rooms with beach view

Joker; Mexico 1, eight km south of town (Ejido Chapultepec); tel. 6-72-01; US$30-50; restaurant, pool, jacuzzi, opposite Cipres Airport

Joya Mar; Av. Veracruz 360; tel. 6-74-30; US$30-40; restaurant, pool, parking, near Playa Hermosa

Las Rosas; Mexico 1, six km north of town (A.P. 316, Ensenada, BCN); tel. 4-43-10, 4-43-20, in U.S. tel. (800) 829-2252, fax 4-45-95; US$101-108; restaurant, pool, jacuzzi, sauna, exercise center, racquetball court, all rooms with ocean view

Punta Morro; Mexico 1, five km north of town (mailing address: P.O. Box 4263, San Ysidro, CA 92073); tel. 8-35-07; US$86 with kitchens, US$116 two-bedroom apts., US$156 three-bedroom apts.; pool

Quintas Papagayo; Mexico 1, three km north of town (A.P. 150, Ensenada, BCN); tel. 4-45-75; US$40-85, US$80 for two-bedroom apts.; restaurant, pool, jacuzzi, tennis courts

01), across the highway from El Ciprés Airport in Ejido Chapultepec, has around 30 full-hookup sites (no tents) with cable TV for US$10-12 a night. RVers are permitted to use hotel facilities, including the pool and jacuzzi.

For information on camping and RV parks at Estero Beach, La Jolla, and Punta Banda—12-20 km south of Ensenada—see "Vicinity of Ensenada."

FOOD

Ensenada features just about every kind of restaurant imaginable, but seafood and Northern Mexican ranchero-style food are the city's culi-nary strong suits. *Tacos de pescado* (fish tacos) are an Ensenada specialty, usually made from fresh yellowtail or halibut fillets cut in strips, deep-fried in a light batter, and served in folded corn tortillas with salsa, guacamole, and a touch of mayonnaise or sour cream.

Seafood stands are scattered throughout the city, many selling *cocteles* (spicy shellfish cocktails) and *ceviche* (a lime-marinated seafood salad). Clams (*almejas*), abalone (*abulón*), shrimp (*camarones*), and oysters (*ostiones*) are the most popular cocktails. The healthiest stands use purified water—usually clearly displayed in large bottles—to wash ingredients and utensils before preparing each dish. One of the best places to sample fish tacos and seafood cocktails is at the

Mercado de Mariscos, next to and a little bit behind the huge Plaza Marina on the waterfront.

Speaking of cocktails, the *clamato*, a beverage made from clams, tomato and lime juice, Mexican spices, and vodka, was probably invented in Ensenada. Ensenadan clamatos are nothing like the pale imitations served north of the border—a good one will come half-filled with fresh clams.

If you don't like seafood on your plate or in your glass, try other Ensenada specialties like *tacos de carne asada* (grilled beef tacos), Sinaloa-style grilled or roasted chicken, or one of the many varieties of burritos available. Several restaurants also specialize in American and continental cuisines.

Seafood

$$ Casamar (tel. 4-04-17), Blvd. Costero 987: Offers a wide selection of reasonably priced, freshly prepared seafood in a tourist-oriented atmosphere. Open daily for lunch and dinner.

$$ Haliotis (tel. 6-37-20), Calle Delante 174: The name sounds Greek but is actually the Latin genus term for abalone, the house specialty. Other seafood here is consistent as well; the family owners frequently fly fresh fish in from Isla Cedros, where they run another restaurant. Open daily except Tuesday for lunch and dinner.

$$ Hussong's Pelicano (tel. 4-45-75), three km north of town, off Mexico 1 at Quintas Papagayo Beach Resort Motel: Juan Hussong of Hussong's Cantina fame opened this restaurant to offer Baja regional cuisine with an em-

phasis on fresh seafood, including lobster, shrimp, clams, and scallops. The Mexican combos are good, too. Open daily for breakfast, lunch, and dinner. A varied Mexican brunch buffet is served Sat.-Sun. 0800-1600.

$$-$$$ La Cueva de Los Tigres ("The Tiger's Cave") (tel. 6-64-50), Calle Acapulco and Las Palmas, Playa Hermosa: Driving south toward Estero Beach, you can't miss the signs for the Tiger's Cave, located about two km out of town. A favorite with old-timers, this beachfront restaurant is famous for its abalone in crab sauce. Some folks rave about the place while others say it's overpriced and overrated. Open daily 0900-2330.

$-$$ Los Manueles, two locations; Calle Sangines at Bucaneros, and Av. Cortés at Belisario Dominguez: Reliable Sinaloa-style seafood with another overriding attraction—both locations are open 24 hours.

$$ Mariscos Bahía Ensenada (tel. 8-10-15), Av. Riveroll and López Mateos: A local favorite for moderately priced seafood, with everything from *pulpo* to *pargo*. Open daily for lunch and dinner.

$ Mercado de Mariscos ("Seafood Market"), Blvd. Costero and Av. Miramar, on the harbor: A real fish market, not a restaurant, where vendors serve fresh shrimp, octopus, squid, clams, lobster, tuna, abalone, halibut, and yellowtail. This is the best, and most inexpensive, place in town for fish tacos. Open daily from late morning until early evening.

mariscos vendor

JOE CUMMINGS

Mexican

$$ Acambero (El Refugio Ensenadense) (tel. 6-52-35), Av. Iturbide 528 off Av. Juárez between Calles 5a and 6a: Traditional northern Mexican dishes—pozole, mole, birria, chilaquiles, chiles rellenos, enchiladas—freshly prepared and served with bowls of limes, oregano, and salsas in a rustic but tasteful wood-and-brick decor. Delicious Mexican *postres* (desserts), too, including homemade flan, *arroz con leche* (rice pudding), *capirotada* (Mexican-style bread pudding), and *pay manzana* (apple pie). The restaurant recently obtained a license to sell beer and wine. Open daily for breakfast, lunch, and dinner.

$-$$ Café Hussong, Upstairs in Plaza Hussong, corner of avenidas Ruíz and López Mateos: This recently opened eatery features freshly made Mexican breakfasts and other *platillos típicos* in a pleasant indoor-outdoor dining area at very reasonable prices. Open daily for breakfast, lunch, and dinner.

$-$$ Domico's (tel. 8-13-75), Av. Ruíz 283 between calles 2a and 3a: Known for authentic Sonoran *machaca* (jerked meat) and seafood. Open daily for breakfast, lunch, and dinner.

$-$$ El Charro (tel. 8-38-81), Av. López Mateos 475: Popular with locals and tourists alike for tasty roast chicken, homemade chicken tamales, *pollo pipián* (chicken cooked in a pumpkinseed mole), grilled seafood, burritos, tacos (three large ones for US$3 with rice and beans) and botanas of all kinds. Fresh tortillas are handmade on the spot. Beverages include *jamaica,* a refreshing Mexican drink made from crushed hibiscus seeds. Open daily for lunch and dinner till 0200.

$ El Pollo Real (tel. 8-31-11), Av. Macheros and Calle 2a: A fast-food spot cranking out its own Sinaloa-style roast chickens—whole or half—for eating on the premises or *para llevar* (to go). Served with tortillas, beans, and salsa. Open daily 1000-2200.

$ Las Brasas (tel. 8-11-95), Av. López Mateos 486 between Av. Gastelum and Ruíz: Sinaloa-style, marinated and mesquite-grilled chicken is the major draw here, but Las Brasas also serves steak, seafood, and Mexican platters, all at reasonable prices. Open daily except Tuesday for lunch and dinner.

$$ Las Cazuelas (tel. 6-10-44), Calle Sangines 6 near Blvd. Costero: An old standby serving border-style cuisine, including *codorniz* (quail), seafood, steaks, ribs, and hearty Mexican breakfasts. Open daily 0700-2300.

$$ Plaza Mexico (tel. 4-06-35), Av. Macheros and López Mateos: A large patio restaurant with a festive atmosphere and lots of tourists. All the typical Mexican dishes and beverages North Americans expect, plus jelly-filled *churros,* deep-fried, doughnut-like Mexican pastries. Open daily for lunch and dinner.

$-$$ Sofia y Alma, Av. Delante and Av. de los Mangos 194, one traffic light east of the Gigante supermarket: A good all-around spot for antojitos, including tacos, burritos, pozole, and chiles rellenos, as well as *desayuno, almuerzo, comida corrida,* and Sunday buffets. Open daily 0730-2100.

$ El Taco de Huitzilopochtli (tel. 4-23-81), Av. de las Rosas 5, Col. Valle Verde: This hard-to-find, hard-to-pronounce spot is open only on weekends but is worth the trouble. Food preparation begins five days in advance; many of the ingredients are grown in back of the restaurant by the family owner-operators, who moved to Ensenada 22 years ago from the State of Mexico. House specialties include *mixiote* (lamb wrapped in maguey and baked in a mesquite-fired oven), *barbacoa, chancla* (thick corn tortillas with beef fillet and grilled *nopales*), *romeritos* (*nopal,* potato, and shrimp fritters in mole), *huauzontle* (a pepper-like vegetable filled with cheese and cooked like a chile relleno), *tlacoyos* (thick corn tortillas filled with beans and served with grated cheese and *chile verde*), and *cuitlacoche* (corn fungus) cooked with chile strips (*rajas poblanas*).

To find the restaurant, follow Av. Reforma north about three km (two miles) to Calle Ambar, then turn right (east) just before a small bridge. Follow Ambar to its end, then turn left for two blocks; make another left and you'll see the brightly painted restaurant on the left side of the street. Open Sat.-Sun. 0900-1700 only.

$$ Viva México Taquería (tel. 7-21-51), Av. López Mateos 2184: Great *tacos de carne asada* and *tacos al pastor* in clean surroundings with sharp service. Open daily 1000-2300.

European

$$$ El Rey Sol (tel. 8-17-33), Av. López Mateos 1000 at Av. Blancarte: The renowned Doña Pepita, a native of Santa Rosalía, opened this

Ensenada fish market

elegant French restaurant in 1947 after spending 16 years in France, where she studied French cuisine at the famous Cordón Bleu cooking school. Recently renovated, the kitchen prepares a variety of seafood, poultry, and meat dishes served with herbs and vegetables grown on the family's farm in Santo Tomás. The menu also includes a few Mexican dishes. Open daily for breakfast, lunch, and dinner.

$$-$$$ **Enrique's** (tel. 8-24-61), on Mexico 1 about a km north of town: Advertising "the smallest bar in the world," Enrique's is an old-time favorite with a romantic atmosphere and a reputation for consistent quality. The mostly continental menu features chateaubriand, lobster Newburg, quail, frog's legs, and abalone prepared to order. The small dining room is a good spot for a quiet celebration. Open daily for breakfast, lunch, and dinner.

$$$ **La Embotelladora Vieja,** Bodegas de Santo Tomás building, Av. Miramar and Calle 7a: High-quality French cuisine served in a wine-cellar ambience. At least 20 different wines from Mexico, the U.S., France, and Italy are available each month by the glass. Open Tues.-Sun. for dinner.

$$-$$$ **La Mafia,** Plaza Blanca, López Mateos and Alvarado: Overseen by a Guadalajara native who spent several years in Italy, this recently opened spot in the tourist zone serves fresh pasta and other Italian specialties as well as breakfasts in a cozy setting Thurs.-Tues. 0830-2230.

American And Pizza

$$ **Alfonso's** (tel. 4-05-70), Av. Macheros 499 at Blvd. Costero: Good pizza, seafood, and Mexican breakfasts at reasonable prices. Open daily for breakfast, lunch, and dinner.

$$ **Cha-Cha Burger** (tel. 6-54-51), Blvd. Costero at Calle Sangines: This American-owned-and-operated burger joint is also a headquarters for Amigos de Ensenada, a gringo service club. Besides burgers, the offerings include corn dogs, fish, chicken, french fries, milkshakes, tacos, and ice cream. Open daily 1000-2200.

$$ **Denny's,** Plaza Marina, Blvd. Costero: Offers a range of soups, salads, sandwiches, Mexican standards, burgers, and ice cream. Open 24 hours.

$-$$ **La Fábula Pizza** (tel. 6-55-22), Blvd. Costero and Av. Riviera: Part of a Mexican chain that serves American-style pizza in a family atmosphere. Open daily for lunch and dinner.

$$ **Pizza Hut** (tel. 8-18-88), Centro Comercial Plaza Palmira, Blvd. Costero; also Plaza Marina: Two locations offer the American standby. Both make pizza deliveries. Open 1100-2300 daily.

Oriental

$-$$ **China Land** (tel. 6-86-44), Av. Riveroll 1149 between calles 11a and 12a: Good selection of Sichuan, Mandarin, and Cantonese dishes at reasonable prices. Open daily for lunch and dinner.

$$ **Ebisu** (tel. 6-05-11), Av. López Mateos and Balboa: A decent, reasonably priced Japa-

BAJACALIFORNIO WINE

Ensenada is the unofficial capital of Mexico's finest winemaking region, northern Baja. Most North Americans are unaware of the quality of Mexican wines and assume rum and tequila are all the place has to offer. Bajacalifornio wines are, in fact, shipped all over Mexico and western Europe, but because of current U.S. trade policies, they're not exported to the United States. This may change now that NAFTA has passed. In the meantime, if you want to taste wines produced in northern Baja, you can always go to the source.

History

Although the first wine produced on the peninsula came from Jesuit monks at Misión San Javier near Loreto in the early 1700s, as the missionaries moved northward it became clear that the best areas for viniculture were the temperate valleys of northern Baja.

In 1791, Dominican Padre José Lorieto founded Misión Santo Tomás, planting the first Spanish vinifera in the Valle de Santo Tomás 45 km south of Ensenada. The product, a variety simply called "Mission," was used mainly for sacramental purposes but was highly regarded by padres throughout the mission system. Following secularization of the mission, Bodegas de Santo Tomás took over the vineyards and in 1888 started selling wine by the barrel in booming Ensenada. In 1906, some 500 Russian immigrants settled the Valle de Guadalupe and cultivated extensive vineyards; other winemakers, including the Italian family of oenologist Angel Cetto, followed the success of the Santo Tomás and Guadalupe operations with viniculture in valleys near Tecate, San Vicente, Guadalupe, Mexicali, and Ensenada.

Wines And Winemakers

Today some 28 viniculturists and labels compete in northern Baja, among them Bacco, Calafia, Cetto, Domecq, Santo Tomás, Valmar, San Antonio, Monte Xanic, Don Miguel, Sol de España, Champbrulé, and Viña Real. The highest-producing valleys, in descending order, are Ensenada, Guadalupe, San Vicente, Mexicali, Tijuana, and Tecate. Smaller *ejido* operations exist in El Porvenir, Ajusco, and Chapultepec.

Among the varietals produced in Baja are Mission, Zinfandel, Cabernet Sauvignon, Barbera, Valdepeñas, Cariñana, Grenache, Ruby Cabernet, Petit Sirah, Merlot, Pinot Noir, Gamay, Chenin Blanc, Palomino, French Colombard, Muscatel, White Riesling, and Pinot Blanc. It is said the best Bajacalifornio wines are made from grapes cultivated in the Guadalupe and San Vicente valleys, where red varietals predominate.

To learn more about Baja wines, and to sample some vintages, join one of the daily tours offered at Bodegas de Santo Tomás or Cavas Valmar in Ensenada.

Festival De La Vendimia

Every year in late August/early September, six Baja wineries collaborate on a nine-day winemaking festival in Ensenada and the Valle de Guadalupe that includes winetasting, paella cookoffs, fireworks, music, dancing, and other bacchanalian activities. For information on upcoming festivals, contact the Santo Tomás winery in Ensenada (tel. 627-8-33-33).

nese place with fresh sushi, sashimi, tempura, and teppanyaki. Open daily except Wednesday for lunch and dinner.

Groceries

The **Gigante** at Av. López Mateos and Calle Delante is a huge supermarket with just about anything you might need for picnics, camping, or an epic Transpeninsular road trip. The store also offers a takeout buffet with tasty Mexican dishes you won't find in most Ensenada restaurants, including spicy moles and Oaxacan cheese. There are eight other Gigantes in town.

Scattered along Av. Diamante are a number of inexpensive panaderías, tortillerías, and dulcerías. For European-style baked items, you could investigate **La Baguette** (tel. 8-28-14) on Blvd. Costero near Av. Blancarte. Prices at La Baguette are about double what you'd pay in an Av. Diamante bakery; if you're pinching pesos, stick with the latter.

On Mexico 1, a few km south of town between Estero Beach and La Bufadora, is a row of vendors selling fresh tamales stuffed with corn (*elote*), olives (*aceitunas*), or red chiles. Vendors along this road also sell jars of olives, chiles, and honey.

La Milpa (tel. 6-10-05, Calle 4a 1329, between Espinoza and Floresta) is a health-oriented store carrying natural foods, nonalcoholic wine and beer, herbs, dried fruits, baked goods, and natural remedies.

ENTERTAINMENT

Bars And Discos

Many of the hotels and motels in the main tourist district, along Av. López Mateos and Blvd. Costero between Calle Sangines and Av. Macheros, feature bars or lounges with occasional live music—usually *trovadores* (troubadours) or mariachis playing Mexican standards. **Bananas** (tel. 8-20-04, Blvd. Costero 277) and **Ibis** (tel. 6-14-40, Blvd. Costero and Av. Alvarado) offer nightly dancing to recorded music and light shows—not on a par with Tijuana's high-tech discos but good enough.

West of Av. Macheros, the city leaves behind the middle-class tourist zone and revels in cheap seafood joints, bars, and dance halls with a slightly seedy air. In this area is one of Baja's most famous landmarks, **Hussong's Cantina** (tel. 8-32-10, Av. Ruíz 113), quite justifiably advertised as "the bar that built a town." This could be amended to "the bar that built a shopping center" now that the neighborhood is studded with Hussong's souvenir shops.

the fabled Hussong's Cantina

At the same location since Johan Hussong, a German immigrant, opened shop in 1892, and still owned by his son Juan, hardly anything about the clapboard structure has changed in a hundred years but for the addition of electricity. Always crowded, on any given night tourists are outnumbered two to one by regulars, a mixture of expats and Bajacalifornios. Unamplified norteña ensembles sometimes play polkas and *rancheras* as *gritos* (shouts) pierce the smoky air. Come in the early afternoon if you hope to claim a table.

Across the street from Hussong's is **Papas and Beer,** a slightly more sedate bar with recorded music and a collegiate atmosphere. It lacks character but is a reasonable alternative for folks who find Hussong's too rowdy. Another favorite watering hole for the young and boisterous is **Plaza Mexico** at Blvd. Costero and Av. Macheros, an outdoor restaurant-bar that packs them in on warm weekend nights.

A wander north along Av. Ruíz or especially Av. Gastelum will turn up a number of Mexican-oriented bars and cantinas, many of the red-light sort. **Anthony's** (Blvd. Costero and Av. Miramar), a classic in this category, is a large bar-dance hall with a bawdy, boy's-town reputation. Beyond the curtained entrance revolves a merry-go-round of ranchers, surfers, painted ladies, and other lost—at least for the night—souls.

EVENTS

February
Carnaval (Mardi Gras): Ensenada has observed this pre-Lenten festival since 1918, and the celebration seems to get bigger every year—over 300,000 visitors attended in 1993. Usually held for six days before Ash Wednesday, the second week in February, festivities start with the Quema de Mal Humor, or "Burning of Bad Humor," in which an effigy is hanged and burned. The victim is usually modeled after an unpopular politician.

Throughout the week, a nightly street fair stretches for 12 downtown blocks, offering food vendors, carnival rides, live music, and a steady flow of Mexican beer, brandy, and tequila. Carnaval parades, consisting of flowered floats and legions of costumed dancers, wind through the streets every afternoon amid clouds of confetti.

Events with a local flavor include a *juegos florales* contest, in which poets compete to see who can compose the best "flowery verse"; Spanish students shouldn't miss this one. Another local highlight is the selection of the Reina de Carnaval ("Carnaval Queen") and El Rey Feo ("Ugly King") at a mid-festival coronation ball on Saturday night. The Monday following this weekend is El Día del Marido Oprimido, the "Day of the Oppressed Husband," in which married men are allowed 23.5 hours of symbolic freedom to do whatever they wish.

Carnaval's grand finale is a masquerade ball held on the Tuesday night before Ash Wednesday. Prizes are awarded for best costumes as well as for other attainments over the course of the week—best float, best dance troupe, etc. For specific information on Carnaval scheduling and venues for individual events, pick up a copy of the *Baja Sun*.

SUCRO Motocross Series: An off-road motorcycle race usually held the last weekend of February. Sponsored by SUCRO. For informa-

tion, contact Alberto Herediu, tel. 6-47-47, Av. México 843.

March
Three Sister Cities Bike Ride: On the last weekend of the month, cyclists race along a triangle course between Ensenada, Rosarito, and Tijuana; sponsored by Monday International (tel. 619-275-1384 in the U.S.).

April
Taco, Tamal, and Mole Fiesta: A culinary event the last weekend in April attracting the best antojitos chefs. Sponsored by CANIRAC (tel. 4-04-48, 4-04-35) and the Amigos de Ensenada.

May
Tecate-Ensenada Bike Ride: Third week in May. Sponsored by Monday International (tel. 619-275-1384 in the U.S.).

June
Baja 500: A 500-mile offroad race out of Ensenada, held in early June by SCORE International and Tecate. See November entry for **Baja 1000.**

July
Gran Carrera de Ensenada: Yet another offroad race, this one sponsored by Baja Promotions (tel. 818-340-5750 in the U.S.) and extending 250 miles out of Ensenada.

August
Hobie Cat Fleet Four Todos Santos Regatta: A Hobie-sponsored catamaran regatta held on Bahía de Todos Santos the first weekend of August.

Fiesta de la Vendimia (Wine Harvest Festival): Wineries in Ensenada and Valle de Guadalupe co-sponsor 10 days of winetasting, music, and gourmet cooking at various venues in both locales; usually commences the third week of the month.

Corona Cup Regatta: A new multi-lap yacht race held in the bay. For information contact the state or city tourist offices.

September
Seafood Fair: Usually held the last weekend of the month, this is one of the city's best-attended fiestas. Many local restaurants participate. Sponsored by CANIRAC (tel. 4-04-48, 4-04-35).

BAJA 1000

Every November desert rats from around the globe gather in Ensenada for the grueling Baja 1000 ("Baja Mil"), the world's most prestigious offroad race. The first organized contest took place in October 1967, though dirtbikers had informally raced from Ensenada to La Paz since the '50s. In 1962, Dave Ekins and Bill Robertson, Jr. were the first to record their efforts when they raced two Honda 250 motorcycles from Tijuana to La Paz, establishing their times by stamping sheets of paper at telegraph offices in Tijuana and La Paz. Ekins pulled into La Paz after 39 hours, 54 minutes; Robertson made it an hour later.

From 1967 to the present, the event has occurred yearly except in 1974, when the National Off Road Racing Association lost Mexican permission to operate the race. Since 1975, SCORE International has organized the race, most recently with the sponsorship of Mexico's Presidente Brandy. Participants can enter in one of 23 categories—15 car and truck, six motorcycle, and two ATV classes. The course alternates year to year between a straight 1,000-mile Ensenada-La Paz run and a shorter 1,000-km loop beginning and ending in Ensenada; the latter course offers more spectator opportunities and pit stops.

SCORE recently added a separate Baja 1000 Endurance Safari on a course parallel to, but rougher than, the usual 1,000-mile Ensenada-La Paz route. A rally rather than a race, in this event contestants aren't rated on their time achievements but rather on endurance—a quality of obvious interest to automotive manufacturers and marketers seeking the imprimatur "Baja-proven."

October

SUCRO Supercross Series: Another offroad motorcycle race sponsored by SUCRO; see May entry for contact. First weekend of the month.

Juan Hussong International Chili Cookoff: A cookoff sanctioned by the International Chili Society (ICS) and one of Ensenada's biggest events, usually held the second weekend in October. The cookoff winner is eligible to compete in the annual ICS World Championship Chili Cookoff in Alta California.

In addition to chili cooking competitions for individuals, clubs, and local restaurants, the day's activities typically include chile-pepper-eating and tequila "shoot-and-holler" contests, live music and dancing, and the selection of Ms. Chile Pepper and Mr. Hot Sauce. You can extinguish the fire with beverages provided by Cuauhtémoc Brewery, brewers of Tecate, Carta Blanca, and several other popular Mexican beers; tequila purveyors Viuda de Romero; and winemakers Bodegas de Santo Tomás. A small admission fee is charged; part of the proceeds goes to charity. For current information on scheduling and venue, contact Juan Hussong (tel. 4-41- 55) at Quintas Papagayo Resort.

Fiesta Viva: A four-day exposition the second week of October. Exhibitors come from all over the Ensenada *municipio*.

November

SCORE-Presidente Baja 1000: The grand-daddy of all offroad races takes place over a four-day period during the first or second week of the month. For a race schedule, consult the Ensenada tourist office or pick up a current issue of the *Baja Sun*.

SPORTS AND RECREATION

Fishing

Although commercial fishing (both local and foreign) has depleted the overall supply of game-fish in the Ensenada area, sportfishing here can still be rewarding, especially from June through mid-September when several species make coastal runs from the south. Bahía de Todos Santos catches include lingcod, rockfish, calico bass, sand bass, barracuda, bonito, and occasional yellowtail. Though this was once known as the "yellowtail capital of the world," yellowtail catches now are generally rare and rather puny.

Long-range fishing trips from Ensenada—to Punta Colonet, Isla San Geronimo, or Isla San Martín—yield bluefin, yellowfin, and albacore tuna; skipjack; white seabass; salmon grouper; and the occasional dorado.

Several companies operate sportfishing trips from the Ensenada Sportfishing Terminal, off Blvd. Costero near the end of Av. Macheros. **Ensenada Clipper Fleet** (tel. 8-21-85, 8-20-62, fax 8-19-63; mailing address 2630 E. Beyer Blvd., Suite 676, San Ysidro, CA 92143-9011) runs day-trips for US$40 a person, overnights for

US$80, and multi-day, long-range trips by charter. Rates for local trips (day and overnight) include license and tackle; live bait and added services, like cleaning and fish-filleting, cost extra.

Gordo's Sportfishing (tel. 8-35-15, 8-23-77, fax 4-04-81) is slightly cheaper at US$35 per person for local day-trips, US$75 for long-range party boats. Gordo's also offers a package deal that includes one night's motel room, a fishing trip (including license and tackle), and breakfast for US$84 for two people. Gordo's also operates its own smokehouse for fish preservation.

Tackle: Ensenada Clipper Fleet maintains a tackle shop at the sportfishing pier that's open to the public 24 hours a day. Just north of town in El Sauzal, **Anzuelos Universales de Ensenada** (tel. 4-62-29, Mexico 1, Km 102) carries a full line of fishing tackle, including its own Baja-tested Anzuelos gear.

Boating

For the moment, Ensenada's public anchorage is little more than a set of breakwaters, a section of rickety piers, and a parking lot. As Ensenada is an offical Mexican port of entry, arriving boaters must check in with the COTP. See "Sports and Recreation" under "Out and About" for details on check-in procedures.

A new marina with 220 slips is currently under construction; daily rates are expected to fall in the US$5-7 range. A nearby boatyard, **Baja Naval,** offers a few slips and accepts foreign boats for servicing or repair. The rates are lower

than for comparable work done in the United States. Fuel is also available here.

For outboard motor repairs, inquire at **Motores de Baja California Norte** (tel. 6-30-25, Calle 6a 1990), which specializes in sales and service of American-made motors.

Surfing

The nearest consistent surfing areas are at Punta San Miguel, several kilometers north of Ensenada off Mexico 1, and Islas de Todos Santos, 20 km west by boat. (For details see the "San Miguel" and "Islas de Todos Santos" sections, respectively.) Playa La Jolla, approximately 16 km south of town via Mexico 1 and BCN 23, occasionally benefits from the winter northwest swell.

You can purchase surf gear, including Ensenada-made San Miguel boards, at **San Miguel Surf Design** in Plaza Hussong, a small shopping center on the corner of Av. López Mateos and Calle Ruíz, near Hussong's Cantina. San Miguel boards run around US$210-220. Locally made, full-length wetsuits cost US$125-135.

Diving

The best local diving spots are at Punta Banda and Islas de Todos Santos. Ensenada offers four dive shops: **Almar** (tel. 8-30-13, Av. Macheros 149), **El Yaqui** (tel. 6-63-44, Blanco Shopping Center, Fracc. Valle Dorado), **Baja Dive Expeditions** (tel. 3-02-20, Baja Beach and Tennis Club, Punta Banda), and **La Bu-**

San Miguel
surfboard factory

fadora Dive Shop (Punta Banda, A.P. 102, Maneadero, BC).

Cycling
Baja Montaña, in Plaza Hussong at the corner of Calle Ruíz and Av. López Mateos, sells bicycles and biking supplies, with an emphasis on mountain bikes.

Baja Cycling Adventures (tel. 8-18-79), at Blvd. Costero 609-14, offers one-day guided mountain biking trips to La Bufadora (US$29), Laguna Hanson (US$39), and Valle de Guadalupe (US$39). Prices include lunch; bike rentals are available.

Bullfights And *Charreadas*
During the summer, bullfights and Mexican rodeos are occasionally held at a modest **Plaza de Toros** on Calle Sangines between Av. Pedro Loyola and los Bucaneros. For current scheduling, contact the state tourist office.

Race And Sports Book
LF Race and Sports Book maintains an outlet at the Hotel San Nicolás, Av. López Mateos and Blancarte. **Caliente Foreign Book** has a branch on Av. López Mateos behind the Riviera del Pacífico and another in the new Plaza Marina.

Cruises
Over the past few years Ensenada has become Mexico's biggest port of call for cruise ships, measured in numbers of visitors per year. **Sea Cruise San Diego** (tel. 619-595-1695, toll-free 800-848-3836) offers day cruises aboard the *Pacific Star* for US$99, often discounted to US$69-79, depending on the day of the week and the booking source. The ship leaves San Diego at 0900, arrives in Ensenada at 1400, leaves Ensenada at 1730, and docks at San Diego at 2230. As part of a multi-day cruise along Mexico's Pacific coast from Los Angeles, Royal Caribbean's *Viking Serenade* arrives in Ensenada at 0730 and leaves at 1600.

Bay Cruises: Baja Fiesta (tel. 4-04-79) offers two-hour and four-hour dining cruises aboard the *Royal Pacifico* yacht. Boats leave from the sportfishing piers behind Plaza Marina at 1000 (four hours, US$15 per person), 1600 (two hours, US$12 per person), and 1900 (two hours, US$12).

SHOPPING

You'll find the usual assortment of tourist-oriented souvenir and beachwear shops along Av. López Mateos and Blvd. Costero. The government-operated **FONART,** next to the state tourism office on Av. López Mateos, offers a collection of Mexican handicrafts. The **Centro Artesanal** on Blvd. Costero caters mostly to cruise-ship passengers in town for a few hours, but is worth a look for Oaxacan folk art and neo-Casa Grandes pottery from Chihuahua's Valle de Casas Grandes. The new **Plaza Marina** is also slated to become a big shopping venue for cruise passengers, but so far it offers very few shops.

Galaría de Pérez Meillon, in Plaza Hussong (avenidas Ruíz and López Mateos) and in the Centro Artesanal, carries a high-quality selection of Paipai and Casas Grandes pottery, Kumiai basketry, and contemporary art by up-and-coming Latin American artists.

The best bargains for everyday items are found deeper in the downtown area, away from Blvd. Costero and Av. López Mateos. The locals do much of their shopping in the vicinity of the Av. Juárez and Ruíz intersection, where bookstores, record shops, and zapaterías are particularly numerous. Ensenada's zapaterías specialize in boots made from "exotic" skins like lizard or ostrich—don't buy anything prohibited by U.S. Customs if you plan on taking it across the U.S.-Mexico border. **Librería El Spaña** (Av. Ruíz 217) and **Librería Banuelos** (Av. Ruíz 370) carry English-language books and magazines.

A large flea market called **Los Globos,** on Calle 9a three blocks east of Av. Reforma, features vendor stalls selling everything from housewares to sandals. It's open daily 0900-1800. A similar market at Calle 6a and Av. Riveroll is open only on weekends.

SERVICES

Moneychanging
Most banks in Ensenada refer visitors to a casa de cambio for foreign-exchange services. **La Moneda** casa de cambio in the Blanco Bahía shopping center, at Juárez and Reforma, offers one of the best exchange rates in town.

ATM machines are available at several **Banamex** branches, including one at Av. Juárez and Riveroll. **Banco Serfin** at Av. Ruíz 290 also offers an ATM.

Post And Telephone
The most convenient post office for visitors staying near the waterfront sits at the corner of avenidas López Mateos and Club Rotario (Riviera), opposite Hotel La Pinta. Open Mon.-Fri. 0800-1900, Saturday 0800-1300.

The **Message Center** (tel. 8-29-83, fax 4-07-61), next door to Hussong's Cantina (Edificio Hussong, Av. Ruiz 105, No. 13), also handles U.S. mail service. Open Mon.-Fri. 0900-1900, Saturday 0900-1700.

Ensenada features a number of public telephones in the downtown area. For both local and long-distance calls, these are less expensive than hotel phones. If you need a phone line installed, pay a visit to the municipal telephone office at the intersection of Blvd. Ramirez Mendez and Av. Reforma, near the Blanco Bahía shopping center.

Ensenada's area code is 617.

Immigration Office
The Ensenada immigration office occupies a nondescript building just around the corner from COTUCO's information booth, near the waterfront at the northern entrance into town. If you haven't validated your tourist card yet and plan to travel farther south than Maneadero, this is the place to do it. The office is usually open daily 0900-2000; on Sunday afternoons the office may close for about an hour while the only officer on duty goes to the pier to meet a cruise ship from San Diego.

Language Schools
Two private institutes in Ensenada offer intensive Spanish-language courses. The long-established **International Spanish Institute of Ensenada** (tel. 6-01-09, 6-65-87, or 619-472-0600 in the U.S.) is at Blvd. Rodriguez 377, near the Gigante shopping center. ISIE's program includes six hours of classroom instruction per day, plus a Mexican family homestay. Tuition is a reasonable US$20 per day, plus US$20 a day for a homestay and three meals. ISIE's U.S. mailing address is P.O. Box 536, Bonita, CA 92002.

Another institute, the **Center of Languages and Latin American Studies** (tel. 6-70-76, or 619-279-0996 in the U.S.), operates a similar program but offers one hour less of classroom instruction per day. Tuition at CLLAS is US$25 per day (US$65 for a weekend course), plus US$20 daily for private homestay and meals (US$15 in a shared room). CLLAS is located at Calle San Carlos 242, Fracc. Buenaventura near Av. Reforma and Calle Diamante; the institute's U.S. mailing address is 5666 La Jolla Blvd., Suite 116, La Jolla, CA 92037.

Amigos De Ensenada
This service club, consisting mostly of resident norteamericanos, organizes fundraising community events throughout the year—Juan Hussong's Chili Cookoff, the Christmas parade—for charitable purposes. The club meets twice monthly at Calle Mazatlan 526, Playa Hermosa; for information, contact John Dixon (tel. 6-54-51, 6-79-31).

Real Estate
Century 21 (tel. 4-46-48, fax 4-45-36, Km 108; mailing address: P.O. Box 309, Ensenada, BCN) provides information on houses, condos, and lots for sale in the Ensenada area.

Emergency
The **public hospital** (tel. 6-17-01, 6-17-05) at Calle Sangines and Av. Pedro Loyola has 24-hour emergency services, as does the new, state-of-the-art **Hospital Las Americas** (tel. 6-03-01) at Av. Arenas 151, off Calle Sangines. For medical problems requiring emergency treatment at San Diego medical facilities, contact **Transmedic** (tel. 8-14-00, Av. Obregón at Calle 11a), a 24-hour ambulance service providing either air or surface transport to San Diego.

ENSENADA INFORMATION

Tourist Offices
The SECTUR-sponsored state tourism office (tel. 2-30-22, fax 2-30-81) occupies a new office at Blvd. Costero and Calle Las Rocas that dispenses information on Ensenada events, dining, and hotels as well as BCN travel. The English-speaking staff is very competent and helpful; the Attorney for Tourist Protection also works

USEFUL ENSENADA TELEPHONE NUMBERS
(Ensenada area code: 617)

Police 134
Red Cross 132
Highway Patrol 6-13-11
IMSS Hospital 6-17-01, 6-17-05
Tourist Attorney. 6-36-86
State Tourism Office 2-30-22
Customs 8-24-77
Immigration 4-01-64

out of this office. Open Mon.-Fri. 0900-1900, Saturday 0900-1500, Sunday 1000-1400.

The city-sponsored Convention and Visitors Bureau (COTUCO, tel. 8-24-11) is located at Blvd. Costero 540, opposite the PEMEX station at the north entrance to town. It distributes much of the same information as the state tourist office and can also make hotel bookings. Open Mon.-Sat. 0900-1900, Sunday 0900-1400.

Business Offices
Ensenada has an active chamber of commerce (CANACO, tel. 4-09-06, Av. López Mateos 693) and a restaurant association (CANIRAC, tel. 4-04-48, Av. López Mateos 885-7) with many North American members.

Newspapers
The English-language *Baja Sun,* a free monthly newspaper, is full of information on current Ensenada events, local businesses, beaches, entertainment, and dining establishments. It's available at several locations throughout the city, including tourist offices and the larger hotels. For information on subscriptions or advertising, drop by the office at Calle Obregón 1099 (at Calle 11a), open Mon.-Fri. 1000-1800, or call 8-73-33.

Bilingual visitors, or those who want to practice their Spanish, should pick up a copy of *Vivir en Ensenada* ("Living in Ensenada"), a free Spanish-only weekly covering cultural events from a local perspective.

Consulates
Most countries with consulates in Baja staff them in Tijuana or Mexicali. Daring to be different, Denmark maintains a consulate in Ensenada at Av. Virgilio Uribe 496 (tel. 6-60-35, 6-62-49).

TRANSPORT

Getting There
Air: There are currently no regularly scheduled flights in or out of Ensenada, although Air L.A. may soon initiate regular service from Los Angeles. Aeropuerto El Ciprés (tel. 6-63-01), just south of town off Mexico 1, is an official Mexican airport of entry with a paved airstrip suitable for small-plane arrivals and departures (Unicom 119.75).

Bus: Intercity buses (ABC, Transportes Norte de Sonora, Tres Estrellas de Oro) use the bus terminal at Av. Riveroll and Calle 11a (tel. 8-67-70). For details on scheduling and fares, see "Ensenada Bus Departures."

ABC's new *servicio plus* offers deluxe buses to Tijuana (US$7.50) and Mexicali (US$14) several times daily.

Driving: Ensenada is the southernmost terminal for Mexico 1-D, the four-lane toll road from Tijuana. Beyond Ensenada, Mexico 1 is, for the most part, a two-lane highway with road conditions varying from kilometer to kilometer.

Mexico 3 from Tecate also terminates in Ensenada, then reappears east of town winding across the Sierra Juárez to join Mexico 5 for San Felipe. Finding Mexico 3 east out of Ensenada can be difficult, as the route is not well signposted in the city. The simplest way to get there is to follow Av. Juárez until it meets Av. Reforma at the Benito Juárez statue. The street directly across Av. Reforma is Calzada Cortés; after crossing Av. Reforma, follow Calzada Cortés until it curves to the left and feeds into Mexico 3.

Getting Around
City Bus: Several varieties of buses and vans ply the main avenues of the city; e.g., López Mateos, Juárez, Ruíz, Diamante, Delante, Reforma, and Calle 9a. The route—designated by street name—is usually whitewashed on the windshield or printed on a marquee over it. Fares are roughly US$.45, depending on the size of the vehicle; bigger is cheaper. Buses to outlying districts like Ejido Chapultepec leave from Av. Juárez.

Bus Tours: Viajes Guaycura (tel. 8-37-18) offers a three-hour "Discover Ensenada" tour of the city and nearby countryside for US$15 per person. Guaycura's air-conditioned bus departs daily from Alvarado near Scorpio's Rent-A-

ENSENADA BUS DEPARTURES

DESTINATION; DEPARTURES; DURATION; FARE

Tijuana; hourly 0500-2300; one and a half hours; US$4.60-5.30

Mexicali; 2nd class every 30 minutes; four hours; US$7.30
ejecutivo: 0530, 0630, 0800, 1100, 1320, 1700, 1930, 2000 one and a half hours; US$14

San Felipe; 0800, 1800; four hours; US$3.30

San Quintín; hourly 0600-2100; three hours; US$2.50

El Rosario; 0600, 0900, 1600; four hours; US$3.30

Guerrero Negro; 1000, 1900, 2130; nine hours; US$7.30

La Paz; 0930, 1230, 1600, 2000, 2230; 22 hours; US$17-50

Tecate; two hours; US$4

Car; the tour includes stops at Santo Tomás Winery and La Bufadora.

Taxi: Most of the city's taxis park along López Mateos or Juárez, or near the bus depot at Calle 11a and Av. Riveroll. Fares are negotiable; most trips in the city cost around US$3-4. A taxi to La Bufadora costs US$10-15.

Car Rental: Ensenada is an expensive place to rent a car compared to Tijuana or Los Cabos. The highest rates are charged by the independents: **Ensenada Rent-A-Car** (tel. 8-18-96) and **Scorpio Rent-A-Car** (tel. 8-32-75), both on Av. Alvarado just off Av. López Mateos. Rates for a Nissan Sentra at these two agencies run around US$65 per 24 hours plus US$.42 per km. Two-to four-day rentals come down to US$56 per day plus US$.33 per km, US$50 per day plus US$.20 per km for rentals of seven days or more. A special weekly rental for US$1000, including 4,000 free km, is available from Ensenada Rent-A-Car.

Hertz (tel. 8-37-76, 800-654-3001 in the U.S.), in the Bahía shopping center at Calle 2a and Av. Riveroll, offers considerably lower rates—US$39 a day, plus US$.22 per km, for a VW bug—if you reserve in advance, but you must return the car to one of the company's Tijuana offices.

Scooter Rental: A vendor at the south end of the Plaza Civica (Three Heads Plaza) on Blvd. Costero, **Chavo's Sport Rentals,** rents Yamaha motor scooters for US$10 per hour.

Driving your own Vehicle: Driving in Ensenada is fairly straightforward as long as you're prepared to stop at *every* intersection. Even when you don't see a stop sign, chances are a stop is required. The Ensenada traffic police don't go out of their way to hassle visitors, but fines are stiff for speeding, running stop signs, or drinking while driving. Fines must be paid in cash at the municipal police station, Calle 9a and Av. Espinoza.

VICINITY OF ENSENADA

Estero Beach

This huge, estuarial beach at the junction of Bahía de Todos Santos and Río San Carlos lies about 12 km south of the center of Ensenada via Mexico 1, behind Ejido Chapultepec. The turnoff from Mexico 1 is 7.5 km/4.7 miles south of the Gigante at avenidas López Mateos and Delante. Except during July and August, the beach is surprisingly uncrowded.

The **Estero Beach Museum**, part of the Estero Beach Resort complex, offers natural-history exhibits and a display of Mexican folk art. Nominal admission fee; open daily 0900-1700.

Punta Banda And La Bufadora

This rocky peninsula juts into the Pacific at the south end of Bahía de Todos Santos and is largely undeveloped except for a few campgrounds and the Baja Beach and Tennis Club. Hikers can explore the peninsula's windswept spine on a number of unmarked trails leading from turnouts along the only paved road, BCN 23. From lookout points on Punta Banda, you can often see spouting gray whales as they pass by during their annual Jan.-March migration.

One of the Ensenada area's prime tourist sites, the scenic blowhole at the tip of Punta Banda, is about 25 km (16 miles) from the city via Mexico 1 and BCN 23. During incoming tides, waves rush into an underground cavern and force spumes as high as 25-30 meters through a hole in the top of the cavern. Loosely translated, La Bufadora means "Buffalo's Snort," referring to the sound created as water spews from the blowhole.

La Bufadora is a favorite weekend excursion among local Ensenadenses as well as visiting gringos. Vendors selling snacks and souvenirs line the road from the parking lot to the blowhole. This spot could be nicknamed "Baja's *churro* capital" since there are probably more churro vendors here than anywhere else on the peninsula. Below the blowhole is Bahía Papalote, a bay and small residential-recreational community.

Scuba Diving: Detached rocks, underwater pinnacles, sea caves, and kelp beds below the cliffs on Punta Banda's south shore are popular among scuba enthusiasts, and accessible by boat or from the shore. Easiest access is at the bay below La Bufadora, Bahía Papalote, which is sheltered enough for intermediate divers or supervised novices; an underwater hot springs at a depth of 25-30 meters warms the bottom of the bay.

Off the northwest tip of Punta Banda lies an underwater ridge—accessible by boat only—topped by a 1.5-mile chain of small islands. The ridge is dotted with underwater cliffs, caves, rock reefs, and kelp beds. Cold-water upwellings along the ridge stimulate marinelife and help maintain good visibility. Because of swells and currents in the area, only divers with open-ocean experience should consider diving here unless accompanied by someone who knows local diving conditions well. Dive shops in Ensenada can arrange guided trips to any Punta Banda dive spot; there are also a couple of dive shops along the Punta Banda road (BCN 23).

Kayaking: Challenging sea kayaking routes include following the peninsular shore from La Jolla around to La Bufadora, or crossing over to the Isla Sur of the Islas Todos Santos. The latter is a fairly straightforward 6.4-km (four-mile) paddle from Punta Banda.

Getting There: To drive to Punta Banda from Ensenada, take Mexico 1 south to BCN 23 (just north of Maneadero), then follow this road west through olive orchards and the La Jolla community onto the peninsula. After La Jolla, the road begins to climb, winding its way toward La Bufadora and ending at a parking lot for the blowhole.

You can also hire a taxi from the city to La Bufadora for US$10-15.

Camping And RV Parks
The deluxe **Estero Beach Trailer Park** (tel. 6-62-65) is adjacent to the Estero Beach Resort Hotel. RVers can use all the hotel facilities, including boat ramp, tennis courts, and clubhouse. Full-hookup sites are US$16.

At Ejido Chapultepec, eight km south of town between Estero and Hermosa beaches, are **Corona Beach, Playa Mona Lisa,** and **El Faro,** all with full hookups for US$12-15 a night depending on the season, with weekly and monthly rates available. Mona Lisa has the best facilities and ambience; there are also several two-bedroom beach cottages here for US$50-120 a night, less for long-term stays. From the highway, follow signs for "Estero Beach." Frequent buses, marked Chapultepec, ply the route between this neighborhood and the city center.

A short distance along the road to La Bufadora (BCN 23), in the North American retirement enclave of La Jolla, is the large, secure, and well-kept **La Jolla Beach Camp,** facing Bahía de Todos Santos. Electric-water hookups or tent sites cost US$6 for two, plus US$1 for each additional person. Additional facilities include hot showers, boat ramp, tennis court, disposal station, market, and restaurant.

JOE CUMMINGS

La Bufadora

Mexico 3

JOE CUMMINGS

The adjacent **Villarino Camp** (tel. 6-13-09) offers tent/camper sites with electricity for US$6, full hookups for US$10. Other facilities include hot showers, boat ramp, and market. A couple of ejido-operated campgrounds with minimal facilities (toilets and water only), **Tres Hermanas** and **Rancho La Bufadora,** lie farther out on Punta Banda en route to La Bufadora; look for signs along BCN 23. Rates are usually US$5-6 night for tent or RV, less for long-term stays.

ENSENADA TO SAN FELIPE (MEXICO 3)

Mexico 3 stretches 198 km (123 miles) between Ensenada and San Felipe. The first two-thirds of the highway traverses high chaparral along the gradually ascending western slopes of the Sierra Juárez. Just past Km 39 is a short paved road leading north into **Ojos Negros,** a small farming center with a PEMEX station, a couple of cafés and markets, an auto parts dealer, and a pharmacy. A network of dirt roads out of Valle Ojos Negros links farms, the old mining settlement of Real del Castillo, and a longer road to Parque Nacional Constitución de 1857.

A natural spring flows from a steep hillside on the east side of the highway between Km 73 and 74—a good place to stock up on drinking water.

Parque Nacional Constitución De 1857
The most commonly used road to this national park branches northeast off Mexico 3 at Km 55.

Although ungraded much of the way, the 35-km (22-mile) dirt road is usually traversable, if caution is taken, by ordinary passenger car all the way to the park entrance. As the road climbs, passing a number of ranchos, the chaparral gradually gives way to conifer forests and the temperature drops. At the park entrance, rangers collect a fee of US$3 adults, US$.75 children.

Most of the 5,000-hectare park encompasses a subalpine plateau at the center of the Sierra Juárez with an average elevation of around 1,200 meters (3,950 feet); several granite peaks reach over 1,500 meters (5,000 feet). Laguna Juárez, more commonly known as Laguna Hanson (named for an American settler who disappeared here in 1880; legend has it he was cooked in a cauldron by a friend), is for all intents the center of the park. In years when rainfall is plentiful, the scenic lake is filled with bass and catfish; in the fall, ducks are common. Fishing is permitted; hunting isn't. A campground at the lake features raked grounds and neat firepits, some furnished with firewood and grills. Except for a 10-km path around the lake, there are no established hiking trails in the park. A smaller lake within the park limits, Laguna La Chica, is less visited.

Most of the year the park receives few visitors. This changes at Easter, when enough jeepsters arrive to dispel all peace and quiet. Snow occasionally falls in the winter.

The road from Mexico 3 continues northeastward through the park and ends at Mexico 2—60 km (30 miles) from Laguna Hanson—

near La Rumorosa. See "Vicinity of Mexicali" for details on the northern approach to Laguna Hanson.

Independencia
This pueblo of around 500 ejidatarios, at Km 92 on Mexico 3, is part of Ejido Héroes de la Independencia. It makes a good rest spot if you're driving Mexico 3 straight through, as it's roughly halfway between Ensenada and the Mexico 5 junction. Among the scattered buildings, some abandoned, are a Conasupo, a PEMEX station, a church, an auto shop, and a couple of handicraft shops.

The latter sell pottery and other crafts made by the Paipai who live in nearby **Santa Catarina,** a former mission settlement eight km east of Independencia via a graded dirt road. The adobe ruins—foundations only—of Misión Santa Catarina de los Paipais, founded by Dominican padres in 1797 and destroyed by Yumanos in 1840, are still visible in the village. The Paipai, who may be related to the Yavapai and Walapai of Arizona, make rustic coil pots prized by collectors for the orange-and-black swirls or "fire clouding" created during the firing process.

Valle De La Trinidad-Mike's Sky Ranch
A paved road south to Valle de Trinidad branches south from Mexico 5 at Km 121. This farming community of around 5,000 offers a PEMEX station, a bank, and several markets, cafés, and auto shops. Southwest of Valle de la Trinidad, a dirt road suitable for sturdy, high-clearance vehicles only continues southward some 48 km (30 miles) past a few ranchos to the northern boundary of Parque Nacional Sierra San Pedro Mártir.

Just beyond Km 138, a dirt road leads 35.5 km (22 miles) south to **Mike's Sky Ranch,** a remote resort at the northwestern edge of Parque Nacional Sierra San Pedro Mártir (elevation:

1,200 meters/ 3900 feet). Named for its late founder, Mike Leon, the ranch has long served as a checkpoint for the Baja 500 and Baja 1000 off-road races; nearby are hiking trails to year-round waterfalls and Río San Rafael. Ranch accommodations include rooms for US$20 per person per night (includes swimming pool access) and campsites for US$6 a night (water and shower privileges only). Guests eat family-style meals together, paying US$12 for dinner and US$6.50 for breakfast and lunch. Information or reservations: Mike's Sky Ranch (tel. 66-85-49-95 in Tijuana; 619-428-5290 in the U.S.), P.O. Box 1948, Imperial Beach, CA 92032.

The road to Mike's is rough in spots, though drivers with passenger cars and RVs can make it with patience. Beyond the ranch, this road continues southwestward to join the better, graded road between Mexico 1 and the national park. For more information on this route, and Parque Nacional San Pedro Mártir, see "Ensenada to San Quintín."

San Matías Pass To Crucero La Trinidad
Southeast of Valle de la Trinidad, Mexico 3 climbs through the 900 meter (2,950 foot) San Matías Pass, and, as the road descends the eastern escarpment of the Sierra San Pedro Mártir, the scenery shifts from chaparral to desert. Between Km 160 and 170, ocotillos increase rapidly in number and size.

At Km 164, a dirt road leads southeast toward Rancho Villa del Sol, than south through the dry Laguna Diablo to the eastern approach to Picacho del Diablo, via Cañon del Diablo. This road also connects with a dirt track east to San Felipe.

Mexico 3 meets Mexico 5 at Crucero La Trinidad (PEMEX, café); from here it's 109 km (65 miles) north to Mexicali, 48 km (29 miles) south to San Felipe.

ENSENADA TO SAN QUINTIN

Maneadero

This farming community 20 km (12 miles) south of Ensenada is unremarkable except for the fact that it's the southernmost limit of Baja's "free zones." Beyond Km 23, every visitor is supposed to possess a valid tourist permit or visa. The immigration checkpoint at Km 23 has been closed for several years now, so be sure to validate your tourist card in Ensenada.

Restaurants, small grocery stores, auto parts shops, and other small businesses line Mexico 1 in the middle of Maneadero. A car wash on the east side of the highway performs an excellent exterior and interior cleaning for US$4, something to consider if you're on the way north after extensive offroad driving in the interior.

Ejido Uruapan

Just south of Km 41 (19 km south of Maneadero) is the turnoff for Ejido Uruapan, a farming village set in a deep valley. During quail season, Nov.-Feb., Uruapan is popular among North American hunters, most of whom stay at a hunting lodge operated by the regional wildlife inspector, Billy Cruz. During the rest of the year, non-hunting visitors may stay here as well. Guests can explore the Uruapan Valley, visit nearby vineyards and dairy farms, or make daytrips to beaches at Punta Santo Tomás, 31 km west of the village.

Uruapan itself offers little to see. A stream on the valley floor is linked to a hot springs where *ejidatarios* bathe and wash clothes at a cement structure built for this purpose. The ejido also operates a sea-urchin processing plant. Established with Japanese assistance, the plant prepares the tiny marine creatures for export to Japan, where they're a popular sushi ingredient.

Accommodations: Cruz's simple, red-brick lodge is built around a courtyard; guests dine in front of a huge fireplace. During the off-season, the spartan rooms cost US$15 per person, including the use of a modern kitchen. A cook can be arranged at extra cost. During hunting season, the lodge rents for US$130 a day, which includes a hunting guide, transport to hunt sites, and a large evening meal. For further information on staying at the lodge, contact the state tourist office in Ensenada.

At the junction of Mexico 1 and the turnoff for the village is a campground with well-shaded tent/camper sites and a few firepits. Campers can bathe at the village hot springs.

La Bocana-Puerto Santo Tomás

Off Mexico 1 at Km 48, an unpaved graded road follows the Río Santo Tomás 29 km west to the

seaside fishing villages of La Bocana and Puerto Santo Tomás, both on the south side of Punta Santo Tomás. The Río Santo Tomás drains into the Pacific at La Bocana ("The Mouth"); during the Dominican era, Puerto Santo Tomás served as a supply port for nearby Misión Santo Tomás.

The scenic coastal topography along Punta Santo Tomás and the coves to the south have attracted a small gringo settlement, but for the most part you'll have the beach all to yourself. Camping is free; you can rent rustic cabins at either village. The villagers also rent fishing pangas.

The shoreline in front of La Bocana offers occasional beach and reef breaks. Determined surfers can brave an ungraded dirt road that runs south off the graded road from Mexico 1—the turnoff is approximately 20.5 km west of the highway—and straggle 11 km southwest to Punta San José, where there are often good reef and point breaks.

Santo Tomás

The Valle de Santo Tomás, cleft by the Río Santo Tomás, is one of Baja's prime agricultural regions and a visual highlight of any transpeninsular journey. Winding up, down, and around olive-green hills, the highway repeatedly suspends drivers over vignettes of tidy olive groves, vineyards, fields of flowers, and the occasional herd of goats. For some visitors, a day's stopover turns into weeks or months, perhaps because Santo Tomás offers the ambience of Alta California's Sonoma or Napa valleys without the tourists and high prices. The valley community of around 1,500 is friendly and welcoming.

History: The valley was originally settled in 1790 by Dominican missionaries as an intermediate point between Misión San Miguel to the north and San Vicente to the south. In 1791 the Dominican padres established **Misión Santo Tomás de Aquino,** which by 1800 boasted over 3,000 cattle, sheep, and goats, plus an estimated 200 acres of grapes, corn, and wheat. The Mission wine produced at Santo Tomás was famous throughout the California mission system, and is now one of several wines produced by Ensenada's Bodegas de Santo Tomás. The Santo Tomás mission was secularized in 1849.

Mission Ruins: The mission ruins lie in two locations. The original site is on a low mesa off the unpaved road to La Bocana-Puerto Santo Tomás; the second site, where the mission was moved in 1794, is just off the east side of Mexico 1 in the village of Santo Tomás, north of El Palomar Trailer Park. At both sites, the only remains are a few ruined adobe walls and a foundation.

Accommodations and Food: The family-owned **El Palomar** (tel. 617-8-23-55, A.P. 595, Santo Tomás, BCN) in Santo Tomás began as a restaurant in 1948 but now includes a motel, trailer park, and PEMEX station. Comfortable, heated rooms at the motel are US$35 s, US$45 d. Full-hookup RV sites in the trailer park cost US$12 a night for two people. El Palomar's dining room offers a full list of Bajacalifornio wines and home-cooked meals starting at US$5. The swimming pool at El Palomar is a treat during the summer months; it's open 1000-1900 daily.

Ejido Eréndira-Puerto San Isidro

At Km 78 a paved road leads west off Mexico 1 to the fishing and farming community of Ejido Eréndira. Although the village is far from attractive, the beaches north of town offer plenty of opportunities for camping and surf or boat fishing. The road to Puerto Isidro (two km north of Ejido Eréndira) and beyond is unpaved, ungraded, sandy, and potholed—a passenger car can manage it, but very slowly. Surfers will find a number of decent point and reef breaks in the vicinity of Puerto Isidro.

Castro's Place (tel. 617-6-28-97, A.P. 974, Ensenada, BCN) near Puerto Isidro is a fish camp with simple cabins that sleep up to six people in bunkbeds for US$20-25 a night. The owner, Fernando Castro Ríos, leads guided fishing trips in the vicinity for US$22 per person per day. Reservations are necessary on weekends. Camping is permitted at Castro's for a nominal fee; a few kilometers north are plenty of free camping spots. Ejido Eréndira has a small grocery store, but the PEMEX station is abandoned. The nearest working pumps are in Santo Tomás and San Vicente.

A new RV park with electricity and water has reportedly opened near Castro's. US$10 per night with discounts for longer stays.

San Vicente

The scenic Valle de San Vicente and adjacent Llano Colorado ("Colorado Plain"), like the Río Santo Tomás valley, are heavily cultivated with olives, grapes, wheat, and corn. Just south of the Km 88 marker, a dirt road leads west off Mexico

1 to the ruins of **Misión San Vicente Ferrer,** a Dominican mission in use from 1780 to 1833. During its half-century tenure, the mission came under repeated attacks by Yumano warriors living in the Sierra Juárez. On a small mesa near the adobe walls of the mission are a mission-established cemetery—still in use—and the remains of a Spanish presidio.

Along Mexico 1 in the small town of San Vicente are a sprinkling of cafés, markets, a PEMEX station with Magna Sin (usually), and the **Motel El Camino,** a 10-room motel near the south end of town with basic accommodations for US$12 a night.

San Antonio Del Mar

At Km 126, just north of Colonet, an unpaved graded road leads 12.5 km northwest to this seaside settlement, little more than a collection of trailers, rustic beach houses, and a couple of beach camps that charge US$5-8 a night. The beach at San Antonio del Mar, wedged into a large gap between high cliffs created by a tidal estuary, is wide, windy, and backed by sand dunes. If you can stand the wind, you can camp for free on the beach. Surfcasting and clamming are usually excellent here; the estuary is an added attraction.

The main road in from Mexico 1 becomes softer as it gets closer to the beach. Unless you have 4WD, stick to the most well-worn, hardened tracks and leave the many branching roads to drivers with SUVs or ATVs.

Restaurant Chely, just north of the San Antonio del Mar turnoff, offers simple Mexican meals.

Colonet

Like San Vicente, Colonet is a small farming center with a PEMEX station and a couple of cafés and markets. Travelers spending time at San Antonio del Mar, Rancho Meling, or Parque Nacional Sierra San Pedro Mártir often use the town as a supply depot.

A graded dirt road leads southwest out of town 14 km to a fish camp on Bahía Colonet. Cabo Colonet, at the north end of the bay, offers a point break during winter northwest swells. The town, bay, and cape are reputedly named for Captain James Colnett, a British sea captain who explored this section of the Pacific coast in the late 18th century. At **Cuatro Casas,** about 4.5 km south of Cabo Colonet on the bay, campsites are available for US$4 a day. Surfcasters will find plenty of barred surfperch, halibut, and bass.

San Telmo-Rancho Meling

Between Km 140 and Km 141, an unpaved graded road branches east to San Telmo, Rancho Meling, and Parque Nacional San Pedro Mártir. San Telmo, six km (3.5 miles) east of Mexico 1, is a small farming-ranching settlement with little of interest to the traveler; supplies for extended trips into the interior, including gas, should be procured in Colonet or Colonia Vicente Guerrero on Mexico 1.

tamal stand

JOE CUMMINGS

Rancho Meling, also known as Rancho San José, lies 42 km farther southeast along the road, at an elevation of 670 meters (2,200 feet). Founded in 1893 by Texas miner Harry Johnson as a base for his gold-mining operations in the western Sierra San Pedro Mártir, the ranch was destroyed by Magonistas during the 1911 border rebellion. A Norwegian family, the Melings, helped rebuild the ranch shortly thereafter, turning it into a 10,000-acre cattle ranch.

Today, in addition to raising cattle, the ranch takes in paying guests who want to experience Baja's high country. Visitors are accommodated in a comfortable lodge for US$50 s, US$90 d (US$30 for children ages 8-11, US$20 four to seven) per day, including three family-style meals. Optional activities include swimming in a spring-fed pool, horseback riding, quail and dove hunting, and excursions into the Sierra San Pedro Mártir—an excellent opportunity to see the national park with experienced guides. Guests with their own planes may use the 1,064-meter (3,500-foot) airstrip. For reservations or further information, write Rancho Meling, A.P. 1326, Ensenada, BCN, or 1777 Knapp Dr., Vista, CA 92084 (tel. 619-758-2719) in the United States.

Another recreational spot run by the Meling family is **Rancho La Cienega,** at Km 73 on the observatory road about four hours from Ensenada and 51.5 km/32 miles from Mexico 1. The main activity occurs on weekends in late summer/early fall when Andy Meling fires up a deep-pit barbecue for a Saturday afternoon feast. Guests generally arrive Friday afternoon to camp overnight; facilities are limited to toilets and hot-water showers. For information, contact the Rancho Meling.

A new guest resort, **Rancho Los Manzanitos,** under construction at Km 74 off the observatory road, will offer an RV camp, cabins, and restaurant. Call (116) 6-22-68 in Colonia Vicente Guerrero for information.

Punta San Jacinto-Camalú

Between Km 149 and Km 150, a dirt track suitable in good weather for ordinary passenger vehicles proceeds west nine km to a sandy beach at Punta San Jacinto. A somewhat popular point break, known as "Freighters" because of the nearby wreck of the huge freighter *Isla del Carmen,* led to the establishment of the rustic **El Parador Surf Camp.** The camp offers few facilities—water, sometimes, and a couple of firepits. You can camp for free among the dunes behind the beach.

Camalú, beginning at Km 157, offers a variety of markets, pharmacies, cafés, a mechanic's shop, and a PEMEX station. An unpaved side road leads west to Camalú Via la Mar, a fish camp, and areas suitable for overnight camping. Reef and point breaks at Punta Camalú to the north attract surfers; a recently established surf camp provides minimal facilities.

Misión Santo Domingo-Colonia Vicente Guerrero

Colonia Vicente Guerrero is a growing agricultural center with post office, Conasupo, motel, two banks, restaurants, police station, panadería, PEMEX station, *butano* (butane/propane) plant, Banamex, clinic, and two trailer parks. The surrounding fields produce a variety of vegetables and fruit.

The ruins of **Misión Santo Domingo,** named for the founder of the Dominican Order, lie north of town, eight km east of Mexico 1, in a canyon formed by Arroyo de Santo Domingo. An earlier mission, established in 1775, lay eight km farther east along the arroyo. Moved to the current site in 1782, the mission closed in 1839 after most of the Indians in the area either died in battle or succumbed to smallpox. The meter-thick adobe walls at Santo Domingo are more extensive than those at Santo Tomás or San Vicente; the outline of the mission quadrangle and several rooms are clearly visible.

The mission road parallels Arroyo de Santo Domingo for several kilometers beyond the ruins, offering a scenic, if rough, drive past two ranchos. Originating in the high reaches of the Sierra San Pedro Mártir, this arroyo is said to carry the largest volume of water of any stream on the peninsula.

Accommodations: The **Motel Sánchez,** in the middle of town on the west side of Mexico 1, offers basic rooms for US$15-21 a night. At the south end of town, on the west side of the highway next to the butane facility, is the nicely landscaped **Mesón de Don Pepe RV Park** (tel. 616-6-22-16). Tent sites, on green grass—a Baja rarity—are US$4-6 a night; full-hookup sites cost US$7.50-9 for two people (US$1 for each additional person); rates vary according to the time of year and discounts are readily granted for long-term stays. Don Pepe's restaurant serves Mexican standards and seafood.

Follow the same turnoff to Don Pepe's farther west, toward the beach, and you'll come to the quiet **Posada Don Diego Trailer Park** (tel. 616-6-21-81). Full hookups are US$8-9 a night, tent space US$5-6, with discounts for long-term stays. The park also has a few small trailers for rent (US$20), in case you didn't bring your own. Coin-operated washers, but no dryers, are available. If you dig up your own pismo clams on the beach, ask Señora Martinez, who operates the park with her husband José, to steam them for you.

Camping on the beach among the dunes is a possibility, but the sandy track gets a bit dodgy once you pass Posada Don Diego. Passenger cars can make it, but RVs—except those with 4WD—risk getting stuck.

PARQUE NACIONAL SIERRA SAN PEDRO MARTIR

Founded in 1947, this 170,000-acre national park is centered on the Sierra San Pedro Mártir—the highest mountain range in the peninsular cordillera. Like other Baja sierras, the San Pedro Mártir tips toward the west, with its highest peaks thrusting out along the precipitous eastern escarpment. The peninsula's highest peak, Picacho del Diablo, or "Devil's Peak"—also known as Cerro de la Encantada, "Enchanted Mountain," and La Providencia, "Providence"—looms over the San Felipe Desert at 3,086 meters (10,154 feet), a challenging Class 3-5 climb.

Three prominent canyons radiate eastward from the base of the mountain—Cañon del Diablo, Cañon Providencia, and Cañon Teledo, providing magnificent bouldering and scrambling opportunities, sheer cliffs, waterfalls, fan palms, Indian petroglyphs, and several approaches to Diablo's twin granitic summits. Hikers interested in these eastern canyons, which lie just outside the park boundaries, usually approach them from Mexico 3 to the northeast.

Within the park, hikers and backpackers can choose from a network of trails and campsites on a pine-and-juniper forested plateau—approximately 70 km by 15 km—at the heart of the range. Because much of the park exceeds 1,800 meters (6,000 feet) in elevation, annual precipitation averages 60 cm (24 inches); thus water sources are abundant and shady conifers predominate. Only a few hundred people visit San Pedro Mártir each year, making it one of the most undervisited national parks in Mexico and an extraordinary opportunity for wilderness solitude. The mountain hiking conditions enjoyed here are similar to those in Alta California's Sierra Nevada, but attract far fewer people.

MOUNTAIN OF MANY NAMES

Devil's Peak, Enchanted Mountain, Providence, and Mt. San Pedro Mártir are a few of the map designations given Baja's highest peak over the last four centuries. Whether the Yumano or Cochimí Indians had a name for the soaring peak isn't known, but they must have been acquainted with its serrated profile, visible from 160 km (100 miles) away in Sonora, on the Mexican mainland.

The first recorded mention of the jagged, sparsely vegetated, twin-summited mountain dates from 16th-century Spanish explorations of the Sea of Cortez. As the Spanish sailed into the thirsty upper reaches of the Cortez in late spring, the snowcapped peak hanging over the searing San Felipe Desert to the west must have seemed a mirage, a gift from God. Hence they called it La Providencia, a name sustained through the early 1900s.

La Providencia's semantic opposite, El Picacho del Diablo, or "Devil's Peak," surfaced during the missionary period, probably in reference to the peak's formidable appearance when viewed from the west. Misión San Pedro Mártir, perhaps the most remote mission on the peninsula, was established some 25 km to the southwest. Anyone approaching the mountain from its western side is met with a deep chasm, Cañon del Diablo, at its base; the geographical separation makes Diablo seem all the more unassailable. Another possible semantic explanation is the mountain might have been revered by local Indians; to divert Indian attention away from the peak and toward the mission, the San Pedro Mártir padres may have consigned it to the Devil.

The padres called a large, open valley meadow between the mission and the mountain La Encantada, "The Enchanted," perhaps because it appears in the midst of heavy pine and juniper forests as if cleared by supernatural forces. The meadow appeared on Spanish maps thereafter, and Mexican cartographers in the 1920s, whether by mistake or intention, applied the name to the mountain.

Other names have made brief appearances this century, including El Picacho Blanco, a reference to both the peak's mostly white coloring and its snowbound condition in the winter. But El Picacho del Diablo is the most common term used among Sierra San Pedro Mártir residents and mountaineers; it's also the most common name found on English-language maps of Baja. The official Mexican government name, however, remains Cerro de la Encantada.

The Climbers

Called "the unchallenged retreat of lions and mountain sheep, the unscaled lookout of eagles and mighty condors" by author A.W. North in 1910, Devil's Peak was successfully challenged by American cartographer Donald McLain the very year following this colorful statement. The next recorded climb was by a U.S. Sierra Club group in 1932, who bestowed the names Campo Noche and Arroyo Noche ("Night Camp" and "Night Wash") to the area in Cañon del Diablo where they were forced to spend the night after struggling with the mountain's west face.

The peak was ascended by another American climber (Randall Henderson, editor of *Desert* magazine) in 1937, by several more in the '50s, and by the early '70s over 50 people a year (both Mexicans and foreigners) were scaling the heights—with as many attempting the climb and turning back short of the summit. Today the Class-3 Slot Wash approach is a straightforward but challenging ascent for experienced climbers, while the other six proven approaches comprise some of the toughest climbing in Mexico.

National Observatory

Because the air is exceptionally clear and potential sources of light pollution are remote, the Mexican government selected the San Pedro Mártir Plateau in 1967 as the site for its Observatorio Nacional. The observatory facilities are at the end of the park access road (20 km past the park entrance), at an elevation of 2,830 meters (9,286 feet). A locked gate just before the observatory means visitors must park and walk two km to reach the domed buildings. Several telescopes are in use at the observatory, including Mexico's largest, a 2.11-meter (83-inch) reflector.

Observatory tours occur every Saturday at 1100. A viewpoint nearby offers an inspiring glimpse of the eastern escarpment and canyons. At night, stars appear over the plateau like a sea of diamonds—who needs a telescope?

Climate

Temperatures on the plateau, 1,800 meters above sea level, average 26° C (80° F) in July and August during the daytime, down to 4.5° C (40° F) at night. From December through March, temperatures run from 4.5° C (40° F) down to -12° C (10° F). Freezing nights sometimes occur in the spring and fall, with daytime temperatures in the 15-21° C (60-70° F) range.

Snowfall is common above 2,000 meters during the winter; Picacho del Diablo is often snow-capped Nov.-April. While occasional heavy rains fall in late summer, it's usually dry in spring, early summer, and fall.

The best hiking seasons are mid-April through mid-June, good for wildflowers; and late September through early November, when quaking aspen puts on a show. For backpackers, April-June is optimal because water sources from the snowmelt are most abundant. Late summer rains can cause flash floods in the arroyos.

Flora And Fauna

About 53 km east of Rancho Meling the San Telmo road begins ascending rapidly, the terrain changing from arid coastal plains to scrubby high chaparral. At 900 to 1,500 meters (3,000 to 5,000 feet), stands of pine, oak, and juniper appear, mixed with a dwindling number of desert and chaparral species—sagebrush, verbena, yucca, and fan palm. Above 1,500 meters, thickly forested glens leave the Baja desert mythos behind. Here you'll find piñon and Jeffrey pine, incense cedar, white fir, sugar pine, and at least three species not found elsewhere in Baja—quaking aspen, lodgepole pine, and the endemic San Pedro Mártir cypress.

Streams in the sierra's western canyons carry an endemic trout species, the Nelson rainbow trout (*Salmo nelsonii*, named for E.W. Nelson, who discovered the fish in 1905). In the early '80s, a group of Mexico City naturalists transplanted Nelson rainbows to several other canyon streams in the park. Today, fishing without a license is permitted. Mule deer, mountain lion, coyote, and the rare *borregon* (bighorn sheep) inhabit some of the canyons.

Domestic animals—cattle and sheep—are often seen in the park, especially along the east side where two ranches lie within park boundaries. Unfortunately, overgrazing is destroying much of the vegetation in this portion of the park, with the full consent of the Mexican government. On the positive side, the Mexican park service—unlike its U.S. counterpart—forbids logging in all national parks.

Park Facilities And Regulations

The park entrance is 78 km (47 miles) from Mexico 1 via an unpaved but graded roadway; follow signs marked Observatorio. In winter, the occasional snowstorm may force temporary road closure, but during most of the year the road is passable by passenger car. The entrance station, at a forested meadow called La Corona de Abajo (Lower Crown), is open daily 0700-1900, with an entry fee of US$1.50.

A number of established campsites and trails are minimally maintained by park staff. Overall, the park is most suited to wilderness hiking and camping. Although there are no facilities for car or trailer camping, it's safe to leave a vehicle parked anywhere within the park boundaries.

On the edge of the park boundaries near the observatory, a private concern is building a new facility with campground (estimated US$5 a night) and cabins (US$25-30); to make reservations, inquire at the real estate/tourist office in Col. Guerrero.

Neither hunting nor the possession of firearms is permitted within park boundaries. When the occasional sanctioned deer hunt is held in adjacent Cañon del Diablo, the canyon may be closed to hiking and backpacking. Offroad driving is banned at all times. Fires, using fallen deadwood, are permitted only within established fire-rings at a few campsites on the plateau; backpackers should carry portable camp stoves. Before leaving on an overnight hike, let park rangers know where you're going and how long you intend to be gone.

Preparations And Precautions

Park trails are not well-marked; don't consider even a day hike without carrying a compass. The observatory road bisects the park east to west and makes a useful mental landmark. When embarking on a hike, note whether you're heading north or south of the road. If you get lost anywhere west of the eastern escarpment, simply head directly north (or south) from your current location and you should intercept the roadway.

Canyon hiking along the eastern escarpment is rugged and should only be attempted by experienced climbers or those in the company of someone who knows the terrain. You may be able to arrange for a guide through Rancho Meling (A.P. 1326, Ensenada, BCN).

Maps: The Mexican government publishes two topographic maps (20-meter contour), *San Rafael H11B45* and *Santa Cruz H11B55,* that cover an area that includes the park. They're available by mail from the Map Centre (tel. 619-291-3830, 2611 University Ave., San Diego, CA, 92104).

More up to date and easier to use is a 1988 topo map published by Centra Publications (4705 Laurel St., San Diego, CA 92105) and titled *Parque Nacional San Pedro Mártir: Topographic Map and Visitor's Guide to Baja's Highest Mountains.* This well-designed, readable map is based on the Mexican topos but adds many physical features never mapped before. Also printed on the map are brief descriptions of

17 different hiking trails, including seven Picacho del Diablo climbing routes.

Water: Except during midsummer, streams are abundant on the plateau, and are generally considered clean enough to drink from. In the eastern arroyos and canyons, water is usually available year-round, though it may be contaminated by livestock. Whether on the plateau or in the canyonlands, always treat local water, just to be sure. Wherever you go in the San Pedro Mártir, carry extra water and a water-purification system—filter, iodine, or halazone.

Trails

The park is honeycombed with footpaths and hiking trails, particularly in the vicinity of Picacho

SIERRA SAN PEDRO MARTIR (PLATEAU)

del Diablo at the edge of the eastern escarpment. Longer, more isolated trails connect the large meadow areas of Vallecitos, Los Llanitos, La Encantada, La Grulla, and Rancho Viejo in a 50-km loop. The three trails described below, on the park's scenic northeastern edge, are well-traveled and thus relatively easy to follow. For a more complete inventory, obtain Centra Publications' detailed topo map of the park.

Vallecitos-Blue Bottle Peak (9.5 km): Vallecitos (literally, "Little Valleys") is the name given to a complex of little flats southeast of the observatory road reached via a dirt track that begins 16.5 km from the park entrance. About 3.5 km from the observatory road, a footpath branches left (east) up an arroyo for 1.7 km, then into an aspen-studded meadow. A smaller path leads north from the meadow to an excellent escarpment-edge view of Cañon del Diablo.

Two km farther southeast on the main trail is north-branching path that leads to Scout Peak (2,850 meters), where you'll find primitive campsites and an unobstructed view of Picacho del Diablo's western face. From this point, climbers can scramble down the side of the Cañon del Diablo to Campo Noche below, and continue on to Blue Bottle Peak via the arroyos at the southern end of the canyon.

Meanwhile, the main trail below Scout Peak continues south and then east a couple of kilometers to a point just northwest of Cerro Botella Azul ("Blue Bottle Peak"); a smaller trail ascends the peak itself. At 2,950 meters (9,680 feet), Blue Bottle is the highest point on the plateau and a reasonable alternative to Picacho del Diablo for the less adventurous. On a clear day—perhaps 85% of the time—you can see both the Pacific and the Sea of Cortez.

Observatory-Cañon del Diablo (5.3 km): Just below the observatory gate, a trail branches east from the main road and leads into Cañon del Diablo, the deepest and longest canyon in the Sierra San Pedro Mártir. Along the way, this trail passes through a scenic aspen meadow at 2,500 meters, where a short path branches north to a rocky viewpoint over the canyon. Beyond the meadow, the trail becomes a demanding Class 3-4 descent that requires hikers to negotiate brush and boulders along an arroyo intersecting with the larger canyon. Water is available at several streams and waterfalls in the canyon.

Near the bottom of the canyon this trail joins the Cañon del Diablo-Campo Noche Trail, the beginning of one of the eastern approaches to Picacho del Diablo. This latter trail, though rated Class 2-3, involves a four-day hike in desert conditions, and is best undertaken with a guide who knows the terrain.

Slot Wash Ascent of Picacho del Diablo: This is the easiest—Class 3—of the seven routes used to climb Baja's highest mountain. To reach Slot Wash, an arroyo that descends Diablo's west face, follow the Vallecitos-Blue Bottle Peak Trail until you've passed the saddle northwest of Blue Bottle; then continue along the peak's north flank until the trail narrows and descends into Cañon del Diablo.

Near the bottom of the canyon, on the east side, is Campo Noche, a large campsite with a fire-ring and nearby pools. The ascent to Slot Wash begins at a shallow arroyo, next to Campo Noche, called Arroyo Noche or "Night Wash," which segues into Slot Wash at an elevation of 2,240 meters. The way is well marked with ducks (stone trail markers). At about 2,500 meters, the route forks. The little-used southern branch leads out of Slot Wash, through a brushy side ravine, to the lower of Diablo's twin peaks (3,094 meters). The northern route, which most climbers take, continues through Slot Wash, and over large stone slabs, until ducks point out a sharp left (north) up a rocky slope. This leads to a steep-walled arroyo nicknamed "Wall Street," which in turn proceeds directly to the higher of the peaks (3,095 meters). Continuing straight up Slot Wash, instead of taking the north branch, leads to the saddle between the two summits.

Starting at Blue Bottle Peak on the plateau, the trip to Picacho del Diablo and back usually takes three days—one night at Campo Noche in each direction, plus one night in the vicinity of the summit. Fit hikers with good orienteering skills can make it to Campo Noche in less than a day, but you really should spend the night for a fresh morning start on the peak.

Approaching Picacho Del Diablo From Mexico 3

You can approach the network of trails below Picacho del Diablo from Mexico 3 (the section between Ensenada and Crucero La Trinidad), to the northeast of the park, via Cañon del Diablo. The road to the canyon area is 164 km southeast of Ensenada (or 34 km northwest of Crucero La Trinidad, if you're driving from Mexicali or San Felipe), south off Mexico 3. The road is graded as far as Rancho Villa del Sol, about eight km south of the Mexico 3 junction, then joins vehicle tracks southeast across the saltflat Laguna Diablo.

Approximately 24 km south of Mexico 3, another set of tracks branches straight west toward Rancho Santa Clara. At Rancho Santa Clara, a dirt track passes just south of the ranch and leads nine km west until it ends at Cañon Diablito. You can park here, but don't leave valuables in the vehicle.

From Diablito, a three-km trail heads northeast to the mouth of Cañon del Diablo. Perhaps the greatest obstacle in the canyon is only about 800 meters into the mouth—a sizable waterfall tumbling down smooth granite walls. A cable bolted to the wall allows hikers to scramble up one side; sometimes accumulated sand creates a temporary platform high enough for you to surmount the wall without the assistance of the cable. The canyon itself is mostly a Class 2 hike with a few Class 3 bouldering exercises along the way; there are plenty of year-round pools and waterfalls to cool off in along the way.

Campo Noche lies 11 km (seven miles) into the canyon, at an elevation of 1,915 meters (6,300 feet). A roundtrip hike at a comfortable pace from the end of the vehicle track to Picacho del Diablo usually takes four days, including stops at Campo Noche each way. See "Slot Wash Ascent of Picacho del Diablo" for a description of the usual route from Campo Noche.

VALLE DE SAN QUINTIN-BAHIA DE SAN QUINTIN

The Valle de San Quintín, actually more a coastal plain than a valley, is a broad flat between a row of seven extinct volcano cones to the west—six on the peninsula, one on Isla San Martín just offshore—and the Sierra San Miguel to the east. Two small rivers, Río San Miguel and Río Santa María, bisect the flat east to west and feed an irrigation system that makes the valley an important vegetable-farming center. Many Indians from the interior of Mexico, espe-

cially Oaxaca and Chiapas, work on the farms and live in shacks on the outskirts of San Quintín.

For visitors, San Quintín's main attraction is a complex coastal environment, the chief features of which are three large, interconnecting bays: Bahía San Quintín, Bahía Falsa, and Bahía Santa María. The innermost bay, surrounded by tidal flats and saltmarshes, is referred to both as Bahía San Quintín and Puerto San Quintín. The outermost bay, facing the Pacific, is called Bahía Santa María as far south as the tip of Cabo San Quintín; beyond it's usually referred to as Bahía San Quintín.

The town of **San Quintín** itself is little more than a collection of shops, motels, restaurants, and other businesses clustered along Mexico 1. Useful services include a long-distance telephone booth, 24-hour medical clinic, and two banks. Five km south of San Quintín is another town of similar size, **Lázaro Cárdenas**, consisting of Mexico's 67th Infantry battalion camp, the intercity bus terminal, a few shops and restaurants, and two motels.

Most visitors remaining more than one night in the area are anglers or hunters. Although the beaches are pristine, an almost-constant summer fog has prevented San Quintín from becoming a popular beachgoing spot.

History
In the 1880s, a British land company with plans for a wheat empire purchased much of the San Quintín area from the U.S.-based International Land Company; at the time, ILC owned most of northern Baja. In response to promises of agricultural wealth, around a hundred English colonists purchased subdivided land tracts from the parent company, planted wheat, and constructed a grist mill. For flour transport, the English built a pier on the inner Bahía San Quintín and began constructing a railway to link up with the Southern Pacific tracks in Alta California. Thirty km of track were laid, including a rail causeway from the west bank of inner Bahía San Quintín, before the colony failed.

A drought devastated one of the first wheat harvests, and by 1900 all colonists had abandoned San Quintín. Although individual farmers were economically ruined, the U.S. and British land companies walked away all the richer, a pattern that would recur several times in northern Baja. Remains of the grist mill, railroad

causeway, pier, and English cemetery still stand along the perimeter of the inner bay. The English names on the cemetery's heavily weathered wooden crosses have faded from sight, and more recent Mexican graves are beginning to crowd out their neglected English counterparts.

In recent years a small community of American retirees has moved into the area, leasing bayfront property and building homes. The most concentrated area is Pedregal, where some houses are built of volcanic rock. Around San Quintín these days are many lots "for sale"; actually available only through lease or *fideicomiso* arrangements.

Climate

While most of northwestern coastal Baja features a climate similar to San Diego's, San Francisco is a better comparison for Valle de San Quintín. As in the San Francisco area, Pacific influences combine with the insulating effect of a large bay—in this case, three bays—to keep average temperatures within a narrow year-round range: from 12° C (54° F) Dec.-Jan. to 20° C (68° F) Aug.-September.

Annual precipitation averages 31 centimeters (12 inches); December usually records the most rainfall (average six centimeters), with Feb.-March second (four to five centimeters); summer months are usually rain-free but foggy.

Beach And Bay Access

Several dirt roads south of Lázaro Cárdenas lead directly west from Mexico 1 to the inner bay; follow signs to the Old Mill Motel and Old Pier Restaurant. You can launch cartopped or trailered boats here, or from a boat launch on the west shore of the bay. To reach the latter site, drive west out of Lázaro Cárdenas on a gravel road that leaves Mexico 1 between the PEMEX station and a military camp; a sign here reads Bahía Falsa. This is a long, rough ride. Fourteen km from Mexico 1, just past Monte de Kenton with a cinder cone immediately to the west, a lesser dirt road forks left and leads to Pedregal, a bayside settlement suitable for boat launching. The marshes and tidal flats at the north end of Bahía Falsa make an excellent birding venue.

If, instead of turning south to Pedregal, you continue west along the road from Lázaro Cárdenas, you'll pass an oyster farm on Bahía Falsa and reach the road's end at a fish camp on the Pacific.

To reach Bahía Santa María or the larger, Pacific-facing Bahía San Quintín, drive 16 km south of Lázaro Cárdenas and turn right (west) on the paved road to Santa María. The turn is marked by signs advertising Hotel La Pinta and Motel Cielito Lindo. Follow the signs along this pine-tree-lined road to Hotel La Pinta; Playa Santa María, the largest, longest beach in the area, is behind the hotel.

Hotels And Motels

Motel Chávez (tel. 5-20-05, A.P. 32, San Quintín, BCN) and **Motel Uruapan** (tel. 5-20-50, Km 190) are the only places to stay in the town of San Quintín. Although far from bays and beaches, if you're just stopping for the night Motel Chávez is a clean, economical choice, with well-maintained rooms for US$21 s, US$24 d, US$27 t/q. Some rooms feature kitchenettes; weekly and monthly rates are available. Motel Uruapan is a poor second choice.

In Lázaro Cárdenas, near the military camp, are **Las Hadas** and **Hotel Romo,** both offering basic, nondescript motel rooms for US$12-18. The Romo is the better of the two; consider crumbling Las Hadas only as a last resort.

Southwest of Lázaro Cárdenas, on the inner bay next to the Old Pier Restaurant, is the **Motel San Carlos** (P.O. Box 11, Valle de San Quintín,

BCN). Simple rooms, all with bay views, cost US$17-25. The San Carlos is usually quieter than the **Old Mill Motel** (tel. 619-428-2779, toll-free 800-479-7962 in the U.S./Canada), which lies farther north along the same dirt road, on the site of a former grist mill and next to the main public boat launch. This longtime favorite among hunters and anglers features newly renovated brick cottages at US$30 for a room with two twin beds or one double bed with private bath; rooms with kitchenettes cost US$38 d, US$42 t. There are also "sleeping rooms," each with four twin beds and private bath, for US$50. In a newer section, rooms with a fireplace and one queen-size bed go for US$60; a two-bedroom suite costs US$85, or US$90 with bay view. In this same section rooms with complete kitchens cost US$53 d, US$62 t, US$70 q. The electricity at the Old Mill is usually turned off midnight-0530. A new RV park is attached; fishing and hunting trips can be arranged. Although accommodations at the Old Mill are comfortable and well-maintained, the din from partying anglers—especially on weekends—means nights here are anything but tranquil.

Farther south, next to Bahía Santa María, is the **Motel Cielito Lindo** with large but dingy rooms for US$30 s, US$36 d; the electricity is turned off 1100-1500. A restaurant, bar, and RV park are adjacent to the motel. Also on Bahía Santa María is **Hotel La Pinta** (tel. 617-6-26-01 in Ensenada; 800-336-5454 in the U.S.). Spacious heated rooms, all with sea views and terraces, cost US$55 s, US$60 d. Hotel facilities include a restaurant, bar, tennis court, and private airstrip.

Bed And Breakfast

Rancho Sereno Bed and Breakfast (tel. 909-982-7087 in the U.S., 1442 Hildita Ct., Upland, CA 91786) is a welcome addition to the San Quintín lodging scene. Owned and managed by the friendly Atkinson family, this charming ranch house not far off the highway offers three quiet rooms for US$40/45 s/d (with outside bath) and US$55 s/d (with private bath) per night, including full breakfast. One of the US$55 rooms is attached to a large rec room where extra guests are accommodated for an additional US$10 per person. All rooms have private entrances; power is generated 0800-1200 and 1800-2200. The family owns several horses and will lead trail rides in the vicinity for US$10 per hour. Rancho Sereno is 1.9 km (1.2 miles) from the highway; the turnoff is south of Lázaro Cárdenas, just south of the agricultural inspection station, on the west side of the highway—the same turnoff as for the Old Mill. The public boat ramp at the Old Mill is only about three km (two miles) farther west.

Camping And RV Parks

Primitive beach camping is available at a number of spots in the San Quintín area, including Playa Santa María south of Hotel La Pinta. More secluded cobble beaches are found south of Santa María from Km 18 onwards—a good number of dirt tracks lead west from the highway almost all the way to El Rosario.

If you're planning to stay awhile, you can check the west side of inner Bahía San Quintín at Pedregal or the Pacific shore (Playa Médano) below the cinder cone Picacho Vizcaíno. The latter area can be cold and damp, and the road is quite long and rough; this is a place best enjoyed by hardcore Robinson Crusoes. The clams here are huge and plentiful.

Motel Cielito Lindo maintains a beach campground where self-contained tent or trailer camping runs US$5 per night. The toilet/shower facility is in quite poor condition.

On the east side of inner Bahía San Quintín, the American-owned **Old Mill Motel** offers 15 RV spaces, with more planned for the future. Full hookups cost US$15 for up to four people, plus US$1 for each additional person. Hot showers are available. Tent/camper sites cost US$10 for up to four people.

At the **Old Pier/Motel San Carlos** self-contained camping costs US$4 per person. RVs can park nearby for no charge. Farther north along this same shore, beyond the Old Mill, **Campo Lorenzo** has sites with full hookups for US$7 a night. Tent/camper sites on the beach, with no hookups, run US$5. A more remote choice, **El Pabellón RV Campground,** lies on a secluded beach 15 km (nine miles) south of Lázaro Cárdenas and 1.6 km west of Mexico 1 (the turnoff is near Km 16). Sites with water and sewage, but no electricity, cost US$6 per night for tents or RVs. Other facilities include hot showers and flush toilets. The road to El Pabellón—two rutted tracks—could be a bit much for some rigs.

Food

The tourist-oriented **Restaurant-Bar Quintín** (tel. 5-23-76), next door to the Motel Chávez, serves good Mexican dishes and seafood for US$9-14 per meal. The restaurant doubles as the local tourist office; near the entrance is a table of printed information on San Quintín.

Also in the town of San Quintín, **El Alteño** and **Costa Azul** offer fresh continental- and Mexican-style seafood respectively; both accept credit cards and are open for breakfast, lunch, and dinner. Food usually isn't served at the Costa Azul on Sunday evenings, when the restaurant becomes a disco. El Alteño has a small bar.

On the east side of the highway a bit south of the Costa Azul, the friendly, clean **Asadero El Alazán** serves tasty and relatively inexpensive *carne asada* and *pollo asado* with a delicious *salsa casera.*

Restaurant Misión Santa Isabel, at Km 190 toward the north end of San Quintín, specializes in *carne tampiqueña* and *machaca.* This is also a popular breakfast stop. Major credit cards accepted.

The Old Mill has a new, larger restaurant and bar called **Gaston's Cannery** that serves very good seafood and Mexican meals, including home-raised chicken and goat. Prices are relatively high but portions are large.

The well-known **Old Pier,** next to Motel San Carlos on the inner bay, offers rather expensive—for Mexico—seafood, from unimpressive clam dinners for around US$10 to abalone or lobster for US$16. Meals include a generous appetizer tray, but the entrees themselves can be disappointing.

If you're driving to either the Old Mill Motel or the Old Pier Restaurant/Motel San Carlos in the afternoon with plans for an evening meal, be sure to note each turn along the way so you can find your way back. At night it's very easy to become lost on the maze of sandy roads.

The seafood at the **Motel Cielito Lindo** restaurant is as good as any in San Quintín and prices are fairly reasonable. Though the restaurant is open for dinner only, an adjoining coffee shop serves breakfast and lunch. **Las Cazuelas,** the restaurant at Hotel La Pinta, features the usual La Pinta menu for breakfast, lunch, and dinner.

The highway through Lázaro Cárdenas and San Quintín is lined with taco and *mariscos* stands. One of the best for *tacos de pescado* is **Marshall Fish Tacos,** a modest stand just north of the PEMEX station in Lázaro Cárdenas. For fresh clams, **Cocteles Fito** on the west side of the highway in San Quintín can't be beat. It's one of the fancier vendors, with a boat-shaped stall and places to eat. The *almejas ahumadas* (smoked clams) here are especially good.

Groceries: There are a number of tiendas in San Quintín; **Mercado Indio,** on the highway, is the best. In Lázaro Cárdenas try **Mercado Avigal.** There are also a couple of panaderías in San Quintín and a tortillería in Lázaro Cárdenas.

Sports And Recreation

Fishing: The unusually varied marine environment, created by the intersection of the Pacific and the three bays, makes the San Quintín coast an excellent area for surfcasting and inshore fishing. Because the entrance to the two inner bays, Bahía Falsa and Bahía San Quintín (Puerto San Quintín), is blocked by steady surf year-round, the bays are inaccessible to commercial fishing fleets. This means more gamefish available for casual anglers, who can launch small boats from inside or from the Pacific shore.

In general, San Quintín attracts the same fish species found north to Ensenada—except they're more highly concentrated here. Flatfish are common in the shallows of the inner bays, bottomfish in the deeper sections. The channel near the bay entrance is reportedly good for large halibut; live mackerel is the recommended bait. Perch and croaker run along the Pacific beaches. According to Tom Miller, author of *Angler's Guide to Baja California,* nowhere in their range are croakers as large as the ones typically caught along San Quintín's beaches. **El Socorro,** 27 km (17 miles) south of Lázaro Cárdenas, is known for surf fishing and has attracted a small group of devoted gringo anglers who maintain homes there.

Farther out in the Pacific, particularly near the south end of volcanic Isla San Martín and at the tip of Cabo San Quintín, yellowtail, yellowfin, white and black seabass, rock cod, and lingcod are common—in season, of course, and to properly equipped anglers. Tuna and dorado are occasionally caught. Isla San Martín features a fish camp and mussel farm; sheltered anchorages are possible in two coves, one at either side of a rocky cape at the southeast end of the island. If you plan to camp on the island, bring all the supplies and fresh water needed for your stay. Sturdy hiking shoes are necessary if you plan to explore San Martín; volcanic rock and cactus thorns will destroy the average pair of sneakers.

The Old Mill, the Old Pier, or Campo Lorenzo can arrange guided fishing trips. You can rent light fishing tackle at the Hotel La Pinta.

Clamming: All three bays are well-endowed with clams and mussels. The easiest and most scenic spot for digging up large pismo clams is Playa Santa María, behind Hotel La Pinta. If you come here at low tide, you'll most likely join a legion of local clamdiggers. You can use your fingers to dig the huge clams out of the sand, or bring along a mesh bag and pitchfork—available in Lázaro Cárdenas—as the locals do. A pro threshes the sand at the surf line with a pitchfork, tossing the clams into a bag tied around the waist. A mesh bag works best because it holds the clams but allows water and sand to drain away. Remember not to take more clams than you can eat that day, and don't take clams smaller than your hand.

Boat Rentals: The Old Mill is the best place to rent a boat for bay fishing. Eighteen-foot aluminum pangas rent for US$15 a day and will carry up to three people. You can charter a 22-

clam diggers, Playa Santa María

JOE CUMMINGS

foot, outfitted fishing cruiser for US$225 a day. The Motel Cielito Lindo also rents pangas and is appropriate for Bahía Santa María launches.

Hunting: The tidal flats and marshlands around the inner bays attract migrating duck and Pacific brant (a small, black goose) during the winter, and quail most of the year. The Old Mill and Cielito Lindo hotels organize local hunting trips.

Scuba Diving: Johnston's Seamount, nine km southwest of Cabo San Quintín, is a renowned site for underwater photography and spearfishing. Sixteen km northwest of Cabo San Quintín, Isla San Martín is surrounded by kelp beds, several rock reefs, and underwater pinnacles. Roca Ben, five km south of the island, rises within three meters of the surface, with intermediate depths of 30 meters. Encrusted with hydrocoral formations, the rock is a habitat for abundant abalone, scallop, lobster, and other shellfish. Due to cold-water upwellings, visibility ranges 15 to 25 meters (50 to 80 feet).

Although San Quintín has no dive shop, a small, American-owned outfit called **Neptune's,** on the road between Rancho Sereno and the Old Mill Hotel, offers guided dive trips. **Diving Charters** (see "Sports and Recreation" under "Out and About" for phone and address) leads periodic dive trips to Isla San Martín and Johnston's Seamount. The latter was named for a Diving Charters skipper who pioneered diving in this area.

Surfing: There are at least two spots along Valle de San Quintín's Pacific coast. Both require tackling the long and bumpy coastal road from Lázaro Cárdenas to Bahía Falsa, then continuing to the coast on a lesser road. Follow the main road around Bahía San Quintín as far as Chapalita and the oyster farm, then continue west to the coast until the road forks south toward Cabo San Quintín. At the top of the cape a strong northwest swell produces a good beach break, while at the tip of the cape a couple of *puntas* catch both northwest and southern swells for long-riding point breaks. The beach along the west side of the cape, known as Playa Médano (or Playa Oeste Médano), is suitable for camping. Just be sure you're well supplied, as it's a relatively long haul back to civilization.

Transport

Fuel: Three PEMEX stations offer regular and unleaded gas, one each in San Quintín and Lázaro Cárdenas, and one at Hotel La Pinta. Diesel is available at the San Quintín station only.

Buses: Intercity buses arrive and depart from a bus depot in Lázaro Cárdenas, on the west side of Mexico 1. The San Quintín area is not a suitable destination for travelers arriving without their own vehicles, however, since everything is rather spread out and there is virtually no public transport to the bayshores and beaches. **ABC** runs a new *servico plus* bus, with air conditioning, toilets, and beverage service, between Tijuana and Lázaro Cárdenas for US$14.

TECATE

During his 1964 presidential campaign, Gustavo Díaz Ordaz referred to Tecate as *la ventana mas limpia de México*, "the cleanest window of Mexico." He may have been fishing for the Tecate vote—which he didn't get; Díaz was unpopular in northern Baja—but as Mexican border towns go, this one is easily the most inviting.

Set in a bowl-shaped valley in the lower Sierra Juárez—known as the Laguna Mountains on the Alta California side—Tecate is insulated from industrial Tijuana and Mexicali to the west and east. The fresh, unpolluted air in the valley lured the developers of North America's first and longest-running health spa, Rancho La Puerta. Tecate's other claim to fame is its namesake *cerveza,* brewed here for nearly 50 years.

The border crossing, four blocks north at the end of Calle Lázaro Cárdenas, is one of Baja's most relaxed. Savvy Alta Californians use this crossing instead of Tijuana's when returning from an Ensenada holiday; the wait is much shorter, and the drive along Mexico 3 between Ensenada and Tecate provides an alternative to Mexico 1's coastal scenery. The town on the U.S. side of the border is also called Tecate.

Town life is centered around **Parque Hidalgo,** a shady plaza at the intersection of Av. Juárez and Calle Lázaro Cárdenas, Tecate's main thoroughfares. At the southeast corner of the park is a statue of Miguel Hidalgo, the Dolores priest who issued the call for Mexican independence in 1810. In the vicinity of the small plaza are a number of restaurants, taco stands, *paleterías y neveterías* (popsicle and ice-cream stands), craft shops, and the tourist office.

Tecate's general ambience is more that of a provincial Mexican town than a border town. Yet in spite of the many pleasantries Tecate has to offer, the area receives relatively few tourists compared with Tijuana, Mexicali, Rosarito, or Ensenada.

CLIMATE

Tecate is famous for its mild summers, thanks to an elevation of 514 meters (1,690 feet) and distance from both cold Pacific breezes and the high temperatures of the San Felipe Desert. The average temperature in the warmest months, July-Aug., is 22° C (72° F); on a particularly hot afternoon, temperatures may approach 38° C (100° F), but by nightfall temperatures will drop to the low 20s C (70s F).

In winter, Tecate records lower temperatures than either Tijuana or Mexicali; during the coolest months, Dec.-Feb., the average temperature is 10° C (50° F), with an occasional frost. Average annual precipitation in the Valle de Tecate is 49 centimeters (19 inches). Typically, over half the rainfall occurs Dec.-February.

HISTORY

Tecate is the oldest border town in Baja, though in terms of peninsular history it's still relatively young. In the early 1800s, a few mestizo farmers began working the valley lands, and, as word got around the valley was fertile and water—supplied by the Tecate and Las Palmas rivers—was abundant, more followed. In 1831 Peruvian Juan Bandini received a land grant of 4,500 hectares from the Mexican government, and two years later laid out a town to serve the budding farming community.

Long before Bandini's arrival, the valley surrounding Tecate had been sporadically inhabited by Yuma Indians, who called it Zacate. The Yumas revered 1,520-meter (5,000-foot) Monte Cuchumá, the valley's most outstanding geographic feature, which today straddles the U.S.-Mexico border. Surviving Kumyais, a subtribe of the Yumas, still revere the mountain, and in 1982 they successfully obtained a U.S. agreement to dismantle radio towers on Cuchumá's Alta California side.

Most likely the name Tecate developed from a Spanish corruption of the Indian name for the valley, Zacate. Another theory, rather unlikely, has it that Tecate comes from the English "to cut," since Anglos to the north often came to the valley to cut wood in the late 19th century—though the vegetation in the valley has always consisted mostly of treeless chaparral. The settlement became the capital of a new Mexican municipality in 1892, following completion of a railroad built to connect Tijuana, Tecate, and Mexicali with the national rail system.

Tecate became a household word in Mexico after the founding of the Tecate Brewery in 1943. This is the town's only real industry, however, and Tecate today remains primarily dependent on agriculture. Tourism, though relatively limited, is also a source of local revenue.

Tecate Brewery

Tecate beer, the only beer in Mexico named for a town, was first brewed by Tecate entrepreneur Alberto Aldrete in 1943. Aldrete started the brewery as a sideline to his *maltería* (malt factory). The first bottles distributed to the public carried a label that read "Rubio Tecate" over a silhouette of Monte Cuchumá. Although the beer sold well locally, Aldrete went bankrupt after 10 years. In 1954 the brewery was sold to Cervecería Cuahutémoc, brewers of two other well-known Mexican beers, Carta Blanca and Bohemia.

Today, Cuahutémoc operates breweries in six other Mexican cities and has added the Chihuahua, Indio, and High Life labels to its output, with Dos Equis and Sol as subsidiaries. The Tecate brand, however, is brewed only in Tecate and Monterrey. The Monterrey brewery produces canned Tecate—in the red-and-silver can familiar to many North Americans—much of it

for export; the Tecate plant produces only bottles and kegs. Mexican beer drinkers mostly consume Tecate in long-necked deposit bottles or liter-size *ballenas* ("whales"). On both cans and bottles, every label still carries the profile of Cuchumá, the Kumyai's sacred mountain.

Beer aficionados claim the best Tecate comes from Tecate; the water used at the brewery there, tapped directly from local springs, is considered the purest in Mexico. According to Cuahutémoc brewers, Tecate is brewed as a lager, with an alcohol content of 3.6% and sufficient hops to rate a 20 on the international bitterness scale. Tecate exported to the U.S. is reduced to 3.2% alcohol—a major reason the brand tastes so different north of the border (along with the fact that U.S.-consumed Tecate is usually canned product from Monterrey). The hops level for export Tecate is also reduced.

Carta Blanca, the only other label produced at the Tecate brewery, is a lighter pilsner with a bitterness grade of 16 and an alcohol content of 3.5%. Bajacalifornios overwhelmingly prefer Tecate to Carta Blanca, partially out of loyalty to Baja California—Carta Blanca originated in Monterrey—but also because they believe the latter a bland brew. Incidentally, the custom of drinking Tecate with salt and a squeeze of lime, now part of Cuahutémoc's Tecate advertising campaign, was probably introduced by gringo Baja hands —

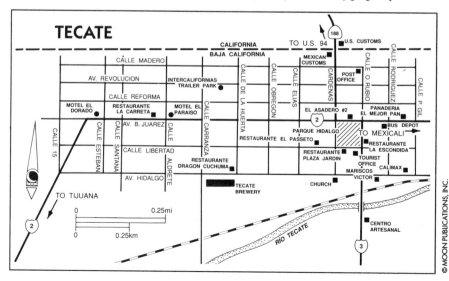

who squeeze lime over everything they consume in Mexico—concerned with killing bacteria on the top of the can. Lime juice also tends to neutralize the "can" taste. Follow the *mexicano* example and drink bottled Tecate; it's cheaper, if you return the bottles for a deposit refund, better-tasting, and more ecologically responsible.

Tours: Brewery tours are offered only on Saturday mornings and only for groups of 20 or more. Sometimes individual visitors are permitted to join a scheduled group tour—contact the state tourist office on the plaza or call the brewery (tel. 665-4-17-09). The usual tour takes around 45 minutes and includes a look at all stages of the brewing and bottling process. A few facts, in case you miss the tour: the present brewery complex stands on the same site as Aldrete's original keg brewery; high-tech German equipment is used to produce 250,000 hectoliters per month (6.6 million U.S. gallons); and the brewery employs around 850 people, who have their own recreational and cultural center south of town.

ACCOMMODATIONS

Hotels And Motels
El Dorado (tel. 4-11-01, 4-10-84; fax 4-13-33, Av. Juárez 1100), a wood-and-stucco motel near the western entrance to Tecate at Av. Juárez and Calle Esteban, offers rooms with TV, air conditioning, and phone for US$43 s, US$48 d, or US$80 suite. Just west of town on the north side of Mexico 2, **La Hacienda** (tel. 4-12-50, Av. Juárez 861) offers clean rooms with TV and air conditioning for US$35-40. Both hotels feature motel-court parking.

Two blocks east of Motel El Dorado at Calle Aldrete and Av. Juárez, closer to the center of town, is the inexpensive **El Paraíso** (tel. 4-17-16). The rooms are basic but clean, with a/c (old window units) and attached hot shower for US$18 s, US$23-28 d. In winter, if necessary, you can ask for a space heater (*calentador*). Guests can park in the garage beneath the hotel.

Ranch Resorts
The luxurious **Rancho Tecate Resort Country Club** (tel. 4-00-11, fax 4-02-11, 619-234-7951 in the U.S.), 9.5 km (six miles) southeast of Tecate off Mexico 3, is a sprawling ranch resort with a nine-hole golf course, tennis courts, a swimming pool, and a lake stocked with freshwater gamefish. Rates for standard rooms, in a building constructed in the typical Tecate hacienda style, are US$60 s, US$65 d. Suites cost US$70-115 a night (depending on the floorplan—each is unique) and include kitchens.

Hacienda Santa Veronica (tel. 66-85-97-93 in Tijuana, 619-341-9811 or 619-298-4105 in San Diego) is a newish ranch resort off Mexico 2, about 30 km east of Tecate near Km 98. Guest rooms, in mission-style condos, cost US$55 and come with fireplace and patio. Recreational facilities include six tennis courts, offroad racetracks for motorcycles and four-wheelers, equestrian trails, swimming pool, volleyball court, and basketball court. Originally a *ganadería,* or breeding ranch for fighting bulls (*ganados bravos*), the Hacienda also offers elementary bullfighting lessons for ranch guests. Other facilities include a restaurant, bar, and RV park open to the public. Hacienda Santa Veronica's mailing address is 74818 Vellie Dr., Suite 4, Palm Desert, CA 92260.

Rancho La Puerta
The most famous spa in North America, La Puerta ("The Door") is not open to the public as simple lodgings; the prices, in fact, tend to limit the clientele to CEOs and Hollywood celebrities. Enrolled guests participate in an all-inclusive, week-long health regime designed for physical and spiritual rejuvenation. The regimen includes mountain hiking, low-impact aerobics, yoga and t'ai chi, swimming, and weight-training. The site was chosen for its location in one of the Californias' last "safe zones" for the environmentally sensitive, and for its proximity to Monte Cuchumá, viewed by the spa's founders as a source of spiritual power.

Hungarian Edmond Szekeley and his wife Deborah opened the Essence School of Life in 1940, with guests paying US$17.50 a week to pitch their own tents, talk philosophy, climb Monte Cuchumá, receive massages, and eat organic food. In the '50s, the spa inspired Michael Murphy to found Big Sur's Esalen Institute. Today Szekeley's son Alex oversees the ranch, which has been transformed into a beautifully landscaped, 300-acre health resort. Alex Szekeley also runs its sister spa, the Golden Door in Escondido, Alta California.

The hacienda-style architecture includes cottages and suites for a maximum 150 guests, most with fireplaces, each with its own garden. A recently renovated dining hall serves organic fruits and vegetables grown at the subsidiary Rancho Tres Estrellas, along with occasional fresh fish. State-of-the-art recreational facilities include six aerobic gyms with sliding glass walls, a weight-training gym, four swimming pools, five whirlpools, three saunas, and gender-separated centers for massage, herbal wraps, and private sauna-steam baths.

All-inclusive prices for the daily health program, meals, and accommodations range from US$1,700 per week (US$1,350 double occupancy) in a studio cottage to US$1,900 (US$1,700 double occupancy) for a villa with separate living room, bedroom, and kitchen. In other words, it costs about the same as a deluxe seven-day cruise but is probably a good deal healthier. Summer rates—late June to early September—are lower. For reservations or more information, contact Rancho La Puerta, P.O. Box 2548, Escondido, CA 92033 (tel. 619-744-4222 or 800-443-7565, fax 619-744-5007).

Camping And RV Parks
The **Intercalifornias Trailer Park** (tel. 4-08-61), on Av. Revolución, 3.5 blocks west of Calle Lázaro Cárdenas, offers 10 trailer sites with full hookups, including cable TV. When spaces are vacant, the daily rate is US$11.60. Facilities include restrooms and a telephone.

Costa RV Park at Rancho Santa Veronica (30 km east of Tecate at Km 98, Mexico 2) features full-hookup slots for US$15, tent spaces for only US$2.50. Guests have access to all the ranch recreational facilities.

FOOD

For its size, Tecate offers an unusually high number of places to eat. Among the most renowned culinary attractions are the long-established *taquerías* surrounding Parque Hidalgo, which serve a variety of better-than-average tacos, burritos, and tostadas. Each has its unique way of assembling the basic ingredients, but you can hardly go wrong if you choose one of the following: **La Escondida** (facing the east side of the plaza on Calle Ortiz Rubio), **El Asadero No. 2** (facing the north side of the plaza on Av. Juárez), or **Doña Magi** (a half block east of the plaza on Av. Juárez, next to the bus terminal). The taquerías are typically open from after morning till late evening; the Doña Magi usually opens around 0600 to serve waiting bus passengers craving breakfast tacos. **Victor's,** next door to Doña Magi, is open 24 hours.

For quick, inexpensive, sit-down meals, try the **Plaza Jardin Tecate.** This tiny diner on the south side of the plaza, a few doors west of the tourist office, offers Mexican standards at reasonable prices for lunch and dinner, plus a large variety of breakfasts. During warm weather, the Jardin places a few tables outside and instantly becomes the only sidewalk café in Tecate.

downtown Tecate

JOE CUMMINGS

Another inexpensive, diminutive place is **El Serape,** next door to Motel El Paraíso on Av. Juárez. The short menu includes Mexican breakfasts, tacos, enchiladas, and mole poblana. Open daily for breakfast, lunch, and dinner.

Mariscos Victor (Av. Hidalgo 284) serves very reasonably priced Mexican-style seafood, including ceviche tostadas, fish tacos, seafood cocktails, and shrimp, as well as ranchero standards like *burritos de machaca, gorditas,* quesadillas, and *bistek* (steak). A choice of nine different full breakfasts is available, starting at 0700, for US$2.20-2.35. Open for breakfast, lunch, and dinner.

For more elaborate meals, **La Carreta** (tel. 4-04-62, Av. Juárez 270, at Calle Santana) is often recommended by the locals, who favor the dark, brick-walled interior. The menu features all kinds of Mexican food, with an emphasis on norteña cooking, at moderate prices. It's open daily for breakfast, lunch, and dinner. One block west of La Carreta, attached to Motel El Dorado, is the slightly more expensive restaurant-bar **El Tucán,** specializing in Mexican and continental; open daily for breakfast, lunch, and dinner.

On an alley to the west of the plaza is **El Passetto** (tel. 4-13-61, Callejón Libertad 200), which serves mostly Italian pasta, along with seafood and a few Mexican dishes. Prices are moderate; open for lunch and dinner.

Noodle addicts can switch from Italian to Chinese in **El Dragón Cuchumá,** at Av. Hidalgo and Calle Obregon, opposite the brewery. The Cantonese cuisine here won't win any awards, but portions are huge and the table sauce is hotter than most Mexican salsas by several degrees. Open daily for lunch and dinner.

Groceries: A number of tiendas on Av. Juárez and Av. Hidalgo sell basic foodstuffs; there's also a medium-size supermarket on Av. Juárez near the Calle Carranza intersection. For excellent pan dulce, bolillos, and other Mexican bakery items, grab tray and tongs at **Panadería El Mejor Pan,** on the north side of Av. Juárez between Calles Rodriguez and Portes Gil. Some folks claim it's the best Mexican bakery in all of Baja; it's certainly a contender, and is open 24 hours.

ENTERTAINMENT AND EVENTS

Tecate is not big on nightlife; the main source of evening entertainment seems to be promenading back and forth along Av. Juárez until around 2100, when the streets become practically deserted. Perhaps the healthy air sends everyone to bed early.

El Passetto and **El Tucán** restaurants each have attached bars; the bar at El Passetto usually stays open till after midnight. Tecate has only one movie theater, **Cine Variedades** on Av. Juárez.

Although it almost seems out of place in this low-key town, **LF Race and Sports Book,** at the corner of Calle Rodriguez and Av. Juárez, offers the usual betting lounge, restaurant, and bar; it's open Wed.-Sun. 0900-2300, Tuesday 0900-2030.

The **Tecate-Ensenada Bike Ride,** sponsored by Monday International (tel. 619-275-1384, P.O. Box 99120, San Diego, CA 92109), has been a tradition since 1969; it usually takes place the third Sunday of April. Participation is limited to 10,000 entrants. The hilly, 116-km (72-mile) Mexico 3 route, some of it through valley farmlands, is one of the better bike rides in northern Baja.

The Santa Veronica Offroad Park and Roadway, a series of dirt racetracks at Hacienda Santa Veronica, 30 km east of Tecate off Mexico 2, is the site of several racing events throughout the year. The biggest is the three-day **Gran Carrera de Tecate,** held in late May and sponsored by Baja Promotions (tel. 818-340-5750, P.O. Box 8938, Calabasas, CA 91302). Several classes of four-wheelers, as well as motorcycles and ATVs, participate in a series of multi-lap races scheduled over the three-day interval. Most of the entrants are from Alta California or Arizona. The Tecate Brewery also sponsors smaller offroad races at Santa Veronica in March, July, and October; contact Baja Promotions for information.

More popular among Bajacalifornios is Santa Veronica's **Gran Carrera de Caballos,** also sponsored by Baja Promotions, which takes place the last weekend in March. The 80-km horse race features mounts (horse with rider) entered by weight in heavy, medium, and light classes; riding tack must be either *charro* or *texana* (Mexican or Western) style. A fiesta is held at Hacienda Santa Veronica on the Saturday evening following the race.

The **SCORE Tecate Baja 500** occurs in June (see "Ensenada" for information on SCORE activities).

During the second week of October, local residents celebrate the Fiesta de la Fundación de Tecate, honoring the founding of the city with parades, music, dancing, and fireworks.

Until recently Tecate hosted a *pamplonada* (running of the bulls) inspired by the famous fiesta in Pamplona, Spain. As in the original, a herd of bulls was loosed to chase participants through the streets of the town. The August event drew as many as 50,000 people, almost twice the population of the town. With each year the crowds grew increasingly unruly, until pressure from local merchants in 1990 led municipal authorities to cancel the event. The state tourist office in Tecate suggested the pamplonada might be resurrected in the future under a new set of guidelines, but for the moment, it's gone.

SHOPPING

A few *alfarerías* (pottery and tile works) and *vidrierías* (glassworks) sell products in local stores. As in Tijuana and Rosarito, several shops in town depend on sales to U.S. residents crossing the border for bargains on tile and other building materials.

Visitors crossing into Baja at Tecate can't miss the highly visible **Patio del Sol** on the east side of Calle Lázaro Cárdenas, two blocks south of the gateway. The outdoor display features a large selection of unglazed pottery, plus a smaller number of decorative sculptures.

The government-sponsored **Centro Artesanal,** south of the railway and Río Tecate on Mexico 3 (about 1.5 km south of Av. Juárez), houses two shops, **Tecate Handicraft Center** and **Artesanías Mexicanas**. Besides glasswork and pottery, the vendors offer blankets, rugs, folk art, and other crafts from elsewhere in northern Mexico. **Rosita's Curios,** west of Calle Lázaro Cárdenas on the south side of Av. Juárez, is a private shop with an interesting collection of handicrafts.

INFORMATION

The **state tourist office** (tel. 4-10-95) faces the south side of Parque Hidalgo and is open Mon.-Fri. 0900-1900, Saturday 0900-1500, Sunday 1000-1400. There is also a **tourist information** booth near the border crossing at Calle Lázaro Cárdenas and Calle Madero. Next to the state tourist office is a **police station**.

Tecate's **post office** is located on the corner of calles Madero and Ortiz Rubio. The telephone area code for Tecate and vicinity is 665. Probably the best place to make a long-distance call is from the staffed *caseta* at the bus depot.

Across the border in Tecate, California, **The Home Office** (tel. 619-478-9560, fax 478-9482, toll-free 800-358-3004), at 443B Tecate Rd. next to the U.S. post office, offers mail, fax, and message services, along with Mexican insurance and Mexico tourist information. It's open Mon.-Fri. 0800-1700, Saturday 0600-1600.

TRANSPORT

The railway that passes through Tecate now carries freight trains exclusively; the nearest passenger railway begins in Mexicali. Most visitors arrive by bus or private vehicle.

Tecate's bus depot is on Av. Juárez at Calle Rodriguez; on the premises are a snack bar and long-distance telephone service. Departures include ABC buses to Mexicali (every hour 0630-1930, US$3.50), Tijuana (every half-hour 0530-2100, US$2), Ensenada (five times daily, US$4), and Puerto Peñasco, Sonora (twice daily, US$17).

To drive to Tecate from San Diego, take U.S. 94 east 66 km (41 miles) to the Tecate turnoff near the border. From Arizona and points east, take I-8 west to the U.S. 94 junction at Jacumba or Boulevard, then follow U.S. 94 west to the Tecate turnoff. The Tecate border gate is open 0600-midnight.

Tecate lies at the intersection of Mexico 2 (to Tijuana or Mexicali) and Mexico 3 (to Ensenada). A new toll road between Tijuana and Tecate, Mexico 2-D, was recently completed; the toll is US$6. Within the next year or so the tollway will extend all the way to Mexicali.

TECATE TO ENSENADA (MEXICO 3)

The two-lane highway between Tecate and Ensenada winds through the rolling, boulder-studded western slopes of the Sierra Juárez. Traffic is generally light, and the boulders offer plenty of opportunities to view modern rock art, including political slogans, evangelical exclamations—*"Cristo viene pronto!"* or "Christ is coming soon!"—declarations of love, and Catholic iconographs.

Except for the occasional valley, the terrain along Mexico 3 is mostly uninhabited chaparral. Valle de las Palmas, a small farming community at kilometers 27-28, features a café and a PEMEX station. Roll up the windows at Km 32, location of a large, smoldering trash dump.

Valle De Guadalupe

The next settlement of note along Mexico 3 is historic Guadalupe (Km 77), centered in a large valley created by the Río Guadalupe. Dominican padres established the last and shortest-lived of the Baja California missionary efforts, **Misión Guadalupe,** west of the current village in 1834. In 1836 the mission was successfully defended against an attack by 400 Yumanos; four years later a much smaller force, led by a Neji Indian baptized at the mission, chased away the last Dominican padre. The remains of the mission were incorporated into other buildings and are now difficult to identify.

Vineyards: Although a variety of grains, fruits, and vegetables are grown in the Valle de Guadalupe, grapes have been the major crop ever since a colony of Russian immigrants established the valley's first vineyards early this century. Guadalupe grapes are sold to a number of wineries and fruit distributors throughout northern Baja, including the valley's own Domecq winery. The section of the Valle de Guadalupe devoted to viniculture is sometimes called **Valle de Calafia.**

Colonia Rusa: A small Russian cemetery and around 25 Russian-style homes occupy a part of the village known as Colonia Rusa. The original Russian immigrants were Molokans (the word means "milk-drinkers," presumably in reference to the sect's abstinence from alcohol), a strait-laced Christian sect that broke from the Russian Orthodox Church. Around 105 Russian families of approximately 500 individuals migrated to Guadalupe in 1905, fleeing religious persecution in czarist Russia.

The group purchased 13,000 acres of valley land from the Mexican government. There they planted grapes and wheat, raised geese, kept honey bees, and built whitewashed adobe and wood homes, complete with thatched roofs and glass windows. As in their Russian homeland, the Molokans built their houses along a main street with the front doors facing away from the street. The simple chapel contained no religious decorations or icons, but the Molokans worshiped with such fervor that to the local Mexicans they were known as "the Spirit Jumpers."

In 1938, following President Cardenas's seizure of all foreign-owned lands, the community was engulfed by 3,000 Mexican squatters and renamed Francisco Zarco. Many of the Russians left the valley. Of those that stayed on, most ended up marrying Mexicans; today only four families of pure Russian lineage remain. In almost every respect they've become ordinary Mexican citizens; Russian is the first language only among a few elders.

Physical, if not cultural, evidence of the Russian colony remains. Around 25 of the original Molokan houses are intact. In the cemetery, the older tombstones at the back are engraved in Russian, while later stones toward the front show a combination of Russian and Mexican names—e.g., Juan Samarin, Pedro Pavloff. A small **community museum** containing an exhibit of Russian memorabilia from the former colony—clothing, old photos, tools—recently opened in Guadalupe. To find the cemetery and museum, take the turnoff for Guadalupe and follow the paved road to its end, then turn right and drive about 150 meters; the cemetery should appear on your left.

Wineries: In the Valle de Guadalupe you can now tour **Vinicola L.A. Cetto,** run by descendants of Italian immigrants. The Cettos' modern facility produces Chardonnay, Colombard, Muscat, Sauvignon Blanc, Chenin Blanc, Cabernet Sauvignon, Merlot, Nebbiolo, Zinfandel, and Petite Sirah. It's best to call in advance (tel. 668-5-30-31) although the winery will soon open a new tasting room intended to serve the public on a daily basis.

Group tours and tastings at **Pedro Domecq** can also be arranged through Baja California Tours (tel. 619-454-7166 in the U.S.).

RV Park: Rancho Sordo Mudo Trailer Park, at Km 75 on Mexico 3, offers full hookups for US$12 a night. Proceeds from the park aid a school for deaf children near Ensenada; the nightly fee is tax deductible.

Food: Around 22 km (14 miles) northeast of Ensenada on Mexico 3, just north of the small community of San Antonio de las Minas, is **Restaurant Mustafa,** a Moroccan-owned eatery which serves good Mexican and Moroccan food. In San Antonio itself, **El Mesón** is popular for breakfast and lunch stops; it's closed on Thursday. The owner is an admirer of British aviation artist Robert Taylor, and displays Taylor's work upon the restaurant walls.

Guadalupe-El Sauzal

At Km 96 is a gravel road west to the Valle San Marcos, a scenic area of cattle ranches and small farms. This gravel road meets paved Mexico 1, the "free road," after 12 km (7.5 miles). Mexico 3 links with Mexico 1-D, the toll road, at El Sauzal (Km 105), a tiny coastal community supported by a fish cannery. No toll is charged for the final nine km south to Ensenada.

NORTHEASTERN BAJA

MEXICALI

Driving or walking into Mexicali from Calexico, a visitor's first impression of the city focuses on the congested downtown area—the "old" Mexicali. Like other large Mexican border districts, it's chockablock with street vendors, souvenir shops, and *casas de cambio* (moneychangers). But a few blocks away from the border in any direction are broad, palm-lined boulevards and tidy residential areas reminicent of San Diego or Phoenix. Definitely not Tijuana or Cuidad Juárez.

The only Mexican border town that's also a state capital, Mexicali boasts Baja's largest population; 850,000 is the official count. (Probably more people, uncounted by the federal census, actually live in Tijuana, where the official count is only 800,000.) City promoters make much of the fact that the city is considerably less tourism-dependent than Tijuana; you won't find any zebra-painted burros on Mexicali streetcorners, or any place resembling Tijuana's Bar San Marcos.

As citizens of Baja Norte's capital, Mexicalienses view themselves as a step closer to Mexico City, while at the same time true *cachanillas*. Like the cachanilla, a sturdy desert plant that flowers in arid, saline soil, Mexicali has flourished at the edge of the harsh San Felipe and Sonora deserts and bloomed as one of Mexico's most prosperous communities. Today, any northern Bajacalifornio can claim to be a cachanilla, but as the verse from Antonio Valdez's famous corrido "El Cachanilla" says, "Mexicali, fue mi cuna" ("Mexicali was my cradle").

THE LAND

The nearly flat Valle de Mexicali extends westward from the Río Colorado delta to the Sierra de Cucapá. Millenniums ago the entire area was covered by a northern extension of the Sea of Cortez; Alta California's Salton Sea and Baja Norte's Laguna Salada are vestiges of the Cortez trapped by the gradual silting of the Colorado delta. The city of Mexicali, in fact, is a foot below sea level.

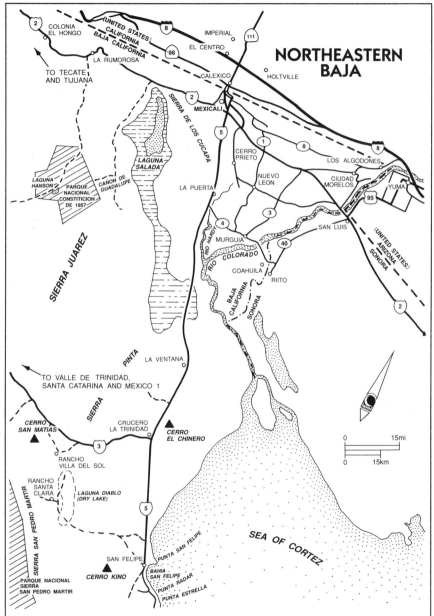

NORTHEASTERN BAJA

South of the valley lies the San Felipe Desert, an extension of the Sonora Desert. The valley itself can be classified as desert since it averages less than 25 cm (10 inches) of rainfall a year. Quite unlike most deserts, centuries of river silting have made the soil here nutrient-rich; earth that once filled the Grand Canyon was carried into the delta at a rate of 160 million tons per year. Yet the overall lack of water sources meant that agriculture outside the Colorado floodplain was almost impossible before U.S. land companies established a canal system early this century to irrigate Alta California's Imperial Valley and the Valle de Mexicali.

Before the damming of the Colorado River in the U.S., the floodplain was enormous; in fact, the tidal bore at the mouth of the river, where it fed into the Cortez, was strong enough to sink ships. The outflow slowed with the U.S. dams and was then reduced to a trickle by the 1950 construction of Mexico's Morelos Dam near Los Algodones, which diverts water into the Valle de Mexicali to supplement the American-built canal system.

With irrigation, a 2.5-km-thick layer of river silt, and an abundance of sunshine, most of the valley today is under intensive cultivation, producing cotton, wheat, grapefruit, lemons, oranges, carrots, corn, asparagus, onions, broccoli, potatoes, lettuce, cauliflower, and grapes.

CLIMATE

During December and January, Mexicali's coolest months, temperatures average 12° C (54° F). In July, temperatures reach 35-38° C (95-100° F) in the daytime (occasionally as high as 48° C/120° F), dropping to around 24° C (75° F) at night. The lack of humidity means that perceived temperatures in the summer are significantly lower, and since the Mexicali area is primarily agricultural, air pollution is not an appreciable problem. Rainfall averages a scant 12 cm (4.7 inches) a year.

The best overall months for a Mexicali visit are Sept.-Oct., when the temperature averages 23° C (73° F) and desert plants are usually in bloom. March through late May are also quite pleasant. Peak periods for visitors from the north are Nov.-Feb., especially for those on their way to San Felipe. July and August are the least hospitable months, as soaring temperatures bring the city to a standstill.

HISTORY

Pre-Hispanic Indian Cultures

In pre-Columbian times, the Río Colorado delta—which, at the time, included the Valle de Mexicali—was inhabited by a centuries-long succession of Yumano tribes. When the Spanish first stumbled upon the delta after traversing, with great difficulty, the Sonora Desert's Camino del Diablo ("Devil's Road"), a sophisticated Río Colorado culture was cultivating squash, melons, peas, and five colors of corn: yellow, blue, white, red, and blue-white. The Indians also possessed an impressive knowledge of medicinal herbs and employed desert plants like mesquite and agave in a wide variety of uses. Like their neighbors the Kiliwas, the Cucapás' numbers were greatly reduced by Spanish missionization in northwest Mexico.

Among the major Yumano groups in the region were the Cucapás, who navigated the difficult Río Colorado on reed rafts. Today Cucapá descendants inhabit a small government-protected corner of the delta near the junction of the Hardy and Colorado rivers, an area marked by names like Colonia Indigena, Colonia Cucapá El Mayor, Terrenos Indios, and Mestizos. For the most part, the Indians work on agricultural ejidos or fish the rivers, although many have migrated to Mexicali. Few indigenous customs survived both the Spanish and Mexican eras; both the Kiliwas and the Cucapás continued to practice cremation rituals, for example, until they were banned by the Mexican government early this century.

The Building Of An Agricultural Empire

After the Jesuits left, the Spanish and later the Mexicans had little to do with northeastern Baja, perceiving it as an untamable, flood-prone desert delta. Around the time of the American Civil War, a Yale geologist, while surveying a route for the Southern Pacific Railroad, wandered into the delta and discovered what the dwindling population of Yumanos had known for centuries: the 2.5-km-thick sediment was prime farming soil. The sediments extended far to the west of the river itself, accumulating in a shallow basin

MEXICALI CHINESE

Mexicali has one of the highest per capita concentrations of Chinese residents in Mexico, but the current population of 5,000, in a city of 850,000, hardly compares with the Chinese colonies in cities like San Francisco. Earlier this century, however, Mexicali was actually more a Chinese than a Mexican town.

Early Chinese Settlement

The first Chinese to arrive in the area came as laborers for the Colorado River Land Company, which designed and built an extensive irrigation system in the Valle de Mexicali. Some immigrants arrived overland from the U.S., fleeing officially sanctioned anti-Chinese policies; others sailed directly from China via the Pacific Ocean and the Sea of Cortez. As in Alta California, thousands of Chinese coolies were lured to the area by the promise of high wages that never materialized.

A 200-meter desert peak near Crucero La Trinidad is named El Chinero in memory of a group of 160 Chinese laborers who perished while crossing the San Felipe Desert in search of work in the valley. The desert itself was known for a time as El Desierto de los Chinos, "Desert of the Chinese." An unscrupulous boatman landed the group at a fork in the Río Colorado, telling them Mexicali was only a short distance away; actually 65 km of burning desert lay between them and their goal, which they never reached.

Many of the Chinese laborers who survived the building of the irrigation system stayed on after it was finished, congregating in an area of Mexicali known as Chinesca ("Chinatown"). During the Prohibition years, Chinesca housed many of the city's casinos and bars; an underground tunnel system led to bordellos and opium dens, and under the border to Calexico. The latter route was used by bootleggers. By 1920 Mexicali's *chinos* outnumbered the *mexicanos* 10,000 to 700. A group of 5,000 single Chinese males started the Asociación China, a Mexicali social organization at least partly devoted to the procurement of Chinese wives from overseas; the association still exists.

The Anti-Chinese Movement And Overseas Refugees

In 1927 a series of Tong wars in northern Mexico erupted over control of gambling and prostitution rings. Mexican alarm over the Chinese control of

below the Sierra de Cucapá. All it needed was the addition of water to become an overnight agricultural miracle.

In 1900 the U.S.-based California Land Company received permission from the Porfirio Díaz government to cut a canal through the delta's Arroyo Alamo, thus linking the dry basin with the Colorado River. To attract farmers to the area, the developers named the basin the Imperial Valley. In March 1903, the first 500 farmers arrived; by late 1904, 100,000 valley acres were irrigated, with 10,000 people settled on the land and harvesting cotton, fruits, and vegetables. A collection of huts and ramadas that straddled the border was named Calexico on the U.S. side, Mexicali on the Mexican side.

Seeing that the equally fertile Valle de Mexicali lay undeveloped, another American land syndicate, the Colorado River Land Company, moved in. Led by Harry Chandler, then publisher of the *Los Angeles Times,* the syndicate controlled some 800,000 acres of northern Baja and in 1905 began constructing a Valle de Mexicali irrigation system. Instead of using Mexican labor, as the Imperial Valley developers had, Chandler imported thousands of Chinese coolies. After a major 1905 rainfall, the channel dug from Arroyo Alamo ended up diverting the entire outflow of the Colorado River into the Imperial Valley, taking Mexicali with it—unknowingly, the syndicate had tapped into one of the river's original routes. The Salton Sink, a dried-up remainder of the Sea of Cortez, became the Salton Sea virtually overnight.

Neither the U.S. nor Mexico wanted to take responsibility for the growing "New River" created by Chandler's mistake. As both valleys became increasingly inundated, the Southern Pacific Railroad stepped in and, to protect its tracks, dumped a sufficient amount of rock into the river to head the Colorado back into the Cortez, leaving a canal to the Valle de Mexicali. From then on, both valleys became highly productive agricultural centers.

organized crime led to the government-encouraged Movimiento Anti-Chino in the late 1920s. The wave of anti-Chinese sentiment that swept the country led to the torture and murder of hundreds of Chinese in northern Mexico—a tragic echo of what happened on a larger scale in Alta California in the 1880s. To Mexico's credit, the government never enacted an equivalent to the U.S. Chinese Exclusion Act, which prevented all persons of Chinese heritage from holding U.S. citizenship.

Mexicali quickly became a refuge for Chinese fleeing the violence, since in that city chinos predominated. As the anti-Chinese movement faded away, still more Chinese arrived in Mexicali, where it became the Mexican headquarters for the Kuomintang, Sun Yat-sen's nationalist Chinese party. During WW II, the nationalists were pushed out of China first by the Japanese and then by the Communists; the Mexican government loosened its immigration policies to allow a large number of refugees into Mexico. Until Mexico severed diplomatic relations with the nationalist Taiwan government, Mexicali harbored a Taiwan consulate. The consulate promptly moved across the border to Calexico; when the U.S. in turn withdrew its recognition of Taiwan, the consular office continued operations under the name Coordinating Council for North America.

Hybridization

Postwar Mexicali featured two cinemas; both showed Chinese movies almost exclusively. But as the city recovered from the post-Prohibition recession, a steady influx of Mexicans diluted the local population until the Chinese became a minority. Mexicali still boasts more Chinese restaurants per capita than anywhere else in Mexico, and Chinesca survives in part of the downtown area. Local Chinese associations struggle to preserve the arts and culture of the homeland through the sponsorship of Chinese festivals, calligraphy clubs, and language classes.

But in most aspects, Chinese cultural life has blended with local traditions to create a unique, hybrid culture. Only in Mexicali will you find banners of the Virgin of Guadalupe hanging side by side with Chinese paper lamps, or a café called Mexburger where Chinese elders kibitz over hamburgers and green tea, speaking a mixture of Cantonese and Spanish. Surfers, note: Mexicali is probably the only place in the world where you can enjoy the revenge of eating shark-fin tacos.

A New Capital, Prohibition, And The Postwar Boom

In 1911, both Mexicali and Tijuana were briefly occupied by American and Mexican *filibusteros* (see "Tijuana"). To defend the border from similar threats, the Mexican government moved the Baja California Norte capital from Ensenada to Mexicali. That same year, the U.S. government passed Prohibition, forbidding the manufacture, sale, and consumption of alcohol; although Mexicali received fewer of the Hollywood high-rollers than did Tijuana, Americans nonetheless developed a romance with the city, as embodied in the popular song of the time, "Mexicali Rose".

Many of the Prohibition-era businesses were operated by *chinos,* Chinese laborers and farmers who moved into the city and spent their hard-earned savings to open bars, restaurants, and hotels. With people from both sides of the border drawn to the burgeoning town, Mexicali's urbanization accelerated.

Like Tijuana, Mexicali suffered an economic recession with the repeal of Prohibition in 1933 and the Mexican ban on casino gambling in 1938. But with a flourishing agricultural base and a federal presence, Mexicali bounced back sooner than its border counterpart. After Baja California Norte attained statehood in 1952, the capital began receiving a steady rotation of *chilangos* (Mexico City residents), some of whom stayed on and started new businesses after completing their terms of office. Although local residents might hesitate to admit it, part of Mexicali's postwar success in shedding its border-town image should probably be credited to the influx of outsiders—from the coming of the Chinese in the early 1900s to the postwar arrival of the chilangos.

Today the main source of Mexicali income remains agriculture, primarily cotton, wheat, alfalfa, and vegetables. Other moneymakers are the geothermal plants at nearby Cerro Prieto, the world's third-largest producer of geothermal power. Electricity generated here powers most of northeastern Baja and is even sold north of the border. A third major industry is the growing complex of in-bond plants, or *maquiladoras,* which currently number around 160 in 11 different industrial parks. Major multinational firms with Mexicali in-bond plants include Rockwell International, Hughes Aircraft, Emerson Electric, ITT, and Goldstar.

The economic symbiosis evident all along the U.S.-Mexico border is especially visible in the Mexicali-Los Algodones area. Laborers alternately work at Imperial Valley or Valle de Mexicali farms on either side of the border. And, like Tijuana, Mexicali is a free-trade zone. Television and radio stations in El Centro (Alta California) and Yuma (Arizona) broadcast ads for pharmacies in Mexicali and Los Algodones, where generic equivalents for American drugs are available without prescription at prices sev-

eral times lower than those in the United States. In return, the small Alta California town of Calexico (pop. 15,000) serves as a convenience mart for Mexicalienses shopping for discounted American-made apparel and housewares.

Tourism is important to Mexicali but is for the most part limited to short American shopping trips or brief stopovers by San Felipe-bound visitors. A tally of the Mexicali Holiday Inn guest register for 1990 showed that only 26% of all hotel guests hailed from the U.S.; 73% were from Mexico, with the rest a mix of visitors from Japan, Central and South America, and Eu-

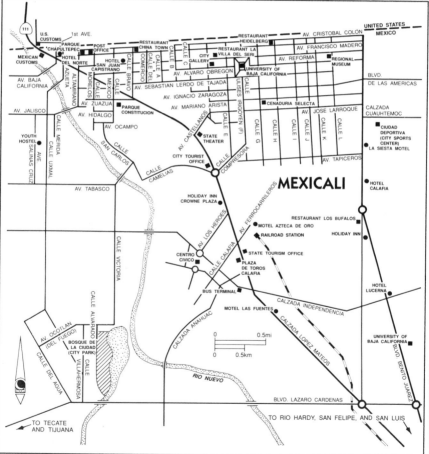

rope. According to hotel management, most guests come to Mexicali on business.

SIGHTS

Mexicali is not a city with a long list of tourist attractions, nor is it a particularly festive city by Mexican standards. The city seems to focus on creating an amenable environment for government- and business-oriented activities, while trying to make the community as comfortable a place to live as possible. As a result, it's one of the cleanest cities in northern Mexico. There are also a number of modern cultural venues of interest.

The city has two hearts. First is the old downtown area, pushed up against the border and featuring turn-of-the-century architecture. A prime example is the Hotel del Norte, almost Texan or New Mexican in appearance. Then there's the newer **Mexicali Civic-Commercial Center** (Centro Civico-Comercial de Mexicali), southeast of downtown along Calzada Independencia. Ambitiously dubbed the *Zona Rosa* after Mexico City's chic business-entertainment district, the center is a renovated warehouse district containing offices, restaurants, bars, and utilitarian shops selling paint, furniture, stationery, and office supplies. Although it's near the bullring, and the bus and train stations, the Centro Civico has become more of an attraction for Mexicali residents than for foreign visitors.

Linking the various city sectors is a system of wide avenues and *glorietas* (traffic circles), many encircling statues of Mexican national heroes.

Museo Regional De UABC

This University of Baja California-sponsored museum of anthropology and natural history is unequaled on the peninsula. In spite of its compact size, the exhibits manage to pack in a wealth of information on northern Baja's pre- and post-Columbian history as well as the flora and fauna unique to the region. Exhibits are labeled in Spanish only; if you're familiar with the language, you can learn much about northern Baja ethnology, especially regarding the Yumano and San Dieguito cultures.

The museum is located away from the main UABC campus, at Av. Reforma and Calle L. Hours are Tues.-Fri. 0900-1800, Sat.-Sun. 1000-1600. Admission is free. For more information, call 52-57-17 or 54-19-77.

Galería De La Ciudad

This privately owned gallery exhibits works by painters, sculptors, photographers, and other artists from both the region and around Mexico. Open Mon.-Fri. 1400-2000; admission is free. At Av. Obregón 1209, between calles D and E (tel. 53-50-44, ext. 23).

Bosque De La Ciudad

An oasis of green in a dry city, this park in southwest Mexicali offers picnic areas, a playground, a botanical museum, and a zoo. At Av. Ocotlán and Calle Alvarado; open Tues.-Sun. from 0900-1700.

Colleges And Universities

Mexicali has four institutes of higher learning, including the respected **University of Baja California** (Universidad Autonomía de Baja California). UABC's main campus is off Blvd. Juárez between Calzada Independencia and Blvd. Lázaro Cárdenas. The university rectory and administrative offices (tel. 54-04-00) are housed in the former governor's palace, in an older section of the city between Av. Reforma and Calle S.L. de Tajada, off Calle Irigoyen. Anthropology is one of the university's stronger disciplines.

Other tertiary institutions include the **Instituto Tecnologico Regional** (tel. 61-85-22, Blvd. Lázaro Cárdenas), a federal institute specializing in engineering studies, and the **Centro de Enseñana Tecnica y Superior** (tel. 65-01-16, Calzada Compuertas), a private school that combines upper high-school and college levels.

ACCOMMODATIONS

Hotels And Motels

Room rates for Mexicali hotels and motels range from around US$20 s (Motel El Indio) to US$84 for a suite at the Holiday Inn, the city's top property. For details, see the accompanying "Hotels and Motels" chart. If you can't find a room to your liking in Mexicali, try the historic **Hotel De Anza** (tel. 619-357-1112, 233 4th St.) across the border in Calexico; rooms in the 1930-vintage hotel run US$27-34.

Hotel del Norte

JOE CUMMINGS

Youth Hostel
The **Instituto de la Juventud y el Deporte** (tel. 57-61-92), at Calle Coahuila 2050 and Av. Salinas Cruz in the western part of the city (Parcela 36), offers dorm beds for US$5 a night. Unlike most government-sponsored youth hostels, the Mexicali facility has no cafeteria.

Camping And RV Parks
The nearest camping area is a cluster of rustic hunting and fishing camps 30-35 km (18-21 miles) south of the city, off Mexico 5 in the Río Hardy area. Tent/camper sites usually go for about US$4-5 a night; no hookups.

FOOD

Mexicali has more restaurants in the *turística* category—125 out of over 550 total—than any other city in Baja. The older downtown area near the border offers the least expensive, most authentic northern Mexican food—vendors and cafés every other block or so. Another good area for cheap eats is opposite the bus station on Av. Independencia, where a number of taco and torta stands vie for the patronage of arriving and departing passengers. Other recommended dining venues include the following.

Mexican
$ **Restaurant Del Norte,** Hotel Del Norte, corner of Av. Madero and Calle Melgar: This restau-rant wedged onto a downtown corner near the border crossing is popular with tourists and locals alike for its large *platillos típicos*. Prices are very reasonable. Open daily 0700-2200.
$-$$ **Cenaduría Selecta** (tel. 52-40-47), Calle G 1510 at Av. Arista: In a slightly less congested downtown area, the renowned Selecta has crowded them in since 1945 for some of the best tacos and burritos in town. Open Tues.-Sun. 0800-2300.
$$-$$$ **La Parroquia** (tel. 54-23-13), Av. Reforma and Calle D: This large restaurant is oriented toward visiting gringos—a branch of the Caliente Foreign Book is attached—and the prices are a bit high, but the all-Mexican menu is dependable. Open daily for breakfast, lunch, and dinner.

Steak/Carne Asada
$$-$$$ **Los Búfalos** (tel. 66-31-16), Blvd. Juárez 1616: Along the Blvd. Juárez hotel strip, steak and carne asada are the clear favorites and are usually served in pseudo-rustic, ranch-style surroundings. Los Búfalos, typical of the genre, is a short walk north of the Holiday Inn; its steak platters are highly rated, but the menu also features a few seafood and less meat-oriented Mexican dishes. Los Búfalos has a second location at Plaza La Cachanilla, Calzada López Mateos. Both are open daily for lunch and dinner.
$$ **Cachanilla's** (tel. 66-23-01), Blvd. Juárez 1990: Although the restaurant is billed as "international," the house specialty is carne asada.

MEXICALI HOTELS AND MOTELS

Note: Add 10% hotel tax to all rates unless otherwise noted (some hotels may charge an additional 10% service charge). Area code: 65

Azteca de Oro; Calle de la Industria 600 (diagonally opposite train station); tel. 57-21-85; US$23 s, US$29 d; a/c, parking, near train and bus stations

Boulevard; Calzada López Mateos (Mexico 5 south, Km 4.5); tel. 57-06-12; US$27 s, US$33 d; a/c, restaurant, bar, parking

Calafia; Calzado Justo Sierra 1495; tel. 68-33-11, fax 68-2010; US$61 s or d, tax included; a/c, pool, restaurant, 24-hour coffee shop, bar

Casa Grande; Av. Colón 612; tel. 53-66-51; US$30 s, US$33 d, US$36 t; a/c, pool, restaurant, bar, parking, walking distance from border gate

Cosmos Posada; Calzada Juárez 4257 (south of town on Mexico 5); tel. 6-67-08; US$26 s, US$30 d; a/c, parking

Del Norte; Calle Melgar and Av. Madero; tel. 52-81-01; US$38 s, US$42 d; a/c, restaurant, bar, parking, walking distance from border gate

El Indio; Calzada López Mateos and Av. Fresnillo; tel. 57-22-77; US$22 s, US$32 d; a/c, parking

Holiday Inn; Calzada Juárez 2220; tel. 66-13-00, toll-free in Mexico tel. 91-800-00-999, in U.S. tel. (800) 465-4329, fax 66-49-01; US$65 (tax included); a/c, pool, restaurant, coffee shop, bar, disco, parking

Holiday Inn Crowne Plaza; Blvd. López Mateos and Av. de los Héroes 201; tel. 57-36-00, in U.S. tel. 800-HOLIDAY; US$100-140; a/c, heat, pool, spa, tennis courts

La Siesta; Calzado Justo Sierra 899; tel. 68-20-01; US$40 s, US$53 d; a/c, restaurant, parking

Las Fuentes; Calzada López Mateos 1655; tel. 57-15-25; US$23 s, US$32 d; parking

Lucerna; Calzada Juárez 2151; tel. 66-10-00; US$71 s, US$74 d; a/c, refrigerator, pools, restaurants, coffee shop, bar, disco

San Felipe Marina Resort; south of marina, on beach; tel. 7-15-68, in U.S. tel. (619) 558-0295; US$45 up; a/c, one to three bedrooms with kitchens, pool, tennis courts, jacuzzi

San Juan Capistrano; Av. Reforma 646 (downtown); tel. 53-66-16; US$38 d; a/c, heat

Other menu items alternate between American and northern Mexican dishes. Open daily for lunch and dinner.

$$ La Villa del Seri (tel. 53-55-03), Av. Reforma and Calle D: Well removed from the hotel strip, this good Sonoran-style steakhouse offers lower prices and longer hours; open for breakfast, lunch, and dinner.

Chinese

Mexicali has more Chinese restaurants per capita than any other city in Mexico—well over a hundred at last count. Cantonese cooking predominates, but with few exceptions it's not the sort you'd recognize from Canton or Hong Kong—or Vancouver or San Francisco, for that matter. As in many Chinese restaurants outside of China, Hong Kong, Singapore, and Taiwan, immigrant cooks have adapted their native cuisine to local tastes. Almost every Chinese restaurant in Mexicali, for example, serves each dish with a small bowl of what tastes like generic steak sauce, a distinctly *norteño* touch. Still, the city's Chinese restaurants are among the most economical places to eat, and are worth visiting for their interior decors alone—some represent the ultimate in Chinese restaurant kitsch.

$-$$ El Dragón (tel. 66-20-20), Blvd. Juárez 1830: As is typical in Mexico, "Dragon" appears in a good number of local Chinese restaurant names. This Dragon is in a small shopping center just north of the Holiday Inn and features one of the most elaborate Chinese interiors in town. Large portions and fresh ingredients make it one of Mexicali's most popular restaurants; the huge menu features several regional styles. Open daily 1100-2300.

$-$$ **Palacio Imperial** (tel. 61-73-91), Blvd. Juárez and Lázaro Cárdenas: Similar to El Dragón. Open daily 1100-2300.

$-$$ **La Misión Dragón** (tel. 66-44-00), Blvd. Lázaro Cárdenas 555: More of the same, with the Chinese-style gardens and fountains a bonus. Open daily 0700-midnight.

$ **China Town** (tel. 54-02-12), Av. Madero 701: A good choice if you're touring *Chinesca*. Open daily for lunch and dinner.

Vegetarian

$ **Mesón Vegetariano** (tel. 57-12-19), Arcade Chapala 1096 (Centro Civico): One of the few vegetarian restaurants in Baja specializing in Mexican dishes. Open Mon.-Sat. 0800-1800.

$-$$ **El Oasis** (tel. 68-33-11), Calzada Justo Sierra 1495: International vegetarian cuisine. Open daily for breakfast, lunch, and dinner.

American

$ **Mi Burger** (tel. 66-03-02), Blvd. Juárez 221: Homesick already? Burgers, fries, and shakes. Open daily 1500-2300.

$-$$ **Pizza Hut** (tel. 53-46-34), Plaza Cachanilla, Blvd. Lázaro Cárdenas: A branch of the famous American pizza franchise—and they deliver. Open daily for lunch and dinner.

Miscellaneous

$$ **Café-Bar-Restaurant Mandolino** (tel. 52-95-44), Av. Reforma 1070: The place to go for Italian food in Mexicali. Piano bar attached. Open daily for lunch and dinner.

$-$$ **Denny's** (tel. 57-05-51), Blvd. López Mateos 1048 at Blvd. Calafia: The extensive menu here features many well-prepared Mexican standards as well as soups, salads, and sandwiches. Open 24 hours a day year-round.

$$ **Restaurant-Bar Heidelberg** (tel. 54-20-22), Av. Madero and Calle H: German and continental dishes; close to downtown. Open Tues.-Sat. for lunch and dinner.

$$ **Sakura Kotubyi** (tel. 66-48-46), Blvd. Lázaro Cárdenas 200 at Calzada Montejano: Teppanyaki, tempura, and sushi are among the offerings at Mexicali's only Japanese restaurant. Open daily for lunch and dinner.

ENTERTAINMENT

Live Music

Bars at the Lucerna, Holiday Inn, and Calafia hotels are popular local meeting spots where you can usually count on a *botanas* lay-out most weekdays around 1800, with live music—norteña, Latin pop, international—later on in the evening. **Casa Carmina** (tel. 52-56-48, Av. Reforma and Calle C) also has live music and is one of the most congenial non-hotel bars in town for both *mexicanos* and *norteamericanos*.

Every Sunday afternoon during warmer weather, mariachi groups play outdoors at **Parque Constitución,** a small downtown park bordered by Av. Zuazua, Av. Hidalgo, Calle Mina, and Calle México.

Discos

Top dance spots include **Tempo's Laser Disco** (tel. 57-29-70, Calle Alfareros), **Forum Video-theque** (tel. 52-40-91, Av. Reforma and Calzada Justo Sierra), and **Little Rock** (tel. 56-06-32, Calle da la Libertad 990). Expect to pay cover charges of US$5-6 Thurs.-Sunday.

State Theater ("Teatro Del Estado")

A variety of local and visiting theatrical, dance, and musical performances are held year-round at this modern, 1,100-capacity building at Calzada López Mateos and Av. Castellanos. Ticket prices vary according to the performance but are usually quite reasonable. For information on the latest theater schedule, call 52-96-30 or contact the city tourist office.

Events

The 350-mile (563 km) **Gran Carrera de Mexicali** offroad race is held yearly in mid-May by Baja Promotions (tel. 818-340-5740, P.O. Box 8938, Calabasas, CA 91302).

In mid-November the Chamber of Restaurants (CANIRAC) sponsors the **Muestra Gastronómica,** a food fair featuring Mexican, seafood, and Chinese cuisines. Call CANIRAC at 56-47-27 for scheduling and venues.

Radio And Television
Mexicali broadcast media receive a wide variety of transmissions from Mexican, Arizonan, and Alta Californian stations. One of the better local radio stations is XED (1050 AM), which mostly broadcasts Mexican folk music.

SHOPPING

Mexicali features the usual border-town assortment of souvenir shops, many clustered along Calle Melgar in the downtown area, near the border crossing. **El Sarape** and **Campo's Curios,** both on Calle Melgar, carry a broad selection of Mexican handicrafts. As the name suggests, **Taxco** (Calle Melgar, next door to Campo's Curios) offers silverwork from the Valle de Mexico.

El Armario (tel. 68-19-06), Calle Justo Sierra 1700 (Plaza Azteca, at the junction with Blvd. Juárez), stocks a selection of rustic furniture, glassware, ceramics, sculpture, and other handicrafts.

Something you might not expect to find in Mexicali is a shop specializing in *guayaberas,* the pleated men's shirt characteristic of Mexico's Yucatán Peninsula. **Merida Guayaberas,** in the 700 block of Av. Madero near the post office, does a good business selling these shirts to locals and visitors during Mexicali's furnace-like summers. In Mexico, the light, short-sleeved guayabera is considered appropriate apparel for any occasion, even in place of coat and tie.

A bit farther from downtown is another Mexican handicraft dealer, the government-sponsored **Desarrollo Artesanal de Mexicali** (tel. 61-64-44, Blvd. Lázaro Cárdenas 1190).

SPORTS AND RECREATION

Bullfights
In Baja, Mexicali's **Plaza de Toros Calafia** (tel. 65-07-81) is second in size only to the Plaza Monumental in Playas de Tijuana. At Blvd. de los Héroes and Calle Calafia near the Centro Civico, the stadium hosts corridas two or three Sundays a month, Sept.-November. Current

schedule information is available from the city tourist office.

Charreadas
Mexicali has two charro rings: **Lienzo Charro de Mexicali** (tel. 66-55-45), six km east of Calzada Justo Sierra on Calle Compuertas (the airport highway); and **Lienzo Charro Zaragoza,** west of Mexicali on Mexico 2. Regular charreadas are scheduled about once a month Sept.-April, but may also be held during a fiesta any time of year. Contact the city tourist office for the latest charreada schedules.

Baseball
Mexicali has its own baseball team, Los Aguilas ("The Eagles"), and their local stadium is known as El Nido de las Aguilas ("Eagles' Nest"). The stadium, in the **Ciudad Deportiva** (City Sports Complex) on Calzada Cuahutémoc east of Calzada Justo Sierra, periodically hosts other teams in the Mexican-Pacific League, as well as the occasional visiting team from North or Central America. The season lasts from the end of the American World Series through late January. Seats cost around US$3; to find out when home games are played during the season, contact the city tourist office or call the stadium (tel. 68-30-25).

Sports Centers
Several sports centers in the city feature tennis courts and swimming pools open to public use for nominal day fees. **Casino de Mexicali** (tel. 52-58-93, Av. J.M. Suarez and Calle L) is open Mon.-Fri. 0600-2200, Sat.-Sun. 0700-1900, while **Club Raqueta Britania** (tel. 57-13-07, Blvd. Anahuac and Calle Mar Baltico) is open 0600-2200 daily. The latter also offers a gym, sauna, and steam room. The **Mexicali Country Club** also has a pool and tennis courts.

The city-sponsored **Ciudad Deportiva** (tel. 55-30-25, Blvd. Cuahutémoc) features tennis courts, swimming pool, jogging track, baseball stadium, and a *frontón jai alai* (jai alai court) open to the public Mon.-Fri. 0700-2300, Sat.-Sun. 0700-1700. The **Instituto de la Juventud y El Deporte** (tel. 57-61-92), at Av. Salinas Cruz and Coahuila, also has public tennis courts, basketball courts, and a pool. It's open 0700-2300.

Golf

The **Club Social y Deportivo Campestre,** or Mexicali Country Club (tel. 61-71-30), at Km 11.5 on Mexico 5, Fracc. Laguna Campestre, is an 18-hole, par 72, 6,628-yard golf course open to the public Tues.-Sat. 0900-1700 and 1800-2200. Greens fees are considerably lower than in Tijuana, about US$12.

Race And Sports Book

The ubiquitous **Caliente Foreign Book** has two branches in Mexicali: at Calle Melgar 116 (downtown near the border crossing) and Restaurant La Parroquia, Av. Reforma and Calle D. Hours for each: daily 0900-2230.

Hunting

The Río Hardy area south of Mexicali is popular among visiting hunters for dove and waterfowl (see "Vicinity of Mexicali"). Mexicali has one of only three stores on the peninsula authorized to sell ammunition to the public (the other two are in Tijuana and La Paz): **Tienda Alcampo Aceves** (tel. 52-27-82, Av. Zuazua 515).

INFORMATION AND SERVICES

Tourist Offices

The Mexicali Tourism and Convention Bureau (COTUCO) maintains an office at Calzada López Mateos and Calle Compresora (tel. 52-23-76, 52-58-77; U.S. mailing address: P.O. Box 7901, Calexico, CA 92231). The information counter—with a helpful, English-speaking staff—is open Mon.-Fri. 0830-1400 and 1530-1700.

The State Secretary of Tourism (SECTUR) office (tel. 56-10-72) has moved to Calle Calafia and Calz. Independencia, at Plaza Baja California. SECTUR's legal assistance department (Attorney for Tourist Protection) is headquartered here and can be contacted by calling 56-11-72, faxing 56-12-81, or hailing CB channel 40. SECTUR is open Mon.-Fri. 0800-1900, Sat.-Sun. 0900-1500.

Mexican Consulate In Calexico

The Mexican government maintains a conveniently located consular office in Calexico, just across the border, at 331 W. Second St. (tel. 619-357-3863). If you're entering Mexico via Mexicali, you can save a stop in San Diego for

MEXICALI TELEPHONE NUMBERS

(Mexicali area code: 65)

U.S. Customs	95 (619) 357-3863
Mexican Customs	52-40-18
Green Angels	54-04-43
Municipal Police	134 or 52-44-44
Highway Patrol	54-29-09
Red Cross	132
Chamber of Commerce (CANACO)	54-11-81, 53-46-61
Department of Fishing	52-97-32
State Secretary of Tourism	56-10-72
Attorney for Tourist Protection	56-11-72
Railway Station	57-23-86
Mexicali International Airport	52-23-17
Central de Autobuses (Bus Depot)	57-24-10

information on tourist cards, visas, and other Mexican immigration or customs information. The consulate is open Mon.-Fri. 0800-1400.

Border Crossing

The Mexicali border gateway is open 24 hours. Although the crossing here is less congested than Tijuana's, it's still wise to avoid morning and afternoon commute hours. If you're planning to drive east into the state of Sonora, or to other points east of Baja, and don't already possess a temporary vehicle-import permit, obtain one from the Mexican customs office at the border.

Changing Money

Bancomer, Banco Internacional, Multibanco, and several other large Mexican banks maintain branches in Mexicali; as in most Mexican cities, the foreign exchange service closes around noon each day. For better hours, shorter lines, and competitive rates, use any of the several casas de cambio in the vicinity of the Hotel Del Norte downtown. As in most border towns, the best rates are given for cash rather than traveler's checks.

Downtown Calexico, near the border crossing, also features several small moneychangers. The dollar-to-peso rate is sometimes a bit higher here than in Mexicali, but check to see whether there's a commission charge before exchanging currencies.

Post And Telephone

Mexicali's **main post office,** at the corner of Av. Madero and Calle Morelos downtown, is open Mon.-Fri., 0800-1700. Mail to the U.S. will move more quickly if deposited at a post office in Calexico; the main p.o. is at Birch St. and George Ave., four blocks west of Imperial Avenue.

The Mexicali area code is 65.

GETTING THERE

By Air

Mexicali International Airport (MXL), 20 km (12 miles) east of the city via Blvd. de las Americas, fields Mexicana flights from Guadalajara and Mexico City, and Aviación del Noroeste flights from Mazatlán, Ciudad Obregón, La Paz, and Hermosillo. **Mexicana's** city office is at Av. Madero 833 (tel. 53-54-01); **Aviación del Noroeste** (tel. 52-58-87, 53-67-41) maintains an office at the airport. Although it schedules no flights out of Mexicali, **Aeromexico** (tel. 57-25-51) also runs a ticket office at Callejón Alamo 1008, Centro Civico.

Air L.A. (tel. 800-933-5952 in the U.S./Canada, 95-800-10-04-13 in Mexico) recently announced a daily flight schedule from Los Angeles (US$69 one way, US$138 roundtrip).

By Bus

Mexicali's intercity bus depot (Central de Autobuses, tel. 57-24-22) is on the south side of Av. Independencia, between Calzada López Mateos and Centro Civico. Buses bound for northern Baja destinations leave every hour from around 0600-2100 to Tijuana (US$4.50), Ensenada (US$5.50), Tecate (US$3.40), and San Felipe (US$4.60). Southbound buses, less frequent, go to La Paz (US$25) via Santa Rosalía (US$16), Mulegé (US$17), and Loreto (US$18), as well as to these mainland des-

tinations: Hermosillo, Sonora (US$12.60-14.60); Culiacán, Sinaloa (US$25-28); Guadalajara (US$38-44); and Mexico City (US$50-55).

Autotransportes de Baja California (ABC) (tel. 57-24-40) operates a deluxe *servicio plus* commuter bus, complete with beverage and movie service, to Tijuana (US$7.50) and Ensenada (US$14) several times daily.

Golden State buses run between Mexicali and Los Angeles several times a day between 0900 and 1430 for US$25.

To/From Calexico: The Greyhound station in Calexico (tel. 619-357-1895), a few steps from the pedestrian border crossing on First St., has frequent daily bus service to/from Los Angeles (US$23), San Diego (US$14), Tucson (US$39), El Centro (US$1.50), Yuma (US$14.50), Phoenix (US$29), and El Paso (US$83).

By Train

Mexicali is the northwesternmost terminal for Ferrocarriles Nacionales de México (FNM), the country's national rail system. The passenger station is on Calle Ulises Irigoyen, north off Calzada López Mateos, near the Centro Civico. For advance ticket reservations, you can call 57-23-86, or write El Jefe de Estación, P.O. Box 231, Calexico, CA 92231 (in Mexico: A.P. 3-182, Mexicali, BCN). The station's advance ticket window is open daily 0700-1400.

Two Guadalajara-bound trains leave Mexicali daily, Tren No. 2 (Tren Estrella) at 1000 and Tren

---

TRAIN FARES FROM MEXICALI (ONE WAY)

Note: Children ages 5-11 ride for 50% of adult fares; children under five ride free.

DESTINATION; DISTANCE (KM); 1ST-CLASS*; 2ND-CLASS
Puerto Peñasco, Son.; 250; US$15.65; US$9
Benjamin Hill, Son.; 534; US$34; US$19
Hermosillo, Son.; 660; US$41; US$23
Ciudad Obregón, Son.; 919; US$58; US$33
Culiacán, Sin.; 1,340; US$84; US$47
Mazatlán, Sin.; 1,559; US$98; US$55
Tepic, Nay.; 1875; US$118; US$66
Guadalajara, Jal.; 2,149; US$135; US$76
Mexico City; 2,753; US$173; US$97

* (includes three meals)

No. 4 (Tren Nocturno) at 2150. The faster No. 2 connects at 2255 with a train to Mexico City, which arrives in Mexico City at 0910 the following day. The first-class fare to Puerto Peñasco, Son. is US$10, second-class US$2.50.

The **Mexicali-Guadalajara** line also connects with rail lines to Nogales, at Benjamin Hill, Sonora, and Chihuahua, at Sufragio, Sinaloa.

GETTING AROUND

Bus
Mexicali's city buses are large converted school buses; districts or main streets (e.g., Centro Civico for the civic center/zona rosa area, Justo Sierra for Calzada Justo Sierra) marked on the bus marquee indicate the final destination. Many city buses start from Calle Altamirano downtown, just two blocks from the border crossing. Fares are around US$.30.

Taxis
Large *taxis de ruta* (route taxis) compete with city buses along popular routes and cost just a few pesos more. A private hired taxi costs US$3-5 within the downtown area, US$6-8 to the Centro Civico area or the Blvd. Juárez hotel strip from the border crossing. Taxis are most concentrated near the pedestrian border crossing and at the Lucerna, Calafia, and Holiday Inn hotels.

Tours
The Mexicali Tourism and Convention Bureau (COTUCO) recently began offering van tours of the city for only US$1 per person. Tours leave from the COTUCO office at Calzada López Mateos and Calle Compresora on the hour Thurs.-Sun. 1000-1700, wheel through the downtown area, then stop at shopping centers (Plaza Cachanilla, Plaza

---

MEXICALI AUTO RENTAL AGENCIES

Budget; Blvd. Juárez 2220; tel. 66-48-40

Central; Calzada López Mateos 655; tel. 52-22-06

Dollar; Blvd. Juárez 1000; tel. 65-62-62

Hertz; Blvd. Juárez 1223; tel. 68-19-73

National; Blvd. Juárez 1004; tel. 68-39-63

Fiesta, and/or Plaza Universidad). You can arrange to be dropped off anywhere along the tour route, then get picked up later in the day. For more information, call 52-97-95 or 52-43-91.

Driving In Mexicali
Except for the congested downtown area near the border, the traffic in Mexicali moves fairly easily. Parking is sometimes a problem near the border but elsewhere in the city is plentiful. The *glorietas* (traffic circles) are a bane for timid visiting drivers; lanes within the circles aren't generally marked, and drivers jockey for position according to where they plan to exit the circle. It's important to stay alert while maneuvering, always counterclockwise, round the circle so that when the desired spoke approaches you're in a position to take it.

To get onto Mexico 5 south for San Felipe, drive southeast on Calzada López Mateos until it meets Blvd. Juárez; follow the signs to the right (south). Just south of this intersection, Mexico 5 crosses Mexico 2, the highway west for Tecate and Tijuana or east to Sonora.

Vehicle Insurance: Oscar Padilla Mexican Insurance (tel. 619-357-4883), at 747 Imperial Ave., Calexico, is a reliable source for auto and boat policies.

VICINITY OF MEXICALI

Southeast of Mexicali lies the agricultural Valle de Mexicali and Río Colorado Delta area. Before the Mexican government's expropriation of foreign-owned lands in the '30s, much of the delta belonged to the U.S.-based Colorado River Land Company. Since then, it's been divided among ejidos, many named for mainland Mexican states and cities. A network of two-lane state highways connects the ejidos with the small farm towns of Nuevo León, Murguia, Victoria, Ledón, Coahuila, Ciudad Morelos, and Los Algodones.

The state border between Baja California Norte and Sonora runs along the Río Colorado as far south as Coahuila. Mexico 2 east enters Sonora at the town of San Luis; once you cross the state line eastward, a temporary import permit is required for any vehicle not bearing Mexican license plates. Auto permits are available at the Mexican customs office at the Mexicali border crossing; in Baja, no permit is necessary. Remember to set your watch an hour ahead when crossing the Colorado—Sonora is on Mountain Time.

One of the more interesting ejido towns in the delta, if only because it straddles the BCN-Sonora line, is **Coahuila.** At the southeast end of BCN 4, past a toll bridge spanning the Colorado, this Baja outpost sits smack in the middle of the delta; the bumpy streets are paved with clay blocks. The popular **Restaurante India Bonita,** renowned for *milanesa* and carne asada, is almost reason enough to make the trip. The only other reason is to say you've crossed the Colorado River in Mexico; in Coahuila, when you stroll over the state line you pay a visit to Sonora.

Southeast of Coahuila, about 69 km (43 miles) into Sonora via SON 40, is **El Golfo de Santa Clara,** the northernmost town on the Sea of Cortez. This small fishing town features a couple of cafés, markets, a church, motel (Motel Marcia, US$12-15), PEMEX station, and three campground/RV parks (US$3 tents/campers, US$10 full hookups). A sandy road to the southeast leads into an area of dunes popular with ATV riders. At high tide, dunes become sandy beaches; low tide exposes broad mudflats where large clams are plentiful. Anyone bringing a boat

to El Golfo should also possess a current set of Cortez tide tables, as the tidal range is extensive. From May through mid-September, the desert delta becomes an inferno.

Further Travels: If you're planning to continue on to Sonora, Sinaloa, Chihuahua, or points farther east in northern mainland Mexico, you might want to read Moon's *Northern Mexico Handbook,* which covers the country's nine northernmost states. Highlights of the region include the splendid Chihuahua al Pacífico train ride through the Barrancas del Cobre ("Copper Canyon"), the beaches of Sonora and Sinaloa, the Pueblo-style ruins at Casas Grandes, fishing along the Gulf of Mexico coast in Tamaulipas, backpacking in the two Sierra Madres (Oriental and Occidental), and the colonial capitals of Zacatecas and San Luis Potosí.

LOS ALGODONES

This friendly *poblado* of around 2,000 inhabitants in the northeast corner of Baja Norte, eight km (five miles) west of Yuma, Arizona, is named for the main cash crop in the region—cotton. In the town itself, however, the biggest business is dentistry for gringos; fees for dental services run 30-50% less than in the United States. Two or three dental clinics appear on virtually ever commercial block.

The most common Baja gateway for Arizona residents, Los Algodones also receives a steady stream of day visitors from Yuma County, one of the top three "snowbird" communities in the U.S.—along with Dade County, Florida and the Rio Grande Valley, Texas—where retired Americans choose to spend their winters.

Sights
The southern tip of the huge **Algodones Dunes** complex straddles the U.S.-Mexico border just west of town. To reach it, drive west along Mariano Ma Lee until it ends about eight blocks from the border crossing. Formed at the northeast banks of an extinct Pleistocene sea, the 650-square-km Algodones Dunes are the driest spot in North America save for Death Valley

SAND FOOD AND SIDEWINDERS

In spite of the fact that the Algodones Dunes average less than 7.5 cm (three inches) of rainfall a year, the dunes aren't entirely barren. **Evening primrose, sand verbena, desert lily, creosote bush,** and other long-rooted plants grow in the hollows between the dunes, lending shape and structure to the landscape. Even during long rainless periods, extensive root systems enable these plants to survive by tapping into pockets of moisture deep below the sandy surface.

Living in symbiosis with these plants is the hidden **sand food** (*Ammobroma sonorae*), a root unique to the Sonoran Desert. It grows beneath the dunes, tapping moisture and sugar from the other vegetation through a network of root hairs barely touching the host plants. It is not quite a parasite, for in times when the host plants lack moisture, they receive nourishment from the sand food. The Sonoran Papago Indians, or Hiach-eD-O'odham (Sand People) as they called themselves, depended on the sand-colored, melon-flavored root as part of their desert diet, and it was known to early European desert travelers as well—hence, its odd English name.

Animate life in the dunes includes the common **desert iguana;** the **sidewinder** (*Crotalus cerastes*) a rattlesnake whose means of locomotion—tossing its body in side-to-side loops—is uniquely suited to sandy environments; and the rare **fringe-toed lizard,** the only reptile species totally limited to sand dunes.

and the Mojave Desert. Iron-bearing minerals lend a reddish tinge to some of the dunes.

The **Presa Morelos** ("Morelos Dam"), constructed in 1950 as part of the Valle de Mexicali irrigation system, lies about 6.5 km south of town via Calle 6a. This is Mexico's only dam on the Río Colorado, which runs roughly 160 km (100 miles) south of the border before emptying into the Sea of Cortez. Considering the All-American Canal System and the 10 major dams on the U.S. side, it's a wonder any water is left in the river by the time it crosses the border—a sore spot in U.S.-Mexico relations since early this century. Recently the U.S. government proposed cementing the bottom of the All-American Canal to stop underground seepage—an action that would further decrease Mexico's supply of the Colorado runoff.

Restaurants

The most popular restaurant in town among day visitors is **Pueblo Viejo** (tel. 4-78-90), a combination Mexican restaurant, souvenir shop, and bar at Calle 2a and Mariano Ma Lee. At **Plaza del Sol,** Av. A 14, seafood and Mexican dishes are served on a pleasant garden patio from 0700 to 1600.

Shopping

Los Algodones pharmacies and liquor stores, concentrated along Calle 1a directly opposite the border crossing, do a booming business serving Yuma snowbirds. The **Mercado de Artesanías,** at the Parque de la Ciudad at Calle 4a and Av. B, offers a variety of Mexican handicrafts, as does **Curios El Sahuaro,** opposite Restaurant La Cabana at Calle 2a and Av. A.

Information And Services

A Mexican insurance company at Calle 1a and Mariano Ma Lee distributes tourist information on Los Algodones and northern Baja. It can also recommend dental clinics.

The border crossing, along with Mexican **immigration** (tel. 4-78-21) and **customs** (tel. 4-78-30) offices, is open 0700-2000.

You can change money at **Los Algodones** casa de cambio on Av. B, between calles 2a and 3a near the church and telegraph office. The **post office** is at Calle 5a and Av. D.

Transport

A bus depot at Av. A and Calle 2a serves buses west to Mexicali (US$3) and Tijuana (US$7.50). Yuma, Arizona, eight km east of Los Algodones, offers a Greyhound station and a regional airport.

A PEMEX station at the corner of Av. B and Calle 5a pumps diesel and unleaded gasoline.

MEXICALI TO TECATE (MEXICO 2)

West of Mexicali, Mexico 2 skirts the northern edge of the Sierra de los Cucapá and flattens out along the top of **Laguna Salada,** a huge dry salt lake extending southward nearly 100 km (60 miles).

At Km 24, an unpaved, ungraded road leads south to the northern shore of the lake, where a small fish camp survives on accumulated runoff from the Río Colorado delta; visitors are permitted to camp overnight. A PEMEX station near this junction offers a chance to gas up before proceeding farther along Mexico 2 or south along Laguna Salada. The next gas station is 53 km (33 miles) west, in La Rumorosa.

Palm Canyons

At Km 28, another unpaved road to the south, this one graded (a mixed blessing, since it means washboard surface much of the way), threads between the western edge of Laguna Salada and the eastern escarpment of the Sierra Juárez. Several steep-walled palm canyons cut deeply into the escarpment; the larger Tajo, El Carrizo, Guadalupe, and El Palomar canyons contain year-round streams and tinajas, and are highly desirable hiking and backpacking destinations from November through mid-April. Late April-Oct., temperatures often exceed 37° C (100° F)—not the best of conditions for desert hiking.

The Laguna Salada road is adequate for ordinary passenger vehicles as far south as the turnoff for Cañon de Guadalupe; beyond that a 4WD vehicle is usually necessary. For overnight hikes, come prepared for wilderness camping.

Cañon Tajo, the most spectacular of the palm canyons, is reached by a dirt road that branches west off the Laguna Salada road 34.5 km (21.5 miles) south of Mexico 2. From this point, most vehicles can only make it 2.5 km (1.5 miles) or so before the track contours become too extreme; after that it's 5.5 km (3.5 miles) of hard slogging across sandflats to the mouth of the canyon.

Your reward is a wide canyon studded with thousands of fan palms and watered by freshwater pools below 450-meter (1,500-foot) granite walls. It's 6.5 km (4 miles) to the head of the canyon, where an old Indian trail leads north; you can see—but not touch—a number of petroglyphs and Indian relics along the way. *Borregos* (desert bighorn sheep) and deer occasionally wander into the canyon.

The turnoff west to **Cañon de Guadalupe** is 44 km (27.5 miles) south of Mexico 2 and signed Alta Guadalupe. Unlike the approach to Tajo, this side road is passable by car or truck all the way to the mouth of the canyon (12.5 km/8 miles), where you'll find a public campground and hot mineral springs. Average driving time is 45 minutes. A nominal fee is charged for use of the hot springs (41.5° C/107°

F); campsites are US$10 per night, each with its own cement hot tub. Sodas and beer are sold at a small snack stand.

Although not as large as Tajo, Cañon de Guadalupe is quite impressive, with tiered waterfalls, pools, and plenty of blue fan palms. The main stream through the canyon leads to the "Pool of the Virgin," surrounded by white granite walls and fringed with ferns, *alamo* (cottonwood), and *sauz* (willow). As in Cañon Tajo, there are signs of an earlier Indian presence. Both canyons were used by the Cucapás and Paipais during seasonal pilgrimages to collect piñon nuts on the Sierra Juárez plateau.

La Rumorosa

At around Km 44, Mexico 2 begins climbing the Juárez escarpment along the steep Cantú grade (also called Cuesta de La Rumorosa). The town of La Rumorosa, topping the grade at Km 68, is named for the constant murmuring of winds through the 1,275-meter (4,200-foot) mountain pass. Many Tijuana and Mexicali residents own summer homes in the vicinity, but the town itself is little more than a wide spot in the road with a café and self-serve PEMEX station.

Descending along the more gradual western slope of the Sierra Juárez, the environment changes rapidly from the arid, scrubby vegetation east of the mountains to piñon stands and chaparral.

La Rumorosa To Laguna Hanson

West of La Rumorosa at Km 73 is a dirt road that leads 63 km (39 miles) south to **Laguna Hanson** (also known as Laguna Juárez), part of the Parque Nacional Constitución de 1857. The road is graded for the first 37 km (23 miles) or so but rapidly deteriorates as it approaches the national park's northern boundary. High-clearance vehicles, preferably with 4WD, are recommended for this route.

The more popular and easier route into the national park is via Mexico 3, southeast of Ensenada. For information on this road, and on the national park itself, see "Ensenada to San Felipe."

El Condor To Tecate

At **El Condor** (Km 83), 14.5 km (9 miles) west of La Rumorosa, another unpaved road heads south to Laguna Hanson, passing the ranchos of Cisneros, Jacaranda, El Encanto, Tres Pozos, and others. Although this route proves slower going than the La Rumorosa road, there's more to see, including several abandoned mines. Just beyond Rancho Jesayo and Mina Margarita ("Margarita Mine"), about 30 km from Mexico 2, the road joins the La Rumorosa-Laguna Hanson road.

The ejido settlement of **El Hongo** appears off Mexico 2 at Km 99, where a paved road leads southwest toward Hacienda Santa Veronica and a network of unpaved roads and vehicle tracks in the western foothills of the Sierra Juárez. The largest is an 83.5-km (52-mile) road, mostly ungraded, that winds southward to join the Mexico 3-Laguna Hanson road near Rancho El Coyote. Along the way are several ranchos and abandoned mines, including **La Rosa de Castilla,** a former gold-mining center that served as the territorial capital (1870-82) before Ensenada. This road is suitable for high-clearance vehicles only.

Beyond El Hongo, Mexico 2 dips through rolling dairy farms and olive groves, a relatively uneventful ride until you arrive in **Tecate** at Km 130.

MEXICALI TO SAN FELIPE (MEXICO 5)

Mexico 5, the paved, mostly two-lane highway (some parts have four lanes) between Mexicali and San Felipe, is flat all the way and features one of the more durable roadbeds in Baja. Gringo rumor says the road was originally built by the U.S. Army Corps of Engineers following WW II to provide access to a radar station at Bahía de San Felipe's south end; local authorities insist it was 100% Mexican-built. It's odd how the highway immediately deteriorates south of San Felipe.

The first 45 km (27 miles) of the highway is flanked by ejido lands with irrigated vegetable and dairy farms. You'll find several *nopal* (prickly-pear cactus) farms along the highway around Km 15; fresh and pickled cactus is sold from roadside stands.

Just south of **La Puerta,** at Km 38, BCN 4 branches east to Coahuila and the Sonoran state border. La Puerta offers a PEMEX station, market, and café. At about Km 48, the pastureland gives way abruptly to desert lands as you reach the southern limit of the delta irrigation system.

Río Hardy

Beginning at around Km 50 off Mexico 5, the marshy Río Hardy is easily accessed by a number of dirt tracks heading east off the highway. Several rustic *campos,* mostly catering to hunters and anglers, lie along the river to its junction with the Río Colorado (about 15 km southeast).

The Río Hardy attracts a number of migrating bird species, including pintails, green-wing teals, egrets, pelicans, coots, cranes, and a dozen or more duck species. The main quarry for visiting hunters are quail and white-wing and mourning doves. Dove-hunting season generally runs Sept.-December.

Local Cucapá Indians fish the river for carp, flathead catfish, largemouth and striped bass, and, more recently, *mojarra* (tilapia), a prolific African species that has come down into the Río Hardy through locks in Colorado River dams. Reportedly, the best fishing is at the junction of the Hardy and Colorado rivers, near Campo Los Amigos. This area is accessible by vehicle track from Río El Mayor (Km 55) or San Miguel, about 12 km farther south, just before the causeway over Laguna Salada.

Camps in the Río Hardy area open and close from year to year depending on river conditions. They include Sonora, Las Cabañas, Mosqueda, Río Hardy, Club BBB, El Mayor, Muñoz, and Los Amigos. *Campos* **Sonora, Mosqueda, Río Hardy,** and **El Mayor** are usually open and can accommodate RVs; rates are around US$6 a night.

La Ventana-San Felipe

Kilometer 105 marks the one-pump, one-café town of **La Ventana;** sneeze and you'll miss it. Farther south at Km 122 is an unpaved, graded road to the west leading to three abandoned mines in the Sierra Las Pintas: La Fortuna, Buena Vista, and La Escondida. A fourth, Jueves Santo, is still a working gold mine.

South of this turnoff, the highway crosses the **Llano El Chinero** ("Chinese Plain"), where a large group of Chinese immigrants died of heat and thirst while trying to reach Mexicali on foot early this century. The lone peak east of the highway is 200-meter **Cerro El Chinero.**

Mexico 5 intersects with Mexico 3, the highway to Ensenada, at **Crucero La Trinidad** (Km 140). Just south of the junction is a PEMEX station. A string of signs for beach camps on the east side of the highway, beginning at around Km 172, marks the final approach to San Felipe, reached at Km 189.

SAN FELIPE

This unlikely beach community of 11,000 squeezed between the San Felipe Desert and the Sea of Cortez received its name from Jesuit Padre Fernando Consag, who briefly landed four canoes here in 1746 and named the gently curving bay San Felipe de Jesús. In 1797, a padre from Misión San Pedro Mártir de Verona established a supply port at Bahía San Felipe, but it failed, along with the mission, in 1806. In

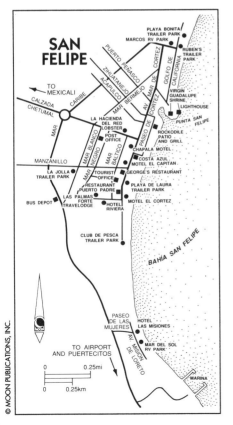

the late 19th and early 20th centuries, virtually the only people who knew of San Felipe's existence were nomadic fishermen working the eastern Sea of Cortez coast.

The post-WW II construction of a paved road to a radar station at the south end of the bay finally linked San Felipe with the outside world. In the late '40s and '50s, North American anglers came in droves to compete for the *totuava* (*Cynoscion macdonaldi*), a strong-fighting, copper-silver-gray croaker with a weight range of 16-115 kilograms (35-254 lbs.). Old-timers say it's one of the tastiest fish in the Cortez, but since they fished the species onto the endangered species list, most of us will never get a taste. Mexican law now forbids the taking of totuava.

The bay is protected from north-northeast winds by Punta San Felipe, a jutting headland topped by 240-meter Cerro El Machorro at the north end of the bay. The summit offers a good view of the bay and bears a shrine dedicated to the Virgin of Guadalupe. Below the headland are an estuary and boatyard. At the south end of the bay, an artificial harbor shelters the local commercial shrimping fleet, one of five such fleets licensed to net shrimp along Mexico's west coast. The tidal range in the northern Cortez is extreme, so only the outer section of the harbor is suitable for larger craft.

San Felipe today is a beach playground for Alta Californians and Arizonans who camp or park their RVs on the many beaches extending north and south of the bay. The nearby dunes attract dune-buggy and ATV enthusiasts who scream up and down the sloping sands with Cerro Juan (1,025 meters/3,369 feet) and Cerro Kino (1,304 meters/4,290 feet) to the west as a backdrop. A number of North Americans have retired in San Felipe but, for most people, the best San Felipe has to offer is a cheap beach and/or fishing vacation within two to three hours' drive of the Alta California-Arizona border—and possibly the best fish tacos on the peninsula.

Climate And Tourist Season
Peak tourist season in the San Felipe area is Nov.-April, when temperatures are mild, although in Dec.-Feb. the northern Cortez may be a bit chilly for most swimmers. May-Oct., daytime air temperatures frequently break 38° C (100° F), but it doesn't get quite as hot as Mexicali. During the summer, many North Ameri-

cans residing in San Felipe go elsewhere—usually the Pacific coast—to cool off. Rainfall, at any time of year, is virtually nil.

Accommodations

Hotels and Motels: Because San Felipe is so popular and so close to the U.S. border, hotel and motel rates tend to be a bit on the high side, at least for Baja. The cheapest hotels are US$23-30 a night and overpriced at that; if you spend a little more, you'll get a better value. See the "San Felipe Hotels and Motels" chart for specifics.

A recent development in the San Felipe area are "condotels" and resort villas—often part time-share, part hotel, and part year-round condo complex. Ask at the tourist office about renting local condos or apartments by the night; in some cases they're a better deal than the local hotels and motels. Since sales are slow, developers are desperate to get what money they can.

A Mexico City contractor is developing an extensive marina and resort complex south of the current commercial fishing marina. A 180-space RV park is planned for the first phase, opening in the mid-'90s, along with a handful of waterfront villas. Eventually this development may include a hotel wing. Then again, it might never get built at all; it wouldn't be the first San Felipe development to falter.

Several kilometers south of the semifunctional San Felipe airport, on the way to El Faro beach, is **La Hacienda** (tel. 7-13-81), a resort development with homes for sale or rent.

Camping and RV Parks: Over two dozen beachfront operations in San Felipe, and to the north and south of town, tout themselves as campgrounds or RV parks. Some—mostly those out of town—offer few facilities beyond a graded road between the highway and beach. Others come with full RV hookups, restaurants, bars, hot showers, and flush toilets.

Prices have jumped a bit over the last two years. Those in town generally cost US$12-17 nightly per site for two people, plus US$2 for each additional person. The beach camps farther north and south of town typically run US$5-10 for two per site, depending on the facilities, plus US$1 for each additional person. An exception is **El Faro Trailer Park** at Punta Estrella 16 km south of town, which has full hookups (including 24-hour electricity), tennis courts, and a pool, but no restaurant and no telephone.

SAN FELIPE HOTELS AND MOTELS

Note: Rates quoted are for peak season; November to April. Off-season rates drop as much as 20-30%. Add 15% hotel tax to all rates; some hotels may charge an additional 10% service charge. Area code: 657

Chapala Motel; Av. Mar de Cortez 142 (A.P. 331, San Felipe, BCN); tel. 7-12-40; US$35-40; a/c, some rooms with kitchenettes

El Capitán Motel; Av. Mar de Cortez 298 (P.O. Box 1916, Calexico, CA 92231); tel. 7-13-03; US$40 midweek, US$45 weekends (rates valid for one to four persons); a/c, pool

Motel El Cortez; 1 km south of town on bay, Local 5, Mexicali, BCN (in U.S., P.O. Box 1227, Calexico, CA 82231); tel. 7-10-55; US$46-56; a/c, pool, boat launch, palapas, restaurant

Motel El Pescador; Calzada Chetumal and Av. Mar de Cortez; 7-10-44US$27

Hotel Las Misiones; 2.5 km south of town near marina, Av. Misión de Loreto 148 (in U.S., P.O. Box 120637, Chula Vista, CA 92012); tel. 7-12-84, in U.S. tel. (800) 336-5454, fax (619) 422-6910; US$65; a/c, satellite TV, pools, tennis courts, basketball court, restaurant, bar, includes buffet breakfast

La Hacienda del Red Lobster; Av. Chetumal 125; tel. 7-15-71; US$30-40 midweek, US$35-45 weekends

Las Palmas Forte Travelodge; Av. Los Cedros; tel. 7-13-33; US$37 midweek, US$50 weekend; a/c, tennis and volleyball courts, pool, restaurant, bar

Hotel Riviera; Av. Los Cedros; tel. 7-11-85; US$32; a/c, satellite TV, pool, includes breakfast

Cost: US$17 per site per night. All camps and RV parks in the San Felipe area grant generous discounts for long-term stays.

The most popular campgrounds among the RV crowd are those along the beach just north of Punta San Felipe, on the outskirts of town. This area generally receives a good sea breeze and is thus cooler than parks on the bay itself. In this northern zone, running from north to south, are Playa Bonita, Ruben's, Costa Azul, La Posada del Mar, Marcos, Numero Uno, and Vista del Mar, all decent places to park awhile. If you don't like the first one you try, you can always move to another. **Playa Bonita** (tel. 7-12-15 in San Felipe, 213-413-4272 in the U.S.) and **Ruben's** (tel. 7-10-91) are particularly popular for their large deck-topped palapas; some people might complain about the sound level of the music emanating from Ruben's restaurant, however. Playa Bonita takes phone reservations; Ruben's doesn't. Cheaper spots in the area include **Marcos** and **Vista del Mar,** both back from the beach with rates of US$8-10 per vehicle.

South of town next to Hotel Las Misiones is San Felipe's top trailer park, **Mar del Sol** (tel. 7-12-80 in San Felipe; 800-336-5454 or 619-422-6900 in the U.S.). The management doesn't allow motorcycles, ATVs, or dune buggies, so it's one of the quietest trailer parks in San Felipe. Facilities include hot showers, flush toilets, pool, restaurant, palapas, boat launch, coin laundry, and groceries. RV sites are US$25 beachfront, US$20 back row per night while tent sites cost US$13. Discounts are given for Good Sam members and long-term stays.

Farther south on the bay, the new **San Felipe Marina Resort and RV Park** (tel. 657-7-15-68 in Mexico, 619-558-0295 in the U.S./Canada) features 143 spots with full hookups, including cable TV, for US$20 per night. Facilities include pool, showers, laundry room, and clubhouse. This resort plans to construct boat slips and condo villas over the next few years.

Other camping and trailer parks in town include **La Jolla** (tel. 7-12-22, Av. Manzanillo and Mar Bermejo), US$12 for RVs or tents; **Campo San Felipe** (tel. 7-10-12, Av. Mar de Cortez), US$11 for tents, US$16 for RVs; **Club de Pesca** (tel. 7-11-80), US$17 for RVs; and **Playa de Laura** (tel. 7-11-28), US$15 for tents, US$18 for RVs. All offer full hookups, showers, and flush toilets; La Jolla takes phone reservations.

Food

Seafood is what San Felipe restaurants do best. Vendors sell fresh seafood cocktails and fish tacos along the *malecón* (waterfront) at the intersection of Calzada Chetumal and Paseo de Cortez. Right on Calzada Chetumal, a block and a half east of the malecón, is the **Red Lobster Inn,** the only restaurant in town with a patio receiving full sun all day during the winter. Seafood entrees are moderately priced, delicious ceviche tostadas cost only US$1, and the beer is served in chilled mugs. Open for breakfast, lunch, and dinner.

trailer park,
San Felipe

JOE CUMMINGS

George's (tel. 7-10-57), at Av. Mar de Cortez 336, is a favorite among gringo regulars who come for the dependable seafood dinners and American breakfasts. For something less touristy, try the homey Puerto Padre (tel. 7-13-35), at Av. Mar de Cortez 316, next to George's. Puerto Padre's Cuban owners try hard to please with a variety of fresh seafood entrees and a large selection of Mexican and American breakfasts; the real brewed coffee is a nice change from the Nescafé served in many Baja restaurants. Both George's and Puerto Padre are open for breakfast, lunch, and dinner.

Wherever you find a heavy concentration of gringos in Baja, you can be sure there's an El Nido steakhouse nearby. San Felipe's is on Av. Mar de Cortez (tel. 7-10-49), in the same area as George's and Puerto Padre. The menu features the usual steak and ranchero standards; dependable, but not particularly inspiring. Open for breakfast, lunch, and dinner.

Also on Mar de Cortez is Green House, a restaurant-bar with Mexican food and gringo prices. The pleasant sidewalk tables at the front only receive sun in the morning; a patio was recently added in the back. Open 0730-0300 daily.

To the north of Calzada Chetumal are several small, inexpensive cafés, including Petunia's Café at the corner of Calle Puerto de Acapulco and Av. Mar de Cortez. The main draw: tacos and burritos, along with Mexican and American breakfasts. El Club, between Rockodile and Rock N'Roll Plaza on the malecón, is very popular for Mexican breakfasts, including chilaquiles, one of Mexico's best hangover remedies.

La Perla (tel. 7-10-39), on Mar de Cortez opposite Petunia's, serves Mexican-style seafood and, in the afternoons, a reasonable comida corrida. Los Gemelos, next door to La Perla, features the cheapest and greasiest comida corrida in town: US$3 for chile relleno, enchilada queso, taco dorado, beans, and rice. The taco-burrito-hamburguesa stand farther north on the same side of Mar de Cortez serves better.

The dining room at Hotel Las Misiones has an international menu; the all-you-can-eat breakfast buffet is a bargain, and complimentary for hotel guests.

Rockodile Patio and Grill, on the malecón, serves very tasty fish tacos along with a tray of six different condiments. They also have burgers, fries, and huge beef tacos, called "tacodiles."

Food is served from around noon till midnight.

Away from the waterfront, and from the bulk of the tourist dining crowd, is John's (Av. Mar Baltico 150), a steak and seafood place open for lunch and dinner only.

Groceries: Several tiendas along Calzada Chetumal, on the way into San Felipe, sell fresh vegetables, ice, canned goods, and camping/household supplies. Two bakeries on Av. Mar de Cortez compete for local business: Panaficadora Singapur, opposite Motel El Pescador, with the town's widest selection of baked items, and Pandería El Buen Gusto, north of Calzada Chetumal near Petunia's.

To buy fresh, locally harvested finfish and shellfish, pay a visit to the Pescadería Los Temos, a fishing co-op on Calle San Felipe reached by making a left turn off Av. Mar de Cortez just north of Punta Santa Felipe. The co-op is open daily 0700-1900.

Entertainment

At night, the young and not-so-young shake it at Rockodile or Plaza Club, both large dance clubs on the malecón. Weekdays are usually on the dead side, while the weekends are packed. Rockodile is the more popular of the two, with a better sound system and a sand volleyball court. The Green House restaurant-bar also brings in a loud crowd, especially now that a patio has been added. All three bars offer happy hours from noon till around 1700.

Gamblers can wager on race and sports events at Caliente Foreign Book, in the Plaza Cortez next to the El Cortez Hotel on Av. Mar de Cortez.

Events

Most of San Felipe's yearly events calendar revolves around desert or Sea of Cortez racing. The Gran Carrera de San Felipe, a 250-mile offroad race, is held in early February by Baja Promotions (tel. 818- 340-5790, P.O. Box 8938, Calabasas, CA 91302) and usually runs northwest around the Sierra San Felipe, south through Laguna Diablo and Arroyo Chanate, and east around the Sierra Santa Rosa.

Late February or March winds bring the Hobie Cat Regatta, a catamaran race on Bahía de San Felipe.

Navy Day ("Día de la Marina"), observed on June 1, is celebrated in San Felipe with a street festival, music, and dancing. Also in June is an all-terrain cycling race between San Felipe and Puertecitos; contact the tourist office in San Felipe or Mexicali for information on this new sporting event.

Sports And Recreation

Fishing: Although the San Felipe fishery is not what it used to be, with the magnificent totuava now a protected species, fishing is still one of the primary local tourist activities. The high fishing season is March-June, when white seabass runs are common. Croakers are available year-round, corvinas late March-November. Cabrilla, yellowtail, sierra, and grouper are plentiful May-October; in the fall months, you can catch pompano.

Generally, the best onshore fishing area runs from Punta San Felipe north, while inshore fishing is good from Punta Estrella south. The best offshore fishing and the best overall is found around Roca Consag, 27 km (17 miles) east of Punta San Felipe. This is a particularly good area for croaker and white seabass.

Two sportfishing services at the north end of the malecón, **Alex's** (tel. 7-10-52) and **Tommy's** (tel. 7-11-20), plus a new place in town, **Flota Pelicanos** (tel. 657-7-11-88, Av. Mar del Cortez 122), offer a variety of guided fishing trips aboard eight-meter (24-foot) pangas. A 0700-1200 bay fishing trip costs US$50-60 for two (US$80-90 for four), including bait, guide, license, and tackle. Bay angling usually nets calico bass, small croaker, sierra, or triggerfish. An all-day trip to Roca Consag (45 minutes away by boat) costs US$100-120 for two to four anglers, US$40 for each additional person. Depending on the season, a Roca Consag trip brings back sierra, yellowtail and large croakers and corvina. On either type of trip, anglers must bring their own lunches. Flota Pelicanos accepts credit card payments. Hotel Las Misiones offers room and fishing packages for US$140 per person for two nights' hotel, two breakfasts, a day's fishing, and discount coupons for drinks and meals.

You can purchase fishing tackle at **Proveedora de Equipos de Pesca** on Av. Mar de Cortez near the estuary. Tony's and Alex's small offices sell hooks and sinkers. You can buy live bait from the shrimpers at the commercial marina south of town. As elsewhere in Mexico, every person in every boat that carries fishing tackle needs a valid fishing licence. You can legally fish from shore without a license.

Windsurfing: Sailboards—but not exactly state-of-the-art gear—can be rented at the Motel El Cortez. Spring is the best wind season on the bay, but there are breezes year-round. The shoreline north of Punta San Felipe receives the best wind.

Boating: Experienced, self-sufficient small-boaters and kayakers often put in at San Felipe for the 258-km (160-mile) coastal cruise to Bahía de los Angeles. Although there are plenty of coves along the way, only a few places—Puertecitos, Punta Bufeo, and Bahía San Luis Gonzaga—offer limited supplies.

Information And Services

The **state tourist office** (tel. 7-11-55), at Av. Mar de Cortez and Calle Manzanillo, is open Mon.-Fri. 0900-1900, Saturday 0900-1500, Sunday 1000-1400. In addition to handing out the usual hotel brochures and city maps, the staff can help with suggestions on how to spend your time in the area.

Changing Money: The Banamex on the corner of Calzada Chetumal and Mar Blanco offers foreign currency exchange service Mon.-Fri. 0900-1100. Bancomer and Banco Internacional each maintain branches on Av. Mar de Cortez with similar exchange services.

Post and Telephone: San Felipe's post office is on Mar Blanco, a block south of Calzada Chetumal. Hours are Mon.-Fri. 0800-1300 and 1400-1800. The San Felipe area code is 657.

Bathhouses: On Calle Puerto de Acapulco, just off the malecón, are a couple of small public *baños* (bathhouses). A hot shower costs US$1.

Transport

Air: Although the sign at the airport, nine km south of San Felipe, reads Aeropuerto Internacional de San Felipe, there are no regularly scheduled international flights to San Felipe. **Air L.A.** (tel. 800-933-5952 in the U.S./Canada, 95-800-10-04-13 in Mexico), however, recently announced it will begin daily flights from Los Angeles to San Felipe for US$149 roundtrip midweek, US$174 weekends. This is the third airline in the last five years to announce a San Felipe schedule; neither of the previous two panned out, so be sure to call Air L.A. for confirmation.

Bus: San Felipe's bus depot is on Av. Mar Caribe, south of Calzada Chetumal. ABC operates buses to and from Mexicali (US$7, four times daily) and to and from Ensenada (US$9 second class, twice daily; US$15 first class, also twice daily). Bus tickets go on sale an hour before departure.

Taxi: Local taxis wait on Av. Mar de Cortez and at the Hotel Las Misiones for the occasional fare. You can order a taxi by dailing 7-12-92. Fares in central San Felipe should run under US$5; from the malecón to Hotel Las Misiones costs around US$7.

SAN FELIPE TO
BAHÍA SAN LUIS GONZAGA

The road from San Felipe to Puertecitos (85 km/53 miles), though paved, is in a fairly constant state of disrepair, especially south of the turnoff for El Faro Trailer Park. In many places, a sand track parallels the paved road and provides a smoother ride for vehicles that can handle sandy surfaces. In some places, giant chunks of the road are missing, or there's heavy washboarding. Still, the road is passable by ordinary passenger vehicle—slowly. The *vados*, or places where dry culverts intersect the road, bear mention, as they're some of the most treacherous in all Baja. Road signs are mostly in English, as only gringos seem interested in driving this desert road.

Indications of human habitation grow increasingly sparse the farther south you proceed. Three km south of San Felipe lie a handful of condo developments, then the Hotel Aquamarina 10 km farther south. Just past the El Faro turnoff is a huge, unsightly trash dump right off the highway, used by El Faro Trailer Park and other beach camp owners. Around this point begins an enchanting desert landscape of mesquite, ocotillo, cholla, elephant trees, cenizo, and sage. **Punta Estrella,** a good beach for clamming, is six to seven km south of El Faro.

All the way to Puertecitos, every so often a beach camp is signed on the left. The going rate to park on the beach is around US$5, with facilities usually limited to drinking water and outdoor toilets. Between Km 38 and 40 is **Playa Mexico,** a more elaborate beach camp with restaurant and airstrip.

Puertecitos is little more than a cluster of breeze-block buildings and rusting trailers ensconced around a shallow cove. At one time probably a beautiful spot, today it's a jumble of mismatched shelters and discarded auto parts only a dune-buggy or fishing fanatic could love. At the hot springs at the northeast side of the cove, prudish local norteamericanos have been known to scold visiting skinny-dippers. The PEMEX station is closed more often than not; a palapa restaurant and bar provide meager sustenance. Groceries are available from unmarked shacks around town; ask at the restaurant for suggestions.

South of Puertecitos the road is appropriate only for vehicles with sturdy tires and shocks. About 29 km (18 miles) south along the coast is a small beach camp/retirement community called **El Huerfanito**; after another 30 km there are several more fish camps, with cabins for rent, at **Punta Bufeo.** The onshore fishing here and at the nearby **Islas Encantadas**—five islands and several islets close to shore—is reputedly good for yellowtail, croaker, corvina, and sierra. Several of the Encantadas—San Luis, Pomo, Encantada, Lobos—are of volcanic origin, displaying pumice and lava deposits. The islands constitute a good kayaking destination although offshore winds can blow quite strong in the winter.

Punta Willard And
Bahía San Luis Gonzaga

About 12 km (seven miles) south of Punta Bufeo is Punta Willard, home of **Papa Hernandez Resort,** a campground with gas, meals, and fishing pangas for rent. Just a few kilometers below Punta Willard, at the south end of Bahía Willard on a sandspit connected to Isla San Luis Gonzaga during low tide, is **Alfonsina's,** the main supply point for visitors and residents enjoying large, pristine Bahía San Luis Gonzaga, the next bay south. Many visitors and residents are pilots and almost every house has a plane nearby; along the main unpaved road, airplanes have the right of way over cars and trucks.

Climb Punta Final (actually a small cape with five points and a small lagoon) at the south end of Gonzaga for a good bay view. Fishing pangas are available for rent at Alfonsina's. A cot in one of the rustic rooms here costs US$10 a night with no showers and shared toilets. The fresh seafood dinners are a definite highlight. The camp is famous for its annual Memorial Day bash, which draws visitors from all over the peninsula.

The entire 72.5 (45-mile) trip from Puertecitos to Alfonsina's takes five to six hours by car. From Bahía San Luis Gonzaga, a mostly graded but unpaved road leads southwest 64.5 km (40 miles) to meet Mexico 1 at Km 229/230; this drive generally takes about three hours. About 38 km (24 miles) from Bahía San Luis Gonzaga, near Rancho Las Arrastras, the same road intersects an unpaved, partially graded road east to **Bahía de Calamajué,** another nearly untouched bay.

Reportedly, the Mexican government has plans to extend the paved road from San Felipe all the way to Bahía San Luis Gonzaga and eventually to Mexico 1. This would provide an alternative route to Baja Sur, along the east coast via Mexicali, for drivers of ordinary, low-clearance vehicles.

BOB RACE

NORTH-CENTRAL BAJA
EL ROSARIO AND VICINITY

Near the mouth of a deep valley formed by Río del Rosario is the town of El Rosario, a market center for farms and ranches in the valley as well as fish camps along the nearby Pacific coast. Although the valley has been continuously inhabited for at least 300 years, El Rosario today is little more than a cluster of modest homes, a rustic baseball field, hospital, school, town hall, several markets, two motels, two PEMEX stations, and a few taquerías and cafés. It is, however, the largest town for 356 km (221 miles) southward, and as such it's an important supply and reconnaissance point for anyone exploring north-central Baja.

El Rosario actually consists of two communities: the larger El Rosario de Arriba, along the highway in the upper part of the valley, and the smaller El Rosario de Abajo, south of the highway and the Río del Rosario, toward the coast.

History

Little is known about the Cochimí Indians who lived here when the Spanish arrived except that they subsisted mostly on Pacific shellfish and wild desert plants, and called their valley community "Viñadaco." In 1774, the Dominican Order established its first and southernmost California mission, **Nuestra Señora del Rosario,** on the east side of the valley facing the Pacific; the mission was moved downstream in 1802 to take advantage of a better water supply. The adobe ruins of the latter mission can be found by turning right—west—at the supermarket, where Mexico 1 curves east, then left at the first road. After crossing the riverbed to El Rosario de Abajo, the minimal ruins lie on the right.

At first the mission community thrived, producing the most abundant crops of any northern Baja mission; the valley was perfectly suited for agriculture. As elsewhere in the Californias, the Indians eventually succumbed to diseases brought by the missionaries and, left without converts or laborers, the mission closed in 1832.

A Spanish land grant in the 1840s brought Carlos Espinosa to the valley, where he and

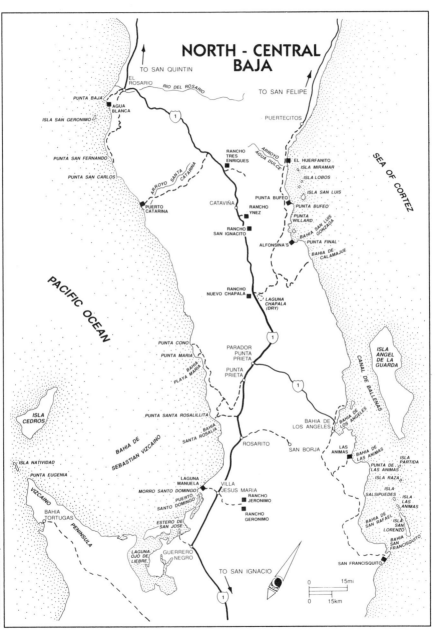

NORTH - CENTRAL BAJA

TO SAN QUINTIN

EL ROSARIO

RIO DEL ROSARIO

TO SAN FELIPE

PUNTA BAJA

AGUA BLANCA

ISLA SAN GERONIMO

PUERTECITOS

PUNTA SAN FERNANDO

RANCHO TRES ENRIQUES

ARROYO AGUA DULCE

EL HUERFANITO

ISLA MIRAMAR

ISLA LOBOS

PUNTA SAN CARLOS

ISLA SAN LUIS

CATAVIÑA

PUNTA BUFEO

SEA OF CORTEZ

PUERTO CATARINA

RANCHO YNEZ

PUNTA BUFEO

ARROYO SANTA CATARINA

PUNTA WILLARD

RANCHO SAN IGNACITO

BAHIA SAN LUIS GONZAGA

ALFONSINA'S

PUNTA FINAL

BAHIA DE CALAMAJUE

PACIFIC OCEAN

RANCHO NUEVO CHAPALA

LAGUNA CHAPALA (DRY)

PUNTA CONO

PARADOR PUNTA PRIETA

ISLA ANGEL DE LA GUARDA

PUNTA MARIA

BAHIA MARIA

PLAYA MARIA

PUNTA PRIETA

ISLA CEDROS

PUNTA SANTA ROSALILLITA

CANAL DE BALLENAS

BAHIA DE LOS ANGELES

BAHIA DE LOS ANGELES

ISLA NATIVIDAD

BAHIA DE SEBASTIAN VIZCAINO

SANTA ROSALIA

BAHIA SANTA ROSALIA

LAS ANIMAS

BAHIA DE LAS ANIMAS

PUNTA EUGENIA

ROSARITO

SAN BORJA

PUNTA DE LAS ANIMAS

ISLA PARTIDA

ISLA RAZA

VIZCAINO

LAGUNA MANUELA

VILLA JESUS MARIA

ISLA SALSIPUEDES

ISLA ANIMAS

BAHIA TORTUGAS

PENINSULA

MORRO SANTO DOMINGO

PUERTO SANTO DOMINGO

RANCHO JERONIMO

RANCHO GERONIMO

BAHIA DE SAN RAFAEL

ISLA SAN LORENZO

ESTERO DE SAN JOSE

BAHIA SAN FRANCISQUITO

LAGUNA OJO DE LIEBRE

GUERRERO NEGRO

TO SAN IGNACIO

SAN FRANCISQUITO

0   15mi

0   15km

his family became successful ranchers and farmers. Italian copper miner Eduardo Grosso arrived at the turn of the century. The union of the two families has been a prime source of El Rosario history ever since.

In the '60s, El Rosario became a checkpoint for the Baja 1000 offroad race and the first landing for the Flying Samaritans, a group of North American doctors who provide volunteer medical service by plane to several northern Baja settlements. El Rosario's Doña Anita Grosso de Espinosa, proprietor of Espinosa's Place café, acted as a liaison between gringos and the local community and was largely instrumental in the initial success of both endeavors.

Punta Baja-Agua Blanca
Sixteen km (10 miles) southwest of El Rosario de Arriba, via an unpaved but all-vehicle road, is **Punta Baja,** a fish camp and headland at the north end of Bahía del Rosario. You can rent pangas here, or launch your own; the perch and rock cod fishing is good year-round. Farther offshore, tuna, croaker, bonito, and yellowtail are abundant. During northwest swells, the surfing off Punta Baja is excellent.

Agua Blanca is another fish camp, eight km (five miles) south of Punta Baja toward the middle of the bay. Between Punta Baja and Agua Blanca you may notice piles of sea urchin shells at the roadside. The harvesting of sea urchins constitutes the bulk of the local fishing industry; 90% of the catch is exported to Japan, mostly for sushi. The orange-colored "roe" consumed by the Japanese isn't the sea urchin's eggs, as is commonly believed, but the sex organs.

Agua Blanca is also a launching point for scuba excursions to **Isla San Geronimo** (sometimes spelled Jeronimo) and Sacramento Reef.

Accommodations And Food
El Rosario has two motels, **Motel El Rosario** on the east side of the highway as you enter town from the north, and **Motel Sinai,** around the bend in the highway to the east. Both offer adequate rooms; El Rosario costs US$15-18 a night, the Sinai charges US$25. One drawback of Motel El Rosario is its location at the bottom of a grade leading into town (and next to a PEMEX station); decelerating truckers make quite a roar as they pass, even more when they stop for fuel.

Yet Motel El Rosario is but a short walk from the legendary **Espinosa's Place (Mama Espinosa's).** This small restaurant, operated by the family of Doña Anita Grosso de Espinosa, has hosted Baja 1000 drivers, Flying Samaritans, and thousands of other Baja travelers since before the completion of the Transpeninsular. The small dining room was refurbished a few years back with plastic, McDonald's-style chairs and tables, but the burritos—from beans to lobster—are as tasty as ever. Profits from the restaurant help support a local orphanage. Doña Espinosa is also happy to accept donations of food staples and clothing for distribution among the community's poor.

More or less in the center of town and along the highway, the standard-issue **Restaurant Grullenses** specializes in fresh seafood while the relatively new **Pueblo Viejo** serves carne asada and antojitos in an old-west setting.

Around the bend toward Motel Sinai is **Restaurant Yiyo's,** a popular local hangout with a variety of egg dishes, fish, lobster, beef machaca, breaded shrimp, and steak. Prices at these restaurants set the standard for just about every café and rancho between El Rosario and Guerrero Negro: US$3-4 for breakfast, US$5-8.50 for lunch or dinner.

Camping: Beach camping is free along Bahía del Rosario. **El Rosario de México,** in town, offers 50 camper/RV slots with full hookups for US$8 a night. The Motel Sinai also charges US$8 a night for RV parking.

Supplies
Several tiendas offer fresh vegetables, baked goods, and a variety of automotive and household items. The supermarket at the first bend in the highway, near Espinosa's Place, has the largest selection, including vaquero hats.

El Rosario has two PEMEX stations but only the northernmost station, at the town entrance, is open these days. It dispenses both Nova and Magna Sin.

EL ROSARIO TO BAHÍA DE LOS ANGELES JUNCTION

After El Rosario, the Transpeninsular Highway drifts southeast, toward the center of the peninsula. For many Baja aficionados, this is where the "real" Baja begins. The population thins out rapidly, revealing 200 km (120 miles) of the peninsula's most classic desert scenery.

Once across the Arroyo del Rosario (Km 62), spindly cirios or "boojums" begin appearing, gradually increasing in number as you move farther inland. Cardón are also prolific, along with barrel cactus, yucca, and a whole pantheon of Baja desert plants.

A graded road leaves the highway at Km 78, traveling 56 km (35 miles) southwest to **Bahía San Carlos,** a well-known spot among Baja windsurfers and surf anglers.

Misión San Fernando Velicatá

A dirt road at Km 114 leads west off the highway to the ruins of the only mission built by the Franciscans in Baja. The secluded site was first discovered in 1766 by Jesuit Padre Link, but the Jesuits were expelled before they could found a mission. Father Junípero Serra, on his way north, established San Fernando in 1769. Due to its location at a midpoint between the Gulf and Pacific coasts, it became an important way station on the Camino Real. The mission community was wiped out by a 1777-80 epidemic.

Although the adobe ruins themselves aren't much, the arroyo setting is dramatic and the short side trip (eight km/five miles) affords an opportunity for desert solitude and a chance to get closer to the regional flora and fauna. Two families operate rancherías at the site, living off

the slim bounty of the arroyo. Rock walls near the arroyo bear petroglyphs and pictographs, some created by the Cochimís in the 17th-18th centuries, others possibly older.

Just south of the mission road, at Km 116, is **Rancho El Progreso,** the first of many ranchos along the Transpeninsular that offer food to passing motorists. The menu includes whatever's on the stove that day, usually simple ranchero fare like enchiladas, chiles rellenos, frijoles, and rice.

El Mármol

This abandoned onyx quarry, accessible via a 15-km (nine-mile) graded dirt road branching east off Mexico 1 at Km 143, makes another interesting side trip. *Mármol* means "marble" in Spanish, and for the first half of this century onyx—a brown-and-red-veined calcite or tufa that can be polished to a high gloss—was a popular marble substitute. A San Diego mining company began the El Mármol operation in the early 1900s; by the late '50s, when it closed due to the advent of cheaper synthetics, much of the world's onyx inkstands, bathroom fixtures, floor and wall panels, statues, and other decorative objects had come from this site. Onyx's peak was the art deco period, when celebrities like actress Theda Bara ordered custom-made onyx bathtubs.

The onyx at El Mármol is easy to quarry, since layers of it sit right on the desert surface. The problem lies in transporting the stone from

JOE CUMMINGS

onyx schoolhouse, El Mármol

this isolated site: onyx slabs had to be trucked to Puerto Catarina (80 km east on the Pacific coast), loaded through the surf one by one, and shipped north to San Diego by boat.

Banded onyx blocks remain strewn about the old quarry site. The ruins of a schoolhouse built entirely of thick onyx blocks sit to one side of the quarry. About midway between the highway and the old quarry a huge mesquite tree stands next to a well and an antique Aermotor windmill, a scene right out of West Texas.

Off the El Mármol road, between the highway and the quarry, **Rancho Tres Enriques** offers meals and rustic accommodations. **Rancho (Lonchería) Sonora,** between Km 144 and 145 on Mexico 1, also serves food.

Cataviña-Parque Natural Del Desierto Central

This Mexico 1 waystation at Km 174 lies in the middle of possibly the most spectacular desert scenery on the peninsula, a vast area of Volkswagen-sized boulders, cardón, elephant trees, cirios, and a hundred other desert oddities. The north end of the Desierto Central is marked by the Cataviña Boulder Field, honeycombed with trails and an excellent area for hiking—except in summer when the heat is deadly.

A *cueva pintada* above Arroyo Cataviña (also known as Arroyo El Palmarito because of the fan palms growing here) is a short hike from the highway. From the Hotel La Pinta, walk or drive three km (two miles) north along the highway to the second dirt track past a prominent *vado* where the arroyo crosses the highway, near the Km 171 marker. Proceed down the dirt road to the edge of the arroyo, which is usually dry at this point. If driving, park here. Before hiking across the arroyo, look for a white wooden sign on the other side, high up on a bouldered bluff a bit south of your position at the edge of the arroyo. This marks the way to the nearby cave. If you can't locate the sign, start hiking in the described direction and *maybe* you'll stumble on it. It's much easier to spot from the west side of the arroyo.

No one knows who painted the geometric patterns and humanoid figures on the rock face, though the Cochimí have been suggested due to the presence of equestrian images.

During times of rain you might find enough water in the arroyo for a refreshing swim.

Mission Ruins: A very tough vehicle track—experienced dirt bikers or four-wheelers only—leads 23 km (14 miles) east of Rancho Ynez, just south of Cataviña, to the adobe ruins of Misión Santa María de los Angeles, the last New World mission (1767-69) founded by the Jesuits. The site was known among the Cochimí as Cabujakamaang, "place where spirits dwell," when the Franciscans arrived in Baja. Though Father Junípero Serra refused to close the nonproductive mission simply because he found himself "addicted to the place," the mission was totally depopulated by 1800. As the original roofs were palm thatch, only the walls stand today. A *palma azul* oasis near the ruins is almost worth the ordeal of negotiating steep grades, switchbacks, and melon-sized rocks—definitely a destination best reserved for obsessed historians or offroaders.

Practicalites: Accommodations, food, and fuel are available at Cataviña's **Hotel La Pinta** (tel. 617-6-26-01 in Ensenada; 800-336-5454 in the U.S.). Large, clean guest rooms surround a small pool. Opposite the hotel is a second PEMEX station, open 24 hours and offering mechanical services. At last pass, only the PEMEX at La Pinta pumped Magna Sin.

Adjacent to the hotel the **Parque Natural de Desierto Central** operates a trailer park of 60 spots with full hookups; rates are US$7 a night.

A kilometer south of Cataviña is a turnoff east to **Rancho Santa Ynez (Inés),** where ranchero food, hot showers, and bunkhouse accommodations (US$8) are available. RVers can also park here; it's much quieter than the trailer park on the highway. The ranch was originally founded by a Spanish mission soldier stationed at the now-ruined Misión Santa María further inland.

Cataviña To Parador Punta Prieta

About 30 km (18.5 miles) south of Cataviña, off the west side of the highway between Km 207 and 208, is **El Pedregoso,** a massive natural rock formation 610 meters (2,000 feet) high that looks as if it were constructed from a pile of boulders.

Rancho San Ignacito, at Km 187, is yet another rancho food stop. A nearby plaque commemorating the completion of Mexico 1 is located at the spot where road crews from the north and south finally met. Between Km 229 and 230, a graded road heads northeast to Bahía San Luis Gonzaga and Bahía de Calamajué on the Sea of Cortez coast. At this junction, **Rancho Nuevo Chapala** offers traveler's meals. The cirio, cardón, yucca, and cholla in the area are often exemplary specimens.

Parador Punta Prieta is a government-established rest stop at Km 280 with a PEMEX station and a large, now-defunct cafeteria. Mexico 1 splits here, with the east fork leading southeast 68 km (42 miles) to Bahía de los Angeles.

BAHIA DE LOS ANGELES AND VICINITY

The highway to Bahía de los Angeles passes thick stands of copalquín (elephant tree) as it winds through the Sierra La Asamblea. At Km 44 a 4WD-only track leads southwest 35 km (21 miles) to the restored Misión San Borja; a better road of similar distance is accessible from Rosarito, off the west branch of Mexico 1. The final descent to the bay from the sierra affords an inspiring view of the island-studded blue waters.

Beginning in the late '40s, North American sportfishing enthusiasts began flying private planes into Bahía de los Angeles; a few hardy souls even drove down here from San Diego and points north. Old Baja hands say in those days the village was nothing more than thatched-roof huts. But novelist John Steinbeck, who sailed into the bay in early 1940 with marine biologist Ed Ricketts, described his feeling of resentment at finding "new buildings, screened and modern, and on a tiny airfield a plane. . . ." Even then, Steinbeck wrote, there were Americans in Bahía de los Angeles.

The town really hasn't grown much since the pre-Transpeninsular days; telephone service is still nonexistent, with the nearest phone in Guerrero Negro, 197 km/119 miles away by road. Modern concessions to tourism include a small power plant, three trailer parks, a couple of motels, a few cafés, a PEMEX station, and a small park. The major leisure activity remains fishing.

Behind the park is the small but well-curated **Museo de Naturaleza y Cultura** (open Sunday, Tuesday, and Friday 1400-1600), displaying gold- and silver-mining exhibits, shells and fossils, two whale skeletons, ranch life re-creations, and a collection of Seri and Cochimí Indian artifacts. The toy-like locomotive in front of the museum once ran on the San Juan mine railway, 17.5 km (11 miles) south of the current town. The museum is staffed by volunteers and is open 1400-1600 in the winter, 1500-1700 in

summer. Postcards, books, and monographs on Baja are available for sale.

MARINELIFE

Mammals
Canal de Ballenas—the channel between Isla Angel de la Guarda and the peninsula—often features a variety of whales and dolphins, including Bryde's, Minke, gray, finback, blue, sperm, humpback, orca, pilot, common dolphin, and bottlenose dolphin. Bryde's (summer) and finback (winter) are the most common whales here, although every one of the aforementioned species is spotted year after year by visiting marine biologists. Dolphins are most numerous in summer and early fall.

Along island shores the California sea lion is common year-round; during spring, northern elephant seals are occasionally seen.

Sea Turtles
The Sea of Cortez and lower Pacific coast are prime breeding areas for sea turtles, specifically the Pacific varieties of the green, loggerhead, hawksbill, and leatherback. At one time Bahía de los Angeles was one of Mexico's principal turtle fisheries, but overharvesting in the '60s and '70s placed every species under threat of extinction. A sea turtle conservation and research station lies along the north shore of the bay; cooperative local fishermen bring in sea turtles in hopes their chances of survival will increase and that someday there will again be a viable turtle fishery.

ACCOMMODATIONS

Motel Villa Vitta is a clean, modern little motel in the center of town. Room rates vary according to the occupancy rate; sometimes a fine value at

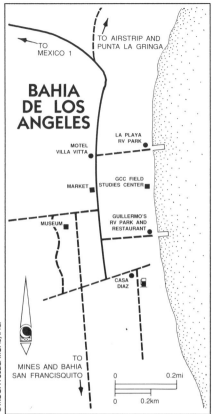

BAHIA
DE LOS
ANGELES

TO
MEXICO 1

TO AIRSTRIP AND
PUNTA LA GRINGA

LA PLAYA
RV PARK

MOTEL
VILLA VITTA

GCC FIELD
STUDIES CENTER

MARKET

GUILLERMO'S
RV PARK AND
RESTAURANT

MUSEUM

CASA
DIAZ

TO
MINES AND BAHIA
SAN FRANCISQUITO

0   0.2mi

0   0.2km

© MOON PUBLICATIONS, INC.

launch (fee for nonguests), showers, toilets (sometimes they flush, sometimes they don't; no seats), and a small market/gift shop. Guillermo's also rents five rooms, each with two king-size beds and one double bed, for US$50 d, US$60 t.

At the south end of town, the long-established **Casa Díaz** offers large, funky, bay-front rooms for US$20 s, US$25 d, less for longer stays. The Díaz family operates a fishing and bird-watching guide service to the bay islands, as well as a small market and the town's only PEMEX pump. RV sites with full hookups are available at Casa Díaz for US$5 a night.

Camping

Just north of town, near the paved airstrip, is the rustic **Brisa Marina,** a trailer park with its own generator, located right on the water; the area receives a good bay breeze and is a good spot in hot weather. Campsites cost US$5, showers US$1.50. North of Brisa Marina lies a string of minimal campgrounds for US$2-5 per person per night.

A graded road follows the bayshore as far as **Punta La Gringa,** the end of the bay and a fish camp/retirement community. Along the way are a number of open campsites where camping is free.

About eight km (five miles) south of town is **Camp Gecko,** a unique spot featuring huts with rock walls and palapa roofs as well as simple open-sided palapas. The huts cost US$10, tent/camper sites are US$5, with an additional US$5 for each additional vehicle whether you stay in a hut or on the beach. During the summer you can probably negotiate rates of US$8 and US$4 respectively. The offshore breeze is very refreshing here and the beach is kept exceptionally clean. "Doc," the man who runs the camp, leads panga and whale/porpoise-watching trips.

Farther southeast of Camp Gecko you can find a number of bayshore areas suitable for camping.

FOOD

Ostensibly because of Bahía de los Angeles' relative isolation, food—whether bought in local markets or at restaurants—is pricier here than in many places in Baja. If pinching pennies, stock up in Guerrero Negro before coming.

US$20 s, US$25 d, other times an overpriced US$45. Motel facilities include swimming pool, restaurant/bar, and access to a boat launch. The nearby **Mini Hotel** only has three rather basic rooms; when available, they cost US$25 a night. **Motel Las Hamacas,** a small collection of rooms recently developed by the owners of the Las Hamacas restaurant, rents at similar rates.

La Playa RV Park, across the road on the bay, is under the same ownership as the Villa Vitta and costs US$10 for unshaded tent/RV sites with morning and evening electricity. Showers, flush toilets, and a boat launch are available.

Next to La Playa is the fairly well-run **Guillermo's,** a trailer park and restaurant operation with palapas, tent sites, and full hookups for US$4 per person per night. Facilities include a boat

Las Hamacas, just north of the Mini Hotel, serves seafood and ranchero dishes for breakfast, lunch, and dinner; meals are in the US$5-12 range, with beer US$1. The restaurant also sells used paperbacks; proceeds reportedly go to the town museum.

Guillermo's nicely appointed restaurant-bar offers breakfasts for around US$4, dinner US$8, beer US$2. Specialties include fresh fish, shrimp, and lobster; the palapas out front are a nice spot for a margarita.

The dining room at **Casa Díaz,** once the only place to eat in town, is open only intermittently these days.

TRANSPORT

Bus service to Bahía de los Angeles is nonexistent; to get here you need your own wheels or plane, or must hitch from the Parador Punta Prieta junction. Once you've arrived, all of Bahía de los Angeles is accessible on foot. For trips to the Punta La Gringa airfield, or farther afield, you can hire a VW van taxi at Restaurant Las Hamacas.

A paved, 1,460-meter (4,800-foot) airstrip serves small planes; buzz the town once for taxi service. The local Unicom frequency is 122.8.

SPORTS AND RECREATION

Hiking
Arroyos east of the bay lead into the Sierra San Borja; for a good day-hike, pick out a dry wash and follow it. As long as you keep the bay in sight, it's impossible to get lost.

Mina Santa Marta, a nearby abandoned mine, makes an interesting hike. Along with the more successful Mina San Juan farther south, Santa Marta operated during the 1890s using a cable- and-bucket system to transfer gold and silver ore (mostly the latter) from steep hillsides to a miniature railway below. Access to Mina Santa Marta begins about 3.5 km (two miles) south of Casa Díaz next to the town dump. Once you've located the dump alongside the graded road south, walk west until you come across the remains of the railway grade, then follow the grade west to the remains of the mine itself. The roundtrip hike can be completed in one day, though many hikers spend a night at the mine.

The San Juan (also known as Las Flores) mine is reached by following the same road 17.5 km (11 miles) southwest of the bay to Valle Las Flores. You'll see the remains of a smelter and boiler along the west side of the road. This same road can be followed farther south into the Sierra San Borja, where there are several major Indian rock art sites; inquire at local ranches for trail guides. The graded road continues southward through the sierra all the way to **Bahía San Francisquito,** approximately 131.5 km (81 miles) south of Bahía de los Angeles.

Fishing
Due to heavy local gill-netting, Bahía de los Angeles fishing is not what it once was. The best bets are onshore angling for sand bass, guitarfish, and triggerfish, or, at Punta La Gringa in spring, croaker and halibut. Farther out at nearby islands—especially near **La Ventana, Cabeza de Caballo,** and **Coronado**—you can try for yellowtail, white and black seabass, dorado, tuna, and grouper. Most of the offshore fish run in the summer months, though yellowtail runs are sometimes seen in Jan.-March.

Guillermo's, Camp Gecko, and Casa Díaz arrange guided fishing trips to the islands for US$75 a day. Bring your own tackle; it's scarce in Bahía de los Angeles.

Boating And Kayaking
Guillermo's, La Playa, and Casa Díaz each feature boat launches. You can rent pangas at the latter. The bay is protected by the 67.5-km-long **Isla Angel de la Guarda,** but strong northeasterlies set up a nasty chop on occasion. Make local weather inquiries before venturing any considerable distance from shore.

Bahía de los Angeles is popular among kayakers, who paddle to the nearby coves and islands, including the larger **Isla Coronado** (also known as Isla Smith, three km/two miles northeast of Punta La Gringa) and **Isla Angel de la Guarda** (19 km/12 miles from Punta La Gringa). Landings are usually easiest on the westward side of the islands; this is also generally where the best camping spots lie. On Angel de la Guarda, **Puerto Refugio,** at the northern tip (64 km/40 miles from Bahía de los Angeles), is the usual landing. Explorations on Isla Angel de la Guarda can take in cirio stands, 1,200-meter (4,000-foot) peaks, and beaches with basking sea lions.

An easier two- to three-day kayaking circuit involves paddling from the bay to Isla Coronado and back, stopping at smaller islands Ventana, Pata, and Cabeza de Caballo along the way.

East and south of Bahía de los Angeles you'll find several coves worth visiting. Those with beaches and camping areas include **Puerto Don Juan, Ensenada del Quemado,** and **Ensenada del Pescador.**

It's possible to complete a "stepping stones" kayak route from Bahía de los Angeles (or from farther south at Bahía San Francisquito) to Isla Tiburón and Bahía Kino on the Mexican mainland. The usual route, once followed by Seri Indians in reed canoes, is Partida-San Lorenzo-San Esteban-Tiburón-Kino, but navigating the currents requires advanced kayaking abilities and knowledge of the local geography. The University of Arizona Sports and Recreation Department, probably your best source of information on the route, sponsors a yearly Bahía de los Angeles-Bahía Kino crossing by kayak.

Because many novice kayakers have experienced problems in the Bahía de los Angeles area, an Alta Californian kayaking club called San Diego Sea Kayakers has printed a set of Bahía de los Angeles kayaking guidelines, distributed free at Guillermo's Restaurant, the mayor's office, and the museum.

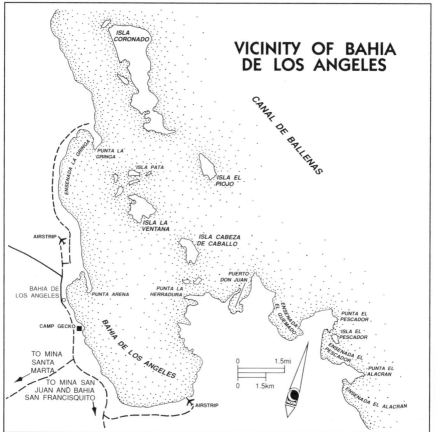

VICINITY OF BAHIA DE LOS ANGELES

© MOON PUBLICATIONS, INC.

Windsurfing

Bahía de los Angeles is a good bay for novice board-sailors because of the lack of large swells. Prevailing northeasterlies are strongest in the northern parts of the bay. A 10- to 12-km (six- to seven-mile) downwind run through the small islands west of Isla La Ventana, then all the way to the town waterfront, can be accomplished from Punta La Gringa.

Birdwatching

The shores of Bahía de los Angeles and the bay islands host a wide variety of birdlife, including terns, pelicans, gulls, egrets, herons, cormorants, petrels, boobies, and ospreys. The most renowned local marine bird rookeries are **Isla Partida** and **Isla Raza.** The latter, a tiny, guano-covered, sparsely vegetated island of 250 acres, is the site for annual territorial wars between approximately 100,000 Heermann's gulls and 200,000 elegant terns, who battle for nesting grounds on the small island. The conflict—including "war formations" and egg-smashing—takes place in April; Casa Díaz can arrange special boat trips to view the annual event.

A number of rare royal terns and tropic birds also inhabit Isla Raza, declared a national wildlife sanctuary in 1964 to stop egg-hunters from destroying the bird populations. It's possible the gull-tern wars are related to the elimination of egg-hunting, which local Indians had practiced—albeit at a slower pace than their Mexican successors—for centuries.

Baja California Field Studies Program

Alta California's **Glendale Community College** sponsors a special field-studies program every summer at Bahía de los Angeles. Courses include Introduction to Marine Biology, Natural History Field Studies, and Introduction to Marine Vertebrates, plus Basic Spanish Conversation. Students stay in the Field Studies Center, a building at the center of town on the bay. For information, contact Dr. José Mercade, GCC, 1500 N. Verdugo Rd., Glendale, CA 91208.

BAHIA DE LOS ANGELES JUNCTION TO GUERRERO NEGRO

Southwest of the Bahía de los Angeles junction, the main section of Mexico 1 is marked by a new kilometer sequence beginning at Km 0. The ranch community of **Punta Prieta** is at Km 13; between Km 38 and 39 a graded gravel road heads west 13 km (eight miles) to **Santa Rosalillita,** a fish camp below Punta Santa Rosalillita.

The Santa Rosalillita area is a well-known surfing destination; in a northwest swell, the point break at the north end of the bay reportedly offers Baja's longest ride (much depends on current bottom conditions). Windsurfers also enjoy the breaks and the bay's steady breeze. At the bay's south end, **Punta Rosarito** produces decent reef breaks in swells from any direction. If the waves aren't tipping right at either of these spots, breaks at **Punta Negra, Punta Maria,**

state border sign

and **Punta Cono**—all positioned perfectly to catch winter swells—can be reached by following the dirt road north out of Santa Rosalillita for 24-30 km.

The wreck of the double-masted schooner *Jennie Thelin* (built in 1869, stranded in 1912) lies buried in the sand dunes along Bahía Santa Maria. The schooner and her captain Alexander McLean were the inspiration for the infamous ship *Ghost* and skipper Wolf Larson in Jack London's novel *The Sea Wolf*. The ship was reputedly often used to transport illegal immigrants and untaxed merchandise between the U.S. and Mexico.

Rosarito-San Borja

Rosarito, a small ranching center, appears on the east side of Mexico 1 at Km 52. The **café** at the northeast end of town, on the highway, is a favorite stop for passing truckers. The ranchero food is good, and reasonably priced, but best of all is the real coffee, filtered through a cloth strainer in the old Mexican style. There are other cafés in town as well.

A dirt road, suitable for high-clearance vehicles only, leads 34 km (21 miles) east from Rosarito to San Borja, a small farm settlement in the foothills of the Sierra San Borja. **Misión San Francisco Borja de Adác** was founded here by Jesuit padres in 1759, then handed over to the Franciscans in 1767 along with large numbers of sheep, goats, cattle, horses, and mules. In 1773, the Dominicans took charge of the mission property and over 1,600 Indian parishioners in the Adác (the original Indian name for the site) community. Although the mission was officially secularized in 1818, it has since been restored and offers weekly services for local residents. The fig, pomegranate, olive, and date orchards planted by the missionaries continue to provide a livelihood.

Northeast of San Borja are at least two major Indian rock art sites, Las Tinajitas and Monte-video. They're difficult to find; inquire in San Borja for a guide.

Villa Jesus Maria-Puerto Santo Domingo

The town of Villa Jesus Maria, at Km 94-95 on Mexico 1, has a PEMEX station and a couple of cafés, including the dependable **Restaurant Ejidal**. A paved road runs northwest from town to Ejido Morelos, connecting with a graded dirt road southwest to **Laguna Manuela**, a fish camp on the bay of Puerto Santo Domingo.

The occasional point break off volcanic **Morro Santo Domingo**, at the north end of Puerto Santo Domingo, draws a few surfers. A solar-powered lighthouse stands at the end of the point. Fishing is said to be good in the bay—corvina, croaker, and halibut inshore, and grouper, yellowtail, and white seabass offshore. You can easily launch trailered or cartopped boats on the beach, or rent pangas at Laguna Manuela. The laguna itself can be difficult to navigate due to high winds and unpredictable tidal surges. About 2.8 km (1.7 miles) northwest of the fish camp is a long sandy beach known locally as "Playa Arcos."

Paralelo 28

The northern border of Baja California Sur, at 28° N latitude, is reached at Km 128. A 43-meter-high (140 feet) steel monument—a stylized eagle that looks more like a giant tuning fork—marks the border and the change from Pacific to Mountain Time. South of the 28th parallel, kilometer markers on the Transpeninsular Highway begin at Km 220 and descend toward Km 0 (at Santa Rosalía).

Between the border and the town of **Guerrero Negro** (seven km south of the state border) is an agricultural inspection station. The inspectors usually wave gringos in passenger vehicles through without an inspection or even a query. Trucks and larger vehicles may be stopped briefly.

SOUTH-CENTRAL BAJA

GUERRERO NEGRO

This town of around 10,000 took its name from the *Black Warrior,* a Hawaii-ported whaling barque that foundered in Laguna Guerrero Negro in 1858. Too overloaded with whale oil to leave the lagoon under its own power, the barque sank while being towed out to sea. This was just a year after Charles Melville Scammon "discovered" the Baja lagoons where migrating gray whales came to calve.

Within 20 years, tens of thousands of gray whales had been slaughtered and the whalers moved on to other Pacific hunting areas. But the gray made a remarkable comeback from the brink of extinction, and currently numbers around 21,000. Once again the whales of Scammon's Lagoon are attracting visitors.

More important to the local economy than whalewatching tourists is the local saltworks, a large solar-evaporative operation producing around six million tons of salt a year. Exportadora de Sal, S.A. (ESSA), the town's largest employer, maintains a huge system of diked ponds southwest of town which take in seawater from the lagoons and impound it, at a depth of about one meter, until the fierce Vizcaíno Desert sun turns it into thick layers of salt. The salt is then scooped into trucks and driven to Puerto El Chaparrito at the north end of Laguna Ojo de Liebre (Scammon's Lagoon), where it's loaded onto barges and shipped 80 km northwest to Isla Cedros. From Isla Cedros the salt is shipped by freighter to the Mexican mainland, the U.S., Canada, and Japan.

About 9.5 km (six miles) from town or four km (2.5 miles) from Mexico 1 near Paralelo 28 are the **Dunas de Soledad,** a large system of coastal sand dunes as high as eight meters (26 feet) tall. Along the other side of the dunes facing the Pacific is **Playa Don Miguelito,** a pristine beach named for the man considered the "father of Guerrero Negro." In 1926 fisherman Don Miguelito came to the lagoon by burro all the way from Sonora and stayed in the area till his death in 1992 at age 96. You can reach the dunes by taking the wide sand-salt road that veers to the right off Blvd. Zapata just before the canal (past the PEMEX, before Banamex).

CLIMATE

Temperatures in Guerrero Negro remain fairly steady year-round, due to the overall Pacific influence and the insulating effect of bays and lagoons to the west. Daytime highs are 21°-24° C (70°-75° F) in summer, 15°-18° C (59°-65° F) in winter. Rainfall is very scarce, but an almost-constant fog keeps the air moist during the summer months.

ACCOMMODATIONS

Hotels And Motels

Except for La Pinta, all of Guerrero Negro's hotels and motels are located on or just off Blvd. Zapata, the main street through town, west of Mexico 1. Right below the state border, just off Mexico 1, the **Hotel La Pinta** (tel. 617-6-26-01 in Ensenada; 800-336-5454 in the U.S.) offers large, comfortable rooms for US$55 s, US$60 d, not including tax. If you're just stopping off for the night, La Pinta is conveniently situated for getting on and off the highway. It's a seven-km (four-mile) drive into town; if you plan to spend a few

GUERRERO NEGRO

TO DUNAS DE SOLEDAD

TO PUNTA PRIETA

HOTEL LA PINTA

THE DUNES RV PARK

PARALELO 28 MONUMENT

AIRFIELD
(FLIGHTS TO ISLA CEDROS, BAHIA TORTUGAS)

CANAL

BANAMEX

MOTEL GAMEZ

IMSS CLINIC

MOTEL BRISA SALINA

SUPERMERCADO CALIMEX

RESTAURANT LUPITA

COCINA ECONOMICA LETY

TORTILLERIA

DUNAS MOTEL

MERCADO LA BALLENA

MOTEL EL MORRO

MOTEL LAS BALLENAS

MOTEL SAN IGNACIO

MOTEL SAN JOSE

BUS DEPOT

MALARRIMO RESTAURANT/ RV PARK

RESTAURANT PUERTO VIEJO

CALLE MADERO

RESTAURANT FIGON DE SAL

POST OFFICE

BLVD ZAPATA

SHRINE

TO SAN IGNACIO

NOT TO SCALE

© MOON PUBLICATIONS, INC.

(top) bakery, San Felipe; (bottom) fruit vendor, Cabo San Lucas

(top left) Bajacalifornio, Tijuana; (top right) Guadalupe Cathedral, Tijuana;
(bottom) open-top kayaking in Bahía Concepción

days exploring Guerrero Negro, you might look for something in the town itself.

In town, next to the Malarrimo Restaurant, prefab trailer-style units at **Cabañas Don Miguelito** (tel. 7-02-50, 7-0020) rent for US$22 s, US$25 d, US$28 t. More amenable and less expensive is the **Motel San Ignacio,** farther west on the same side of the street; cozy rooms here cost US$18 s, US$22 d. **Motel El Morro** (tel. 7-04-14) next door offers spacious rooms with ceiling fans for US$25-27 s, US$31-33 d.

Between Malarrimo Restaurant and Motel San Ignacio is the recently established **Motel San José,** a US$15-a-night place catering to bus traffic (the bus depot is across the street).

West one block, behind Motel El Morro, the quiet **Motel Las Ballenas** offers five simple rooms with TV and private baths for US$17 s, US$20 d. Knock US$2 off the rates if you pay in pesos. Farther north along Blvd. Zapata is the slightly cheaper **Dunas Motel** (tel. 7-00-57), where off-the-street rooms cost US$14-16 s, US$18 d.

Even cheaper digs are available at the **Motel Gamez,** west toward the ESSA buildings; rooms are just US$10-12, but they're very basic and the hot water supply is inconsistent. In this same general vicinity are the **Motel Salparaíso** (turn right at Frutería Loma Bonita) and **Motel Brisa Salina,** both with adequate rooms for US$15-20.

Camping And RV Parks

Coastal areas around Guerrero Negro offer plenty of free camping spots, but few are accessible by ordinary passenger vehicle. Camping is permitted along the lagoon in the Parque Natural de la Ballena Gris; a daily parking fee of US$3 is usually collected during whalewatching season, Jan.-March. A few RVers set up camp at a dirt lot near the old salt wharf, about 10 km (six miles) northwest of town via a graded road that meets Blvd. Zapata just past the Banamex.

The Dunes RV Park, just south of Hotel La Pinta next to the state border off Mexico 1, has 18 electricity/water hookups (no shade) plus toilet and shower facilities for US$6-8 for two people, US$2 per each additional person. In town, Malarrimo Restaurant/Cabañas Don Miguelito runs an RV park with electricity/water hookups at similar rates.

FOOD

Guerrero Negro has several places to eat and a couple of supermarkets that supply residents as far away as Bahías de Los Angeles and San Francisquito. Like the hotels and motels, most are spread out along Guerrero Negro's main avenue, Blvd. Zapata.

The most popular restaurant in town, especially for gringos, is **Malarrimo,** on the north side of Blvd. Zapata just as you enter Guerrero Negro. The pismo clams, deep-sea scallops, lobster, and other fresh seafood are always good; breakfasts are another highlight here, including lobster omelettes, homemade chorizo and eggs, and other diet-busters, served with beans, chilaquiles, and tortillas. It's open daily for breakfast, lunch, and dinner; prices are higher than average. A new restaurant on the edge of town, **Puerto Viejo,** offers a similar menu at slightly lower prices.

Another restaurant on Blvd. Zapata competing for the tourist business is **Restaurant Lupita,** serving seafood and open for breakfast, lunch, and dinner. Prices are moderate.

For something more local in price and ambience, try the **Cocina Económica Lety,** a small eatery on the east side of Blvd. Zapata next to the Secretaría de Pesca trailer. Simple home-style meals run US$3-4, about half the average price at tourist restaurants here; in addition to regular menu items for breakfast, lunch, and dinner, Lety offers a daily *comida corrida.* No alcohol is served, but the banana *licuados* are excellent.

In the old town toward the post office and *salinero* (salt worker) residences, the long-established **Figón de Sal** still serves moderately priced Mexican and seafood *platillos* for lunch and dinner in a tiny dining room. To find it, follow Blvd. Zapata until it ends at Calle Madero. Turn left onto Madero and you'll come to Figón de Sal a few blocks down on the left.

Groceries

Guerrero Negro has the only supermarkets south of Ensenada and north of Santa Rosalía. **La Ballena** is the largest and most popular of the pair on Blvd. Zapata, and is the only store in town that accepts traveler's checks. They stock an amazing variety of things, including full picnic supplies.

Panadería Hermanos (Hnos.) Aguiar, on the south side of Blvd. Zapata west of Malarrimo Restaurant, offers a good selection of Mexican pastries, including fresh bolillos daily.

Frutería Loma Bonita, on the west side of Zapata just south of Supermercado Calimex, carries a good selection of fruit and vegetables; the family that runs it also makes great *licuados* and *aguas frescas*. **Frutería El Triunfo,** closer to the main hotel zone, is also quite good.

SERVICES

Changing Money

A Banamex near the ESSA buildings, near the end of Blvd. Zapata, offers a currency exchange service Mon.-Fri., 0900-1200. It also contains an ATM, very convenient for travelers with cash cards. On weekends or at other times of day, the only other choice for cashing traveler's checks is La Ballena supermarket. Naturally, the clerks prefer you make a purchase and accept change in pesos. **Novedades Ely,** a sundries store on the east side of Blvd. Zapata near Lety, will change cash dollars into pesos.

Telephone

Guerrero Negro has the only public telephone service in a 200-km (120-mile) radius. Several privately operated phone offices in town add service charges to the cost of any call. Collect calls can be made at the public phone booth in front of Malarrimo Restaurant for no charge (dial 02 or 09, or 92 for collect to the U.S.). The area code for Guerrero Negro is 115.

GETTING THERE

Air: Aerolineas California Pacíficos operates flights to Bahía Tortugas and Isla Cedros several times weekly. For fares and schedules, see the appropriate sections below under "Vicinity of Guerrero Negro."

Aerotaxis del Vizcaíno (Aero Vizcaíno) (tel./fax 7-10-00) has small planes for charter at US$400 per hour. The company can be contacted at the Paralelo 28 airfield or at its office on Blvd. Zapata in town.

Guerrero Negro has two airfields. The one used by California Pacíficos is near the north end of town; follow Blvd. Zapata north and west past the PEMEX station and make a right turn onto the wide sand-salt road just before the canal. The airfield is less than a half kilometer down the road on the right. A larger airfield, Aeropuerto Federal Paralelo 28, lies just off Mexico 1 near the Paralelo 28 monument; the turnoff is between Km 125 and 126. The latter facility is used by ESSA planes and Aero Vizcaíno only.

Buses: Transportes de Aguila and **ABC** use a small depot on the east side of Blvd. Zapata between Malarrimo Restaurant and Motel San José. Three or four first-class buses head north daily to San Quintín (US$17.30), Ensenada (US$22), and Tijuana (US$27), while four or five daily departures travel south to San Ignacio (US$6), Santa Rosalía (US$9), Mulegé (US$11), Ciudad Constitución (US$22), and La Paz (US$29).

GETTING AROUND

Yellow city buses, marked Infonavit-Centro, run frequently between the Paralelo 28 monument and the old town via Blvd. Zapata and Calle Madero; the fare is the peso equivalent of US$.35. You can hire taxis at the bus depot; a cab ride to anywhere in town costs US$3.

VICINITY OF GUERRERO NEGRO

Whalewatching At Scammon's Lagoon
During the season, January through March, Scammon's Lagoon offers several whalewatching options. The Malarrimo Restaurant organizes small group tours of up to eight people for US$30 per person; prospective participants should book at least a day in advance. During the height of the season, vans leave daily from the restaurant at 0800 and 1100 and drive, via ESSA-owned road, to a shore of the lagoon, where a panga takes participants out on the water for about two hours. Lunch, included in the tour fee, is eaten on Isla Arena, a large sandbar island covered in dunes.

You can book a similar tour through **Grupo Mario's** (tel. 115-7-07-88) for the same price. Mario's can be contacted at the Restaurant Bar

close encounters of the big and barnacled kind

Mario's next to Hotel El Morro or at the Agencia de Viajes Mario's office on Blvd. Zapata.

A less expensive alternative is to drive on your own to the shore of the lagoon and deal directly with the *pangeros.* To do this, take Mexico 1 south of town nine km (5.5 miles) to the turnoff marked **Parque Natural de la Ballena Gris** and turn right (southwest). This 24-km (15-mile) road alternates between washboard and sandy surfaces that sometimes require slow driving. After about six km (3.5 miles), the road reaches a salt company checkpoint where you must usually wait for an attendant to open the gate. After the checkpoint, the road runs between two salt evaporation flats; the drying salt looks like packed snow. The road ends at the edge of the lagoon, where a US$3 parking fee is collected.

Once you're at the shore, you can watch the whales from land or sign on with a boat tour. With a good pair of binoculars you can see the whales from shore, but you get much closer to them on the water, and can hear them blowing. From January through March, two or three boats are usually on hand at the park for charters. The going rate is US$10 per person; boats leave 0900-1500 only and stay out about an hour and 15 minutes. After 1500, the wind comes up, fog comes in, and whalewatching conditions are poor.

Private boats, kayaks, sailboards, inflatable rafts, or other floatables aren't permitted anywhere in Scammon's Lagoon during the whale season. The *pangeros* who take tourists out to see the whales are granted seasonal permits to do so. They're also very skilled at running the pangas so as not to frighten or threaten the whales, most of whom are mothers and babies. The males, for the most part, cavort near the entrance of the lagoon, farther from shore.

Vizcaíno Peninsula

Jutting northwest into the Pacific, the coast of this huge desert peninsula is renowned among beachcombers, anglers, surfers, and scuba divers for the abundant opportunities to participate in their favorite recreational activities far from "civilization." The isolation and long distances involved in navigating the peninsula's interior deter the casual visitor, despite the fact that the roads aren't really all that bad. The greatest distance between PEMEX stations on the Vizcaíno Peninsula is 166 km (100 miles). More critical is the lack of automotive and/or medical assistance along lengthy stretches of road.

Although most visitors head straight for the peninsular shores, a leisurely drive through the interior affords close, uninterrupted views of the Vizcaíno Desert. Rainfall is scant and the desert vegetation mostly survives on Pacific fog; yucca trees (*datilillos*) are particularly abundant. Several of the cactus and succulent species chosen for Biosphere II—an experimental dome environment in Arizona—were borrowed from this desert. Less than 100 rare *berrendo* (desert pronghorn) survive on the peninsula.

Fuel, food, and other supplies are available at four cannery towns along the southwest coast of the peninsula and, to a much lesser extent, from a handful of fish camps and ranchos

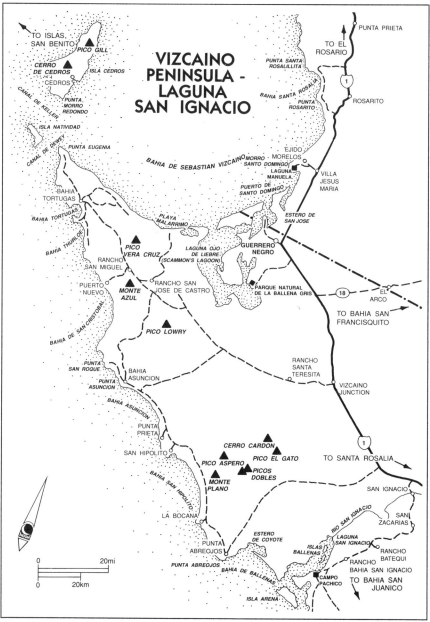

VIZCAINO PENINSULA - LAGUNA SAN IGNACIO

TO ISLAS SAN BENITO
PICO GILL
CERRO DE CEDROS
ISLA CEDROS
CEDROS
PUNTA MORRO REDONDO
ISLA NATIVIDAD
CANAL DE KELLER
CANAL DE DEWEY
PUNTA EUGENIA

PUNTA PRIETA
TO EL ROSARIO
PUNTA SANTA ROSALILLITA
BAHIA SANTA ROSALIA
PUNTA SANTA ROSALIA
PUNTA ROSARITO
ROSARIO
ROSARITO

BAHIA DE SEBASTIAN VIZCAINO
MORRO SANTO DOMINGO
EJIDO MORELOS
LAGUNA MANUELA
PUERTO DE SANTO DOMINGO
VILLA JESUS MARIA

BAHIA TORTUGAS
BAHIA TORTUGAS
BAHIA THURLOE
PLAYA MALARRIMO
ESTERO DE SAN JOSE

PICO VERA CRUZ
RANCHO SAN MIGUEL
PUERTO NUEVO
MONTE AZUL
RANCHO SAN JOSE DE CASTRO
LAGUNA OJO DE LIEBRE (SCAMMON'S LAGOON)
GUERRERO NEGRO
PARQUE NATURAL DE LA BALLENA GRIS

PICO LOWRY
BAHIA DE SAN CRISTOBAL

EL ARCO
TO BAHIA SAN FRANCISQUITO

RANCHO SANTA TERESITA
VIZCAINO JUNCTION

PUNTA SAN ROQUE
PUNTA ASUNCION
BAHIA ASUNCION
BAHIA ASUNCION

PUNTA PRIETA
SAN HIPOLITO
BAHIA SAN HIPOLITO

CERRO CARDON
PICO ASPERO
PICO EL GATO
PICOS DOBLES
MONTE PLANO

TO SANTA ROSALIA

SAN IGNACIO
SAN ZACARIAS
RIO SAN IGNACIO

LA BOCANA
ESTERO DE COYOTE
PUNTA ABREOJOS
ISLAS BALLENAS
LAGUNA SAN IGNACIO
RANCHO BATEQUI
RANCHO BAHIA SAN IGNACIO
TO BAHIA SAN JUANICO

PUNTA ABREOJOS
BAHIA DE BALLENAS
CAMPO PACHICO
ISLA ARENA

0   20mi
0   20km

© MOON PUBLICATIONS, INC.

between these settlements. **Bahía Tortugas,** 166 km (100 miles) from Mexico 1 (Vizcaíno Junction), is the largest, with a population of around 3,000. Aside from a cannery and PEMEX station, the town offers several markets, cafés, a clinic, a post office, a modest motel, and an airfield.

North of Bahía Tortugas, 26.5 km (16.5 miles) by graded dirt road, is **Punta Eugenia,** a small fishing village and jumping-off place for boat trips to Islas Natividad, Cedros, and San Benito.

Bahía Asunción, 56 km southwest of the Vizcaíno Junction-Bahía Tortugas road, is less than half the size of Bahía Tortugas, and has a PEMEX station, airstrip, cannery, clinic, market, and café. **La Bocana** and **Punta Abreojos,** farther southeast along the coast, are smaller yet; both may have gasoline available in barrels, leaded only. The best onshore/inshore fishing areas are generally found between Bahía Asunción and Punta Abreojos; typical catches include Cortez halibut, corvina, croaker, and sand, calico, and pinto bass.

A loop trip involves driving west from Vizcaíno Junction (Mexico 1, Km 144) to Bahía Tortugas and/or Bahía Asunción, then southeast to Punta Abreojos and back to Mexico 1 at Km 98. Beach camping is possible at numerous spots between Bahía Asunción and Punta Abreojos, and rustic rooms are available in Bahía Tortugas for around US$10 a night. **Vizcaíno Junction,** also called Fundolegal, has several cafés and small markets.

Those with 4WD vehicles can make a side journey to **Malarrimo Beach.** The challenging track to Malarrimo branches north off the Vizcaíno Junction-Bahía Tortugas road 116 km (72 miles) from Mexico 1, at Rancho San José de Castro. It then winds through arroyos and around mesas for 44 km (27 miles) before fading out at the dunes behind the beach. Malarrimo receives the brunt of northwest Pacific currents, and is therefore a beachcomber's paradise. It takes a hardened beachcomber to appreciate the beach, since much of the flotsam washed ashore consists of the dregs of civilization—styrofoam and plastic, and garbage jettisoned from ships throughout the North Pacific.

Air Transport: Aerolineas California Pacíficos flies to Bahía Tortugas from Guerrero Negro on Mondays, Thursdays, and Saturdays for US$20 each way. Soc. Coop. de Producción Pesquera ("Cannery Airlines") also flies from Ensenada. Bahía Tortugas's harbor is the best between Ensenada and Bahía Magdalena.

Isla Cedros

Baja's largest Pacific coast island not of oceanic origin is 20 km (12 miles) north of the tip of the Vizcaíno Peninsula, or about 72 km (43 miles) northwest of Guerrero Negro. The two main industries on the 24-km-long (14.5-mile) island are fishing and off-loading salt from Guerrero Negro's saltworks for long-distance shipping. Because of the salt business, Cedros ranks as Mexico's third-largest port after Veracruz and Tampico, carrying over nine percent of all offshore cargo.

Among naturalists, Isla Cedros is known for its small stands of scrub juniper and pine in the center of the island between its tallest peaks, Pico Gill (1,060 meters/3,488 feet) at the north end and Cerro de Cedros (1,200 meters/3,950 feet) toward the south. Like cedars, the island's mistaken namesake, junipers belong to the cypress family. Even more impressive are the Cedros Island oak, (*Quercus cedrosensis*) and Cedros Island pine (*Pinus radiata* var. *cedrosensis*), both endemic to this island. A rare variety of mule deer reportedly inhabits the island's center. Date palms stand along the northeast coast; no one remembers who planted them.

To reach Cerro de Cedros, follow the road northwest out of town till it ends at a trail that follows a water pipe most of the way up the hill. Keep an eye on the hill's radio towers and you'll have no problem following the trail. The hike from town to summit takes around three hours and is rewarded by very good views of the surrounding island.

From the town and airport, the nearest good beach is at **Punta Prieta** at the southwest end of the island; locally this beach is referred to as "Playón." Taxis cost a standard US$13 for the 10-km (six-mile) trip from town, though some drivers will go as low as US$10. Though after Punta Prieta the vehicle road ends, a rough track continues along the coast. You can also reach Playón by traversing the island via Cerro de Cedros, but this requires an overnight at the beach—carry plenty of water. Surfing is possible at **Playa Elefante,** an empty stretch of sand north of Cabo San Agustín; the only way to get there is by panga from town or from one of the fish camps. The going rate for a complete coastal circuit by panga is US$100. A panga to nearby Isla Natividad also costs US$100; these boats take up to five passengers.

Fish camps are located at **Cabo San Agustín,** on the southwest corner of the island, and at **Punta Norte** to the north. The largest settlement on the island, **Cedros,** is a village of around 5,000 on the southeast coast facing the peninsula. Along the main street leading from the harbor are a port captain's office (COTP), Conasupo, fish cannery, post office, church, bank (traveler's checks can't be cashed here), school, a couple of cafés, and a sizable residential area. South of the village along the same coast are the docks where salt from Guerrero Negro is off-loaded.

Accommodations: Basic lodging in town can be arranged for US$7-15 per night; ask a taxi driver for recommendations or look for signs on the main street reading Se Rentan Cuartos. Primitive camping on a rocky beach north of town is also an option.

Food: La Pacenita, a block south of the main drag and two blocks inland from the harbor, offers a good, basic menu of Mexican fish, chicken, and beef dishes daily 0600-2000. The nearby **Restaurant El Marino,** on the north side of main street three blocks from the harbor, has more inexpensive—though not necessarily tastier—Mexican dishes and seafood.

Transport: Aside from sailing over in your own boat, the easiest way to reach the island is by plane. Aerolineas California Pacíficos flies from Guerrero Negro Mon.-Fri. at 1000 for US$25 each way; the flight takes around 40 minutes. The return trip leaves at 1230 but you need to be at the airfield early in the morning to be sure of securing a seat. The same airline flies between Bahía Tortugas and Cedros on Thursday and Friday for US$17.30 each way. Soc. Coop. de Producción Pesquera ("Cannery Airlines") also flies periodically from Ensenada. The island's paved airstrip lies south of Cedros village at Punta Morro Redondo. It's sometimes possible to charter a boat to the island from either Bahía Tortugas or Punta Eugenia.

A taxi from the airfield into town costs US$5 per car. Up to five passengers can split the fare.

Time: Isla Cedros occupies the same time zone as Baja California Norte; i.e., an hour behind Guerrero Negro.

Isla Natividad

During the Spanish missionary period, a Cochimí subtribe lived on this arid island 10 km (six miles) northwest of Punta Eugenia, calling it Afegua, or "Island of Birds." Eventually a Jesuit padre from Misión San Ignacio convinced them to leave the island and live at the mission. Renamed "Christmas Island," today it's one of the most famous surfing destinations along the Pacific coast of the Americas.

The most popular Natividad break, "Open Doors," is off the southeast tip and catches summer swells from the southwest—peak time is generally July through September. Waves here typically run four to six feet, with occasional sets up to 15 feet. In winter, large breaks—for pros only—are found at the northwest and southwest tips; the former break can only be reached by boat. A small village along the southeast shore of the 22.5-square-km island houses around 200 fishermen during the summer. In winter many visit relatives on the peninsula or work on farms in the Ensenada area. Thus boats out to the northwest shore break should be arranged in Punta Eugenia. Or bring your own.

Transport to and from Isla Natividad can be difficult in the winter, when the island is mostly deserted. In summer, and when there are enough passengers, Soc. Coop. de Producción Pesquera flies to the island from Ensenada via Isla Cedros. You can charter boats from Punta Eugenia in the summer; it's less easy in winter. The simplest way to arrange a Natividad surfing vacation is through **Baja Surf Adventures,** an Alta California-based organization that has operated Natividad surf tours every summer since 1984. See "Surfing" under "Out and About" for tour details.

What else is there to do on the island besides surf? According to BSA, the surf and inshore fishing is good, and if surfing the best tubes on the coast isn't thrilling enough, cliff diving—from 10- to 15-meter-high ocean precipices—might be. Then there's "surging," an activity invented by bored surfers in which you jump into a deep tidal pool and then allow the wave action to pump your body six to nine meters (20-30 feet) up and down. The island has a clinic to handle small injuries.

Islas San Benito

This group of three small islands (Isla Benito

del Este, Centro, and Oeste), about 25 km north-west of Isla Cedros, has the best yellowtail fishing on the Pacific coast. Boats usually anchor along the leeward (southeastern) shore of Isla Benito del Oeste, opposite the tiny village of Benito del Oeste. Elephant seals, the world's largest pinnipeds, often sun themselves along the coves north of the village.

Rock reefs along the western shores of all three islands provide the best diving and fishing opportunities. Divers may be interested in the wreck of the U.S. tanker *Swift Eagle*, which went aground in 1934 off the north shore of Isla Benito del Oeste; parts of the wreck lie within two meters of the ocean surface.

SAN IGNACIO

In pre-mission days, local Cochimí Indians called the sheltered arroyo formed by the Río San Ignacio *Kadakaamán* or "Creek of Reeds." Fed by an underground stream, this fertile palm oasis on the southeastern edge of the Vizcaíno Desert has supported mission crops of wheat, figs, grapes, pomegranates, oranges, corn, and dates for over 200 years. The sleepy town of San Ignacio (pop. 4,000) is a cluster of stuccoed, pastel-colored, colonial-style buildings and small rancherías centered around **Misión San Ignacio Kadakaamán** and the adjacent plazuela. Hemmed in on all sides by mesas, the town's palm-oasis ambience and ongoing resistance to change have made it a favorite among Baja travelers for decades.

Climate
San Ignacio is very pleasant in the winter months, when daytime temperatures are 18° C (65° F) to 21° C (70° F), nights a bit cooler. During the summer, the surrounding desert sizzles as high as 40° C (105° F), although the valley floor may be a few degrees less. Rainfall is nearly nil year-round.

Misión San Ignacio Kadakaamán
Jesuit records indicate the Cochimís of Kadakaamán sent several requests for mission assistance to Padre Píccolo of Misión Santa Rosalía de Mulegé in the early 18th century. Píccolo first visited the area in 1716 and stayed in a brush cabaña for a month, apparently converting

and baptizing a willing Indian population. In 1728 Jesuit Padre Juan Bautista Loyando constructed a church and mission house on the present site, then proceeded to build a number of visiting chapels at nearby rancherías. He was succeeded by Padre Sigismundo Taraval, who brought Indians from the Pacific islands off the tip of the Vizcaíno Peninsula into the mission community. Eventually the San Ignacio mission became the largest and most successful in Baja California, with a parish of over 5,000 Indians.

After the Jesuits were expelled from New Spain, Dominican Friar Juan Crisostomo Gomez took charge of the mission, building a grander church on the original site in 1786. The walls, 1.2 meters (four feet) thick, were constructed of local volcanic stone without the use of mortar. The lumber for the wooden beams was transported from Misión Guadalupe in the high sierra; the carved doors at the front of the church were brought from the Mexican mainland. According to Jesuit records, the Queen of Spain paid 1.5 million pesos for the church's construction.

Today the venerable church stands largely in its original condition, thanks to a 1976 restoration, and is used by the local community for masses, weddings, funerals, and daily worship. The church's elaborate facade, with its engraved stone plaques and plaster ornamentation, makes it the most impressive of all Baja's mission

© MOON PUBLICATIONS, INC.

churches. The plaque to the left of the main doors, above the lower left window, is emblazoned with two crowned lions (symbol of the Kingdom of León in Spain), two castles (for the Kingdom of Castile), and the crown of Spain. To the right of the portal, over the corresponding lower window, is a simpler plaque with two overlapping globes (representing the Old and New Worlds), flanked by the twin Hercules pillars of Spain and North Africa; the pillars are topped by the crowns of Spain and Portugal, while the globe motif features a hybrid crown combining aspects of both the Portuguese and Spanish crowns.

Inside the church, the statue at the center of the main viceregal-style altar is of the mission's patron saint, St. Ignacius Loyola. Surrounding the statue are paintings of St. Joseph and the infant Jesus (upper left), St. Bernard (lower left), Virgin de Pilar (above the statue), St. John the Baptist (upper right), and St. Dominio (lower right). The two side altars, while not as impressive, also date from the mission period.

A sign in the church foyer requests that visitors dress with respect and refrain from chewing gum.

Accomodations

Hotels and Inns: Hotel La Pinta (tel. 617-6-26-01 in Ensenada; 800-336-5454 in the U.S.),
3.5 km (two miles) off Mexico 1 on the edge of town, has clean, comfortable a/c rooms for US$55 s, US$60 d, not including tax. Facilities include restaurant, pool, billiards room, and PEMEX station.

A more modest choice in town, **La Posada,** offers rooms for US$20 s, US$25 d; each room has two beds, dressers, a hot-water shower, and a fan. La Posada can be a bit difficult to find: walk or drive away from the church along Av. Hidalgo with the plazuela on your left, turn right at Callejón Ciprés, and then, after 200 meters, turn left; after passing a street to the right, you'll come to La Posada on the right-hand side of the road.

Camping and RV Parks: On the highway at the turnoff for San Ignacio (Km 74), behind the PEMEX station, is the **El Parador Trailer Park.** Sites with electricity and water, but no shade, cost US$5.

Two smaller campgrounds near the Hotel La Pinta are located in palm groves on the Río de San Ignacio. **El Padrino** charges US$2 for tent/camper sites, **Palapa Asadero La Presa** (formerly La Candelaria) costs US$3. At both, mosquitoes and/or *jejenes* (no-see-ums) are sometimes a problem.

Food

Restaurant Tota, a palapa hut just east of the

THE DATILES OF SAN IGNACIO

The lush date palm of Arroyo de San Ignacio, a welcome sight to those who've driven the Transpeninsular Highway south across Baja's Central and Vizcaíno deserts, has multiplied considerably since its introduction to the valley by Spanish missionaries over 200 years ago. At last count, some 100,000 of the creatures now call Baja home.

First cultivated in Mesopotamia around 1,000 B.C., dates (*dátil* in Spanish) were originally brought to Spain during the Moorish occupation of the Iberian Peninsula. The Middle East is currently the second-highest date producer after the U.S.; Mexico is a distant third.

Although mature date palms are easy to maintain, palm shoots must be planted near the mother tree for several years before they can be separated. If moved too soon, they'll perish. From germination, it takes an average 12 years for a date palm to mature and begin to produce commercially. It can then yield fruit for 85 years. Dates are very rich in potassium and proteins—the protein content of two dates equals that of one egg.

The annual date harvest is celebrated in San Ignacio on 31 July, which also happens to be the feast day for the town's patron saint, San Ignacio Loyola. During the fiesta, all manner of date products are displayed in the town plaza. La Reina del Dátil (the "Date Queen") is crowned, and music and dancing keep things lively well into the night.

BOB RACE

Misión San Ignacio

Bonfil (Km 53, 21 km/12 miles south of San Ignacio), are the **Café Tuxpan** and **Lonchería Sinaloense,** serving mainly antojitos and beer for passing truckers. Farther south at Km 39, **Rancho El Mesquitál** serves whatever's on the woodfired stove that day; if the family's had hunting luck, it might be *venado guisado* (deer stew).

Groceries: A couple of small tiendas in town, including a Conasupo, supply the basics. As might be suspected, dates are plentiful, typically costing around US$2 per kilo.

Entertainment
Around 15 km (nine miles) southwest of town via the road to Laguna San Ignacio, near Rancho San Joaquín, is a large palapa dance hall called **La Trampa**—"The Trap," named for a deep vado across the road nearby. It's usually open only on weekends and holidays, when you may be fortunate enough to hear San Ignacio's famous norteña group Tata Viejo.

Banking
A new Bancomer facing the plaza is open Mon.-Fri. 0830-1330; traveler's checks cashed here 0830-1200 only.

Transport
ABC and **Aguila** buses traveling north and south stop in front of the Conasupo next to the PEMEX station on the highway. As there are no bus depot or ticket offices in town, you can't make reservations or buy tickets in advance; when the bus arrives, you buy your ticket inside the Conasupo. Seats are usually available except during Holy Week in April.

VICINITY OF SAN IGNACIO

Indian Rock Art
San Ignacio is in the middle of what Indian cave painting expert Harry Crosby has termed the "Great Mural Region" of Baja California. The most extensive and numerous pictograph and petroglyph sites are found in caves and arroyos north of San Ignacio in the sierras of San Francisco and San Juan. The closest to San Ignacio are those in the Sierra de San Francisco, including the highly developed **Cuesta Palmarito** and **El Batequi** sites, in the arroyos of Palmarito and Batequi respectively.

plaza next to an irrigation pond built by the Spanish, has very tasty and reasonably priced seafood and antojitos served in a congenial atmosphere. The owner-chef, Tota, is renowned for her excellent cooking; her nephew Victor, who usually works as a waiter in the evenings, speaks some English. Tota is open Mon.-Sat. from around 0800 till 2100 or 2200, on Sundays for dinner only.

On the plazuela, the small **Restaurant Chalita** serves typical enchiladas, tacos, burritos, chilaquiles, breakfasts, and, occasionally, fresh seafood; it's open Mon.-Sat. from 0800 till around 1700 or 1800, Sunday 1300-1800.

Other than the aforementioned and the Hotel La Pinta's restaurant, **Las Cazuelas,** there is nowhere else in town to get a meal. Out on Mexico 1, about three km (two miles) north of town, **Restaurant Quichules** has a very good menu of breakfasts, antojitos, and seafood. The meat, milk, and cheese served at Quichules comes from the owners' Rancho El Carricito (often cited as "the cleanest ranch in Baja"). It's open daily 0800-2200.

Also on Mexico 1, in nearby Ejido Alfredo V.

JOE CUMMINGS

THE PREHISTORIC MURALS OF BAJA CALIFORNIA

BOB RACE

In hidden palm oases and remote canyons throughout the sierras of Baja California, far from the Transpeninsular Highway and most of the peninsula's larger towns, the artistic heritage of a lost Indian culture arcs across rock walls. Dubbed the "Painters" by Baja rock art expert Harry Crosby, these anonymous Indian artists painted thousands of figures in hundreds of murals that rival the cave paintings of Lascaux and Altamira in Europe. Most are concentrated in the central peninsular sierras of San Francisco, San Borja, San Juan, and Guadalupe. Paleolithic paintings are also found in northern Baja at San Jose de Tecate, Palmas de Cantú, Pilitas, and Arroyo Grande and in the south at Sierra de Cacachillas and Miraflores.

The Paintings

Central Baja's prehistoric murals are actually larger and more numerous than those found at Lascaux and Altamira. Between Bahía de los Angeles and Comondú alone, there are over 400 mural sites. Most paintings are placed high—as high as 10 meters (33 feet)—on the walls or ceilings of arroyos, canyons, and rock overhangs. Scaffolds, probably made of cardón ribs or palm trunks, were used to reach these heights. Styles were codified to such an extent that all human figures feature arms extended upwards, all four-legged animals are depicted running or leaping, fish are always shown from a dorsal view, and birds are in flight as seen from below, with their heads turned in profile.

Ritual purposes are implied by the fact that only the outlines of painted figures are representational, while interiors contain conventionalized abstractions. In some areas of the sierras, human figures are occasionally bicolored, with the left half of the body painted red and the right half painted black. Figures

may also wear headdresses or top-knotted hair. Rock-art experts have discerned several different schools within the Great Mural Region of central Baja: in the Sierra San Borja, monos are painted in red; Sierra San Francisco paintings show red-black bicolors; the Sierra de Guadalupe features monochrome, bicolor, and checkerboard color schemes, along with monos filled in with vertical lines.

One of the more awesome examples of prehistoric rock art is a 166-meter (500-foot) by 10-meter (30-foot) mural at Cueva Pintada in Arroyo de San Pablo (Sierra de San Francisco) consisting of overlapping images of men and women, deer, bighorn sheep, rabbits, and birds. At Arroyo de San Gregorio a four-meter (12-foot) whale is painted onto a rock overhang.

The Painters

Little is known about the Painters except that they belonged to the only culture, in a succession of central peninsula cultures, to leave behind artifacts borne not of economic necessity but from the realms of art and ritual. Ancillary evidence discovered at the rock-art sites—metates (grinding plates), manos (grindstones), bows and arrows, choppers, scrapers, carved bone, woven fibers, and firepits—identify the Painters as paleolithic. The artwork itself, ritualistic paintings of human and animal figures, correlates with art styles found in paleolithic sites the world over.

Eighteenth-century missionary documents from Baja refer to a few mural sites, but the Cochimí Indians living in the central peninsula at the coming of the Spanish padres had no knowledge of the significance of the symbols or motifs in the paintings, nor of the techniques of painting; they themselves didn't paint. Cochimí legends said the paintings were the work of a race of giants who inhabited the region well before the time of their ancestors. The Painters must have been giants, according to the Cochimí, because many of the paintings appear on rock walls up to 10 meters above the ground.

Because archaeological and anthropological research in Baja has been so scant, scholars haven't a clue whether the Painters were a separate cultural group that migrated from the north or an early phase of the Cochimí culture. That the Painters were migratory—like all early Indian cultures in Baja—is certain since they left behind no permanent dwellings or pottery.

The desert conditions of central Baja meant the Painters had to move with the migrations of game and the seasonal changes in surface water. Such a culture required highly portable materials made mostly of wood, hide, and fibers. The minerals used for painting, as well as materials for building the scaffolds, could be gathered on site.

Rock-art Research

Although the Spanish missionaries of the 18th and 19th centuries were aware of the murals, the first systematic study of the paintings awaited Leon Diguet, a French naturalist working at El Boleo copper-mining company in Santa Rosalía near the turn of the century. Diguet visited several mural sites in 1893-94 and published his findings in a few French journals; he missed the Painters' most extensive sites in San Francisco.

The next person to delve into the mysteries of the murals was American mystery writer Erle Stanley Gardner of "Perry Mason" fame. Gardner began traveling to Baja in the 1940s and was first led to El Batequi and other Sierra San Francisco sites in 1962 by local ranchers. Realizing he'd viewed sites of great archaeological significance, Gardner devoted a considerable part of his income to the study of the murals and wrote about them for *Life* magazine and in his book *The Hidden Heart of Baja*.

In 1972, Baja historian Harry Crosby succeeded Gardner in the search for undiscovered sites, making extensive forays into the San Borja, San Francisco, San Juan, and Guadalupe mountain ranges. Crosby printed the results of his explorations in *National Geographic*, as well as in his excellent 1984 book, *The Cave Paintings of Baja California*, the most authoritative general reference work on Baja rock art.

Based on an assortment of facts and artifacts—including what appears to be a mural rendering of the supernova birth of the Crab Nebula in A.D. 1054—Crosby speculates that the Painters' artistic output extended over a thousand-year period from around A.D. 500 to 1500.

To verify or refute this dating, more research is needed in the fields of archaeology, anthropology, geology, and meteorology.

UNESCO recently designated Baja's Great Mural Region a "World-Class Rock Art Site," an honor that will allow mural researchers to apply for UNESCO grants.

Viewing these rock-art sites requires a guide, not only because of the difficulties involved in finding the sites, but because the state requires it. Wandering around on your own—unless you're a recognized researcher, and even most researchers employ local guides—usually isn't done. The Fischer family at San Ignacio's La Posada offers guided trips from San Ignacio for minimum eight-person groups at US$20 per person; during whale season, it also leads a combined Laguna San Ignacio whalewatching and rock-art trip for US$40 per person.

An alternative involves driving to the village of San Francisco de la Sierra and arranging for a guide there; ask at the tienda or seek out federal *delegado* Enrique Arce Villa. The village is approached by a 37-km (22-mile) graded dirt road branching east off Mexico 1 at Km 118, 45 km (27 miles) north of San Ignacio. **El Batequi** is also known as Gardner's Cave,

since it was discovered by mystery writer Erle Stanley Gardner during one of his many Baja sojourns. It is located in magnificent Cañon San Pablo, and can be reached by mule from the village, usually requiring a three-day trip. Also accessible from San Francisco is the **Serpent Cave** of Arroyo del Parral, with its eight-meter-long (26-foot) deer-headed serpent and bicolored, rabbit-eared *monos* (human figures). Closer but much less impressive is **Cueva Ratón,** just west of the village.

Recently SEDESOL constructed a cluster of breeze-block huts south of town near Km 61 for the use of visiting archaeologists studying rock art in the Sierra de San Marta. It was also meant to serve as an information center for visitors interested in the cave murals. As seems all too common with Mexican government projects, it is now an abandoned facility serving little or no purpose. At the moment there is an ongoing dispute between government officials, who want to take over stewardship of the rock art, and local ranchers, who have successfully operated a guide program for decades without raising unsightly buildings in the middle of the desert. Depending on the outcome of the dispute, it may be that in the near future anyone who wants to visit the caves will need a government permit.

Laguna San Ignacio

Southeast of San Ignacio is a large bay used by calving gray whales January through March every year. The grays are closer to shore here than at Scammon's Lagoon to the north or Bahía de Magdalena to the south, and seem to exhibit friendlier behavior here than at other calving lagoons. Many mothers and calves at Laguna San Ignacio actively seek out tactile encounters, i.e., petting and scratching.

During the calving season, only boats with whalewatching permits are allowed on the bay. At **Campo Pachico,** where the road from San Ignacio meets the bayshore, licensed *pangeros* take visitors out to meet the whales for US$20 per person. The tour lasts about four hours; you must be at the camp by around 0900 to get on one of the boats. Since the 59-km (35-mile) drive from San Ignacio takes up to three hours due to road conditions (most passenger vehicles can make it—slowly), you must leave town early in the morning or spend the previous night at the camp.

Farther south along the bay is **Punta Piedras,** also known as Punta Peñasco, a camp often used by adventure-travel organizations for Laguna San Ignacio expeditions. High-clearance vehicles can reach Punta Piedras by road—a stream must be crossed along the way—or you can arrange to be dropped off by boat from Campo Pachico. You can also arrange food service at Punta Piedras, and there's radio contact with Campo Pachico. The road to Punta Piedras continues south all the way to Bahía San Juanico, but is recommended only for 4WD vehicles.

In the northern section of the bay lies **Isla Pelicano**, nesting grounds for ospreys and a variety of other birds. Though the island is closed to visitors during the whale season, you can visit by boat the remainder of the year.

SANTA ROSALIA

At Santa Rosalía, the Transpeninsular Highway completes its 215-km (129-mile) journey from Pacific to Cortez coasts. As in San Ignacio, the town is wedged into a deep arroyo between mesas, but the similarity between the two towns ends there. Whereas San Ignacio's architecture is strongly Spanish-flavored due to the mission influence, the buildings along Santa Rosalía's narrow streets—many of them wood-frame houses fronted by long verandas in the French colonial style—were designed by a French mining company in the 19th century.

Other Gallic touches include a French bakery and the only Eiffel-designed church in Mexico. One of the most impressive French-built structures in town, the Palacio Municipal, was once a school. Although many of the town's current residents certainly appear as if they could be of French or part-French ancestry, the locals claim most French citizens left town when the mines closed in 1954.

A new *malecón* (waterfront promenade) with benches, cement sidewalk, and street lamps was recently completed along the bayfront near the PEMEX station and bus depot, south of the ferry pier. Though not particularly scenic, this is a good spot to catch a refreshing offshore breeze.

Santa Rosalía is a terminus for the SEMATUR ferry to Guaymas, eight hours across the Sea of Cortez, and is the capital of the Município de Mulegé.

History

Copper-bearing deposits, in blue-green globules called *boleos,* were discovered near here in 1868, and in 1885 a French mining company calling itself El Boleo acquired mineral rights to the area for 99 years. To help build over 600 km (375 miles) of mine tunnels, a large copper-

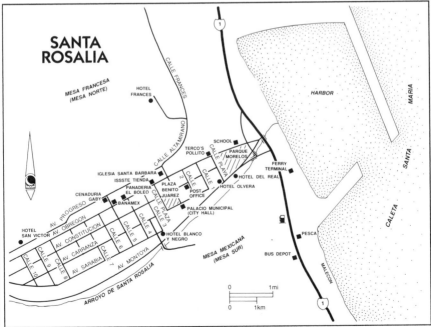

smelting foundry (imported by ship from Europe), a pier, and a 30-km (18-mile) mine railway, the French brought in Yaqui Indians from Sonora; fresh water was piped in from the Santa Agueda oasis, 16 km (10 miles) west. Two thousand Chinese and Japanese laborers, told they would be able to plant rice, also came to work at El Boleo. When they found that rice wouldn't grow in central Baja, almost all of them left; many ended up in Sinaloa across the Cortez.

After smelting, the copper ore was shipped to Tacoma, Washington, for refining. Instead of returning empty, copper-transport ships brought lumber from the Pacific Northwest to Santa Rosalía, and, as the town grew, the French filled the arroyo and mesas on either side with wooden buildings to house workers, company officials, and Mexican soldiers. During El Boleo's heyday in the 1940s, a sooty cloud issued constantly from the foundry's smokestack, hanging over the town. Eventually the ore began to run out, and in 1954 the French company sold its mining facilities back to the Mexican government. Copper ore from the Mexican mainland is smelted in Santa Rosalía on occasion, but the mines closed in 1985.

Without the mines in operation, Santa Rosalía (pop. 10,200) is probably a far more pleasant place to live than ever before. Today it serves as a government, transport, and market center for central Baja. It's also an important tourist crossroads for visitors making the ferry trip to the mainland or stocking up on supplies for further peninsular explorations.

The **Mahatma Gandhi Public Library** in Parque Morelos, at the east end of town near the harbor, features an exhibit of historic photos from Santa Rosalía's mining days.

Iglesia Santa Bárbara De Santa Rosalía

A novelty in Baja—or anywhere for that matter—is this prefabricated, iron-walled church designed by famous French architect Alexandre Gustave Eiffel in 1884.

Eiffel, who earned his reputation by designing locks for the Panama Canal and the frame for the U.S.A.'s Statue of Liberty, originally constructed this church in France in 1887 to serve as a prototype for missionary churches built to withstand the climate in France's equatorial colonies. Two years later it was exhibited in Paris, together with the Eiffel Tower, at the 1889 Paris World Exposition, where Eiffel took first

JOE CUMMINGS

Iglesia Santa Bárbara

prize for his modular, tropics-proof design.

When a French official at Compañía El Boleo later heard the church had been warehoused in Brussels, he purchased it and had it shipped in sections to Santa Rosalía, where it was reassembled in 1897. The exterior is modern, even minimalist, in tone, while the interior resembles that of any Catholic church. Except for two side wings added locally, the entire structure is made of galvanized iron. The church is still very much in use, with an Italian priest in residence.

Accommodations

Hotels: The tourist-oriented **Hotel Morro** (tel. 2-04-14), overlooking the Sea of Cortez about 1.5 km south of town on Mexico 1, features large a/c rooms for US$23 s, US$25-28 d. Facilities include a restaurant, bar, and filthy swimming pool.

Several hotels in town offer more basic, but comfortable, accommodations at lower rates. The **Hotel Blanco y Negro** (tel. 2-00-80), an old French wooden building with friendly proprietors at Av. Sarabia and Calle 3, provides clean rooms with shared bath for US$10 s/d; with private bath for US$11.60 d (two or three beds); with TV for US$15. There is also one single room with private bath upstairs for US$10. To reach this hotel through the town's one-way street system, head southwest on Av. Obregón, turn left at Calle 4 (in front of Panadería El Boleo), and follow Calle 4 until it ends at Av. Sarabia; turn left at Av. Sarabia and after two short blocks you'll find the Hotel Blanco y Negro on your right.

Hotel Olvera (tel. 2-00-57), at the corner of Calle Playa and Av. Montoya, is similarly priced but more exposed to dust and noise. The large, wooden **Hotel Central,** on the corner of Calle Plaza and Av. Constitución adjacent to Plaza Juárez, recently added a new coat of paint. Rooms come with *baño colectivo* only and cost US$10 s, US$12 d.

Nearby on Av. Montoya is the spruced-up **Hotel del Real** (tel. 2-00-68), with small a/c rooms for US$17-23; ask for a room in back (*al detrás*) for more quiet and less road dust. **Restaurant Terco's Pollito,** on Av. Obregón at Calle Playa, recently opened a few small rooms attached to the restaurant for US$17 s, US$22 d.

Farther west from the harbor is the **Hotel San Victor** (tel. 2-01-77) at Av. Progreso 36, where not very well-kept a/c rooms cost US$20. Over-looking the copper smelter on Mesa Norte is the venerable **Hotel Frances,** once the best hotel in town but closed down in 1991. New owners recently began restoring the French colonial-style building and a limited number of rooms are now open for a bargain US$20 a night.

Camping and RV Parks: Just south of Santa Rosalía off Mexico 1, the **Las Palmas RV Park** offers hot showers and a dump station, but no hookups, for US$6.60 per person per night.

Fifteen km (nine miles) south of town off Mexico 1, on the pretty bay of Caleta San Lucas, is the secluded **San Lucas RV Park** (mailing address: A.P. 131, Santa Rosalía, BCS). Tent/camper sites (no hookups) cost US$6 per vehicle. Facilities include a restaurant, usually open for breakfast only, hot showers, disposal station, and boat ramp.

Food

Most of the town's restaurants and cafés are spread out along Av. Obregón. **Restaurant Terco's Pollito,** on Av. Obregón at Calle Playa

opposite Parque Morelos, specializes in mouth-watering barbecued chicken as well as a wide variety of moderately priced breakfasts, seafood, soups, and Mexican standards. There is a pleasant palapa eating area between the main dining room and the attached hotel rooms.

Cenaduría Gaby, at the corner of Calle 5 and Av. Progreso, has operated for many years and offers very well-prepared and inexpensive enchiladas, tostadas, tacos, gorditas, burritos, and *almuerzos* Mon.-Sat. 0900-2100.

Restaurant Tokyo, run by a descendant of a Japanese laborer who worked for El Boleo, offers inexpensive seafood and tacos—but no Japanese food. It's on Av. Obregón between calles 3 and 4 and is open daily for breakfast and lunch only.

Pepe's, a cart vendor usually parked along the north side of Parque Morelos on Av. Obregón, makes delicious fish and shrimp tacos, triggerfish ceviche, and shrimp cocktails.

Around 14 km (8.5 miles) south of town on Mexico 1 at Km 182 (near the San Lucas RV Park) is the **Restaurant Sara Reyna,** a funky roadside café with good, reasonably priced food.

Groceries: The **ISSSTE Tienda** on Av. Obregón at Calle 3 purveys a wide selection of foodstuffs and household supplies at government-subsidized prices. Just west of this store, on the same side of the street, is the famous **Panadería El Boleo,** which typically draws a long line out front when it opens at 1000. The baguettes here are legendary; they also offer a good variety of other Mexican- and French-style baked goods.

Semillas del Sur, at the corner of Calle 6 and Av. Obregón, sells a variety of grains, dried pastas, beans, and lentils—all excellent camp foods—in bulk. For fresh tortillas, visit the **Tortillería Cachanía** on Av. Obregón near Calle 6.

Fishing

Corvina, pompano, grouper, and snapper are usually plentiful at **Caleta San Lucas,** 15 km (nine miles) south of town. You can launch small boats here at low tide. Farther offshore in the Canal San Marcos (between Caleta San Lucas and Isla San Marcos), sierra is available, especially in the winter months.

Events

Santa Rosalía's biggest festival is **Carnaval,** a pre-Lenten celebration held six days before Ash

Wednesday, usually in mid-February.

During the **Fiesta de Santa Rosalía,** held annually around 4 September, the townspeople organize concerts, food fairs, and fishing tournaments to honor their patron saint, Santa Rosalía. There is also a founder's day celebration during the second week of October.

Money And Communications

You can exchange foreign traveler's checks or cash for pesos at the **Banamex** at Calle 5 and Av. Obregón, Mon.-Fri. 0830-1200.

The **post office** is east of the plaza at Calle 2 and Av. Constitución. On the south side of the plaza a **public telephone** is available for local and long-distance calls. There is also a *caseta* at the bus depot. Santa Rosalía's area code is 115.

Transport

Bus: Santa Rosalía's intercity bus depot lies on the west side of Mexico 1, just south of the ferry terminal. Two or three first-class buses a day travel north to San Ignacio (US$3), Guerrero Negro (US$8.60), San Quintín (US$21), Ensenada (US$29), and Tijuana (US$34), as well as south to Mulegé (US$2.60), Loreto (US$2.60), and La Paz (US$22). Less expensive second-class buses are also sometimes available to San Ignacio, Guerrero Negro, Mulegé, and La Paz.

Ferry: The Santa Rosalía-Guaymas ferry leaves the SEMATUR ferry pier in Santa Rosalía every Wednesday and Sunday at 0800. You can purchase tickets at the SEMATUR office (tel. 2-00-13, fax 2-00-14) in front of the pier on Tuesday and Friday 0800-1300 and 1500-1400, Thursday and Saturday 0800-1500, Wednesday and Sunday 0600-0730. For further information on fares and departure times, see "Getting There" under "Out and About."

Boat: A marina in the breakwater-protected harbor has a few moorings for rent, and the city has plans to add more in the near future. Fuel is available. As Santa Rosalía is an official port of entry, the harbor features COTP, immigration, and customs offices.

VICINITY OF SANTA ROSALIA

South of Santa Rosalía, on the way to Mulegé via Mexico 1, are two side roads into the Sierra de Guadalupe suitable for high-clearance vehicles. At Km 188, just beyond the state prison, a graded road branches 12 km west to **Santa Agueda** and beyond to several ranchos. Local ranchers may be willing to act as guides to Indian murals at La Candelaria, San Antonio, or Los Gatos. The Guadalupe "school" of Indian rock art shows more variation than the paintings found farther north in the Sierra de San Francisco, and known sites are more numerous. According to Crosby, more sites are found in the Guadalupe than in any of Baja's other sierras. Murals here are typically smaller than those in the San Francisco area.

An even more scenic side road leaves Mexico 1 about 20 km (12 miles) south of the Santa Agueda turnoff, and heads 14 km (8.5 miles) west to the isolated farming community of **San José de Magdalena.** The winding, rocky road climbs several steep grades with inspiring views of palm-studded canyons, healthy stands of cardón, mesquite, and ocotillo, and picturesque rock outcroppings—you almost expect to see the Lone Ranger and Tonto around the next bend. San José de Magdalena is known as Baja's garlic capital and many visitors purchase long *ristras* (strands) of linked garlic bulbs here.

Beyond San José, the road continues another 48 km (30 miles) to several ranchos. There's a number of Indian mural sites accessible in this area, assuming you can find a guide at one of the ranchos; you can also reach the adobe ruins of **Misión Guadalupe de Guasinapi** (1721-95), one of the peninsula's most remote mission sites.

San Bruno, a small fishing community just before the turnoff to San José de Magdalena, has a PEMEX station, bus stop, church, *tienda rural,* and **Costa Serena Trailer Park,** where basic tent/camper sites are sometimes available for US$5 a night. A storm in 1993 blew several spaces away and the remaining sites are usually full up with semi-permanent residents. The turnoff for the town is just north of Km 173. The village ambience is enhanced by wandering cows and chickens, along with fishing nets hanging out to dry or awaiting mending. On the highway near the bus stop, the **Restaurant Peninsular** serves delicious home-cooked seafood platters, meatballs, spaghetti, and Mexican dishes.

MULEGE

The town of Mulegé (pop. 6,000) straddles a wide arroyo formed by the Río Santa Rosalía (also called Río Mulegé), an estuarial river that feeds into the Sea of Cortez. The abundance of water made it a desirable mission location in the early 1700s, and today the agricultural legacy of the Jesuit padres—dates, figs, bananas, olives, and oranges—comprises most of the local livelihood, along with fishing and tourism.

Steinbeck and the crew of the *Sea of Cortez* passed up Mulegé on their 1941 coastal journey because they'd heard "the port charges are mischievous and ruinous" and "there may be malaria there." The quaint mission-style buildings, narrow streets, and riverside palms, however, have made Mulegé a favorite stopover among modern Transpeninsular travelers. The local facilities, including a first-class dive shop, laundromat, five auto mechanics, two auto parts stores, markets, restaurants, hotels, and campgrounds, provide all the necessities and amenities for a long-term bivouac. Mulegé offers enough activities to occupy visitors for at least a couple of weeks, including hikes to nearby Indian cave paintings, snorkeling, scuba diving, fishing, clamming, birding, and kayaking.

Although it's well above the Tropic of Cancer, Mulegé is the first point south along the peninsular coast where the climate and ambience begin to feel tropical. Winters are mild, summers are hot and humid, and mosquitoes appear along the river when the wind is still.

Climate

Weather conditions along the coast from Mulegé to Loreto are subtropical. From December through March, daytime temperatures average 15°-21° C (60°-70° F); April through July, daytime temperatures run 26°-35° C (80°-95° F); and August through October the thermometer ranges 32°-43° C (90°-110° F). Annual rainfall is 10 centimeters (four inches), with much of the precipitation occurring in the late summer and early fall. These weather patterns mean that, for most prospective visitors, divers and anglers excepted, Aug.-Nov. is low tourist season.

Misión Santa Rosalía De Mulegé

Mulegé's original mission was founded on the riverbanks in 1705. In 1770, a flood destroyed most community structures, and shortly thereafter the church was rebuilt at its current site, on a bluff overlooking the river. Although not one of Baja's most striking mission churches, it's worth a visit just for the unobstructed views of the town and palm-lined river below. The church is usually locked except when services are held.

JOE CUMMINGS

Misión Santa Rosalía de Mulegé

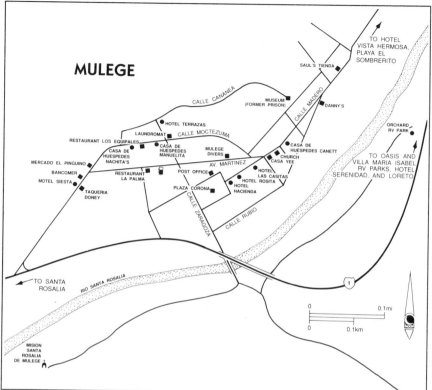

The church is best approached by following Calle Zaragoza southwest beneath the highway bridge, then west (right) until the road climbs the bluff by the church, about three km (1.8 miles) from the bridge.

Museum

The prison on the hill overlooking town functioned as a criminal detention facility from 1907 until 1975. During much of that time the prison operated on an honor system; trustee prisoners were permitted to walk into town from 0600 each day as long as they returned when the conch shell blew at 1800.

The walled facility stood empty until recently, when a local historian and a group of volunteers established a small museum inside. In addition to the old cells, visitors can view a collection of local historical artifacts—many marine-related—and a desk used by mystery writer Erle Stanley Gardner while researching central Baja's prehistoric murals.

Although hours are supposed to be 0900-1300 daily, in reality the museum is open only sporadically. If you're intent on seeing the museum and find it closed, look up curator Homero Yee at Casa Yee market. Admission is by donation.

Accommodations

Hotels: Mulegé has five hotels in town, plus two east of town. Except for the Serenidad, all are among Baja's least expensive hotels. One of the most popular is **Hotel Las Casitas** (tel. 3-00-19) on Calle Madero, the town's main east-west street. Formerly the home of Mexican poet Vicente Gorosave, this eight-room establishment offers modest a/c accommodations for US$23-28; facilities include a very nice patio restaurant and bar.

A bit farther west on Calle Madero, the rambling, colonial-style **Hotel Hacienda** (tel. 3-00-21, toll-free 800-464-8888 in the U.S./Canada) has come under new management and offers rooms surrounding a flagstone courtyard for an economical US$20 a night with ceiling fan, US$25 a night with a/c. The courtyard is planted with banana, citrus, and palm, and the hotel pool, long lying in ruin, is operational again. A bar off to one side of the courtyard is the most popular evening gathering place in town. Although it usually closes around 11 p.m., the bar could be a potential source of irritation for anyone trying to turn in for an early night's rest. The hotel also maintains mountain bikes for rent.

Just west of Las Casitas on the same street is **Hotel Rosita** (tel. 3-02-70), where budget two-bedroom apartments, complete with kitchenettes, cost US$20 per night for up to four persons.

The recently opened **Motel Siesta** (tel. 3-05-55), on the main access road into town and opposite Taquería Doney, offers five American-style motel rooms with reliable air conditioning and hot water for US$25 a night. The owners plan to add a second floor if/when room demand increases.

Hotel Terrazas (tel. 3-00-09), at the north end of Calle Zaragoza, has seen better days but is still the quietest place to stay in town. Good-size, clean rooms with two double beds, fan, and private bath cost US$20, or only US$17 per night for stays of two nights or more; with air conditioning rates run an additional US$5-10. Hot water showers are on-again, off-again but the rooms are still a bargain. Free coffee is provided every morning; take it on the palapa terrace on the second floor with pastries purchased in town and you'll have breakfast with a view for pennies.

Hotel Vista Hermosa (tel. 3-02-22) has a river view, a pool (often empty), restaurant, and bar. During the winter of 1993-1994 the hotel was closed and there's no word as to when—or whether—it will reopen. When last the hotel was operating, room rates fluctuated with hotel occupancy from as low as US$25 to as high as US$55. At the lower rates, it was

a good value.To get to the hotel, follow Calle Madero-Calle Playa east along the river toward the coast and you'll see the sign for the hotel after three km (two miles).

Four km (2.5 miles) east of town off Mexico 1 is Mulegé's largest inn, the **Hotel Serenidad** (tel. 3-01-11, fax 3-03-11, mailing address A.P. 9, Mulegé, BCS). The Serenidad even operates its own paved, 1,200-meter airstrip (Unicom 122.8); it's a favorite among *yanqui* pilots, many of whom fly in for the Saturday night pig roast. The spacious hotel grounds, which include pool, tennis court, boat ramp, restaurant, and bar, are impressive-looking, but some of the a/c units need replacing and the hot water supply can be weak. Noise from the bar is sometimes a problem, continuing well past midnight. Rooms are US$38 s, US$50 d; two-bedroom cottages cost US$90.

Casas de Huéspedes: Mulegé supports three guesthouses, or *casas de huéspedes*. **Casa de Huéspedes Canett,** on Calle Madero opposite a church, is the most livable of the three; clean rooms, some with private toilet and shower, cost just US$5-6. A minor (or major, depending on your sensibilities) drawback is that the church bells across the street ring most mornings at around 0600.

Casa Manuelita, opposite Restaurant Los Equipales on Calle Moctezuma, is a fair second choice, although the US$15 rate is overpriced. **Nachita's** was barely functioning when last I checked; the caretakers tend to send gringos across the street to the Hotel Terrazas.

Camping and RV Parks: Several well-run trailer parks compete for Mulegé's campers and RVers. Best of the bunch is the attractively landscaped **Orchard (Huerta Saucedo),** on the river about a kilometer east of town off Mexico 1. Riverfront tent sites on grass are US$6.50 for two persons, full hookups US$12 (US$15 riverfront) for two, plus US$2 for each additional person. For all sites, every seventh night is free. Monthly RV rates range from US$216 to US$245 depending on the number of consecutive months. Facilities include a boat launch, canoe rentals, storage (US$25 a month), free fruit (mangoes, dates, oranges, limes, figs), picnic areas, an *asador* (Mexican-style grill), hot showers, toilets, and a dump station. The showers are among the best campground showers in southern Baja, and are open to the general public for US$1.50 per person.

In the same vicinity, also along the river, are **Poncho's, Oasis Río Baja,** and **Villa María Isabel,** all decent, well-kept spots with rates slightly lower than the Orchard's. The Villa María Isabel also has a pool. Discount rates are generally granted travel club members and long-term stays.

The **Hotel Serenidad** has an RV park with full-hookup slots for US$12 for two people, plus US$2 for each additional person. It's rather like a large parking lot, with none of the ambience of the riverfront parks.

Free Camping: Playa El Sombrerito, the beach between the estuary and the Sea of Cortez and next to Café La Almeja, is a fine place to spend a few nights. Just take care not to pitch a tent too far toward the lagoon side, which cars and trucks use as a road to the fishing marina. Southeast of Hotel Serenidad, just past the big PEMEX station on the highway, is a dirt road that leads to **Playa El Gallito,** a sandy, fairly clean beach that few people seem to know about.

Food

Mulegé boasts several good restaurants; like the town's hotels, they're generally less expensive than those in most other Baja resort towns. During the off-season (anytime outside Nov.-Feb.), they look rather empty, but this doesn't mean they're no good—it's typical outside "the season."

The tastefully decorated **Los Equipales,** a second-floor dining room overlooking Calle Moctezuma next to Casa de Huéspedes Nachita's, features the tastiest Mexican specialties and seafood in town. Though a bit on the pricey side, it's worth every peso.

The service at **Restaurant El Candil,** on Calle Zaragoza opposite Plaza Corona since 1961, is somewhat slow, as everything is made from scratch. But the food is generally worth the wait and the prices are reasonable. The specialty of the house is the *combinación mexicana,* a huge plate of well-prepared taquitos, enchiladas, chiles rellenos, beans, rice, and tortillas.

When it's open, the family-run **Restaurant La Palma,** on Av. Martínez near the PEMEX station, is hard to beat for inexpensive, well-prepared meals. Breakfast selections include oatmeal, cream of wheat, corn flakes, omelettes,

huevos rancheros, chilaquiles, and good coffee. For lunch and dinner, the tiny restaurant serves fresh seafood, cheeseburgers, and a few Mexican standards. It was closed throughout most of 1993 but the owners said they would try to reopen in 1994.

Another cheap place for breakfast is **La Michoacana,** a truck stop on the highway next to the town entrance. It opens at 0700 and offers hearty ranchero-style plates of eggs and chorizo or machaca with beans and real brewed coffee.

Another find is **Café La Almeja,** a palapa hut on the beach at the mouth of the Punta El Sombrerito estuary. Exemplary tacos and fresh seafood are reasonably priced, especially considering the location. The restaurant is generally open from around 0900 to 2000.

The restaurants at the **Hacienda, Las Casitas** and **Serenidad** hotels are popular among the tourist crowd and serve decent, moderately priced Mexican fare. The Hotel Hacienda specializes in spaghetti and features a Sunday evening pig luau. Las Casitas' garden patio offers the best all-around ambience in town and the delicious daiquiris—especially the "bango" banana/mango concoction—are legendary. Las Casitas also hosts a mariachi night on Fridays. The Serenidad offers a pig roast every Saturday night; Wednesday night brings mariachis and a Mexican buffet.

Mulegé has three very good taco stands. Next to the now-defunct El Nido Restaurant on Calle Romero Rubio is a place called **Danny's,** also known as the "no name place" since owner-cook Daniel has yet to hang his sign. The place makes very good tacos de carne asada and quesadillas, and is open daily from around 0700 to 2200. This is also a good spot for brewed coffee in the mornings. On Saturdays and Sundays Daniel cooks up a batch of mouth-watering *carnitas* which can be purchased as tacos or by the kilo.

Great fish tacos are available from **Taquitos Mulegé,** a taco vendor on Plaza Corona, usually open 0900-1300 or until the fish supply runs out. **Taquería Doney,** on the road in from Santa Rosalía, has good tacos de carne asada, quesadillas, and tostadas (here called *mulitas*); it's open only in the evening. Also on the menu are *frijoles charros* and *horchata.*

Excellent *nieve* (Mexican-style, no-milk ice cream) is available from **Nevería La Purísima (Blanca's)** on Plaza Corona.

Groceries: Several tiendas stock fresh, locally produced meats, poultry, fruits, and vegetables, along with smaller supplies of canned goods. Generally the best stocked are **Casa Yee** (Calle Madero near Las Casitas), **El Pinguino** (on the road in from the highway, near Motel Siesta), and **Saul's Tienda** (on Calle Madero where it becomes Calle Playa). Saul's caters to the gringo market; owner Saul Davis speaks English and can get just about anything grocery-related—Thanksgiving turkeys, for example—if given enough advance notice. Block ice and purified water are available from the **Hielera Mulegé** on "Ice House Road," the road signed San Estanislao just north of town west off the highway. It's open 24 hours.

Oddly enough for a pueblo of Mulegé's size, there is no bakery in town.

Sports And Recreation

Fishing: Las Casitas, The Hacienda, Serenidad, and Vista Hermosa hotels can arrange guided fishing trips to nearby islands, Punta Chivato, and Bahía Concepción. Onshore fishing near the estuary—the south side is best—sometimes lands winter catches of yellowtail, roosterfish, sierra, and pargo; farther offshore are summer runs of dorado, yellowfin, and various billfish. Typical rates are US$120 per day in a panga for up to three persons, US$180 in a small cruiser that holds four anglers, or US$200 per day for a five-person diesel cruiser.

Diving: The marinelife in the Sea of Cortez off the coast of Mulegé and Santa Rosalía is more prolific and colorful than in the upper Cortez. Many of the tropical or Panamic species appear in reef areas, including the green moray eel (much less shy than its Pacific counterpart), angelfish, damselfish, parrotfish, triggerfish, flag cabrilla, several wrasses, and three varieties of lobster (red, spiny Cortez, and slipper). Generally speaking, the best diving season is Aug.-Nov., when visibility extends up to 30 meters (100 feet) and water temperatures near the surface are in the mid-20s C (mid-80s F). Full wetsuits are necessary in the winter; in the summer a Lycra skin is good protection against jellyfish.

Islas Santa Inés, three small islands in the northern part of Bahía Santa Inés, offer good snorkeling along their eastern shores, where rock reefs with soft corals lie at depths of around 4.5 to 12 meters (15-39 feet). Reefs and rock pinnacles extending from the north end of these islands are excellent scuba diving spots, with depths of six to 25 meters (20-85 feet). Scuba diving is also good at a reef at the north end of the bay, about a kilometer northeast of **Punta Chivato.** Other possibilities, farther north toward Santa Rosalía, include **Caleta San Lucas** and **Isla San Marcos.**

The islands and reefs of **Bahía Concepción,** south of Mulegé, provide plenty of diving and snorkeling opportunities, including **Pelican Reef, Isla Santispac, Isla Guapa, Isla Requesón,** and **Roca Frijole.**

Mulegé Divers (tel. 3-00-59, 3-01-34) on Calle Martínez in Mulegé offers just about everything scuba and free divers need, including air, equipment, and boat charters. One of the best-operated dive centers in Baja, it's also one of the least expensive. Guided dive trips start at US$30 if you supply the equipment, US$40 with weight belt and two tanks, US$50 for all equipment except wetsuit. Add US$5 for a jacket, US$5 for a farmer john.

For those requiring scuba instruction, Mulegé Divers offers a four-hour basic resort course for US$60, including all equipment and transport. Equipment rentals are very reasonable, from US$3 a day for a weight belt to US$8 for a regulator or power-inflated buoyancy compensator; air fills are available for US$3 (2250 psi) and US$4 (3000 psi). You can rent or buy snorkeling equipment as well, and arrange guided snorkeling trips for US$25, including mask, snorkel, and fins, or US$20 if you supply your own gear. Of possible interest even to those not planning an immediate dive trip are the shop's selection of fishing and diving guidebooks, waterproof fish charts for identifying marinelife underwater, and fishing tackle. The shop is open Mon.-Sat. 0900-1300 and 1500-1800.

Kayaking: You can launch kayaks at the estuary for excursions into Bahía de Santa Inés to the north or Bahía Concepción to the south. Most kayakers intending to paddle in the latter launch farther south—for more details see "Vicinity of Mulegé."

Experienced kayakers enjoy the well-known Mulegé to Loreto coastal trip, a 135-km (84-mile), five- to seven-day paddle. Because shore campsites are few and far between, you should only attempt this route in the company of someone who's made the trip before.

Baja Tropicales operates half-day trips on easy-to-paddle, open-cockpit kayaks, in the estuary area and at Bahía Concepción—see "Bahía Concepción" under "Vicinity of Mulegé" for details. Baja Tropicales also rents kayaks to experienced kayakers for US$30 a day, less for overnight or long-term rentals.

Other Recreation: The small lagoon where the river meets the sea is a good birdwatching site. For a view of the lagoon, river, fishing marina, and town, climb to the top of **El Sombrerito,** the hat-shaped hill topped with a cross at the south end of Mulegé's beach. Mornings are best for photography.

Information And Services

Post and Telephone: A post office and public phone with local and long distance service are located on the plaza off Calle Zaragoza. There are other public phone booths around town but this is the only one that works; sometimes you must stand in line and the circuits are often busy all day Saturday and Sunday. If Mulegé civic leaders really want to please visitors from the north they should install a Ladatel office or at least another functioning phone or two.

There is also a small private long-distance telephone office in the tienda at the corner of Calle Zaragoza and Av. Martínez. As usual, a substantial service charge is added to the phone charges. The area code for Mulegé and vicinity is 115.

Money: A new Bancomer was constructed in February 1993 and sat unopened through October of that year. Rumor has it the bank won't open until the streets are paved; spokespersons for the city say they won't pave the streets until the bank opens. How this Mexican standoff will end is anyone's guess. For the time being you can cash traveler's checks at the Hotel Las Casitas and Hotel Hacienda, or use the Banamex in Santa Rosalía, 61 km (38 miles) north.

Fuel: The PEMEX station in town, on Av. Martínez, sometimes has vehicles waiting for gas backed up all the way to the end of the block.

A quicker alternative—in spite of the drive—is the large, new **Mulegé PEMEX Centro** on Mexico 1, about 15 minutes south of Mulegé by car. Reportedly the most modern in Mexico, this station offers 13 self-service pumps, six containing Magna Sin. Attached to the station are a small café and mini-market with ice.

Other: There is no longer a U.S. consul in Mulegé; the State Department plans to open a new consulate farther south in La Paz, San José del Cabo, or Cabo San Lucas.

A very clean and efficient **laundromat** at the corner of calles Zaragoza and Moctezuma is open Mon.-Sat. 0800-1800.

Getting There

Air: The nearest commercial airport is Loreto, where Aero California fields daily flights from Los Angeles and La Paz.

Next to the Hotel Serenidad is a 1,200-meter (4,000-foot) dirt strip (Unicom 122.8) popular with North American pilots; aviation fuel is usually available.

Buses: ABC and **Aguila** buses on the way north and south stop at the town entrance on Mexico 1. Although they follow no strict schedules, three buses in either direction generally pass by every day: two southbound buses usually arrive in the late morning and one in the mid-afternoon, while northbound buses arrive one in the mid-afternoon and one each in the early and late evening, though this is highly variable from year to year.

As there are no bus depot or ticket offices in town, you can't make reservations or buy tickets in advance. When the bus arrives, buy your ticket on board.

Getting Around

You can easily reach every point in town on foot, even from the riverfront RV parks.

You can rent **mountain bikes** at the Hotel Hacienda for US$2 per hour, US$6 per four hours, US$10 per day, or US$20 for three days.

Downtown Mulegé possesses a system of narrow one-way streets that might seem a bit confusing at first but is pretty easy to figure out. Some streets are marked with arrows; some aren't. A policeman usually stands at the main intersection of Av. Gral. Martínez and Calle Zaragoza to make sure motorists drive in the correct direction. They're easygoing fellows there to direct traffic, not catch and fine gringos. Still, a flagrant traffic violation can result in a trip down to the station; drive carefully.

The streets of Mulegé are too narrow for large RV rigs; RVers can walk into town from the riverfront RV parks.

VICINITY OF MULEGE

Cave Paintings

The Sierra de Guadalupe, east of Mulegé, contains the largest number of known prehistoric mural sites in Baja California. Several hotels in Mulegé can arrange excursions to the more accessible sites for US$25-35 per person.

La Trinidad: One of the best trips involves a canyon site near Rancho La Trinidad, about 29 km (18 miles) west of Mulegé. As with other sites encompassed by central Baja's Great Mural tra-

dition, those at La Trinidad are federally protected and you're only supposed to visit with a licensed guide. Viewing the major sites at La Trinidad means a challenging canyon hike of around 6.5 km (four miles) that includes several river crossings—at least two and sometimes three usually require swimming. Although the hike isn't particularly difficult or dangerous, it requires good overall fitness, the ability to swim up to a hundred meters (300 feet) through calm waters, the strength to hoist oneself out of the water onto stone riverbanks up to a meter high, and a fair sense of balance for walking along narrow paths.

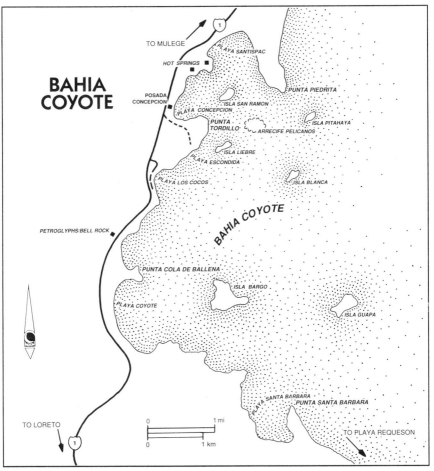

You should also carry at least two liters (roughly a half gallon) of drinking water per person, preferably in canteens or other containers slung over the shoulder. You can float a limited amount of camera gear up the river on small, impromptu rafts made of inflated inner tubes and any flat, sturdy material used as a platform over the tube. Everything else you bring along—including shoes (Teva-style sports sandals are the perfect footwear for this trip)—should be submersible. Count on a half-day to complete the canyon hike itself, although some visitors prefer to spend an entire day in the canyon. Others may want to spend some time at the various ranchos along the way.

The trip begins with a scenic desert drive to Rancho La Trinidad, a large goat and cattle ranch at the foot of the mountains. Some guides stop at other ranches along the way to allow visitors to observe leather tanning, cheese-making, and other ranch crafts. After you arrive at Rancho La Trinidad, you hike about 800 meters (a half mile) to a four-meter (12-foot) stone dam, which you must climb to enter Cañon La Trinidad. These are reportedly the headwaters of the Río Mulegé, though the river drops underground before resurfacing near town. Once inside the mouth of the canyon, you make one river crossing before reaching the first and largest group of murals. Among the many red and black animal representations on the canyon walls is a large ocher deer silhouette, considered one of the best prehistoric deer paintings in Baja; others throughout the peninsula are often compared to the "Trinidad deer." Among humanoid representations in this group is a shamanistic figure sometimes referred to as a "cardón man," though there's no real evidence to suggest the image is linked to local legends about cardón cacti coming to life at night. Arrows pierce the figure's neck, chest, and groin. There are also a couple of vulva drawings and a painting of a fish skeleton, thought to be the only such work in Baja; other fish paintings in Baja appear to represent whole fish.

To reach the second group of murals you must ford the river several more times. Depending on river height, at least one crossing requires a swim of up to 100 meters through a narrow stone gorge. For many people this is the high point of the trip. The water is safe to swim in but should be boiled or treated before drinking. The canyon scenery is spectacular, with cactus and wild fig trees clinging to the sides of high tuff (volcanic ash) cliffs.

The final site is reached by ascending a sloped canyon wall affording long views of the canyon, which splits in two here. The paintings at this site are neither as numerous nor as impressive as the first, but the hike/swim through the canyon makes it a worthwhile objective.

There are five guides in the Mulegé area licensed to lead this trip. Any of the hotels in town can arrange for a guide; the usual price is US$33 per person when using the guide's vehicle, US$25 per person with your own. High road clearance is required and a cache of spare parts is suggested. The fee usually includes a

swimming in Cañon La Trinidad

JOE CUMMINGS

simple lunch, sodas, and beer. Recommended guides include Salvador at Hotel Las Casitas, Chichu at Hotel Serenidad, and Kerry ("El Vikingo," the only gringo guide in town—and perhaps in all of Baja—licensed to lead visitors to prehistoric murals), who can usually be contacted through the Hotel Hacienda. Most tours include an interesting stop in the desert to learn about medicinal plants.

You can also drive to Rancho La Trinidad and arrange for someone at the ranch to take you to see the murals. Although this is much less expensive—no more than US$5 per person—the drive to the ranch involves several unsigned turns. Ask at one of the hotels for detailed directions. The turnoff for the main road from Mexico 1, known locally as "Ice House Road" for the ice factory alongside it, is just a few miles north of Mulegé; it's signed San Estanislao. Continue following signs to San Estanislao until you see a sign for La Trinidad.

San Borjitas: This site has been known to local residents since mission times; Leon Diguet visited San Borjitas in the 1890s, Erle Stanley Gardner in the 1960s, Harry Crosby in the 1970s. To get there from Mulegé, drive north on Mexico 1 to the Km 157 marker near Palo Verde at the turnoff for Punta Chivato, then take the dirt road east into the sierra. This route is appropriate for high-clearance vehicles only. Keep left at all forks, pass two abandoned ranchos (when you reach a gate, go through it and close it after you), and continue until you arrive at Rancho Las Tinajas (about 30 km/18.5 miles from the highway), where you should be able to hire a guide. This area is also known as Cerro Gordo. From Las Tinajas, it's a two-hour mule ride and walk to the cave.

The paintings at San Borjitas are unique among Baja rock-art schools in several respects: at least a dozen of the more than 50 large *monos* (human figures) in the rock shelter are apparently transfixed with arrows; some exhibit male genitalia; and about a dozen are filled in with longitudinal stripes. Colors employed at San Borjitas include black, red, ocher, gray, white, and combinations of all five, painted in monocolor, bicolor, and checkerboard patterns. Along the tuff side walls of the cave is a collection of petroglyphs (rock carvings) depicting female genitalia; the fire-blackened back wall shows fish and deer.

Punta Chivato

At the north end of Bahía Santa Inés, 48 km (30 miles) northeast of Mulegé (24 km north via Mexico 1, then another 20 km/13 miles east on a graded, unpaved road), is the secluded but popular **Punta Chivato Resort** (tel./fax 115-3-01-88, mailing address A.P. 18, Mulegé, BCS). The hotel has its own 1,219-meter (4,000-foot) airstrip (Unicom 122.8), boat ramp, small desert golf course, pool, and lovely nearby beaches. Large, attractive, and well-maintained rooms with a/c, fireplace, and private garden patio cost US$55 s/d facing the Sea of Cortez, US$45 s/d one row back. Extra adults are charged US$10, children US$5. The restaurant is quite good and overall service is excellent.

The resort also maintains a clean campground along a sandy cove a bit north of the hotel with pit toilets, showers, fresh water, trash receptacles, palapas, and soft boat launch for US$5 per day. The Islas Santa Inés lie just southeast of the point; fishing and diving excursions can be arranged.

Bahía Concepción

From this point south to the Cape Region, the Sea of Cortez and its many bays begin matching the tourist-brochure description of a "desert Polynesia." This huge bay, open to the north and sheltered on the east, has a string of sandy beaches along its west side and a number of small islands anchored in the middle—a perfect setting for anglers, small boaters, windsurfers, divers, and especially kayakers.

The entire bay, recently declared a national marine preserve, is reportedly one of the cleanest marine bay systems in the world. It's home to an amazing variety of marinelife, from blue-footed boobies and magnificent frigates to whales, porpoises, and abundant shellfish. Commercial fishing is prohibited within the bay—if you spot any fishing boats working in Concepción and feel like doing something about it, report your sighting to Mulegé authorities immediately. If you plan to sail a yacht into the bay, please refrain from dumping the head until north of Punta Concepción.

Mexico 1 parallels the west bayshore, providing inspiring views of the blue-green bay and conical, flat-topped islands to the east and Sierra Coyote peaks to the west, as well as access to several beaches and coves along the way.

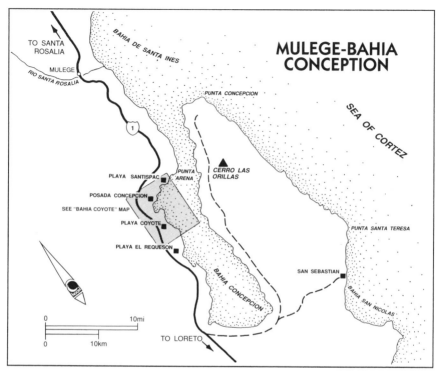

MULEGE-BAHIA CONCEPTION

© MOON PUBLICATIONS, INC.

Most of the beaches are ejido lands where the local ejidatarios collect camping fees of US$3-5, regardless of whether you're parking a motor home or sleeping on the sand.

Beaches: Bahía Concepción attracts a loyal following of Canadians, Mexicans, Americans, and Europeans who return year after year to the beaches—staying in tents, palapa huts, and motor homes—for intervals ranging from two weeks to six months. So far only one permanent settlement, Posada Concepción, has developed along the bayshore. Now that the bay is a national preserve, perhaps it will be the last.

For the most part Concepción's sandiest beaches are concentrated along the northwest shore in a bay subsystem sometimes called Bahía Coyote (not to be confused with Playa Coyote, near Bahía Coyote's south end).

At the top of the bay's western shore, a signed, four-km (2.5-mile) road leads to **Punta Arena,** a sandy, rather windy point with a string of palapas and palapa huts—many of them permanent homes—for US$5 a night. This area offers the best windsurfing along the bay's west shore; the winds also make this one of the more comfortable camping beaches in the summertime. The turnoff for Punta Arena is 13.2 km (8.2 miles) from the Motel Serenidad turnoff from Mexico 1.

Farther south (entrance between Km 115 and 114) is the largest and most popular beach, **Playa Santispac** (Km 118), where tent and trailer camping next to shade palapas is available for US$5 per vehicle per night. This is the most developed camping beach along the bay, and many sites are occupied year-round by motor homes. Satellite dishes and solar batteries are common. Facilities include toilets, showers, and the famous **Ana's Restaurant Bar,** where fresh-baked goods, meals, and beverages are available daily. As Baja Tropicales is headquartered at the north end of Santispac, this is a popular put-in point for kayakers. You can reach several nearby islands by small boat or kayak, including **San Ramón, Liebre, Pitahaya** (Luz), and **Blanca.** Between Liebre and Pitahaya is a reef known as **Arrecife Pelicanos,** or Pelican Reef. On the point at the south end of Santispac are a couple of thermal springs.

Posada Concepción, access at Km 112, is a somewhat congested development of houses and trailer homes along Playa Concepción, offering a market and tennis courts. Full-hookup slots, when vacant, cost US$10. You can sometimes rent houses on **Punta Tordillo,** a steep, rocky point southeast of the beach community; inquire at Posada Concepción.

About 50 meters south of the Posada Concepción entrance, an 800-meter (half-mile), bumpy, narrow road unsuitable for larger RVs parallels the highway and provides access to other beaches. Follow the road over some hills to **Playa Escondida,** a scenic, uncrowded beach with a few palapa campsites for US$3 a day. The clamming is very good here and as a result the beach is rather shelly.

Farther south is **Playa Los Cocos,** at Km 111, with one of the prettiest beaches along this section of the bay; the limestone in the surrounding cliffs lends a turquoise hue to the bay. Camping is permitted here for US$4; the only facilities are a few two- and three-sided, well-spaced palapas and pit toilets. Behind the beach is a small, pristine lagoon lined with mangrove.

Two kilometers farther along the shore is **Playa El Burro,** a public beach with palapas and trash barrels next to a scrappy-looking residential section. Separated by **Punta Cola de Ballena** ("Whale's Tail Point") is the adjacent **Playa Coyote,** with a campground/RV park (pit toilets, well-spaced palapas, showers, drinking water) that charges US$5 a vehicle. The **Restaurant Estrella del Mar,** opposite Playa Coyote, serves breakfast, lunch, and dinner.

On the opposite (west) side of the highway from Playa El Burro is an arroyo containing hundreds of prehistoric **petroglyphs.** This site may have been sacred to Indians in the area because of a large, horizontal "bell rock" lying in the arroyo; when struck with a stone or hard stick, the rock resonates with a bell-like tone. A few hundred meters east of Playa Coyote is **Isla Bargo** (Coyote Island), an elbow-shaped island with a sandy beach suitable for camping in the "elbow."

Around 2.4 nautical km (1.5 nautical miles) southeast of Playa Coyote is the idyllic **Playa Santa Bárbara,** also known as "Honeymoon Cove." This is a sandy, palm-fringed inlet accessible only by boat. Santa Bárbara makes an excellent kayak camp for those paddling the bay circuit.

After El Coyote, Mexico 1 veers away from the coast for a short distance, returning at Km 94.5 to **Playa Buenaventura,** a half-sand, half-rock beach with a market, restaurant/bar, showers, toilets, and well-kept palapas, including walled palapas on short stilts with cots that cost US$15 per night—a bit exorbitant for this beach. Ordinary palapa sites are US$5.

A kilometer or so farther south is the nicer **Playa El Requesón.** Tent and RV camping (pit toilets, palapas, no drinking water) is permitted along the broad, sandy beach here for US$3 per vehicle; at the north end a sandbar connects the shore with Isla El Requesón, forming sheltered coves on either side.

South of Requesón the bayshore becomes a bit rocky and swampy. **Península Concepción,** on the east side of the bay, is visited less than the western shore because access requires a sturdy, high-clearance vehicle, preferably with 4WD. Although there are plenty of camping areas along the peninsula's usually deserted bayshore, none have toilet or water facilities. The 60-km (37-mile) road north along the bayshore ends just southeast of Punta Concepción at an abandoned manganese mine. The beaches and coves of Península Concepción are best visited by boat from Punta Arena, west across the bay. The access road for Punta Arena branches off Mexico 1 at Km 118.

Kayaking: Scalloped with sandy beaches, dotted with islands, and protected from winds on three sides, Concepción is the perfect Sea of Cortez kayaking destination. While many other Baja kayaking spots may be blown out several months per year, kayakers in Concepción typically lose less than a cumulative two weeks—spread out over a year—to high winds. **Baja Tropicales,** based at palapa number seven on Playa Santispac toward the north end of the beach, rents open- and closed-topped kayaks for US$30 per day; less for multi-day rentals. The American couple who run the concession also lead very well-organized paddle-and-

JOE CUMMINGS

open top kayaks for rent in Bahía Concepción

snorkel tours of Bahía Concepción that include basic kayaking instructions, no-roll, open-top kayaks, snorkeling equipment, a visit to at least one nearby island, informative descriptions of flora and fauna, a snorkeling stop, and a lunch of fresh clams and beer. The kayakers themselves gather the clams (*chinitas* and *chocolates*) from the sandy bay bottom while snorkeling.

Participants meet at Playa Santispac at 0800 and finish lunch by around 1430. The fee for the trip is US$38.50 per person, including federal tax. Other kayaking programs offered include moonlight paddles, Río Mulegé explorations, and multi-day trips between the Mulegé estuary and Caleta San Lucas, as well as to nearby islands. A typical six-day trip costs US$275-300 per person, including experienced guides and all kayaking and snorkeling gear; paddlers contribute to a common food kitty and prepare meals together along the way. Tropicales, incidentally, is the only Baja kayaking concession that runs year-round. You can make reservations through Hotel Las Casitas in Mulegé or by calling or writing Baja Tropicales (tel. 115-3-00-19, fax 115-3-03-40, A.P. 60 Mulegé, BCS, 23900).

San Isidro-La Purísima-Comondú

Southeast of Mulegé lies a series of volcanic valleys, isolated from the rest of Baja California Sur by the rugged Sierra de la Gigante, that supports the historic farm/ranch communities of San Isidro, La Purísima, and Comondú. Although a journey to this region is easiest via the paved and gravel roads heading north from Cd. Insurgentes, the road from Mexico 1, from a point south of Bahía Concepción, is shorter and more scenic.

The turnoff for this rough byway into Old Baja branches west from Mexico 1 just below the Km 60 marker, 75 km (47 miles) south of Mulegé. The first 18 km (11.5 miles) is graded, threading through a series of steep-walled arroyos before meeting a four-way junction.

Left is an unpaved, ungraded, 40-km (25-mile) road southwest to San José de Comondú, the larger of the two villages comprising Comondú. The second half of the Comondú road is very rough and features steep grades; except for 4WD vehicles, a better approach would be from San Isidro to the northwest or La Poza Grande to the southwest.

The road to the right at the four-way junction is abandoned. Take the unpaved, ungraded road straight ahead to arrive, via a series of switchbacks into Valle de la Purísima, at **San Isidro** (37 km/23 miles west of the junction). San Isidro (pop. 1,500) offers rustic accommodations, a café, clinic, market, and drinking water, but most visitors continue another five km (three miles) west to the slightly larger **La Purísima.**

Set amidst ponds, date, citrus, and mango orchards, surrounded by high volcanic cliffs, and backed by a sloped butte (El Pilón), La Purísima represents the quintessential interior Baja settlement. Originally established as a mission community in 1719, the village was abandoned in 1822 and revived in the late 19th century by Mexican farmers. The ruins of Misión de la Purísima Concepción, incorporated into a private residence, lie several kilometers north of the village,

Before the completion of Mexico 1, Todos Santos, San Ignacio, and Mulegé must have resembled this place. If a second highway along the east side of the peninsula, as proposed by a La Paz consortium, becomes a reality, it will most likely pass just west of here. Facilities in La Purísima include gasoline (probably Nova and diesel only), guesthouse accommodations, post office, market (with ice), auto parts store, drinking water, and medical clinic. Following the late summer rains, it's possible to canoe or kayak—with a few portages—the Arroyo de la Purísima west to the Pacific Ocean at Punta San Gregorio. A 47.8-km (27.9-mile) graded road leads west and then north to Bahía San Juanico, a little-known surfing destination; from San Juanico another graded road heads northwest to Laguna San Ignacio.

The twin communities of **San José de Comondú** and **San Miguel de Comondú** (known collectively as "Comondú") lie 23 km (14.5 miles) southeast of San Isidro via an unpaved, ungraded road. The well-watered, 11-km-long (seven-mile) Arroyo Comondú, wedged between barren volcanic mesas, produces dates, figs, citrus, corn, grapes, sugarcane, and a variety of vegetables. A small plaza in San José is surrounded by stone and adobe buildings, including a surviving Jesuit missionary house from Misión San José de Comondú (1737-1827), now used as a church. A church bell dating to 1708 is on display next to the edifice.

San Miguel de Comondú, about three km (two miles) west of San José, was originally

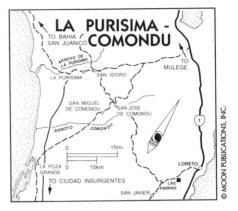

the site of a **capilla de visita** (visiting chapel). Locally grown sugarcane is still processed in San Miguel using traditional donkey-powered presses. Although smaller than San José, the village offers more local services because it's on the road southwest to Cd. Insurgentes. San Miguel has gasoline, a post and telegraph office, and a general store; drinking water is available at either village.

One of the best times of year for a Comondú visit is on the feast day for San Miguel (29 September), when tiny San Miguel de Comondú bursts with music and dancing.

LORETO

At first sight, it's difficult to believe this unassuming seaside town of 10,000 was the first European settlement in the Californias, and served as the Californias' secular and religious capital for 132 years. Superseded by La Paz following an 1829 hurricane, Loreto all but vanished for three-quarters of a century, until Mexican fishermen again began frequenting the area. As word of the prolific fisheries spread, a handful of North American anglers started flying to Loreto fish camps in private planes.

Although Loreto never regained its former glory, the 1973 completion of the Transpeninsular Highway finally brought the area within range of the average tourist. Today Loreto is part of a 27-km (17-mile) coastal segment, including **Nopoló** and **Puerto Escondido** (soon to be renamed **Puerto Loreto**), slated by the Mexican government for development as a major tourist resort. In the town itself, a restored cobblestone plaza adjoins the historic mission church and museum, and a new malecón has transformed the old seawall into a picturesque promenade. A small marina with a concrete boat ramp was recently completed at the north end of the malecón.

Offshore fishing remains the principal tourist attraction. Other major assets include an international airport and a world-class tennis center; recent additions include an 18-hole golf course at Nopoló and a recreational marina at Puerto Escondido. Not entirely reliant on tourism, Loreto

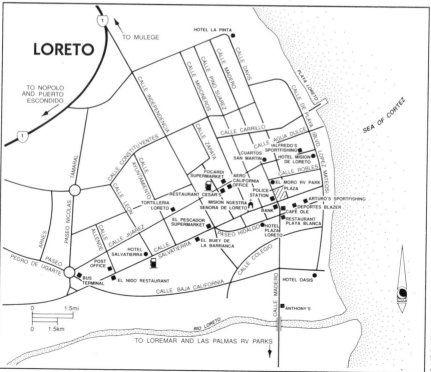

LORETO

TO MULEGE
HOTEL LA PINTA
TO NOPOLO AND PUERTO ESCONDIDO
SEA OF CORTEZ
© MOON PUBLICATIONS, INC.

also benefits from the saltworks on **Isla del Carmen,** opposite the peninsular coast, where 40,000 tons of salt per year are harvested from a salt basin formed by an extinct volcano crater. Other important local sources of livelihood include commercial fishing and agriculture.

In spite of FONATUR (Fondo Nacional de Fomento del Turismo, the National Foundation for Tourism Development) accomplishments, Loreto for the moment remains a somewhat sleepy port town when compared with La Paz or Los Cabos. The expected tourist invasion has yet to appear—a bonus for Baja visitors looking to get away from the crowd.

History

After several unsuccessful attempts over a 167-year period to establish a permanent Spanish settlement on the peninsula, Jesuit Padre Juan María Salvatierra founded the first mission in the Californias at Loreto in 1697. As the Loreto colony grew, it served as a base for California exploration and for the expansion of the mission system throughout the peninsula. Franciscan Padre Junípero Serra started his journey north to Alta California from here in 1769, eventually founding Alta California's first mission at San Diego Bay.

As the "mother of the California missions" and Spanish California capital, Loreto prospered until a hurricane destroyed much of the town in 1829. The mission church survived, but damage was so extensive, and fear of future hurricanes so high, the capital was moved from Loreto to La Paz the following year.

The town remained virtually deserted until the 1850s and 1860s, when a small group of intrepid immigrants resettled the area. Several among this second wave of settlers were English immigrants; a surprising number of Loreto residents today bear surnames such as Green, Davis, Cunningham, and Drew. Loreto remained a backwater, frontier village until after WW II, when it began developing a small commercial and sportfishing industry.

Misión Nuestra Señora De Loreto

The first chapel at Loreto was a large tent erected at the mouth of Arroyo San Dionísio in October 1697. The building of the mission church proper proceeded in three stages, beginning in 1699 with a simple rectangular chapel with pre-

sidio near the current site. The foundations for a larger church, with a cruciform floor plan, were laid in 1704, and the church as it now appears attained its basic form in 1752.

After weathering the 1829 hurricane and several subsequent earthquakes, the church was restored in 1976 and is currently in use as a place of worship. A sign over the massive front doors reads Head and Mother of the Missions of Lower and Upper California. Despite its history, however, it's not a particularly impressive Spanish mission church.

Of equal or greater interest is the adjoining **Museo de los Misiones,** a small but well-endowed historical and anthropological museum with exhibits on regional history and culture, Baja California mission history, and religious art. An anthropological library and small bookstore offer a variety of literature on Baja and Mexican history. The museum is open Mon.-Fri. 0900-1700. Admission is US$1.70.

On the first weekend of every September, the church and town cosponsor a Virgin of Loreto festival with plenty of feasting, music, and

Misión Nuestra Señora de Loreto

dancing. Another big fiesta is celebrated during the last week of October to commemorate the founding of the city. Activities for both events are centered around the plaza.

Nopoló-Puerto Loreto (Puerto Escondido)
Loreto—along with Cancún, Huatulco, Ixtapa, and Los Cabos—was slated for tourist development on the recommendation of a computer study carried out by the Mexican government during the oil-rich '70s. The prime criterion in Loreto's selection was the fact the area enjoys an average of 360 sunny days per year. Most of the completed and ongoing projects in the Loreto area have been entirely or partially funded by FONATUR, which has invited investors from around the world to participate in the area's future. Even gringos looking for an inexpensive vacation home in the Loreto area can receive FONATUR assistance in the form of low-interest, low down-payment loans.

The focus of most ongoing local development is **Nopoló,** eight km (five miles) south of Loreto. Nopoló consists of a hotel zone (so far only one hotel, the Loreto Inn, has opened), a recreation zone (tennis center and golf course), and a residential zone, linked by wide, palm-lined boulevards. The Loreto Inn is one of the most pleasant hotel stops along the entire peninsula, but what wasn't entered into the computer equation, or so it seems, is the lack of sandy beaches at Nopoló—although Playa Notri and Playa Juncalito, both several kilometers south, fill the bill. Another factor apparently not taken into consideration is the proximity of Loreto, already a destination in its own right. With taxi rides between the two locales costing a steep US$30, most people choose to stay in Loreto, where there's more to do.

Now that the marina at **Puerto Loreto/Escondido,** 16 km south of Loreto, is completed, FONATUR hopes to attract boaters; fishing and boating are, and always have been, Loreto's major strengths. Rumor has it the Paraíso-Radisson hotel chain may soon build at Puerto Escondido.

Accommodations
Cuartos San Martín, on Calle Juárez between Madero and Davis near the plaza, is the cheapest sleep in town. Spartan rooms with two or three beds, floor fans, and private bathrooms cost US$8.30.

Away from the waterfront is the slightly less basic **Hotel Salvatierra** (tel. 5-00-21) at Calle Salvatierra 125. Room rates vary according to occupancy rate but usually run US$15 s, US$23 d. The Salvatierra features a/c rooms with hot showers but little else in the way of amenities.

The new 29-room, neocolonial-style **Hotel Plaza Loreto** (tel. 5-02-80, 5-08-55) recently rose on Paseo Hidalgo a block from the mission church. During the hotel's first year of operation rates were only US$30 s/d—a bargain for clean, well-furnished rooms with hot water, a/c, and cable TV—but these rates may rise in 1994. A small cafetería-bar is attached.

At the north end of Calle de Playa (López Mateos), facing the sea, is the **Hotel Misión de Loreto** (tel. 5-00-48, mailing address A.P. 49, Loreto, BCS), with a pool, two restaurants, and a/c rooms surrounding a courtyard for US$37-42. Now that the malecón is finished, this is the classiest location in town—even if the rooms are rather ordinary.

A favorite among anglers, the **Hotel Oasis** (tel. 5-01-12, 5-02-11, fax 5-07-95, mailing address A.P. 17, Loreto, BCS) started as a fish camp many years ago but has since been transformed into a nicely landscaped, palapa-roofed hotel facing the Sea of Cortez. At the south end of Calle de la Playa (Blvd. López Mateos), the hotel's large, clean, a/c rooms cost US$40 per day without meals, US$68-90 with three meals. Facilities include a restaurant and bar, pool, tennis court, and the hotel's own sportfishing fleet.

Farther north along the waterfront, on Calle Davis, the **Hotel La Pinta** (tel. 5-00-25, 800-336-5454 in the U.S.) offers spacious a/c rooms with sea views and terraces at US$55 s, US$60 d; a limited number of rooms are available for US$49. Facilities include a restaurant, bar, and pool.

Nopoló Hotels: The **Loreto Inn Hotel** (tel. 5-07-00, fax 5-03-77, 310-943-6233, fax 943-4078 in the U.S./Canada or toll-free 800-472-3394) is on Paseo Costero in Nopoló's hotel zone, eight km (five miles) south of Loreto. Formerly the Stouffer Presidente, the hotel is now owned by a French corporation with an interest in the harbor facilities at Puerto Loreto (Puerto Escondido).

Large, bilevel rooms come with separate sitting areas and all the amenities of an international-class hotel for just US$56 s/d. Rates may rise, however, once the new management begins filling the rooms. Set among spacious, immaculate,

(top) ruins, Misión San Fernando Velicatá; (bottom) city hall, San José del Cabo; (following page) Puerto Balandra

palm-shaded grounds, the hotel features a restaurant, outdoor café, bar, disco, two pools, and tennis courts. Also available: instruction and equipment for windsurfing, boating, and fishing. The Loreto Inn is the only hotel in the Loreto area with telephones in the guest rooms.

Although FONATUR hopes eventually to place several hotels in Nopoló's hotel zone, so far Loreto Inn is it. Most visitors prefer to stay in Loreto, where there's a selection of restaurants; taxi fares between Nopoló and Loreto are also rather prohibitive.

Puerto Loreto (Escondido) Hotels: The **Tripui Motel** (tel. 5-08-18, 512-749-6070 in the U.S.), part of the Tripui Resort complex 24 km (15 miles) south of Loreto, has rooms with a/c, TV, patios, and tiny showers for US$40. Facilities include a pool and tennis courts, with fishing charters available.

Camping and RV Parks: El Moro RV Park (tel. 5-05-42) on Calle Rosinda Robles just off Calle Davis between the plaza and the malecón offers full hookups and hot showers for US$10.

The popular, American-owned **Loremar RV Park** (tel. 5-07-11, A.P. 56, Loreto, BCS 23880), 1.5 km (a mile) south of town via Calle Madero, has full-hookup RV spaces for US$10 a night for two people and tent sites for US$8; beyond two per site, add US$3. Facilities include hot showers, laundry service, boat launch, and palapas along the waterfront. There are discounts for long-term stays.

Also in the vicinity is **Las Palmas RV Park** (tel. 5-02-02), with full hookups for US$10 a night, tents for US$4, laundry, and showers. In 1993-94 Las Palmas only opened Nov. 1-April 1.

Although officially prohibited, many folks still camp at Playa Juncalito, 22.5 km (14 miles) south of town, a small, brown-sand cove backed by date and Washington palms. North of Juncalito, toward Nopoló, you should be able to camp on the beach for free.

The trailer park at **Tripui Resort** (tel. 5-08-18, 512-749-6070 in the U.S.) in Puerto Loreto contains 129 "permanent" yearly spaces and only 31 overnight slots. A full-hookup slot costs US$12 a night for two people, plus US$5 for each additional person. Discounts for long-term stays are available. Facilities include boat launch, boat storage, pool, tennis, restaurant, bar, and grocery store. For reservations, call one of the numbers above or write Tripui Resort, A.P. 100, Loreto, BCS (or P.O. Box 839, Port Aransas, TX 78373).

Food

Loreto doesn't count among its attributes a great number of restaurants, but in those that do exist, quality is high. **Café Olé,** at Calle Madero 14 on the plaza, serves a variety of inexpensive breakfasts and lunches, including seafood omelettes, *huevos con nopales* (eggs with cactus), tacos and other antojitos, plus burgers, ice cream, and milkshakes. It's open 0700-2200 daily.

For more leisurely, atmospheric meals, one of the most popular places in town is palapa-roofed **Cesar's** (tel. 5-02-03), on Calle Juárez and Zapata. The house specialties are moderately priced and include fresh seafood, Caesar salads, and *carnes rojas* (barbecued steaks); the bar, to one side of the dining room, is one of Loreto's nicest. Open daily for lunch and dinner.

Restaurant Playa Blanca (tel. 5-04-28), Hidalgo and Madero, is a more casual spot with an upstairs, open-air dining area decorated with whale vertebrae, lacquered turtle shells, and other marine memorabilia. Prices are fair; breakfast is served. You can order food in the downstairs Bar Playa Blanca as well.

El Nido (tel. 5-02-84), at Calle Salvatierra 154, features the usual menu of mesquite-grilled steaks and seafood, but this restaurant is generally considered one of the better links in the Baja chain. Open daily for breakfast, lunch, and dinner.

Anthony's Casa de la Pizza, on Madero just north of the arroyo in the general vicinity of the Loremar and Las Palmas trailer parks, advertises "the world's worst pizza" and doubles as a sports/video bar. It's open daily 1000-2200.

Two small thatched-roof eateries on Calle Salvatierra east of El Pescador supermarket serve a variety of antojitos and breakfasts—**El Buey de la Barranca** and **La Fuente.** The latter also serves a few seafood dishes, including fish tacos.

Another good choice for quick, inexpensive snacks is **McLulu's,** a taco stand just west of Calle Colegio on Calle Salvatierra. McLulu's fish tacos are legendary; other offerings include tacos de carne asada, homemade chorizo, and *picadillo* (spicy meat-and-chile salad). Lulu, the cook, doesn't mind if you buy beer

SIERRA CEVICHE

Ceviche (sometimes spelled "cebiche" or "sibiche") is a seafood appetizer in which fish or shellfish is marinated in lime juice until "cooked." It's very popular throughout Baja and there are as many recipes as there are cooks—it can be a wonderful experience in one restaurant and a bad excuse for getting rid of fish scraps in another.

Since it's easy to make even while camping on the beach (no fire necessary), ceviche offers an excellent alternative to the usual fried, baked, or grilled fish dishes. One of the best fish to use for ceviche is the sierra, a common type of mackerel usually caught inshore/offshore; John Steinbeck, during his 1941 Sea of Cortez expedition, pronounced it "the most delicious fish of all." Other great candidates for ceviche are halibut, shark, shrimp, lobster, or just about any other fish whose flesh is not too dry. The oilier the better, since the lime juice counteracts the oil. Always use only the freshest fish available.

Recipe:
Serves four
$1/2$ pound fresh sierra fillets, thinly sliced
$1/2$ cup fresh lime juice
one avocado, peeled and cut
  into half-inch cubes
eight ripe, red cherry tomatoes cut in half
  (or one large ripe tomato)
one serrano chile, minced (or more if you want it
  really hot)
two tablespoons fresh cilantro leaves, minced
one tablespoon olive oil
$1/2$ teaspoon salt (optional)

Put the sliced sierra in a large bowl, mix with the lime juice, and marinate in a cooler for a half-hour. Drain; then gently toss the remaining ingredients. Best served with fresh tortilla chips (or spread over *tostadas,* whole fried corn tortillas) and cold cerveza.

---

at the nearby supermarket to drink while eating at her tables. Usually open in the afternoons and early evenings.

Groceries: Loreto has two supermarkets, one each on Calle Salvatierra **(El Pescador)** and Calle Juárez **(Focardi Supermarket). Tortillería Loreto,** on Calle Juárez between Ayuntamiento and Independencia, sells fresh tortillas as well as bolillos and Mexican pastries. A number of small tiendas and *ultramarinos* are scattered around town.

Sports And Recreation

Fishing: Although commercial gill-netting has to some extent affected Loreto's coastal fisheries, this section of the Sea of Cortez is still considered one of Baja's hottest sportfishing destinations, and the Mexican government is taking steps to keep commercial operations out of the area. Offshore fishing is best east of Isla del Carmen, where you'll find yellowtail and sierra in winter, dorado, snapper, cabrilla, grouper, tuna, sailfish, and marlin in summer. Inshore fishing, between Loreto and Isla del Carmen (particularly at the north end of Carmen), nets smaller yellowtail, snapper, white seabass, and, in spring, roosterfish.

Fishing trips can be arranged at the Oasis, Misión, La Pinta, and Loreto Inn hotels, or at one of the sportfishing outfits in town. **Arturo** (near Restaurant Playa Blanca on Calle Madero) and **Alfredo's** (tel. 5-01-65, fax 5-05-90, Calle Juárez and Callejón 2) are two of the oldest sportfishing fleets. The going rate for a panga trip is US$80-90 per day for up to three anglers. Fishing cruisers run US$250-350.

Boating: You can launch small boats at the north end of the malecón, at the Loremar RV Park, or farther south at Playa Juncalito and Puerto Loreto (more commonly known as Puerto Escondido). Jaunts to Isla del Carmen (18 km from Loreto, eight km from Puerto Escondido) are popular; the island has several good beaches, with the best anchorages at Puerto Balandra and Bahía Marquer on the island's west shore or at Bahía Salinas on the east.

Any of the hotels that organize fishing trips can arrange pangas by the day. You can also rent pangas at the harbor at the north end of Loreto's waterfront. The Loreto Inn Hotel rents Hobie catamarans for fun sailing. **C & C Ground Services** (tel./fax 5-01-51, mailing address P.O. Box 1, Loreto, BCS) organizes picnic trips to Isla del Carmen and Isla Coronado beaches, as well as whalewatching excursions for blues, humpbacks, and fins.

Sea cruisers generally anchor at the sheltered, deep-water marina at Puerto Escondido. With a COTP office recently established at the marina, Puerto Escondido became an official marine entry point.

Kayakers can put in at Loreto for excursions to Isla Coronado or the north end of Isla Carmen. For the southern or eastern shores of Isla Carmen, as well as for Isla Danzante and Los Candeleros, Puerto Escondido is the most convenient starting point. Setting out from Puerto Escondido, the ambitious, experienced sea kayaker can paddle out to Isla Monserrate or even Isla Santa Catalina. A logical run begins at Puerto Escondido, then paddle south with the currents to Bahía Agua Verde (described in "Vicinity of Loreto") by way of Danzante (13 km/eight miles) and Monserrate (24 km/15 miles). You can rent open-top kayaks at **Deportes Blazer** (see "Diving").

Diving: The islands off Loreto's coastline offer numerous diving opportunities, including rock reefs, seamounts, and underwater caves. The best local diving areas include the north end of Isla Coronado; the north and east shores of Isla del Carmen; the 120-foot sunken freighter near del Carmen's Bahía Salinas; Playa Juncalito, with its wreckage of a small, twin-engine plane; and the smaller islands of Monserrate, Santa Catalina, and Danzante (northern and eastern shores). South of Isla Danzante is a string of granite islets called Los Candeleros; the vertical walls make an awesome underwater sight.

You can arrange guided excursions, scuba equipment rentals, and air fills through **Deportes Blazer** (tel. 5-00-06), Paseo Hidalgo 18.

Tennis: The **Loreto Tennis Center** (tel. 5-04-08), attached to the Loreto Inn Hotel, has nine lighted courts, a clubhouse, bar, and pro shop; John McEnroe is a touring pro for the center. Loreto Inn hotel guests may use the courts at no charge; non-hotel guests pay a court fee of US$3 during the day, US$5 after dark.

Golf: The 18-hole **Campo de Golf Loreto** at Nopoló is finally completed and it's a beauty. So far few tourists seem to know about the place, making it probably the least crowded coastal golf course in North America.

Information And Services
Tourist Office: FONATUR (tel. 5-06-50) runs an office in Nopoló where you can pick up tourist info on the area.

Post and Telephone: On the plaza sit the post office, a Bancomer (exchange services Mon.-Fri. 0830-1100 only), and a public phone with long-distance service. There is also a public phone with long-distance service inside Mercado El Pescador. The area code for Loreto, Nopoló, and Cd. Constitución is 113.

Travel Agencies: Viajes Pedrin (tel. 5-02-04), a travel agency on Paseo Hidalgo, can book air tickets, bus tickets, and hotel reservations. **Loretours** (tel. 5-00-88) on Blvd. López Mateos next to the Hotel Misión, offers these same services as well as car rentals, fishing excursions, dive trips, and tours to San Javier.

Transport
Air: Aero California (tel. 5-05-00, 5-05-66), currently the only international airline with service to Loreto, schedules daily nonstop flights from Los Angeles and La Paz. The airline has an office in town at Calle Juárez and Zapata.

An official port of entry, the airport features a 2,200-meter (7,200-foot) paved runway (Unicom 118.4). Aviation fuel is usually available.

Bus: Loreto's bus terminal sits at the junction of Paseo Ugarte, Calle Juárez, and Calle Salvatierra. Aguila and ABC operate several first-class buses daily to Mulegé (US$5), Santa Rosalía (US$US$7), San Ignacio (US$9.30), Guerrero Negro (US$14) San Quintín (US$30), Ensenada (US$38), Tijuana (US$42), Cd. Insurgentes (US$4.60), Cd. Constitución (US$5.30), and La Paz (US$13.30). Departures change frequently but there are usually six buses per day in either direction.

Taxis: Loreto may have the most expensive taxi fleet in all of Baja. Taxis between Loreto and Nopoló cost US$30; Loreto-Puerto Escondido costs US$40; a trip to the airport is US$12. In town you shouldn't pay more than US$4; walking is free and the town isn't very large.

Car Rental: Cars and jeeps can be rented through the **Thrifty** office (tel. 3-07-00, ex. 430) at the Loreto Inn Hotel in Nopoló or at the airport. Rates are anything but thrifty but it's the only game in town.

Loreto has several mechanics and auto parts shops.

VICINITY OF LORETO

Las Parras-San Javier

The 36-km (22-mile) road to San Javier, one of Baja's most scenic interior drives, is a section of the old Camino Real ("Royal Road") used by Spanish missionaries and explorers. Access to the road is off Mexico 1 at Km 118, south of Loreto. Only drivers with sturdy, high-clearance vehicles should attempt the trip, as surfaces are stony and, except in the driest years, it's necessary to ford a winding stream in several places. Following heavy rains, this road shouldn't be driven at all for a few days, unless you have a 4WD vehicle and are skilled at driving through mud. Grades approach 15% in places; the average driving time is two hours.

Along the way, the road winds around Cerro La Gigantica (1,490 meters/4,885 feet), passing several palm oases hidden away in narrow arroyos, *zalates* (wild fig trees) clinging to cliffs, and other rewarding vignettes. **Rancho Las Parras**—an oasis settlement consisting of a stone chapel, small dam, and orchards of grape, olives, figs, and citrus—appears about midway to the mission (20 km/12.4 miles from Mexico 1) in the Arroyo de Las Parras. This arroyo provided water and a way into the Sierra de la Giganta for Indians and later missionaries; in the vicinity are a number of old Indian trails and Indian rock art.

About 9.2 km (six miles) beyond Las Parras, the San Javier road meets a lesser branch road leading 42 km (26 miles) northwest to Comondú. This route to Comondú is in poor condition, with grades of 20-23%, and hence is recommended only for 4WD vehicles.

San Javier, a village of thatched-roof, stone houses and around 300 inhabitants, contains one of the peninsula's most well-preserved Jesuit mission churches. Misión San Francisco Xavier de Viggé-Biaundó, nowadays simply called Misión San Javier, was originally founded by Padre Francisco Píccolo in 1699, two years after the establishment of the peninsula's first mission in Loreto. In 1701, Padre Juan de Ugarte arrived at Arroyo de San Javier from Mexico City, bringing with him a number of seeds and seedlings for the Californias' first cultivated fruit orchards. Many of the mission varieties of grapes, olives, figs, oranges, and lemons now grown throughout the

Californias are descended from Ugarte's original San Javier plantings.

To make room for the orchards, the mission church was moved to its current site in 1720 and rebuilt by Padre Miguel del Barco sometime between 1741 and 1768. Although the church facade is not as ornate as that of Misión San Ignacio to the north, the side windows are splendid—no two are alike. The gilded altar and statuary inside the church were probably transported from Mexico City by boat and burro in the mid-1700s; two of the bells in the church tower are dated 1761, the third 1803.

A good time to visit is during the week leading to 3 December, San Javier's patron saint day. Pilgrims sometimes number in the hundreds.

Practicalities: The only amenities in the village are a couple of small tiendas with beverages and limited foodstuffs. For those without their own vehicles, or without the right kind of vehicle, it's possible to arrange a car and driver from Loreto to San Javier for about US$35. Inquire at any Loreto hotel.

Primer Agua

The graded, unpaved road to Primer Agua, a FONATUR-owned palm oasis, begins at Km 114 on Mexico 1. A road sign is posted just south of a highly visible electric transformer station next to the highway. The Primer Agua road, a bit better than the San Javier road, reaches the oasis after 6.5 km (four miles); ordinary passenger vehicles can make it in dry weather. This fenced-off section of arroyo, a branch of Arroyo de San Javier, serves as a nursery for propagating plants to be used at nearby FONATUR projects. Recently a picnic area, complete with tables and barbecue grills, opened near a natural pool at the bottom of the arroyo. If the gate to the facility is locked—and it sometimes is, even in the middle of the day—a hike into nonfenced sections of the arroyo, west of the orchards, is still worthwhile. The FONATUR office in Nopoló says that, if given a day's notice, it will provide a visit permit and ensure that the park is open.

Bahía Agua Verde

Between Km 64 and 63, where Mexico 1 veers inland from the Cortez coast, a part-graded, part-ungraded, gravel-and-dirt road heads southeast for 40 km (24 miles) to the fish camp of

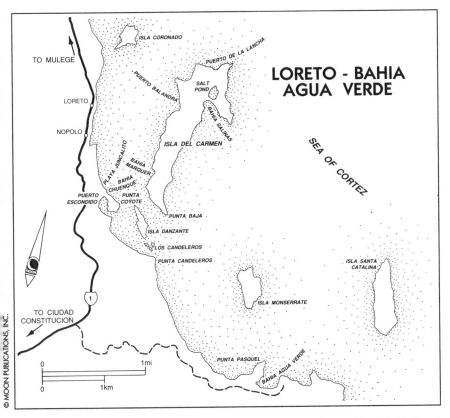

LORETO - BAHIA AGUA VERDE

Agua Verde. The roadbed is steep and winding in places, not at all suitable for trailers or motor homes. As the road approaches Agua Verde, it flattens out and divides into several tracks running to five small coves scalloped into the bayshore. The turquoise waters are framed by Islas Monserrate and Santa Catalina to the north and east, and hillsides of palo verde, palo blanco, cardón, palm, and mesquite to the west. Very picturesque.

Local residents make a living herding goats, fishing for small shark (*cazón*), or servicing a steady trickle of outside visitors who brave the road in from Mexico 1. Rocky bayshore campsites, with palapas, cost US$3-5. **Rancho El Carricalito,** a goat ranch, boards visitors for a few dollars a night and can also provide meals. Panga fishing trips can be arranged for US$50-60 a day.

Isla Santa Catalina, 17.5 km (11 miles) east of Isla Monserrate, is known for its endemic "rattleless rattlesnake" (*Crotalus catalinensis*), and for the largest barrel cactus species in Baja, *Ferocactus diguettii,* named for French naturalist Leon Diguet. Individuals of this variety may reach four meters (13 feet) in height and a meter (3.28 feet) in diameter. *Ferocactus diguettii* is also found on Islas Cerralvo, Monserrate, Danzante, and del Carmen.

Ciudad Insurgentes

At Cd. Insurgentes (pop. 8,500), the kilometer marker countdown from Santa Rosalía reaches Km 0 and starts over again at Km 236. The town itself has little to recommend it except as a fuel and food stop or as a transit point for the "easy" road north to La Purísima (102 km/61 miles) and

Comondú (101 km/60.5 miles). About a third of the road is paved; the remainder is graded as far as La Purísima and San Miguel de Comondú.

From La Purísima, an ungraded road leads northwest 48 km (30 miles) to **Bahía San Juanico** on the Pacific coast. Gas and limited supplies are available at San Juanico. Fishing is said to be good here, and surfers can catch a great point break during summer swells. Winter surfing isn't too shabby either. The road continues north from San Juanico all the way to San Ignacio via Laguna San Ignacio. Portions of the road between San Juanico and Laguna San Ignacio require 4WD vehicles and skilled driving.

CIUDAD CONSTITUCION

Even though it has more hotels than any other town between Santa Rosalía and La Paz, few Baja travelers stop over in Cd. Constitución (pop. 45,000), the capital of Município de Comondú and the second-largest population center in Baja California Sur. Founded in the '60s to serve as a market center for the irrigated Llano Magdalena ("Magdalena Plain") agricultural basin, the town features two PEMEX stations, three banks, three bicycle shops, supermarkets (including Conasuper and Tienda ISSSTE), a hospital, an Aero California office, panaderías, tortillerías, auto shops, and a number of other small businesses.

Accommodations
Of the nine hotels in town, the best value is the clean and friendly **Hotel Conchita** (tel. 2-02-66), Blvd. Olachea and Hidalgo. Air conditioned rooms with phones and color TV cost only US$16 s and US$24 d. Nearby, the **Maribel Hotel** (tel. 2-01-55), next to Banco Internacional on Blvd. Olachea at Victoria, offers similar rooms at US$26 s, US$30 d.

Other Cd. Constitución hotels include the **Hotel Conquistador** (tel. 2-25-25, Calle Bravo 161) at US$21 s and US$27 d, and the economical **Hotel Reforma** (tel. 2-09-08, Calle Obregón 125), US$15-18.

The **Campestre La Pila** RV park (tel. 2-05-62), south of town near the power plant, has full hookups, a pool, cold showers, and a picnic area for US$7 for two people, plus US$2 for each additional person.

Food
The main boulevard—part of Mexico 1—through Cd. Constitución is dotted with restaurants, *asaderos* (grills), and *taquerías*. In the northern part of town, before the turnoff for BCN 22 west to San Carlos, good choices along the boulevard include the **Dragón** (Chinese), **Rincón Jarocho** (seafood and antojitos), and **Super Pollo** (Sinaloa-style barbecued chicken).

Restaurant Queratana, at the center of town on the east side of the boulevard and within walking distance of the Maribel and Conchita hotels, features inexpensive *comidas corridas* and various *platillos típicos*. **Lonchería La Laguna,** north of the plaza on the main boulevard just north of Calle Olachea, serves tortas, tacos, chilaquiles, carne asada, and a decent cup of *café de olla.*

The Maribel and Conchita hotels each include restaurants open for breakfast, lunch, and dinner. Opposite Super Pollo on the boulevard is a supermarket; the town also offers several *tiendas de abarrotes* and *ultramarinos*.

Misión San Luis Gonzaga
Cd. Constitución is a convenient departure point for an excursion to this surviving mission settlement 42 km (26 miles) southeast of Mexico 1. The best of two secondary roads leading from Mexico 1 starts at Km 195 where a sign reads La Presa Iguajil. Founded in 1737 and rebuilt in 1751, the simple mission church is well-maintained by local ranchers and farmers. The surrounding arroyo is planted in figs, dates, pomegranates, citrus, grapes, and olives.

BAHIA MAGDALENA

This unique marine environment is only a 45-minute drive from Cd. Constitución, yet many transpeninsular voyagers pass it by. Where the flat Llano Magdalena has sunk lower than the Pacific, the ocean has intruded and created a string of barrier islands over 209 km (130 miles) long, separated from the peninsula by a series of shallow bays with an average depth of less than 18 meters (60 feet). Arroyos that sank under the Pacific have become *bocas* or "mouths" that let the sea in; these bocas now form channels between the barrier islands.

Starting at Boca de las Animas in the north,

the most prominent barrier islands are **Isla Santo Domingo, Isla Magdalena, Isla Santa Margarita,** and **Isla Creciente.** The largest of the bays between the islands and peninsula, **Bahía Magdalena** and **Bahía Almejas,** are linked by Canal Gaviota to form a vast, protected waterway—the best on Baja's Pacific coast for kayaking and windsurfing. Naturalists could spend a lifetime exploring the mangroves and estuaries along the eastern bayshores, which support an astounding variety of marine- and birdlife.

History
Because of the proximity of Bahía Magdalena's natural harbor to the fertile Llano Magdalena, several groups of colonists attempted to settle the coastal plains here. In 1879 the Chartered Company of Lower California, an American land syndicate, settled 5,000 Americans along the bayshore. For a time the colony made money harvesting orchilla, a lichen growing on plants on the Llano Magdalena rendered for use as a commercial dye. The introduction of synthetic dyes killed the orchilla industry, and the colony along with it.

The shore remained unpopulated throughout the first half of this century except for the occasional visit by Bajacalifornio anglers and a few unplanned visits by passing mariners. Several ships foundered on the barrier islands, including the famous steamer *Independence* in 1853. Of the 400 passengers aboard, 150 perished in fires on the ship or by drowning after jumping into the breakers.

In 1920, the U.S. submarine *H-1* ran aground on Isla Santa Margarita. What the sub was doing in Mexican waters—at a time when relations between the two countries were tense—has never come to light. Although all but four of the crew were rescued by a passing vessel, the sub was mysteriously looted of all logs and other classified material before U.S. Navy rescue ships could approach it; the Navy scuttled the sub at a depth of nine fathoms just off the island coast and erased virtually all records of its existence. More submarine lore: during WW II, Japanese submarines used Bahía Magdalena as a hiding place. Max Miller, author of *Land Where Time Stands Still,* spotted a Japanese sub in the bay when he made an overland journey to the edge of the Llano Magdalena in 1941.

In the '60s, after Mexico recovered full own-

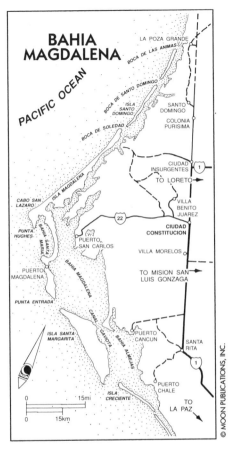

ership of the Llano Magdalena basin from foreign investors, the valley was irrigated and farmers began moving in. The harbor settlement of **Puerto San Carlos** soon developed as a relay point for the shipping of agricultural products, principally cotton and alfalfa, from the plains to mainland Mexico and abroad.

Puerto San Carlos
From Cd. Constitución, paved highway BCN 22 leads west 57 km (34 miles), then crosses a causeway onto a small hooked peninsula. Mangroves fringe the peninsula; a long wharf stretches from the western shore to the only other deepwater port besides Ensenada on the Pacific

coast. Often simply called San Carlos, this small port town of 5,000 residents includes a PEMEX station, tiendas, a café, and COTP, customs, immigration, and fishery offices. The **Hotel Las Brisas** (tel. 6-01-52), **Hotel Marlín** (tel. 6-01-10), and **Motel Palmar** (tel. 6-00-35) offer basic rooms; camping and RV parking at the north and south ends of the small peninsula costs around US$4 per vehicle. The most developed is the southern camp, **Magdalena Fishing Village.**

Sports and Recreation

Boating: Trailered or cartopped boats can be launched from a concrete boat ramp in San Carlos; you can easily launch pangas from the beach. Other launching points for small boats or kayaks are **Puerto López Mateos** to the north (reached via Cd. Insurgentes), **Puerto Cancun** to the south (accessible from Mexico 1 at Km 173), and **Puerto Chale** (via Santa Rita, Km 157, Mexico 1).

Fishing: The bay fisheries provide steady sportfishing due to the relative lack of commercial fishing interests. Onshore catches, near the mangroves, include halibut, occasional yellowtail, red bass (mangrove snapper), corvina, and snook. Farther out in the bay, anglers take grouper, black bass, and yellowtail; offshore, beyond the 100-fathom line, are sailfish, marlin, dorado, wahoo, and giant seabass. Although most of these gamefish frequent the area in lesser or greater numbers year-round, July through November are generally the most productive fishing months. Best places to get live bait are the mackerel holes off Punta Entrada.

You can gather clams in the shallows of both bays, although Bahía Almejas lives up to its name with the most extensive clam grounds. In the latter bay, clamming is easiest at Puerto Cancún.

Windsurfing: Mag Bay, as gringo board-sailors usually refer to Bahía Magdalena, offers the best windsurfing on Baja California's Pacific coast. A strong year-round breeze, together with the relatively calm bay surface, create perfect conditions for novice and intermediate windsurfers; experienced wave-sailors can experiment at or near the bocas, where breakers and stronger winds increase the challenge.

A protected run of 88 km (52 miles) begins at Puerto López Mateos and ends at Puerto Cancún; you can lengthen this run to 113 km (70 miles) by staying in until Puerto Chale.

Whalewatching: During the annual gray whale migration, Jan.-March, the canals, bays, and bocas of the Bahía Magdalena complex are practically filled with the whales' undulating forms. Puerto López Mateos and San Carlos are the usual centers for whalewatching activities. Often you can spot grays from shore at Puerto López Mateos as they come and go via Boca de Soledad to the north; a public parking and viewing area lies north of the port's fish-processing plant. Pangeros offer two-hour boat tours from this area for US$25 per panga per hour; a panga can take up to five passengers.

While pregnant female grays venture into shallower parts of the bay for calving, males tend to loiter near bay entrances, where they cavort with other males and nonpregnant females, often breaching and spyhopping—but not "mating," as myth would have it. One of the best viewing spots is **Punta Entrada,** at the southern tip of Isla Magdalena, which forms the north end of the wide channel between Magdalena Bay and the Pacific. The island is only accessible by boat, with the best anchorage on the southeast side of the point, or via small plane (a landing strip is situated just north of Punta Entrada). You can camp at the fish camp near the tip or farther north near the village of **Puerto Magdalena.** A San Carlos pangero will drop you off on the island and pick you up the following day; the usual hourly rates apply.

You can book Magdalena Bay whalewatching tours in La Paz through several travel agencies, including **Turipaz** (tel./fax 112-5-47-77, Km 4, Carretera Transpeninsular, at El Cardón Trailer Park). The agency charges US$83 per person, including guide, boat, lunch, and roundtrip transport from La Paz.

During the whalewatching season, **Baja Expeditions** (tel. 619-581-3311, 800-843-6967, 2625 Garnet Ave., San Diego, CA 92109) offers five- and eight-day kayaking trips for US$750 and US$1,150 respectively. Rates include all gear, ground transport to and from La Paz, and meals.

Transport

The road to Puerto San Carlos (57 km/35 miles from Cd. Constitución), one of Baja California Sur's only official state highways, is an easy drive of less than an hour. Buses ply the

Cd. Constitución-Puerto San Carlos route several times daily for a fare of about US$1 per passenger.

El Cien-Punta Conejo

At Km 100, about midway between Cd. Constitución and La Paz, lies the tiny roadside settlement of El Cien ("One Hundred"). As a pit stop, El Cien offers the **Lonchería El 100**, a Conasupo, and a PEMEX station—the only one between Cd. Constitución and La Paz. A nearby fossil reef reportedly contains whale vertebrae and other marine skeletons; inquire at the loncheria for a guide.

Farther south at Km 80, a good dirt road branches west 19 km (12 miles) to **Punta El Conejo.** El Conejo ("The Rabbit") is well known among surfers for steady point breaks in both northwest and southwest swells. Near the coast, the road to El Conejo intersects a lesser dirt road heading south 17 km (12.5 miles) to another surfing spot, **Punta Marquez.** This road continues southward along the coast all the way to Todos Santos (124 km/77 miles from El Conejo), passing a number of good beach breaks. Recommended for 4WD vehicles only.

BOB RACE

CAPE REGION
LA PAZ AND EAST CAPE

Ensconced along the southeastern crescent of Baja's largest Sea of Cortez bay, La Paz is a city of 150,000 noted for its attractive *malecón* (waterfront) backed by swaying palms and pastel-colored buildings, splendid sunsets, easygoing pace, near-perfect climate, and the proximity of uncrowded beaches and islands. Many Baja travelers—Mexicans and gringos alike—cite La Paz ("Peace") as their favorite city on the peninsula; a few even go as far as to pronounce it their favorite in all of Mexico. Nowadays Cabo San Lucas, 221 km (137 miles) farther south, receives more attention than La Paz in the North American press, which suits La Paz fans fine since it means fewer tourists.

La Paz is also arguably Baja's most Mexican city due to the longtime influx of Mexican mainlanders and its status as the first major European settlement on the peninsula. Many *paceños* (La Paz natives) are descendants of mainlanders who sailed to La Paz to avoid the political turmoil of 19th and early 20th century mainland Mexico. It's not uncommon to meet more recent Mexican emigrés who have resettled in La Paz after becoming fed up with modern-day political machinations in Mexico City, Guadalajara, or Monterrey. Paceños are proud of the many ways in which their city lives up to its name.

For travelers and tourists, this city of around 180,000 offers a variety of accommodations and dining venues, well-stocked supermarkets, marine supplies, and a ferry terminal with daily departures for Mazatlán and Topolobampo across the Sea of Cortez. Traffic snarls are common in *el centro,* the downtown area, but can be avoided by using Blvd. Forjadores, a wide avenue skirting the southern section of the city. Along the bay, La Paz remains much as John Steinbeck described it in 1941:

La Paz grew in fascination as we approached. The square, iron-shuttered colonial houses stood up right in back of the beach with rows of beautiful trees in front of them. It is a lovely place. There is a broad promenade along the water lined with

THE PEARLS OF LA PAZ

Pearls develop from sand grains or other small particles that manage to get between an oyster's mantle and its shell. The oyster secretes a substance that cushions it from the irritation of the particle—if the grain moves freely during the secretion buildup, the pearl is more or less spherical; if it stays in one place or is embedded in the shell, it becomes a "baroque" pearl. Even when an oyster doesn't contain a pearl, the interior of the shell is valued for its rainbow luster, known as mother-of-pearl. Only particular mollusk varieties within the family Pteridae, found only in certain coastal areas off East Asia, Panama, and Baja California, can form pearls.

Pearl gathering in the New World goes back at least 7,000 years. When the Spanish found Indians along the Sea of Cortez coast wearing pearls and pearl shells as hair ornaments in the early 16th century, they quickly added pearls to the list of exploitable resources in Mexico. Finding the source of the luminescent, milky-white spheres—oyster beds—became a priority of marine expeditions off Mexico's west coast.

After a Spanish mutineer reported the presence of pearls in Bahía de la Paz in 1533, harvesting them became one of Cortés's primary interests in exploring Baja's lower Sea of Cortez coast. Between 1535, when Cortés finally managed to establish a temporary settlement at Bahía de la Paz, and 1697, when Jesuit padres began missionizing the Baja peninsula, untold thousands of pearls were harvested. The Jesuits, however, strongly objected to any secular exploitation of the peninsula, preferring to keep Baja within the domain of the Church. Hence during the mission period (1697-1768), pearling was restricted to sporadic illegal harvests; still, many pearls found their way to Europe, where they encrusted the robes of bishops and Spanish royalty.

In the mid-19th century, following the secularization of Baja missions, the Baja pearl industry was revived by *armadores* (entrepreneurs) who hired Yaqui divers from Sonora to scour the shallow bays, coves, and island shores between Mulegé and La Paz. The invention of diving suits in 1874 revolutionized pearling by allowing divers access to deeper waters. By 1889 the world pearling industry was dominated by Compañía Perlífera de Baja California, based in La Paz.

Intensive harvesting rapidly depleted the oysterbeds, and between 1936 and 1941 most of the remaining pearl oysters were wiped out by an unknown disease. Many La Paz residents today believe the disease was somehow introduced by the Japanese to eliminate Mexican competition in the pearl industry, but it's more likely the disease simply took advantage of an already weakened population.

The mystique of La Paz pearls continued long after the industry's demise. John Steinbeck based his novella *The Pearl* on a famous pearl story he heard while visiting La Paz in 1941.

---

benches, named for dead residents of the city, where one may rest oneself. . . .[A] cloud of delight hangs over the distant city from the time when it was the great pearl center of the world. . . . Guaymas is busier, they say, and Mazatlán gayer, but La Paz is antigua.

CLIMATE

The most pleasant time of year for a La Paz visit is mid-October through May, when days are balmy, evenings cool. In January, maximum temperatures average 22° C (72° F), minimum temperatures 14° C (57° F). Temperatures for July average 35° C (96° F) maximum, 24° C (75° F) minimum. Hot summer afternoons are somewhat moderated by the daily arrival of the *coromuel*, a strong onshore breeze that bedevils yachties trying to escape the harbor but cools down the rest of the population.

La Paz and vicinity average only around 15 cm (six inches) of rainfall per year, over half generally falling during the Aug.-Sept. *chubasco* (tropical storm) season. Full-fledged chubascos with gale-force winds actually reach La Paz only every couple of years. Most of the time the area receives only the remote influences of storms centered along mainland Mexico's lower west coast.

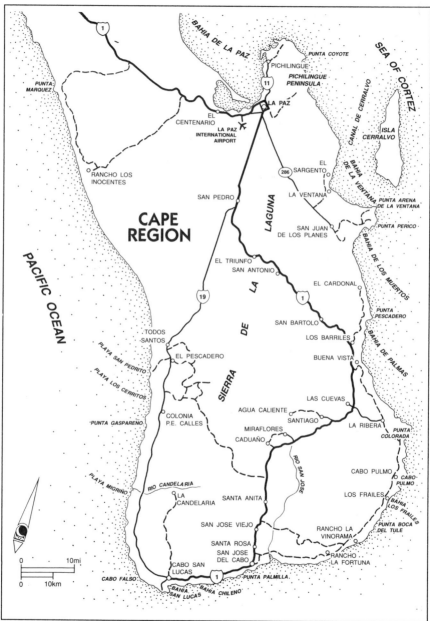

ENGLISH PIRATES ON THE SEA OF CORTEZ

Sir Francis Drake, Thomas Cavendish, William Dampier, Woodes Rogers, Thomas Dover, and other English privateers left behind a colorful Baja legacy. In spite of Spain's repeated attempts to colonize the peninsula, throughout the Spanish colonial period the pirates probably gained more wealth in the Californias than the Spanish themselves. For 250 years they plagued the Manila galleons off the coast of the Californias, finding the bays and lagoons of Baja's Cape Region perfect hiding places from which to launch attacks on treasure-laden ships.

In La Paz, using their knowledge of the strong breeze that blows into the harbor every summer afternoon, the pirates attacked Spanish galleons while the vessels were effectively trapped in the bay. Four centuries after the first Manila-Acapulco voyages, this afternoon wind is still known as *El Coromuel*, named for the Puritan Cromwells—father and son—who ruled successively as Lord Protectors of England.

The Disappearance Of The *Desire*

The most notorious of the Pacific privateers was Sir Thomas Cavendish, whose greatest feat of plunder occurred at Cabo San Lucas in 1587. There his two English vessels, *Desire* and *Content*, commandeered the Spanish galleon *Santa Ana* following a protracted sea battle. After looting the *Santa Ana's* cargo holds and setting its crew and passengers ashore, Cavendish set fire to the ship. The Spanish crew later retrieved the burned hulk, and restored the galleon for a return to Acapulco.

The plundered treasure, meanwhile, was divided between the *Desire* and *Content*. The ships set sail for England immediately, but during the first night of their triumphant voyage, the *Desire* disappeared. Cavendish reported in England that the captain and crew of the *Desire* must have scuttled the ship on a nearby island and disappeared with the loot. Neither the wreckage of the vessel nor the treasure was ever discovered; some historians speculate that at least part of the missing wealth remains buried near the Cape.

A Visit By Robinson Crusoe

In 1709, famed corsair Woodes Rogers landed in La Paz after rescuing a seaman who'd been marooned five years on a deserted island off Chile's coast. The rescued man was Alexander Selkirk, whose island sojourn became the inspiration for Daniel Defoe's *Robinson Crusoe*, published in 1719. Selkirk was aboard Rogers's *Dover* when the crew captured the Spanish galleon *Encarnación* off Cabo San Lucas in 1709; he served as sailing master on the ship's return voyage to England the following year.

HISTORY

Early Spanish Contact

When the Spanish first landed on the shores of Bahía de la Paz in the early 16th century, the area was inhabited by migrating bands of Guaycura and Pericú Indians. Hunters and gatherers, these Indian groups lived mostly on shellfish, small game, and wild plants. As artifacts on display at La Paz's Museum of Anthropology demonstrate, they were also skilled weavers and potters.

Into this peaceful scene entered the first European, a Basque mutineer named Fortún Jiménez who commandeered the Spanish ship *Concepción* on the Sea of Cortez in 1533. Originally under the command of Capt. Diego Becerra, the *Concepción* had been sent to explore the sea on behalf of Spain's most infamous conquistador,

Hernán Cortés. After executing the captain, Jiménez landed at Bahía de la Paz in early 1534, where he and 22 of his crew were killed by Indians while filling their water casks at a spring. The survivors sailed the *Concepción* back to the mainland, where the ship was immediately captured by Cortés's New Spain rival, Nuño Guzman. At least one crew member managed to escape and returned to Cortés with descriptions of a huge, beautiful bay filled with pearl-oyster beds.

Cortés himself landed at the northeast end of the bay, probably at Pichilingue, in May 1535, naming it Puerto de Santa Cruz. Cortés was able to effect a truce with local Indians, but his attempt at establishing a permanent Spanish colony lasted only through 1538, when the colonists were forced to abandon the peninsula due to supply problems.

The next Spaniard to visit the bay was famed explorer Sebastián Vizcaíno, who landed here in

1596 during his long voyage around the peninsula's perimeter and north to Alta California. Because he and his crew were treated so well by the Pericús, Vizcaíno named the bay Bahía de la Paz ("Bay of Peace").

Pirates And Colonization

Baja California remained free of Spaniards another 100 years before the successful establishment of a mission colony at Loreto to the north. By this time, English and Dutch pirates were plundering New Spain's Manila galleons as they returned from the Orient weighted down with gold, silks, and spices. One of the freebooters' favorite staging areas was Bahía de la Paz, which

contained numerous *ensenadas* (coves) and inlets perfect for concealing their swift corsairs. When Spanish crews put in for water, the pirates raided the galleons, often using their knowledge of strong bay winds to attack the ships when they were effectively pinned down.

Increased pirate activity in the late 17th and early 18th centuries created the need for a Spanish presence in the Cape Region. In 1719 Padre Juan de Ugarte, then President of the Missions, contracted a master shipbuilder to construct a ship for the specific purpose of exploring the Sea of Cortez coast and improving supply lines with the mainland. The barque *El Triunfo de la Cruz,* assembled of native Baja

LA PAZ

BAHIA DE LA PAZ

TO HOTEL PALMIRA AND PICHILINGUE

TOURIST INFORMATION OFFICE
CITY HALL
CUSTOMS
POST OFFICE
PLAZA CONSTITUCION
HOTEL LOS ARCOS
IMMIGRATION
RESTAURANT EL TASTE
LA CALETA
MARINA DE LA PAZ
RESTAURANT ESTRELLA DE MAR
ABAROA BOAT YARD
BAJA EXPEDITIONS
HOTEL MEDITERRANE
SEE "DOWNTOWN LA PAZ MAP"
MERCADO MUNICIPAL
MUSEUM OF ANTHROPOLOGY
STADIUM
RESTAURANT EL MAR
CITY THEATER (TEATRO DE LA CIUDAD)
TO AIRPORT AND LORETO
YOUTH HOSTEL (INSTITUTO DE LA JUVENTUD Y DEPORTE)
CENTRAL BUS STATION
TO CABO SAN LUCAS

CALLE SALVATIERRA
CALLE VICTORIA
CALLE BELISARIO DOMINGUEZ
CALLE MORELOS
CALLE HIDALGO
PASEO ALVARO OBREGON
CALLE 5 DE MAYO
AV INDEPENDENCIA
AV CONSTITUCION
CALLE REFORMA
CALLE 16 DE SEPTIEMBRE
CALLE DEGOLLADO
CALLE OCAMPO
CALLE BRAVO
CALLE ROSALES
CALLE JUAREZ
CALLE ALLENDE
CALLE MARQUEZ DE LEON
CALLE LEGASPI
CALLE PINEDA
CALLE NAVARRO
CALLE 5 DE FEBRERO
CALLE ENCINAS
CALLE GRAL FELIX ORTEGA
CALLE ISABEL LA CATOLICA
CALLE MEXICO
CALLE ABASOLO
CALLE RANGEL
CALLE JALISCO
CALLE FRANCISCO MADERO
CALLE REVOLUCION DE 1910
CALLE AQUILES SERDAN
CALLE GUILLERMO PRIETO
CALLE IGNACIO RAMIREZ
CALLE IGNACIO ALTAMIRANO
CALLE VALENTIN GOMEZ FARIAS
CALLE HEROES DE LA INDEPENDENCIA
CALLE JOSEFA ORTIZ DE DOMINGUEZ
CALLE LIC PRIMOS VERDAD
CALLE SONORA
CALLE CUAUHTEMOC
CALLE VERACRUZ

0   0.2mi
0   0.2km

© MOON PUBLICATIONS, INC.

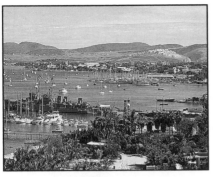

JOE CUMMINGS

Bahía de la Paz

hardwood at the Mulegé estuary, made its first sailing to Bahía de la Paz in 1720 with Ugarte and Padre Jaime Bravo as passengers.

Ugarte and Bravo founded the mission community of Nuestra Señora del Pilar de la Paz at the current city site. The padres didn't find the Pericús to be as friendly this time around; the mission lasted only until 1749, when it was abandoned following a series of Indian rebellions. By this time, another mission, along with a presidio, had been founded farther south at San José del Cabo—a better location for monitoring pirate activity.

La Paz Reborn

Left with European diseases and without the support of the mission system, the local Indian population dwindled quickly. By 1811, Mexican ranchers and *pescadores* who had settled along the Bahía de la Paz started their own town, which they named La Paz after the bay. After Loreto was severely damaged during a hurricane in 1829, the capital of Baja California Sur was moved to burgeoning La Paz, where it's remained ever since.

During the Mexican-American War (1846-48), the city was occupied by U.S. troops; the soldiers left when the Californias were split by the 1848 Treaty of Hidalgo. But American General William Walker, dissatisfied with the treaty and hoping to add another slaveholder state to counter the growing U.S. abolitionist movement, formed his own army and retook La Paz in November 1853. Proclaiming himself "President of the Republic of Lower California," Walker lasted only six months before he and his mer-

cenaries fled upon hearing that the U.S. wouldn't back their claims, and that the Mexican Army was on its way to La Paz from the mainland. Walker was tried in the U.S. for violation of neutrality laws, acquitted, and two years later was executed by the Nicaraguan army for attempting a similar takeover of Nicaragua.

La Paz remained a sleepy tropic port, known only for pearl fishing, until it was declared a duty-free port following WW II. During Mexico's postwar economic boom, mainland Mexicans crossed the Sea of Cortez in droves to buy imported merchandise; enchanted by La Paz itself, many stayed on. In the '50s, La Paz became well-known as a fishing resort and was visited by a succession of North American literati and Hollywood celebrities, thus initiating the city's reputation as an international vacation spot. But until the Transpeninsular Highway was completed in 1973, the city remained for the most part a tourist destination for mainland Mexicans.

Statehood was bestowed on the Territory of Baja California Sur in 1974, with La Paz as its capital. Linked by air, ferry, and highway to mainland Mexico and the U.S., the city has grown considerably yet managed to maintain its tropic port ambience.

SIGHTS

Museo De Antropología

Baja history buffs shouldn't miss this well-designed museum (tel. 2-01-62) at Calle 5 de Mayo and Altamirano. Three floors of exhibits cover Cape Region anthropology from prehistoric to colonial and modern times. On display are fossils, minerals, Indian artifacts, dioramas of Indian and colonial life, and maps of rock-painting sites throughout central and southern Baja. Labels are in Spanish only. Next to the museum is an older building that has served La Paz as a hospital, prison, and, more recently, the **Biblioteca Justo Sierra,** a children's library. Behind the library is a recently completed sculpture garden.

Admission to the museum is free; daily hours are 0900-1800.

Plaza Constitución (Jardín Velazco)

La Paz's tidy downtown *zócalo* is enclosed by calles 5 de Mayo, Independencia, Revolución de 1910, and Madero. At the southwest side of the

Catedral Nuestra Señora de la Paz

JOE CUMMINGS

of the plaza is the post-missionary-style **Catedral de Nuestra Señora de la Paz,** which replaced La Paz's original mission church in 1861. Although the twin-towered brick edifice looms over the plaza, it has none of the charm of earlier Jesuit missions.

At the northwest side of Plaza Constitución, opposite the cathedral, is the **Biblioteca de História de las Californias** ("History of the Californias Library"). Housed in the former Casa de Gobierno ("Government House"), the library is filled with Spanish- and English-language volumes on Alta and Baja California history. The general public is welcome to use the library for research purposes; it's open Mon.-Fri. 0900-1800, Saturday 0900-1500. For library information, call 2-01-62.

La Unidad Cultural Profesor Jesus Castro Agundez

This cultural center at Calle Farías and Legaspi, in the area of the city known as Cuatro Molinos ("Four Windmills"), includes an art gallery, community art school, and city archives. Also part of the complex is the **Teatro de la Ciudad** (City Theater, tel. 5-02-07), a 1500-seat performing-arts facility that hosts musical, theatrical, and dance performances throughout the year.

The four windmills next to the theater pay tribute to a time when La Paz relied on windmills to pump water and generate electricity. Another symbolic display in the complex is **La Rotunda de los Sudcalifornianos Illustres,** a circle of sculpted figures representing Baja California Sur's most illustrious heroes. Most of the historical personages honored at the Rotunda are former teachers or soldiers.

Malecón

One of the city's major attractions is the pleasant malecón, a seawall promenade along the northwest side of Paseo Alvaro Obregón extending from Calle 5 de Febrero (Mexico 1 south) to the northeastern city limits. Palm-shaded benches are conveniently situated at intervals along the walkway for watching sailboats and yachts coming in and out of the bay.

The best time of day for people-watching is around sunset, when the city begins cooling off, the sun dyes the waterfront orange, and paceños take to the malecón for an evening stroll. Snacks and cold beverages are available at several palapa bars along the way.

Universities

As Baja California Sur's educational center, La Paz supports a large number of schools at the primary, secondary, and tertiary levels. Most prominent among the latter is the **Universidad Autonomía de Baja California Sur** (University of South Baja California) on Blvd. Forjadores, with an enrollment of around 2,000 and reputable programs in agriculture, engineering, and business. The **Instituto Tecnologico de la Paz** (Technological Institute of La Paz), also on Blvd. Forjadores, enrolls approximately 3,000 students and is primarily known for its commercial fishing department.

ACCOMMODATIONS

Hotels And Motels

In 1941 Max Miller, author of *Land Where Time Stands Still*, wrote:

The Hotel Perla is the place to stay. For an American there's no other choice unless he wishes to rent a room with a Mexican family or live in a Mexican board-and-rooming house.... [T]he Mexicans themselves expect an American to stay at the Hotel Perla. If he doesn't stay there when he first arrives, then he's in La Paz for no good reason. He's under suspicion.

Time hasn't stood still in La Paz, and although the malecón's **Hotel Perla** is still one of most popular hotels in the city, it's now only one among many.

Hotel rates in La Paz are quite reasonable for a resort area, with most rooms falling in the US$25-65 range. Another standby around since the dawn of La Paz's tourist industry is **Cabañas de los Arcos.** Built in 1954, during La Paz's heyday as an exotic playground for Hollywood celebrities, Los Arcos became the city's first center for sportfishing trips. Paceño-owned Los Arcos now has a hotel section which, like the cabañas, faces the malecón and bay. For specifics on these hotels and others, see the "La Paz Hotels and Motels" chart.

Pensiones, Casas De Huéspedes, And Hosterías

La Paz offers more budget accommodations— *pensiones, hosterías,* and *casas de huéspedes*—than any other city in Baja. Doubles with a private shower are readily available for under US$12—a steal by modern Baja standards. Long-term visitors can often get a room for around US$5 a night. On the downside, accommodations in this price range come without air-conditioning, a significant inconvenience July-Oct., and since most of them are located in the downtown area they can be a bit noisy, with open windows and vented doors contributing to the influx of noise. But if you can do without air-conditioned silence, these are fairly clean, friendly, safe, and economical choices.

As old as the city itself is **Pensión California** (tel. 2-28-96), housed in a former 18th-century convent at Calle Degollado 209 between Revolución de 1910 and Madero. The interior courtyard of this rambling Moorish-style building contains a tropical garden of sorts and a display of old and new paintings. Some by local artists, some from the mainland—including an 18th-century Silva in a 17th-century baroque frame—they lend a distinctly Bohemian feel to the atmosphere. Rooms are very basic, little more than a few worn sticks of furniture, fan, and hot shower. Rates are US$8 s or d, US$10 for up to four people, or US$13 for a room sleeping six. Discounts are possible for long-term stays.

Just around the corner at Calle Madero 85 is another former convent, operated by the same family that owns Pensión California. At the **Hostería del Convento** (tel. 2-35-08) room rates are roughly the same as at Pensión California, although the place is more funky and faded. Even less expensive is **Casa de Huéspedes Miriam** (tel. 2-11-04), Calle 16 de Septiembre 202 between Calles Domínguez and Madero, where a cell-like but clean room costs US$6.60 s, US$8 d. The water supply can be iffy.

One of the better values in this category is the **Posada San Miguel** (tel. 2-18-02), Calle Domínguez 15140, a colorful colonial-style villa built around a tiled courtyard. The basic, almost bare rooms cost US$10 s, US$12 d, but the courtyard entrance is a major plus.

Although in name it's a hotel, **Hotel Yeneka** (tel. 2-03-35), Calle Madero 1520 between Degollado and 16 de Septiembre, looks and operates much like a guesthouse. Long known on the backpacker circuit, the Yeneka is built around a courtyard filled with tropical vegetation, a rusting Model T, and an amazing collection of other items giving the appearance of an ongoing garage sale. Almost everything is painted green; a pet monkey swings from tree to tree. Basic, scruffy rooms cost US$15 s, US$18 d, US$22 t.

La Paz has an official youth hostel at the **Instituto de la Juventud y El Deporte** (tel. 2-46-15), a sports complex on Blvd. Forjadores (Km 3) near Calle 5 de Febrero. A bed in a gender-segregated, four-person dorm costs US$6 a night, US$5 with a Hostelling International card; all ages welcome. Facilities include pool, gym, cafeteria, and volleyball and basketball courts.

LA PAZ HOTELS AND MOTELS

Note: Add 10% hotel tax to all rates; some hotels may charge an additional 10-15% service charge. Area code: 112

Cabañas de los Arcos; Paseo Obregón 498 (A.P. 112, La Paz, BCS); tel. 2-27-44, in U.S. tel. (213) 583-3393 or (800) 347-2252; US$75 s, US$77 d, US$81 t; a/c, cabaña section with fireplaces, (junior suites—same rates, no fireplace), telephones, pool

Club El Moro; La Paz-Pichilingue Rd., Km 2 (A.P. 357, La Paz, BCS); tel. 2-40-84; one bedroom US$60, two bedroom US$80, weekly and monthly rates on request; a/c, refrigerators, pool, restaurant, bar

Hotel Acuario's Mar de Cortés; Calle Ignacio Ramirez 1665; tel. 2-92-66; US$35-40; a/c, telephones, pool, restaurant, bar

Hotel Cristina; Revolución and Delgollado; tel. 2-66-23; US$13 s, US$18 d, US$22.30 t; a/c

Hotel El Mesón; Ortega 2330; tel. 5-74-54, fax 5-74-64; US$30 s/d; complimentary continental breakfast, a/c, telephones, pool, garden, restaurant/bar

Hotel Gardenias; Av. Serdán Norte 520; tel. 2-30-88; US$22-36; a/c, pool, restaurant

Hotel La Posada de Engelbert; Calle Nuevo Reforma and Playa Sur (A.P. 152, La Paz, BCS or P.O. Box 397, Bonita, CA 91908); tel. 2-40-11, in the U.S. (619) 421-2062, fax 2-06-63; US$55 suites, US$75 cottages; a/c, cottages w/fireplaces, pool, tennis court, restaurant, bar

Hotel La Purísima; 16 de Septiembre and Serdán; tel. 2-34-44; US$18.30 s, US$23 d, US$26 t; a/c, telephones

Hotel Lorimar; Calle Bravo 110; tel. 2-18-19; US$18 s, US$22 d US$25 t; a/c

Hotel Los Arcos; Paseo Obregón 498 (A.P. 112, La Paz, BCS); tel. 2-27-44, in U.S. tel. (714) 476-5555 or (800) 347-2252; US$75 s, US$77 d, US$81 t, add US$2 for bay-view rooms; a/c, telephones, pool, massage, sauna, coffee shop, restaurant, bar, gift shop

Hotel Mediterrané; Allende 36-B; tel./fax 5-11-95; US$35-40; restaraunt, half block from malecón

Hotel Miramar; Calle 5 de Mayo and Domínguez; tel. 2-06-72, fax 2-06-82; US$29 s, US$33 d; a/c, TV w/VCR, bar, refrigerator, restaurant

Hotel Palmira; La Paz-Pichilingue Rd., Km 2.5 (opposite Marina Palmira); tel. 2-40-00, in U.S. tel. (800) 336-5454, fax 5-39-59; US$66 s/d; a/c, telephones, pool, tennis court, restaurant, bar, disco

Hotel Perla; Paseo Obregón 1570; tel. 2-07-77, fax 5-53-63; US$42 s, US$48 d, US$52 t; a/c, telephones, pool, restaurant, coffee shop, nightclub

Hotel Plaza Real; Callejón La Paz and Esquerro; tel. 2-93-33; US$29.30 d; a/c, restaurant

Hotel San Carlos; Calle Revolución and 16 de Septiembre; tel. 2-04-44; US$11-15; ceiling fans

La Concha Beach Resort; La Paz-Pichilingue Rd., Km 5; tel. 2-65-44, in U.S. tel. (213) 943-1369 or (800) 528-1234, fax 2-62-18; US$77 s/d, US$128 suite; a/c, telephones, bay views, beach, pool, restaurant, bars, gift shop, aquatic sports center

At **Hospedaje Mareli** (tel. 2-15-17), Av. Serdán Sur 283, you can rent adequate a/c rooms by the month for US$166.

Camping And RV Parks
Free beach camping is available north of the Pichilingue ferry terminal at Playa Pichilingue, Playa Balandra (Puerto Balandra), Playa El Tecolote, and Playa El Coyote. At none of these beaches are there sources of fresh water; all

supplies must be brought from La Paz.

In and around La Paz are six trailer parks—five at the western edge of the city off Mexico 1 and one to the south off BCS 286. Starting from the west (Mexico 1 south), the first is **Los Aripez (Oasis de Aripez) RV Park,** just before Km 15 in El Centenario. Popular among Transpeninsular voyagers making short La Paz stopovers, full-hookup slots here cost US$8 for two, plus US$2 per each additional person; facilities include showers, flush toilets, laundry, restaurant, bar, and access to the shallow Ensenada de Aripes, where you can launch boats. There are no tent sites available.

Next along Mexico 1, five km (three miles) west of the city near the state tourism office, is the well-maintained **Casa Blanca RV Park** (tel. 2-51-09, fax 5-11-42), where full hookups are US$10 a night for two persons plus US$2 for each additional guest. The facility includes showers, flush toilets, a pool, tennis courts, spa, laundry, restaurant, and a small market. **El Cardón Trailer Park** (tel. 2-12-61; mailing address: A.P. 104, La Paz, BCS), at Km 4, has well-tended palapa sites with full hookups for US$9 for two, plus US$1 each additional person. Tents permitted. El Cardón offers a pool, groceries, flush toilets, hot showers, dump station, and laundry.

Just before the defunct Hotel Gran Baja, off Av. Abasolo (Mexico 1) near the VW dealer, is the upscale **La Paz Trailer Park** (tel. 2-87-87; mailing address: A.P. 482, La Paz, BCS). Full hookups or tent sites cost US$12 for two plus US$2 per additional guest; facilities include showers, flush toilets, pool, jacuzzi, tennis court, laundry, restaurant, and bar.

A bit farther east toward the city center, off Calle Nayarit on the bay, is the **Aquamarina RV Park** (tel. 2-37-61; mailing address: A.P. 133, La Paz, BCS). A favorite among boaters and divers, Aquamarina features its own marina, complete with boat ramp, storage facilities, and air for scuba tanks, plus showers, flush toilets, pool, and laundry facilities. Full-hookup sites are US$13 for two people, plus US$1 per additional guest.

El Carrizal RV Park is about two km south of La Paz off BCS 286, the state highway to San Juan de los Planes. Full hookups at El Carrizal cost US$9; facilities include a large pool, showers, flush toilets, and laundry.

FOOD

La Paz offers dining venues for all tastes and budgets; as might be expected in a coastal city, the seafood selection is particularly good. In the evenings, the downtown area centered around the malecón and Calle 16 de Septiembre features a number of street vendors serving fish tacos and *cocteles*. One of the best stands for

fish, shrimp, and clam tacos is at the corner of Calle Arreola and Esquerro, opposite the bank.

During the daytime, the cluster of loncherías in the **Mercado Municipal Francisco E. Madero**, Revolución and Degollado, serve as a very inexpensive grazing spot for antojitos and comidas corridas.

Seafood
$$-$$$ **Restaurant Bermejo**, Los Arcos Hotel, Paseo Obregón: One of the better hotel restaurants, enhanced by its location overlooking the malecón—ask for a window table—and presided over by an Italian chef. The menu features mostly seafood, steak, and pasta; open daily for lunch and dinner.

$$ **Bismark II** (tel. 2-48-54), Degollado and Altamirano: A casual, family-run restaurant specializing in lobster, abalone, and carne asada. All meals start with the restaurant's unique *totopos*—instead of chips, they're fried whole tortillas—with a smooth guacamole. The ceviche is also very good. Open daily 0800-2230.

$$ **Restaurant Camarón Feliz** ("Happy Shrimp") (tel. 2-90-11), Obregón and Bravo: A small, cutesy seafood place on a traffic island near Hotel Los Arcos; very good *cocteles de camarones* (shrimp cocktails). Open daily noon to midnight.

$$ **Restaurant La Mar** (tel. 2-99-49), 16 de Septiembre between Isabel la Católica and Albañez: Operated by local seafood wholesalers Mar y Pina, this small air-conditioned restaurant has a terrific menu that features practically everything that swims, including several *machaca* (dried and shredded) versions. Credit cards accepted. Open daily for lunch and dinner.

$-$$ **Palapa Adriana** (tel. 2-83-26), on the beach at Paseo Obregón, between 5 de Mayo and Constitución: One of the malecón's original palapa restaurant-bars, with fresh seafood, *carnes rajas* (grilled steak), and Mexican standards. Casual and very reasonable. Open weekdays 1000-2300, weekends till 0200 (with live music).

Mexican
$ **Café San Francisco**, next to the Hotel Mediterrané on Calle Allende: Very inexpensive but tasty Mexican meals served in a clean, bright, airy café. Open 0800-2300 daily; comida corrida available 1300-1600.

$$-$$$ Carlos 'n Charlie's, Paseo Obregón and 16 de Septiembre: One of the latest installments in the Grupo Anderson chain that includes Squid Roe and Señor Frog's. The atmosphere is much more low-key than the usual Anderson enterprise, with the interior decor featuring old Mexican movie posters. More of an emphasis on good Mexican fare, seafood (try the *ceviche paceño*), and steak dishes; much of the clientele is Mexican. The terrace tables usually catch a breeze. Open daily noon-midnight.

$ Mr. Taco (tel. 3-01-88), Paseo Obregón and Salvatierra: Though a bit removed from the central malecón action, you won't find a larger selection (18 kinds) of tacos in La Paz. Open daily 1100-2200.

$$ PAS, Paseo Obregón and Independencia, on the malecón: This relatively new, upmarket spot on the waterfront features a wide selection of well-prepared Mexican standards for breakfast, lunch, and dinner.

$-$$ Restaurant Plaza Real (tel. 2-93-33), Hotel Plaza Real, Calle Esquerro and Callejón La Paz: A very popular coffee-shop-style place with moderate prices, efficient service, and good Mexican food. Open Sun.-Fri. 0700-2300, Saturday 0700-1300.

$ Super Pollo, three locations: Calle 5 de Febrero and Gómez Farías; 5 de Maya and Gómez Farías; Blvd. Forjadores and Loreto: A good, economic choice for *pollo asado al carbón estilo Sinaloa,* Sinaloa-style grilled chicken, sold with tortillas and salsa. Eat in or take out; open daily 1100-2200.

American
$-$$ The Dock Café, Marina de la Paz, at the bay end of Calle Legaspy: Visiting and resident yachties crowd this small, casual diner for fried chicken, hamburgers, fish and chips, salads, steaks, American breakfasts, and homemade apple pie. A three-man blues band occasionally performs in the evening. Open Sun.-Tues. and Thursday 0800-2200, Fri.-Sat. 0800-midnight; closed Wednesday.

$$ El Molino Steak House (tel. 2-61-91), Legaspy and Topete, near Marina de la Paz: Although the house specialty is American-style steaks, this large palapa restaurant is very popular with local residents; most nights there are mariachis. Open daily 1100-2300.

$$ Restaurant Grill Campestre (tel. 5-63-34), opposite the FIDEPAZ building on Mexico 1 North, near Km 5.5: Popular with gringos and Mexicans alike for barbecued ribs, Cobb salad, and other American specialties. Open daily for lunch and dinner.

International
$$-$$$ El Taste (tel. 822-8121), Paseo Obregón and Juárez: An old-timer featuring steaks, Mexican, and seafood, patronized by a mostly tourist and expat clientele. Open daily for breakfast, lunch, and dinner.

$-$$ Restaurant Dragón (tel. 2-13-72), Calle 16 de Septiembre and Esquerro: La Paz's tiny Chinatown harbors five or six Chinese restaurants, of which this is usually considered the best. Basically Cantonese, with Mexican influences; open daily for lunch and dinner.

$$ La Fabula Pizza, three locations: Obregón and Independencia; Obregón and Altos; La Católica and Allende: American-style pizza and Italian specialties. Very popular with young paceños. Open daily for lunch and dinner.

$$ La Terraza (tel. 2-07-77), Paseo Obregón 1570: This outdoor cafe beneath the Hotel Perla has an extensive menu of seafood, Mexican, steak, and Italian dishes that attracts a steady crowd of both tourists and locals. It's the best place in town for people-watching, and the food is reasonably priced and reasonably tasty.

$ Los Arcos Cafetería, Hotel Los Arcos, Paseo Obregón: A self-service coffee shop with inexpensive Mexican and international dishes; open daily 0600-2200.

$$ Trattoria La Pazta (tel. 5-11-95), Hotel Mediterrané, Calle Allende, a half block off the malecón: A Swiss-run restaurant specializing in pasta and other Italian specialties. Open Wed.-Mon. 1300-2200.

$$ Sushi Loco, Calle Ortega between Rosales and Juárez: With all the fresh seafood available, it's about time someone opened a sushi joint in La Paz. The sushi is good, but will it be able to compete against *ceviche paceño?* Open daily 1100-1600.

Vegetarian
$ El Quinto Sol (tel. 2-16-92) Calle Domínguez and Independencia: This natural food/vegetarian store includes a café section serving

tortas, comida corrida, pastries, salads, granola, fruit and vegetable juices, and yogurt. Open daily 0800-2200.

Ice Cream
Downtown La Paz is packed with tiendas selling *nieves* (Mexican-style ice cream) and *paletas* (popsicles). **Mr. Yeti** is a big one, with branches on Paseo Obregón and Calle Madero. A personal favorite is the tiny **La Fuente** on Obregón between Degollado and Muelle; though small, this place offers an amazing variety of flavors, including *capirotada* (Mexican bread pudding), licuados, aguas frescas, and all-fruit *paletas.*

Groceries
The **Mercado Municipal Francisco E. Madero,** at Revolución and Degollado, houses a collection of vendor stalls purveying fresh fish, meats, fruit, vegetables, and baked goods at nonsubsidized free-market prices. Since prices are usually posted, no bargaining is necessary. Opposite the market on Revolución, **Panaficadora Lilia** sells fresh bolillos and pan dulce daily. Nearby at the corner of Revolución and Bravo is a tortillería. Other traditional markets include **Mercado Bravo** (at calles Bravo and G. Prieto) and **Mercado Abastos** (Blvd. Las Garzas).

La Paz features several supermarkets, including the large **CCC** (Centro Comercial California) outlets at Av. Abasolo and Calle Colima and at La Católica and Bravo. These carry American-brand packaged foods as well as Mexican products, but prices are about twice what you'd usually pay elsewhere in town. The government-subsidized **ISSSTE Tienda** at Calle Altamirano and Bravo has the best grocery prices in the city, although the selection varies according to what ISSSTE purchased cheaply that week. The **Tienda Militar** ("Military Store") on Calle 5 de Mayo at Padre Kino offers a larger selection than ISSSTE Tienda and is almost as inexpensive.

Two stores in La Paz specialize in natural foods. **El Quinto Sol** (Domínguez and Independencia) offers natural juices, wheat gluten, soybean meat substitutes that include soybean chorizo, whole wheat flour, herbs, yogurt, and ice cream, as well as a few ready-to-eat items like tortas and salads. **Los Girasoles** (tel. 2-55-90, Calle Revolución between Hidalgo and Morelos) operates a bakery and sells veggie

sandwiches, yogurt, granola, vitamins, and various whole grains.

At the other end of the nutritional spectrum are two *dulcerías* (sweet shops) on the corner of Calle Ocampo and Serdán. **Dulcería Perla** has a complete selection of traditional and modern Mexican sweets, while **Dulcería La Coneja** on the opposite corner specializes in candy-filled *piñatas,* including a few in the shape of Teenage Mutant Ninja Turtles.

ENTERTAINMENT AND EVENTS

Bullfights
The municipal stadium at Calle Constitución and Verdad hosts *corridas de toros* in the late winter months, usually Feb.-March. For information on the latest schedule, contact the state tourism office (see "La Paz Information and Services," below).

Bars And Cafés
The **Bar Pelicanos,** overlooking the malecón in Hotel Los Arcos, is a large, sedate watering hole popular among tourists and Old Hands. It's worth at least a visit to peruse the old photos along the back wall; subjects include a motley array of unnamed vaqueros and revolutionaries, as well as Pancho Villa, General Blackjack Pershing, President Dwight Eisenhower, Emiliano Zapata, and Clark Gable posing with a marlin. The bar is open daily 1000-0100.

On the beach side of Paseo Obregón, three blocks west of Hotel Los Arcos, is the casual and sometimes lively palapa bar **La Caleta,** where the clientele is predominantly local. Drinks are reasonably priced, with a 1600-2000 happy hour, and there's usually live guitar music after 2100 or so.

The recently opened **Café Chamate,** opposite Calle 16 de Septiembre on the malecón, is a European-style coffeehouse with espresso drinks, light meals, and recorded music, mostly jazz, blues, and Latin from the '20-'40s. On Wednesday evenings the café's "Cine Club" screens art films. It's open Mon.-Thurs. 1600-2200, Fri.-Sat. 1800-midnight.

Discos And Nightclubs
Living up to its laid-back reputation, La Paz isn't big on discos. The most popular dance spot

among young Paceños is the two-story **5to Patio (Quinto Patio)** on Paseo Obregón between Muelle and Degollado; often the music is live. An older, mixed tourist/local crowd patronizes the Hotel Palmira's disco, **El Rollo,** which features a mix of international and Latin recordings and occasional live music. The **Cabaña Club,** at the Hotel Perla, usually offers live music and attracts a more local, good-time crowd.

Events

La Paz's biggest annual celebration is **Carnaval,** held for six days before Ash Wednesday in mid-February. Carnaval is also held in the Mexican cities of Santa Rosalía, Ensenada, and Veracruz, but Carnaval connoisseurs claim La Paz's is the best—perhaps because the city's malecón makes a perfect parade route.

As at all Mexican Carnavals, the festival begins with the Quema de Mal Humor, or "Burning of Bad Humor," in which an effigy representing an unpopular public figure is burned. Other events include the crowning of La Reina del Carnaval ("Carnaval Queen") and El Rey Feo ("Ugly King"), colorful costumed parades, music, dancing, feasting, cockfights, and fireworks. The festival culminates in El Día del Marido Oprimido, the "Day of the Oppressed Husband"—23.5 hours of symbolic freedom for married men to do whatever they wish—followed by a masquerade ball on the Tuesday evening before Ash Wednesday.

© MOON PUBLICATIONS, INC.

Also prominent on the city's yearly events calendar is the **Fiesta de la Paz,** held 3 May, the anniversary of the founding of the city. The state tourist office can provide up-to-date details on festival scheduling and venues.

SHOPPING

Until recently, imported merchandise could be purchased in La Paz free of import duties and sales tax. The city's duty-free status was recalled in 1989, however, and sales tax is now commensurate with the rest of Mexico's. But the city still offers some of Baja's best shopping in terms of value and variety, starting with the downtown department stores of **Dorian's** (calles 16 de Septiembre and Esquerro) and **Perla de la Paz** (calles Arreola and Mutualismo).

Along Paseo Obregón in the vicinity of the Hotel Perla and Hotel Los Arcos are a number of souvenir and handicraft shops of varying quality. One of the better ones is **Artesanías La Antigua California,** at Paseo Obregón 220, which sells quality folk arts and crafts from the mainland. Away from the downtown area, the **Centro de Arte Regional** (calles Chiapas and Encinas) produces and sells pottery, while **Artesanía Cuauhtémoc** (Av. Abasolo between Jalisco and Nayarit) weaves rugs, blankets, wallhangings, tablecloths, and other cotton or wool items. Custom orders are available, and customers are welcome to watch the weavers at their looms in back of the shop.

For tourist-variety souvenirs, especially T-shirts, **Bye-Bye** (four blocks east of Hotel Perla on Paseo Obregón) is a good choice. **Soko's Curios** (Obregón and 5 de Septiembre) is strictly for collectors of Mexican kitsch.

For bottom-dollar bargains on clothing and housewares, browse the **Mercado Municipal Francisco E. Madero** at Revolución and Degollado.

SPORTS AND RECREATION

Beaches
Bahía de la Paz is scalloped with nine public beaches. At the northwest end of the bay are **Playa El Comitán** and **Playa Las Hamacas,** both shallow beaches tending toward mudflats

in low tide. More inviting are the seven beaches strung out east of the city along the Pichilingue Peninsula—they get better the farther you get from the city. **Playa Palmira,** around four km (2.5 miles) east of downtown La Paz via the La Paz-Pichilingue Rd., is now monopolized by the Hotel Palmira and Marina de Palmira. A kilometer farther, the small but pleasant **Playa El Coromuel** offers restaurant-bar service, palapas, and a waterslide.

Playa del Tesoro, 14 km (8.5 miles) from the city, is another casual, semi-urban beach with palapas and a restaurant. At Km 17, just beyond the SEMATUR ferry terminal, is **Playa Pichilingue,** the only public beach in the La Paz vicinity with restrooms available 24 hours for campers. The beach also has a modest palapa restaurant.

After Pichilingue the once-sandy track has been replaced by pavement as far as Playa Tecolote. The turnoff for **Playa Balandra** appears five km (three miles) beyond Pichilingue, then it's another 800 meters (half-mile) to the parking area and beach. A couple of palapas and trash barrels were recently installed by the city.

Depending on the tide, the large, shallow bay of Puerto Balandra actually forms several beaches, some of them long sandbars. Ringed by cliffs and steep hills, the bay is a beautiful and usually secluded spot, perfect for wading in the clear, warm waters. Clams are fairly abundant; a coral reef at the south end of the bay offers decent snorkeling. Climb the rock cliffs—carefully—for sweeping bay views. Camping is permitted at Balandra, but oftentimes a lack of breeze brings out the *jejenes* (no-see-ums), especially in the late summer and early fall. The beaches sometimes draw crowds on weekends.

About three km (1.5 miles) beyond the Playa Balandra turnoff is **Playa El Tecolote,** a wide, long, pretty beach backed by vegetated dunes. Because Tecolote is open to the stiff breezes of Canal de San Lorenzo, the camping here is usually insect-free. The palapa-style **Restaurant El Tecolote** offers seafood, cold beverages, and panga rentals. The concession also rents noisy jet skis, waverunners, and three- and four-wheel ATVs. If you visit during the week the place is almost deserted. Isla Espíritu Santo is clearly visible in the distance; you can hire a panga from the restaurant to cross the channel for around US$40-50. Two smaller palapa restaurants have also opened for business along the beach—apparently the *municípío* government has decided to allow beach development.

From Tecolote the road returns to sand as it winds across the peninsula for about 13 km (eight miles) before ending at remote **Punta Coyote.** Along the way shorter roads branch off to rocky coves suitable for camping. Don't tackle this road expecting to find the perfect white-sand beach; the farther northeast from Tecolote you go, the stonier and browner the beaches become.

Tecolote or the smaller beaches just east of Tecolote are good put-in points for kayak trips to **Isla Espíritu Santo,** 6.5 km (four miles) away. Because of winds and tidal currents, this isn't a trip for the novice sea kayaker. Even experienced paddlers on a first voyage to the island should accompany someone who knows the tricky interplay of currents, shoals, tides, and winds.

Islands

The 22.5-km-long (14-mile-long) **Isla Espíritu Santo** and its smaller immediate neighbor to the north, **Isla Partida,** are excellent destinations for all manner of sailing craft from sea kayaks to yachts. Sandy beaches and large coves along the western shores of both islands offer an abundance of opportunities for small-craft landings and camping. **Punta Lupona,** on the southern tip of Espíritu Santo, is just 6.5 km (four miles) from Pichilingue Peninsula, and the shallow channel between Espíritu Santo and Partida is only a few hundred meters across.

At the south end of Isla Partida are a couple of fish camps where drinking water and food might be available—but don't count on it. There are usually plenty of yachts in the vicinity. Just north of Partida is **Los Islotes,** a volcanic rock island popular among divers, anglers, and sea lions.

Getting to the Islands: Several travel agencies in La Paz arrange two-hour jaunts to Isla Espíritu Santo and Isla Partida for around US$40 per person including lunch. Remember to inquire about the quality and contents of the lunch. Aguilar's Baja Diving Service, for example, serves a lousy sandwich of white bread glued to two slices of processed American cheese—and that's it. If the lunch situation sounds iffy or awful, demand more food or carry your own lunch. Life preservers are another variable worth inquiring about; some boats don't carry them.

Fishing

Outer bay and offshore fishing in the La Paz area are very good; a boat is mandatory since there's little onshore or surf fishing. In the bay or the canals west of the islands live roosterfish, pargo, cabrilla, needlefish, bonito, amberjack, jack crevalle, yellowtail, sierra, and pompano. Beyond Isla Espíritu Santo are the larger gamefish, including dorado, grouper, marlin, tuna, and sailfish. Yellowtail usually run in the area Jan.-March, while most other gamefish reach peak numbers April-November. Canal de Cerralvo, around the other side of Pichilingue Peninsula, provides excellent fishing for roosterfish and pargo colorado Jan.-July.

Any of the major La Paz hotels will arrange fishing trips; one of the oldest operations is **Dorado Velez Fleet** (tel. 2-27-44, 5-47-94, A.P. 402, La Paz, BCS), which maintains a desk at Hotel Los Arcos. Another established outfit is **Fisherman's Fleet** (tel. 2-13-13), also with a desk at Los Arcos. You can arrange guides and boats at the pier just east of the Pichilingue ferry terminal. Panga fishing trips in the bay generally cost US$80-90 a day for two people, beyond Isla Espíritu Santo or to Canal de Cerralvo figure around US$160. Long-range fishing cruises run US$200-300 a day and usually accommodate up to four anglers.

Fishing tackle is available at **Deportiva La Paz** (tel. 2-73-33), Paseo Obregón 1680.

Boating

With a huge, protected bay, one private and four public marinas, and several boatyards and marine supply stores, La Paz is Baja California's largest and best-equipped boating center. Northeast of town, on the Canal de la Paz at Km 2.5, the well-planned **Marina Palmira** (tel. 2-42-77, fax 5-39-59; mailing address: A.P. 34, La Paz, BCS) currently offers 146 slips with electricity for yachts up to 42.5 meters (140 feet), as well as dry-storage facilities, a market, laundry, marine supplies, fuel, and boat launch. This marina also offers crewed and bareboat yacht charters. Daily slip rates range US$25-100 depending on the size of the boat, with discounts for long-term moorings; boats up to 90 feet are charged US$8.50 per foot per month, larger craft cost US$10-12 per foot per month. Condos adjacent to the marina are also available for rent by day, week, or month.

At the west end of the malecón (calles Topete and Legaspy) is the **Marina de la Paz** (tel. 2-16-46, fax 5-59-00; mailing address: A.P. 290, La Paz, BCS), owned by panga designer Malcolm "Mac" Shroyer. Facilities include a launch ramp, fuel dock, market with groceries and marine supplies, water and electricity, laundry, showers, restrooms, chandlery, boat and vehicle storage, and 68 slips. Daily rates range from US$14 for a six- to nine-meter (20- to 30-foot) craft to US$50 for anything over 20 meters (63 feet), up to a maximum of 22.8 meters (75 feet). The daily rate is discounted June-Oct.; monthly rates start at US$237. Showers cost US$1. Marina de la Paz is by far the most popular marina in the bay and is often full Nov.-May; call or write in advance to check for vacancies before sailing in.

The well-established **Abaroa Boat Yard,** at the end of Calle Navarro near the Marina de la Paz, offers mooring facilities for up to 25 boats but is usually full; the rates are the lowest in La Paz. Still under construction is La Paz's fourth docking facility, the government-financed **FIDE-PAZ Marina** on the waterfront near the state tourist office at the west end of Canal de la Paz. According to FIDEPAZ officials, the facility—if ever actually completed—will eventually offer over 400 slips. Yet another pipe dream is a marina called **Costa Baja** north of the Marina Palmira.

You can launch trailered and cartopped boats at Marina de la Paz, Marina Palmira, Abaroa Boat Yard, Aquamarina RV Park, and Pichilingue. Smaller boats and kayaks can put in at any of the public beaches.

Pangas: If you're in the market for a new panga, La Paz is the panga capital of Mexico. American Mac Shroyer, the first person to design and build the molded fiberglass panga, produces them at his panga factory at Calle Navarro 960. Until 1968, when Mac started his small factory, many Sea of Cortez fishermen still used dugout canoes of Indian design; Shroyer's glass pangas are now sold all over Mexico.

The standard panga is sold in 18-, 20-, or 22-foot lengths, but the factory can accommodate special orders as long as 36 feet. The standard panga outboard motor is a "cinco-cinco caballos," 55 horsepower. Prices run US$3200-4200 each, depending on whether canopy, stowage compartment, or other options are included. To arrange for a tour of the factory or to inquire about panga sales, call Mac or his wife Mary at Marina de la Paz (tel. 2-16-46).

Kayak Trips: The only area outfit operating guided kayak trips is **Baja Expeditions** (see "Dive Shops" below). The basic programs include five- and eight-day itineraries in the vicinity of Isla Espíritu Santo (March-May and Oct.-Jan. only) and an eight-day trip from Loreto to La Paz (Oct.-April only). Rates range from US$695 for the five-day Espíritu Santo trip to US$1,195 for the Loreto-La Paz paddle.

Parts and Repairs: Marina de la Paz is the best local source of information for boating needs. A booklet by Janet Calvert entitled *La Paz Boater's Guide to Goods and Services,* available at the marina, contains a thorough list of all boatyards, outboard-motor shops, and marine supply stores in La Paz. Boaters at the marina can also offer recommendations for the best places to acquire boat parts and repairs.

Diving

Some of Baja's best dive sites lie in the La Paz vicinity, but most are accessible only by boat. As elsewhere in the Sea of Cortez, the optimum diving months are May-Aug., when visibility reaches 30 meters (100 feet) or more. In September tropical storms are an obstacle and during the late fall and winter months high winds and changing currents reduce visibility. A light wetsuit is necessary any time except June-August.

One of the most popular diving spots is the wreck of the *Salvatierra,* a 91-meter (300-foot) La Paz-Topolobampo ferry that went down in the Canal de San Lorenzo in 1976. The hull lies about 2.5 km (1.5 miles) southeast of the southern tip of Isla Espíritu Santo at a depth of approximately 10 fathoms (18 meters/60 feet). Encrusted with sponges, sea fans, mollusks, and gorgonians, the wreck attracts numerous varieties of tropical fish, including groupers, barracuda, angelfish, goatfish, parrotfish, moray eels, and rays.

Along the western shores of **Isla Espíritu Santo** and **Isla Partida** are several good diving reefs. Bahía San Gabriel, a large cove along Espíritu Santo's southwest shore, features a shallow boulder reef (San Rafaelito) at its northern end suitable for both scuba diving and snorkeling. A similar reef is found farther north off Espíritu Santo's western shore, extending from the west side of **Isla Ballena.**

The most colorful dive site in the vicinity is **Los Islotes,** the tiny islet group off the north end of Isla Partida. Boulder reefs and underwater pinnacles off the north and northeast draw large marine species, including schools of hammerhead sharks, manta rays, and other pelagic (open-ocean) fish. A nearby cove is home to around 300 sea lions who seem to enjoy swimming alongside divers and performing tricks for the camera. Late in the breeding season (Jan.-May) is the best time to visit the colony, since this is when the adolescent pups are most playful.

To the southwest of Los Islotes is **El Bajito,** a large rock reef that extends to within six meters (20 feet) of the sea's surface; the base of the reef meets a sandy bottom at about 24-28 meters (80-90 feet). The diverse marinelife frequenting the reef includes grouper, cabrilla, and an unusually large number of morays; attached to the rocks are gorgonians, sea fans, and a variety of other invertebrate creatures.

A group of three sea pinnacles called **El Bajo** (also known as Marisla Seamount), about 13 km (8.2 miles) northeast of Los Islotes, is renowned for the presence of large pelagics such as marlin; hammerhead, blacktip, tiger, and silvertip sharks; dorado; corvina; and manta rays. Mantas frequent El Bajo from July to mid-October, and for unknown reasons often allow divers in this area to "hitch" rides by holding onto their backs near the pectoral fins. Whale sharks, the largest fish in the world, are occasionally seen near El Bajo during the same months, as are pilot whales.

Due to strong tidal currents, Los Islotes, El Bajito, and El Bajo are best left to experienced open-ocean divers.

Southeast of Península de Pichilingue, the somewhat more remote **Isla Cerralvo** offers several additional diving opportunities. Even more remote—generally reached by live-aboard trips—are **Isla Santa Cruz** and **Islas Las Animas** to the north. The former is known for rock reefs at depths of around 17 meters (35 feet) with a profusion of seahorses, while the latter reportedly offers the greatest variety of diving experiences—caves, hammerheads, whale sharks, sea lions—of any site in the Sea of Cortez. Only Baja Expeditions leads Santa Cruz and Animas dives at the moment.

Dive Shops: The granddaddy of all dive outfits in La Paz is Fernando Aguilar's **Baja Buceo y Servicio ("Baja Diving Service")** (tel. 2-18-26, fax 2-86-44) at Av. Independencia 107-B. Besides offering equipment sales and rental, Aguilar organizes dive trips to the *Salvatierra,* El Bajo, and Los Islotes for US$70 a day including guide, transport, lunch, unlimited sodas and beer, weight belt, and two tanks. Add US$10 for full gear. Basic scuba certification costs US$90; a complete open-water diving certification course is available for US$280. In addition, BBS offers snorkeling trips for US$40 to Playa Encantada and the sea lion colony, as well as windsurfing equipment and instruction.

Baja Expeditions (tel. 5-38-28), at Calle Sonora 586 just off Abasolo, offers a variety of day-long and live-aboard dive programs in the La Paz vicinity. Most of these—particularly the live-aboard trips on the 86-foot *Don José*—are booked out of the U.S. office (tel. 619-581-3311, 800-843-6967, 2625 Garnet Ave., San Diego, CA 92109) but it's occasionally possible to sign up in La Paz when space is available. A seven-day excursion costs US$1,495.

Day excursions aboard Baja Expeditions' 50-foot *Río Rita* dive boat can be booked in La Paz at a rate of US$95 per day, which covers weights and tanks, up to three separate dives, breakfast, lunch, and afternoon snacks. US$299 buys a three-day package that includes three nights of hotel accommodations, usually at Los Arcos.

Diving equipment and air fills are available at **Deportiva La Paz** (tel./fax 2-73-33), Paseo Obregón 1680. This shop doesn't organize dive trips.

LA PAZ
INFORMATION AND SERVICES

Tourist Offices

Baja California Sur's SECTUR office (tel. 2-11-99, fax 2-77-22) lies between Km 6 and 5 on Mexico 1 (Av. Abasolo) opposite the FIDEPAZ Marina. The friendly staff speaks English and can assist with most tourist inquiries; the Attorney for the Protection of Tourists is also stationed here. The office maintains an information booth for the distribution of maps and brochures on the malecón near Calle 16 de Septiembre. Office and booth are open Mon.-Sat. 0800-1900.

USEFUL LA PAZ TELEPHONE NUMBERS
(La Paz area code: 112)

Police	2-07-81
Red Cross	2-11-11, 2-12-22
Highway Patrol	2-03-69, 2-87-98
IMSS Hospital	2-73-77
Tourist Attorney	2-59-39
State Tourism Office	2-11-99
Immigration.	2-04-29
Ferry Office	5-38-33, 5-51-17

Newspapers
Two Spanish-language dailies are published in La Paz: *Diario Peninsular* and *El Sudcaliforniano.* The *Los Cabos Times,* a bilingual, biweekly paper based in Cabo San Lucas, usually carries a few tourist-oriented features on the La Paz area.

Librería Contiempo, a bookstore on Calle Arreola at Paseo Obregón, carries *The News* from Mexico City.

Changing Money
Several banks and moneychangers are located in the area around Calle 16 de Septiembre. As elsewhere in Baja, the foreign-exchange service at banks is only open Mon.-Fri. before noon. Both Bancomer and Banamex have ATMs.

Moneychangers *(casas de cambio)* stay open till early evening and on Saturday, but are closed on Sunday, when your only alternative is to change money at a hotel at lower rates. Pesos are a must for everyday purchases in La Paz; city merchants are not as receptive to U.S.-dollar transactions as their counterparts in Ensenada or Cabo San Lucas simply because they're not as used to them.

Post Office
The main post and telegraph office is at Calle Revolución and Constitución, a block northeast of the cathedral; it's open Mon.-Fri. 0800-1300 and 1500-1900, Saturday 0800-1300.

Immigration And Customs
If you're planning to cross the Sea of Cortez by ferry and haven't yet validated your tourist card,

stop by the immigration office (tel. 2-04-29), on Paseo Obregón between Allende and Juárez. It's usually open Mon.-Fri. 0800-1500. The immigration office at the Pichilingue ferry terminal is open only an hour or so before each ferry departure.

The Customs office sits in a building opposite the Muelle Fiscal ("Public Pier") on the malecón.

TRANSPORT

Air
La Paz International Airport (LAP) is 12 km south of the city; the airport access road leaves Mexico 1 at Km 9. Although it's a small airport, facilities include a couple of gift shops, two snack bars, rental car booths, LADATEL phones (cards available for purchase from the snack bar), and a fax/telegraph service.

Aeroméxico (tel. 2-00-91, 2-16-36, Paseo Obregón between Hidalgo and Morelos) offers daily nonstop flights between La Paz and Los Angeles, Culiacán, Guaymas, Tijuana, and Mexico City, as well as connecting flights to San Francisco, Tucson, Indianapolis, Baltimore, and a number of Mexican cities.

Aero California (tel. 2-11-13, 2-83-92, Paseo Obregón 550 at Bravo) flies daily nonstops to and from Culiacán, Loreto, Los Mochis, Mazatlán, and Tijuana, plus connecting flights to Los Angeles via Loreto and Mexico City via Mazatlán.

Airport Transport: A company called **Transporte Terrestre** operates yellow-and-white vans between the city and the airport. The standard fare is US$10 *colectivo* (shared), US$20 private service. A regular taxi to the airport should be US$15. Some hotels operate airport vans that charge around US$3 per person.

Land
Intercity Bus: La Paz has two intercity bus terminals. From Terminal Malecón, Paseo Obregón 125, Transportes Aguila runs buses between La Paz and Pichilingue (US$1.20, every two hours 0800-1200, hourly thereafter till 1800), San José del Cabo (US$7.60, six buses a day), and Cabo San Lucas (US$9.30, five buses a day).

The Central Camionera, used mainly by Aguila, is located at Calle Jalisco and Independencia. From here, northbound buses depart twice daily (late morning and early evening) for Cd. Constitución (US$7.60), Loreto (US$13.30), Mulegé (US$18), Santa Rosalía (US$22), Guerrero Negro (US$29), Ensenada (US$51), and Tijuana (US$56); there is also a single daily departure for Mexicali in the late afternoon for US$64.

Southbound, Transportes Aguila runs buses from this terminal four times daily to the central Cape Region towns of El Triunfo (US$2), San Antonio (US$2), San Bartolo (US$3), Santiago (US$5), and Miraflores (US$5), then continues on to San José del Cabo (US$7.60) and Cabo San Lucas (US$8.60). More direct buses to Cabo San Lucas via Todos Santos operate six times daily between 0630 and 1900 for US$9.30. The fare as far as Todos Santos is US$7.60.

Driving: For now, Mexico 1 is the only federal highway leading to La Paz. A local consortium sponsored by CANACINTRA (National Chamber of Manufacturing Industries) has announced plans to develop a new four-lane toll road that would run along the west coast from Ensenada to La Paz—instead of turning inland at El Rosario as does Mexico 11—but so far the project is still in the discussion stages.

Fuel: La Paz is blessed with seven PEMEX stations, all offering Magna Sin (unleaded), Nova (leaded), and diesel.

Sea

The ferry port at Pichilingue, 16 km (9.5 miles) northeast of downtown La Paz via Mexico 11, serves vehicle and passenger ferries between La Paz and two mainland destinations, Topolobampo (for Los Mochis) and Mazatlán. **SEMATUR** (tel. 5-38-33, 5-46-66, fax 5-65-88) runs passenger and vehicle ferries to and from both cities; the company also has tentative plans to begin a new route between La Paz and Puerto Vallarta, replacing the old Cabo San Lucas-Puerto Vallarta ferry discontinued several years ago.

You can book SEMATUR ferry tickets in advance at the ferry terminal (tel. 2-94-85), the city ticket office (tel. 5-38-33, 5-46-66) at Calle 5 de Mayo and Guillermo Prieto, or Turismo La Paz (tel. 2-76-76, 2-83-00) at the Hotel Perla.

For fares and schedules, see "Getting There" under "Out and About."

Vehicle Permits: Tourist cards must have a special endorsement (a temporary vehicle-import permit) for vehicular travel on the Mexican mainland. These permits aren't needed

for Baja California travel, but if you've driven down to La Paz and decide you'd like to take your wheels on a mainland-bound ferry, you'll need to get one before buying a ticket. The whole process operates more smoothly in Tijuana, so if you anticipate using the ferry service, doing the paperwork in advance will save time and hassle.

If for whatever reason you decide to take the ferry and haven't done the paperwork in advance, you can arrange the proper permit in La Paz. Simply apply at the customs office (aduana) near the downtown pier—*not* the Pichilingue ferry pier—a day or two in advance of departure. Bring your vehicle plus all immigration and registration papers, quadruple photocopies of your driver's license, proof of a U.S. insurance policy valid for six months from the date of application, and a credit card to post a "bond" of US$10. Without a temporary vehicle-import permit, SEMATUR will not sell vehicle tickets to non-Mexican citizens. For further information, read the section on vehicle permits in "Getting There."

Private Boats: La Paz is an official Mexican port of entry and, as such, the COTP office at the Muelle Fiscal has authority to clear yachts for movement throughout Mexican waters. The easiest way to arrange this is to check in at the Marina de la Paz and let the marina staff process all port clearance papers. For Marina de la Paz clients, clear-in service is free, clear-out is US$10; for nonclients charges are US$5 in, US$15 out. Only one clearance in and out is required for entering and exiting the country; between Mexican ports the same papers can be presented. See the "Boating" section of "Out and About" for information on the five La Paz marinas.

Local Public Transport

You can reach most points of interest downtown on foot. For outlying areas, you can choose city buses, hire taxis, or route taxis.

Bus: As in other towns on the peninsula, a La Paz city bus bears the name of either the principal street along its run or the district where the route begins and ends. Any bus marked El Centro, for example, will end up near the Mercado Municipal at Revolución and Degollado. Bus fare anywhere in town is around US$.30. Buses to Pichilingue depart from the Terminal Malecón (Paseo Obregón 125) regularly 0800-1800; the fare is US$1.20.

Taxi: Taxi stands are found throughout El Centro, the downtown area between calles 5 de Mayo and Degollado, and in front of the tourist hotels. The average taxi hire downtown costs around US$3-4; La Paz taxis don't have meters, so it's sometimes necessary to haggle to arrive at the correct fare.

Route taxis (*taxi de ruta*) operate along the main avenues parallel to city buses for about US$.45 per person.

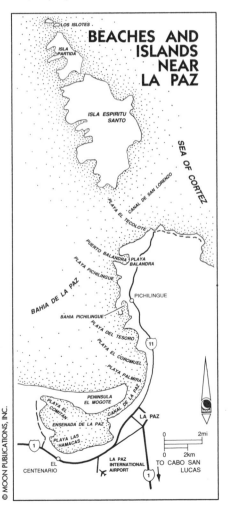

BEACHES AND ISLANDS NEAR LA PAZ

Car Rental: Several La Paz travel agencies can arrange auto rental, but rates are generally lower if you deal directly with a rental agency. **Avis** (tel. 2-26-51) at Paseo Obregón between Pineda and Marquéz de León; **Servitur Autorento** (tel. 2-14-48, calles 5 de Febrero and Abasolo); **Autorentos del Pacífico (Hertz)** (tel. 2-53-00, Paseo Obregón 2130); **Thrifty** (tel. 5-96-96, Paseo Obregón and Lerdo de Tejada, also at Hotel Palmira and La Concha Beach Resort); and **Budget** (tel. 2-10-97, Paseo Obregón and Hidalgo) offer Volkswagen bugs, vans, and Jettas for US$25-40 per day, plus a per-kilometer charge. Nissan Tsuru IIs and Jeeps are much more expensive, running US$65-83 per day plus kilometer charges or US$90-100 including free kilometers, tax, and insurance. All companies offer significant discounts for rentals of six days or more.

Avis, Thrifty, and Hertz operate service counters at La Paz International Airport.

VICINITY OF LA PAZ

San Juan De Los Planes- Punta Arena De La Ventana

State highway BCS 286 begins south of La Paz off Mexico 1 (at Km 211) and leads southeast 43 km (26 miles) to the agricultural center of San Juan de los Planes. Along the way this paved road climbs over the northwestern escarpment of the Sierra de la Laguna, then descends toward the coastal plains with a panoramic view of aquamarine Bahía de la Ventana and Isla Cerralvo in the distance. At Km 38 a graded road branches northeast off BCS 286 eight km (five miles) to the fish camps of La Ventana and El Sargento on **Bahía de la Ventana.**

Windsurfing is good here due to the strong northeasterlies channeled through Canal de Cerralvo to the north. Free beach camping is available along the bay just south of La Ventana.

San Juan de los Planes, or Los Planes, as it's usually called, has several markets, a café, and around 1,500 inhabitants supported by farming (cotton, tomatoes, beans, and corn) or by fishing at nearby bays. From Los Planes, a graded road runs east 21 km (13 miles) to **Bahía de los Muertos,** a pretty, curved bay with primitive beach camping.

A lesser road branches northeast about three km before los Muertos and leads eight km (five miles) to beautiful Punta Arena de la Ventana. The defunct **Hotel Las Arenas** was once a fishing and diving resort with its own 1,820-meter (6,000-foot) airstrip; it's up for sale now.

The waters off Punta Arena de la Ventana reputedly offer Baja's best roosterfish angling; wahoo, amberjack, grouper, dorado, and billfish are also reportedly in abundant supply. Guided panga trips are available locally for US$50-75 per day. A bit south of the abandoned hotel, at **Punta Perico** ("Parakeet Point"), is a lively reef with varied depths of 3-25 meters (10-82 feet).

Isla Cerralvo

Across Bahía de la Ventana and Canal de Cerralvo lies **Isla Cerralvo,** one of the largest islands in the Sea of Cortez at about 30 km (18 miles) from north to south. At the time of early Spanish exploration, the island featured large pearl-oyster beds and was inhabited by a small group of Pericú Indians. Later the rugged island reportedly became a favored final resting place for *vagabundos del mar,* Mexican-Indians who roamed the Sea of Cortez in dugout canoes until well into this century.

Today Cerralvo remains one of the least visited of Baja's large coastal islands, simply due to its location on the far side of the Pichilingue Peninsula. Coral-encrusted **Roca Montaña,** off the southeastern tip of the island, is an excellent diving and fishing location, as is **Piedras Gordas,** marked by a navigation light at the southwestern tip. Depths at these sites range 3-15 meters (10-50 feet). Other good dive sites include the rock reefs off the northern end (average depth 18-21 meters/60-70 feet), which feature a good variety of reef fishes, sea turtles, and shipwrecks. One of the reefs, **Arrecife de la Foca,** features an unidentified shipwreck with "Mazatlán" marked on the hull. **La Reina,** another reef at the north end of the island, is the site of a large steel-hulled freighter that sank half a century ago. Barely a hundred meters off the island's west shore are two adjacent rock reefs known as **La Reinita.**

Access to Isla Cerralvo is easiest from Bahía de la Ventana or Punta Arena, where beach launches are possible. From La Paz, it's a long haul around the Pichilingue Peninsula via Canal de San Lorenzo.

CENTRAL CAPE

Along Mexico 1 between La Paz and San José del Cabo are a number of mining-turned-farming towns with cobblestone streets and 19th-century stone-and-stucco architecture. Nestled among well-watered arroyos of the Sierra de la Laguna, these neglected settlements now support themselves growing citrus, avocado, mangoes, corn, and sugarcane, and, to a lesser extent, serving the needs of passing travelers. Many of the families living in the central Cape Region are descended from Spanish settlers of the 18th and early 19th centuries. Others are newcomers—including a few *norteamericanos*—drawn by the area's solitude and simplicity.

San Pedro appears—and quickly disappears—just before the junction of Mexico 1 and Mexico 19. Carnitas connoisseurs swear by **El Paraíso de San Pedro,** an unassuming roadside café on the highway's west side. The junction itself is reached at Km 185; if Cabo San Lucas is your destination, you must decide whether to take Mexico 19 via Todos Santos or the Transpeninsular Highway (Mexico 1) via El Triunfo, San Antonio, San Bartolo, Santiago, and Miraflores.

For trailers, RVs, and other wide or lengthy vehicles, Mexico 19 is the better choice since it runs along relatively flat terrain. South of San Pedro, Mexico 1 winds through the Sierra Laguna and features a succession of dizzying curves and steep grades. Unless you're in a hurry to reach Cabo San Lucas, Mexico 1 is the most scenic choice for drivers of autos and light trucks.

El Triunfo-San Antonio

During the Jesuit missionary period, this section along the lower northern slopes of the sierra was earmarked for cattle ranching. Mining concessions moved in following the discovery of silver near San Antonio in 1748, and the settlement quickly grew into a town of 10,000 people. When Loreto was heavily damaged by a hurricane in 1829, San Antonio briefly served as capital of the Californias before the capital was transferred to La Paz in 1830.

Gold and silver were discovered at El Triunfo ("Triumph"), seven km (4.5 miles) north of San Antonio, in 1862. By 1878 the large Progreso mining concern had established a gold and silver mine that attracted a number of Mexican, French, English, Italian, German, and North American immigrants. The company paid for the first post office in the region, and also installed the first electrical and phone lines to La Paz.

Both towns bustled with frontier commerce through the end of the 19th century, when the ore began running out; then a hurricane in 1918 flooded the mines, and by 1925 both towns were virtually abandoned. Today El Triunfo has only around 500 residents, San Antonio around 1,000. A number of historic adobe buildings in both towns have been restored, including El Triunfo's **Casa Municipal** and San Antonio's unusual 1825 church exhibiting train and paddle-wheeler motifs. **Restaurant Las Glorias,** on the east side of the highway through El Triunfo, is a good food stop.

San Antonio, set in a lushly planted valley that descends eastward all the way to the Sea of Cortez, boasts a PEMEX station with Magna Sin, a post office, and a few markets. A fun time to visit San Antonio is 13 June, the feast day of St. Anthony, when the whole town (and El Triunfo) turns out for music and dancing.

San Bartolo

Beginning just past Km 128, San Bartolo is the greenest and lushest of the central Cape settings, thanks to a large spring gushing straight out of a mountainside into the arroyo. To complete the tropical picture, many homes sport thatched roofs. Mangoes, avocados, and other fresh fruits are available at roadside stands or in town. **Restaurant Los Burritos, Restaurant El Paso,** and two other unnamed eateries on the east side of the highway serve meals.

San Bartolo's patron saint day is 19 June, conveniently close to San Antonio's.

Santiago

The largest of the central Cape Region towns (pop. 2,500), set in the Arroyo de Santiago among stands of blue fan palms, Santiago was founded as a mission community in 1723. The mission was abandoned in the latter half of the 18th century following a series of Pericú rebellions, and only in relatively recent times has agriculture revived the arroyo community. A handful of *tiendas* line the town plaza; the town also offers a PEMEX station, hotel, supermarket, church, and the only zoo on the peninsula south of Mexicali.

Among the residents of the small but nicely landscaped **Parque Zoologico** are a peccary, bear, coyote, fox, monkey, parrots, and ducks. Some of the animals are Cape Region natives. The park is open daily 0600-1800 and admission is free, though donations are gladly accepted. To bypass the town center and proceed directly to the zoo, take the left fork just after crossing the dry arroyo near the town entrance, then take the next left fork onto a levee road that curves along the south end of town to the zoo.

Santiago celebrates its patron saint day, the feast day of St. James, on 25 July.

Accommodations and food are available at **El Palomar,** south of the plaza. This eight-room casa de huéspedes charges US$20-25 a night; meals—primarily seafood and Mexican standards—are served Mon.-Sat. 0830-2000.

The dirt road to the zoo continues westward nine km (5.5 miles) to the village of **Agua Caliente,** where a hot spring in a nearby canyon (about seven km/four miles west of the village) has been channeled into a concrete tub for recreational purposes. Camping is permitted in the canyon.

At the north end of Santiago, another dirt road leads northwest to **Rancho San Dionísio** (23.5 km/14.5 miles), where the Cañon San Dionísio approach to Picacho la Laguna begins.

Three km south of Santiago is a large cement sphere marking the Tropic of Cancer (23.5° north latitude), south of which you are "in the tropics." As if to sanctify the crossing, an impressive Guadalupe shrine has been built next to the rather unattractive marker.

Miraflores

A 2.5-km (1.5-mile) paved road to Miraflores branches west off Mexico 1 at Km 71 next to a PEMEX station. This ranching and farming community is known for leatherwork; **Curtiduría Miraflores** ("Miraflores Tannery"), just off the access road between the highway and town, sells handmade leather saddles, bridles, whips, horsehair lariats, and other ranching gear as well as a few souvenir items such as leather hats, belts, and bags. Custom orders are accepted. Look for a small sign on the right-hand side of the access road reading Leather Shop. **Restaurant Bar Bugambilias** in town provides simple Mexican meals.

A dirt road northwest of Miraflores leads to **Boca de la Sierra** ("Mouth of the Sierra"), a settlement at the mouth of Cañon San Bernardo—the second of the three canyons providing access deep into the Sierra de la Laguna. Another dirt road southwest of town leads to the mouth of Cañon San Pablo, a third Laguna hiking route. Inquire at the tannery about guided trips into the sierra to view Indian rock-art sites.

SIERRA DE LA LAGUNA

The mountainous heart of the Cape Region extends southward from the Llano de la Paz (the plains just south of La Paz) to Cabo San Lucas, a distance of around 135 km (81 miles). Originally named Sierra de la Victoria by the Spanish, it was renamed Sierra de la Laguna in the early Mexican era. These peaks are unique among sierras in the southern half of Baja California in that they're granitic rather than volcanic. Unlike the sierras to the north, the entire Laguna range is tilted eastward instead of westward, i.e., its steepest slopes are on the west side of the escarpment rather than the east. They're also lined up along a north-south axis instead of in a northwest-southeast direction, the only mountain range on the entire peninsula with this orientation.

Picacho de la Laguna (elevation 2,155 meters/7,090 feet), roughly in the sierra's center, is usually cited as the highest peak in the range, although according to some sources Cerro las Casitas—approximately 6.5 km (four miles) southeast of Picacho de la Laguna—may be higher. Between these two peaks is a large, flat meadow called La Laguna (elevation 1,700 meters/5,600 feet). This depression held a moun-

tain lake until around 1870 when Cañon San Dionísio became sufficiently eroded to drain away accumulated water.

Islands In The Sky

This meadow and other flats and high canyons in the Sierra de la Laguna contain a number of "relict environments" preserving flora and fauna long ago lost to the arid plains below. La Laguna's highlands, in fact, receive more annual precipitation—up to 89 centimeters (35 inches) per year in some microclimates—than any other place in Baja California.

These "islands in the sky" have gathered together a rare mix of desert, tropical, and subalpine species seen growing side by side nowhere else in North America. Included are mosses and cacti, madrone and monkey flower, palm and willow, and other unlikely combinations. Of 390 plant species known to grow in the sierra, at least 70 are reportedly indigenous. Undisturbed by human progress, deer, coyote, mountain lion, Pacific tree frog, and dozens of hummingbird species also thrive in the highland areas of the sierra.

A growing number of naturalists and outdoor enthusiasts are clamoring for the upper Sierra de la Laguna to be declared a national park. Some Baja maps even optimistically add green shading to the area as if it already had park status. On the darker side, one rumor has it the state government has plans to allow development in La Laguna meadow. Several ranchers graze livestock in the area. Anyone interested in expressing support for a Sierra de la Laguna national park should contact the offices of Mexico's SEDESOL (Secretaría de Desarollo Social) and SECTUR (Secretaría de Turismo) in La Paz.

BOB RACE

Hiking And Backpacking

The Sierra de la Laguna is a popular hiking area for Cape residents, as it offers the opportunity to leave behind the fig trees and palms of the arid-tropical environment for a walk among cottonwoods and subalpine meadows. Three lengthy east-west canyons provide the principal access into the sierra: Cañon Dionísio, Cañon San Bernardo, and Cañon San Pablo. All three routes enable hikers to traverse the sierra's spine from east to west—or vice versa, although the western escarpment is considerably more precipitous. Primitive campsites are available along each of the three routes.

The best backpacking season for La Laguna is late fall, after the rainy season has passed and sierra streams and tinajas are full. In January and February, temperatures above 1,500 meters (5,000 feet) can dip close to freezing at night; July-Oct. rains may wash out trails and flood the canyons. A compass and good topo map are musts for any trip into the Sierra de la Laguna. To cover all three routes, you should possess copies of Mexico's F12B23, F12B24, F12B33, and F12B34 50,000-scale topos. (See "Hiking and Backpacking" in "Out and About" for recommended map sources.) Bring warm clothing and sleeping bags for the summit; morning frost isn't uncommon even in fall and spring. Long pants and sturdy hiking shoes—even at lower elevations—are recommended as a defense against the abundant cactus and nettles.

The northernmost route, via **Cañon San Dionísio,** leads directly to La Laguna, the range's largest and most impressive meadow. La Laguna also lies between Picacho de la Laguna and Cerro las Casitas, the sierra's tallest peaks, hence the scenery on this hike is impressive. The eastern mouth of the canyon is reached via a dirt road to Rancho San Dionísio from Santiago (19 km/12 miles). From there it's a 13-km (eight-mile) hike west through the canyon mouth, then into a side arroyo and finally along the southern rim of the canyon to La Laguna, at just under 1,800 meters (6,000 feet). Pine and oak began appearing about two-thirds of the way. This trail is not that easy to follow and is intersected by potentially confusing animal paths; a guide, available at Rancho San Dionísio or in Santiago, is highly recommended. If you decide to go it alone, be sure to carry a topo map and compass, and pay very close attention to your position on the trail.

Those wishing to explore a bit can follow the canyon four km straight west of the ranch into a steep area of boulders; where the arroyo forks there's a waterfall and deep pools suitable for swimming. Don't attempt to follow the canyon all the way to the meadow unless you're into some very serious bouldering and scrambling.

Near the northwest edge of the meadow itself are a couple of herder's shacks; just past these the trail cuts into the forest and divides; the southern branch descends to La Burrera, while the north branch ascends Picacho de la Laguna. Easy to climb, the latter peak is bare of trees and provides splendid views of the surrounding terrain. A nearby hill surmounted by radio towers is also a good vantage point.

Those wishing to traverse the sierra can descend westward from La Laguna another 11 km (seven miles) to La Burrera. Also known as San Juan del Aserradero, this village on the sierra's western slopes lies around 17.5 km (11 miles) northeast of Todos Santos. From the east side of the sierra, count on three days to La Laguna and back with time to explore the area; from the west side a roundtrip can be completed in two days since the distance between La Burrera and La Laguna is a bit shorter, though the route is steeper. A straight traverse, starting from either side, is possible in three days. Roads from La Burrera meet Mexico 19 south and north of Todos Santos; the area east of these junctions is honeycombed with other dirt roads, but if you continue in a westerly direction you'll eventually come to the highway.

On the Todos Santos side, the road to La Burrera leaves Mexico 19 about 100 meters south of the Punta Lobos turnoff. Past an old water tower, take the first left and continue straight through several intersections till the road ends at a gate and parking area. From here hikers can follow posted signs to the main trail to La Laguna.

The next route south, via **Cañon San Bernardo,** is a relatively easy hike that crests at around 900 meters (3,000 feet). The canyon trailhead is accessible via an eight-km (five-mile) dirt road from Miraflores to Boca de la Sierra, where the trail skirts a dam and follows the canyon to the crest, 16 km (10 miles) northwest. Several pools along the way provide fresh water year-round. From the 900-meter mark, the trail continues over the sierra to the village of Santo Domingo on the western side, for a total traverse of 22.5 km (14 miles). The Cañon San Bernardo crossing makes a good four- to five-day hike, although it's possible to make a quick overnight to the crest and back from the eastern approach.

Cañon San Pablo provides the southernmost route into the sierra, reaching an elevation of around 1,000 meters (3,250 feet). The canyon mouth is best approached by taking a 6.5-km (four-mile) dirt road west from Caduaño, a village four km (2.5 miles) south of Miraflores, to Rancho El Salto. From Rancho El Salto, it's approximately 10.5 km (6.5 miles) to the crest; the trail continues over the ridge and along a steeper 4.8-km (three-mile) westward descent to the village of El Guerigo on the other side, where a network of dirt roads leads west to Mexico 19. A leisurely El Salto-El Guerigo hike takes four to five days.

Guides

Those unsure of their backpacking and orientation skills should consider hiring a local guide for Sierra de la Laguna trips, since Laguna trails are often obscured and junctions not always obvious. A guide can also prepare simple camp meals and point out items of natural interest—Indian rock art, flora and fauna—that first-timers might otherwise miss. Guides are available in Santiago, Miraflores, and Todos Santos; simply ask around. For the Cañon San Dionísio route, you can sometimes arrange a guide at Rancho San Dionísio, just before the eastern trailhead.

The going rate for guides is US$15-25 per day per person, depending on whether pack animals like horses or burros are used. Rancho San Dionísio charges US$20 for a guide without mules, no matter how many people are hiking.

EAST CAPE

The Cabo del Este ("East Cape") consists of a succession of scenic tropical coves and beaches extending from the northern end of Bahía de Palmas south to San José del Cabo, at the tip of the cape.

Beach camping is available along almost the entire length of the coast, although the area is developing gradually and some of the prettiest beaches now bear rather tasteless housing developments. Coastal development, in fact, is ongoing from Buena Vista all the way around the Cape to Cabo San Lucas, with land prices skyrocketing in recent years. Fortunately, there are still a few choice spots left where the fishing and camping are free.

Bahía De Palmas

The gently curving shore of Bahía de Palmas, stretching 32 km (20 miles) from Punta Pescadero south to Punta Arena, is a Baja fishing and windsurfing mecca. In many places along the bay, anglers can reach the 100-fathom line less than a mile from shore, especially toward Punta Pescadero (Fisherman's Point) at the north end. Billfish frequent the area June-Dec., yellowtail Jan.-June, and roosterfish, wahoo, tuna, and dorado year-round. Inshore catches include pargo, cabrilla, grouper, amberjack, wahoo, and pompano, plus the occasional yellowtail or rooster.

The world-famous "Tuna Hole," about 6.5 km (four miles) directly south of Punta Pescadero, reaches depths of 50 fathoms and has a year-round population of sizable yellowfin tuna; rocks along the Tuna Hole's submerged canyon walls tend to cut the lines of all but the most skilled sportfishers. You can arrange guided fishing trips at any of the hotels along the bay—generally US$80-150 a day for a panga, US$200-300 a day aboard a fishing cruiser. You can launch trailered or cartopped boats off sandy beaches or at the boat ramp just north of the Hotel Spa Buena Vista.

With such favorable fishing conditions, it's little wonder legions of gringo anglers are buying up property along the bay to build vacation and retirement homes. Although the area is still without telephone service, the Barriles-Buena Vista area is starting to look like a San Diego

*Vela-O'Neill
Baja Championships*

suburb. Because there are no real zoning regulations, construction varies from flimsy palapa extensions to impressive beach homes. Construction trash is unfortunately a common sight; in some spots the unmistakable stench of sewage indicates improper installation of cesspools.

Windsurfing: Board-sailors flock to Los Barriles Nov.-April when sideshore winds—aided by thermals from the Sierra de la Laguna—blow 18-30 knots for weeks at a time. The rest of the year, you'll have to settle for around 12-14 knots—not too shabby. During the high-wind season, inshore water temperatures average around 22-24° C (72-75° F), with air temperatures in the 25-29° C (78-85° F) range.

Several hotels on the bay rent windsurfing equipment and provide basic instruction. During the high-wind season, two windsurfing centers in the Barriles-Buena Vista area can arrange package deals that include use of state-of-the-art equipment, lessons geared to your level, air transportation, and accommodations. Bring a wetsuit, harness, and booties—the centers supply the rest. **Baja Surf Club** (tel. 800-551-8844 in the U.S.) is based at the Hotel Palmas de Cortez, while **Vela Highwind Center** (tel. 800-223-5443 in the U.S.) uses both Hotel Playa del Sol (formerly Playa Hermosa) and Hotel Palmas de Cortez.

During the second week of January, Vela Highwind Centers and surf-gear manufacturer O'Neill co-host the annual Baja Championships sailboard race at Los Barriles. Non-windsurfing spectators are welcome to watch the event from shore. The center also offers a race clinic, staffed by world-class instructors, the week before the competition. For more information, contact Vela Highwind Centers, 125 University Ave. No. 40, Palo Alto, CA 94301, or call (415) 322-0613.

Surfing: One of Baja's least-known surfing spots—simply because no one expects surf along the Sea of Cortez—is Punta Arena, at the south end of Bahía de Palmas just below Punta Colorada. A left point break can crop up here anytime during the March-Nov. southwest swell, but the peak surf usually comes around in late summer or early fall—chubasco season.

Hotels, Central Bay (Los Barriles/Buena Vista): Several dirt roads branch east off Mexico 1 between Kms 110 and 105 to hotels and trailer parks—most owned by North Ameri-

cans—scattered along the central section of Bahía de Palmas. None have local phone service, so reservations must be made through U.S. reservations offices. In the center of the bay at Los Barriles are the **Hotel Playa del Sol** (tel. 408-375-4755, toll-free 800-347-6847 in California, P.O. Box 1827, Monterey, CA 93942) and **Hotel Palmas de Cortez** (tel. 818-222-7144, P.O. Box 9016, Calabasas, CA 91372). Hotel Playa del Sol features a restaurant, bar, and rental fishing tackle; rooms cost US$55 s, US$80 d. The hotel is closed in September.

South of Hotel Playa del Sol—and just a half-mile off the highway—the Hotel Palmas de Cortez offers air-conditioned rooms for US$55 s, US$85 d; facilities include a restaurant and bar, pool, tennis court, a 1,000-meter (3,250-foot) landing strip (Unicom 122.8), windsurfing gear, and equipment for both fishing and hunting. The dove and quail hunting in the nearby Sierra de la Laguna is reportedly good.

About 6.5 km (four miles) south of Los Barriles, at Buena Vista, is the **Rancho Bueno Vista** (tel. 818-303-1517, 800-258-8200 outside CA, P.O. Box 673, Monrovia, California 91016). The resort has a nice restaurant and bar facing the sea, a pool, tennis courts, fishing tackle that includes fly-fishing equipment, cruisers, windsurfing gear, a boat ramp, and air-conditioned cottages for US$60-130 per night for two, plus US$45 for each additional guest.

Hotel Spa Buena Vista (tel. 310-943-0869, 800-752-3555 in CA only, 16211 E. Whittier Blvd., Whittier, California 90603), about a kilometer farther south, offers rooms in a converted hacienda as well as condo-style units for US$65 s, US$90 d, or US$130 t, including three meals. Additional people pay US$25 each. Facilities include pool, tennis court, mineral spa, and equipment for fishing and hunting. The Spa Buena Vista also offers special package deals that include accommodations, all meals, and several days of guided fishing.

Hotels, North and South Bay: At the extreme north end of Bahía de Palmas (13 km/eight miles north of Los Barriles via an unpaved road from Mexico 1 signed El Cardonal) is the **Hotel Punta Pescadero** (tel. 415-948-5505, 800-426-2252, P.O. Box 1044, Los Altos, CA 94022), a small fishing resort on 125 palm-studded acres overlooking a sandy beach. A room costs US$85 s/d and comes with sea views, a private veranda, television, and refrigerator; some also have fireplaces. The resort features restaurant and bar, pool, tennis court, golf course, landing strip (1,160 meters/3,500 feet, Unicom 122.8), and rental equipment for scuba and free diving, boating, and fishing. The unpaved road to Punta Pescadero is not recommended for RVs or trailers.

Farther north along this same road (23 km/14 miles from Los Barriles), a French Canadian recently established **El Cardonal Resort** (no phone), which offers apartments as well as spaces for RV or tent camping. Early reports say it's well-run and pristine, and there are supposed to be some prehistoric cave paintings nearby. The sandy, washboard road to El Cardonal crosses a couple of arroyos that could be problematic in heavy rains.

Punta Colorada, at the south end of the bay (16 km/10 miles east of Mexico 1 via the La Ribera road), features the **Hotel Punta Colorada** (tel. 818-222-5066, 800-368-4334, P.O. Box 9016, Calabasas, CA 91372). Roosterfish fanatics often choose to stay here since the roosterfishing off nearby Punta Arena is usually the best in Baja. Large rooms cost US$50 s, US$80 d; like the competition to the north, Hotel Punta Colorada has its own airstrip (1,060 meters/3,300 feet, Unicom 122.8). Guided hunting and fishing trips are available. The hotel is closed September and the first week of October.

North of Punta Colorada lies the palapa-style, 12-room **Inn at Rancho Leonero** (tel. 619-428-2164, 800-696-2164, 223 Via de San Ysidro, Suite D, San Ysidro, CA 92143) with restaurant and bar, jacuzzi, fully equipped dive center, and rental fishing gear. Rates are US$60 s, US$95 d, US$125 t, US$150 quad. All rooms offer sea views. Rancho Leonero's restaurant is considered one of the best on the East Cape.

Casa de Rafa (tel. 112-5-36-36, ex. 163) is a new bed and breakfast with six rooms in Buena Vista, just off the highway near Km 109.

Camping and RV Parks: North of Hotel Playa del Sol in Los Barriles are **Martin Verdugo's Trailer Park** (A.P. 17, Los Barriles, BCS 23501) and **Playa de Oro RV Resort** (tel. 818-336-7494 in the U.S., 3106 Capa Drive, Hacienda Heights, CA 91745). Both have flush toilets, showers, laundry, boat ramps, and full hookups for US$8-9 for two, plus US$1.50 for

each additional person; tent sites cost US$5 a night at Verdugo's, US$6.50 at Playa de Oro. Verdugo's operates a restaurant; Playa de Oro features an ocean view and bonded boat storage. Both parks can arrange fishing trips. On the west side of the dirt road north, the smaller **Juanito's Garden** has trailer spaces without hookups for US$6-8 a night.

Free primitive camping is available in the area north of these two parks, usually referred to by gringos as the "North Shore."

About two km south of Hotel Spa Buena Vista is the modest **La Capilla Trailer Park,** with flush toilets, showers, and full hookups for US$8 a day.

Food: The modest but popular **Restaurant Gaviota**, out on the highway in Buena Vista, offers a standard list of fresh seafood (including fish tacos), antojitos, and breakfasts, and is open daily 0800-2100. The Gaviota also sports a jukebox stocked with norteña tunes. **Restaurant Calafia**, on Mexico 1 near the Buena Vista police station, offers good shrimp tacos and tables with views of Bahía de Palmas. Usually open for lunch and early dinner only.

Los Barriles has but one restaurant, **Tío Pablo**, a large palapa-style structure with a mostly American menu and Taco Bell-like decor; it's open daily 1130-2200.

El Camino Rural Costero ("The Rural Coastal Road")

About halfway down the infamous Coastal Road is a brass plaque commemorating the road's May '84 grading. For first-time drivers who have braved washouts and sandpits to read it, the sign never fails to elicit a few chuckles. Big plans claim the road will soon be paved—such claims have been around for several years now. In spite of the rough access, certain areas along the Coastal Road—e.g., Cabo Pulmo and Los Frailes—are filling up with small, half-finished housing developments. Yet plenty of open space for beach camping is still available.

Contrasting strongly with the budding resort development are several ranchos along the road that raise cattle, goats, pigs, and sheep—mostly without fencing. If you substitute fiberglass pangas for dugout canoes, the ranchos today appear much like they must have in 1941, when John Steinbeck described Cabo Pulmo:

On the shore behind the white beach was one of those lonely little rancherías we came to know later. Usually a palm or two are planted nearby, and by these trees sticking up out of the brush one can locate the houses. There is usually a small corral, a burro or two, a few pigs, and some scrawny chickens. The cattle range wide for food. A dugout canoe lies on the beach, for a good part of the food comes from the sea. Rarely do you see a light from the sea, for the people go to sleep at dusk and awaken with the first light.

In general, driving conditions along the Coastal Road are suitable for passenger cars of average road clearance; even smaller RVs sometimes manage to make it all the way. Sand can be a problem in places, and shoulders are invariably soft. Weather plays an important role in day-to-day conditions; following late-summer or early-fall storms, parts of the Coastal Road can be impassable. Make inquiries before embarking on the trip and be prepared to turn back if necessary. The 88.5-km (55-mile) stretch between La Ribera and San José del Cabo can take up to four hours.

La Ribera-Cabo Pulmo: To reach the Coastal Road from the north, take the paved road signed La Ribera east at Km 93 off Mexico 1. This 12-km (7.5-mile) road terminates in La Ribera (La Rivera), a small town of around 2,000 with markets, houses, PEMEX station, church, and **Restaurant Las Tres Banderas.** Another paved road branches south from La Ribera, meeting the unpaved road east to Punta Colorada and the Coastal Road. The section of the Coastal Road from here to Cabo Pulmo, 26.5 km (16.5 miles) south of La Ribera, is usually in fair condition.

Extending south from Cabo Pulmo is **Bahía Pulmo,** noted for its reef-building corals. The bay's **Pulmo Reef,** one of only three coastal reefs in North America, is rich with Panamic marinelife and hence a favorite snorkeling and scuba-diving destination. Adding to its attraction is the fact that it's easily accessible from shore.

The reef has eight fingers that extend northeastward from the bay shore. The reef system here is very delicate; reef corals can't tolerate temperatures lower than 21° C (70° F) and must

have clear water since debris settling on their disks and tentacles will kill them. The Mexican government has declared Pulmo Reef an underwater nature preserve—no fishing or anchoring at the reef is permitted. Shore development remains the reef's biggest ecological challenge, since the corals rely on unpolluted and unimpeded runoff. If resorts or housing developments are permitted along Bahía Pulmo, the reef will perish quickly.

Another system, **Outer Pulmo Reef,** lies roughly 3.2 km (two miles) east of Cabo Pulmo (the cape, not the village). Ask for José Luis Purrieta or Juan Castro in Cabo Pulmo if you're interested in a guided dive or boat service. Their **Pepe's Dive Center** (tel. 114-3-05-05, A.P. 532, Cabo San Lucas, BCS, 619-489-7001 in the U.S.) offers a complete diving service, including PADI certification, to 14 dive sites in the area.

Bahía Los Frailes-San José Del Cabo

About eight km (five miles) south of Cabo Pulmo village is a sandy spur road east to Bahía los Frailes. This is one of the best camping beaches along the East Cape in spite of the conspicuous hotel/housing development underway behind the beach. Onshore and inshore fishing is usually good—surfcasters even reportedly land tuna here. Windsurfers will find a steady cross-shore breeze at the bay's south end. The bay plummets here as deep as 210 meters (688 feet).

South of Los Frailes, the Coastal Road deteriorates rapidly but those with sturdy vehicles and steady nerves will be rewarded by secluded arroyo campsites and vignettes of disappearing ranch life. About 12.5 km (7.5 miles) south of Los Frailes is **Rancho Tule,** followed after 5.5 km (3.5 miles) by **Rancho Boca Vinorama,** then another five km (three miles) and 1.5 km (one mile) respectively to **Rancho San Luis** and **Rancho Santa Elena.** Following another 5.5-km (3.5-mile) section is the small dairy farm of **La Fortuna,** after which the road improves a bit for 24 km (15 miles) before terminating at **Pueblo la Playa,** a fishing village on the eastern outskirts of San José del Cabo. On the coast before Pueblo la Playa is **Punta Gorda,** known for fishing and, in a southwest swell, surfing.

The last couple of kilometers between Pueblo la Playa and San José del Cabo is more tropical than the entire East Cape, with mango trees, huge banyan trees, and wild sugarcane.

Accommodations and Food: Pepe's Diving Service can arrange accommodations in small houses with hot water, refrigerator, stove, and bath for US$25 per night.

Pulmo Beach Resort (tel. 208-726-9233, fax 726-5545, P.O. Box 774, Ketchum, ID 83340) rents one- and two-bedroom houses for US$50-65 per night for two people, US$12.50 per extra person, with discounts for stays of three nights or more. All units come with kitchens or kitchenettes, plus bed and bath linens.

The new **Hotel Bahía Frailes** (tel. 415-956-3499, toll-free 800-762-2252, 220 Montgomery St., Suite 1019, San Francisco, CA 94104) charges US$90 per adult (children 5-13 US$50, under five free) with three meals. One-bedroom suites cost US$110 per adult (same rates for children as regular rooms), while two-bedroom suites with four queen-size beds and two baths go for US$400 for four guests including meals. Pangas are available for rent from US$80 per day.

Just north of La Ribera, in a large mango orchard near the beach, is the tidy and well-run **Correcamino RV Park** (no phone, CB channel 66) where shady tent/camper/RV spaces cost US$6 per day. Facilities include hot showers and flush toilets.

Tito's, a casual palapa restaurant in the small settlement of Cabo Pulmo, can provide meals and drinking water. Beach camping is permitted along the bay—a nominal fee is collected at camp.

SAN JOSE DEL CABO

Los Cabos ("The Capes") is a marketing term of rather recent origin applied to the twin resort towns of San José del Cabo and Cabo San Lucas at Baja California's southernmost tip. Although closer to Los Cabos International Airport, San José represents the quieter, more traditional resort of the two. A somewhat older tourist crowd frequents San José (pop. 22,000), leaving Cabo San Lucas to partying singles and young couples.

HISTORY

Spanish galleons first visited Estero San José, at the mouth of the Río San José, to obtain fresh water near the end of their lengthy voyages from the Philippines to Acapulco in the late 17th and early 18th centuries. As pirate raids along the coast between Cabo San Lucas and La Paz became a problem, the need for a permanent Spanish settlement at the tip of the cape became increasingly urgent. The growing unrest among Guaycura and Pericú Indians south of Loreto also threatened to engulf mission communities to the north; the Spanish had to send armed troops to the Cape Region to quell Indian uprisings in 1723, 1725, and 1729.

In 1730 Jesuit Padre Nicolás Tamaral traveled south from Misión La Purísima and founded Misión San José del Cabo on a mesa overlooking the Río San José, some five km north of the current town site. Due to the overwhelming presence of mosquitoes at this site, Tamaral soon moved the mission to the mouth of the estuary, on a rise flanked by Cerro del Vigía and Cerro de la Cruz.

Tamaral and the Pericús got along fine until he pronounced an injunction against polygamy, long a tradition in Pericú society. After Tamaral punished a Pericú shaman for violating the anti-polygamy decree, the Indians rebelled and burned both the San José and Santiago missions in October 1734. Tamaral was killed in the attack. Shortly thereafter, the Spanish established a presidio, which served the dual purpose of protecting the community from insurgent Indians and the estuary from English pirates.

By 1767, virtually all the Indians in the area had died either of European-borne diseases or in skirmishes with the Spanish. Surviving mission Indians were moved to missions farther north, but San José del Cabo remained an important Spanish military outpost until the mid-19th century when the presidio was turned over to Mexican nationals.

During the Mexican-American War (1846-48), marines from the U.S. frigate *Portsmouth* briefly occupied the city. A bloody siege ensued, but the Mexicans prevailed under the leadership of Mexican naval officer José Antonio Mijares. Plaza Mijares, San José's town plaza, is named for him. As mining in the Cape Region gave out during the late 19th and early 20th centuries, San José lost population along with the rest of the region. A few farmers and

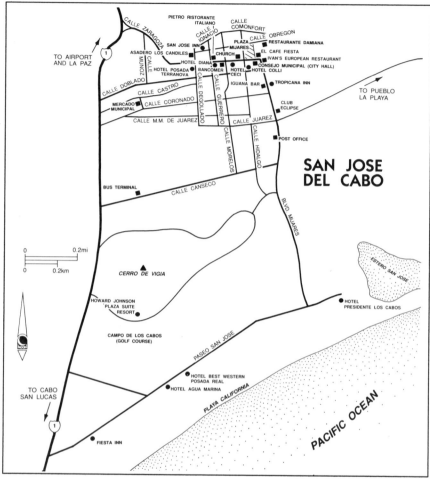

© MOON PUBLICATIONS, INC.

fishermen began trickling into the San José area in the '30s, and in 1940 the church was rebuilt.

San José remained largely a backwater until the Cape began attracting sportfishers and later the sun-and-sand set in the '60s and '70s. Since the late '70s, FONATUR (Fondo Nacional de Fomento del Turismo, or National Foundation for Tourism Development) has sponsored several tourist development projects along San José's shoreline. Fortunately, the development has done little to change San José's Spanish colonial character, and local residents take pride in restoring the town's 18th-century architecture and preserving its quiet, laidback ambience.

In November 1993 a severe rainstorm wreaked havoc on beachside condos near San José but the town itself was little damaged.

SIGHTS

Plaza Mijares
The shady town plaza at the intersection of Blvd. Mijares and Zaragoza—San José's two main

WHAT'S A GRINGO?

The Latin-American Spanish word *gringo*, reportedly a corruption of the Spanish word *greigo* or "Greek," has different meanings in different parts of Latin America. In Argentina or Uruguay, for example, it is used to refer to anyone of Italian descent. In Mexico and Central America, it's almost always reserved for persons of northern European descent, especially North Americans. In Cabo Pulmo, I once heard a naive, newly arrived white Canadian archaeologist comment that it would be easy for him to carry out his research in Baja because he wasn't a gringo. (Sorry pal, but you're a gringo, too.) In spite of everyday linguistic evidence to the contrary, many non-Spanish speakers insist that only Americans are gringos. The Mexicans, however, have a more precise epithet for Americans: *yanquis* or "Yankees."

Is *gringo* a derogatory term? It can certainly be used that way. Most of the time, however, it's simply an unconscious racial identification of neutral value. Educated Mexicans tend not to use it; instead they would typically say *norteamericano* or *americano* for Americans. Some Mexicans insist on the former even though the term is a slight to Canadians who, after all, are North Americans, too. *Canadiense* is used for Canadians, *alemán* for Germans, and so forth. Expatriate North Americans and Europeans living in Baja frequently refer to themselves and their expat friends as gringos.

and marshgrasses, a habitat for over 200 species of birds. Canoes can be rented at the Presidente for paddling around the lagoon.

Zona Hotelera
FONATUR has developed 4,000 shoreline acres adjacent to San José into a hotel-recreation zone. Thus far, the zone contains six resort hotels, a nine-hole golf course, and several condominium developments. The wide, sandy beach here, known either as Playa Hotelera or Playa California, is perfect for sunbathing, but the undertow is very strong.

La Playita
Just east of San José via Calle Juárez is a beach area called the La Playita ("Little Beach"), adjacent to the village Pueblo La Playa. An ocean beach away from the hotel zone, La Playita offers pangas for rent, a reputable seafood restaurant, and free camping. Along the dirt road from here to Pueblo la Playa and beyond to the East Cape are a number of large banyan (*zalate*) and mango trees as well as wild sugarcane. Earlier this century much of the Río San José valley was planted in sugarcane.

Gringo home development has recently begun in the area. FONATUR supposedly has plans to develop a marina at La Playita, a ridiculous scheme that would involve building a huge semi-enclosed breakwater and completely dredging the beach to create a harbor.

ACCOMMODATIONS

Hotels In Town
Besides the major hotels and condotels in the Zona Hotelera, San José offers a number of smaller, moderately priced inns in the town itself. Top of the list is the hospitable **Hotel Posada Terranova** (tel. 2-05-34, fax 2-09-02) on Calle Degollado (just south of Zaragoza), a converted home with 18 clean, air-conditioned rooms for US$35 s/d. The inn also features an intimate dining room with an outdoor eating section and a bar.

The very basic **Hotel Ceci**, at Calle Zaragoza 22 opposite the church, offers rooms for only US$10 s, US$15 d, US$18 t. At night, busy Calle Zaragoza might make this small hotel an economical but noisy choice. Around the corner

streets—is a well-tended expanse of brick with a number of benches and a gazebo. At the west end of the plaza is the twin-towered **Iglesia San José,** built in 1940 on the site of the original 1730 Misión San José del Cabo. A mosaic over the main entrance depicts a scene from the infamous 1734 Pericú uprising, with Indians shown dragging Padre Tamaral toward a fire, presumably to be burned alive.

During the Dec.-March tourist season, the town holds a fiesta every Saturday evening in Plaza Mijares.

Estero San José
The freshwater Río San José meets the Pacific Ocean at this estuary, just east of the Presidente Hotel. A sandbar at the mouth of the river forms a scenic lagoon surrounded by tall palms

the **Hotel Colli** on Calle Hidalgo, between Zaragoza and Doblado, is a mostly residential hotel with occasional rooms—simple but comfortable—for US$20-25.

Hotel Diana, on Calle Zaragoza a bit west of the Hotel Ceci, has spartan but comfortable rooms with a/c, TV, and hot water for US$23 s/d/t—a much better deal than the Colli.

Farther off the beaten track is the **San José Inn** (tel. 2-09-24) on Calle Obregón between Degollado and Verde. Formerly the Hotel Pagamar, the inn has large, somewhat bare rooms with basic furnishings and hot showers for US$20 s, US$25 d. If the Ceci and Colli are full, you can usually count on finding a room here.

The **Tropicana Inn** (tel. 2-25-80, fax 2-25-90, 415-652-6051 in the U.S.) was built around the Tropicana Bar and Grill on Blvd. Mijares in 1991. Room rates are US$75 s/d Nov.-March, US$65 s/d the rest of the year. All rooms come with air-conditioning and telephones; other hotel facilities include a swimming pool and complimentary transport to La Playita and Playa Palmilla.

Beach Hotels
Four major hotels widely spaced along Playa Hotelera are seldom full except in the peak months of December and January. Friendly negotiation can often net a savings of as much as 40% off the usual rack rate.

Best of the bunch is the **Hotel Presidente Los Cabos** (tel. 5-25-00, fax 2-02-32, toll-free 800-468-3571 in the U.S./Canada), a well-designed place next to the Estero San José with large pool, tennis courts, jacuzzis, beach palapas, poolside restaurant, coffee shop, and auto/ATV rental. Spacious rooms with air conditioning, satellite TV, and telephones cost US$70-110 s/d mid-April through late December, US$110-170 late December through mid-April.

Next west along the beach is the well-maintained **Hotel Best Western Posada Real** (tel. 2-01-55, toll-free 800-528-1234 in the U.S./Canada), where rooms with a/c, telephone, and satellite TV run US$60 s/d in the low season, US$90 s/d in the high season. Hotel facilities include pool, tennis court, jacuzzi, and restaurant. Most rooms offer ocean views.

A bit farther west, the **Hotel Aguamarina** (tel. 2-01-10) features rates and facilities similar to those at the Posada Real.

The last place within the beach hotel zone is the **Fiesta Inn** (tel. 2-07-93, toll-free 800-343-7821 in the U.S./Canada), where rooms with a/c, TV, and phones cost US$70 s/d in the off-season, US$100 s/d at the peak. The Fiesta Inn provides a restaurant and pool.

On the Campo de Golf, a 10- to 15-minute walk from the beach, **Howard Johnson Plaza Suite Resort** (tel. 2-09-99, toll-free 800-654-2000 in the U.S./Canada) offers one-, two-, and three-bedroom apartments with kitchens for US$90-129 in the low season, US$90-140 in the high.

Condos
Several condominium complexes in the golf course and beach area, and on the hill west of Mexico 1, rent vacant units to visitors for anywhere from US$65 a night for a studio or one-bedroom unit to US$300 for a deluxe two- or three-bedroom unit. Local companies that help arrange condo rentals include **Baja Properties** (tel. 2-09-88, fax 2-09-87, Doblado and Morelos) and **Laguna Vista Real Estate** (tel./fax 2-05-23, A.P. 66, San José del Cabo, BCS).

Camping And RV Parks
Brisa del Mar Trailer Park (mailing address A.P. 45, San José del Cabo, BCS), 3.2 km (two miles) southwest of San José off Mexico 1 at Km 28, is so far the only beachfront RV park in the Cabos area. As such, it's often full in the high tourist season, mid-November through mid-February. For two people/one vehicle, full-hookup RV slots run US$13 and tent spaces US$6, plus US$1.50 per additional guest. Facilities include flush toilets, showers, laundry, pool, restaurant, and bar.

You can camp free on the beach at La Playita between San José and Pueblo La Playa and between Brisa del Mar Trailer Park and the water.

FOOD

Almost all of San José's fashionable restaurants are found along Blvd. Mijares and Calle Zaragoza in the vicinity of the plaza. As a general rule, the closer a restaurant to the plaza, the more expensive the menu. To save money and/or experience local flavor, seek out the spots where San José residents eat—most are in the western part of town toward Mexico 1. At the west end of Calle Doblado are several inexpensive taco stands and *fruterías*. The Mercado Municipal features a section of side-by-side *loncherías* open 0700 till around 1600 or 1700.

Boulevard Mijares

$$ El Café Fiesta (tel. 2-28-08): Right on the plaza on the premises of the former Café Europa, this friendly, cozy café-bistro offers espresso coffees, omelettes, salads, burgers, pastries, desserts, and daily specials of "light Mexican food." Open daily 0700-2200.

$$-$$$ Damiana (tel. 2-04-99): Named for the Cape Region's legendary herbal aphrodisiac, and housed in a restored 18th-century townhouse, this is one of the most romantic settings in either San José or San Lucas. The front room is a tastefully decorated bar, followed by an indoor dining area in the middle room, and a patio dining area—candlelit in the evening—in the lushly foliated rear courtyard. House specialties include shrimp, lobster, abalone, and steak. A complimentary taste of *damiana* liqueur is served to guests upon request. Open daily 0900-midnight, serving *almuerzo,* lunch, and dinner.

$$ Iguana Bar (tel. 2-02-66): Although more of a bar than a restaurant, the Iguana serves a variety of well-prepared seafood, ribs, chicken, and Mexican dishes. In the evenings, the restaurant transforms into a nightclub with live music. Open daily 1100-0100.

$$$ Ivan's European Restaurant (tel. 2-12-18): Just south of the plaza, this semi-elegant upstairs restaurant is decorated with historic photos of San José. The music tends toward historic French *chansons.* The changing menu features a variety of Greek, Italian, and French dishes, all well-prepared. Open 1800-2300 daily.

$-$$ Sandrick's (tel. 2-12-70): Informal late-lunch, aprés-beach kind of place, specializing in fajitas, burgers, and chimichangas. Open daily except Tuesday 1400-2100.

$$ Tropicana Bar & Grill (tel. 2-09-07): Large, touristy restaurant-bar with outdoor patio, big-screen sports TV, and music and dancing at night. The menu is basic Tourist Mex/Fake Caribbean, but the drinks are strong. Open daily for lunch and dinner.

Calle Zaragoza

$-$$ Asadero Los Candiles (no phone), on Calle Degollado just north of Calle Zaragoza: A recently established outdoor grill with excellent mesquite-grilled *arrachera* (skirt steak, often called fajitas in the U.S. and in some parts of northeastern Mexico). Also serves quesadillas, vegetarian *brochetas, tacos machos* (mild chile pepper stuffed with chopped *arrachera* and cheese inside a folded tortilla), Costilla-style barbecued ribs, *frijoles charros,* grilled onions, fresh guacamole, potatoes baked with cheese and sour cream, and other delights. Not to be missed. Open daily from around 1900 till around 2300.

JOE CUMMINGS

Calle Zaragoza, San José del Cabo

$$-$$$ La Fogata: Despite the name, this well-touristed restaurant specializes in steaks and seafood, plus a few Mexican dishes. Popular for its huge, gringo-style portions. Opposite Bancomer; open daily for breakfast, lunch, and dinner.

$$ Posada Terranova (tel. 2-05-34), on Calle Degollado just south of Zaragoza: This family-run inn features a small dining room and bar, plus outdoor seating; good, high-quality variety of Mexican and American breakfasts. Open daily for breakfast, lunch, and dinner.

$$-$$$ Pietro Ristorante Italiano (tel. 2-05-58): This tastefully decorated restaurant-bar near La Fogata serves Italian food for lunch (1145-1545) and dinner (1745-2315).

$-$$ Restaurant Diana: Just off Calle Zaragoza, this tiny dining room is popular among locals and visitors alike for its reasonable prices and authentic Mexican food, including fresh mariscos. The TV in the corner is tuned to Mexican variety shows and novellas, always a good sign. Open daily for breakfast, lunch, and dinner.

$-$$ Tacos Indio, off Mexico 1 on Calle Malvarrosa in the Colina de los Maestros neighborhood: Very similar to Asadero Los Candiles; very good *papas y ceballas asadas.* Generally open 1800-midnight.

$ Cafetería Arco Iris: Next door to Restaurant Diana, this diner-style place serves inexpensive licuados, tortas, and burritos.

Other Locations

$$ La Playita, La Playita, Pueblo la Playa: Many people swear this big palapa-roofed restaurant has the best seafood in San José. Try the barbecued shrimp and become an instant rooter. Also good are the grilled cabrilla and snapper. The bar is a great spot for a casual drink. Open daily 1100-2200.

$$ Pizza Fiesta (tel. 2-18-16), Degollado and Coronada: A decent pizzeria on a San José backstreet, with a mix of local and tourist clientele. Open daily 1300-2200; delivery orders accepted.

Groceries: The **Mercado Municipal,** between calles Castro and Coronado in the west part of town, provides fresh fruits and vegetables, fish, meats, a licuado stand, and a cluster of loncherías; it's open daily from dawn to dusk.

More expensive canned and imported foods, plus beer and liquor, are available at **Almacenes**

Goncanseco, Blvd. Mijares 14-18 (opposite city hall); this supermarket accepts credit cards. A couple of smaller grocery stores are located along the west end of Calle Zaragoza.

Cha Cha Cha's Delicatessen, on Calle Doblado a block south of the hospital, began as a meat market specializing in Sonoran beef but now carries gourmet coffee beans, lamb, duck, turkey, and other Alta California-deli-style items.

Also toward the west end of Calle Zaragoza is **Pastelería y Panadería La Princesa,** with a good selection of Mexican cakes, pastries, and bread. Pricier European-style baked items are available at **La Baguette,** Blvd. Mijares 10, on the east side of the plaza, near Café Europa.

ENTERTAINMENT AND EVENTS

Bars And Discos

While San José doesn't offer as much of a nighttime party scene as Cabo San Lucas, neither does the town close down at sunset. The current hot spot is the **Iguana Bar** (tel. 2-02-66) on Blvd. Mijares, where live bands play a mix of Latino and international pop. Also popular is the **Tropicana Bar & Grill** (tel. 2-09-07) across the street, although the music isn't as good, with lounge-lizard folk music in the front room and canned music in the back. Both bars host a two-drinks-for-the-price-of-one happy hour in the late afternoon.

The **Club Eclipse,** near the Iguana on Blvd. Mijares, is a sizable video disco pushing "Daks" (daiquiris) and "Margs" (margaritas). The Presidente has its own **Bones Video Disco** for folks who don't want to leave the Zona Hotelera.

Events

On most Saturday evenings during the Dec.-March high tourist season San José hosts a fiesta in Plaza Mijares. Although mostly held for the benefit of tourists, lots of locals attend as well. Typical events include folk dances, mariachi performances, cockfight demonstrations, and piñata breaking, with food vendors and arts-and-crafts sales. Profits from food and beverage sales go to local charities and service clubs.

San José's biggest annual festival is held 19 March, the feast day of its patron saint. In addition to music, dancing, and food, celebratory activities include horse races and parades.

SHOPPING

Near the intersection of Blvd. Mijares and the road to Pueblo la Playa, about halfway between the Zona Hotelera and the plaza, is a large open-air market selling inexpensive Mexican handicrafts; it's generally open 1100-2100. Higher-quality and higher-priced arts and crafts are offered in shops along the east end of Calle Zaragoza and north end of Blvd. Mijares, including **Copal** (handmade furniture, antiques, rugs, folk art, and ceramics), **Bye-Bye** (T-shirts and souvenirs), **La Casa Vieja** (folk art, jewelry, beachwear), **Galería El Dorado** (modern sculpture), and **La Mina** (silver jewelry).

Galería Los Cabos, on Calle Obregón one block north of Zaragoza, sells a unique assortment of antique furniture, stoneware, crafts, decorator items, and locally made barrel-back chairs. Also on this street is **Zapatería Evelyn,** a shoe store with a good selection and reasonable prices.

Killer Hook Surf Shop, on Calle Hidalgo between Zaragoza and Doblado, stocks a variety of surfing, snorkeling, and other water sports equipment.

La Botica, a shop opposite the Tropicana Inn, offers a small selection of English-language magazines and paperbacks.

A new shopping mall, **Plaza Los Cabos,** recently opened opposite the Fiesta Inn along the beach hotel strip.

SPORTS AND RECREATION

Fishing

All hotels in the Zona Hotelera can arrange guided fish trips. Since San José has no harbor or marina, all trips use pangas, fiberglass skiffs with outboard motors. You can also hire pangas directly from the pangeros at the beach next to Pueblo la Playa, in front of Restaurante La Playita.

Onshore and inshore catches include cabrilla, grouper, roosterfish, sierra, snapper, toro, pompano, and occasional yellowtail. Farther offshore offers tuna, dorado, and sailfish. One of Baja's best marlin and wahoo grounds is Bancos Gordos (Gordo Banks), about 16 km (10 miles) southeast of San José. Striped marlin are seen year-round in Cape Region waters; angling for dorado, roosterfish, and sailfish is best in the late summer and early fall.

Golf And Tennis

Surrounded by FONATUR condotel projects, the **Campo de los Cabos** ("Los Cabos Country Club," also known simply as "Campo de Golf") features a well-groomed, 18-hole golf course with a sea view. Another nine holes are planned for the future. This is a fairly challenging course; the third hole extends 540 yards, with a lake in the middle of the fairway. The greens fee is US$18; carts (US$14) and clubs (US$12) are available for rent. Tee-offs can be scheduled daily 0700-1600.

The club also features tennis courts, pool, clubhouse with changing rooms, pro shop, restaurants, and a bar.

Race And Sports Book

A branch of Tijuana's **LF Caliente,** attached to the Fiesta Inn, offers off-track and sports betting using Vegas odds in a bar-restaurant setting. You don't have to gamble to enjoy a drink or a meal while watching the club's bank of closed-circuit TVs. Hours are 0900-2200 Sun.-Thurs., 0900-midnight Fri.-Saturday.

SERVICES

Changing Money

Two banks in town offer foreign exchange services, open Mon.-Fri. 0830-1130. The lines at **Bancomer,** one block west of the plaza, are generally the longest; if you're not in line by 1100, you might not make it to the foreign-exchange window before it closes. On the other hand, Bancomer offers an automatic teller, so if you've brought along a debit card you can avoid the lines altogether. **Banco Serfin,** two blocks west of Bancomer, usually has shorter lines. There don't appear to be any casas de cambio in San José, although the major hotels will gladly take your dollars at a low exchange rate.

Post And Telephone

San José's post and telegraph office, on Blvd. Mijares, is open Mon.-Fri. 0800-1700. The public telephone office on Calle Doblado, opposite the hospital, offers direct-dial long-distance phone service. There are also several private long-distance services in town. San José's area code is 114

TRANSPORT

Air

Los Cabos International Airport (SJD), 12.8 km (eight miles) north of San José del Cabo, services both San José and Cabo San Lucas. The airport includes several snack bars, souvenir shops, and a money exchange service. There are no seats in the waiting area for arriving flights, a minor inconvenience for those meeting incoming passengers. An official port of entry, Los Cabos' paved, 2,200-meter (7,200-foot) runway is tower-controlled (Unicom 118.9), offers fuel, and can receive DC-10s and 747s. Auto rental agencies with airport booths include Avis, Hertz, Dollar, and Thrifty.

Three airlines—Aero California, Alaska, and Mexicana—fly into Los Cabos. **Aero California** (tel. 3-08-27, 3-08-48) has daily nonstop flights to Los Cabos from Los Angeles and Phoenix. **Alaska** (tel. 95-800-426-0333 in Mexico) schedules nonstop flights to Los Cabos from Los Angeles and San Diego, plus connecting flights from Anchorage, Bellingham, Fairbanks, Portland, San Francisco, Seattle/Tacoma, Spokane, Victoria (B.C.), Walla Walla, and Yakima. **Mexicana** (tel. 2-02-30) offers nonstop flights to Los Cabos from Denver, San Francisco, Guadalajara, and Mazatlán, with connecting flights from Chicago, Los Angeles, Sacramento, San Diego, Mexico City, Monterrey, Puerto Vallarta, and Tokyo.

Mexicana maintains a ticket office on Paseo San José in the Zona Hotelera; Aero California's office is in the Centro Comercial Plaza in Cabo San Lucas. Alaska handles ticket sales only at the airport.

For San Francisco Bay Area residents, one of the best air deals around is offered by Suntrips (tel. 800-786-8747), a charter company with roundtrip air fares between Oakland International Airport and Los Cabos for US$179-309 depending on the length of stay, with a seven-night maximum.

Airport Transport: A taxi from the airport to any destination in San José del Cabo costs US$4 pp or US$11 for an entire taxi.

Departure Tax: the Los Cabos airport collects a US$12 departure tax from every passenger, payable in cash only.

Bus

From San José's bus station (tel. 2-11-00) on Calle Valerio Gonzales, there are nine buses per day to La Paz (US$7.60) and 10 buses to Cabo San Lucas (US$2). The last bus to Cabo San Lucas leaves around 2000. Each morning a first-class bus also leaves for the 24-hour trip all the way to Tijuana (US$115).

The bus station provides a small cafeteria and a licuado stand.

Vehicle Rental

Several auto rental agencies—Dollar, Hertz, Thrifty, Avis—maintain desks at Los Cabos International Airport. Rates average US$27 a day for a VW bug (plus US$.21 per km), US$38 for a Golf (plus US$.25/km), US$41 for a Nissan Tsuru II (plus US$.27/km), US$47 for a Jetta or Jeep (plus US$.30/km), US$61 for a Combi van (plus US$.35/km), and US$56 for a Caravelle (plus US$.33/km). According to the price lists, you'll add around 40% of the basic rental fee to obtain 200 free kilometers; the supply of cars, however, is usually large enough so you can obtain free kilometers for the lower basic fee.

In town, Dollar runs an office at the corner of Guerrero and Zaragoza; Thrifty has one on the highway near the town entrance, next to a Nissan dealer. **Vagabundos** (no phone), next to the Presidente, rents motor scooters and ATVs for US$8-10 an hour or US$22-30 per day.

SAN JOSE DEL CABO-CABO SAN LUCAS

The Transpeninsular Highway's 29-km (18-mile) stretch between San José del Cabo and Cabo San Lucas provides access to numerous beaches, points, and tidal pools along the Pacific Ocean. Most of the roads branching south of the highway are unpaved; almost all can be negotiated by ordinary passenger vehicles. To locate beaches, follow the SEDUE signs along Mexico 1 marked Acceso a Playa. Sometimes these signs include the name of the beach, sometimes not. The accompanying key lists all those beaches accessible from the highway.

A November 1993 rainstorm heavily damaged the almost-completed four-lane highway between San José and Cabo San Lucas, but repairs and/or alternate routes were completed within weeks. When the road is finished, this strech will constitute one of the finest non-toll highways in Mexico.

Hotels

Three of Los Cabos's priciest and best-situated hotel properties grace the coast along the corridor. Even if you have no plans to stay in the area, the hotel bars are worth a visit for a drink and the ocean view.

Covering 900 acres of Punta Palmilla (Km 27) is the **Hotel Palmilla,** the Cape's first major resort, built in 1956 by "Rod" Rodríguez, son of former Mexican President Abelardo Luis Rodríguez. Coconut palms, clouds of hibiscus, and sweeping sea views dominate the grounds; facilities include a chapel used for weddings, 1,500-meter (4,500-foot) illuminated airstrip (Unicom 122.8), pool, tennis courts, croquet court, giant outdoor chessboard, horse stables, restau-

Playa Palmilla

JOE CUMMINGS

rant, and bar. The hotel maintains its own sportfishing fleet, offering panga trips (one to three anglers) for US$75-150 per day or long-range cruises (one to four anglers) for US$395 per day.

A Jack Nicklaus-designed 27-hole golf course at the Palmilla is about to open and by all accounts is a splendid course. Nicklaus himself, though admitting his bias as the designer, claims the 17th and 18th holes are the best finishing holes in the world. Gray water is used to irrigate the fairways and greens, easing the strain on the Los Cabos water supply.

The Palmilla's room rates vary from US$125 s, US$155 d in winter in the Garden section to US$250 s, US$305 d for a Vista Suite in summer. Two-bedroom suites sleeping up to four are also available for US$345 (summer) or US$700 (winter); five-bedroom villas cost US$650-1090. For information contact Hotel Palmilla Reservations (tel. 714-833-3033 or 800-637-2226 in the U.S; mailing address: 4343 Von Karman Ave., Newport Beach, CA 92660-2083). In Baja, dial (684) 2-05-83.

If even the Hotel Palmilla's La Cantina bar seems beyond your budget, you might at least enjoy the beach below by stopping in at **Restaurant-Bar Pepe's** on Playa Palmilla, where the first drink is on Pepe; if he's not in attendance, the first *two* drinks are on the house.

Farther southwest at Km 15-14 is the **Hotel Cabo San Lucas** (tel. 213-205-0055 or 800-733-2226 in the U.S.), on Playa Chileno. Another heavy hitter in the colonial-luxury league, the Cabo San Lucas, features its own hunting ranch, as well as sportfishing excursions, horseback riding, a three-level swimming pool, a dive center, a 1,200-meter (3,600-foot) airstrip, and an Asian art gallery. The reef below the hotel is suitable for snorkeling and surfing. Rooms cost US$80-100 in summer, US$120-180 in winter. One- and two-bedroom apartments that sleep up to four guests are available for US$260 a night, three- to seven-room villas cost US$920-1410.

The third and most expensive of the corridor's royal triumvirate is the **Twin Dolphin Hotel** (tel. 3-04-96 in Los Cabos; tel. 213-386-3940 or 800-421-8925 in the U.S.) at Km 11. Like the Palmilla, the Twin Dolphin offers splendid ocean views. Playa Santa María, to the immediate north, is one of Los Cabos's best snorkeling/diving beaches. The hotel has its own fishing fleet, an 18-hole putting green, dive center, pool, ten-

BEACHES BETWEEN SAN JOSE DEL CABO AND CABO SAN LUCAS

Beach	Km marker	plus number (of meters*)
Costa Azul	29	(+500)
Acapulquito	27	(+800)
Arroyo Seco/ Punta Palmilla	26	(+400)
Punta Bella	24	(+400)
Buenos Aires	22	(+400)
El Mirador	20	
San Carlos	19	
El Zalate	17	(+500)
Costa Brava	17	(+100)
Canta Mar	16	(+700)
Del Tule	15	(+400)
Punta Chileno	14	
Santa María	12	(+200)
Twin Dolphin	11	(+500)
Barco Varada ("Shipwreck")	9	
Cabo Bello	6	(+200)

* refers to the approximate number of meters west of the kilometer marker, with San José as the starting point

nis courts, horseback riding, restaurant, and bar. Rooms are US$225 s, US$310 d, plus US$20 for each additional guest.

Surfing

Although Los Cabos is less famous than Baja's northern and central Pacific coast for surf, the summer southwest swell brings decent wave action to the tip of the peninsula—when most of the west coast points are flat—reaching peak height during the chubasco season, late summer to early fall. Probably the best surfing area between San José and Cabo San Lucas is **Playa Costa Azul,** at Km 29-28, where a grinding shore-breaker called "Zippers" is sometimes backed by Hawaii-style outside breaks in heavy swell. **Punta Palmilla,** below the Hotel Palmilla at Km 28-27, whips out a decent point break, while the bay to the point's immediate north offers a good reef break in heavy swell.

Reef breaks sometimes occur at **Playa Buenos Aires,** at Km 22, and **Playa Cabo Real,** at Km 20; then there's a gap until **Playa Canta Mar** at Km 16 and **Punta Chileno** at Km 14, both offering workable point breaks. **Playa Cabo Bello,** Km 6-5 (near the Hotel Cabo San Lucas), is known for a consistent reef break nicknamed "Monuments" for the H-shaped concrete monument that used to stand next to the highway near here. This break is fueled by northwest swell refracted off Cabo San Lucas, and is the easternmost break for winter surfing.

Most of these beaches now feature some sort of condo or resort development in progress but there's always a way to drive through or around them: it's illegal to restrict public beach access.

Diving

Several beaches along the corridor feature rock reefs suitable for snorkeling and scuba diving, particularly **Playa Santa María** (Km 12) and **Playa Barco Varado** (Shipwreck Beach, Km 9-10). Santa María offers rocky reefs at either end of a protected cove at depths of 13 meters (40 feet) or less. The north point displays sea fans and gorgonians, along with the usual assortment of tropical fish. The south end has sea caves, coral outcroppings, and large rocky areas inhabited by reef fish and lobster.

The remains of the Japanese tuna boat *Inari Maru No. 10,* stranded on rocky shoals in 1966, is the main diving destination at Shipwreck Beach. The hull and other wreckage lie within 2-26 meters (6-78 feet) of the bay surface; there are also scenic rock reefs in the vicinity. Tidal pools containing starfish and sea urchins are located along the beach.

CABO SAN LUCAS

The resort town of Cabo San Lucas, named for the slender cape extending eastward from Baja's southernmost tip, only gradually developed into a tourist hot spot. During the Spanish colonial era, its natural harbor was periodically used by passing mariners, but since it offered no source of fresh water and scant protection during the late-summer storm season when chubascos rolled in from the southeast, it was largely ignored by the Spanish. Although English pirates used the harbor as a hiding place for attacks on Manila galleons, many of the historical incidents ascribed to Cabo San Lucas may actually have occured near present-day San José del Cabo, where ships often watered at the Río San José estuary.

By the 1930s, a small fishing village and cannery occupied the north end of the Cabo San Lucas harbor, inhabited by around 400 hardy souls. The Cape sportfishing craze of the '50s and '60s—when the waters off the peninsula's southern tip earned the nickname "Marlin Alley"—expanded the population to around 1,500 by the time the Transpeninsular Highway was completed in 1973. Following the establishment of the highway link between North America and Cabo San Lucas, the town transformed from a fly-in/sail-in resort into an auto-and-RV destination.

The construction of Los Cabos International Airport near San José del Cabo in the '80s brought the area within reach of vacationers who didn't have the time for a six-day drive from border to Cape and back. The establishment of a water pipeline between San José and San Lucas further loosened the limits on development. Los Cabos—the area stretching between and including San José del Cabo and Cabo San Lucas—is currently the seventh most popular tourist destination in Mexico and the second fastest growing resort in the country. With a permanent population of only 25,000, many of them retirees, the tourist-resident ratio is quite high, especially during the peak Nov.-Feb. tourist season.

San José del Cabo and Cabo San Lucas enjoy equal access to the great beaches along the corridor between the two towns, but be-cause the Cabo San Lucas harbor provides shelter for a large sportfishing and recreational fleet, the preponderance of the 250,000-plus yearly Los Cabos visitors center themselves here rather than in San José or along the corridor. In spite of all the tourists, Cabo manages to retain something of a small-town feel.

Besides the harbor, Cabo San Lucas's main attractions include an underwater nature preserve only a few minutes' boat ride from the harbor, and the striking Land's End rock formations at one end of the bay, with a pristine beach right around the corner. Without the tenacity of a few of the town's original residents, who demanded this land be preserved, hotels and condos would probably fill the town's entire perimeter. San Lucas is the only coastal resort in Mexico with a nature preserve within its city limits.

Outside this area, however, hotel and condo development marches ahead. Pedregal, a fashionable hillside district to the west, the marina, and Playa El Médano to the east are all chock-ablock with condos and villas. Next to undergo development will probably be the large section of unused harborfront property near the inner harbor entrance, where an old cannery and ferry pier sit abandoned. Rumor has it this will become a new docking area for cruise ships; in 1993 five cruise lines—Princess, Carnival, Royal Cruise, Bermuda Star, and Seabourn—featured Cabo San Lucas on their itineraries.

While Cabo nightlife isn't on par with Acapulco's, the town attracts a young, energetic crowd that creates a more vibrant ambience than is found at relatively staid San José del Cabo, 29 km (18 miles) northeast.

CLIMATE

Cabo San Lucas is sunny and mild year-round. The town's location at the confluence of the Pacific Ocean and the Sea of Cortez means ocean currents and airstreams from both sides of the peninsula tend to moderate the general climatic influences of each; neither the cool Pacific nor the warm Cortez completely dominates in

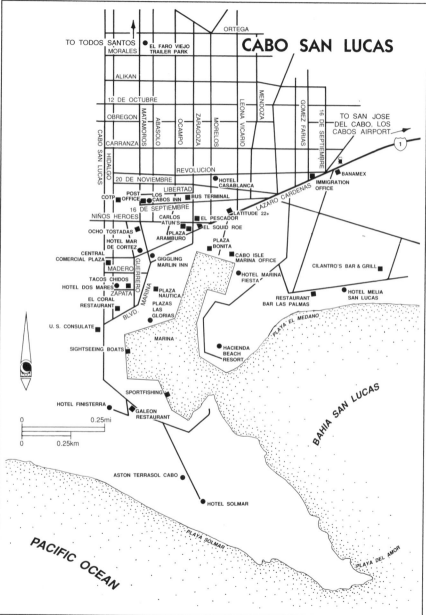

any given season. Hence summers aren't as hot as in La Paz (220 km north on the Cortez side), and winters aren't as cool as in El Pescadero (62 km north on the Pacific).

The average temperature in August is 27° C (81° F), in January 18° C (64° F). Maximum temperatures rarely exceed 33° C (92° F) and minimum readings seldom fall below 13° C (56° F).

Cabo San Lucas boasts an average of 360 days of sunshine a year. Annual rainfall averages a scant 19 cm (7.5 inches), most falling Aug.-Oct. Brief showers are sometimes encountered as late as November or early December.

SIGHTS

Cabos San Lucas offers virtually nothing of historical or cultural interest; people fly, drive, and boat here to soak up the plentiful sunshine and enjoy fishing, diving, and other aquatic activities.

Beaches
Beachgoers can choose between four beaches close to the downtown area, plus a string of beaches and coves along the San José del Cabo-Cabo San Lucas Corridor.

Playa El Médano: The most popular and easily accessible local beach, Playa El Médano ("Dune Beach") extends several kilometers northeast from the inner harbor's southeast corner along Bahía San Lucas. This heavily used beach is Baja's closest equivalent to Hawaii's Waikiki Beach in terms of the concentration of swimmers and sunbathers during peak vacation periods. Besides swimming—Médano is one of the few local beaches where swimming is safe year-round—and lying on the sand, a variety of other activities entertain beachgoers. Beach vendors rent pangas, jet skis, inflatable rafts, sailboards, snorkeling equipment, volleyball equipment, palapas, and beach furniture. Several palapa bars and restaurants—Playa Brujita Beach Club, El Sinaloense, El Delfin, and Las Palmas—strung out along the beach offer cold beverages and seafood.

Minor annoyances at Playa El Médano include the jewelry and rug vendors who plod up and down the beach although they won't persist if you show no interest. Then there are the condo developments in the background, marring the view of the Sierra de la Laguna foothills.

Playa del Amor: Cabo's next most popular beach can only be reached by boat or by a difficult climb over two rock headlands along the ocean. Playa del Amor ("Love Beach," also known as Playa del Amante, "Lover's Beach") lies near the tip of Cabo San Lucas—the cape itself, not the town—just northwest of the famous arch-shaped rock formation featured in virtually every Los Cabos advertisement. The wide, sandy, pristine beach actually extends across the cape behind the arch to the other side, forming two beachfronts—one on the Bahía San Lucas and one on the Pacific. The latter is sometimes whimsically called "Divorce Beach."

Only the beachfront facing the bay is generally safe for swimming. Bring along a cooler full of beverages, as the entire area is free of vendors and commercial enterprises. Unless you have a portable beach umbrella, go early in the day to command one of the shady rock overhangs. The southeast end of the bay features a series of coral-encrusted rocks suitable for snorkeling; a deep submarine canyon lying only 45.5 meters (150 feet) offshore is a popular scuba-diving site.

You can reach Playa del Amor by water taxi from the marina for US$3, or take a glass-bottom boat tour (US$5) and arrange a drop-off at the beach. Any tour boat in the vicinity will give you a ride back to the marina upon presentation of your ticket stub; the last tour boat leaves the marina at 1500. Those skilled at bouldering can reach the south side of the beach by climbing from the east end of Playa Solmar (in front of the Hotel Solmar) over two rocky points that separate the two beaches. The climb is best attempted during low tide, when the cove between the rock formations reveals a sandy beach useful as a midway rest-stop. The second set of rocks, to the east, is more difficult than those to the west; turn back after the first set if you've reached the limit of your climbing skills.

Playa Solmar: This huge beach running along the southwestern edge of the cape is accessible via the road to Hotel Solmar. The strong undertow makes it a sunbathing-and-wading-only beach. Solmar's biggest advantage is its lack of people, even during peak tourist seasons.

Corridor Beaches: Northeast of Cabo San Lucas—on the way to San José del Cabo—are a number of uncrowded, relatively pristine beaches suitable for swimming, fishing, camping, snorkeling, and scuba diving. See "San José del Cabo-Cabo San Lucas" for names and locations.

Rock Formations
El Arco ("The Arch"), a rock outcropping at the tip of the cape, has become Cabo San Lucas's most immediately recognizable symbol. Also called **Finisterra**, or Land's End, the 62-meter (200-foot) rock formation features an eroded passage through the middle. Just offshore are **Los Frailes** ("The Friars"), two rock islets frequented by sea lions.

A smaller, bird-limed rock pinnacle off the northeast side of the cape, **Roca Pelicanos** ("Pelican Rock"), serves as a crowded pelican roost. The base of the pinnacle, about six meters (20 feet) down, is richly endowed with marinelife, including coral, sea fans, gorgonians, sea urchins, and numerous tropical fish. Recent reports from divers say visibility at the rock is declining, however, due to discharge from boats moored in the outer harbor.

ACCOMMODATIONS

Hotels And Condominiums
Cabo San Lucas offers a greater number and variety of hotels than neighboring San José. Most are in the US$50-110 range although four hotels charge under US$35 a night and several cost well over US$100 in winter and early spring. Some of the best deals for families or small groups are in rental condos, which usually sleep up to four for US$80-125 per night. For names, addresses, rates, and facilities, see "Cabo San Lucas Hotels and Condos."

Condo units not listed on the chart can be rented through real estate or property management companies. Companies with a broad variety of rental units in the Los Cabos area include **Pinal y Associados** (tel. 3-04-58, fax 3-01-34, A.P. 68, Cabo San Lucas, BCS), **Ogden Gutiérrez Realty** (tel. 3-25-58, A.P. 427, Cabo San Lucas, BCS), **Baja Properties** (tel. 3-25-60, fax 3-25-61, A.P. Box 273, Cabo San Lucas, BCS), and **Los Cabos Property Management** (tel. 3-11-64, fax 3-11-62, A.P. Cabo San Lucas, BCS 23410).

Camping And RV Parks
El Faro Viejo Trailer Park, at Matamoros and Morales in the northwestern section of town on the way to Todos Santos, offers full hookups for US$9 for two, flush toilets, showers, laundromat, and a reputable restaurant-bar. This park tends to fill up Nov.-May.

Three km northeast of Cabo San Lucas off Mexico 1, the **Vagabundos del Mar RV Park** (tel. 3-02-90; 707-374-5511 in the U.S.), has full hookups for US$15 for two plus US$3 per additional guest; discounts are available for members of the Vagabundos del Mar travel club. Facilities include flush toilets, showers, a

El Arco,
Cabo San Lucas

JOE CUMMINGS

CABO SAN LUCAS HOTELS AND CONDOS

Note: Rates quoted are for peak season; November through May. Some hotels may offer a 15-20% discount March through October. Add 10% hotel tax to all rates; some hotels may charge an additional 10-15% service charge. Area code: 114

Bahía Condo/Hotel; Playa El Médano; tel. 3-18-88, in U.S. tel. (800) 932-5599, fax 3-18-91; US$95-120; a/c, kitchenettes, pool, bar, ocean view, beach access

Aston Terrasol Cabo; Playa Solmar; tel. 3-03-83, in California tel. (800) 794-6835, elsewhere in the U.S. tel. (415) 652-6051, fax 3-18-04; studio US$110, one bedroom US$160, two bedroom US$220 (up to four people); a/c, full kitchens, pools, sauna, health club, restaurant, bar, ocean view, beach access

Giggling Marlin Inn; Blvd. Marina at Matamoros; tel. 3-06-06, in U.S. tel. (818) 907-7219; US$75-100 s/d; a/c, kitchenettes, restaurant, bar

Hacienda Beach Resort; Playa El Médano; tel. 3-01-22, in California tel. (213) 655-2323, elsewhere in the U.S. tel. (800) 733-2226; US$92-175 s/d; a/c (some rooms), pool, tennis court, aquatic center, anchorage, restaurant, bars, ocean view, beach access

Hotel Casablanca; Calle Revolución at Morelos; tel. 3-02-60; US$15 s, US$20 d, US$23 t

Hotel Calinda Quality Cabo San Lucas; Km 6, Playa Cabo Bello; tel. 3-00-44, in U.S. tel. (800) 228-5151; US$100-125 s/d; a/c, telephones, pools, jacuzzi, tennis courts, ocean view, beach access

Hotel Dos Mares; Calle Zapata s/n; tel. 3-03-30; US$20 s/d fan, US$30 s/d a/c

Hotel Finisterra; Blvd. Marina; tel. 3-00-00, 3-01-00, in U.S. tel. (714) 476-5555 or (800) 347-2252; US$70-110 s, US$75-120 d, US$90-140 t, one-bedroom suites US$130-150, two-bedroom suites US$240-250; pools, tennis courts (charge for night play), spa, horseback riding, travel agency, wedding chapel, restaurant, bars, ocean and marina views

Hotel Mar de Cortez; Calle Lázaro Cárdenas and Guerrero; tel. 3-00-32, in U.S. tel. (408) 375-4755, in California tel. (800) 347-6847; US$29-41 s, US$33-48 d, suites US$41-51.50; a/c, patios, pool, restaurant, bar

Hotel Meliá San Lucas; Playa El Médano; tel. 3-10-00; US$152-182 s, US$162-182 d; a/c, telephones, in-room safe, pool, tennis court, restaurants, bars, ocean view, beach access

Hotel Solmar; Playa Solmar; tel. 3-00-22, in U.S. tel. (213) 459-9861 or (800) 878-4115; US$130-180 s/d, suites US$142-196; a/c, pool, tennis court, restaurant, bar, gift shops, aquatic center, ocean view, beach access

Los Cabos Inn; Calle Abasolo and 16 de Septiembre; tel. 3-05-10; US$25 s/d; fans

Marina Cabo Plaza; Blvd. Marina; tel. 3-08-98, in California tel. (800) 794-6835, elsewhere in the U.S. tel. (415) 652-6051; US$75 s/d, US$85 s/d with kitchenette; a/c, pool, gift shop, marina view, Playa El Médano access

Marina Fiesta; Cabo Isle Marina; tel./fax 3-26-88, in U.S. tel. (800) 332-2252; US$100-140 s/d; a/c, pool, sauna

Plazas Las Glorias; Blvd. Marina; tel. 3-12-20, in U.S. tel. (713) 448-2829 or (800) 342-2644, fax 3-10-18; US$70-120 s/d; a/c, telephones, refrigerators, in-room safety box, pool, restaurants, bars, shopping center, travel agency, beach club at Playa El Médano, marina view

Pueblo Bonita Resort; Playa Médano; tel. 3-19-76, in U.S. tel. (800) 262-4500; US$180-220; a/c, telephones, pool, beach views, kitchenettes

Siesta Suites Hotel; Calle Zapata; tel./fax 3-27-73, tel./fax in U.S. (909) 945-5940; US$41 s/d; full kitchens, weekly and monthly rate available

Villa Alfonso's; Playa El Médano (P.O. Box 3, Cabo San Lucas, BCS); tel. 3-07-39; US$100-135 s/d; complimentary breakfast, a/c, pool, jacuzzi, beach access, restaurant, bar

pool, and laundry. The nearby **San Vicente Trailer Park** (tel. 3-07-12) has full hookups for US$10-12, plus showers, a rec room, bar, and restaurant.

Also northeast of town, at Km 4 on the south side of Mexico 1, is **Cabo Cielo RV Park**, with full hookups for US$9, flush toilets, and showers. On a rise at Km 5.5 on the highway, **El Arco Trailer Park** (tel. 3-06-13) commands a view of the town and Bahía San Lucas even though it's on the north side of the highway. Full hookups cost US$10, tent sites US$5; the park features flush toilets, pool, and a large palapa restaurant with distant bay views.

Just a bit farther east along the highway, the **Villa Serena RV Park** (tel. 3-05-09), next to the Villa Serena Motel, offers 85 full hookups for US$14 per vehicle with two persons, US$2 for each additional guest. Facilities include showers, flush toilets, pool, fitness center, jacuzzi, restaurant, and bar.

Beach camping is possible at beaches farther northeast along Mexico 1 (see "San José del Cabo-Cabo San Lucas") or northwest along Mexico 19 (see "Todos Santos to Cabo San Lucas").

FOOD

Downtown Cabo San Lucas is riddled with restaurants and bars, most of open-air design, with menus that attempt to cover all the bases—seafood, Mexican, and steak. Because Cabo is Baja's number-one resort town, prices are above what you'd find in La Paz, Ensenada, Tijuana, or other tourist areas. Quality is also generally high since Cabo attracts chefs from all over Mexico and beyond. One complaint: Cabo restaurants sometimes hold back on the chiles in Mexican dishes and table salsas, hence picante-lovers may be forced to request extra chiles or fresh salsa cruda to bring things up to the proper level of heat.

Mexican And Seafood

$$ **Cilantro's Bar & Grill** (tel. 3-07-44), Playa El Médano: One of the better tourist-oriented Mexican restaurants, featuring mesquite-grilled seafood and homemade tortillas. Open daily for lunch and dinner.

$-$$ **El Coral**, opposite Plaza Las Glorias on Blvd. Marina: This rambling outdoor restaurant serves reasonably priced meals from early till late. The food's not bad, and nowhere else in town can you consume huevos rancheros for US$2 or a lobster dinner for US$12. Open daily for breakfast, lunch, and dinner.

$-$$ **El Pescador:** Zaragoza and Niños Héroes: A humble palapa restaurant with very good Baja-style seafood—oysters, shrimp, and red snapper are specialties—at low prices. A piece of the old Cabo, and still patronized by locals. Open daily 0800-2100.

$ **La Perla**, Calle Lázaro Cárdenas at Guerrero: Like El Pescador, one of the few Cabo restaurants that has maintained a local flavor, with inexpensive desayuno, comida corrida, tortas, tacos, burritos, quesadillas, and licuados. Open daily for breakfast, lunch, and dinner.

$$ **Giggling Marlin** (tel. 3-06-06), Calle Matamoros near Blvd. Marina: Better for appetizers and booze than entrees. Most tourists come here to snap photos of themselves hanging upside down—like landed marlins—from the restaurant's block-and-tackle rig. Others come for the big-screen satellite TV.

$$ **Las Palmas** (tel. 3-04-47), Playa El Médano: This was the first palapa restaurant on Médano, and most residents agree it's still the best, in spite of the ugly concrete addition. The grilled seafood is always a good choice. Open daily for lunch and dinner.

$$$ **Mi Casa** (tel. 3-19-33), Calle Cabo San Lucas opposite the plaza: Often cited as the most authentic Mexican restaurant in Cabo, Mi Casa is tastefully designed with a half-palapa, half-open-air dining room encircled by pastel murals intended to look like a small central Mexican village. The menu lists dishes from all over Mexico, including fajitas, *mole verde, mole poblano, pipián, carne asada a la tampiqueña, pollo borracho,* and *cochinita pibil.* The food is good but doesn't always match menu descriptions. Open daily for lunch and dinner.

$$ **Pancho's** (tel. 3-09-73), Calle Hidalgo off Blvd. Marina: Specializes in huge Mexican platters at reasonable prices, plus over 40 brands of tequila. Mexican beer costs US$1 a bottle, house tequila shots US$.30. Open daily 1100-2300.

$$-$$$ **Río Grill** (tel. 3-13-35), Blvd. Marina, near Calle Zapata: One of the nicer outdoor restaurant-bar combinations in the central marina area, with live music nightly and well-prepared steak, lobster, shishkebab, and Mexican

rina area, with live music nightly and well-prepared steak, lobster, shishkebab, and Mexican combos. Open daily 1200-2400.

$$ **Salsitas** (tel. 3-17-40), Plaza Bonita, Blvd. Marina: This mall restaurant is mostly a tourist scene, serving Mexican food adapted for gringo palates, but is one of the only restaurants outside Plaza Las Glorias with marina views. Nice terrace tables. Open daily 0630-2230.

$-$$ **The One That Got Away**, Calle Hidalgo at Zapata: A casual, second-story place overlooking the street with reasonably priced breakfasts, sandwiches, seafood, and licuados. Open daily for breakfast, lunch, and dinner.

$$-$$$ **Señor Sushi** (tel. 3-13-23), Blvd. Marina and Guerrero: Don't be fooled, no sushi here. Instead the energetic staff serves seafood platters, ribs, fajitas, and huge drinks from the Tai Won On Bar. Open daily 1030-0100.

$$$ **Villa Alfonso's** (tel. 3-07-39), Playa El Médano: The elegant dining room at this small hotel specializes in *nacional novelle,* or Nouvelle Mexicain cuisine, served a la carte or as a seven-course, fixed-price meal. The changing menu also features several international dishes. Open Mon.-Sat. 1800-2230; reservations suggested.

European

$$$ **Da Giorgio:** (tel. 3-29-88), Km 5.5 on the corridor, adjacent to the Misiones del Cabo complex: This well-designed palapa restaurant with long-distance views of Land's End has upstaged all other local Italian venues with high-quality pasta and seafood entrees. Open daily 0800-2300.

$$$ **Galeón** (tel. 3-04-43), Blvd. Marina, just south of the Hotel Finisterra entrance: Elegant restaurant with harbor views, specializing in Neapolitan cuisine and pizzas baked in wood-fired ovens. Open daily 1600-2300.

$$$ **Pavo Real** (tel. 3-18-58), next to Hotel Meliá Cabo: Highly regarded continental kitchen presided over by a German chef. The changing menu features creative delights such as blackened tuna with tomato-almond chutney, dorado in pecan crust, and other original recipes. Open daily 1800-2230 only.

$$-$$$ **Romeo y Julieta** (tel. 3-02-25), Blvd. Marina near Hotel Finisterra: An Italian menu featuring fresh pasta and wood-fired pizzas. Open daily for dinner only.

Tacos And Fast Food

The local food scene is concentrated along Calle Morelos, where a string of stands offers tacos, carne asada, and mariscos at the lowest prices in town. Tamal fans shouldn't miss the Yucatán-style, banana-leaf-wrapped chicken tamales at the small stand diagonally opposite Castro's Market on Morelos. From December to March a trolley cart at the corner of Calle Lázaro Cárdenas and Guerrero assembles delicious custom fruit salads for US$1.30 a cup, including your choice of sliced papaya, watermelon, cucumber, mango, orange, cantaloupe, and jicama, with a squeeze of lime. Salt and chile powder optional.

$-$$ **Ali's Burger,** Calle Morelos and 16 de Septiembre: Quick American breakfasts, burgers, and North African couscous. Open daily 0700-2300.

$ **Carlos Atún's Wahoo Saloon,** Calle Zaragoza and Niños Héroes: Formerly Paty's Tacos, this large open-air grill specializes in chicken, pork, and beef tacos and grilled seafood of all kinds, plus US$1 beers. Open daily 1100-midnight.

$ **Latitude 22+,** Blvd. Lázaro Cárdenas between Morelos and Vicario, opposite the boat ramp: More of a bar than a restaurant, with the cheapest breakfasts in town (starting at US$1 for one egg with toast). Other American fare available throughout the day. Open 0700-midnight daily.

$ **El Pollo de Oro,** Blvd. Lázaro Cárdenas at Morelos: A longtime favorite for Sinaloa-style barbecued chicken. Open daily 1200-2200.

$ **Ocho Tostadas,** corner of Matamoros and Niños Héroes: This street vendor specializes in tasty seafood tacos stuffed with oysters, shrimp, scallops, or octopus; the ceviche is also good. Usually open midday till mid-evening.

$$ **Taquería Sonora,** Calle Niños Héroes and Zaragoza: Good tacos de carne asada, Sonora-style. Open daily 1800-2300.

$ **Tacos Chidos,** Calle Zapata: A tiny diner with excellent fish tacos, *torta milanesa, sopes,* and chicken tamales at low prices. Open daily 0900-2200.

$$ **Wabo Grill,** Calle Guerrero: This Van Halen-owned nightclub serves excellent taco platters, tortas, tortilla soup, burgers, and breakfasts on its outdoor patio. Open daily 0800-2200.

$ **Super Pollo** (tel. 3-07-88), Calle Morelos and Ortega: Part of the Sinaloa-style chicken chain found throughout Baja. Very reliable. Open daily 1100-2200.

Trailer Park Restaurants
$$ **El Arco**, Km 5.5, Mexico 1: A large, airy restaurant with a distant view of Bahía San Lucas. The menu includes a variety of seafood, Mexican, and American dishes. Open Wed.-Mon. for breakfast, lunch, and dinner.
$$ **El Faro Viejo** (tel. 3-19-27), Calle Matamoros and Morales: Renowned for steak, seafood, and ribs. Open daily 1700-2200.

Groceries
Cabo's several supermarkets stock a variety of Mexican and U.S. foodstuffs—from fresh Mexican cheeses to Sara Lee frozen cheesecake—plus cooking and cleaning supplies, and even motor oil. Ranging from small to huge, they include **Almacenes Castro** (Calle Morelos and Revolución), **Sánliz Supermarket** (Blvd. Marina and Madero), **Chany's Supermarket** (Plaza Bonita), and **Supermercado Plaza** (at Plaza Aramburo, calles Lázaro Cárdenas and Zaragoza). Chany's has the longest hours, 0600-2400.

Panadería San Angel (Calle Morelos between Niños Héroes and 16 de Septiembre) carries all your favorite Mexican bakery items, including *bolillos* and *pan dulce*, plus dairy products.

If it's European or American-style baked goods you're looking for, **Mo'be'so's** (named for partners Monica, Bernard, and Sonja) offers European-style pastries, bagels, and breads. All of the latter are baked without oil, sugar, eggs, or milk. Gourmet coffee too. The bakery is located just inside the old entrance to Pedregal.

Frutería Lizarraga (tel. 3-12-15), at Morales and Av. de la Juventud, stocks a very good selection of fruits and vegetables; several local hotel and restaurant chefs shop here.

The best shopping area for beer and liquor is the string of *subagencias* and *licores* along Calle Matamoros.

ENTERTAINMENT AND EVENTS

Bars And Discos
Nightlife in Cabo starts in the bars downtown near the marina and after midnight moves to the discos, which stay open till 0300 or 0400. Tourists bent on getting well-primed for the evening pack the **Río Grill** (Blvd. Marina at Zapata), **Giggling Marlin** (Calle Matamoros and Blvd. Marina), or the two-story **El Squid Roe** (Calle Lázaro Cárdenas at Zaragoza). Squid Roe's dance floor, with bleachers, distinguishes it from the surrounding bar scene.

The **Whale Watcher Bar** at the Hotel Finisterra has a somewhat more sedate but well-attended 1530-1730 happy hour that features two drinks for the price of one. An excellent mariachi group Thurs.-Sun., great Pacific views every day of the week.

One of the oldest and funkiest bars in town is **Latitude 22+** ("Lat 22"), on Blvd. Lázaro Cárdenas between Morelos and Vicario opposite the boat ramp. This is a yachtie's hangout with authentic marine decor assembled from salvaged boats. Prices for drinks and food are very reasonable; the bar is open daily 0700-midnight and offers a happy hour 0800-1000 (yes, in the morning).

Cabo's discos begin filling up around 2300 but the crowd doesn't really break a sweat till around midnight or later. The town's first dance club, **Luka's** (formerly El Oasis, on the northeast edge of town near the PEMEX station on Calle Lázaro Cárdenas), is still in vogue but is facing serious competition from the newer **Studio 94** at Plaza Bonita, which features a state-of-the-art laser show and sound system.

Alta Californians tend to prefer **Cabo Wabo** on Calle Guerrero, a dance club owned by the rock group Van Halen; the music here alternates between a recorded mix with video and live bands. Members of Van Halen put in the occasional—make that rare—appearance, as do Los Tres Gusanos, a locally organized trio headed by Van Halen vocalist Sammy Hagar. The atmosphere is loose, though not beachy.

Events
Cabo San Lucas hosts several sportfishing tournaments throughout the year. The largest is the **Black and Blue Marlin Jackpot Tournament,** held for three days each October. The purse for the contest was US$850,000 in 1992, making it the world's richest marlin tournament. Proceeds went to local charities. For information call **Bisbee's** (tel. 3-16-22) or the Hotel Finisterra in Cabo San Lucas.

THE LA BAMBA SYNDROME

In Mexico, all it takes is the right combination of circumstances—a hotel lounge or tourist bar, plus plenty of tequila or Tecate and a table full of sun-burned gringos—and sooner or later someone will be stricken by what might be called the La Bamba Syndrome. Initial symptoms are a desperate urge to hear or sing the song "La Bamba." If a live Mexican band—it doesn't matter whether they're mariachis or norteños—or even a lone guitarist is present, those afflicted by the syndrome will begin shouting at the musician(s) "La Bamba! La Bamba! Play La Bamba!" Victims are convinced they must hear La Bamba or die.

The desperation appears very convincing, as the victim's face becomes increasingly flushed if the strains of "La Bamba" don't ring out immediately. Finally, the músicos give in—perhaps hesitating just a bit longer than necessary to relish the victim's suffering—and begin banging out those three chords that bring relief to the sufferer. To prolong recovery, the LBS victim usually begins singing along with the music, shouting out an unintelligible mixture of mispronounced Spanish, pseudo-Spanish, and improvised English lyrics. The syndrome is sometimes contagious, but if others in the room don't join in on their own, the original victim will often cajole other gringos to follow his (it's almost always a guy) example.

When the song's over, some LBS sufferers are temporarily cured, but in others the condition only becomes aggravated and they may demand other gringo chestnuts like "Guadalajara" or, in the worst cases, even "La Cucaracha." When it goes this far, even the musicians begin to suffer, along with all the gringos—and locals, if they haven't already made hasty exits—who were hoping to hear something a little more authentic or up-to-date, or who hoped they might at least be able to enjoy themselves without the distractions of a raging La Bamba maniac.

If you're ever in a bar or restaurant that has musical entertainment and an organized tour from the States arrives, consider calling in the tab and leaving, as conditions are ripe for a mass LBS outbreak. And should you become afflicted yourself, at least try to get the lyrics halfway right. (Certain variations are acceptable.) "La Bamba," incidentally, is a Veracruz-style song; if you want to hear something local, ask for la música norteña.

Another notable yearly event falls around the Festival of San Lucas on 18 October, part of a week of music, dancing, and feasting in the Mexican tradition.

SHOPPING

The streets of Cabo are filled with souvenir shops, street vendors, clothing boutiques, and galleries—probably more shops of this type per capita than anywhere else in Baja. For inexpensive handicrafts—rugs, blankets, baskets, leatherwork—from all over Mexico, check the outdoor **Mercado Mexicano** on Calle Hidalgo at Obregón; for the best prices you'll have to bargain. Another place where bargaining is useful is the **Tianguis Marina,** an outdoor souvenir market on the southwest side of the inner harbor toward the old ferry pier. Typical items here include black-coral sculptures, T-shirts, and costume jewelry.

Among the better shops in town are **Casas Mexicanas** in front of Restaurant Mi Casa on Calle Cabo San Lucas, with Talavera ceramics, religious art, pewter, wood and wrought-iron furniture; **Gaby's Huaraches** on Lázaro Cárdenas just east of Matamoros, offering all types and sizes of Mexican-made leather sandals as well as cloned sport sandals; **Faces of Mexico** next door to Gaby's, selling Mexican masks and other ethnic art; and **Joyería Albert**, a branch of the reputable Puerto Vallarta jeweler located on Calle Matamoros.

Plaza Bonita, Cabo's newest shopping center, faces the marina and contains a number of shops offering tourist-oriented sportswear, jewelry, and souvenirs. The recently opened **Books/Libros** (tel. 3-31-71) in Plaza Bonita stocks an excellent selection of English-language paperbacks, magazines, maps, books on Baja, children's books, and U.S. newspapers. The bookshop is open daily 0900-2100.

SPORTS AND RECREATION

Fishing

After swimming and lying on the beach, sportfishing is Cabo's number-one outdoor activity. Known as the marlin capital of the world, an average of 10,000 billfish—marlin, sailfish, and swordfish—a year are hooked off the cape. The biggest trophy of all, the *marlín azul* (blue marlin), can reach five meters (15 feet) in length and weigh close to a ton; in the Cape area, it's not unusual to hook 200- to 400-kilogram (440- to 880-pound) blues. A smaller species, the *marlín rayado* (striped marlin), grows to over 270 kilograms (600 pounds), while the *marlín negro* (black marlin) is almost as big as the blue.

To catch a glimpse of these huge gamefish, stop by the sportfishing dock on the marina's west side around 1500-1600, when sportfishing boats return with their catches. Note the flags flown over the boats; a triangular blue flag means a billfish has been bagged while a red flag with a T means one has been tagged and released. All Cabo sportfishing outfits request that anglers release billfish to fight another day; some even require it. Instead of skinning and mounting these beautiful fish, they recommend bringing a video camera along to record the catch from start to finish.

Good marlin-fishing spots include **Banco San Jaime,** 29 km (18 miles) southwest of Cabo Falso, and **Banco Golden Gate,** 31 km (19 miles) west of Cabo Falso. Dorado and wahoo are also common in the same areas. Sportfishing cruisers—power boats equipped with electronic fish-finders, sophisticated tackle, fighting chairs and harnesses, and wells for keeping live bait—are the angler's best chance for landing large gamefish.

Almost unbelievably, marlin are also somewhat common just beyond the steep dropoffs between Los Frailes and Cabo Falso, an area easily reached by panga or skiff. Without the technology of a fishing cruiser, panga marlin-fishing becomes the most macho hook-and-line challenge of all—the resulting fish stories reach *Old Man and the Sea* proportions. For anglers with more humble ambitions, black seabass, cabrilla, sierra, and grouper are available in inshore waters; surfcasters can take corvina, ladyfish, sierra, and pargo.

Guided cruiser trips are easy to arrange through any major Cabo hotel. Solmar, Finisterra, and Meliá Cabo Real each have their own fleets. **Pisces Fleet** (tel. 3-05-88), opposite Sánliz Supermarket at Blvd. Marina and Madero, will also arrange trips. Rates average US$300 a day on a 28-foot cruiser, US$250 a day on a 26-footer (around US$100 per half-day), or US$175 per couple on a 31-foot party boat. Charter boats generally hold up to six anglers.

Pangas are available in Cabo San Lucas, but most panga-fishing trips operate out of San José del Cabo. When inquiring about rates—panga or cruiser—ask whether the quote includes filleting of edible gamefish. The better outfits include fish preparation among their services at no extra charge.

Minerva's Baja Tackle, next door to Pisces Fleet, is well stocked with lures and other tackle designed specifically for Cabo sportfishing.

yellowfin tuna, Cabo San Lucas

JOE CUMMINGS

Minerva's is also the official IGFA representative in the area.

Boating

Cabo San Lucas is a major Baja California boating center although harbor size and facilities don't match those of La Paz. The outer harbor anchorages are mostly occupied by sportfishing cruisers; recreational boaters can moor off Playa El Médano to the northeast.

Within the inner harbor, first dredged in the early '70s, is the **Cabo Isle Marina** (tel. 3-12-51, 3-12-52, fax 3-12-53, tel. 310-541-3830 in the U.S.), with showers, pool, snack bar, dry storage facilities, chandlery, and 338 slips, complete with electricity and satellite TV cable, that can accommodate boat lengths of up to 45 meters (148 feet). Permanent and monthly renters at Cabo Isle Marina have priority over short-term visiting boaters; daily rentals are available on a first-come, first-served basis for US$20 per day for the first 25 feet of boat length, plus US$.85 for each additional foot, not including IVA. Visiting boaters should call the marina within 15 days of arrival to check on the availability of slips. The marina's condos are occasionally available as rentals and the adjacent Hotel Marina Fiesta usually has vacant rooms.

Also in the inner harbor are two boat ramps, one near the old ferry pier and one at the northeast end of the harbor near Plaza Las Glorias. A fuel dock is located between the old ferry pier and the abandoned cannery, just inside the entrance to the inner harbor. Cabo San Lucas is an official Mexican port of entry; the COTP office is on Calle Hidalgo between Libertad and 16 de Septiembre.

Boat Cruises: Dos Mares operates a fleet of glass-bottom tour boats that depart frequently from the marina and from Playa El Médano between 0800 and 1500 each day. The standard 45-minute tour costs US$5 pp and covers Pelican Rock, the famous Land's End arch, and the sea lion colony. For no extra charge, the crew will let passengers off at Playa del Amor near the arch; you can flag down any passing Dos Mares boat and catch a ride back to the marina later in the day.

Sunset bay cruises with all the beer and margaritas you can drink are also popular and usually last around two hours and 15 minutes. You can make reservations at the marina or at most hotels; tickets cost US$20-40 pp depending on whether dinner is included.

Diving

Cabo is a unique diving destination in that several snorkeling and scuba sites are only a 15- to 25-minute boat ride from the marina. Snorkelers find the base of the cliffs on each side of Playa del Amor, about three meters (nine feet) deep, worth exploring for coral and tropical fish. Nearby Pelican Rock, some six meters (18 feet) deep, is a bit more challenging. Strong divers, on calm days, can swim south around the arch to the seal colony at Los Frailes to frolic with the creatures.

Divers with experience below 30 meters (100 feet) can visit a vast submarine canyon that begins just 50 meters (164 feet) off Playa del Amor. Part of a national marine preserve, the canyon is famous for its sandfalls, streams of sand tumbling over the canyon rim at a depth of around 26 meters (85 feet) and forming sand rivers between rock outcroppings. At a depth of around 40 meters (130 feet), the outcroppings give way to sheer granite walls, where the sand rivers drop vertically for hundreds of meters (to around 2,750 meters/9,000 feet).

The phenomenon was first documented by a Scripps Institute of Oceanography expedition in 1960 and later made famous in one of Jacques Cousteau's television documentaries. The edges of the canyon walls are also layered with colorful coral, sea fans, and other marinelife. These in turn attract schools of tropical fish, including many open-ocean species not ordinarily seen this close to shore.

As with sportfishing, many Cabo hotels can arrange guided dive trips and equipment rentals. Independent outfitters include **Pacific Coast Adventures** (tel. 3-30-76, toll-free 800-491-DIVE in the U.S./Canada, Plaza Las Glorias facing the marina), **Cabo Divers** (tel. 3-07-47, Blvd. Marina at Madero), **Tío Watersports** (at the Meliá San Lucas and Meliá Cabo Real hotels), and **Cabo Acuadeportes** (tel. 3-01-17, fax 3-06-66, VHF radio 69, Playa El Médano or Playa Chileno). Typical rates are US$25-45 pp for snorkeling tours (the more expensive tours go to Playa Santa María), US$40-60 pp for a guided local scuba dive (to Shipwreck Beach or the sand falls), US$110 for a Gordo Banks/Cabo Pulmo dive (including two tanks), US$200 for NAUI/PADI certification.

Operated by the Hotel Solmar, the 34-meter (112-foot) *Solmar V* (tel. 310-546-2464, fax 545-1672, toll-free 800-821-6670 in U.S./Canada) offers luxury live-aboard dive trips to the Gordo Banks, Los Frailes, El Bajo, Cabo Pulmo, and other more remote sites. Prices are US$995 for four-day trips, and US$1495-2375 for six- and seven-day trips, including all land transfers, food and beverages (including wine and beer), accommodations in a/c staterooms (each with TV and VCR), and up to three guided dives per day.

Divers seeking equipment rentals only can expect the following rates in Cabo: wetsuit US$6-10; mask and snorkel US$4-5; fins US$4-5; wetsuit, fins, and mask US$15; weight belt and weights US$4-5; regulator US$12; tanks US$10 each; BCD vest US$6-9; Hawaiian-sling spearguns US$7; underwater camera and film US$20; air fills US$5.

Horseback Riding

Marcos's Horse Rentals (tel. 3-01-23, Hacienda Beach Resort, Playa El Médano) offers horseback riding by the hour or on trail rides. The hourly rate is a relatively high US$15; better value is the three-hour trail ride to El Faro Viejo ("The Old Lighthouse," built in 1890) for US$30, best undertaken in the morning or at sunset for maximum scenic effect. A 1.5-hour, US$20 beach ride or four-hour, US$50 beach and Faro Viejo ride are also available.

ATV Trail Rides

The sandy beaches and dunes in the Cabo San Lucas area are open to ATVs (all-terrain vehicles) as long as they're kept away from swimming areas (Playa El Médano) or turtle-nesting areas (Cabo Falso). Any of the hotels in town can arrange ATV tours for US$40 pp per half-day (four hours), US$70 pp all day (six hours). The basic route visits sand dunes, the ruins of El Faro Viejo, and a 1912 shipwreck; the six-hour tour adds La Candelaría, an inland village known for its mango trees and *curanderos* (traditional healers). Vendors along Blvd. Marina also book these trips.

Whalewatching

A variety of whales pass within a few hundred meters of Cabo San Lucas throughout the year, but the most activity occurs during gray whale migration season, Jan.-March. The Dos Mares tour-boat fleet operates whalewatching trips from the marina during the migration season for US$30 pp. With binoculars you can also see passing whales from the Hotel Finisterra's Whale Watcher's Bar.

Race And Sports Book

The new **LF Caliente** branch in Plaza Naútica near the marina features a full-service bar and restaurant, a bank of closed-circuit television screens tuned to various sporting events, and the opportunity to place bets based on Las Vegas odds on thoroughbred and greyhound races, as well as on American football, basketball, baseball, and other games. You don't have to gamble to watch the TVs or use the facilities. Hours are Mon.-Fri. 0900-midnight, Sat.-Sun. 0800-midnight.

INFORMATION AND SERVICES

Tourist Information

Cabo San Lucas has no government tourism offices or information booths, although FONATUR maintains an office on the marina. FONATUR representatives are always interested in speaking with potential investors but they don't distribute general tourist information. The Los Cabos Tourism Board, a private consortium, has a toll-free information number in the U.S.: tel. (800) 765-2226.

Newspapers

El Tiempo Los Cabos (Los Cabo Times), a bilingual monthly newspaper distributed free throughout the city, contains a number of ads and announcements concerning restaurants, clubs, and recreational events as well as local social and business news. The similar *Los Cabos Magazine* is English-language only and contains information on La Paz as well. The local Spanish-language newspaper is *La Tribuna de los Cabos.*

USA Today and *The News* are usually available at the **Sánliz Supermarket** at Blvd. Marina and Madero, as well as other larger grocery stores catering to gringos. **Books/Libros** in Plaza Bonita carries *The News, USA Today,* and the *Los Angeles Times.*

Post And Telephone
Cabo's post office, on Calle Matamoros just north of 16 de Septiembre, is open Mon.-Fri. 0800-1100, 1500-1800. Public telephone booths are found at various locations throughout town, including the main plaza.

The area code for Cabo San Lucas is 114.

Immigration
Cabo's *migración* office is on Calle Lázaro Cárdenas between Gómez Farías and 16 de Septiembre.

Changing Money
U.S. dollars are readily accepted throughout Cabo, although in smaller shops and restaurants you'll save money if you pay in pesos. Three banks offer foreign exchange services (0830-1200): **Bancomer** (Calle Hidalgo and Guerrero), **Banamex** (Calle Hidalgo and Blvd. Lázaro Cárdenas), and **Banco Serfin** (Plaza Aramburo). Hotel cashiers will also gladly change dollars for pesos, albeit at a lower rate than the banks'.

Except in emergencies, stay away from Cabo's moneychangers, which charge unusually high commissions. **Baja Money Exchange** in Plaza Naútica, for example, charges 7.5% for all transactions of US$500 or less, five percent over US$500, even though the exchange rates are already lower than the bank rates before commisions are deducted. For a cash advance this office levies a surcharge of 10% plus the usual finance charges.

U.S. Consulate
The U.S. State Department has finally terminated the consular position in Mulegé and moved it to Cabo San Lucas. The small office (tel. 3-35-36) is on Blvd. Marina near the west side of the bay and is open Mon.-Fri. 1000-noon. The consular staff can assist U.S. citizens with lost or stolen passports and other emergency situations.

Laundry
Lavamatica Cristy (tel. 3-29-59), behind Restaurant El Faro Viejo on Calle Matamoros, has 40 coin-operated machines for self-service laundry, or you can pay (by weight) to have it done by the staff. There are several other *lavanderías* scattered around town.

Travel Agencies
Cabo's major hotels—Solmar, Finisterra, Hacienda, Plaza Las Glorias—have their own travel agencies for making air reservations and flight changes or arranging local tours. In town, the most reliable and long-running independent is **Los Delfines** (tel. 3-13-96, 3-13-97), next to Panadería San Angel on Calle Morelos; it's open Mon.-Fri. 0830-1800, Saturday 0830-1500.

TRANSPORT

Air
See "Transport" under "San José del Cabo" for details on domestic and international service to Los Cabos International Airport, 12.8 km (eight miles) north of San José del Cabo. **Mexicana** (tel. 3-04-11) has a Cabo San Lucas office at calles Niños Héroes and Zaragoza; **Aero California** (tel. 3-08-27, 3-08-48) is in Plaza Cabo San Lucas, Calle Lázaro Cárdenas.

Sea
The Cabo San Lucas-Puerto Vallarta ferry service was suspended some years ago; SEMATUR, the private corporation that took control of the formerly government-owned ferry line between Baja and the mainland, has no plans to reinstate service anytime soon. The nearest ferry service to the mainland operates from La Paz to Mazatlán (see "Transport" under "La Paz").

Cabo Isle Marina is the main docking facility for visiting recreational boats; bow-stern anchorages are also possible in the outer bay.

Land
Buses to/from La Paz: Autotransportes Aguila operates 13 buses a day (0600-1830) to La Paz from Cabo's main intercity bus depot, Calle 16 de Septiembre at Zaragoza. About half the buses run via Todos Santos, which is the quickest route (about 3.5 hours total), for US$7.60. The fare to Todos Santos (about two hours from Cabo San Lucas) is the same as for La Paz.

Buses to/from San José: Aguila runs around 15 buses a day (0645-2000) to San José del Cabo; the trip takes 30-45 minutes and costs US$3 pp.

Driving: If you've driven down from the U.S. border, congratulations—you've reached "Land's

End." If you're contemplating the drive and have limited time, figure on making it from Tijuana to Cabo in three eight-hour days (Cataviña first night, Santa Rosalía or Mulegé second night) or 2.5 dawn-to-dusk days (Guerrero Negro first night, La Paz second night). If you stretch your itinerary to include a week's driving time each way, you'll have a safer trip and more of an opportunity to enjoy the sights along the way.

Local Transport
Shuttles and Taxi: Shuttle vans from Los Cabos International Airport to Cabo San Lucas cost US$8 per person. A private taxi costs US$50 for the whole cab. In Cabo itself, you can easily get around on foot, bicycle, or scooter, though taxis are available for US$3-4 a trip.

Water Taxi: You can hire harbor skiffs from the marina in front of Plaza Las Glorias to Playa El Médano (US$2.50 pp) and Playa del Amor (US$3). In the reverse direction, skiffs are plentiful at El Médano, but for del Amor, advance arrangements for a pickup are necessary.

Vehicle Rental: You can rent VW sedans or vans at Los Cabos International Airport (see "Transport" under "San José del Cabo"). In Cabo, they can also be rented at **Servitur** (tel. 3-07-37, Prol. F. Villa), **Dollar** (tel. 3-12-55, Blvd. Lázaro Cárdenas and Vicario), and **Thrifty** (tel. 3-16-66, Blvd. Lázaro Cárdenas s/n). Rates vary from around US$24 a day plus US$.18 per km for a no-frills VW bug to US$45 and US$.28/km for a Nissan Tsuru II.

Vendors along Blvd. Marina rent mopeds, ATVs, and motorcycles for US$10 an hour or US$40 per day.

TODOS SANTOS

One of the more lushly vegetated arroyo settlements in the Cape Region, Todos Santos started as a mission community founded by Jesuit Padre Sigismundo Taraval about two km inland from the Pacific in 1734. The Guaycura population in the vicinity was soon wiped out by smallpox and Pericús were brought in to work fields irrigated by springs connected to Arroyo la Reforma. Anglo whalers visiting Todos Santos in 1849 praised the town as "an oasis" with "friendly and intelligent people."

Misión Santa Rosa de las Palmas, later renamed Santa Rosa de Todos Santos, somehow weathered the Pericú rebellions to the southwest in Santiago and San José del Cabo and lasted until secularization in 1854. Unfortunately, the original chapel at Misión Vieja just north of present-day Todos Santos was replaced by a newer one around that same time.

In the post-mission era, Todos Santos thrived as Baja's sugarcane capital, at one time supporting five sugar mills. All but one mill closed when the most abundant freshwater spring dried up in 1950; the remaining mill closed in 1965 though smaller household operations continued into the early '70s. Around 1980 the spring

harbor,
Cabo San Lucas

JOE CUMMINGS

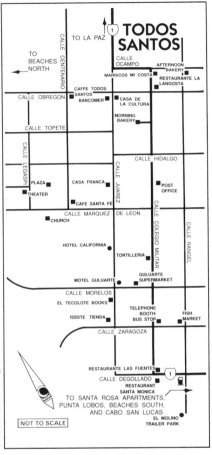

TODOS SANTOS

TO LA PAZ

TO BEACHES NORTH

CALLE CENTENARIO

CALLE OCAMPO

AFTERNOON BAKERY

MARISCOS MI COSTA

RESTAURANTE LA LANGOSTA

CALLE OBREGON

CAFFE TODOS SANTOS

BANCOMER

CASA DE LA CULTURA

CALLE TOPETE

MORNING BAKERY

CALLE LEGASPI

CALLE HIDALGO

PLAZA

THEATER

CASA FRANCA

CALLE JUAREZ

POST OFFICE

CAFE SANTA FE

CALLE MARQUEZ DE LEON

CHURCH

CALLE COLEGIO MILITAR

CALLE RANGEL

HOTEL CALIFORNIA

TORTILLERIA

MOTEL GULUARTE

GULUARTE SUPERMARKET

CALLE MORELOS

EL TECOLOTE BOOKS

TELEPHONE BOOTH/ BUS STOP

FISH MARKET

ISSSTE TIENDA

CALLE ZARAGOZA

RESTAURANTE LAS FUENTES

CALLE DEGOLLADO

RESTAURANT SANTA MONICA

TO SANTA ROSA APARTMENTS, PUNTA LOBOS, BEACHES SOUTH, AND CABO SAN LUCAS

EL MOLINO TRAILER PARK

NOT TO SCALE

© MOON PUBLICATIONS, INC.

signs. With each passing year the town seems to move a little closer toward becoming, if not the next Carmel, then perhaps the next San José del Cabo.

For Cabo San Lucas- or La Paz-bound travelers on Mexico 19, the town makes a good midpoint stopover with several restaurants and cafés, two decent hotels and RV parks, fruit stands, and a PEMEX station. Long-term visitors can explore the nearby as-yet-undeveloped Pacific beaches and the western escarpment of the Sierra de la Laguna.

Accommodations

Hotels and Motels: The Spanish colonial-style **Hotel California** (tel. 4-00-02, fax 5-23-33), on Calle Juárez between Morelos and Marquez de León, has 16 clean, renovated rooms for US$35 s, US$42 d, plus a small pool, bar, and restaurant. The management can arrange pack excursions into the Sierra de la Laguna as well as nearby scuba, fishing, and hunting trips.

Opposite the Hotel California on Calle Juárez is the basic but quite adequate **Motel Guluarte** with recently touched-up rooms for US$10 s, US$17 d.

Near the south entrance to town, in a rather dusty neighborhood, the newish **Santa Rosa Hotel And Apartments** (tel. 4-03-94) on Calle Pedrajo offers eight well-maintained, two-room units with kitchenettes for a bargain US$30 a night, less for long-term stays. The Santa Rosa also has a pool. The signed turnoff for Santa Rosa is three blocks south of the PEMEX station, after which it's another two blocks to the hotel.

Camping and RV Parks: El Molino Trailer Park (tel. 4-01-40, 818-986-7420 in the U.S.), at the southeast edge of town off Mexico 1, rents RV spaces for US$10 a night per vehicle for up to four people, plus US$1 per additional guest. Facilities include flush toilets, showers, laundry, and a café.

San Pedrito RV Park (tel. 4-01-47), about 6.5 km (four miles) south of town off Mexico 1 (3.2 km west of Km 59), has full hookups for US$12.50 (negotiable to US$10 in the off season), and tent sites with simple palapa shelters for US$3 a night. The park has flush toilets, showers, laundry facilities, a pool, bar, and restaurant.

came back to life, and the arroyo now produces avocados, mangoes, citrus, coconuts, papayas, and a variety of other fruits and vegetables. Several small farms in the area specialize in organic produce for the North American market.

Today's Todos Santos is a sleepy town of around 4,000 with semi-historic architecture and a growing artists' colony of Mexicans and North Americans. A rave writeup in the May 1993 issue of *Travel And Leisure* (". . . a new Mexican Oz in the making, destined to become the Carmel of Baja") briefly stimulated outside interest—much of it real estate-focused—and the town's streets are now tacked with For Sale

Free, primitive beach camping is usually possible on Playa San Pedro (2.5 km/1.6 miles west of Km 57). North of town a maze of sandy roads leads to a string of undeveloped beaches suitable for camping. During peak season someone occasionally asks campers for US$2-3 per person.

Food

For a small, relatively undiscovered town, Todos Santos has a surprising number of places to eat, though some seem to flourish and die with each successive tourist season.

Popular among gringos as well as locals for seafood and Mexican dishes is the relatively new **Restaurant Las Fuentes** at the corner of Degollado and Colegio Militar. The seafood is fresh and beer is served with frosted mugs in a well-lighted indoor dining area or outdoors next to a couple of fountains. Prices are moderate. Las Fuentes is open daily 0700-2100.

A notch lower in price is the more rustic **Mariscos Mi Costa** at the north end of Calle Colegio Militar at Ocampo. *Pescado frito* (fried fish) and *camarones al mojo de ajo* (shrimp in garlic butter) are house specialties.

A string of vendors along the south end of Colegio Militar offer inexpensive but tasty fish, usually either shark or dorado, and shrimp tacos. **Pilar's,** at the northeast corner of Colegio Militar and Zaragoza, is the most well known for fish tacos, but a smaller unsigned vendor on the opposite corner, same side of the street, is even better. **Tacos de Pollos Asados,** next to Pilar's, serves fantastic barbecued chicken—by the half or whole, or in chicken tacos.

Restaurant Las Tejitas, in the Hotel California, is open for breakfast 0700-1030 and dinner 1800-2100. In spite of a very competent kitchen, the restaurant is usually empty except when a backpacking or cycling tour is booked into the hotel. During high season the hotel hosts a Tuesday seafood buffet that receives high marks.

Old standby **Restaurant Santa Monica,** just north of the PEMEX station on Mexico 1 (Calle Degollado), serves very tasty shrimp, lobster, and carne asada dinners at reasonable prices. Service can be slow but everything is made from scratch. One of the house specialties is *pollo estilo Santa Monica,* a quarter chicken braised in something akin to barbecue sauce. El

Molino, around the corner next to El Molino Trailer Park on the old mill grounds, is also reportedly good, especially the US$8 Sunday brunch buffet.

Call it chic, call it trendy, but the **Café Santa Fé** (tel. 4-03-40), on Calle Centenario off Marquez de León facing the plaza, has become *the* place to eat and be seen during the Dec.-March tourist season. The changing, mostly Italian menu emphasizes the use of fresh, local ingredients (including organic vegetables) to produce wood-fired pizza, ravioli (a shrimp and lobster version is the house specialty), *pasta primavera,* lasagna, fresh seafood, and the occasional rabbit. Complementing the menu are espresso drinks, a full wine list, *tiramisu,* and fresh fruits. The service is crisp, and prices match the café's aristocratic flair. The Santa Fé is open Wed.-Mon. noon-2100; the restaurant closes each year during the month of October.

Steaks and seafood are house specialties at **La Langosta,** on Calle Colegio Militar near Obregón; in the evening the restaurant becomes the town's only disco.

Two American-operated restaurants on the highway into town from the south cater mostly to the RV/retiree/snowbird/surfer crowd. **Lonchería Paty** specializes in burgers, fries, and shakes, while **Greg's Pizzas del Pacífico** offers the same pizza, beer, and satellite TV.

The new **Caffé Todos Santos,** at the corner of Centenario and Obregón a block west of the Bancomer, is a welcome addition to Todos Santos' early breakfast scene. Housed in a historic corner building with lots of light, the café offers excellent cappuccino and other coffee drinks, hot chocolate, fresh pastries, fruit shakes, and other snacks Tues.-Sun. 0700-2000. During high tourist season the café may stay open later.

Groceries: The usual assortment of staples can be bought at any of several markets in town, including: **Minisuper Salgado** (opposite the Casa Franco furniture store), **Supermercado Guluarte** (next to Motel Guluarte), **ISSSTE Tienda** (Calle Juárez between Zaragoza and Morelos), and **Supermercado Hermanos Castro** (Calle Degollado near Pizzas del Pacífico).

Two unsigned bakeries, one open in the morning and one in the afternoon, sell bolillos, pan dulce, and other Mexican-style baked goods. The **morning bakery** (open 0700-noon) is at the end of an alley off Calle Colegio Militar between Hidalgo and Obregón, while the afternoon bakery (1300 till around 1800 or until they sell out) operates from a house at the north end of Calle Rangel near Ocampo. Per order, the morning bakery will also roast small pigs or lambs in its clay *horno*.

You can buy tortillas by the kilo at the **tortillería** on Calle Colegio Militar between Morelos and Marquez de León. A public **seafood market** on Calle Zaragoza, just south of Mexico 1, sells fresh fish and shellfish. Even fresher seafood can often be purchased from the pangeros at Punta Lobos, south of town.

Events

During the last weekend in January the **Todos Santos Arts And Crafts Show** is held at the Casa de la Cultura. Sponsored by Artosan, a local nonprofit group devoted to the enhancement of local cultural and educational opportunities, the show features sculptures, paintings, ceramics, and other visual works by local artists as well as a few out-of-towners. The show is young, but will probably become an important Cape event over the next few years.

In late February Artosan also sponsors a **Home And Garden Tour** that allows visitors to tour some of the town's more historic or visually notable homes, some restored by resident gringos. For further information on either of the above events, contact Artosan (tel. 5-00-50, fax 5-02-92, A.P. 16, Todos Santos, BCS 23300).

The **feast day** of the town's patrón saint, Virgen del Pilar, is celebrated on 12 October with three days of music and merrymaking centered around the church and town plaza.

Shopping

Although Todos Santos hardly compares with Cabo San Lucas or San José del Cabo as a souvenir hunter's paradise, a couple of interesting shops have opened during the last year or two.

The tiny **Casa Franca,** on Calle Juárez between Hidalgo and M. de León, carries a selection of rustic, handmade furniture, plus regional arts and crafts. Two blocks south on Juárez between the ISSSTE Tienda and Hotel California, **El Tecolote Books** (tel. 5-03-72) carries a surprisingly good selection of foreign and Mexican magazines (including surf magazines), new and used paperbacks (trades welcome), and local arts and crafts. The shop is open Mon.-Sat. 1000-1700. Both shops are also good sources of local tourist information.

Several North American artists live in Todos Santos, some year-round, others only part-time. One of the year-rounders is **Charles Stewart,** who has a home gallery—usually referred to as "Stewart House"—at the corner of Centenario and Obregón. You can't miss this little 1810-vintage house smothered in foliage and singing birds. Formerly of Taos, New Mexico, Stewart works mostly in watercolors and pastels; among his more recently conceived media are small *retablo*-style pieces that feature colorful Bajacalifornio

Todos Santos

JOE CUMMINGS

pictograph motifs on salvaged wood. His work is also displayed and sold at El Tecolote Books.

Beaches

Miles of virgin sand stretch north and south from Todos Santos along the Pacific. A sandy road at the northwest edge of town off Pilar parallels a wide, planted arroyo past a palm-hidden freshwater lagoon (La Poza) to the nearest beach, **Las Pocitas.** This is a great spot for watching the sunset although the undertow and shore break are usually too treacherous for swimming.

A wider network of sand roads crosses the arroyo and runs north parallel to the beach for some 26 km (16 miles) past small coconut and papaya orchards to larger farms at Las Playitas and El Carrizal, then heads inland to join Mexico 19. Several sandy tracks branch west off this road to a lengthy succession of dune-lined beaches. For much of the year the surf isn't suitable for swimming, though you can surf the beach break at **La Pastora.** Look for a large, lone palapa standing over the beach well north of town. The beaches offer secluded sunbathing and beachcombing.

About two km (1.2 miles) south of the town limits via Mexico 1, a signed, unpaved access road suitable for most vehicles leads 2.4 km (1.5 miles) to **Punta Lobos,** a rocky point at the south end of a sandy cove. The surf here is usually okay for swimming but take a good look at the currents before leaping in. This cove is used as a launching point for local anglers, so there's usually a small fleet of pangas toward the point.

Just north of El Pescadero between Km 56 and 57 is an unsigned, 2.5-km (1.5-mile) dirt road west to **Playa San Pedro,** known as Palm Beach to the local gringos. Stretched between two rocky points and backed by Mexican palms and a saltmarsh, this scenic beach offers good camping, fishing, and a steady beach break for surfing. For swimming, the middle 100 meters or so in the center of the cove is usually the safest; toward the north and south ends, the water looks deceptively shallow and inviting but riptides have been known to carry swimmers out of the cove into open ocean or onto the rocks. At the southern end of the cove is a small, semi-permanent encampment of surfers and world travelers seeking *la grande vida* for as few pesos as possible.

In 1993 the most direct road to San Pedro was marked with a sign reading Road Closed; all

the local residents and surfers used it anyway. The road intersects several other sandy tracks; when you see a ruined mansion off to your right, make sure you take the left fork that curves around to the south end of the palm orchard. If you head straight toward the middle or north end of the orchard you'll run into the saltmarsh and have to hike a couple of hundred yards through tall saltgrass and mud to reach the beach.

Around the point at the south end of San Pedro begins the long **Playa San Pedrito** (7.4 km/4.6 miles south of the Todos Santos town limits), stony at the north end but sandy for a long stretch south. Surfing here is sometimes as good as or better than that at San Pedro, and it's a lot easier to find: the access road is clearly marked. San Pedrito also has a campground.

At Km 64 (12.8 km/eight miles south of Todos Santos) a good dirt road branches 2.7 km (1.7 miles) southwest to **Playa los Cerritos,** another fine beach for camping and fishing. A tidy, cactus-landscaped campground charges US$4 per vehicle for tent or trailer camping.

Access to free beach campsites is available via several dirt roads branching off Mexico 19 at Km 70-71, Km 75, Km 86, and between Km 89 and 90. **Punta Gaspareño,** near Km 73, catches a right point break.

For destinations south of Punta Gaspareño, see the "Todos Santos to Cabo San Lucas" section.

Information And Services

Todos Santos' **post office** is on Colegio Militar (Mexico 1) between Hidalgo and Marquez de León. Long-distance phone calls can be made from the **public telephone booth** at Pilar's at Calle Colegio Militar and Calle Zaragoza; for long-distance calls to Todos Santos, the area code is 114.

Several real estate companies handle local property transactions as well as general inquiries on rentals, leases, and sales, including **Amerimex** (tel. 5-00-50, fax 5-02-92, Juárez and Hidalgo, A.P. 16, Todos Santos, BCS 23300) and **San Lucas Pinal y Associados** (tel. 5-03-33, A.P. 68, Cabo San Lucas, BCS).

Transport

Six to seven Aguila buses a day run between Todos Santos and La Paz to the north and Cabo San Lucas to the south. Either bus trip takes about two hours and costs US$7.60 per person; buses depart from the corner of Calle Colegio Militar and Calle Zaragoza.

TODOS SANTOS TO CABO SAN LUCAS

The 140-km (87-mile) stretch of Mexico 19 between Todos Santos and Cabo San Lucas passes several undeveloped beaches and small coastal communities. Wags are fond of saying it's only a matter of time before this area is dotted with resorts; housing developments are already slowly appearing along the southern end of the highway outside Cabo San Lucas. Local resistance to development is growing, so perhaps the area farther north will remain preserved and relatively pristine.

Rancho Nueva Villa, just before Km 60, is a well-known farm producing fruits and vegetables without chemical pesticides or fertilizers. You can purchase organic produce from the farm's roadside stand. **El Pescadero** (pop. 1,500), at Km 62, is little more than a plaza lined with tiendas and a café. East of El Pescadero, a network of dirt roads leads southeast approximately 56 km (35 miles) across the Sierra de la Laguna to Mexico 1 between Santa Anita and Caduaño; parts of the road are graded but the middle section is passable only by sturdy, 4WD vehicles.

Of the many deserted beaches strung out along this stretch of the Pacific parallel to Mexico 19, one of the easiest to reach is **Playa Las Cabrillas** (turnoff at Km 81).

Playa Migriño-Cabo Falso

Playa Migriño, accessed at Km 94 or 97, is a long section of beach next to Estero Migriño, a small estuary linked with Río Candelaría. In winter, surfers can catch a point break at the north end of the beach. Several spots along here are suitable for camping.

After Migriño, a small ranching settlement, the highway begins climbing over the southwestern foothills and coastal plateaus of the Sierra de la Laguna. Southeast of Migriño is an 11-km (six-mile), ungraded dirt road inland that connects with a road north (eight km/five miles) to **La Candelaría.** This small, picturesque village is known throughout the Cape Region for its Indian *curanderos* (healers); tourism flacks in Los Cabos call the curandero culture "white magic." Irrigated by an underground stream, the village produces mangoes, corn, and bamboo. La Candelaría can also be approached from Cabo San Lucas via a 24-km (15-mile), mostly graded dirt road.

About three km before the Cabo San Lucas city limits is **Cabo Falso,** once incorrectly thought to be Baja California's southernmost point. The wide beach along Cabo Falso is protected as a nesting ground for sea turtles; visitors aren't permitted within 50 meters (150 feet) of the surf line. The dunes behind the beach, however, are a popular destination for rented ATVs from Cabo San Lucas. The abandoned lighthouse, **El Faro Viejo,** signaled ships from 1895 to 1961; the original lens is now installed in a newer lighthouse higher on the beach.

BOOKLIST

DESCRIPTION AND TRAVEL

Burleson, Bob, and David H. Riskind. *Backcountry Mexico: A Traveler's Guide and Phrase Book*. University of Texas Press, 1986. Part guidebook, part anthropological study covering Northern Mexico with some relevance to Baja California backcountry travel.

Cudahy, John. *Mañanaland: Adventuring with Camera and Rifle Through California in Mexico*. Duffie and Co., 1928. Provides an interesting glimpse of pre-WW II Baja, with no outstanding revelations.

Cummings, Joe. *Northern Mexico Handbook*. Moon Publications, 1994. A new guidebook—and the first ever published in English—to a largely undiscovered region that shares many geographical and cultural characteristics with Baja California. The book covers mainland Mexico's nine northernmost states—Sonora, Sinaloa, Chihuahua, Durango, Coahuila, Nuevo León, Tamaulipas, Zacatecas, and San Luis Potosí.

Gardner, Erle Stanley. *The Hidden Heart of Baja*. Morrow and Co., 1962. Gardner, the mystery novelist who created Perry Mason, is one of the key people responsible for pulling Baja out of its "forgotten peninsula" status among North Americans in the '60s. The book describes his findings as an amateur archaeologist in Baja's central sierras, including discoveries of El Batequi and other now-famous prehistoric murals. Of Gardner's Baja travelogues, this is arguably the best, in spite of minor inaccuracies.

Mackintosh, Graham. *Into A Desert Place*. Graham Mackintosh Publications, P.O. Box 1196, Idyllwild, CA 92549. A thoroughly engaging report of Mackintosh's walk around the entire coastline of Baja California over the course of two years. Destined to become a classic of gringo-in-Baja travel literature for its refreshingly honest style and insights into Baja fish-camp and village life.

Miller, Max. *Land Where Time Stands Still*. Dodd, Mead, and Co., 1943. A classic travelogue that chronicles Baja life during WW II, when Mexicans alternately fell prey to German and American propaganda.

Miller, Tom, and Carol Hoffman. *The Baja Book III*. Baja Trail Publications, 1987. One of the original "road log"-style guidebooks. The NASA "space maps" aren't always effective, but the authors show a great sensitivity for Baja wildlife.

Steinbeck, John. *The Log from the Sea of Cortez*. Viking Press, 1941. This surprising chronicle of a Baja research voyage with marine biologist Ed Ricketts (the inspiration for the protagonist of *Cannery Row*) reveals Steinbeck as a bit of a scientist himself. Annotated with Latin, the book is full of insights into Pacific and Cortez marinelife as well as coastal Bajacalifornio society. Sprinkled throughout are expositions of Steinbeck's personal philosophy, implicit in his novels but fully articulated here. Also reveals the source for his novella *The Pearl*.

HISTORY AND CULTURE

Crosby, Harry. *The Cave Paintings of Baja California*. Copley Books, 1984. A seminal work on prehistoric Baja California art, written with a poetic perspective. Includes numerous photos and maps.

Crosby, Harry. *The King's Highway in Baja California: An Adventure into the History and Lore of a Forgotten Region*. Copley Books, 1974. Another excellent reference work by Baja historian Crosby, tracing the original trails used by Jesuit, Dominican, and Franciscan missionaries.

Paz, Octavio. *The Labyrinth of Solitude: Life and Thought in Mexico.* Grove Press, 1961. Paz has no peer when it comes to expositions of the Mexican psyche, and this is his best work.

Robertson, Tomás. *Baja California and its Missions.* La Siesta Press, 1978. Robertson was the patriarch of an old Baja California-Sinaloa family of northern European extraction as well as a patron of Baja mission restoration. His useful amateur work synthesizes Baja mission history from several sources; like its sources, the book contains a few minor contradictions and muddy areas.

Weisman, Alan. *La Frontera: The United States Border with Mexico.* University of Arizona Press, 1986. Only the last chapter, "Las Californias," is concerned with northern Baja, but scattered therein are several gems of history and pop sociology.

NATURAL HISTORY

Krutch, Joseph Wood. *The Forgotten Peninsula: A Naturalist in Baja California.* University of Arizona Press, 1986 (reprint from 1961). This work combines natural history and a curmudgeonly travelogue style to paint a romantic portrait of pre-Transpeninsular Highway Baja.

Nickerson, Roy. *The Friendly Whales: A Whalewatcher's Guide to the Gray Whales of Baja California.* Chronicle Books, 1987. A light study, with photographs, of the friendly whale phenomenon in Laguna San Ignacio, where gray whales often initiate contact with humans.

Roberts, Norman C. *Baja California Plant Field Guide.* Natural History Publishing Co., 1989. Contains concise descriptions of over 550 species of Baja flora, more than half illustrated by color photos.

Scammon, Charles Melville. *The Marine Mammals of the Northwestern Coast of America.*

Dover Publications reprint, 1968. Originally published in the 19th century by the whaler who almost brought about the gray's complete demise, this is *the* classic, pioneering work on Pacific cetaceans, including the gray whale.

Wiggins, Ira L. *Flora of Baja California.* Stanford University Press, 1980. For the average layperson with an interest in Baja vegetation, Norman Roberts's *Baja California Plant Field Guide* will more than suffice. But for the serious botanist, this weighty work, with listings of over 2,700 species, is a must.

Zwinger, Ann Raymond. *A Desert Country near the Sea.* Truman Talley Books, 1983. A poetic succession of essays centered around Baja natural history, with sketches by the author and an appendix with Latin names for flora and fauna.

SPORTS AND RECREATION

Fons, Valerie. *Keep It Moving: Baja by Canoe.* The Mountaineers, 1986. Well-written account of a canoe trip along the Baja California coastline; recommended reading for sea kayakers as well as canoeists.

Franz, Carl, with Steve Rogers. *RV Camping in Mexico.* John Muir Publications, 1989. Contains 50 pages—out of 308—on Baja camping. A bit out of date, but the introductory chapters are useful for anyone planning a first RV trip to Mexico.

Kelly, Niel, and Gene Kira. *The Baja Catch.* Apples and Oranges, 1993. The latest version of this fishing guide pushes it firmly to the top of the heap. Contains extensive discussions of lures and tackle, expert fishing techniques, and detailed directions to productive fisheries, plus numerous maps.

Lehman, Charles. *Desert Survival Handbook.* Primer Publishers, 1990. A no-nonsense guide to desert survival techniques; should be included in every pilot's or coastal navigator's kit.

Miller, Tom. *Angler's Guide to Baja California.* Baja Trail Publications, 1984. Contains complete descriptions and sketches of common Pacific and Cortez fishes, as well as extensive commentary on tackle and seasons.

Peterson, Walt. *The Baja Adventure Book.* Wilderness Press, 1987. Packed with information on outdoor activities in Baja, with an emphasis on fishing, hunting, and scuba diving. Contains very little information on towns and cities.

Romano-Lax, Andromeda. *Sea Kayaking in Baja.* Wilderness Press, 1993. This inspiring 153-page guide to Baja kayaking contains 15 one- to five-day paddling routes along the Baja coastline, plus many helpful hints on kayak camping. Each route is accompanied by a map; although these maps are too sketchy to be used for navigational purposes, a list of Mexican topographic map numbers is provided so that readers can go out and obtain more accurate material.

Williams, Jack. *Baja Boater's Guide, Vols. I and II.* H.J. Williams Publications, 1988. These ambitious guides, one each on the Pacific Ocean and the Sea of Cortez, contain useful aerial photos and sketch maps of Baja's continental islands and coastline.

Wong, Bonnie. *Bicycling Baja.* Sunbelt Publications, 1988. Written by an experienced leader of Baja cycling tours, this book includes helpful suggestions on trip preparation, equipment, and riding techniques as well as road logs for 17 different cycling routes throughout the peninsula.

Wyatt, Mike. *The Basic Essentials of Sea Kayaking.* ICS Books, 1990. A good introduction to sea kayaking, with tips on buying gear, paddling techniques, safety, and kayak loading.

GLOSSARY

abarrotes—groceries

aduana—customs service

arroyo—canyon, dry wash, or stream

bahía—bay

basura—trash or rubbish; the sign No Tire Basura means "Don't throw trash."

calle—street

callejón—alley or lane

cañon—canyon

casa de huéspedes—guesthouse

cerro—mountain peak

cerveza—beer

CONASUPO—Compañía Nacional de Subsistencias Populares ("National Company for Popular Subsistence")

correo—post office

COTP—Captain of the Port

ejido—collectively owned agricultural lands

ensenada—cove or small bay

IMSS—Instituto Mexicano del Seguro Social ("Mexican Social Security Institute")

FONATUR—Fondo Nacional de Fomento del Turismo ("National Foundation for Tourism Development")

hostería—hostelry, inn

ISSSTE—Instituto de Seguridad y Servicios Sociales para Trabajadores del Estado ("Security and Social Services Institute for Government Workers")

laguna—lagoon, lake, or bay

llano—plains

mercado—market

palacio municipal—literally "municipal palace," equivalent to city or county hall in the U.S.

palapa—thatched umbrella-like shade shelter or roof

panadería—bakery

parrada—bus stop

PEMEX—Petroleos Mexicanos ("Mexican Petroleum")

pensión—boardinghouse

playa—beach

punta—point

ramal—branch road

SECTUR—Secretaría de Turismo ("Secretariat of Tourism")

SEDUE—Secretaría de Desarollo Urbano y Ecología ("Secretariat of Urban and Ecological Development")

tienda—store

tinaja—pool or spring

topes—speed bumps

ultramarinos—delicatessen-liquor store

SPANISH PHRASEBOOK

As in the rest of Mexico, Spanish is the primary spoken language in Baja California. English is occasionally spoken by merchants, hotel staff, and travel agents in Tijuana, Mexicali, Ensenada, Loreto, La Paz, San José del Cabo, and Cabo San Lucas. Even in these cities, however, you can only count on finding English-speaking Mexicans within each city's tourist district. Outside of tourist areas, and even in smaller border towns like Tecate, it's somewhat rare to encounter anyone who speaks more than a few words of English.

Hence it's incumbent upon the non-Spanish-speaking visitor to learn at least enough Spanish to cope with everyday transactions. Knowing a little Spanish will not only mitigate communication problems, it will also bring you more respect among the local Mexicans, who quite naturally resent foreign visitors who expect Mexicans to abandon their mother tongue whenever a gringo approaches.

This phrasebook should help the non-Spanish-speaking visitor use enough of the language to communicate with the natives in common tourist situations.

PRONUNCIATION GUIDE

Consonants

c—like 'c' in "cat," before 'a', 'o', or 'u'; like 's' before 'e' or 'i',

d—as 'd' in 'dog,' except between vowels, then like "th' in "that"

g—before 'e' or 'i,' like the 'ch' in Scottish "loch"; elsewhere like 'g' in "get"

h—always silent

j—like the English 'h' in "hotel," but stronger

ll—like the 'y' in "yellow"

ñ—like the 'ni' in "onion"

r—always pronounced as strong 'r'

rr—trilled 'r'

v—similar to the 'b' in "boy" (not as English 'v')

z—like 's' in "same"

b, f, k, l, m, n, p, q, t, as in English

Vowels

a—as in "father," but shorter

e—as in "hen"

i—as in "machine"

o—as in "phone"

u—usually as in "rule"; when it follows a 'q' the 'u' is silent; when it follows an 'h' or 'g' it's pronounced like 'w,' except when it comes between 'g' and 'e' or 'i', when it's also silent

USEFUL WORDS AND PHRASES

Greetings And Civilities

¡Hola!—Hello

Buenos dias—Good morning

Buenas tardes—Good afternoon

Buenas noches—Good evening, good night

Buenas—used when you're not sure of the time of day

¿Cómo está?—How are you?

Muy bien—Fine

Así así—So-so

Muchas gracias—Thank you very much

De nada—You're welcome; literally, "It's nothing"

Sí—Yes

No—No

Yo no sé.—I don't know

Está bien—It's fine; okay

Bueno—Good; okay

Por Favor—Please

¡Salud!—(To your) health (used in toasting or after someone sneezes)

Dispénseme—Excuse me

Perdóneme—Pardon me

Lo siento—I'm sorry

Adíos—Goodbye (can also be used as a passing hello)

¿Mande?—What? (as in, "could you repeat that?")

Terms Of Address

yo—I

usted—you (formal)

tú—you (familiar)

él—he/him

ella—she/her

nosotros—we/us

ustedes—you (plural)

ellos—they/them (all males or mixed gender)

ellas—they/them (all females)

señor—Mr., sir

señora—Mrs., madam

señorita—Miss, young lady

Communication Problems

No hablo bien español—I don't speak Spanish well.

No entiendo—I don't understand

Hable más despacio, por favor—Speak more slowly, please

Repita, por favor—Repeat, please

¿Cómo se dice . . . en español?—How do you say . . . in Spanish?

¿Entiende el inglés?—Do you understand English?

¿Se habla inglés aquí?—Is English spoken here? (Does anyone here speak English?)

Obtaining Directions

¿Dónde está . . . ?—Where is . . . ?

¿Qué tan lejos está a . . . ?—How far is it to . . . ?

de . . . a . . .—from . . . to . . .

¿Conduce a . . . este camino?—Does this road lead to . . . ?

la carretera—highway

el camino—road

la calle—street

la cuadra—block

kilómetro—kilometer

milla—mile (commonly used near the U.S. border)

el norte—north

el sur—south

el oeste—west

el este—east

al derecho or *adelante*—straight ahead

a la derecha—to the right

a la izquierada—to the left

At A Hotel

¿Hay un hotel cerca de aquí?—Is there a hotel near here?

posada—inn

casa de huéspedes—guesthouse

¿Puedo (podemos) ver un cuarto?—Can I (we) see a room?

¿Cuál es el precio?—What is the rate?

¿Están incluídos los impuestos?—Does that include taxes?

¿Acepta tarjetas de crédito?—Do you accept credit cards?

solo efectivo—cash only

un cuarto sencillo—a single room

un cuarto doble—a double room

con camas gemelas—with twin beds

con una cama de matrimonio—with a double bed

con baño—with bath

sin baño—without bath

agua caliente—hot water

agua fría—cold water

calentador—heater

aire acondicionado—air conditioning

toalla—towel

jabón—soap

llave—key

cubierta or *manta*—blanket

papel higiénico—toilet paper

hielo—ice

Post Office

la oficina de correos (or *el correo*)—post office

Quiero unas estampillas—I'd like some stamps

Quiero mandar esto . . . —I'd like to send this . . .

por correo aéreo—by air mail

certificado—certified mail

Quiero mandar este paquete—I'd like to send this parcel

¿Hay correo para mí? Me llamo . . . —Is there any mail for me? My name is . . .

Telephone

caseta de teléfono—telephone office

Quiero llamar a . . . —I want to make a call to . . .

por cobrar—collect call

persona a persona—person-to-person

una llamada de larga distancia—a long-distance call

Quiero hablar con . . . —I want to speak with . . .

¿Está . . . ?—Is . . . there?

No está—S/he's not here

La linea está ocupada—The line is engaged

Changing Money

Quiero cambiar dinero—I want to change money

cheques de viajero—traveler's checks

¿Cuál es el tipio de cambio?—What's the exchange rate?

¿Hay comisión?—Is there a commission?

banco—bank

casa de cambio—currency exchange office

Making Purchases

Necesito . . . —I need . . .

Deseo . . . or *Quiero* . . . —I want . . .

Quisiera . . . —I would like . . . (more polite)

¿Hay . . . *aquí?*—Is/are there any . . . here? (Do you have . . . ?)

¿Cuánto cuesta?—How much does it cost?

¿Puedo ver . . . ?—Can I see . . . ?

ésta/éto—this one

ésa/ése—that one

Me llevo éste—I'll take this one

caro—expensive

barato—cheap

más barato—cheaper

Driving

Lleno, por favor—Full, please

Se me ha descompuesto el carro—My car has broken down

Necesito un remolque—I need a tow

¿Hay un garage cerca?—Is there a garage nearby?

¿Puedo pasar con este carro (troca)?—Is the road passable with this car (truck)?

¿Con doble tracción?—With four-wheel drive?

No hay paso—It's not passable

el semáfora—traffic light

el señal—traffic sign

gasolina—gasoline (petrol)

gasolinera—gasoline station

aceite—oil

agua—water

llanta desinflada—flat tire

llantera—tire repair shop

Auto Parts

banda de ventilador—fan belt

batería—battery

bomba de gasolina (agua)—fuel (water) pump

bujía—spark plug

carburador—carburetor

distribuidor—distributor

eje—axle

embrague—clutch

empaque, junta—gasket

filtro—filter

frenos—brakes

llanta—tire

manguera—hose

marcha, arranque—starter

radiador—radiator

regulado de voltaje—voltage regulator

Public Transport

la parada del autobús—bus stop

la central camionera—main bus terminal

la estación de ferrocarril—railway station

el aeropuerto—airport

la terminal del transbordador—ferry terminal

Quiero un boleto a . . .—I want a ticket to . . .

Quiero bajar en . . .—I want to get off at . . .

Aquí, por favor—Here, please

¿Cuánto le debo?—What do I owe?

Hiking And Camping

¿Dónde empieza la vereda (el sendero)?—Where does the trail (path) start?

¿Se puede acampar aquí (allá)?—Is camping permitted here (there)?

¿Hay agua potable?—Is there drinking water?

¿Hay agua allá?—Is there water there?

la tinaja—waterhole

el ojo de agua—spring

el pozo—well

la mochila—backpack

la bolsa de dormir—sleeping bag

la carpa—tent

la leña—firewood

el carbón—charcoal

el fuego—fire

los cerrillos or *los fósforos*—matches

el cruce—crossing

a pie—on foot

a bestia—by horse, mule, or burro

Quiero rentar (comprar) . . .—I want to rent (buy) . . .

un burro—a burro

un caballo—a horse

una mula—a mule

Geography

la isla—island

el cerro or *la colina*—hill

la montaña—mountain

la sierra—mountain range

el bosque—forest

la barranca—large canyon

el cañon—medium-size canyon

el arroyo—streambed, wash, small canyon

el valle—valley

la catarat—waterfall

el río—river

la laguna—lagoon or lake

bahía—bay

el mar—sea

la playa—beach

la punta—point, headland

Numbers

cero—0

uno—1 (masculine)

una—1 (feminine)

dos—2

tres—3

cuatro—4

cinco—5

seis—6

siete—7

ocho—8

nueve—9

diez—10

once—11

doce—12

trece—13

catorce—14
quince—15
diez y seis—16
diez y siete—17
diez y ocho—18
diez y nueve—19
veinte—20
veinte y uno—21
treinta—30
cuarenta—40
cincuenta—50
sesenta—60
setenta—70
ochenta—80
noventa—90
cien—100
ciento y uno—101
doscientos—200
mil—1000
dos mil—2000
veinte mil—20,000
millón—million

Days Of The Week
domingo—Sunday
lunes—Monday
martes—Tuesday
miércoles—Wednesday
jueves—Thursday
viernes—Friday
sábado—Saturday

Time
¿Qué hora es?—What time is it?
la una—one o'clock
las dos—two o'clock

a las dos—at two o'clock
las tres y diez—ten past three
las seis a la mañana—six a.m.
las seis a la tarde—six p.m.
el mediodia—noon
la medianoche—midnight
hoy—today
mañana—tomorrow
ayer—yesterday
esta noche—tonight
anoche—last night
esta semana—this week
la semana pasada—last week
el próximo año—next year
el mes pasado—last month
hace dos años—two years ago

Miscellaneous
más—more
menos—less
mejor—better
un poco—a little
un poquito—a very little
grande—large
pequeño—small
caliente—hot (temperature)
picante—hot (spicy)
frio—cold
rapido—quick
malo—bad
difícil—difficult

For information on Spanish-English dictionaries and phrasebooks, as well as a listing of Baja Spanish-language schools, see the "Language" section of the "Introduction."

INDEX

Italicized page numbers indicate information in captions, charts, illustrations, maps, or special topics.

whalewatching: *26-27,* 246-247, 256, 284, 336
whaling: 25-26, 243
white-breasted nuthatch: 31
white-faced ibis: 31
white fir: 7-8, 18
white oak: 19
white sage: 19-20
white seabass: 28
white-tailed antelope squirrel: 23
white-tailed deer: 21
wildlife preserves: 55
wild lilac: 8
Willard Bay: 230
Willard Pt.: 230-231
willows: 19

windsurfing: 67, 229, 235, 241, 284, 312
wine: 89, 166, *172,* 205-206
woodpecker: 31
wood stork: 31

Y
yellow-bellied sea snake: 32
yellow-eyed junco: 31
yellowfin croaker: 28
yellowfin tuna: 28
yellow snapper: 28
yellowtail: 28
yucca: 7, 15, 247
Yumano Indians: 33

ABOUT THE AUTHOR

Joe Cummings has written about travel and culture for over a decade. Attracted to geographical extremes, his first in-depth journeys involved the river deltas and rainforests of Southeast Asia, where he worked as a Peace Corps volunteer (Thailand) and university lecturer (Malaysia), and later contributed to popular guidebooks on Thailand, Malaysia, Singapore, Burma, Indonesia, and China.

Joe became infatuated with desert terrains while exploring the Sierra del Carmen and Chihuahuan Desert reaches of Texas' Big Bend Country for Moon's *Texas Handbook*. His love of South Texas border culture, including *norteña* music and food, eventually spilled over into Mexico; in preparation for his research travels in Baja California, he undertook an intensive Spanish language course and lived with a Mexican family. Safe and sound after clocking several thousand miles on peninsular roads, Joe is now a confirmed Baja fanatic.

MOON HANDBOOKS—THE IDEAL TRAVELING COMPANIONS

Moon Handbooks provide travelers with all the background and practical information he or she will need on the road. Every Handbook begins with in-depth essays on the land, the people, their history, arts, politics, and social concerns—an entire bookshelf of introductory information squeezed into a one-volume encyclopedia. The Handbooks provide accurate, up-to-date coverage of all the practicalities: language, currency, transportation, accommodations, food and entertainment, and services, to name a few. Moon Handbooks are ideal traveling companions: informative, entertaining, and highly practical.

To locate the bookstore nearest you that carries Moon Travel Handbooks or to order directly from Moon Publications, call: (800) 345-5473, Monday-Friday, 9 a.m.-5 p.m. PST.

THE PACIFIC/ASIA SERIES

BALI HANDBOOK   by Bill Dalton
Detailed travel information on the most famous island in the world. 428 pages.   **$12.95**

BANGKOK HANDBOOK   by Michael Buckley
Your tour guide through this exotic and dynamic city reveals the affordable and accessible possibilities. Thai phrasebook. 214 pages.   **$10.95**

BLUEPRINT FOR PARADISE: How to Live on a Tropic Island   by Ross Norgrove
This one-of-a-kind guide has everything you need to know about moving to and living comfortably on a tropical island. 212 pages.   **$14.95**

FIJI ISLANDS HANDBOOK   by David Stanley
The first and still the best source of information on travel around this 322-island archipelago. Fijian glossary. 198 pages.   **$11.95**

INDONESIA HANDBOOK   by Bill Dalton
This one-volume encyclopedia explores island by island the many facets of this sprawling, kaleidoscopic island nation. Extensive Indonesian vocabulary. 1,000 pages.   **$19.95**

JAPAN HANDBOOK   by J.D. Bisignani
In this comprehensive new edition, award-winning travel writer J.D. Bisignani offers to inveterate travelers, newcomers, and businesspeople alike a thoroughgoing presentation of Japan's many facets. 950 pages.   **$22.50**

MICRONESIA HANDBOOK: Guide to the Caroline, Gilbert, Mariana, and Marshall Islands
by David Stanley
Micronesia Handbook guides you on a real Pacific adventure all your own. 345 pages.   **$11.95**

NEW ZEALAND HANDBOOK   by Jane King
Introduces you to the people, places, history, and culture of this extraordinary land. 571 pages.
$18.95

OUTBACK AUSTRALIA HANDBOOK by Marael Johnson
Australia is an endlessly fascinating, vast land, and *Outback Australia Handbook* explores the cities and towns, sheep stations, and wilderness areas of the Northern Territory, Western Australia, and South Australia. Full of travel tips and cultural information for adventuring, relaxing, or just getting away from it all. 355 pages. **$15.95**

PHILIPPINES HANDBOOK by Peter Harper and Evelyn Peplow
Crammed with detailed information, *Philippines Handbook* equips the escapist, hedonist, or business traveler with thorough coverage of the Philippines's colorful history, landscapes, and culture. 600 pages. **$17.95**

SOUTHEAST ASIA HANDBOOK by Carl Parkes
Helps the enlightened traveler discover the real Southeast Asia. 873 pages. **$21.95**

SOUTH KOREA HANDBOOK by Robert Nilsen
Whether you're visiting on business or searching for adventure, *South Korea Handbook* is an invaluable companion. Korean glossary with useful notes on speaking and reading the language. 548 pages. **$14.95**

SOUTH PACIFIC HANDBOOK by David Stanley
The original comprehensive guide to the 16 territories in the South Pacific. 740 pages. **$19.95**

TAHITI-POLYNESIA HANDBOOK by David Stanley
All five French-Polynesian archipelagoes are covered in this comprehensive guide by Oceania's best-known travel writer. 235 pages. **$11.95**

THAILAND HANDBOOK by Carl Parkes
Presents the richest source of information on travel in Thailand. 568 pages. **$16.95**

THE HAWAIIAN SERIES

BIG ISLAND OF HAWAII HANDBOOK by J.D. Bisignani
An entertaining yet informative text packed with insider tips on accommodations, dining, sports and outdoor activities, natural attractions, and must-see sights. 350 pages. **$13.95**

HAWAII HANDBOOK by J.D. Bisignani
Winner of the 1989 Hawaii Visitors Bureau's Best Guide Award and the Grand Award for Excellence in Travel Journalism, this guide takes you beyond the glitz and high-priced hype and leads you to a genuine Hawaiian experience. Covers all 8 Hawaiian Islands. 879 pages. **$15.95**

KAUAI HANDBOOK by J.D. Bisignani
Kauai Handbook is the perfect antidote to the workaday world. Hawaiian and pidgin glossaries. 236 pages. **$9.95**

MAUI HANDBOOK by J.D. Bisignani
"No fool-'round" advice on accommodations, eateries, and recreation, plus a comprehensive introduction to island ways, geography, and history. Hawaiian and pidgin glossaries. 350 pages.
$14.95

OAHU HANDBOOK by J.D. Bisignani
A handy guide to Honolulu, renowned surfing beaches, and Oahu's countless other diversions. Hawaiian and pidgin glossaries. 354 pages. **$11.95**

THE AMERICAS SERIES

ALASKA-YUKON HANDBOOK   by Deke Castleman and Don Pitcher
Get the inside story, with plenty of well-seasoned advice to help you cover more miles on less money. 460 pages.   **$14.95**

ARIZONA TRAVELER'S HANDBOOK   by Bill Weir
This meticulously researched guide contains everything necessary to make Arizona accessible and enjoyable. 505 pages.   **$16.95**

**BAJA HANDBOOK: Mexico's Western Peninsula
including Cabo San Lucas**   by Joe Cummings
A comprehensive guide with all the travel information and background on the land, history, and culture of this untamed thousand-mile-long peninsula. 362 pages.   **$15.95**

BELIZE HANDBOOK   by Chicki Mallan
Complete with detailed maps, practical information, and an overview of the area's flamboyant history, culture, and geographical features, *Belize Handbook* is the only comprehensive guide of its kind to this spectacular region. 263 pages.   **$14.95**

BRITISH COLUMBIA HANDBOOK   by Jane King
With an emphasis on outdoor adventures, this guide covers mainland British Columbia, Vancouver Island, the Queen Charlotte Islands, and the Canadian Rockies. 381 pages. **$15.95**

CANCUN HANDBOOK   by Chicki Mallan
Covers the city's luxury scene as well as more modest attractions, plus many side trips to unspoiled beaches and Mayan ruins. Spanish glossary. 257 pages.   **$13.95**

**CENTRAL MEXICO HANDBOOK: Mexico City, Guadalajara,
and Other Colonial Cities**   by Chicki Mallan
Retrace the footsteps of Cortés from the coast of Veracruz to the heart of Mexico City to discover archaeological and cultural wonders. 350 pages.   **$15.95**

CATALINA ISLAND HANDBOOK: A Guide to California's Channel Islands
by Chicki Mallan
A complete guide to these remarkable islands, from the windy solitude of the Channel Islands National Marine Sanctuary to bustling Avalon. 245 pages.   **$10.95**

COLORADO HANDBOOK   by Stephen Metzger
Essential details to the all-season possibilities in Colorado fill this guide. Practical travel tips combine with recreation—skiing, nightlife, and wilderness exploration—plus entertaining essays. 416 pages.   **$17.95**

COSTA RICA HANDBOOK   by Christopher P. Baker
Experience the many wonders of the natural world as you explore this remarkable land. Spanish-English glossary. 574 pages.   **$17.95**

IDAHO HANDBOOK   by Bill Loftus
A year-round guide to everything in this outdoor wonderland, from whitewater adventures to rural hideaways. 275 pages.   **$12.95**

JAMAICA HANDBOOK   by Karl Luntta
From the sun and surf of Montego Bay and Ocho Rios to the cool slopes of the Blue Mountains, author Karl Luntta offers island-seekers a perceptive, personal view of Jamaica. 230 pages. **$14.95**

MONTANA HANDBOOK   by W.C. McRae and Judy Jewell
The wild West is yours with this extensive guide to the Treasure State, complete with travel practicalities, history, and lively essays on Montana life. 427 pages.   **$15.95**

NEVADA HANDBOOK   by Deke Castleman
Nevada Handbook puts the Silver State into perspective and makes it manageable and affordable. 400 pages.   **$14.95**

NEW MEXICO HANDBOOK   by Stephen Metzger
A close-up and complete look at every aspect of this wondrous state. 375 pages.   **$14.95**

NORTHERN CALIFORNIA HANDBOOK   by Kim Weir
An outstanding companion for imaginative travel in the territory north of the Tehachapis. 765 pages.   **$19.95**

NORTHERN MEXICO HANDBOOK: The Sea of Cortez to the Gulf of Mexico
by Joe Cummings
Directs travelers from the barrier islands of Sonora to the majestic cloud forests of the Sierra Madre Oriental to traditional villages and hidden waterfalls in San Luis Potosí. 500 pages.   **$16.95**

OREGON HANDBOOK   by Stuart Warren and Ted Long Ishikawa
Brimming with travel practicalities and insiders' views on Oregon's history, culture, arts, and activities. 461 pages.   **$15.95**

PACIFIC MEXICO HANDBOOK   by Bruce Whipperman
Explore 2,000 miles of gorgeous beaches, quiet resort towns, and famous archaeological sites along Mexico's Pacific coast. Spanish-English glossary. 428 pages.   **$15.95**

TEXAS HANDBOOK   by Joe Cummings
Seasoned travel writer Joe Cummings brings an insider's perspective to his home state. 483 pages.   **$13.95**

UTAH HANDBOOK   by Bill Weir
Weir gives you all the carefully researched facts and background to make your visit a success. 445 pages.   **$14.95**

WASHINGTON HANDBOOK   by Archie Satterfield and Dianne J. Boulerice Lyons
Covers sights, shopping, services, transportation, and outdoor recreation, with complete listings for restaurants and accommodations. 433 pages.   **$15.95**

WYOMING HANDBOOK   by Don Pitcher
All you need to know to open the doors to this wide and wild state. 495 pages.   **$14.95**

YUCATAN HANDBOOK   by Chicki Mallan
All the information you'll need to guide you into every corner of this exotic land. Mayan and Spanish glossaries. 391 pages.   **$15.95**

THE INTERNATIONAL SERIES

EGYPT HANDBOOK   by Kathy Hansen
An invaluable resource for intelligent travel in Egypt. Arabic glossary. 522 pages.   **$18.95**

MOSCOW-ST. PETERSBURG HANDBOOK   by Masha Nordbye
Provides the visitor with an extensive introduction to the history, culture, and people of these two great cities, as well as practical information on where to stay, eat, and shop. 260 pages. **$13.95**

NEPAL HANDBOOK   by Kerry Moran
Whether you're planning a week in Kathmandu or months out on the trail, *Nepal Handbook* will take you into the heart of this Himalayan jewel. 378 pages.   **$12.95**

NEPALI AAMA   by Broughton Coburn
A delightful photo-journey into the life of a Gurung tribeswoman of Central Nepal. Having lived with Aama (translated, "mother") for two years, first as an outsider and later as an adopted member of the family, Coburn presents an intimate glimpse into a culture alive with humor, folklore, religion, and ancient rituals. 165 pages.   **$13.95**

PAKISTAN HANDBOOK   by Isobel Shaw
For armchair travelers and trekkers alike, the most detailed and authoritative guide to Pakistan ever published. Urdu glossary. 478 pages.   **$15.95**

STAYING HEALTHY IN ASIA, AFRICA, AND LATIN AMERICA
by Dirk G. Schroeder, Sc D, MPH
Don't leave home without it! Besides providing a complete overview of the health problems that exist in these areas, this book will help you determine which immunizations you'll need beforehand, what medications to take with you, and how to recognize and treat infections and diseases. Includes extensively illustrated first-aid information and precautions for heat, cold, and high altitude. 200 pages.   **$10.95**

TIBET HANDBOOK: A PILGRIMAGE GUIDE
by Victor Chan
This remarkable book is both a comprehensive trekking guide to mountain paths and plateau trails, and a pilgrimage guide that draws on Tibetan literature and religious history. 1104 pages. **$30.00**

MOONBELTS

Made of heavy-duty Cordura nylon, the Moonbelt offers maximum protection for your money and important papers. This all-weather pouch slips under your shirt or waistband, rendering it virtually undetectable and inaccessible to pickpockets. One-inch-wide nylon webbing, heavy-duty zipper, one-inch quick-release buckle. Accommodates traveler's checks, passport, cash, photos. Size 5 x 9 inches. Black.   **$8.95**

**New travel handbooks may be available that are not on this list.
To find out more about current or upcoming titles,
call us toll-free at (800) 345-5473.**

IMPORTANT ORDERING INFORMATION

FOR FASTER SERVICE: Call to locate the bookstore nearest you that carries Moon Travel Handbooks or order directly from Moon Publications:

(800) 345-5473 • **Monday-Friday** • **9 a.m.-5 p.m. PST** • **fax (916) 345-6751**

PRICES: All prices are subject to change. We always ship the most current edition. We will let you know if there is a price increase on the book you ordered.

SHIPPING & HANDLING OPTIONS: 1) Domestic UPS or USPS first class (allow 10 working days for delivery): $3.50 for the first item, 50 cents for each additional item.

Exceptions:
- **Moonbelt** shipping is $1.50 for one, 50 cents for each additional belt.
- Add $2.00 for same-day handling.
- UPS 2nd Day Air or Printed Airmail requires a special quote.
- International Surface Bookrate (8-12 weeks delivery):
    $3.00 for the first item, $1.00 for each additional item. Note: Moon Publications cannot guarantee international surface bookrate shipping.

FOREIGN ORDERS: All orders that originate outside the U.S.A. must be paid for with either an International Money Order or a check in U.S. currency drawn on a major U.S. bank based in the U.S.A.

TELEPHONE ORDERS: We accept Visa or MasterCard payments. Minimum order is US$15.00. Call in your order: (800) 345-5473, 9 a.m.-5 p.m. Pacific Standard Time.

ORDER FORM

Be sure to call (800) 345-5473 for current prices and editions or for the name of the bookstore
nearest you that carries Moon Travel Handbooks • 9 a.m.–5 p.m. PST
(See important ordering information on preceding page)

Name: _____ Date: _____

Street: _____

City: _____ Daytime Phone: _____

State or Country: _____ Zip Code: _____

QUANTITY	TITLE	PRICE

Taxable Total_____

Sales Tax (7.25%) for California Residents_____

Shipping & Handling_____

TOTAL_____

Ship: ☐ UPS (no PO Boxes)   ☐ 1st class   ☐ International surface mail

Ship to: ☐ address above   ☐ other _____

_____

Make checks payable to: **MOON PUBLICATIONS, INC.** P.O. Box 3040, Chico, CA 95927-3040
U.S.A. We accept Visa and MasterCard. **To Order**: Call in your Visa or MasterCard number, or send
a written order with your Visa or MasterCard number and expiration date clearly written.

Card Number: ☐ **Visa**   ☐ **MasterCard**

☐ ☐ ☐ ☐   ☐ ☐ ☐ ☐   ☐ ☐ ☐ ☐   ☐ ☐ ☐ ☐

Exact Name on Card: _____

expiration date:_____

signature_____